PURBECK STONE

Treleven Haysom

FOLLOWING PAGES

Detail from 'Quarrying in a Landscape: Haysom's Quarry, Purbeck'. c. 1961
David Raphael de L. Willis (born 1933), (oil on canvas, 104 x 284 mm).
(Dorset County Museum)

THE DOVECOTE PRESS

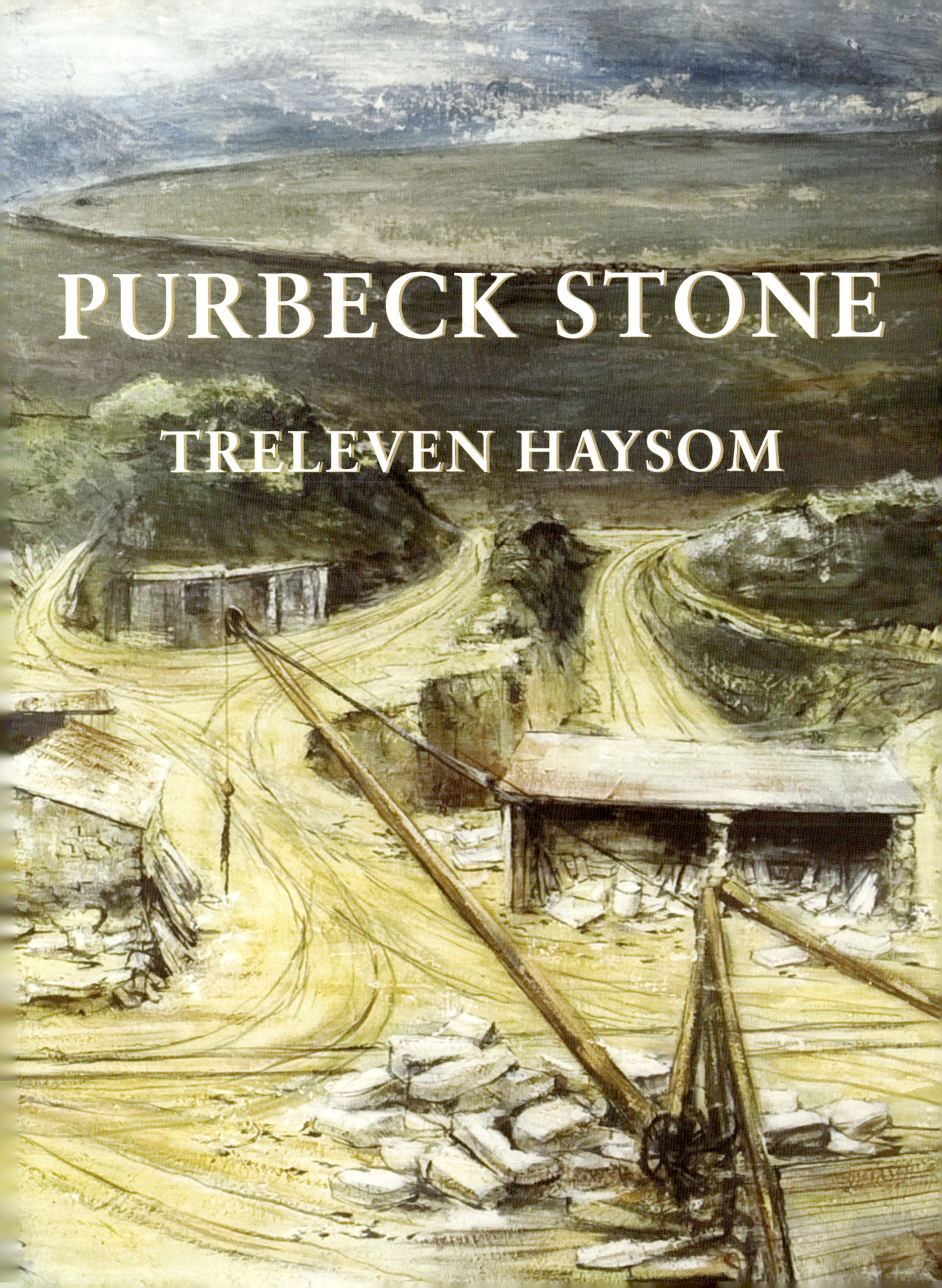

PURBECK STONE

TRELEVEN HAYSOM

To Walter and Sue: this book is an expression of filial piety combined with husbandly gratitude.

The stone quarrying area of the Isle of Purbeck.

First published in 2020 by The Dovecote Press Ltd
Stanbridge, Wimborne Minster, Dorset BH21 4JD

ISBN 978-0-9955462-6-4

© Treleven Haysom 2020

Treleven Haysom has asserted his rights under the Copyright, Designs
and Patent Act 1988 to be identified as author of this work

Designed by The Dovecote Press
Typeset in Sabon
Printed and bound in India by Imprint Press

All papers used by The Dovecote Press are natural,
recyclable products made from wood grown in sustainable,
well-managed forests

A CIP catalogue record for this book is available
from the British Library

All rights reserved

1 3 5 7 9 8 6 4 2

Contents

INTRODUCTION 7

THE STONE 11

MARBLE 31

INLAND QUARRIES 68

PEVERIL POINT AND DURLSTON BAY 93

CLIFF STONE 100

USES 161

TECHNOLOGY 193

TRADE ORGANISATIONS 234

Appendices 276

Glossary 280

Notes 291

Bibliography 299

Index 301

The Illustrations 311

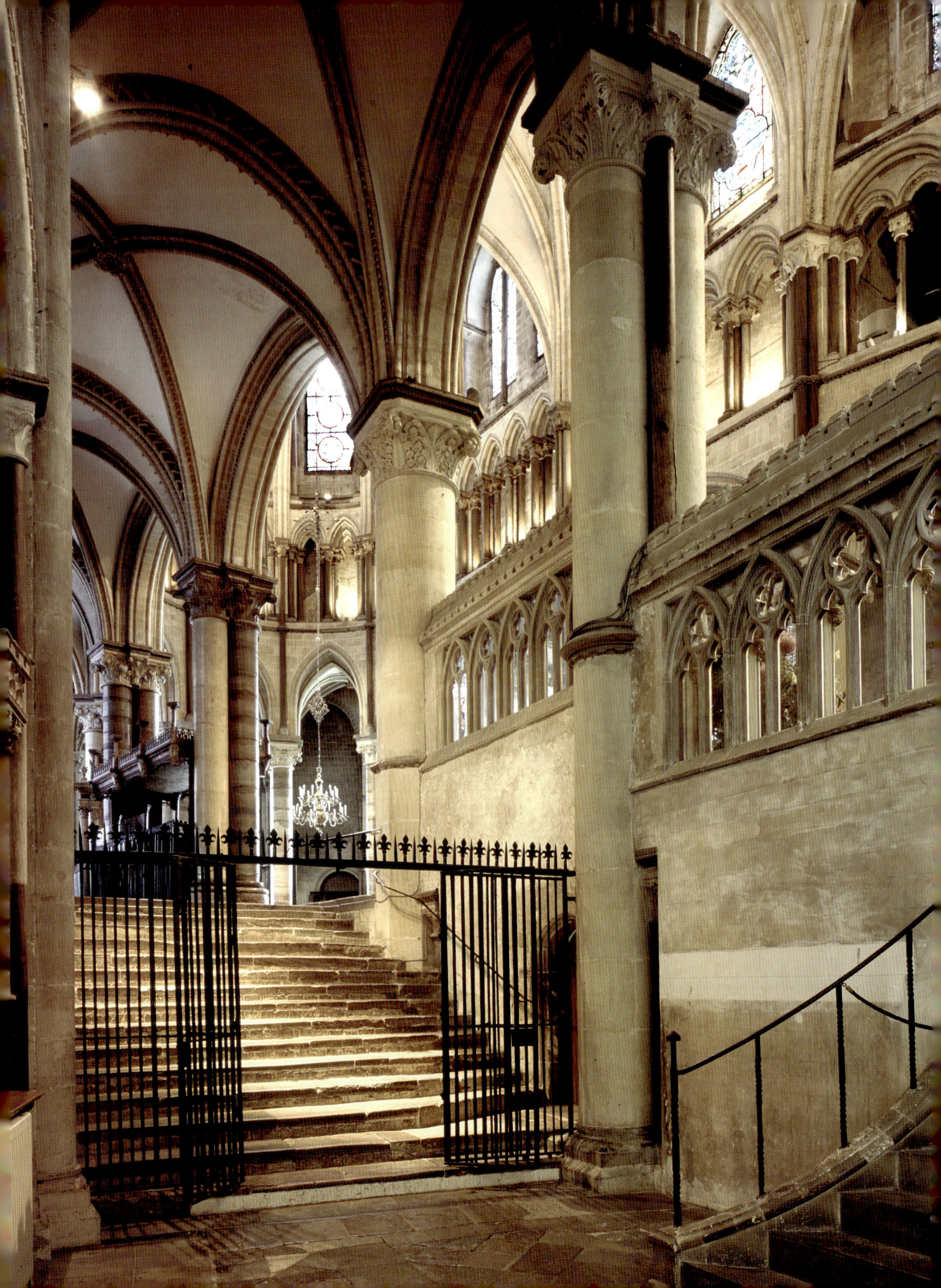

Introduction

In 1969, whilst accompanying Horace Alexander in revisiting some of his former bird watching haunts around Dungeness, we called in at Winchelsea church. I remarked that in my opinion most of the Marble used in the medieval monuments looked more like Purbeck than Sussex, as given in the guide book. He said something like: 'perhaps you should make a note'. Subsequently, when opportunity allowed, my wife Sue and I explored Dorset churches, recording Purbeck stone and Marble where we encountered it, and 'making a note' without any thought of writing a book. However, having read much misleading material on the subject, I thought that it might be realistic to attempt a description of the Purbeck Cliff quarries. Of course, their development is tied up with a wider story, and one thing has led to another.

On holidays or trips to do with work, we ventured further. Sue has remained supportive, in spite of looking at a lot of old, grimy stones and hours frustratingly spent in quest of church keys. Setting the negatives aside, the quest has led us to interesting and beautiful places and to enjoyable encounters. I am sad to relate that just occasionally, and understandably with theft being so common, I have felt a measure of discomfort at being viewed with obvious suspicion. My thanks go out to all those flower arrangers, brass polishers, cleaners, wardens, guides, custodians, friends and clergy who have been so welcoming. In addition thanks must go to others who have provided good company on such excursions and, from time to time, a roof: my sister, Ann Willig for a base in Surrey, sister Mary Haysom when in mid-Dorset, Penny Brooke and cousin Cyril Haysom in Kent, Angela Perkins and Elaine Paget in Devon, Ilay Cooper, John Pickford, Naomi Brooke and her wider family for many convivial excursions venturing into deepest Dorset and beyond.

I count myself lucky to be of a generation which enjoyed childhood before the Health and Safety mantra was heard across the land. My father's approach to us children mucking about in the quarry was 'keep out of the way'. We dug away into an old waste bank or had a go at chiselling as the mood took us, or we ventured off down Pier Bottom; all of which I much preferred to school. That current and future generations cannot enjoy such experiences in their formative years, but instead have blanket bans or bogus 'work experience' foisted upon them; is a shame. When I did begin work properly I was put alongside Thomas Collins. Included in the works we did were a pair of gate piers for the Deanery at Chichester. They were too wide for the planing machine, hence the need to work each one by hand. Similarly, a mensa or altar top for Llandaff Cathedral; at over ten feet, this was too long for the saw machine. Learning from men in the work situation is a form of osmosis; one picks up knowhow and knowledge without overt instruction. I heard 'stone talk' from him and the others working for my father around that time: my brother, Christopher, Ernest Norman, Bill 'Mart' and Ralf Bower, Bert Norman, and the younger men fresh back from National Service: Roger Bonfield, Geoff Hooper and Bill Norman. Later Thomas Bonfield was very informative, on underground work in particular. However he did not 'rattle on' about it. Like others of his ilk who really had done a lot and therefore knew a lot, he kept a certain reticence. Their achievement lay in actual stone dug and work done, not in talking about it. The main product of most of the quarries then was pitched faced walling, which being sold by superficial measurement, was set up, or 'yarded up', in rows nine feet by two feet. Thomas Collins remarked disparagingly 'some of 'em are good at yarding it up at the Square and Compass', which catches to a degree the somewhat scathing approach of men like him, my father and Thomas Bonfield towards people who talk and indeed write about work, as opposed to actually doing it.

I remember a few of their pithy sayings. Evoking the days when winter food stocks were low before anything much was coming on in the garden, Billy Winspit would say: 'March will search, April will try, May will see if we live or die'. Bert Norman's 'Self-praise is no recommendation' puts the deliberately deceptive world of advertising, let alone PR, in perspective! What would he have said about our brave new world of spin, of Local Authorities, the police and utility companies, all telling us by glossy mail shots what a good job they do? 'Ill gotten gains are no man's goods' got the mess house conversation going, as did 'Put

Canterbury Cathedral, North aisle. Steps to Trinity Chapel. Note Purbeck Marble used as abacus and detached shaft out of bed in foremost pillar. Purbeck Marble drums are stacked in bed in pillar, right, at top of steps.

a beggar on horse back and he will ride', said with some of the merchants in mind! From Billy Winspit came: 'Starve gutted money ain't worth a shilling a bushel'; also 'what is born in the bone cain't come out through the skin' and 'If you want to swank, you've got to pay'. Another, from my Uncle Frank was: 'Anyone can start a job', and two from my father: 'If the cap fits, wear it' and 'There are none so deaf as those who won't hear'. Examples of words slipping out of use include Harold Bonfield's reminiscence of George Hancock's response to his unreliable new lorry in the early days of mechanisation, 'At least when we had the donkey we had a pound when we needed it' ('pound' meaning 'work effort'). Similarly, when my father enquired of Bert Norman how he got on delivering a heavy stone, Bertie retorted, 'When I said to this bloke, 'gi'es a pound 'ere 'ut' [would you] he looked at I as if I were talking a foreign language.'

But garrulous or otherwise, everyone has a story to tell. Other men in the trade with whom I have been lucky to talk stone and who have passed on information include Jack Norman, John and Jack Harden, George Brownsea, Ron, Eric, Philip and Glen Bower, Arthur Hancock, John and Edward Pushman, David Glassock, Harry Tatchell, Roy and Bob Cobb, Kevin Keats, Norman Priddle, Harold Bonfield, Jim Norman, Fred Wellman, John and Bob Harris, Mick Samways, Arthur Albin, Alan and Allan Lander. Other locals, all with interesting information, include Bill Bradford, Michael Norman, Bill Carter, Eric Roberts and David White, to all of whom I extend my thanks. Also thanks to Freddy Dowell who taught me masonry at Weymouth College. His clarification of the difference between hen and sparrow – pecked still prompts a smile.

Naturally I heard most from my father, who cautioned about one of the old hands in particular: 'He knows a lot, but what he don't know he will make up.' It is of course easier to make things up than to find them out, which accounts for much of the human condition! When I began work my father and his elder brother Frank would sit in the office during 'dinner'. They both had a great knowledge of old Swanage and Purbeck in general and stone in particular. The talk was often of who dug what, where and when, and where the stone went. On the rare occasions when my two other itinerant uncles returned to Purbeck the conversations were much the same. My perspective therefore has an unintentional Haysom overload, particularly gained from my father. He left school during the Great War before serving in the Navy. After demob in 1919 he worked for a summer on Portland in Hibbs and Barnes' yards, followed by a spell in Webber and Corbin's in London. He also spent time cutting War Grave inscriptions at Burslem's near Tunbridge Wells. It was interesting to discover that his great grandfather, Francis, had quarried in Durlston Bay, a fact he did not know. It illustrates the potential weakness of oral tradition. Grandfather William Haysom's experience had been starting work in the 1870s on Randell's banker, which was managed by his father, John, who had started work in Francis' other quarry, which was about where the Swanage Cottage Hospital has since been built. John had gone to London to work on the rebuilding of the Palace of Westminster. His wife, a Swanage girl, did not like it and they returned. I guess smoke-shrouded London at the time of the big stink was pretty insalubrious. While John was manager in Swanage, Randell's provided stonework for the new Swanage Town Hall, though not, of course, the Portland façade brought down from London. They also did George Burt's gazebo for his Purbeck House, now a hotel, and the chart of the English Channel which he had set up near the Great Globe, made of Acton thornback. At this time Randell's were shipping 'bread and butter work' in the form of paving, kerbing and sinks in quantity, as well as high status, technically-demanding Marble piecing repairs for Salisbury Cathedral and other ecclesiastical work. John, together with his brother James, lettered memorial stones in a distinctive thick-and-thin style. After 'learning the tools' grandfather William had a spell in Trollope & Colls' Vauxhall yard in London, which was managed by his cousin, Frank Tomes.

Most of their work was with Portland stone, but they did other things. My father remembered William talking of an elaborate stair they made in onyx, and of putting 'thumb mould' on Marble washstands. This was sometimes a fall back 'hospital job' when other work was slack. There were more hazards in London than getting a squashed finger. 'Mahogany flats' (bed bugs) inhabited their lodgings. William, like his father, returned to Swanage and had a go at general masonry, deliberately avoiding monumental work, which his cousin Lewis had carried on from the previous generation. Without a quarry, he was dependent on supply from others, a competitive disadvantage. He mostly bought block from Trink (Albert) Bower. Later he worked for Parsons and Hayter, Swanage builders, who had acquired Thomas Steven's yard in Tilly Mead. On Bobby Norman's retirement he took over as manager of the masonry section; the typical Swanage house of the time required decorative masonry.

I regret not making an attempt, using Horace's phrase, to 'make a note' before I did, particularly as the thought of writing a book developed. By the time I began, all three uncles were dead. One of Frank's expressions, referring to the old days, was 'That was before Aaron Bower burnt the books'. It was gratifying when Dr Martin Ayres, local historian, found a letter written by Aaron to his fellow Overseers of the Poor admitting the fact! Exploration of old documents with Martin and other historically minded people has been fun. In particular I am indebted to former County Archivist Margaret Holmes for kindly guiding work colleagues David Burt, Brian Bugler and myself in our first 'amateur' searches and to subsequent staff at the Dorset County archives (now the Dorset History Centre) for continuing assistance, particularly Mark Forrest. Louise Haywood has been very helpful with her work on the Serrell Estate papers and Chris Kaye with information about Swanage bankers. It has been enjoyable to talk stone with, or read the work of, local historians F. D. Pitfield, the late Reg Saville, Dennis Smale, the late David Lewer, Brian Bugler, David Haysom and the late Rodney Legg, all of whom have added to the published canon on the Purbeck Stone Trade. I particularly value Brian Bugler's contributions, coming as they do from a man who can use a mallet and chisel as well computer and camera; he has contributed many good quality images to the book. Parts of some of his fellow authors' works are less worth reading. Cousin John Haysom, who particularly worked on the Swanage merchants and published in *Notes and Queries on Somerset & Dorset*, was helpful in his criticism of early drafts. I would also like to thank Geoffrey Norris who, in his unpublished thesis, has brought an engineer's perspective, and Dr Mark Haysom, who revealed an unexpected vein of information.

I am grateful to James Gaggero for allowing the inclusion of photographs of Encombe. I am indebted to other stone masons, historians, archaeologists and geologists, who have imparted knowledge and encouragement. They include J. Alexander, F. Anderson, Sally Badham, John Bayliss, John Beavis, Claud and John Blair, Tim Connor, Robin Emmerson, Paul Ensom, Jane Fawcett, Ron Firman, Norman Fryer, Moira and Brian Gittos, C. B. Glover, Carolyn Heighway, Michael House, A. Richard Jones, Philip Lancaster, Michael Mandefield, Mike Markey, Michael Marshall, Red Mason, R. K. Morris, John Nunn, Tim Palmer, Ron Roberts, Eric Robinson, James Sabben-Clare, Margaret Sparks, Peter Stanier, Tim Tatton-Brown, Jo Thomas, Harry Tummers, Simon Verity, Ian West, Adam White, N. Woodward-Smith. I apologise to anyone omitted, for possible errors in the spelling of names and omission of current titles, and indeed for all mistakes.

Dot Kerridge took on typing and correction of my first scrawlings twenty years ago. My sister Mary and Mary

Swanage, site opposite Ship Hotel. Randell's banker, 1870-80. L-R back row, Albert Tomes, Septimus Burt, George Norman, Frank Stevens, hidden behind?, John Haysom, Joseph Phippard, Stephen Haysom, James Coleman. Front row, William Haysom sitting,? Turner, standing.

Sparks continued the battle: many thanks to them. Also my thanks to Ildi Clarke for the index: no easy task with so many names virtually the same. I owe a special debt to Sybil Fine King and the Fine Family Foundation for their support.

Identifying differing stones in old masonry is difficult and I admit to changing my ideas about some work as I have looked at it more. Studies such as the examination of thin sections by Peter Bath, and Geoffrey Townson's work on oolites advance identification of stone types, as does Brian Bugler's and Andrew Webster's work on the ostrocods. These have forced a re-thinking of some medieval masonry, though I have stuck to just looking. My approach is that if it looks like a duck then it is a duck. But of course that can be wrong, even when it quacks. I once had the luck to hear that foremost geological authority, Frank Dines, address a gathering of art historians. With a twinkle in his eye he said something like 'knock the nose off the knight you are studying and bring it to me. I like to think that I will be able to tell you whether it is a limestone, a sandstone or something igneous'! The geological field is indeed wide and challenging. I have attempted to 'make a note' about what stone has come out of Purbeck.

Trev Haysom, Langton Matravers, *August 2020*

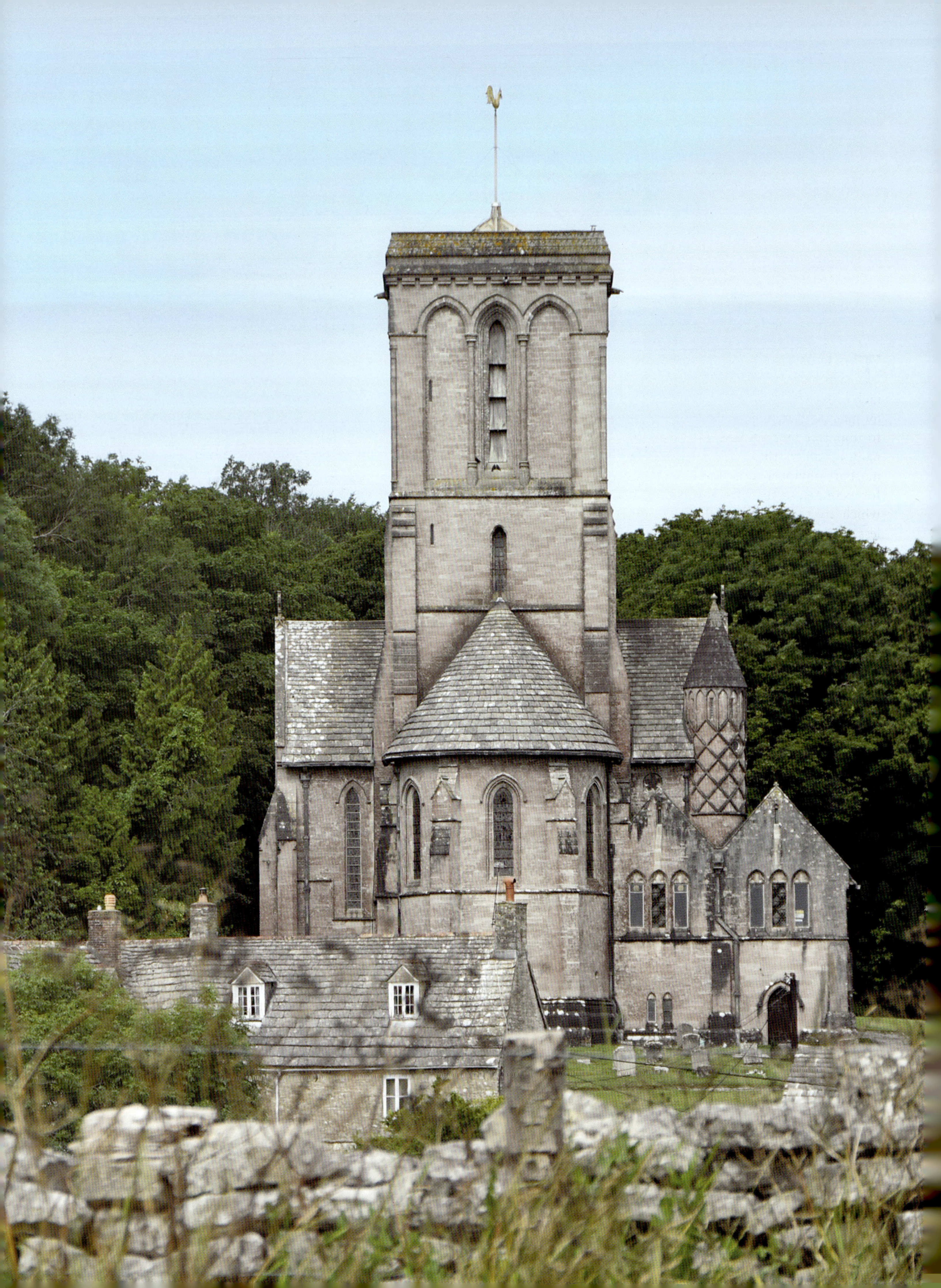

ONE
The Stone

The beds vary in colour, hardness and composition and each has an individual name. Some are no more than an inch or two in thickness, so the naming of them tells of a great intimacy. But then years of toil in a low vein such as the three to four feet high Downs Vein would induce just that. A few names indicate the use to which the particular bed was put; most are obviously descriptive, others mysterious. It is difficult, for example, to see what Purbeck Roach and Portland Roach, which are two entirely different layers, have in common, still less their possible relationship to the roach fish. Some names repeat: there are three or more 'Pon' beds (which sometimes have a 'd' added). In each case they are the upper of a pair of alternatives, the word surely deriving from 'upon'.

Some beds are distinctive enough to be traced over miles, the Cinder being the easiest to follow, all the way from Lulworth to Durlston. It can be pursued beyond Purbeck in the west to the Ridgeway, where it can be seen in the new Poxwell road cutting. In other directions, gypsum mining in Brightling, East Sussex, has also revealed it at depth. Cinder is evidence of a significant event; a marine transgression, whilst the layers above and below are lagoonal. Cinder is something of an exception, but the other beds tend to change in thickness and quality within quite short distances.

One of the less variable in terms of thickness is Downs Vein. It extends from Durlston to Worbarrow at about the same three foot thickness, but thins out to the south, at least above Hedbury. In general the beds thin to the west. Mupe Downs Vein is reduced to only a foot, with the Leper, represented by a mere half inch crust, resting on it. Around Gallows Gore the equivalent, including Underpicking Dirt, is twenty four times thicker! Even more striking is the westward shrinkage of the Freestone/Grub group. At Acton there is about six foot of solid stone, at Mupe about three inches!

Swanage Burr is generally hard and therefore unattractive from a mason's point of view, but around Blashenwell it becomes beautifully workable and a source of the best ashlar. The green Marble bed at Peveril consists of a few thin layers, whilst from Washpond Lane to Dunshay it thickens, providing great slabs, before thinning to insignificance again at Woodyhyde. In the Langton region, between Thornback and Roach, lies a layer of useless scurf. Eastwards at Belle Vue it is still poor, but solid enough for Frank Tomes to use it to build his loading banker, which remains to this day. Still further eastwards it has become a good, durable stone, and is there called 'Grey Bed'.

That sediments accumulating in an enclosed lagoon-like environment change in quite short distances is hardly surprising. The marine Cliff stone beds forming in the open sea change as well, but to a lesser extent. The Under Freestone at Seacombe is coarser and much thicker than that at St. Aldhelm's Head, where it is very fine grained and thin to the point of not being worth digging. At East Winspit and Tilly Whim, but not elsewhere along the Purbeck cliffs, big banks of coarse oysters dominate the Blue Bit level. They result from the formation of discontinuous patch reefs, each one slightly different and productive of a distinctive stone.

There are few references to individual bed names before the earliest systematic list, which appears in the first edition of John Hutchins' *The History and Antiquities of the County of Dorset*.[1] Aubrey's mention of 'Purbac Grubbes' whilst describing his native Wiltshire is therefore particularly interesting.[2] That the names had been coined well before Hutchins' time is evidenced in Article 4 of the 1651 Purbeck Marblers Articles of Agreement. Medieval references, other than to Marble, are scanty and not easy to be sure about. 'Freestones' cropping up in Corfe building accounts are surely Burr rather than what we now call Freestone. 'Hard freestone of Corfe' sent to the Tower of London is probably shelly Cliff stone, for that is what is can be seen there, but who can be sure without documentary evidence? Whoever provided the first list of beds to the Rev. Howel, who communicated it to Hutchins, is not clear, but the informants seem likely to have been James and Robert Scates, who assisted Hutchins with other information about the Purbeck Stone industry. They were surely part of the same family more usually spelled Keates. What they provided is a Swanage section, for it includes Grey Bed, which does not exist in Langton or westwards. Other old lists said to have been set down by Langton quarrymen are re-hashes of Hutchins, if they include this layer. Hutchins' first (1774) list does not include Burr, nor Marble, nor does the later list by 'Mr Bonfield', which

Kingston, St James: commissioned by the the 3rd Earl Eldon, designed by George Street, and built between 1873 and 1880. Purbeck stone and Marble, the church is widely regarded as the 'cathedral' of Purbeck. The workmanship is self-evident. 'Let your deeds be done as well in the dark as they are in the light,' Street's foreman is reputed to have said to the local craftsmen and stone masons who built it.

follows in the third edition of Hutchins in 1861.

Thomas Webster's list of 1825, specific to Durlston Bay, also omits Burr by name. It is what he calls Marble Rag, which points up a difficulty.[3] Webster's is clearly taken from Durlston Bay, men working there providing the details. I like to think one of them may have been my ancestor Francis Haysom, active at Durlston at the time; that is, when he wasn't out in his fishing smack, keeping the White Hart public house (latterly the Purbeck Hotel), or smuggling! Webster alone uses the term 'Shiver' for the useless shales, etc., that separate the good beds. Did he hear it from those men, or, more likely, is it a term he brought with him? Further lists were compiled by the Rev. J. Austen in 1852, and Henry Bristow in 1884, published in Damon.[4] Webster's visit was short, but Austen spent more time here, serving as Rector of Worth for three years. He also tackled Durlston Bay, bed by bed, but his 'economic geology', distilled it would seem from several quarries and quarriers, is perhaps of more interest. His is the only 'Devils Bed Mate' in a list, which probably tells of a Swanage rather than Langton quarry. Conversely his is the only Whetstone and Fustian, both surely to do with Langton rather than Swanage. Bristow's list in Damon, taken from Durlston, omits Thornback entirely, probably including it in 'Sugar'. He calls Grub 'Crab', and is surely in error in including a Brassy bed in the Downs Vein. Such confusion is not confined to the Victorian period: it is astonishing that the recent Building Research Establishment's data sheet about Purbeck Button Bed Limestone describe the Button as 'on top of the Grub bed' and that it is 250 mm deep! How wrong can you get?

A more modern version, R. G. Clements' account of 1969, provides a complete annotated section of Durlston Bay, with each bed numbered. Most of the beds are fairly easy to identify and relate to Hutchins' names, and to quarry exposures westwards to Gallows Gore and beyond, in a limited way.[5] The Corbula and Chief Beef Beds are the most difficult part of the sequence to identify and correlate to Hutchins. These are the layers between the Laining Vein (Clements 144) and Burr (Clements 220). Although of secondary importance, being dominated by worthless shales, they do include some good beds. In my opinion Clements makes the mistake of recording the same bed of Marble twice, 241 and 244 being one and the same. His numbers do not correlate to Ensom's similar work for Worbarrow.[6] William Arkell, a leading authority on the Jurassic Period during the middle part of the 20th century, was intrigued by the bed names and wrote about them, suggesting derivations.[7] What follows is the author's account of the beds in order, the sequence beginning at the top. This account relates Clements' 1969 Durlston section to Hutchins', Webster's and Bonfield's lists, and adds Arkell's comments. Clements' numbers for Durlston are included where present; this is the best known and fullest section. The sequence begins at the top.

MARBLE: So named since the Middle Ages. Three beds, each with subdivisions: blue, green, grey, in descending order, can be recognised at Peveril and westward to Woodyhyde. Quarrying further west at Lynch and Blashenwell only produced the uppermost, but I suspect the others, perhaps attenuated, may occur there also. The distinguishing characteristic throughout

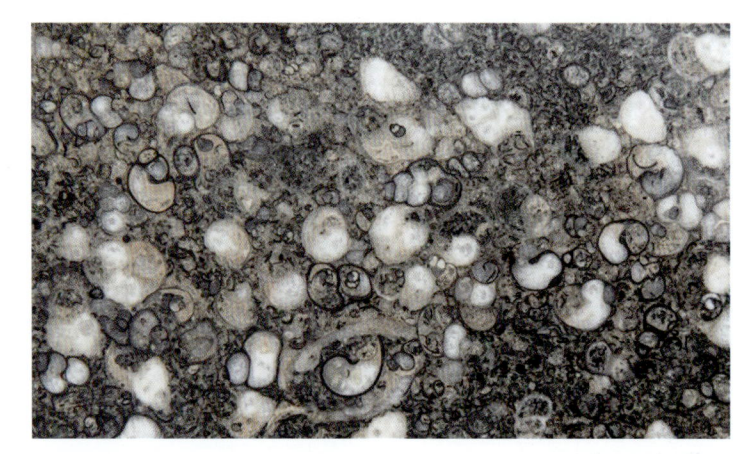

TOP Blue Marble from Quarr.

CENTRE Green Marble. The largest white fossils are unios. Some Green Marble monuments lack them.

BOTTOM Grey Marble.

these beds is viviparous pond snail. Some quarrymen call the topmost bed (Clements 241), Marble Rag. It is current bedded, tougher and less good natured than the lowermost, especially in the Woodyhyde region. The maximum depth of this upper blue bed, which is the thickest, measured at Quarr Farm, is 2ft 9 inches. However, there are invariably beds subdividing this total, with the result that the maximum solid layer is 21 inches thick. Medieval work exceeding this thickness is unknown, but some drums within the composite pillars in Salisbury Cathedral equal it (S.transept, NE column). The middle bed, 239, is

12 / PURBECK STONE

greenish and unio rich. It is of no use at Peveril, but to the west it thickens and provided many monuments, particularly some of the biggest brass indent slabs. Some can become reddish over time. Various authors, particularly Dr. Dru Drury, discuss a red bed.[8] In my opinion it is this middle layer, but the uppermost blue from the Dunshay region can also redden on exposure. However, the same upper blue bed at Lynch does not; nor the bottom bed from any location.

These so-called 'Marble' beds are hard and polishable in a way that the general run of English Freestones are not; hence the application of the name. However, within the Purbeck context many other beds are equally hard and polishable, though known by other names.

Both at Quarr and at Lynch, so probably over a wide area, a fourth thin, similarly viviparous-snail-dominated bed occurs above the blue bed. It is of poor quality, but splits to thicknesses that would lend themselves to use as paving. This prompts the suspicion that the medieval marblers may have used it for such, but this paving may have decayed and been lost. Occasional viviparous snails, which distinguish Purbeck marble, occur as low in the system as the Cap. Some Laining Vein, such as that from the Spyway region include them in abundance. This layer is almost indistinguishable from typical marble. I have encountered no medieval monuments made of this snail-rich Laining Vein. Setting aside niceties such as what scientific geologists (as opposed to medieval masons) call Marble, and the machinations of spin doctors, in my opinion it is correct to call Clements' beds 241, 239 and 237/236 Purbeck Marble and nothing else. Unios are non-existent in the bottom bed, abundant in the middle green bed, particularly the top; present but rare in the top of the upper blue bed from Lynch, and more common in the same bed from Quarr. Therefore, hardly any can be found in the postwar Marble in the Temple Church, which is from Lynch, but quite a lot in recent replacement shafts at Salisbury north door, which come from Quarr.

BURR 220: Along the central and western parts of the outcrop it is mostly relatively soft and hence workable. The suggestion has been made, wrongly in my opinion, that the name therefore derives from the French word for butter; imported stone called 'French Burr' was used for mill stones, because of its extreme hardness. Where Purbeck Burr occurs close to the surface the raw blocks tend to take on rotund worn shapes. Are these not 'burrs' meaning rough, as in Burdock the plant, as Arkell mentions?

No doubt the various subdivisions of its c. 10ft layer once had individual names that were spoken of before Chaucer, but these had been lost by the time of Hutchins' contributors, who had little interest in it. Confusingly, it is what Thomas Webster and John Mowlem call 'Marble Rag', understandable in that in the Swanage/Peveril district it can be hard and blue, quite unlike the good natured Freestone-like stuff from further west.[9] The uppermost part contains unios similar to those in the Marble, but otherwise there is no way the two rocks can be confused. Masons found it hard to cut steps into the raw rock surface of Slippery Ledge, close by Buck Shore; some still remain. In the past Grosvenor Hotel guests used them for sea bathing (*see illustration p. 95*).

TOADS EYE 152: Bonfield's surface earth in Hutchins III must be about 190, but the correlation of his uppermost beds with Clements is difficult before Toads Eye is reached. This has a black rounded shell species obviously suggestive of the animal, but confusingly other beds higher up the succession also contain the same fossil.

LAINING VEIN RAG 147 and 148: My father talked of a Black Bit in the Laining Vein quarried in the inter war years by Fred Bower in Court Cowlease. It does not appear by name in any of the early lists, but would seem to be this bed.

LAINING VEIN 144: Arkell says, charmingly that 'the variety of forms [of the way this word is written, including 'Lane and End', 'Leaning' and 'Lannen'] shows that this has puzzled all recorders'. There was a family of Lanning in Purbeck. Nicholas Lanning appeared in a list of those paying hearth tax for Kingston in 1664. John Lannynge was a yeoman at East Lynch in 1717, but a connection seems unlikely. Arkell's suggestion that it comes from an obsolete term for 'layered' fits very well. Bonfield divides it in descending order:

Pitching Stone Bed [surely for its suitability, pitchers being a Purbeck form of cobbles]

Tombstone Bed, [from its use for such]

White Roach, [see Roach 125]

Leper, [see Leper 114]

White Bed, [presumably descriptive]

Sat Bed, [see 123]

Hard Bed, [descriptive]

Burr.

Laining Vein.

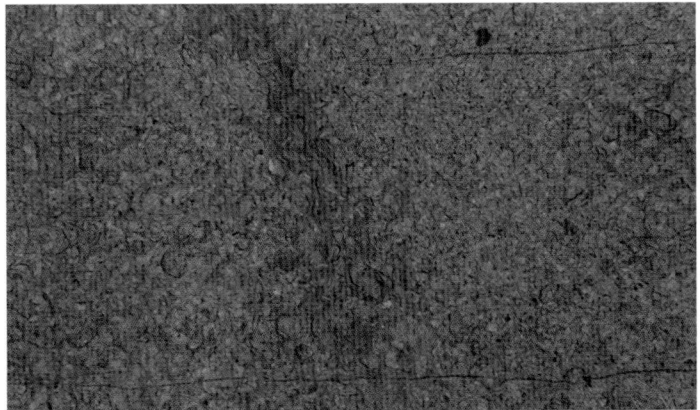

THE STONE / 13

MOCK HARD BED 143: Usually the floor of a Laining Vein quarry. Arkell suggests that it presumably looks like the Hard bed above, as if the two were easy to confuse; but I suspect this is wrong. It tends to be simply called 'the Mock'. For what it is worth, what most people call coppice stools are, or were, in this part of the world called 'Mocks'. Is there a parallel between cutting coppice poles down to the Mock and cutting stone down to its 'base' and calling the base the Mock?

Below the Laining Vein the easternmost Durlston Bay sequence is confused by a fault that makes it difficult to follow the succession of rag beds that come next. To apply Clements' numbers to beds I know best from digging elsewhere is not easy, and I hesitate to do so. RIAL, RYALL or ROYAL is the uppermost of several Rag beds. Arkell suggests 'Royal' derives from its excellent quality, but my experience of quarrying it at Southard it is that it is a very poor stone. 'Royal' becomes 'Ryal' in the dialect.

TOP GALLANT or DEVIL'S BED: Extremely hard, hence Devil. Some square rigged vessels had a top gallant sail course with a royal above and a main below. Is it too fanciful to think of it being seen similarly in relation to the other beds of Rag above and below? To confuse matters, Austen puts his higher, well above the Laining Vein, but this is probably a mistake. These beds figured less in the Langton quarrs, with which he was most familiar, than with those in Swanage.

RAG 133: This is the Rag proper. Like all the others, including one immediately above the Laining Vein and others well above the Toads Eye, and Rags from beyond the bounds of Purbeck (notably Kent), it is bad natured and difficult to work. Hence a derogatory term to a stone mason, but not necessarily to a landscape gardener. It is dramatically current-bedded and the two Durlston Bay sections (North and South) are very different. The upper surface in several of the quarry exposures of one layer is markedly red, hence Webster's name 'Red Rag'.

LEAD or LID BED 131: The lowest Rag, grey, heavy, surely named from the metal. Some way below this lies a distinctive bed of shale called the White Eth / White Earth / White Hearth: possibly Hutchins I's 'smoak coloured earth'. Important to the quarryman in that once he had got down to it he knew the Grub was not much further. Sometimes it has small white calcareous lumps, perhaps suggestive of wood ash in the hearth.

Rag.

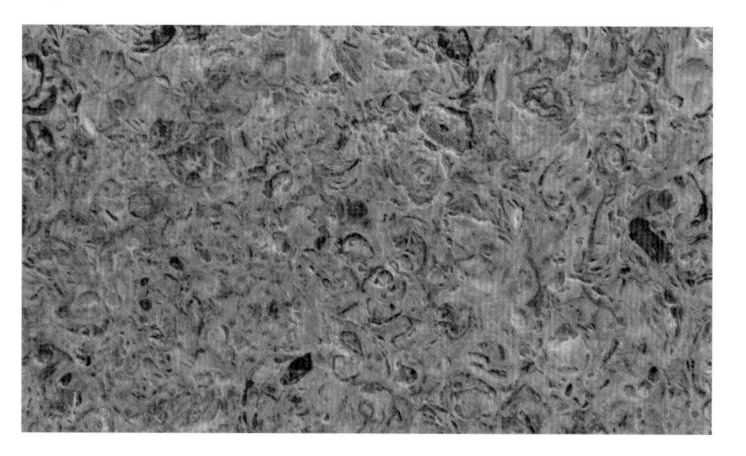

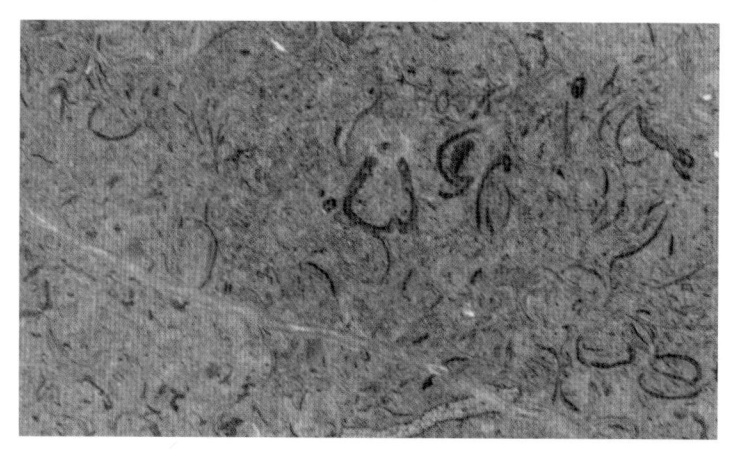

Grub. The white streak is a list; these are common in Purbeck beds in general.

SHINGLE 129a?: Of no use. About this horizon there is a distinctly purple bed. It tends to be called the Raspberry bed.

GRUB 126: Here Bonfield is surprising, for he says that the Shingle formed the ceiling when the freestone group of beds was taken underground. This led Arkell to suggest that Grub earth got its name from the undermining action of grubbing out. But all the freestone undergrounds I have ever heard talked of, and all those that I have ever got into (about a dozen), have the Grub left up as the ceiling.

Aubrey, writing sometime between 1656 and 1691 about Wiltshire says: 'At Swindon are quarries of stones excellent for paving halls, staire-cases etc. being pretty white and smooth and of such a texture as not to be moist or wett in damp weather. It is used at London in Montagu House and in Barkeley House [...] This stone is not inferior to Purbac Grubbes, but whiter'.[10] The second half of the 17th century was exactly when many ledgers of Swanage Grub type were quarried. These were probably got from surface ridden holes, rather than underground. Arkell's suggestion therefore cannot be right, in that the name was probably being applied before the development of underground working, but the dating of that event remains vexed. However he may be right if we consider ridding methods. I suspect it highly likely that men did not dig down layer by layer in the course of surface working but 'underran' on top of the Grub, letting the overburden fall. It is comparatively easy to shovel on a flat layer such as the Grub provides. This method would mean the quarryman adopting a grovelling/grubbing stance.

Below this lies a highly significant bed of clay, the Underpicking Dirt. In most underground Freestone quarrs, this was the layer that was penetrated first. The Grub bed in Durlston Bay is poor, but within half a mile, excellent.

ROACH 125: Bonfield subdivides his into 'Son', which is probably a printer's error for 'Pon', 'Thick Bed' and 'Pink Bed' [Bit]. In some areas there are a lot more partings, at Gallows Gore none. There is another layer called Roach in the Laining Vein and yet another at Portland, which is characterised by big coarse shells, making it undesirable from a mason's point of view. Arkell says the name has basically derogatory connotations, implying brittleness, etc. This could be the clue, now forgotten. Purbeck roach is markedly more brittle than the other vein most productive of roof tile, the Downs Vein, a not insignificant difference *a propos* knocking peg holes through by hand, easily lost sight of now since the introduction of electric drills.

GREY BED 124: This would not appear on a Langton quarryman's list, for in that area it is replaced by useless scurf which, as Eric Benfield put it, is neither stone nor clay. Portland has a worthless bed called Curf, which therefore may have the same root as 'scurf'.[11.]

THORNBACK 123: Surely descriptive of its rough upper surface, as with the ray fish.

Below this, all three contributors miss out what can be, around Acton, one of the best stones in Purbeck, WETSUN BED; also a thin layer between them called SAD or SAT BIT. There are other Sat Beds in the Laining Vein and Downs Vein. Arkell's suggestion of them being made into setts, a sort of cobble, is surely wrong, in that they are so thin, sometimes so much so as to be worthless, but occasionally thickening enough to make a tile. This could suggest a former term for tile in Purbeck, and which continues on Portland as 'slat'. But Austen includes both a Sad bed and a Tile bed, so that seems unlikely. I suggest it is to do with its 'thin to the point of useless' nature. Wetsun bed has no abrasive properties, so the name is not derived from it being a sharpening stone. Swanage men called this same bed Sugar. Some of its partings in the Swanage quarries do suggest granular brown sugar.

FREESTONE 121: Bonfield subdivided his in a curious way. I have never heard the upper part called the White Bed, but simply the 'Top Lift'. Oddly, it tends to be darker than the main part below. Around Acton the lower part, which is hard, usually splits off. This is the White Horse, which is good stone, but the useless Dun Cow adheres to it on the underside. In most Acton undergrounds the White Horse forms the floor, which the cart was run on and the legs built up from. So no Dun Cow rubbish was ever brought up into the light from those quarrs. However things were done differently in some Swanage quarrs where they underpicked beneath the Freestone, as Bonfield describes; those quarrs therefore yielded a bed of which the top half weathers reasonably well, the lower half very badly.

Both Hutchins contributors and Webster follow below the Freestone with a **Lias bed.** This must be the Blue Bed of the Gallows Gore area, sometimes called the River Bed, and distinguished by having the boldest suncracking pattern of any bed in Purbeck. 'Hones' is useless mudstone, generally now called White Rock. I have never heard the term used by quarrymen. Some men called it 'Shards', from it being like broken crockery.

LEPER, probably part of 114: The excellent bed of further west is hard to identify in Durlston. There are other Lepers in and above the Laining Vein which I am not familiar with, but which presumably have a common characteristic. This one from the Langton region is very distinctive when compared with the adjacent Downs Vein in possessing a blistery surface, surely suggestive of the disease, leprosy. It was being dug in the Middle Ages. However, as medieval people did not necessarily distinguish between leprosy and psoriasis, it may be that the name is post-medieval (*see illustration overleaf*).

UNDER PICKING DIRT: The all-important layer of soft

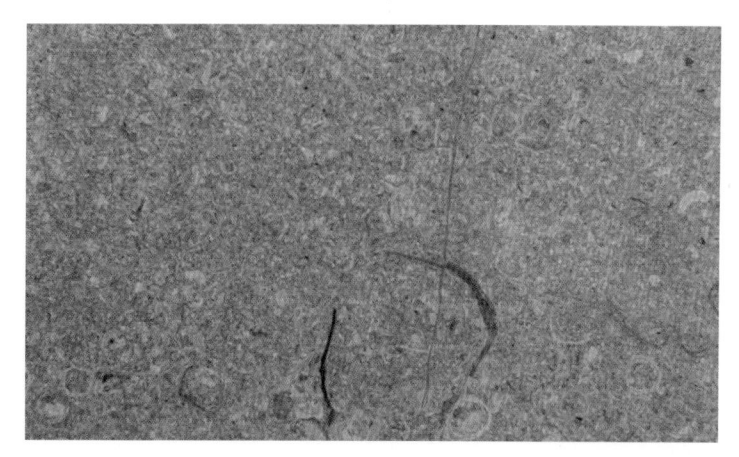

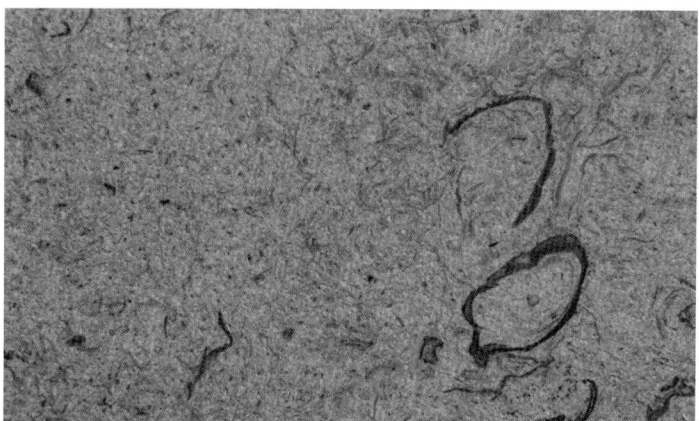

TOP Roach.

CENTRE Thornback.

BOTTOM Freestone.

clay which was penetrated first in Downs Vein undergrounds.

DOWNS VEIN 113: The name is probably of medieval coinage, from its outcropping on the Downs between Kingston and Gallows Gore, as opposed to the location of the other coeval quarries down in the vale. Bonfield subdivided his into eight beds. In places there are more, even as many as twenty two in Eastington Cowlease, whilst south Durlston Bay lies at the other end of the fissile scale, being almost solid. His separations include **Mangy bed**, which has a lot of soft pockets rather like Gorganzola cheese. It is surely the same as Austen's **Fustian Bed**, which he puts at the same level. Where I have quarried the Vein near Swanage these divisions can scarcely be recognised,

Langton Matravers High Street. Leper used as gateposts.

Downs Vein.

Feather.

Cap.

but they clearly apply to stone from the Acton to Gallows Gore area. Within that location the Fustian component is relatively thicker around Acton. Fustian cloth is made from linen and cotton and derivatives include corduroy and moleskin, the latter much worn by the quarrymen in the recent past. It is a close velvet-like fabric, not at all suggestive of the coarse bed of stone, but perhaps the earlier medieval cloth was.

Another parting quite opposite in character, being beautifully fine-grained and almost free of coarse shells, is the **Clear All**. The name is therefore descriptive. My great-grandfather preferred it over all the other beds for letter cutting.

CINDER 111: Apart from a few fairly resistant inches this massive bed readily weathers and breaks up, crumbling into 'cinders'.

BUTTON 110 and 109: Perhaps from the small flints that dot it in a line. Not useless as Arkell says, but sometimes productive of roof tile.

FEATHER 108: Hard and heavy. Not particularly shelly, so Arkell's suggestion that the name derives from the stone having shelly blemishes seems improbable. Some wag may have called it this because it rests on the Cap. There is another Feather bed on the Isle of Wight; perhaps they have something in common. In quarry parlance, very much lumped together with the Cap. A Swanage Nonconformist quarryman preacher addressed his congregation thus: 'There are people who cross the face of this earth possessed of hearts as hard as the Cap and Feather'. A sufficient number knew what he meant.

CAP 106,105,104: Of poor quality in Durlston Bay, where Clements makes these separations, but solid and durable further west. The sense seems to be that of capping other more prized beds, in this case the New Vein.

FLINT 103: The Cap, which lies immediately above, also contains silica nodules, but this bed was specifically called the Flint because of their presence. Fit only for rubble walling at best. The underside exhibits dramatic reptilian footprint casts of several species, including five-toed specimens.

NEW VEIN 101: Probably literal, for it seems not to have been exploited on any scale from as early as the other veins, though of course at outcrops such as the cliffs of Durlston Bay it would have been as easy to get at an early date as any other beds. There are inconsistencies between the two Hutchins accounts in the way the lower part was separated into White Bit, Brassy Bed, etc. The lowermost part of the Vein does not weather well, which leads to a distorted impression of how it was used in the past: decayed stones have been replaced. 'Sheriff' George Burt had a low opinion of it, for in connection with the supply of stone for Swanage Town Hall he said to my Great grandfather 'None of that New Vein mind, John.'

FIVE BED (Vye Bed): George Burt's disparaging assessment was an over-simplification. This part of the New Vein is a good, durable stone. A connection with the quarry family of Vye, which is how it is pronounced, is unlikely. The name comes surely from the tendency to split into five but, where I have quarried it, it only goes into three, the lowest parting, which is thin, being the called the 'Shall', from shell perhaps?

WHITE BIT: Not particularly white, indeed it can be blue-hearted.

BRASSY BED: Arkell's speculation about pyrite seems unlikely, but it does contain yellowish blob-like clasts. I suspect the name is descriptive of its considerable hardness, which is exacerbated by the chert nodules it often contains. Their presence points up a disparity between the two Hutchins lists, for what the first contributor calls Tombstone bed must be this one because of the presence of flints. The beds above and below lack them. His Raw Pudding must therefore equate with Bonfield's Under White bed and/or Tombstone bed and Pudding bed.

I can well understand this sort of confusion for, where I have quarried it, the Brassy bed starts at about eight inches thick at one end of a one hundred foot face and runs to nothing at the other! In effect for part of the quarry the upper and lower White Bit are separated, whilst in another they meet. I have seen a few post medieval ledger slabs made from Brassy Bed, but its concrete-like coarse composition makes it unsuitable for lettering.

The only merit the LOWER WHITEBIT, TOMBSTONE BED (pronounced Tumsun), and RAW PUDDING BED have is that they run big. Being such, ledgers have been cut from them. These have failed to last, particularly box tomb lids from around about 1800. Perhaps Raw Pudding refers to its dull character, both in terms of colour and that it doesn't ring like a decent stone. With regard to different resonances I remember Thomas Collins saying of a stone from an otherwise good bed, but spoilt by a vent: 'Thick thing zounds like a bag of nails'.

FLINT 97: Not to be confused with Flint 103. Almost of only academic interest in that it was not quarried in the eastern part of Purbeck except for backing, being full of flints. But, against the usual trend, it thickens towards the west, and at Bacon Hole, where the flint component is relatively reduced, it was quarried. It is Cap-like, both in its fine grain and flints, which are resistant, and when weathered takes on a characteristic rotund form. They feature prominently in field walls and serve to mark the outcrop over a lengthy distance from West Man to Bradle Down.

Beyond the digging of Gypsum at Durlston Bay and Worbarrow Tout, and some Marl near Kingston and probably elsewhere, the beds that continue below the New Vein do not yield any stone of use in Purbeck. However to the west, along the Ridgeway south of Dorchester, the lower Cypress beds provide rubble walling. Their usage dominates nearby settlements like Dorchester and Puddletown: notable buildings built from it include Wolfeton House and Kingston Maurward old Manor House.

This is perhaps an appropriate place to discuss what were

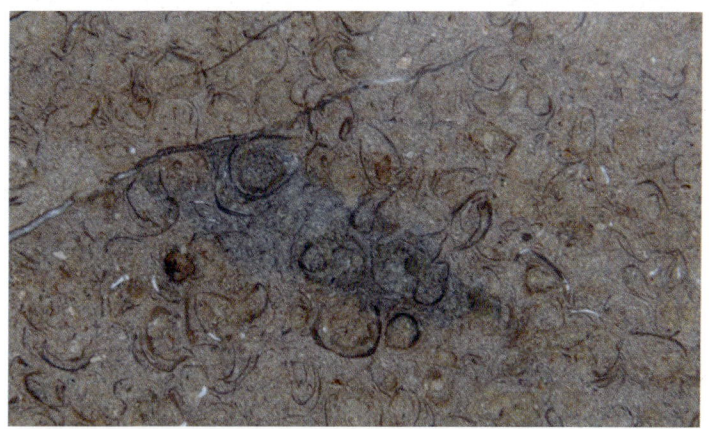

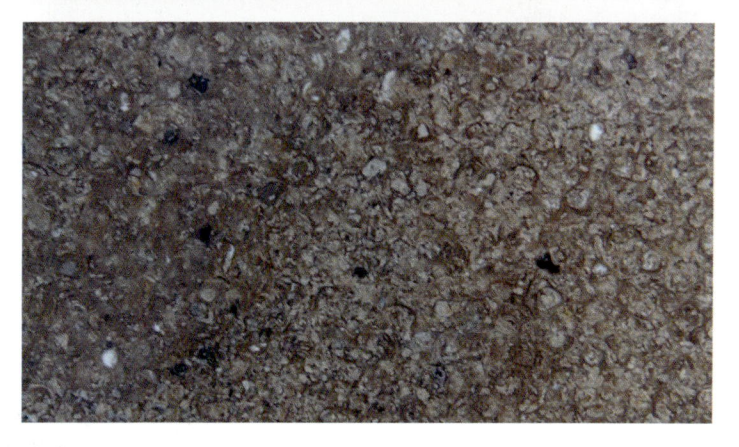

TOP Five Bed.

CENTRE White Bit, which can be blue-hearted, as this sample.

BOTTOM Brassy Bed.

called 'boils'. From a quarryman's perspective they were a nuisance, tending to spoil a more desirable flat shape. Most, perhaps all, are reptile footprint casts. That they are casts is not always obvious, as they may not be seen until the block is dislocated and turned over. Some are spaced out, others in a confused jumble, which may even suggest wallows; some merely nondescript lumps, others beautifully defined so that individual toes are evident. Although some Purbeck footprints do occur pressed into what has become hard stone, more often than not it seems the reptiles walked across shale that has remained soft to this day, but which was then followed by an input of sediment that has lithified into hard stone.

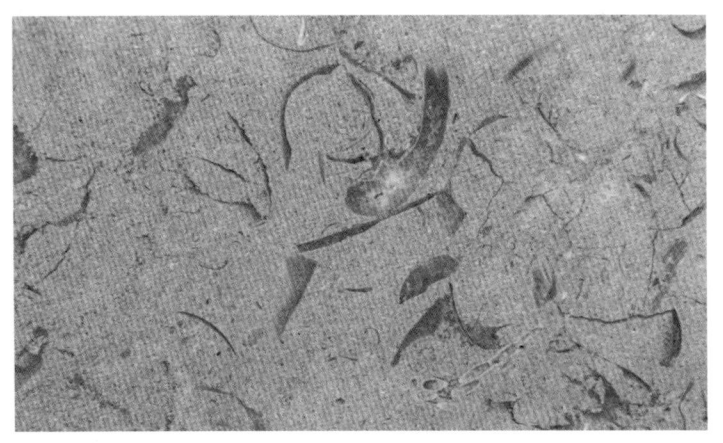

Blue Bit.

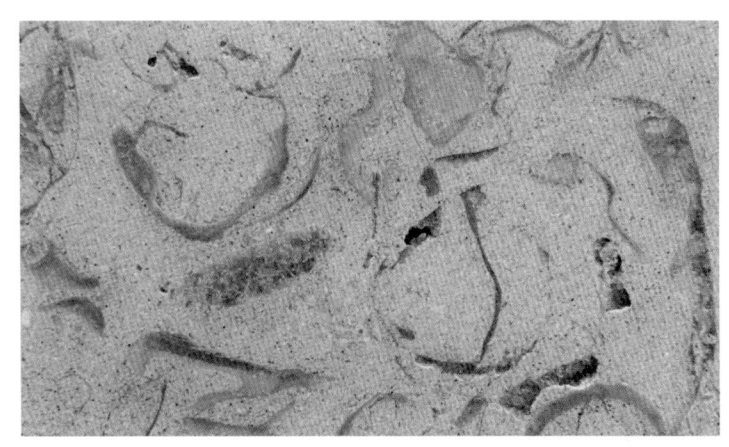

Spangle.

It seems that the depositional sequence was firstly an accumulation of shale in the shallow lagoon, followed by a drying out which allowed for animals big and small to walk over the exposed, sometimes suncracked, surface, sinking to a greater or lesser extent depending on how soggy it was. Sometimes the conditions were obviously very soft with the animals sinking well in, whilst sometimes, conversely, the mud was virtually dry. There are well defined three toed prints in the ceiling of an old Downs Vein quarry with a relief of only a few millimetres. Then came gentle inundation, where large numbers of often just a few species, snails, clams, oysters, water fleas etc swarmed; these were tolerant of the often harsh semi-saline conditions. They died and in due course turned to stone.

All three layers of Marble (plus two more poor quality beds not normally counted), each separated by shale, have casts of some sort on the underside. Most are of rather nondescript lumps but they also include very good specimens, such as that from Woodyhyde, now in the Dorset County Museum. Others occur in at least twelve more levels lower down the stratigraphical column, to the level of the New Vein. They may well occur below, as they certainly do on Portland, where a Purbeck quarryman Roger Bonfield noticed them on discarded blocks of Corbula beds whilst walking the dog. Rock in Purbeck of the same level is of no use and not quarried.

Generations of men have sworn about 'boils' spoiling their otherwise good flat blocks. Generally the boils get knocked off in dressing of the stone, but in some New Vein White Bit there is an effect, presumably caused by compression, whereby footprints within the layer remain harder than the stone around. They are therefore preserved in rather than on the stone. White Bit 'runs big'. A lot was dug around 1800 and used for tops on brick box tombs. These tops have since decayed. One at East Lulworth now has small footprint casts sticking up.

The lower Pink Bit is a layer which has yielded prints rather than casts almost wherever it is quarried; at Gallows Gore, virtually all of Acton plus Swanage quarries. It is of part of the Roach and of poor quality: trackways which have been lifted for exhibition elsewhere have tended to deteriorate quite quickly. However, the prints of the pterosaur (wingspan six metres!) given to the Dorset County Museum by my father, have happily lasted well in spite of years exposed to the weather. This tells us that it was split out from higher up in the Roach.

Paleontologists take note.

Sedimentary deformation caused by heavy animals can present problems for those cutting Thornback headstones now. Some blocks, such as the specimen in the National Trust education centre, Corfe, were trampled on the upper scurfy side. One effect is for the weight of each reptile footprint to press the darker upper sediment down. When we cut at the critical level the face of the slab had footprint sized patches. Many people choose not to commemorate their loved one with such a patchy stone. The underside of both the Inland Freestone and Downs Vein tend to have slightly distorted bedding planes. Typically the shapes on plan are shallow saucers about two feet across with a depth of about one inch. They were formed by giant reptiles, leaving no evidence of toes. Some of the old tiles on my roof are distorted in this way, which makes them difficult to lay. Clearly identifiable prints never occur neatly in a single tile but they result in awkward twisted shapes.

The cliff quarry sequence is as follows:

EARTH ROCK: The uppermost of the Cliff stone group of beds, and therefore, in a typical cliff quarry, lying just beneath the surface. It is silicified, can contain fossil wood and is of no use for masonry.

SHRIMP: I find it hard to believe it is so-called from the fossil crustaceans which do occur, having dug hundreds of tons of the stuff without seeing one! It is full of fractures and highly frost-vulnerable, therefore of no use for masonry.

BLUE BIT: Called by the geologists 'titanites', from the big ammonites that occur at this level. At St. Aldhelm's Quarry it cleaves into four. None are particularly blue by the wider Purbeck standard, but within a Cliff stone context, this bed, particularly the upper two bits and particularly where dug from the deep, is the darkest.

SPANGLE: Surely named from the glitter of the fossils, particularly trigonia, the aragonite shells which have been replaced by crystalline calcite.

PON or POND FREESTONE: The uppermost of two Freestone layers in the cliff. The name derives from 'Upon'. Some blocks are 'callusy'. This is a hard brown outer surface, not an accretion, but a change of the actual stone. It is most marked in the Pond Freestone at Haysoms, St. Aldhelm's Quarry, where it can penetrate to a depth of a few inches. Callus is often associated with the joint being clay-filled, but clay can

Pon Freestone.

be present without any accompanying callus. It is perhaps caused by surface impregnation of the block by silica from the clay. This is apparently unknown at other cliff quarries where the joints are clean of clay. Similar darkening and hardening sometimes occurs at Portland, usually associated with a 'gully', a Portland quarryman's term for an enlarged joint in the general mass of rock, which would also suggest a periglacial effect. There is no parallel in inland quarries, except that the stone near a fault may change in nature throughout, often being harder than normal or 'glassy''.

FLINT: General term for silica nodules in the Cliff stone beds and in some of the lower Purbeck beds. The Flint proper is the layer beneath the Pon Freestone. This solid layer, more correctly called 'Chert', is characteristic of the western quarries; it is much reduced at Tilly Whim.

LISTY BED: Calcite veins in Purbeck are sometimes called 'lists'. Arkell quotes William Jeremiah Bower (known as 'Billy Winspit' and referred to as such throughout this book) as saying that it 'breaks easily', which is odd. Billy liked it for carving his cats, as it is fine grained and soft. Arkell adds its original Old English meaning – streaky, strip, band. Though lists are common in many limestones, including virtually all the Purbeck beds, I am not aware that the term is applied elsewhere in England, such as Bath, where similar veins also occur.

However, in Purbeck lists are common. They can be conspicuous but strong, conversely quite difficult to see but weak. In the Pond freestone at the Head, where they run vertically north and south, weakness can be indicated by a yellow or clay presence. In inland freestone from Acton Common, what is often an open vent in the pinholey main part of the block becomes a tight list in the hard bottom part. They are rare in Marble from Lynch but common in Marble at Peveril, where they are sometimes up to one inch or more wide. Sometimes even these wide lists constitute virtually no weakness at all.

In general, Cliff stone lists differ from typical Portland snail creeps by being straighter and much more sharply defined. However some Portland examples are worryingly similar. Some are pure white (also called glares) some grey; two or more sorts may occur in the same block, sometimes crossing. Such crossings can exhibit lateral displacement which tells of different tectonic episodes.

BROWN CAP, HOUSE CAP, UNDERPICKING CAP: These lie above the Bottom or Under Freestone, and thereby cap it. In driving a cliff quarry underground the initial penetration is effected by cutting or blasting away the Underpicking; this leaves the bed above serving as a ceiling, hence HOUSE.

UNDER FREESTONE: Fine grained and with good working properties. It is probably safe to say that cliff Under Freestone was forming at the same time as Portland base bed, cliff Pond Freestone as Portland Whitbed, and Spangle as Portland Roach.

About another eighty feet of limestone continues below, but it is full of Chert, therefore not much use for masonry. A distinctive layer is called the PUFFIN or PRICKLE BED. Along much of the cliff it is about half way up and the birds laid their eggs in its deep recesses. At Dancing Ledge it slopes to water level and the tracks and swimming pool are cut into it. Layers below it are sometimes called Limpet Rock. The quarrymen used these lower beds to cut in crane post holes.

CLIFF & LAND FORM

The natural contours of the limestone ridge are smooth and flowing. The generally flat terrain of the plateau extending from Chapmans Pool to Durlston around about the 350-400 foot contours suggests a marine peneplain. There are few clues to the wild dipping and faulting of the rock beneath the grass, but quarrying south of Swanage and southwest of Acton reveals dramatic structures. Whilst the Portland rock mass exposed in the sea cliffs has faulted, the more plastic overlying Purbeck beds have both faulted and crumpled, Stair Hole at Lulworth exhibiting a celebrated example. The biggest straightforward fault in the Portland beds is at Dancing Ledge. Here the Puffin bed slopes eastwards down to below sea level, only to reappear 50 feet or so above water level east of the fault, a throw of 80 feet or more. But there is no commensurate bump in the fields inland above it. Nor is there such a bump at the similar faults at West Hedbury or the western end of the Ragged Rocks. Each should have a 'hillock', which has, it seems, been planed off. At Belle Vue the Cinder outcrop is one full field in from the top of the Ware, whilst in the next field west, at Verney, the Rag reaches right out to the brow. This must reflect a throw of 30 feet or more, but again the flat fields give no clues. These faults throw the same way, up on the east side, but others go the other way. Michael's Cove, west of Seacombe, and Crab Hole both throw down to the east and produce rather similar caves. Buttery Corner, also down on the east side, exposes perhaps the same one that cuts across Sheepsleights quarry and which has been such a nuisance to its operation.

If the marine peneplanation idea is correct, then perhaps we should expect evidence of the faults in landforms to the north of the planed area. Is this what we see in forms such as Steps Hill (the Dancing Ledge fault perhaps) and Oak Ridge?

The smooth scarp along the Wares is interrupted by both quarrying and natural land slips. In Belle Vue and westwards, sizable blocks of land have slipped seawards so that there are

THE STONE / 19

outcrops of both Rag and Cinder well over 100 feet below where they 'belong'. One is particularly puzzling, in that the slipped block contains Rag, revealed on its seaward edge, but this bed is absent from the hill above, from where the mass probably originated!

Where the Cinder bed outcrops off the plateau, which means an almost straight line from Dunshay to Worbarrow, it and the beds around it are hard enough to produce a pronounced ridge. A lesser bump, also running east-west, in places defines the Burr outcrop. Swanage High Street at the British Legion is running along this ridge. Westwards it is well marked at Woodyhyde Rookery copse and Pole coppice, Blackmanston.

This bump marking the Burr outcrop under Swanage High Street, at Woodyhyde and West Lynch certainly, and probably along other parts of the outcrop, indicates a structure similar to that exposed in this stone at Peveril Point, the northern limit of the syncline producing the ridge. Secondary faulting of the beds revealed by the sea between Peveril Point and Buck shore is bafflingly complex. Whilst Worbarrow is straightforward enough, the same complexity is probably true for miles of the Burr outcrop.

Durlston Bay is bisected by a fault throwing down on its southern side 90 feet or more. Quarrying reveals that it runs westwards to California Farm (Swanage). All this complexity tells of enormous forces that have broken the rocks. How tortured Purbeck contrasts with the positive serenity of Portland! The result is much more fracturing and generally small blocks, particularly, ironically, of the best quality beds that, because of their 'crisp' nature, have fractured the most. How long ago was it that man first grasped the sequence of rocks?

Thomas Webster remarked about Durlston Bay in 1816: 'the mason recognises among the uppermost beds on the opposite side of the bay, those which are the lowest on this side. I obtained from the quarrymen the thickness of the several beds and the names by which they distinguished them from each other. The quarrymen can point out, in the quarries to the west, as for instance in the one at Worbarrow, beds which they consider to correspond to the veins which they work at Swanwich'. These were unlettered men, but with a stratigraphical grasp years before scientific geology arose.[12] And what knowledge they had! How, for example, did the Squibbs know of the joint in which they sank their shaft close by the Worth Road?

Short, steep, mostly dry combes run inland at Hawcombe, Seacombe, Winspit, Pier Bottom, Chapmans Pool and Encombe. The dip at White Ware is perhaps another incipient combe. Where quarries have been cut in the down slope side, as at Pier Bottom and Sheepsleights, the joints are found to be filled with a periglacial clay the other cliff quarries lack. It seems these clays have entered by lateral movement from the valley scarps. From a quarryman's point of view, to quote my father, 'they are an infernal nuisance'.

Frost shattered scree deposits from the Portland beds above drape the lower Kimmeridge clay slopes in Chapmans Pool where in the 19th century, and probably earlier, this material was used as a source of road metal: at Pier Bottom too. In Hawcombe, Winspit and Seacombe the valley floor has been built up by this secondary material. In Seacombe it is revealed in the cliff immediately west of the way down to the water. This broken rock, consisting of both Cliff stone as well as Purbeck beds that have therefore come some distance, is not the product of quarrying, though at Seacombe quarry waste was tipped over it. Where this went over the cliff the sea has since carried it away, but a few yards inland dumping has altered the configuration of the natural braided defile cut into the valley floor that extends one hundred yards or more landwards. At Winspit quarrying has confused the natural form of the lake, as the stream was called, even more. But it is somewhat like Seacombe with a periglacial deposit containing lower Purbeck beds such as Vie Bed choking the western side of the defile. It is exposed in steep paths descending to the shore. At Hawcombe a deep hollow way has been cut vertically through it, telling of considerable traffic.

For much of the southern cliffs the sea has yet to cut back to the full height of the Portland beds, which would suggest that this scarp did not extend far beyond where we see cliffs now. There is a telling section exposed about 30 yards east from the extreme west end of Dancing Ledge quarry. Best viewed from the west, it reveals that the Portland beds have been cut to a slope. The upper foot or so is severely frost shattered, with the fractures running parallel to the slope. On top lie about ten feet of periglacial clays containing stones which include bits of Vie Bed and biggish lumps of Rag. Since writing this, a particularly big piece has tumbled to the quarry floor, where it remains in two pieces. One wonders just how many freeze-thaw cycles they endured, and which Ice Age it was that brought them to their present position. They bear testimony to what a lasting stone coarse-textured Rag can be. What is odd is that the Rag does not outcrop where the gravitational logic of the current topography demands these stones originated, but it does a short distance eastwards. Also in that direction, at the extreme eastern end of the quarry, the same periglacial mix is exposed, but here it is resting higher up, on the lowermost Purbeck beds, and it only contains small stones, without the big lumps of Rag.

At Cunner Cove and immediately west, the beds dip relatively low to sea level. There the Puffin bed, for much of the cliff about half way up, is below the water line and the water is deep. In heavy weather spray is thrown up to the level of the overlying Purbeck beds, which it has worked away, producing a cliff profile much like that of the Fossil Forest. Conversely, where the rock rises relative to sea level and the Portland Sand reaches the surface, fallen blocks accumulate. The Ragged Rocks, Reform to White Ware, Sutton Rock to Buttery Corner, are like this.

Further evidence of the youth of this cliff is perhaps provided by sloping scoop structures in the cliff face which would seem to be periglacial. Three at West Winspit and a single at West Seacombe have been cut into by the sea at the base and by quarrying at the top, and are not too obvious. But west of the Ragged Rocks there are several, including the boldest, the easternmost, called variously Halfmoon or Pulpit, at a part of the cliff sometimes called Cattle Troughs, for obvious reasons. Were they formed by seepages such as continue to supply the troughs, saturating the rock and thereby making it more

The Simplified Solid Geology of the Isle of Purbeck

Legend:
- BRACKLESHAM GROUP
- THAMES GROUP
- CHALK GROUP
- SELBORNE GROUP
- LOWER GREENSAND GROUP
- WEALDEN GROUP
- PURBECK GROUP
  - DURLSTON FORMATION
    - PEVERIL POINT MEMBER
    - STAIR HOLE MEMBER
  - LULWORTH FORMATION
    - WORBARROW TOUT MEMBER
    - RIDGEWAY MEMBER
    - MUPE MEMBER

British Geological Survey © UKRI. All rights reserved
Contains Ordnance Survey data © Crown copyright and database right 2020

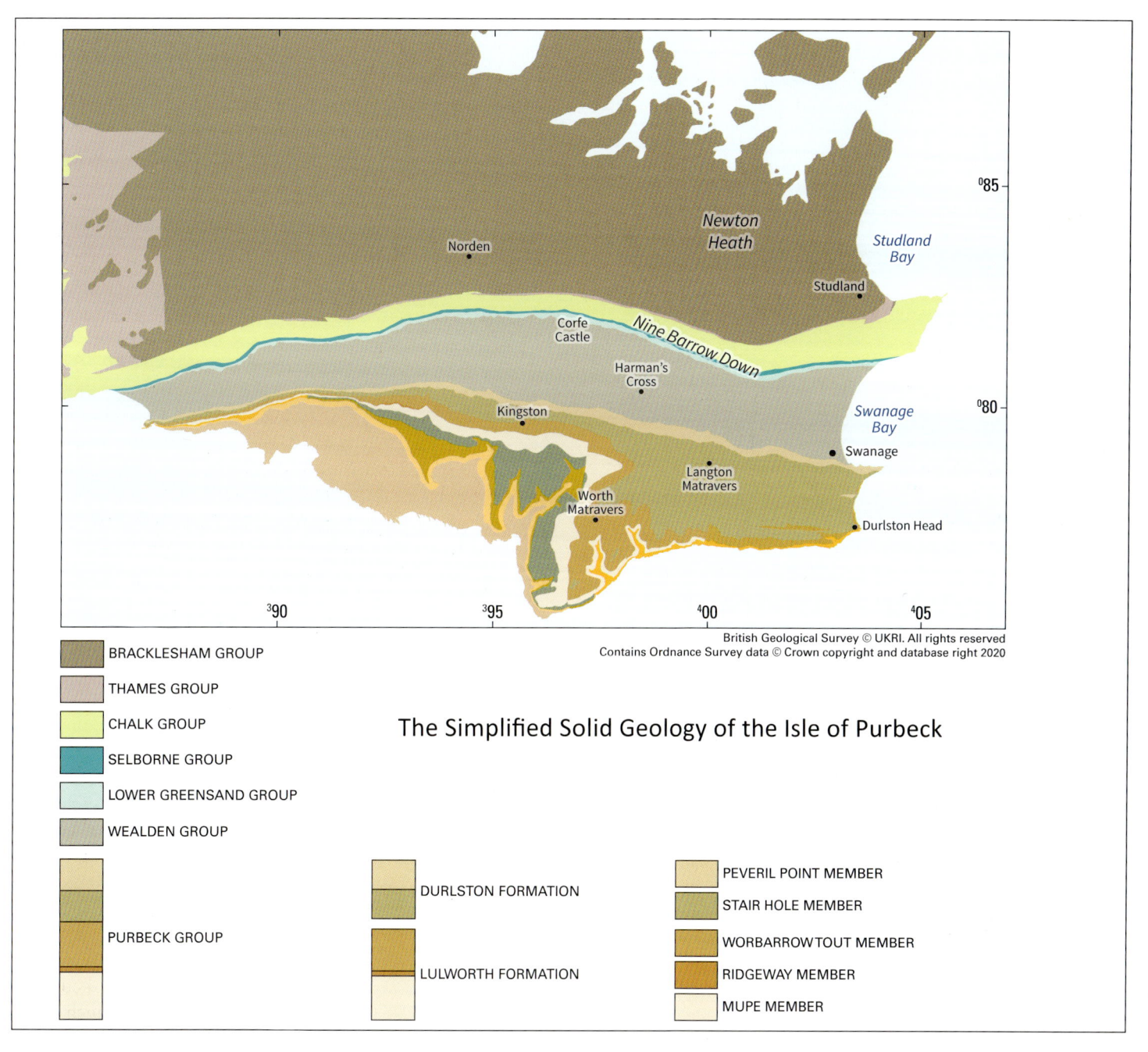

vulnerable to frost action in the hollows? Once the hollow had begun to form the effect would have accelerated, the rock in the bottom fracturing more as the divides between the hollows became better drained until virtually frost-immune.

Happily the cliff quarries remain much as when the men left off work, except that a lot of manageable stuff has been thrown into the sea by idle boys. Inland and Marble quarries are very different, in that there the veins of good stone are relatively thin and separated by many layers of worthless rock, much of it clay. This was dug off and moved just far enough so as not to get in the way. Over time the resulting holes have tended to fill and the waste piles flatten off so that exposures of the workable stone are generally lost. Only Rag and Cinder are at all commonly still visible in situ, the good beds sought beneath them since obscured by slippage. The Marble is revealed in situ in two or three hollow trackways, but not in any quarry face, though the old workings extend for miles. Hollows and mounds are still abundant, marking almost every field productive of stone across the island, but levelling out, and thereby loss of this sort of evidence continues. This has happened from at least as early as the 18th century. Deliberate reinstatement of workings back to a flat condition better for agriculture has gone on since then, on some estates more than others. As with the unequal survival rate of quarry-related documents and the distorted impression of the past that brings, the evidence left in the modern landscape is similarly deceptive when seeking to understand what has happened.

Undergrounds are obviously the most problematic. Nearly all the hundreds of shafts that once existed have been filled in. Many of the loading bankers and scar banks most such quarries developed have also gone, and almost all the sheds. There is often little on the surface left to see. Exploitation of old scar banks was considerable, with tons being taken for projects such as the ferry and valley roads and wartime airfields.

THE STONE / 21

Even after the ready availability of crushed rock, some banks were still being dug as late as the 1950s for, amongst other things, the construction of Swanage Middle School. In a few instances, if close to a road, quarriers got rid of their waste scars by tipping them along it. The highest part of the Langton to Worth road has been raised by Joby Ball Bowers' quarry, latterly the location of the Observer Corps post, in this way. More impressively, a lengthy section of Priests Way at Verney is now fifteen feet or more above the surrounding fields! This is telling evidence of how much stone was worked close by.

Some founders of undergrounds have produced hollows, but these are not very obvious. What is certain is that there are hundreds of square yards of hidden workings, some on one level only, many on two and even a few on three, all now cut off from the surface. Some were driven under the highways. The Langton to Worth road, for example, is undermined by a series of different quarries for most of the stretch from about Court Pound Cottage to the Observer Corps post. A few went under or got close to houses. Almost the only one undermined in Langton is the southernmost house in Arundel Terrace. Acton is different. The occupants of the Shepherd's House, south of Acton, were upset by Sammy Rabbit Bower's close approach. They could hear him underpicking. Other Acton houses have workings beneath them, but they probably pre-date for the most part the cottages in question. Jack Harris's rebuilt house ('Weathertop') must be particularly perilous. It may well stand on a small area of solid ground, but underground workings on two levels extend all around. Trink Bower got close to South Barn. Tommy Bonfield said they could hear the clatter of carthorse hooves on the stone pitched yard overhead. The southward spread of Swanage has taken it over a lot of quarries. A house collapse at the top of Seymer Road was caused by the sudden shift of stuff blocking an old shaft. Sir George Burt is said to have built the Cottage Hospital on solid ground, which it probably is, but buildings to the north exhibit distress whilst a recent extension to the south revealed our family's quarry. Tommy Bonfield said it was possible to get a long way north under Greasehead west of Swanage from his quarry at Verney and that in winter a lot of those workings flooded; an enormous weight of water!

A few pits were dug for material other than stone on or close to the stone outcrop. What was called 'Marrow', surely from Marl (fertiliser) Pit in the plantation west of Kingston, would seem to be one. I guess it yielded beds that lie beneath the building stones and that their outcropping is indicated by holes some yards to the north of it.

A perambulation south to north from about the Anvil Point Lighthouse to the Swanage stream shows Purbeck at perhaps its most complicated, for this route crosses the east to west fault, productive of Sunnydale. It is a fault that causes almost the full Middle Purbeck sequence to be repeated twice.

Leaving the cliff beds behind, the slope is smooth, because these lower beds are not productive of any useful stone. This is different in the west; along the ridgeway between Weymouth and Dorchester some develop into useful building stones. Near the top of the Ware the lowermost workings mark the New Vein and Cap and Feather outcrop. These beds would have been easy to find but, as they disappear into the hill, difficult to pursue other than by underground methods. Such a quarry running in almost on the level has been reopened close by the Lighthouse road. A capstan has been set up at its entrance, necessary because the beds are dipping. Where flat, it would have been possible to work without one. About ten feet above, the Downs Vein similarly runs out, ten feet above that the Freestone, a few feet above that the Rag. The outcropping of these, confused by dips and faults, more or less coincides with the top of the slope, and much has been quarried. One field northwards, on the highest part of the ridge, thickets on the old Townsend Estate obscure another line of workings. Rag is exposed. But it is virtually certain that they dug deeper to the Grub *et al* below. The Rag here tends to split flat; pavings broken in manufacture occur in the walls. To a degree it was worthwhile to quarry on its own account. These old holes seem not to extend eastwards across old Swanage South Field, but this could tell of subsequent restoration rather than less digging. Similarly, evidence of Laining Vein workings running east-west across the southern flank of Sunnydale is stronger on Townsend than on Swanage South Field, but I suspect it was worked to the same degree. The northward dip of the rocks is steeper than the fall of the ground, so logically Burr should come next, but before this can happen the ground begins to rise.

However, in Durlston Bay, where the throw of the fault is greatest, it is revealed. Hundreds of tons have recently slipped down to the shore, carrying away the coast path. This coastal exposure shows the fault not to be a single tear. Whatever its structure, further inland the quarry evidence is of no useful stone occurring near the surface along the northern flank of the valley it creates. However at the northern crest quarry remains are abundant. They stretch more or less unbroken from about the southwest corner of Peveril Downs westwards just to the north of Scar Bank House on towards Mutton Hole, latterly the rubbish tip. At this level the three manors of Sentry, Eightholds and Swanage have all been built up, but Townsend has almost escaped development and the old tumbled workings can be followed well down to the north. As with the south side of Sunnydale, the rate of dip is rather steeper than the land surface, so going downhill the whole succession repeats again. Laining Vein shoals out at about the level of the Cottage Hospital, Burr at the High Street, Marble at the mill pond. Unlike the soft good natured stone of further west, this Swanage Burr can be blue and hard. This is why John Mowlem, who ran into it in his improvements to the High Street, confusingly calls it Marble Rag.[13.]

A similar walk south to north across Langton Matravers produces the same sequence, but only once. Undulations that interrupt the smooth slope down to the cliffs are not the product of quarrying, but are natural landslips. As above the Lighthouse on Anvil Point, quarry evidence only begins at the top of the Ware. At the south end of Queensground the New Vein outcrops right on the brow, allowing for some ridding there. But eastwards it dips down before the big Dancing Ledge fault brings it back up. So, as with Swanage, within quite short distances, beds ranging from as low as New Vein to as high as Rag shoal out on the brow. In contrast to further inland, the Downs Vein is so thin as to be not worth going for. This is clear above east of Hedbury, where the field is flat where it outcrops. If it were thicker the scene would be very different. Gentle undulations west of Spyway farm tell of shallow Laining Vein workings. It continues not far beneath the surface to north of the church. Marble Quarr is actually an exposure of Burr whilst the Marble proper outcrop is evidenced by extensive holes and piles now growing old oaks close by the stream in Talbot's Wood. The people of Langton get buried in the almost stone free gap between Marble and Burr, but if the Crack Lane cemetery is extended northwards or southwards the grave digging will get difficult.

A few fields further west the section is different. Around Acton the beds push up relative to the surface so that the Laining Vein is generally gone. That once it was more extensive is indicated by isolated patches left in hollow saucers or faults, when all around has been planed off. This elevation is most marked at Acton field where not only has the Laining Vein run out, but also the underlying Rag and Freestone. This evidence begs the question of just how much rock was eroded before Purbeck took on its present shape. At Belle Vue we found isolated remnants of Rag left in funnels formed by faults fully 200 yards away from the main outcrop. Would that Purbeck could be stripped bare to just one layer. It would be fantastic in more ways than one!

West of Gallows Gore the outcrop narrows such that the lower and middle building stone veins become restricted to about the width of one field. Their presence is evidenced by an ever narrowing band of workings, extending to Tyneham. In places lower down the slope, another converging line of hollows and bumps marks the Burr and Marble. Possible quarry evidence continues west of Tyneham, but the acute dip has also produced natural slippages which can be confused with human activities. Indeed both are probably mixed, for where a slip exposes a useful layer people would have taken advantage of it.

The amount dug on this narrow outcrop to the west was relatively small, perhaps in places little more than to meet immediate needs such as Worbarrow and Kimmeridge vernacular buildings, but the amount of Burr quarried near Blackmanston was surely more than that required for Steeple church alone. I suspect these are medieval quarries and that they provided stone sent further afield. Similarly the scale of working between Kingston and Gallows Gore must tell of a wider trade, involving other beds, Downs Vein in particular. Returning to the eastern half of Purbeck, Vic Bower remarked: 'There ain't a vield up southard the old hands ain't bin in.' He was not far wrong, but few have been fully worked out; only systematic mechanical surface working, of recent origin, is achieving that.

One legacy from all of this has been the creation of different soils. Many quarries are overlain by heavy clays, but once underground working gets going only stone is brought to the surface, and banks of waste scars accumulate from the dressing of it. In time those can vegetate over but remain lime rich and free draining, so that soils of widely different degrees of acidity arise within a few feet of one another. This outcome is reflected in the occurrence of different plant assemblies. The

Langton Matravers, North Street. Example of weathered 'soapy' Inland Freestone.

Marble working related mounds are different. All are of heavy clay. Where the anemones that like drained soils flourish in Langton West Wood marks the Burr outcrop rather than scar banks.

WEATHERING

All limestones are soluble and slowly dissolve away. When at the surface, the really tough Carboniferous beds become gradually etched by this dissolution, giving rise to celebrated natural pavements such as the Burren, in Ireland. Whilst there is a wide range, an annual loss of 0.01mm is about average.[14] Although there is no equivalent of the Burren in Purbeck, weathering processes of the more resistant beds taking place below the surface can produce similar shapes. Purbeck limestone is much more variable in terms of its durability. Inch by inch, each bed differs in composition, hardness, porosity, etc., which results in differing weathering properties. Whilst further change occurs in quite short linear distances, so a particular layer can vary markedly across just one field. An example is the Edmunds quarry in Burngate. A joint (fault) forced them to sink a second shaft, so the quarry was effectively in two halves. In one the Freestone was pinholey (hence durable), in the other 'soapy', which made it attractive from a working point of view but not so good in terms of lasting well. Langton freestone of this 'soapy' sort that has not weathered well can be seen in some of the mullions at Garfield House, Langton. At the other end of the spectrum the most open or 'pinholey' sort could be seen in 'Everest', Swanage, quarried by Alphaeus Brownsea Bower's family. Cap ranges from being a poor quality mudstone in one area, such as Gallows Gore, to a hard, durable stone in another

Gallows Gore, Worth Matravers, 1992. Downs Vein underground workings revealed in the course of opencast quarrying. The timbers are not part of the original quarry. They support the Leper bed; note very cramped working space. The shovel leans against unquarried Downs Vein.

Gallows Gore, Worth Matravers, 1992. Downs Vein underground. Undug stone at right, excavated area at left. Note Leper ceiling with few joints.

(Herston). When Harold Bonfield reopened Belle Vue after years of dormancy, his father observed: 'Tiz good Blue Cap, not white': an interesting quarryman's assessment. However, durability cannot be reliably assessed from appearances. The Leper and the One Bed provide a good example. They lie almost one on top of the other, but whilst the Leper endures, the One Bed, which looks similar, does not. In most Downs Vein underground workings it lies close to or actually forms the ceiling, so such quarries never produced any; however, opencast workings do. It is tempting to sell, but it rots.

The cracks between blocks are joints, but in addition, where the strata jump or fold is 'a joint'. A quarryman saying 'I've hit a joint' is talking about the latter. Often the stone becomes harder or 'out of nature', near a joint, so a man gets warning of it. Folding joints are a type of fault where the beds fold down into crease-like structures containing a lot of clay and the stone is very broken. Joe Bonfield reckoned that the big folding joints generally ran on the same line as from St. Aldhelm's Head to Old Harry, lesser joints from Tilly Whim to Corfe. They can vary between a dislocation of just a few inches to many feet. A few men did succeed in crossing them underground if the joint was a small one, but any throw of more than a few feet was an impossible obstacle.

Returning to ordinary joints between the blocks: they can be mere fractures, such as occur in the Leper around Gallows Gore, and which allow for it to serve as a secure ceiling, even though the individual stones are generally small. Alternatively they can be as much as four inches wide, such as are found in the Cap at Belle Vue, and which would have made it virtually impossible to keep up as a ceiling. Generally such wide joints are filled with clay which, from a quarryman's point of view, is simply a nuisance. At St. Aldhelm's quarry they are to a degree clay-filled, but some contain deposits of 'congealed water', that is, flow stone or stalactite. This tells of different epochs. After the initial fracturing, the movement of ground water served variously to widen the cracks or to seal them up with calcite before the Quaternary clay arrived. Each bed was fractured into blocks to a greater or lesser extent according to the stresses imposed, and its degree of 'competence'. This geological term does not coincide with what a quarryman would identify as the best rock. 'Competent' does not mean more durable, but does mean more resistant to fracturing. In effect, some of the best, most lasting layers are the most broken up, though the extent varies a lot in short distances. It can be difficult to see the logic: some relatively flat patches can prove to be very broken, whilst others, steeply sloping and on the face of it more stressed, are productive of bigger blocks. This can be important in terms of the value of the stone and the viability of any particular quarry.

Fracturing of the Cliff Beds tells of their 'crisp' nature. At West Winspit the Pond Freestone exhibits calcite surfaces which are great bulbs of percussion, the full height of the Bed. We find similar joints at St. Aldhelm's quarry. Generally a particularly large flint lies at the focal point. These shapes have been mistaken for fossil trees.

Similar variations within a single layer suggest some sort of repeating cycle. It is true of Inland Freestone, Roach and Downs Vein, that the best durable part is the top, whilst the lower part merges into 'rotten' stone that tends to decay and should be discarded. In the case of the Freestone, it is the 'Dun Cow', in the case of the Roach, the Pink Bit, particularly in the areas where it is 'papery'. It seems that, in all three and other cases, as sedimentation began a considerable percentage of clay was accumulating along with the shell debris, but this clay component diminished, leaving a pure shell input which results in a good stone. The Purbeck lagoon environment was marginal marine and given to frequent change, which sometimes meant high salinity levels. Somewhat similar conditions occur adjacent to the Persian Gulf now. The resultant rocks were usually built up from just a few species of clams, oysters or snails. Individual beds therefore often consist of just one or two species that could stand a particular harsh condition.

Perhaps surprisingly, coarse textured Burr, Rag, and the 'pinholey' or open textured part of Langton Freestone are durable and frost resistant even in the most rigorous situations. On the face of it, one would perhaps expect these open textured stones to be readily attacked by frost, and the more fine grained beds not, but it does not work like that. Some Inland Freestone is close-grained and lacking in open pores, and this can be frost damaged in high saturation situations. Swanage Freestone is generally like this. Witchampton church (1832) is of this Swanage sort and whilst the ashlar remains very good, the projecting moulded plinth, which has served to hold rather than quickly shed water, is frost damaged. Voussoirs in St. Julian's Bridge, Wimborne, dating from the widening of 1844 and recently replaced, were also of this sort of fine-grained Inland Freestone, shattered to disintegration.

Such bridges are a tough environment, for they tend to hold a water mass which seeps out through the exposed stones, saturating them where the frost can strike. Kerbs and external paving similarly have a hard time, frequently soaked, then suddenly exposed to sub-zero temperatures, as the typical rain-laden warm front of a winter depression moves across Britain, quickly followed by cold sector frosts. Paradoxically, it is an easier life high in an exposed but free-draining wall, rather than close to sheltering but sodden ground. Frost can act selectively within the same layer. Pinholey Inland Freestone is resistant, but the top couple of inches and the dense, hard bottom part, which is the nature of most Freestone dug in the Acton area, though less absorbent, can be damaged.

The all-important factor is the degree of saturation, which is at its highest when the stone is first dug. In this 'green' condition it is also the most easy to work. This advantage tends to be lost now. Modern machines dig a quantity of block which can be left for months before being used. In the past it was different; stones were generally dug, cut up and worked straight away. Some indication of how they get more difficult to work if left and how quickly this happens, is provided by Thomas Bonfield, who told me that 'Hantney' Haysom would cover up a big Cap with wet sacking overnight when they pulled one out late in the day in high summer. Keeping it wet made it that bit easier to cut next morning. Brian Bugler has recently cut wedge pits in freshly dug Marble, and found it surprisingly easy compared with working the seasoned block he is more used to.

Presumably the sap held within the pores of freshly dug blocks is charged with calcium which crystallises out as the water evaporates away; this crystal growth serves to harden the stone. This process also involves movement and therefore unequal deposition of the hardening mineral. There may actually be more than one benefit in working the stone whilst still green! Simply wetting alone can be a factor, for modern laboratory flextural strength tests produce different results between the same stone wet and dry. Changing working properties become very apparent when stone is frozen. During hard freeze-ups, which prevented sawing, we would spend the time dressing small offcuts into dubbers. Pond Freestone would become 'quick' or 'glassy' so that a pitcher tool blow would 'carry' much more than in the same, but unfrozen stone. For the real cognoscenti a pitched faced dubber worked under such freezing conditions is discernible.

It is of course good practice to fix sedimentary stones 'in bed', that is, as they lie in the ground. With inland Purbeck ashlar the usual result is some etching of the bedding planes over time, visible in the surface of the wall. This is a useful clue when differentiating it from Cliff Stone or Portland. By contrast, when set face-bedded a weak layer may slough off, which is not only unsightly but weakening. However, good stone tends to weather well whichever way it is set. Face-bedded ashlar which is performing well occurs in Durnford Manor (18th century Langton Freestone) as well as much of the medieval Burr in Corfe Castle. Identifying bed direction in homogeneous beds can be difficult. When Bob Harris was supplying the Worth 1950s coastguard houses, an inspector examined the lintels with a magnifying glass to make sure he was putting them in the right way up![15]

Block quarried too late in the summer to allow sufficient time for the drying out of the sap before winter's onset, can be affected. Fine cracks parallel to the bedding develop, sometimes within the heart of the stone. The cracks do not extend to the outside, presumably indicating lesser levels of saturation towards the exterior as the block dries. Such internal damage is not apparent before the block is cut open.

The amount of time required to season stone safely depends

Wareham, the Manor House. Enriched Cliff stone front door lintel.

on weather conditions and the size of block. It has been my dismaying experience to quarry large Langton Freestone blocks at the optimum time of May, followed by a whole summer of drying, only to have them damaged by severe frost the next December. Smaller stuff was quite unaffected, but the really big stones suffered to the exceptional degree of the cracks becoming visible. This happened when the temperature dropped to minus 9C after a relatively wet summer. If the summer had been average or dry, these blocks may have escaped unscathed.

In the 1930s Alfred Norman was supplying Thornback block for the depot from what had been Alfred Benfield's quarry on the Kingston turnpike road. Winter weather kept them underground. 'We had the lane full up with Thornbacks out to mouth,' his grandson Jack told me. This added to the work in that it meant more handling. April arrived and they started to pull the stone out, working the horse hard for days drawing the stones up the slide, tipping them on edge off the cart out onto the loading banker ready for the wagon from Swanage. 'The wind come east, a hard frost set in and spoiled the lot. We walked up from Swanage as usual in the morn. Grandfather tried one or two with a punch, found the damage, was so upset he went on home.' What a blow to those industrious men.

A typical, good Thornback of the Acton district is softer at the bottom, becoming harder towards the scurfy top. If insufficiently dried out, hard frost will cause fine cracks to develop in the upper, harder part, not the soft. Once dried out, Thornback is frost immune. There are miles of lasting kerb which prove it, and this resilience, once dried, may be true of other beds. Typical Roach is not one of them. It requires a low saturation environment in order to endure well, demonstrated by such stones as the Chaffey (1822) headstone in Kimmeridge churchyard, which is frost shattered at saturated ground level. This is like many street kerbs, now laminated (split) though solid when worked. The admixture of good solid kerbs cheek by jowl with badly laminated ones can tell of the same man 'bumping' kerb from the two beds, Roach and Thornback, at the same quarry but with different long term results. The question remains whether any frost-vulnerable beds, once dried, become immune in any conditions. What is almost certain is that some, perhaps all, beds can be well seasoned but then be damaged by frost if it is severe enough, and they are saturated enough.

Inland Purbeck beds can be frost split but still to a degree 'function'. However, the effect on the cliff beds is more disastrous in that frost fractures may run parallel to the surface rather than the bed, which can result in spalling in any direction. East Winspit quarry face displays frost scaling down to the Pond Freestone level, but not below. The damaged beds include the massive shell-packed oyster layer, which occupies the level of the Blue Bit. A splendid block of this, with a row of pits cut in it, lies perched on a heap of waste. The rock in the cliff is badly affected, but this block, lying loose, is undamaged – clear evidence of a stone lasting well in a loose, well drained, situation, but being destroyed when part of a wet mass. To the west at St. Aldhelm's Head this same bed splits and has provided ledgers. Used inside they are fine, but not if fixed on saturated ground outside. One of probably 18th century date outside St. Mary's, Wareham, is shattered into fragments. The Winspit quarry cliff face, from the Pond Freestone down to the floor, shows no evidence of frost damage, but some of these beds, when subjected to sufficiently high levels of saturation, do fail, which monumental masons using Winspit stone learned to their cost. However, it is an oversimplification to conclude that it is no good on the ground. The dressings and external paving supplied for Studland Church Hall are fine, in spite of the paving being laid in the open. I suspect that what is the most vulnerable is the Listy bed, produced from occasional founders. This lies immediately below the flint, is fine-grained and workable. Though it may ring like a bell when fresh dug, it has a relatively low frost resistance. Others have noticed the inferiority of stone from beneath a flint layer at Portland in contrast to the bed above the flint. Cliff stone shortcomings have prompted criticism. My grandfather's succinct assessment was that it was 'alright up off the ground'.

Was this in the mind of the builder of Wareham Manor House (1712) who has set his Cliff stone façade on a Burr plinth with good results? Flint, or more accurately Chert, in Cliff stone can be made to burst by frost. Is it that water movement is impeded by the hard barrier within the stone and saturation increases to a critical level? This is certainly not true of Cap and its flints. The contrast between the effect of frost on the fissile inland beds and Cliff stone is worth emphasising. In the former it has helped to produce thin roof tile, whilst in the latter, awkward slivery shapes of not much use. This can be seen at the west end of Chilmark Quarr, where this weathering from the Quaternary period is evident.

Other processes seem to be at work in the more rapid weathering of the top Blue Bit than in the Spangle and Freestones below. Michael Bower left several such pieces at West Hedbury, skilfully cut with wedges. In the one hundred and fifty years or so since, these are pitting in a curious way. This may well be due to the erosion of whatever mineral it is that gives rise to the darkening of those beds. This alveolian effect requires salt, which can cause either general deterioration or small, pitted holes. Well known from coastal limestones, and more particularly sandstones elsewhere, and possibly the inspiration for archaic Greek vermiculation, it is confined to a quite narrow horizon in the Purbeck Portland. At White Ware the lower part of the Shrimp and Blue Bit exhibit it, but this effect never seems to happen to the other Cliff stone beds.[16.] It would appear that once a small hole has developed it holds salt, which would otherwise get leached away. This then attacks within the hole more rapidly than around it, thereby opening it further. The location in terms of salt arrival and/or flushing rain is all important.

Other Purbeck beds can also develop deep holes in the course of weathering. Some Burr does this markedly: similarly, Thornback, limited to a small area around Worth Matravers. Deep holes, but of small diameter, grow whilst the mass of the stone around endures. St. Aldhelm's Chapel has good examples. In its 12th century work there are holes the depth of a pencil length, which probably follow weak tunnel structures left in the sediment by burrowing animals (shrimps) active when it was still soft. The continuing process is possibly assisted by masonry bees. Both ice and salt crystals damage rock by expanding in confining pores, and it seems that stone vulnerable to one tends to be vulnerable to the other. Fine-grained freestones like Portland or Cliff stone are particularly at risk, but location is all regarding the salt threat. If fully exposed to drenching rain the stone lasts well, for the salt gets flushed away but, paradoxically, if somewhat sheltered, damage occurs. It would seem that when heavy seas break on the coast onshore winds convey airborne salt particles miles inland. Following the October 1987 storm, windows on the sheltered side of houses a mile inland at Langton Matravers were encrusted with salt.

On a geological timescale millions of tons of salt have been and continue to be conveyed inland, even under overhangs that rain does not reach, and are absorbed into porous stonework. Where the salt concentrates crystal growth exerts an expansion pressure which breaks up the stone, but if it is flushed away the stone is fine. South facing 1872 Cliff stone windows at Kimmeridge church show decay in the tracery, which has a measure of protection afforded by the eaves, whilst the fully exposed jambs and sills are good. At Church Knowle the northwest gallery addition of the 1830s has Cliff Freestone windows in the north wall and eastern gable which are as good as new, but the central mullion and tracery to the west window are decaying both inside and out.

On the face of it this would seem not to fit the airborne salt theory in that one would expect plenty of lashing rain on a west window. But at Church Knowle this damaged window is partly protected from the southwest by the tower. Similarly, it must be its location that is causing deterioration of the east facing pilasters on Encombe House's south front, in marked contrast to the splendid pair flanking the central door, rather than a variation in the stone itself. George Burt's globe of Portland stone set on Durlston Head nicely presents every aspect. The somewhat sheltered northeast underside is tending to powder. It is the situation, not the variation in the blocks used that is significant. In the wild confusion of St. Aldhelm's Head undercliff a few fine blocks of Pond Freestone (most have been taken by quarriers), lie beautifully patinated by lichens on the weather side, where they receive plenty of salt spray together with flushing rain. But on their protected underside a white powdering shows damaging salt to be at work. Such patination by algae and lichens indicates relative stability, though these organisms too erode to some extent.

Salt damage can be remarkably localised. A 19th century Thornback headstone in Langton's old cemetery is in a generally good condition, but just in the apex of the sunk face panel an area of a few square inches is blistering. Blown salt has been arriving on a hundred years' worth of southwesterly gales, but never the accompanying rain on that small spot!

Migration of water through stonework can carry a burden of salt to where evaporation causes it to concentrate. This can be on the interior of a building, resulting in more damage inside than out. The arcade of Portland pillars in Langton church is as good as when built, except for the southwestern respond capital, where salt is causing decay, having passed through at least a two foot wall mass, aided, I suspect, by speeded up evaporation caused by the radiator below. Warming of interiors may benefit the congregation but not the stonework!

Interior paving and ledgers often exhibit deterioration around the joints where water is being drawn up. Its extent no doubt relates to the level of salts in the substrate. Where impervious 19th century encaustic tiles are combined with porous stone paving or steps, water can only migrate through the stones, so the problem becomes concentrated. Paradoxically, some beds at least may suffer more when fixed inside than out, where there is the benefit of rain periodically flushing the salt problem away. The distance over which salt can travel and become a problem is illustrated at Fishbourne Palace. Over forty years on from first protecting the mosaics from the elements to allow their exhibition in special buildings, ground water has been moving from outside to the interiors. There it evaporates, concentrating its salt burden at the worst possible place, the Kimmeridge Shale tesserae. Who could have predicted such a dire consequence? Hereford Cathedral has a brass indent of the least durable bed of Marble set in the floor which is almost as good as when laid. Presumably it just happens to have been set in a benign situation. What is dismaying to find are carpeted aisles complete with rubberised underlay, with the concealed ledgers sweating away underneath. Breathable carpets must be better, even if they do allow abrasive dust particles through.

Marble presents its own special problems, of which it is important to be aware as the medieval legacy is so rich. The presence of impurities: iron sulphide, glauconite, aluminium, plus most importantly clay, in addition to the shells, leads to breakdown and decay. But the all important clay component varies a lot, so some Marble beds or parts of beds are much better lasting than others. At Quarr there are two green beds. The upper has a few unios throughout, but with dense clustering at the top, virtually all of these disarticulated and lying round side up, telling of current action. The lower has a scatter of often intact unios, with few or none at the bottom, where there are small dinosaur track casts all over most of the

Corfe Castle village, No 23 West Street. Note asymmetric paired lintel and resolution of relieving arch above.

blocks. This part, with its footprint casts, decays very quickly, but the upper part of the same bed is quite good. Should the underside be selected as the face of a ledger, decay would be rapid; if the other, then the slab would be reasonably well lasting. The upper bed's two alternative faces both last well.

Also at Quarr, the underside of the blue bed is dense, some of it almost slate-like in its absence of big shells. The underside of the same bed at Lynch is pale and washed-out and not so good. At both Quarr and Lynch, though the overall height of the blue bed remains consistent and parallel, 'false' beds within it run out of level, clear evidence of current bedding. Particularly at Quarr this means character change almost from block to block. What can be a well-pronounced free bed in one block fades out as it sweeps out of level and becomes diffuse in the next. It would seem the winnowing action of the current has left a relatively clay free, hence durable, rock compared with that which has formed in calmer regions of the same lagoon at the same time. The lowermost grey bed is of these calmer conditions. The upper blue bed shows signs of being markedly current-bedded at Quarr and Woodyhyde but much less so, or not at all, at Blashenwell. The result is that Blashenwell blue bed tends to look more like the grey from Quarr rather than the blue from Quarr. At Woodyhyde it was only the bottom grey bed the Victorians dug from underground. It is similar in appearance to the underside of some Lynch upper (or blue) bed but is a quite a different layer, which similarly does not weather well. The best of the blue lasts well, even outside. Most of the doorway of No. 23 West Street, Corfe (c.1600), has been cut from it. It remains in good condition, in contrast to the single piece of grey. A similar variation is evident in Corfe Castle's Gloriette (c.1300). It contains a lot of Marble rubble, some quite good after seven hundred years, but a lot badly decayed. Both contrast with the beautiful dressing wrought from fine-grained Burr and atypical Thornback; both retain crisp arrises. The castle exhibits two rather unusual areas of weathering: one, below the garderobe, a result of centuries of acid attack from urine; the other, more worryingly, unusual flushing of ashlar arrises on the lower part of the precarious east wall of the keep. It suggests pressure during severe storms.

Returning to current-bedding, that is, layers exhibiting bedding planes out of horizontal. These are a thorough nuisance to the quarryman/mason but the stone is durable. The Freestone from the Turnpike quarry on the Worth road exhibits this feature, though apparently not the Freestone around it; similarly, the Wetsun bed from a limited area at Southard quarry, Swanage.

Laining Vein Rag and New Vein White Bit seem generally not to endure well. Certainly a number of ledgers of these have been replaced in Salisbury and elsewhere, following serious decay. The problem would seem to be the same as with Marble, i.e. the presence of clays. In sharp contrast the upper layer of the New Vein, the Five Bit (Vie Bed) lasts well. Over time a

Corfe Castle, Gloriette. Window dressings consisting of Burr and Thornback rubble including weathered and unweathered Marble and crisp arris.

characteristic silicified white shell stands up, whether in a rain-blasted field wall or under traffic of feet in a city church.

Different stones of different PH value and pore size support different algae and lichen communities. The one and only sandstone headstone (cut by Fred Bower, who contributed to Paul Hyland's *Written in Stone*, 2009) in Langton Matravers graveyard has a shade-dwelling lichen not to be found on another stone there! The Burr and, to a lesser extent, the Thornback and other Purbeck beds support a reddish algae particularly on shady elevations. Kingston church is a good example. In a mixture of Portland and Purbeck patinated headstones, this reddishness can be a pointer towards Purbeck; its degree of brightness is weather and season-dependent and it likes rain. However, though it is clear that different beds of stone support different lichen species, to use them as identifiers of a particular stone is not easy. Minstead churchyard, Hampshire, has a considerable assembly of Purbeck and Portland headstones, beginning with late 17th century examples. So far, 108 species of lichen have been recorded growing on them, whilst 99 species have been identified on the ruins of Corfe Castle.[17.]

A deleterious characteristic of Cliff stone, as with Portland, is its propensity to stain easily. My father remarked that Isaac Edmunds put the Swanage War Memorial together with a good hard Portland cement. The Winspit Freestone panels went a chocolate brown! Whatever the chemistry the stain

Kingston, St James. Reddish algae on north elevation.

faded, but the Cary/Helier (1607) Blue Bit ledger in Exeter Cathedral appears to be permanently stained, presumably from substrate minerals, an effect which can be confused with Blue heartedness, which that slab also exhibits.

Perhaps the poor performance of much of the Marble was a factor in it going out of fashion. Men must have learnt from early on the varying properties of the different beds. This is hinted at in the 1651 Articles of the Company of Marblers: Article 4 says 'That no man in this Company shall sell or make sale of any stone within this Island unto any man but by its own proper name upon the forfeiture of 5 pounds'. It seems spin is not new, but unchanging: 'Wessex Buff', currently marketed across England, is quarried in the USA.

In 1736 James Keat was paid £3 2s 9d for making Corfe church steps 'which we promise will endure the weather and remain good for 3 years to come'. It seems a modest claim. He was active in Broad Mead around that time: for Thornback from there he could have added noughts. In my opinion selection continues to be a problem. One example might be White Bit paving introduced as part of a village enhancement scheme in Langton Matravers in the recent past. This paving is already beginning to deteriorate in some places, and will not endure for long.

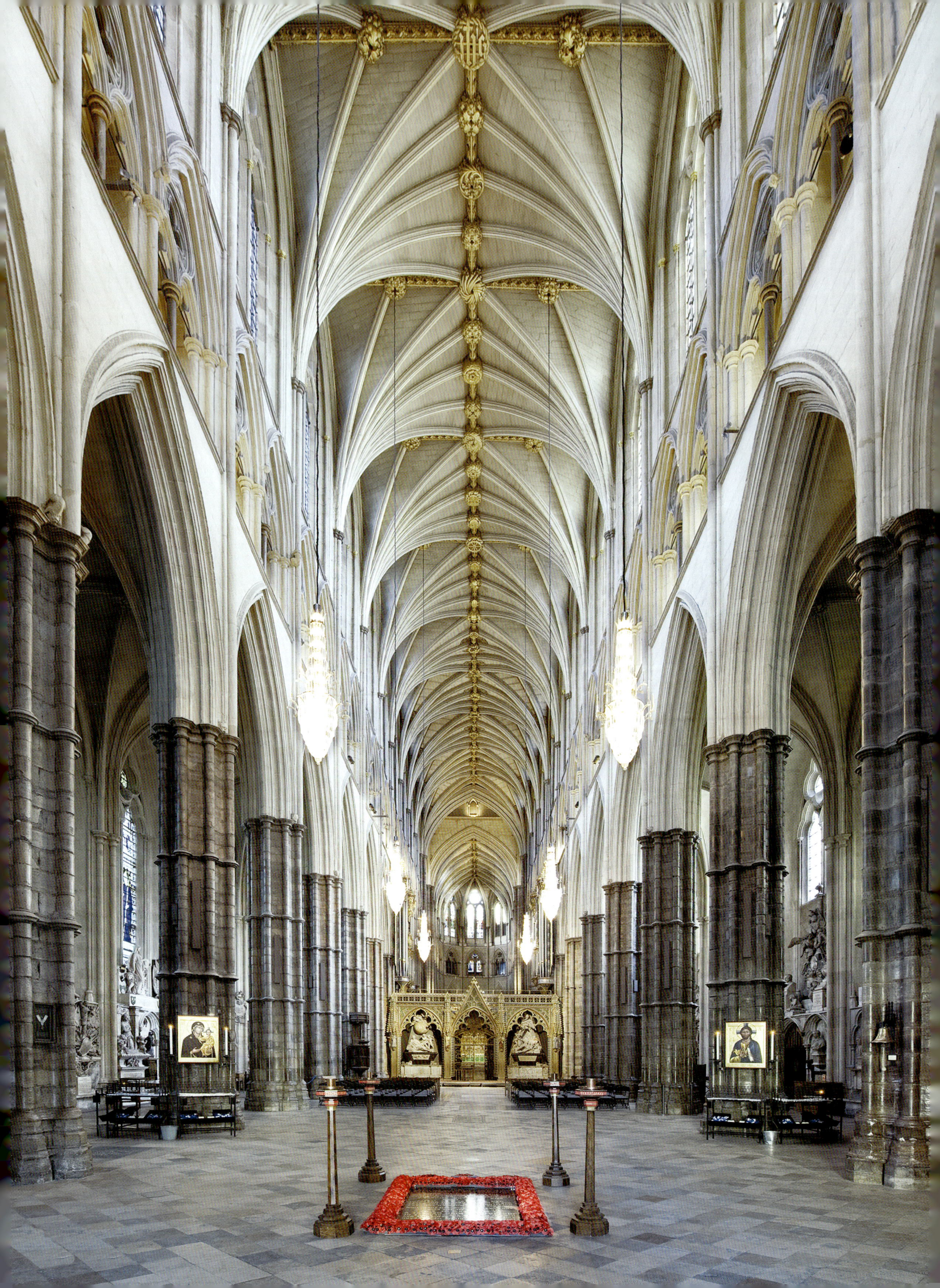

TWO
Marble

The second half of the 12th century saw a rapid development of marble quarrying. A zenith occurred in the 13th century, before a late 14th century reduction and almost complete fizzling out by the end of the 16th century. The high point can perhaps be identified in Henry III's lavish use of marble in his rebuilding of Westminster Abbey in about 1245, complete with Cosmati pavement and Confessor's shrine where more exotic types of stone are set in Purbeck marble. The King was familiar with Wolvesey Palace at Winchester, enlarged by Bishop Henry of Blois, grandson of William the Conqueror, who was 'wealthier, so it was said, than any of the magnates or bishops of England, a man of taste, patron of letters and the arts of illumination, enamelling, jewellery, goldwork and a collector of classical statues.'[1] Purbeck marble appears in work commissioned by the bishop there between 1141 and 1151, after his return to England following exile in Cluny, and after an earlier campaign when he was using Tournai marble. Perhaps in this man of enormous powers of patronage the start of the fashion can be recognised.

Throughout the Middle Ages hard, polishable stones were called 'marble', as against the softer freestones, and the men who worked them 'marblers'. The distinction was such that in London separate guilds of marblers and masons emerged. In England, Purbeck was synonymous with marble in the way that Carrara *et al* have become since the Renaissance. Scientific geology now reserves the term for such metamorphosed limestones only. Though Purbeck dominated, other polishable English stones also called 'marble' were in use. They include Alwalton and Raunds from near Peterborough, Frosterly and Eggleston from Durham, Bletchingdon from north of Oxford (a rarity), Buckingham, Bethersden from Kent, Petworth from Sussex, plus lesser known Laughton and Charlwood stones also from the Weald (these last four often referred to as 'Winklestone'), Wenlock from Shropshire and Lias from Somerset. What may also be Lias was used for the high altar at Tewkesbury and for incredibly long shafts at Bredon, Worcestershire. Another group difficult to identify are dark slabs almost certainly from the East Midlands, perhaps belonging to the Jurassic Lincolnshire limestones which frequently occur as brass indents in East Anglia. The term 'marble' was also used for various Derbyshire stones and geologically similar Nidderdale marble from North Yorkshire.

None compare with Purbeck in terms of wide distribution or numbers of monuments, but within their respective regions can occur more abundantly. Carboniferous Egglestone, quarried in Teesdale near Barnard Castle and characterised by distinctive crinoids that Purbeck entirely lacks, was much used in Yorkshire and Lancashire, reaching southwards into Nottinghamshire and Lincolnshire. The main production period seems to have been later than Purbeck, from about 1400 to 1500. A shrine and some fonts were produced, but most importantly, brass indents including examples of London work. They are surely a case of the brass being taken to the stone. Quarry evidence remains in wedge pits cut in an exposure on a bank of the Tees. Long slabs were produced, such as those at St Michael Le Belfry, which include a 15 foot piece that exceeds any Purbeck examples in length. As with other similar Carboniferous rocks – Irish Kilkenny and Tournai/Belgian Black – it is durable,

LEFT Westminster Abbey, where Henry III made wide use of Purbeck Marble during his rebuilding of the Abbey in the mid-13th century.

RIGHT Westminster Abbey. Edward the Confessor's shrine.

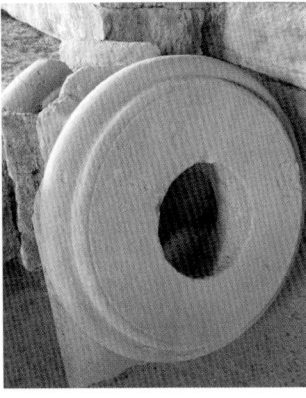

ABOVE LEFT Dunshay Manor, Harman's Cross. Eroded worked Marble pieces from decayed field wall: stiff leaf capital detail (left) and part of a finial (right), both 13th century.

ABOVE RIGHT Haycrafts Farm, Harman's Cross. A 13th century Marble column base dug up at the farm.

and a more southerly location would surely have seen a much bigger scale of quarrying and usage.[2]

I once attended a lecture where the claim was made that many monuments are of Forest marble rather than Purbeck, on the basis that Forest marble extends over several western counties and that there was a compelling logic to use local materials. However, its fossil composition is quite different and, in my opinion, it seems seldom to crop up in medieval tombs or building components. Some 19th century shafts in Sherborne Abbey that replaced Purbeck marble are an exceptional use of Forest marble but do reveal the fact that a few sizable blocks of Forest marble **were** available, but were not commonly found.

MEDIEVAL WORKING PRACTICES

Medieval Purbeck examples of tombs and architectural components in one form or other occur across most of England, the English-controlled part of Wales, the coast of Normandy, northern Brittany, the Channel Islands, Aquitaine and the Pale in Ireland. Ireland has effigies and coffin lids but not column components, as claimed by some authors. In spite of many losses, the remaining legacy is still large. This body of work must have required much labour, not only to dig such an amount of marble out of the ground, but also to cut it into finished shapes. Archeological and documentary evidence shows that a large amount of fine shaping was carried out in Purbeck. The question remains as to what extent shaping work was also done elsewhere. At least in the later medieval period, there were also tomb makers working Purbeck marble in London. Itinerant marblers, as well as and distinct from freemasons, were at work on construction sites such as Westminster Abbey, but it seems most architectural components and tombs were being made at or near the quarries. There may have been a use for some of the resulting waste spalls and scars, so perhaps we should not expect to find too much of that sort of evidence, but some has been found in Corfe. Of course fine finishing work would have produced far less volume of waste than the first rough dressing stage. Practicalities may have meant that highly labour intensive items such as effigies were refined in Corfe, leaving no evidence.

What is certain is that the general run of work was done close by the quarries, where evidence in the form of waste and worked pieces has been found in quantity. Other than mortars, the smallest finished stones being produced were twelve inch square paving, so anything too small even for that was generally discarded. There are exceptions to this: Norwich Cathedral has an astonishing area of five inch squares. Quantities of bits and pieces were left, often of the sort of size and shape suitable for dry stone walling. One at Dunshay, recently rebuilt from a dilapidated state, was found to include several worked pieces of Marble, sadly rather badly weathered. Some column sections are enriched with a bead and therefore puzzling. Another piece is surely part of a 13th century finial, like those on Salisbury Cathedral. Other items include a moulded base fragment, some stiff-leaf carving of about 1200, and abrasive gritstone rubbers.

Years ago Sam Bower, when levelling some bumpy ground in the same vicinity, found that he was digging into rubbly marble waste. Amongst it were pieces of worked mouldings and a splendid 13th century base. Not far away a badger, digging into a waste pile now clothed by mature trees, is bringing out small chips indicative of fine work having been done there. Most tellingly, one piece exhibits a finely chiseled curved surface of approximately seven inch radius on its wide side, punch 'drokes' on another. When cutting a shape such as a quatrefoil base the first step is to produce the plan shape with flat top and bottom beds. The next is to cut the moulding. With a typical section this means first taking out a 'check'. The execution of this produces waste bits exactly like the one dug out by the badger. This particular piece also informs us that the marbler worked fast: to knock off such a piece is a bold act. Such a shape is relatively rare. A man can work for months on straight columns, coffin lids, and indeed moulded bases, and only produce 'ordinary' scars such as others revealed by the badger. Further digging by this industrious animal has produced more scars, including another piece of moulding by-product, and a mortar broken before completion.

Eastwards, in Talbots Wood, north of Langton, medieval waste piles were dug into as a productive source of random

Langton Matravers Museum. Broken medieval mortar from Talbot's Wood.

walling stone during the 1950s. This digging revealed several worked pieces (since lost) and another mortar, also broken in manufacture (now in the Langton Matravers Museum collection). As well as the dominating walling-sized pieces there were drifts of fine scars – sure evidence of fine shaping being done there. The revealed section of waste marble is about three or four feet thick, and lies in such a way as to suggest a workshop floor. Immediately adjacent, the evidence of quarry workings is extensive, whilst the Dunshay badger site is right in the middle of more large scale workings. Cutting a base such as the badger chip came from tells of six weeks work or so. It means highly skilled men were working in close proximity to unskilled labourers who were digging off the overburden, as well as men possessed of intermediate skills such as splitting the blocks. Mortar production possibly suggests training. In the recent past, knocking out a 'dew pond' was the sort of job given to a novice boy.

Deposits of scars, suggesting workshops, were found in Corfe in the 19th century, but subsequent digging of service trenches, foundations, etc. does not seem to have added much more evidence, which is odd. A footnote in the third edition of Hutchins' history of Dorset says:

> 'In many parts of Corfe, particularly the extremity of West Street, on penetrating the soil the rubbish from the mason's banks is frequently found to be ten or twelve feet in thickness. In digging a drain a short time since a thick bed was pierced, which consisted entirely of the *debris* of this marble, largely interspersed with fragments of mouldings, foliations and other ornamental details, some of which has been preserved.'[3.]

Sadly these are lost.

Subsequent finds have been modest. A broken shaft with other bits of masonry have been found in West Street, but are not obviously from a workshop context. A lot of mortars of both Burr and marble, mostly broken in manufacture, some lying in association with waste scars, have been dug up from several gardens in both Corfe streets. A typical find was made in 1999 on removal of a low bank at the rear of No. 47 West Street. It revealed about twelve inches of good earth on top of about twelve inches of small marble scars resting on virgin ground. There were two broken mortars plus worn heath stone rubbers in the scars. The mortars tend to be of a standard pattern similar, and therefore difficult to separate from Romano-British examples: some of medieval date are quite different. Recent excavations at Burtle, a dissolved nunnery in Somerset, have yielded some remarkable jug-like specimens complete with spout and holed handle.[4]

KEY BUILDINGS

The following rough list of surviving buildings that incorporate a significant Purbeck component, not forgetting losses such as Old St. Paul's, London, serves to illustrate the fashion's speedy development and scale. One of the earliest is surely the 12th century Infirmary Cloister at Canterbury Cathedral. It has Purbeck shafts enriched with spiral grooves. This treatment is rare. Only smooth cylinders seem to follow, plus a few

BELOW Canterbury Cathedral. Purbeck Marble paired shafts with spiral grooves in the Infirmary Cloister, *c.*1160.

Temple Church, London. Round Church. The church was badly damaged during the Second World War, and this postcard dates to before the war.

RIGHT Temple Church, London. Round Church.

chamfered examples. Similarities with spirally grooved pillars in the crypt suggest a contemporaneous date of around 1100. However, other aspects of the cloister column design suggest that they are the later work of William of Sens, who began rebuilding the quire using a lot of Purbeck in 1175. But that Purbeck was certainly finding its way to Canterbury before William's great work began has been shown by archaeological finds at St. Augustine's Abbey. They include shafts dating from reconstruction work following a fire in 1168.[5]

Wimborne Minster has such shafts in the central tower (c.1150). John Blair cites font support shafts at Buckfastleigh, Devon, and Kilpeck, Hereford, as also being from this period or 'some decades earlier'.[6] The former are of a rare, slightly bulbous, squashed circular shape on plan, which cannot have been lathe turned. Now about half their former height, they have evidently been reused. However, the source of the stone for the Kilpeck example is disputed, some authorities claiming the font in its entirety to be local stone.[7]

Another early usage, about 1160, is in the Temple Church, London, where six modern replacement columns of Purbeck, each consisting of four separate drums linked at the base, collar and cap, arranged in a circle, support the triforium, clerestory and roof of the Round Church. They are load bearing and resonate when tapped with the knuckles. It is, of course, good masonry practice to set sedimentary stones so that the load is square to the bedding plane, just as the rock lies in the ground. This is impossible with thin bedded stones such as Purbeck, so all long shafts have to be set on end. The original 12th century Temple columns may have been such long pieces; their post war replacements consist of a stack of drums built up in bed. Perhaps architect Walter Godfrey preferred this method, perhaps it was because my father had difficulty in finding enough long blocks from the source available to him. What we see in such a stack of drums, whether 20th or 13th century, is the cutting of each block to its maximum bed height. It is a module imposed by nature, not man. Where the fossil shells are only partially filled with sediment they serve as geopetals, that is, they reveal not only whether the stone is on end or flat, but also which way up it is.

Winchester St Cross lacks much Purbeck in its fabric but has puzzling late 12th century bases (see illustration p. 37).[8] York Minster possibly has earlier Purbeck than any of the above examples. It has what may be Roman work re-used in the 11th century.[9] The Galilee Chapel, Durham, (1175), has long, load bearing, paired shafts of Purbeck combined with local stone apparently added in the 15th century. It would seem the original scheme was too daring. The Purbeck pair in each arrangement of four are original. Perhaps all four were once of Purbeck and possibly unstable.

That same year the commencement of the rebuilding of Canterbury in the new pointed arch style saw Purbeck being used lavishly. Twelve years later it appeared at Chichester, where the leaf crocket capitals in the retrochoir exhibit amazingly bold projections, illustrative of how the carvers mastered this hard stone early on. Lincoln followed in 1185, and continued until about 1260, using a massive amount for bases, shafts, abacus, string and caps, as well as load bearing columns. *The Metrical Life of St. Hugh* provides an insight into the enthusiasm for the material, as well as medieval dance styles:

'With wondrous art he built the fabric of the cathedral, whereunto he supplied not only his own wealth and the labours of his servants, but even the sweat of his own brow; for he oftimes bore the hod load of hewn stone or bonding lime. In this structure, the art equals the precious materials, for the vault may be compared to a bird stretching out her broad wings to fly; planted on the firm columns it soars in the clouds.

On the other hand the work is supported by the precious columns of swarthy stone [Purbeck Marble], not confined to one sole

34 / PURBECK STONE

colour, nor loose of pore, but flecked with glittering stars and close set in all its grain. Moreover it may suspend the mind in doubt whether it be jasper or marble, yet for marble of a most noble nature. Of this are formed those slender columns which stand around the giant pillars, even as a bevy of maidens stand marshalled for a dance.'

In this period some shafts had become purely decorative and incredibly slender. Were the various masters competing with each other, showing off just how delicate they could make them? Lincoln seems to win with a pair of piers at the east end, of about 1186, that consist of the local stone containing Purbeck shafts nine feet three inches long of only three and a quarter inch diameter, well protected in its convolution. Men must have been amazed at this innovation, having previously seen only massive work such as the Durham columns. It seems incredible that such delicate shafts were made by cutting multiple chamfers with mallet and chisel. Even with the aid of modern machinery they are difficult to replicate without mishap. Whether the medieval builders made use of lathes or not remains uncertain. What is sure is that 13th century shafts occupying corner situations in Westminster Abbey include a concealed ridge, so these were certainly not lathe turned. Other medieval shafts are clearly imperfect cylinders, which suggests multiple chamfering rather than lathe turning. However good examples of these imperfect shapes at the east end of Canterbury result from modifications produced by preparations for 19th century *scaglioli* repairs. Not only were slender cyclindrical shafts made; in the case of the Ely Chapter House (1320-49) the panelled pilasters separating the canopied sedilia are Purbeck marble. Also in Ely, Bishop Hotham's contemporaneous tomb chest (1337) includes Purbeck used in a similar way.

Clearly the polychrome effect achieved by setting dark polished Purbeck against contrasting light Freestones, some

Durham Cathedral, Galilee Chapel. Paired shafts of Purbeck Marble combined with local stone.

Ely Cathedral. Canopied Sedilia with Purbeck Marble pilasters in the Chapter House.

ABOVE Ely Cathedral. Bishop John Hotham's tomb, 1337.

LEFT Bedingham, St Andrew, Norfolk. Purbeck Marble shafting in sedilia.

ABOVE RIGHT Exeter Cathedral, nave. Minstrels' gallery. The base is wood, painted to represent unio-rich Purbeck Marble.

RIGHT Ely Cathedral. Purbeck Marble shafts grouped around Purbeck drums. Shaft beds vertical, drums laid in bed. Ely Cathedral, 1229-52. Elsewhere in the Cathedral is a Purbeck Marble pillar entirely in bed, 1323-1345.

moulded elements of which were picked out with coloured paint, was obviously much admired. Nor was Purbeck just for major projects. Hoo, in Kent, Boston, Lincolnshire and Bedingham, Norfolk, have small marble shafts only in their sedilia. Princes Risborough, Bucks, has just two small shafts in a lancet from about 1300. They beg the question of how the integration was achieved. Were these standard products, 'off the shelf'? The fact that Aveton Gifford, Devon, has four shafts in the 'low status' porch whilst all the rest inside are now other stone tells of damage to the main part of the church in the Second World War.[10.]

Sometimes other material was painted to look like Purbeck marble. There are several references to 'marbling' work at Henry III's castles at Ludgershall and Guildford. His son Edmund Crouchback's monument in Westminster Abbey has panels painted to simulate 'typical' marble. By contrast the base of the 14th century minstrels' gallery projecting into the nave at Exeter Cathedral displays big white shapes against a dark background, obviously intending to represent unios as typical of green marble. In Gloucester the pair of Norman capitals either side of Edward II's tomb received a coat of black paint bearing the white hart associated with Richard II. The rest of the Norman arcade remains unadorned. Perhaps the last Purbeck simulation is the treatment of the timber column at the foot of Thomas Sackville's great hall staircase of 1603 at Knole, painted to look like Purbeck marble. The hall's chequered floor is of marble and Downs Vein.

Continuing the list of major projects incorporating significant amounts of Purbeck marble, Ely follows in 1198, Winchester 1202, Rochester 1210, and York in 1220.[11.] What a year that must have been, for it also saw not only the beginning of work on the greenfield site at Salisbury, but also Henry III's rebuilding of Westminster Abbey. Both enormous projects used Purbeck lavishly. All of these dates should be taken with some leeway. It is known, for example, that there were ceremonies of dedication at Salisbury in 1220, but the groundwork no doubt started well before. There are approximately 15,000 tons of

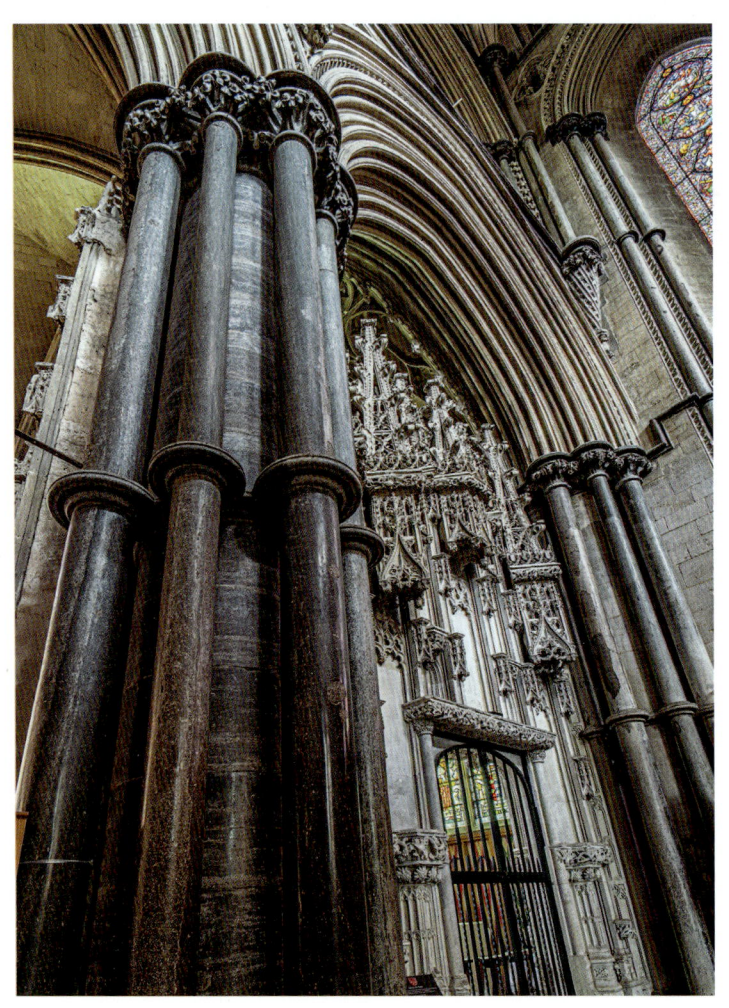

36 / PURBECK STONE

ABOVE Stone, St Mary the Virgin, Kent. Purbeck Marble capital/corbel. This is surely the Master mason with his furrowed brow and protruding tongue. There are strong links with work at this church and contemporary Westminster Abbey.

RIGHT Winchester, Great Hall, 1222.

Purbeck used at Salisbury, combined with about 70,000 tons of the local Wiltshire stone.[12] One wonders where all the labourers toiling with Purbeck were housed, fed and watered. The demand increased with the Great Hall, Winchester (1222). In that year a payment was made to 'a certain cutter sent to the quarry at Corfe.'[13] Further projects were Worcester (1224) and Beverley (about 1230). The latter contains an exception to the cylindrical shaft rule; some in the clerestory are octagons. Finally come Exeter and St. Paul's in about 1275. By this time Salisbury and Lincoln, as far as Purbeck was concerned, were more or less finished. Although Purbeck went on being used at Winchester until about 1340, Exeter about 1342, and Westminster Abbey until even 1500, the tide was on the ebb.

FINISHING TECHNIQUES

Salisbury is unusual in that the clustered columns are entirely Purbeck, although they display different colours. This is because whilst the small diameter shafts are polished, the bigger columns drums are chisel-finished, using a finely serrated claw cutting edge rather than a plain straight edge. The effect of either chisel edge is to 'bruise' the stone, leaving it lighter than its true colour. The art of polishing is to rub this bruising away. Not to rub these pillars saved money, but what was the point? Why not use the local Freestone as was generally done? The colour contrast would have been greater, possibly an aesthetic gain. One reason could be that the hard Purbeck was considered better able to carry high loading. At the crossing this is a lot, for four relatively small Purbeck piers, each about six feet square, carry the entire tower and spire, a mass of about 6,400 tons.[14] Another possible factor is that most of the long shafts are of the lower grey bed. In order to get at it, the upper blue bed has to be dug off. In the Dunshay

Salisbury Cathedral. Clustered Purbeck Marble columns.

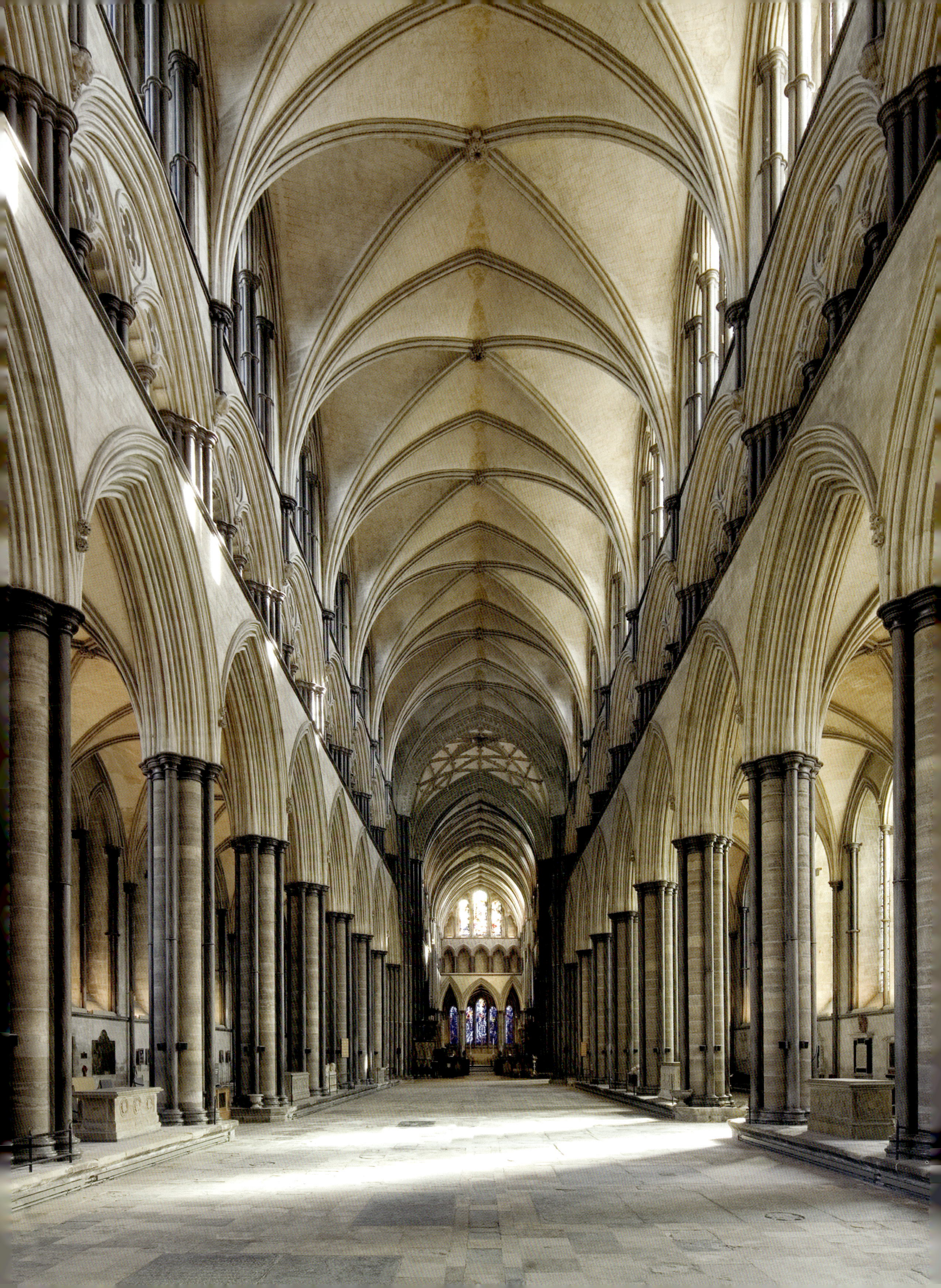

OPPOSITE PAGE Salisbury Cathedral, nave. Showing the use of Purbeck Marble in the arcade, triforium and clerestory.

RIGHT Warwick, St Mary's, Beauchamp Chapel. Purbeck Marble tomb of Richard Beauchamp, Earl of Warwick (d.1439). John Bourde's 1447 specification for the making of the tomb gives a rare insight into how such tombs were constructed, transported and finished.

region, where Salisbury marble originated, this upper bed tends to be more broken, occurring in smaller, more chunky shaped blocks, just right for the load bearing components of the pillars where we see it used. Having got it out of the ground anyway, it made sense to make use of it for a not too distant project, but they fell short of polishing it. Perhaps this idea is quite wrong; perhaps the intention was to polish *in situ*, but limited funds were a constraint. Whatever the reason, Salisbury stands alone as being the only major project with these contrasting surfaces. Lincoln, Exeter, Westminster Abbey *et al* all possess polished/rubbed load bearing columns.

Unpolished architectural components, particularly shafts, are rare, but Wimborne Minster has some, similarly claw chiseled like the Salisbury drums. At ground level they flank the entrances from the transepts to the aisles and support Perpendicular capitals of later date. What story do they tell? Perhaps they arrived on site with others we see in work of the 13th century, but were not built in for another couple of hundred years, and even then were unfinished. It is, of course, easiest to rub a stone on the banker where it can be moved about and got at most comfortably. But there are benefits in finishing off after the work has been put together. Rubbing adjacent stones after they have been set in place can improve an imperfect fit. This was probably common practice. One piece of evidence is in the specification for the Richard Beauchamp tomb in the Beauchamp Chapel, St Mary's, Warwick:

'John Bourde of Corfe Castle in the county of Dorset, marbler, 16 Maii, 35 Hen.VI,[15.] [...] doth covenant to make a tombe of marble, to be set on the said earl's grave; the said tombe to be made well, clean and sufficiently, of a good and fine marble as well coloured as may be had in England. The uppermost stone of the tombe and the base thereof to contain in length ix. foot of the standard, in bredth iv. foot, and in thicknys vij. inches; the course of the tombe to be of good and due proportion, to answer the length and breadth of the uppermost stone. And a pace to be made round about the tombe of like good marble to stand on the ground; which pace shall contain in thickness vi. inches, and in bredth xviij. inches. The tombe to bear in height from the pace iv. foot and a half. And in and about the same tombe to make xiv. principall housings, and under every principall housing a goodly quarter for a scutcheon of copper and gilt to be set in; and to do all the work and workmanship about the same tombe, to the entail, according to a portraicture delivered him, and the carriages and bringing to Warwick, and there to set the same up where it shall stand; the entailing to be at the charge of the executors. After which entailing, the said marbler shall pullish and clense the said tombe in workmanlike sort; and for all the said marble, carriage, and work, he shall have in stirling money xlv li. [...]

The said marbler covenanteth to provide, of good and well-coloured marble, so many stones as will pave the chapell where the tombe standeth; every stone containing in thickness two inches, and in convenient bredth, and to bring the same to Warwick and lay it; and for the stuff, workmanship, and carriage of every hundred of those stones, he shall have xl s. which in the total comes to iv li. xiiis. iv d.'[16.]

This lucky survival of a detailed medieval contract, lost in its original version since Dugdale recorded it, is illuminating on several counts. It shows the order of the working processes in relation to the transport. It also shows that there was close cooperation between Bourde in Corfe and fellow marbler John Essex working in London, who wrought the top slab, as well as with the other metal working artists. It is difficult to get much further away from the sea in England than Warwick. It seems certain that the tomb plus Bourde travelled well over 100 miles by road to reach its destination.

Another reference that certainly indicates rubbing/polishing on site appears in the Vale Royal Abbey records. In 1287 Master John Doget of Corfe, with Ralf of Chichester, were supplying marble columns, capitals, bases and cornice mouldings worked to an 'examplar' (pattern) provided by Walter of Hereford, master of the works. The 'Marble work to be polished sent to Cheshire by sea'.[17.] This shows that it was polished at the final destination and not at source, and suggests that this arrangement was normal procedure.

Polisher as a separate occupation crops up in the mid-13th century accounts for Westminster. Their position in the list of skills as detailed by the medieval account keepers tells something of the work sequence: stone cutters, marblers, layers, carpenters, carvers, painters, plasterers, polishers, smiths, glaziers, plumbers, and scaffolders. It would surely make sense to finish the vault before working down the supporting pillar from top to bottom, giving it its final polish, as the centering and scaffolding were taken away. Over about 20 weeks in 1253 their number remains fairly constant, between 13 and 16. For about half the time the number of marblers was about

MARBLE / 39

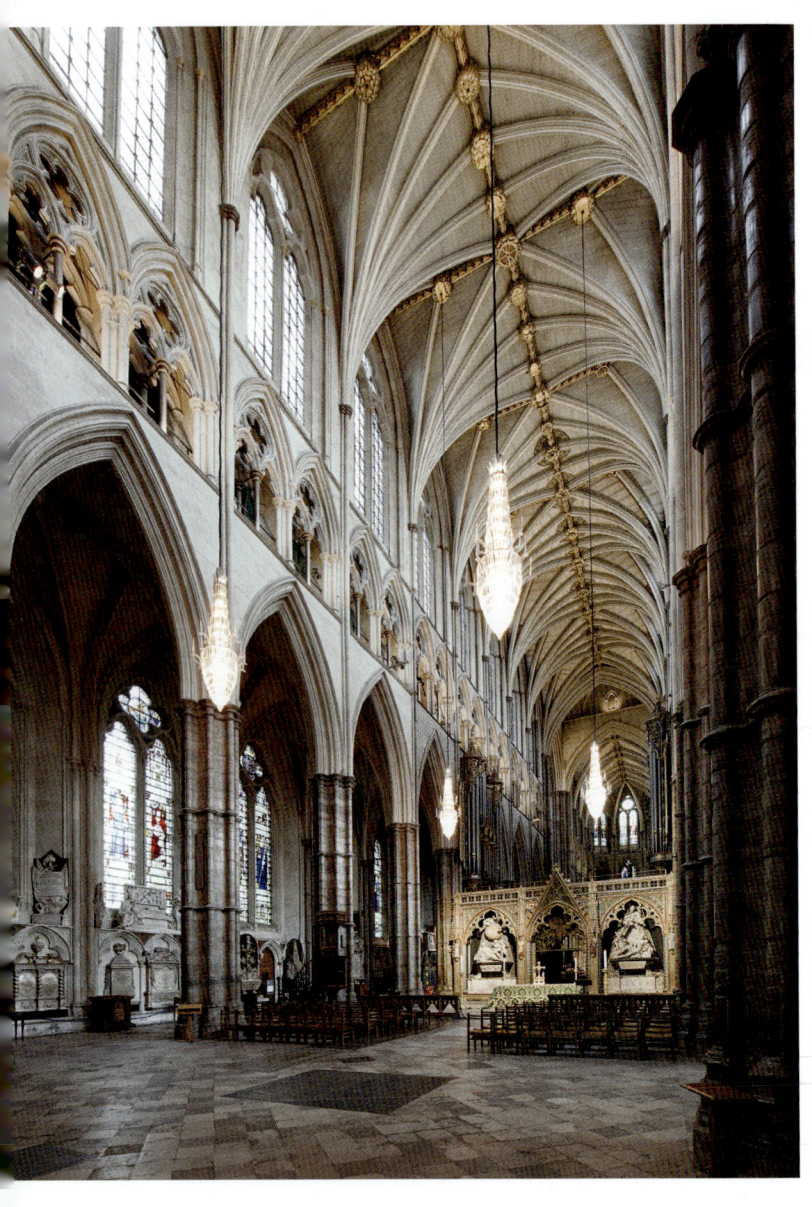

Westminster Abbey, Nave. Note regular jointing in pillars.

the same as the polishers, which is surely more polishers than necessary to keep up. Even though the marblers shoot up to 49 for several weeks, which prompts the question of where they suddenly came from, they remain, it seems to me, rather too few to keep the polishers busy. This imbalance would suggest that the polishers were finishing off chisel faced work sent up from Purbeck as well as that cut on site.

The changing number of marblers working at the Abbey begs the question of how much cutting was going on on site. A lot of the marble is in a form that could easily have been integrated after having been shaped at a distance. Five pairs of nave pillars are like this, each consisting of courses of four similar pieces jointed in the same position. All the builders had to be careful about was to make sets of four all of the same height for each course, but that would not have been a problem. To avoid a weakness the vertical joints are staggered. This was not always done. The Master at Lincoln Cathedral seemed less worried about straight joints, at least with the easternmost pillar (about 1186). The tricky thing they had to watch was making sure each pillar rose to the critical height where it matters, that is at the collar and cap. A weakness in this form of construction is poor adhesion at the beds. Where thrust comes from the side they can slip, which has happened at the crossings in both Westminster Abbey and, more markedly, at Salisbury Cathedral. It is not, as some say, the stone bending.

With regard to whether the polishing was done *in situ* or on the banker, for what it is worth some relatively inaccessible flat surfaces forming part of the complicated configuration of the southwest crossing pier in the Abbey exhibit fine claw tool marks. It does not resolve the question one way or the other for certain, but they suggest a measure of skimping of an awkward place to get at, where they felt it would be out of sight, as the polishers worked their way down the built columns.

Twelfth century Boxgrove, Sussex, has columns that are rubbed, yet light claw and other tool marks remain visible. They did not quite rub enough to get rid of them completely. Warblington, Hampshire, has a 13th century marble arcade in the nave. Caps, shafts and bases, are finished with the claw chisel (except one obvious 19th century replacement at the eastern respond). However original shafts at the chancel arch have been rubbed – I suspect before fixing. Does it suggest that the intention was to rub it all, but for some reason things were never finished? The mystery is compounded by awkward joints in the caps and bases which hardly look intentional. Chiseled octagonal pillars in St. Clement's choir, Sandwich, Kent, (about 1300) are perhaps in a similar category. They did not even get started with the rubbing! This Sandwich marble has big 'lists', suggesting a Peveril provenance.

The recently rediscovered supports for the lost great table in Westminster Hall are remarkable in exhibiting both rubbed and chiseled surfaces. At about three feet square by six inches thick, they were placed crossways, thereby supporting the great slab. The narrow front facing into the hall is enriched with an engaged column. Only this front edge is rubbed. The rest, receding into the shadows, is left off the claw chisel.

In my opinion the regular jointing of the Westminster Abbey nave pillars does not merely suggest manufacture at source, but makes it certain. If they had been shaping the blocks on site the vertical joints would be more irregularly placed within the pillars. Shaping the blocks on site would have allowed for longer stones to be taken advantage of; at the same time, smaller stones complementing them could also have been used. This approach is less wasteful. However, in the case of the Westminster pillars, this consideration must have been outweighed by others, such as savings in freight cost. Other parts of the building with a Purbeck component could surely not have been prepared at a distance. The west side of the south transept has marble engaged with Reigate stone in a quite complicated way. This would have been difficult to achieve other than by a step by step resolution, working the stone and marble together on site. Irregular jointing of the adjacent southwest crossing pillar and the most easterly of the nave arcade suggest a similar story of working on site.

In the Abbey the pillars were fully rubbed, both in the first phase, where the shafts are detached, and later where they are engaged. The prominent master mason to the King, Henry

Yevele, was involved with the 'engaged' phase of this work but did not complete it before his death in about 1400: the nave was finally completed in 1528, without much stylistic change.[18.] In 1375 Henry had been granted the wardship of Langton Wallis until the owner, Joan le Walsh, came of age. We can surely see royal interest in the supply of marble in this appointment. The Westminster Abbey pillars are some of the last in England: one wonders why the fashion passed. The outcrop may have been seriously depleted but not exhausted, for some large slabs for brasses went on being dug for another seventy years or more.

FONTS

In the 12th century Tournai Marble from the Low Countries, (sometimes called Touchstone, or in more recent trade parlance, Belgian Black), was being imported in the form of effigies, fonts and shafts. The trade in these items seems largely to die out as the use of Purbeck begins, but importation of slabs for brasses resumed, with their increasing popularity in the 14th century. Iffley church, Oxford, has octagonal (a Tournai characteristic) shafts of about 1170 at the chancel arch, and a Tournai font. This font is of the typical basic form: a square bowl on a square base, separated by a cylindrical stem flanked by four corner columns, the same plan as the splendid carved Winchester font and the Chichester retrochoir Purbeck pillars. Most of the Early Purbeck examples of fonts are the same basic shape, usually with the sides of the bowl enriched with an arcade of blank round headed arches. This treatment can vary, some have capitals represented; Bruton, Somerset, has rare twisted columns between the panels, etc. There seems to be a standard specification, though some are more expensively carved. Fragments of one later example at Windsor, surely of Henry III's patronage, are enriched by the most elegant stiff-leaf; it is said that Edward III was baptised in it.

Over time, the form of the blank arches became pointed, or trefoil, but before this some bowls become octagonal on plan. Some octagonal examples bear round-headed blank arches but conversely few square examples exhibit pointed arches. The round-headed type must be 12th century, whilst the trefoil and pointed are of later date. The trefoil include two sorts, round-headed and pointed. The 'round' are not often true; some are quite flattened, almost elliptical, drawn without compasses.

Cusped quatrefoil panels appear, some bearing escutcheons, some bearing heraldic roses; detached shafts disappear. One of the later examples reached the Americas. It is in St. Peter's church, Bermuda, built in 1612. It has four quatrefoils on each of its eight sides. Developments in font design therefore parallel architectural development up to about 1500, when the series ends. Purbeck examples form a coherent group spread over a period of three hundred years or so. They are interesting to compare with other English schools, for example Aylesbury, with its quite different, splendid circular bowls. However, there are also a few non-mainstream Purbeck examples, notably Harrow.

I have encountered about 135 Purbeck marble fonts, plus 22 of Purbeck stone. These totals do not include those of uncertain category, such as St. Michael's, Southampton, which is one of the

Chichester Cathedral. Pillar at north side of retrochoir.

Ebbesbourne Wake, Wilts, St John the Baptist. 12th century, Purbeck Marble, Basic Tournai pattern. The other sides are enriched with the more usual scallops or blank arches.

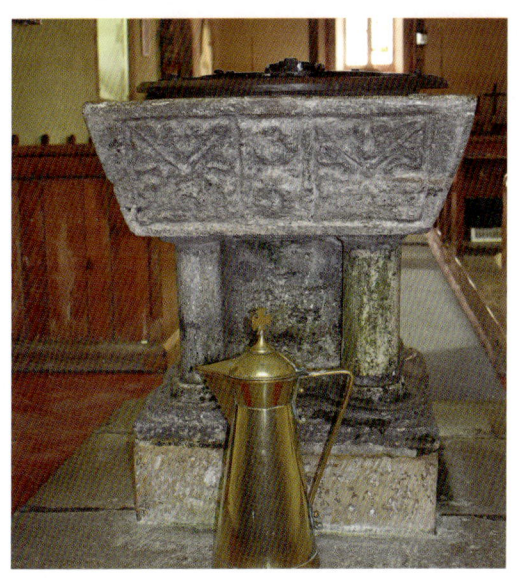

ABOVE Bosham, West Sussex, Holy Trinity. Octagonal, Purbeck Marble. Pevsner says 'c.1200'. Blank arches, crude in execution, pointed or round?

BELOW LEFT St Martin's-by-Looe church, Cornwall. Font.

BELOW RIGHT Lytchett Matravers, St Mary. Purbeck Marble, 15th century. Pevsner says 'Perp'.

12th century Tournai square examples, but with Purbeck corner shafts. These are probably 19th century, when so many restorations and other changes including reworking, were done. The font at Bethersden, Kent, is in a similar odd category. Its plain Portland bowl, clearly a replacement, is supported on Purbeck marble shafts, from which the original bowl must surely have also been made. Another oddity is Lanteglos, Cornwall. It is of the basic Tournai/early Purbeck form, but of Cornish Pentewan stone, with only two of its corner shafts being Purbeck. Some examples consist of more than one original font. St Martin's-by-Looe, Cornwall has a combination of three. A probable 15th century granite bowl stands on what appears to be a Norman base, which in turn stands on a standard (about 1200), Purbeck base with seating for four corner shafts. Almer, Dorset, has an octagonal marble bowl resting on an upturned bowl of some other sort of stone, whilst a loose hexagonal marble base lies outside.

Some bowls now lacking enrichment are, I suspect, the result of reworking, when the medieval blank arches were chiseled off. Peldon, Essex, is probably one; the wall between outer face and inner bowl is narrow. Perhaps all smooth-sided examples are the result of reworking. If any are original, Fifehead Neville, Dorset, must be amongst them, a good quality piece which, if decay and general shabbiness was the reason for reworking, would hardly qualify. Lower Wraxall, Wilts, is probably another. I cannot claim always to be able to tell 19th century from medieval tooling, but the interior of the bowl looks medieval. The well preserved tooling shows punch marks not quite taken out by the chisel: the marbler who made it was right handed and fast, the more work done by use of the punch, so much the quicker. The surviving punch marks show that he left little to be skimmed off by the chisel.

Some fonts are so odd they stand alone. Shroton, Dorset, is one. Is this a 17th century reworking, part of Sir Thomas Freke's additions? Another weird skew-whiff example is at Exbury, Hants. It is out of square, with cut off corners, rather than truly octagonal. Another, on the face of it 17th century oddity, is the hexagonal bowl formerly at Swanage, now in Herston (a loose base outside Swanage church may belong to it). The tooling is extraordinary, surely of 1663, when one pair of round-headed panels was perhaps joined to accommodate the date, but the bowl itself was probably first shaped in the 12th century. From all this confusion it emerges that most were made from the standard 12th century basic Tournai pattern that evolved over time. Brian Bugler has noticed that, whilst variations occur, the basic size of the square bowls often conforms to the length of the hypotenuse of a two foot by one foot right-angled triangle. Does this suggest the size of the standard medieval mason's square?

Fonts surveyed in Dorset include 26 square, 29 octagonal (six of the latter with trefoils, six with pointed arches, four with the later cusped panels). Three are problematic to date, with circular bowls, such as Bincombe, which prompts comparison with similar Burr examples at Steeple and Studland. Some authorities suggest that these are pre-Conquest. Pulham, Dorset, is interesting on several counts: it bears six round blank arches and was clearly never polished. Hampshire has the next highest personal tally, with sixteen fonts, but I must stress how subjective this survey is. The Hampshire group contrasts with Dorset in having proportionately more square bowls, twelve, as against only three octagonal. Curiously the square group includes seven with a variety of motifs, of which Dorset only has two. There are other such single examples in the Isle of Wight, Suffolk, Devon and Cornwall. The last examples, at Hennock and St. German's, respectively, are similar, surely from the same workshop, if not by the same hand. The several arches on one of the sides are treated as scallops (Aylesbury style) rather than squarely cut sunk panels. Other sides bear a triple hour-glass-like decoration, a chain-like series of three rings, and a trio of elementary four-leaf clover-like shapes.

After Hampshire comes Norfolk with thirteen. Only one is square, all the rest octagonal, with nine virtually the same: a pair of pointed arches each side. It is as if the diocese ordered a standard batch. For what it is worth, Ingham (Norfolk), reset on 19th century decorative marbles, has features typical of the blue bed as recently dug at Quarr. The bowl exhibits a false bed merging into a vent, grading into a list. If these features are restricted to the Quarr area, then they suggest its source. The bowl also contains a piece of vertebrate bone. Such pieces, together with teeth, shark dorsal spines, fish scales, turtle carapace and coprolites, are common in the Purbeck beds in general, though articulated vertebrates remain comparatively rare. A paving in Norwich Cathedral north aisle has a bone about three inches long. A similar piece in Dorchester Abbey got me into trouble with a fundamentalist resident.

All but one of the seven Suffolk font examples seen are similarly octagonal. However, this is not true of Cornwall, where all five are square, nor the Isle of Wight or Kent. Kent has a rarity at Elmstone, which has a round bowl contained within 'anvil shaped corner pieces', as Pevsner describes it.

The octagonal one at Dinton, Wiltshire, is of particular interest for it has five round-headed arches on two adjacent sides, whilst the others are enriched with pointed trefoils. Pevsner's suggestion that it was perhaps partly 're-cut about 1300' seems wrong, for the bowl is more or less central.[19.] Perhaps its cutter was trying to keep up with the times even as he made it; I know of no other like it. The two Welsh examples, St. David's, Pembroke, and Llanbadarn Fawr, Cardiganshire, are both of the standard octagonal type with pairs of pointed arches per side.[20.]

Some fonts, now octagonal, were originally square but have had their corners cut off. In the case of Milborne Port, Somerset, this was perhaps done in the 17th century, when the wooden octagonal cover was made. Calbourne, Isle of Wight, is another formally-square bowl, similarly hacked into an octagon, with elementary geometric shapes instead of arches surviving on four sides only. Lustleigh, Devon has a puzzling round example supported on a granite hour-glass-like shape, surrounded by four Ashburton marble shafts of 1891, when, the guide says, it was put together. Pevsner comments: 'primitive Norman font forms centre of an imitation Norman font'. The marble bowl must be medieval, but sits awkwardly on its four corner shafts. I suspect it was once square. However, some round examples, such as Bincombe, Dorset, would appear to be without alteration.

The majority of the marble medieval fonts now stand on modified supports, most dating from the 19th century. It seems that it was common then to keep the old bowl but generally 'do things up'. That often meant renewing the base and shafts and tidying up the bowl by reworking it. However, some rearrangements are much earlier. Honing, Norfolk, has the standard 13th century octagonal bowl, but it rests on an elaborate Perpendicular support that is at least two hundred years later. What of South Hayling, Hampshire? Each corner shaft has a soft stone capital and base of surely medieval date, but are they contemporary with the Norman top? Is there a certain way of knowing when these combinations were put together? A useful clue in differentiating between medieval and 19th century fonts is the presence, or otherwise, of lid fixing clasps. Most, if not all, medieval bowls have them, following Archbishop of Canterbury Edmund of Abingdon's order of 1236 to fix lids 'as a precaution against sorcery'. Another factor that tends to muddy the waters is the differential weathering properties of the marble beds. The Royal Commission ventures that East Lulworth's base to its 15th century font is modern, whilst I suspect it is simply a better quality marble and original.

Goodworth Clatford, Hants, St Peter. Purbeck Marble bowl on later supports. The cut out bowl on all these square examples is cylindrical.

Some fonts are reported as having been rescued from serving as troughs. Church guides for both St German's and Harrow suggest that their fonts were thrown out around 1800, but rescued some fifty years later; one wonders how accurate this sort of information is. The octagonal bowl at Kingston, in Kent, with flattened Norman blank arches each side, was retrieved from serving as a pig trough as early as 1742, which begs the question of when it was first thrown out. Two in Hampshire remain outside yet: Wellow is square with three round arches per side, and Fyfield is of a rare shape suggestive of an outsized mortar. It awaits rescue. I tentatively suggest that a squarish piece of marble which exhibits a drain-shaped hole, built into a post-Reformation wall at Waltham Abbey also containing lots of broken marble shafting, is a quarter of a font base.

Splendid 12th century Harrow stands alone in the decoration of its round bowl, and its twisted single stem, which exhibits a thick list. It owes little to the Tournai/Purbeck mainstream. The only marble effigy in France is at Lisieux, of a cleric, possibly Bishop Arnoul, associate of Becket. It similarly displays a list. Both were probably worked in Canterbury from Peveril Point marble. It comes as no surprise to learn that Canterbury held Harrow estates. At its restoration in 1846 a new top rim was fitted to the Harrow font which explains the absence of clasp holes. The square base with spurs was recut to the round plan we now see. Originally it would have been even more like the splendid Bethersden marble example at Harrietsham in Kent. Their similarity prompts the suspicion that it too was cut in the same workshop.

Sculpted variants in the decoration of bowls are rare. Oare, Kent, has one with four carved heads, but unfortunately is

Lessingham, All Saints, Norfolk. Purbeck Marble bowl.

badly eroded. Minstead, Hampshire, is of the more typical shape but enriched with low relief carving on each side. The piece of marble now built in the internal west wall at Havant, showing an animal between a pair of roundels, is probably a font bowl.

Many fonts have lost the original surface, but where it does remain some reveal that it was chiseled rather than rubbed or polished. Hennock, Devon, and both Barton Stacey and Goodworth Clatford in Hampshire, are early examples (*see previous page*). Lessingham, Norfolk, has an octagonal bowl with pairs of round-headed trefoil sunk panels each side; fine claw tool marks are evident in the sunk panels; fine straight chisel marks define the arrises. Knodishall, Suffolk, is similar but with pointed blank arches, as has Hinton Martell, Dorset, the latter bold enough to suggest a possibility of 19th century retooling. These examples are spread out in date, so the practice of leaving some surfaces chiseled was going on over time. With so many examples badly eroded it is difficult to be always sure of the original treatment. It could well be that, as with coffin lids, in some cases only the salient parts, particularly the top rim, were rubbed and not the whole font. Mappowder, Dorset, looks smooth where the surface endures, but fine chisel marks are evident in the base stooling mouldings.

EFFIGIES

Salisbury has two effigies that predate the Cathedral, one of Tournai with a Purbeck head inserted, and the other entirely Purbeck. More Tournai examples seem not to follow, but Purbeck continues to be used for the greatest magnates, including King John in Worcester Cathedral. There is evidence that some of these were partially painted.[21.] John even had precious stones placed in key places. The royal effigies that follow him are of metal or alabaster, but Purbeck continues to be used prominently in the tomb chests that support the figures. Perhaps in the choice of alabaster for the effigy of Edward II, 1327, even though it rests on an elaborate Purbeck chest, we can see the use of Purbeck beginning to slip. The process was

ABOVE LEFT Salisbury Cathedral. Tomb of Bishop Roger (d.1139): Tournai with Purbeck marble head inserted.

ABOVE RIGHT Salisbury Cathedral. Tomb of Jocelyn de Bohun (d.1184): Purbeck Marble.

BELOW Worcester Cathedral. Tomb of King John (1166-1216) with Purbeck Marble effigy.

LEFT Gloucester Cathedral. Edward II's tomb, with alabaster effigy and Purbeck Marble tomb chest. 1327.

ABOVE Sherborne Abbey, Dorset. Unknown abbot, Purbeck Marble, 13th century.

BELOW Exeter Cathedral. Bishop Henry Marshall (1194-1206), Purbeck Marble.

slow. Henry V's Chantry (1431), includes very high quality Purbeck (better than that used in much of Henry III's work close by), but by Henry VII's tomb, 1518, it has gone as a component of Royal monuments. In considering the different materials used for King John's and Edward II's effigies, I would estimate that hard Purbeck John represents at least four times the man hours of the soft alabaster Edward.

The use of Tournai in England largely died out after the 12th century, giving way to Purbeck's sudden large-scale development. One rather ironical example, given that his name has stuck to two parishes productive of so much Purbeck, is the John Maltravers ledger tomb in Lytchett (d.1365). Perhaps he procured it during his continental banishment? Another is the much altered tomb of Edward IV in St. George's Chapel, Windsor.

In considering where the most highly refined work such as the effigies was done, it would seem reasonable to conclude that some were carved at the source, i.e either at the quarries or Corfe, others at centres such as London or where itinerant carvers gathered to work on major projects. Early examples such as Philip the Priest at Tolpuddle and Abbot Clement at Sherborne, are probably in the first category; later work such as King John at Worcester and Archbishop Walter le Grey at York, possibly in the latter.

A glimmer of light on this question of where things were made is possibly shed by a document describing a dispute which followed the death of Master Ralph, mason of London, in about 1300. It centred on payment for work he had done or failed to do, on Huntingdon Bridge. The result was that his daughter Alice broke into her deceased father's 'tenement' in St Paul's churchyard and carried off a knight carved in marble worth £3 6s 8d (5 marks), and a Latten (brass) effigy of a bishop worth 32 shillings, also small marble columns and other stones. The question remains as to whether Ralph was working in both Purbeck marble and brass in London or stocking items carved elsewhere. What is beyond reasonable doubt is that the brass engraving was being done by these London marblers – were the effigies as well? Considering the cost, the valuation put on Ralph's effigy is not wildly dissimilar from another costing £4 10s. Brian Bugler in his reading of Lethaby and other authors concludes that with wages of about six pence a day such a carving represents about 30 weeks' work.[22]

Romsey Abbey. Purbeck Marble coffin lid (broken). Note 50p coin and confetti for scale. A (c. 12 inches) incised cross of similar geometry is cut into the inner wall of the outer gatehouse at Corfe Castle (c.1282).

early 14th century as the production of plain rectangular tomb slabs bearing brasses commences. Lots of these were produced before they too cease in the early 17th century. Exeter Cathedral has about one hundred Purbeck marble tomb slabs. Dating this secession is difficult due to the problem of re-use, which was common practice.

BRASSES & OTHER USES FOR MARBLE

Medieval brasses have attracted considerable interest and study. This has shown that London workshops dominated, being responsible for about 75 per cent of the existing English figure brasses. From the very earliest, (Sir John D'Aubernoun (1277) at Stoke d'Abernon, Surrey, Robert de Bures (1302) at Acton, Suffolk) the Londoners were setting most, perhaps almost all, of their brasses into slabs of Purbeck, as were at least two provincial workshops at Lincoln and Exeter. During the first quarter of the 14th century the standardised London product had effectively cornered the market.[25]

When I remarked to the churchwarden at Dartmouth that the brass to merchant John Hawley (1408) was set in a slab from Dorset he was quite incredulous. 'Why do that when we have tons of granite just up the back lane?' he said, remaining quite unconvinced. I could have added that the slab probably went first to London before returning westwards. Though the possibility must remain that some London brasses were united with their Purbeck matrices away from the capital, the style that emerged in England of complicated canopies, figures, weepers, heraldic devices, prayer scrolls, individual letters, all in separate outline rather than engraved on a single rectangular sheet of brass, would mitigate against this. John Hawley, complete with his two wives, would have taken a lot of work to fit.

However Branscombe, Devon, may tell a different story. There is evidence of a local mason working in Purbeck marble as well as the local stone. There is a non-Corfe style cross cut on a non-Purbeck coffin lid, of local provenance, as well as the same style cross cut on a Purbeck unio slab. London brasses set in Eggleston Marble, local to the north of England, suggest that the brass travelled to the slab.[26] Of course the real point about the Dartmouth brass *et al* is that Purbeck was coming out of the ground in relatively convenient shapes; contrast that with Dartmoor granite, from which it would have been extremely difficult to produce a large flat slab. The natural shapes, 'like a lot of horses' heads', are a mason's nightmare.

Sir Thomas Windham and wives' chest tomb in Norwich Cathedral (1522) reveals particularly well how the now-missing brasses were fixed. Being on top of the chest, the untrampled matrix retains clear rivet holes, and generous amounts of fixing bitumen in the three figure sinkings. Each rivet is possessed of a groove for the molten lead. In what order was the fixing work done? These sinkings exhibit punch marks as well as chisel, indicative of speed: if you punch close to the finished level, you have less work to do with the chisel.

Some incised slabs were being produced at the same time as the earliest brasses; for example, the civilian figure in the Victoria and Albert Museum, discovered in the course of reconstruction at the Bank of England in 1934.[27] More prosaically, a lot of paving and steps were made, and marble was used for practical rather than aesthetic reasons. At the Tower of London it is combined with timber and Reigate stone in low level courses built in the deepening of the moat attempted by Henry III and recently excavated. Salisbury Cathedral spire has a high level course where its resistance to water penetration may have been the prime consideration.[28] It was also used decoratively as external shafts at Salisbury and Chichester, and semi-externally as mullions in Chichester and Lincoln's eastern windows and Canterbury's Archbishop's Great Hall, begun by Archbishop Hubert Walter, all about 1200. Dunkeswell Abbey ruins, Devon, include plain marble external steps in the Perpendicular gatehouse, perhaps explained by the Brewer family connection. Internal use for steps is much more common. Outside St. Magnus the Martyr, London Bridge, a few pieces of the old bridge remain. Two are of Portland of questionable date but there is a four foot piece of battered marble ashlar complete with holes for leaded cramps at each joint. It almost has Henry Yevele written on it.[29]

Erosion has exposed rough slabs of marble forming footings

Branscombe, Devon, St Winifred. A typical Purbeck Marble coffin lid.

ABOVE Stanton Harcourt, Oxon, St Michael. Detail of Purbeck Marble shrine of St Edburgh, formerly in Bicester Priory. Between 1294-1317. Note use of drill in treatment of hair.

RIGHT Detail from Abbot Litlyngton's missal (1384), showing Edward the Confessor seated on a Purbeck Marble throne (Westminster Abbey Library, MS37 Fol 225v.).

to 13th century work at Corfe Castle, surely selected for their nice flat practical shapes. The loop above bears Alan de Plukenet's arms. He was constable in 1269/70. The slabs appear to be permafrost affected, so dug from just beneath the 'clot', no good for anything special, but an excellent foundation. Current conservation work on the now-inverted bastion to the southwest that has almost tumbled to the stream, exhibits more such slabs of marble. One piece has been split with wedges, which suggests that it is a reject from tomb or architectural masons' work. Corfe also contains quite a few marble lintels. Ready availability in long lengths (unlike Burr) is surely the reason; the same logic for its use as sills in Beaulieu's Refectory's lancets, all but one replaced.

A high percentage of shrines, including heart shrines, as far afield as St. Cuthbert, Durham and St. Thomas Cantalupe, Hereford, contain Purbeck components. The highest quality work exhibited in the best survivals at Stanton Harcourt, Westminster, Winchester and St. Albans, tells that for a while the finest artists and craftsmen were working in Purbeck marble. Each one is a technical *tour de force*, as are some of the chantries and tombs. Archbishop Bouchier's tomb in Canterbury is notable for that reason and that it incorporates two sorts of marble, one certainly from the Weald as well as one that looks to me like Purbeck. I venture the suspicion that the artist who carved the non-Purbeck tomb of Blanche Mortimer (1347) at Much Marcle, is the Stanton Harcourt master.

Other rarer usages include the wonderful 12th century screen from Southwick Priory, Hants (removed and in the care of English Heritage), the fountain at Westminster (its flower-like form is, it seems, unique, but how many other abbeys may have possessed such fountains?), St. Augustine's chair in Canterbury, the great table in Westminster Hall and components in some of the Eleanor Crosses, all 13th century. The expectation that a royal throne should be fashioned of Purbeck marble is displayed in Abbot Litlyngton's Missal of 1384, in which Edward the Confessor is pictured seated on such a throne.

There are several surviving pre-Reformation altar tops. They are typically enriched on the front and ends with a single hollow chamfer. Wrentham, Suffolk, has one reused as a tomb slab in 1651. The altar top at Bere Regis retains a chiseled hollow chamfered edge whilst the top was rubbed. The so-called King

Canterbury Cathedral. St Augustine's Chair, early 13th century, Purbeck Marble.

MARBLE / 49

replacement pillars at St. Aldhelm's quarry, Worth Matravers. Unlike with the originals, machines helped to speed up the first part of the process. That is, the raw blocks were sawn to close to the square containing shape, and top and bottom bed smoothed off by a planing machine. After the preliminary work, the banker masons took over cutting to final profiles, much as their medieval predecessors had worked. Their tools were not so different; tungsten carbide rather than tempered steel chisels do not represent an enormous advance, so long as good blacksmiths are available to keep the steel tools sharp, which, judging from medieval tool marks, they were.

When it came to rubbing and polishing, my father and his men had the benefit of newly invented carborundum, but I suspect that good natural sandstone such as originally used would compare favourably. Another possible difficulty in making comparisons was that my father's masons were almost all past their prime, but they were all proficient and amongst the best in their generation.

The choir pillars in the Temple Church consist of a round drum with four engaged shafts, each resting on a raised quatrefoil moulded base. Moulded base number one, not including the sub-base, is two feet seven inches by two feet seven inches by eleven inches overall. It took Thomas Collins 174 hours, plus my father another 40. I do not know why the two of them worked on this single stone. Perhaps Thomas was off work for some reason. The total hand working hours were therefore 214 before rubbing, which took Thomas and Ralf Bower between them another 140 hours. This rubbing was in stages. First No.1, a coarse grit, to take out the chisel marks. Then No.2, less coarse to take out the rough scratches left by No.1, before finer still, No.3. Lastly came a natural stone called 'snake', which achieved a near polish. Beyond experimenting with various carborundum shapes fitted into an electrical drill, which did not work well, power tools were not used.

My memory of this work going on over several years, was that Ralf Bower rubbed most of it. When we children were at a loose end father would tell us to go and help him. We would beaver away and seem to make progress with the wet marble looking pretty good, only to find stubborn chisel marks or deep scratches as the piece dried off. 'Back to No.1,' Ralf would say, sucking on his pipe of homegrown tobacco.

Base number two took Thomas a little less than 208 hours, somewhat quicker than the first, and Ralf rubbed it more quickly, taking only 87 hours. Pillar number one, again after machine preparation, from base level took Tom Collins 355 hours, Ralf Bower 322 and a half hours, William Tomes 329 and a half hours, and Harry Tomes 378 and a half hours to rise sixteen feet. At one foot eight inches by one foot eight inches over all, this translates as 1,385 and a half hours per 44 and a half cubic feet (the mass of each pillar) or 31 hours per cubic foot, all brought to a chiseled face only. Again for medieval comparisons, more time should be allowed for preliminary work done by machine. After this shaping, it took Tom Collins 129 hours and Harry Tomes 28 hours to rub it, plus other men usually employed on other tasks: Ted Bartlett eight hours, Bert Norman 16 hours, and my father joining in with 24 hours, a total of 205 hours rubbing which adds four and a half hours work to every cubic foot. Probably, in the case of this pillar, Tom Collins and Harry Tomes rubbed their own work. Bert Norman remarked to me years later that they liked rubbing Bill Tomes' work best in that he worked the finest, leaving the least amount of deep chisel marks – a polisher's bane.

The first moulded cap, at two feet seven inches by two feet seven inches by twelve and a half inches over all, took Harry Tomes 201 hours, plus Tom Collins 36 hours. Again I am puzzled why two men were involved with it, as this was not normal practice. Perhaps Harry was off work and Thomas finished it. Certainly my father was under a lot of pressure to get material to London, and I guess that it was not possible to delay delivery of an entire pillar for want of completion of the cap.

He was under more pressure when the supply of block was stopped by flooding of the quarry. Persistent pumping lowered the water level but also caused a nearby well to dry up. Fresh drinking water had to be taken to the tenant of the affected cottage. Harry Tomes, having spent most of his working life in London yards, was nearing retirement. He was a most proficient mason. He and Ralf rubbed this first cap together, taking 100 hours between them. After preliminary cutting out, done in the Middle Ages with wedges, followed by hammer and punch, mallet and chisel but in my father's time by sawing and planing, the preparation of this cap took 336 man-hours. At a guess perhaps another twenty would cover the preliminary work. It therefore probably took the original marblers approximately 356 hours working by hand to achieve a moulded and rubbed cap of approximately seven feet cube out of the raw block, which equals approximately 51 hours per foot cubed. Very roughly therefore, circular moulded work comes out at about 50 hours per foot cubed; straight convoluted columns at about 35.

The original Temple Round Church capitals are of particular interest in that they bear a close similarity to others in Tournai Cathedral, cut from Tournai marble. The same man may have cut both. The pillars supporting the caps consist of quatrefoils of four separate drums, so the replacements were lathe turned, but they are linked at base, collar and cap. These collars were labour intensive, but not too heavy for my uncle Harold to manage in his garden shed in Crayford, Kent. They were first cut to the basic shape before being sent up to him for working. Happily he carefully recorded his hours: the average time taken for cutting and polishing a continuously moulded quatrefoil three feet by three feet by six and a half inches from a sawn-six-sides block, was 330 hours. This represents a rate of very roughly 73 hours per foot cubed, higher than the cap, perhaps because of its differing profile. Like Harry Tomes, Harold was near retirement and past his prime, but still proficient. His lifetime's experience had begun with work on Swanage County Bridge (1910), before leaving for London. Surviving the trenches, he had a spell on the granite of Sydney Harbour Bridge, and taught at Kidbrooke Technical College. Assisted by his nephew, Cyril Haysom, he worked the Beer stone interlaced arcading for the Temple triforium. They had the benefit of a simple power saw, but beyond that all was achieved by hand.

Another garden shed resounded with the bat of mallet and

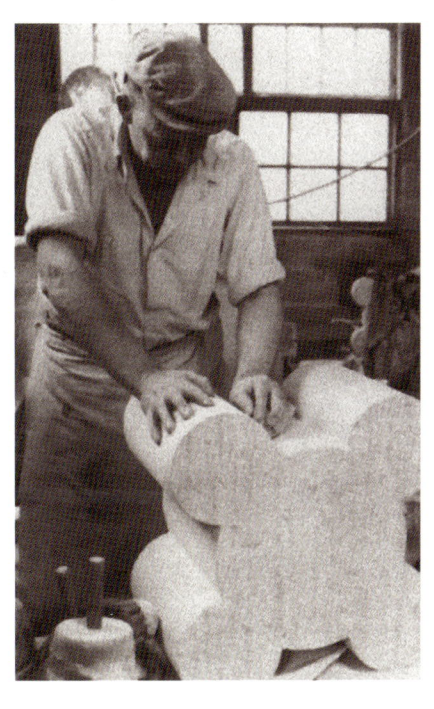

St. Aldhelm's Quarry, a series of photographs dating from the late 1940s to 1950 showing the work for Temple Church.

ABOVE LEFT Thomas Collins with a moulded base, suspended from Dancing Ledge crane. Note dead weight above crane hook to ensure that wire rope does not tangle when not under tension.

CENTRE LEFT Thomas Collins rubbing part of a column..

CENTRE RIGHT Bill Norman handling finished capitals and column drums with rope strops suspended from crane, prior to loading.

ABOVE RIGHT Harry Tomes loading the first moulded capital on to the lorry, June 1950. Note frame saw behind him.

RIGHT Walter Haysom carving a capital.

BELOW Temple Church, London. A modern photograph showing a Capital from St. Aldhelm's quarry in place in the Round Church.

BELOW RIGHT St. Aldhelm's quarry. Stacked triforium capitals for the Round Church.; those on the left have been polished, those on the right not.

MARBLE / 53

Temple Church, London; Chancel (consecrated 1240). Purbeck pillars.

chisel: Arthur Harding, also nearing retirement after years spent on the banker, mostly in Portland, helped out with some of the string return ends in his shed at North Street, Langton. The straight runs were machined by Frank Haysom. He used a coulter planer which cut in both directions, requiring considerable skill to achieve good results. All these masons worked with simple hand tools but pneumatic chisels speed things up. Lots of rapid light blows are an advantage and my father used pneumatic chisels, particularly for the carving of the Round Church capitals, but did not impose them on the other men.

I served part of my time in Benfield and Loxley's Yard at Oxford. After a lapse of a few weeks an old Scotsman who kept himself to himself came over to my banker. 'You are one of those quarry slaves from Purbeck aren't you?' he said. 'Fred Harris was one of the best masons I ever worked with.' He picked up my pneumatic tool; all the bankers were so equipped. 'This is the prostitution of the craft,' he said. His attitude was typical of his generation. However reluctantly, the advantage of air tools has to be recognised.

When attempting to estimate man hours represented in medieval work compared with the 1950s data, it is important to compare like with like. For example, Winchester Great Hall (1222-1236, and therefore contemporary with the Temple Church chancel), has similar Purbeck pillars, but they consist of an arrangement of four engaged shafts plus four more detached, rather than just four, and are therefore more time-consuming. Also, as the girth of a pillar increases, so the surface area reduces in proportion. As it is this surface that requires the work, rather than making per cubic foot comparisons, a better approach may be to 'unwrap' the convoluted surface. But this is still fraught with difficulty. A deeply cut profile means more work than a shallow one, so a large section of relatively shallow convolutions can be quicker to make than a smaller section of deeper convolutions, which characterizes 13th century work. It is interesting to find, on attempting to cut such Early English profiles, how often the depth of the hollows is cut to the maximum. Degrees of hardness dictate the angle of attack by chisel, and those original designers pushed things to the limit. They were practical hands-on men who knew what could or could not be done. I suspect they vied with each other in pushing their technology to the extreme. Some of their slender shafts are almost incredible. Even with modern diamond equipment they are difficult to replicate.

Ignoring the moulding, 'unwrapping' the Temple Church collars produces a surface area of eleven feet by six feet five inches, which equals approximately six foot superficial, so

54 / PURBECK STONE

Winchester Great Hall. Purbeck pillars, 1222-36.

each square foot therefore took 55 hours. Again for medieval comparisons more hours should be added for the preliminary work, perhaps another ten hours. The hours required for this preliminary work would depend on the nature of the raw block. A bed splitting out at about the thickness for the collars would have made life easier than if the nearest thickness nature was producing was larger than necessary, and waste had to be hewed off. This prompts the thought as to what degree the natural material may have influenced the design. Perhaps the most demanding piece of masonry, as opposed to carving, in the rebuilt Temple is the arch over the bishop's effigy recess. Walter Godfrey devised a challenging deeply cut profile. After sawing seven cubic feet, it needed Ralf Bower, my father, plus a third marbler, to work 924 hours.[39]

RECESSION

Marblers engaged in working in brass as well as marble in the late Middle Ages, were sufficiently numerous in London to have their own Company. Its origins are obscure, but it continued until 1585, when its thirteen members 'had beene humble suitors of the Court [of Freemasons] that as wel in respect of the greate decaye and dysabyltye of their said company' they were admitted to the Company of Freemasons.[40] A complaint made by the Corfe marblers 25

Oxford, Christ Church Cathedral. Purbeck Marble soffit detail of canopy for Robert King's tomb, 1557. Note verve of treatment of the bank tracery in pre-Renaissance style.

years earlier illuminates the same recession in Purbeck:

'March 14th, 1560. Grant to the mayor, burgesses and commonality of the borough of Corff in the isle of Purbeck, oc. Dorset, of the right to hold a market every Thursday and two yearly fairs, on the feast of St. Philip and St. James and the feast of St. Luke; rendering yearly 13s. 4d. At their suit: they hold the said town by service of castle-guard, whereby they are to defend the castle adjoining the town for 40 days in time of war at their own costs; but they are impoverished because they live by the working of marble, which art is in decay because it consists in the manufacture of sepulchral monuments and other monuments now not in use.'[41]

Sir William Sydney's (d.1554) Purbeck canopied tomb at Penshurst, Kent, is of this late period and typically conservative in its design. Pevsner remarks: 'untouched by any hint of the Renaissance except for the acanthus scrolls around the brass inscription plate'. Another late example at Milton Abbas, appropriated by Sir John Tregonwell (1565), has similar twisted supports to the canopy but whilst his has separate columns, Sir William's are engaged. The style was slowly evolving but remaining free of Renaissance ideas at this late date. Only in what is perhaps the last marble example, Anthony Forster's

Milton Abbey, Tregonwell tomb, 1565.

MARBLE / 55

LEFT Cumnor, Oxon, St Michael. Marble canopied tomb, Anthony Forster, d. 1572.

CENTRE Blythburgh, Suffolk, Holy Trinity. Example of canopied Purbeck Marble tomb, Sir John Hopton, 1489, serving as Easter sepulchre.

RIGHT Church Knowle, St Peter. Canopied tomb of John Clavil, d.1572.

tomb (1572), in Cumnor, Berks, did its maker give way and incorporate a classical cliché – Ionic corner columns. One at Bisham, Berkshire, removed from Anglesey, hints at Tudor royal patronage. Another of special interest in that it combines Purbeck with Petworth Marble, thereby posing the question of where the workshop was located, is Sir Edward Bayntun's (d.1593) canopied tomb at Bromham, Wiltshire. Tens if not a hundred or more of this canopy type were made, together with similar Easter sepulchres. The most prolific period was 1510-1525. The loss of at least one was revealed by Jerome Bertram describing a chance find in Wytham woods near Oxford : just one small piece of typical cresting found lying in a muddy track.[42]

Curiously the series with canopies finally ends with two Freestone examples: John Clavil (d.1572) at Church Knowle, and John Skerne (d. 1593) at Bere Regis, both in Dorset. In my opinion Clavil is certainly Portland stone, Skerne possibly Cliff, but I am wavering. Both were probably cut before the patron's death. They retain the basic style but take on classical details: egg and dart, fluted columns, etc. One wonders what would have evolved had the style been allowed to continue in isolation, as happened with English fan vaulting.

Around this time Purbeck was also providing more modest marble monuments in the form of rectangular wall plaques. They have a sunk face bearing a brass contained by a round arch or arches producing sunk panels in the spandrels, the arch enriched with very debased egg and dart. Thomas Boys (1584), in St. Mary's Oxford, and William Napper in Puncknowle, Dorset, (16-- the date was never completed) are alike both in style and rather crude treatment. I guess in spite of the apparently rather spread dates, that the same hand cut both.

In 1270, at a time when the marble trade was buoyant, Henry III granted the right to hold a fair and market at Afflington. A chapel existed there until its dissolution in 1553. The chapel's closure is consistent with the fading away of the Purbeck marble industry. The Renaissance was bringing not only new ideas of design but also continental marble. Purbeck, synonymous with the word for generations, was to give way to Carrara *et al*. Full blown grandiose tombs such as Robert Dormer's (1616) at Wing, Buckinghamshire, has Purbeck only occupying a lowly position as sub bases. Interestingly the other similar Dormer monument has Winkle stone in the same location. Sir Charles Reed's splendid alabaster tomb of 1611 in Bredon church, Worcester, is possessed of plain marble panels only in the sarcophagus. It is as if those *arriviste* Southwark School continental artists were making use of odd bits of Purbeck left lying about. There must be quite a human story in all this. Highly skilled men, inheritors of a tradition extending back 400 years, were seeing demand for their craft slip away as new styles and new foreign materials began to dominate.

The Clavil and Skerne canopied tombs with similar mural brasses plus other contemporary lettered inscriptions suggest local provenance for the brass as well as the stone work. With what is known of the London marbler/brass engravers in mind, production of Dorset brasses by Purbeck marblers seems likely. Doris Sibun points out stylistic similarities between some Dorset brasses of that time.[43] Marnhull has a rather coarsely cut brass

56 / PURBECK STONE

LEFT Bredon, Worcester, St Giles. Sir Charles Reed, 1611, Alabaster with a pair of Purbeck Marble panels.

BELOW LEFT Bere Regis, St John the Baptist. Canopied tomb of John Skerne, d.?1596. Freestone.

BELOW CENTRE Oxford, Christ Church Cathedral. Tablet: Henry Dow, 1578. The brass is a palimpsest, which prompts the suspicion that the Marble may be similarly re-worked.

BELOW Oxford, St Mary. Boys monument. Purbeck Marble and brass, 1584.

incorporated in what is probably the local stone, signed 'Anno Domini 1596 by me Lynil Brine'. Several Brines appear in the Worth burial registers around that time and Henry served as Mayor of Corfe between 1605 and 1608.

By this time marble activity was at a low ebb but quarrying in Purbeck did not die out. The production of stone paving was expanding, also the cliff quarries and the exploitation of veins hitherto hardly touched. However some digging of marble continued into the 17th century. Though generally attributed to John Coker of Mappowder, *A Survey of Dorsetshire Containing the Antiquities and Natural History* was actually written by Thomas Gerard of Trent in about 1625.[44] In his account of Purbeck he wrote: 'also quarries of lasting stone and Mines of spotted and blue marble'; mines does not necessarily imply underground working. It seems hardly any marble was dug in the 18th century, one possible exception being columns for Encombe House, about 1734, perhaps sourced from Peveril, which was then part of that estate, but which are more likely to belong to the re-ordering of 1870. This low level of 18th century activity is evident in remarks made by Hutchins: 'In Purbeck is plenty of stone and formerly were some veins of marble' and 'anciently in great repute but now exhausted or neglected.' However, perhaps something was going on for Defoe to say in 1726: 'There are also several rocks of very good marble, only that the veins in the stones are not black and white, as the Italian, but grey, red and other colours.' Defoe seems to be clearly asserting that the decline is a matter of fashion, rather than, as Hutchins suggests, that the Purbeck marble veins were 'exhausted'.

MARBLE / 57

Woodyhyde, Dorset. Author emerging from Squibb's underground quarry in 1986. Note candle and pipe for water pump.

THE NINETEENTH & TWENTIETH CENTURIES

In the 1840s the Benchers sent to Purbeck to obtain marble for refurbishment of the Temple Church. The leading Swanage merchants, Randell's, had some part to play. In the event the marble was dug underground by Robert Squibb of Worth, who sank a shaft in the copse at Woodyhyde. Strahan mentions the quarries active when he explored their geology in 1898: 'Of late years the marble has been raised by means of shafts in a few places only, when occasion arose . . . In a shaft 600 yards west of Downshay [Squibb's] the main bed proved to be two feet thick while an old quarry further on showed three feet of marble'.[45] On quarrying there again in 1986 for Lincoln Cathedral, we reopened their work. They had left the two uppermost beds and only taken out the bottom grey bed. This is sixteen inches thick, overlaid by one foot six inches of shale, resulting in a chamber only two feet ten inches high. We found it flooded to the ceiling in a dry August. However had they coped?

The green unio bed served as their ceiling. Here it is thin and not much use, certainly not productive of the great medieval unio brass indents we see, so none can have come from that region. The blue bed over it is extremely hard, and though some of the blocks were big, all were flawed by innumerable weak calcite veins. This proved a considerable disappointment, but the Lincoln Cathedral requirement was for small pieces for the north choir aisle east window, which we were luckily still able to make. The blue bed here is of high durability, but it seems this 'crispness' has resulted in the abundant fractures. What I do not understand is why these Woodyhyde lists are thin but weak, whilst Peveril Point marble lists can be as thick as your finger, but virtually as strong as the marble itself.

We found hardly any bottom bed left, the Squibbs having taken it in the area to which we were restricted. What we did get was very 'quick' and 'glassy' without being too hard and blocks were of a good straight and parallel shape. But in sharp contrast to the upper blue bed, it has a grey, washed out appearance, indicative of a relatively high clay component, which will accelerate decay.

It is almost incredible how the Squibbs got out large blocks from such a confined space. Pit marks reveal that they sometimes cut lumps with wedges to make the legs, proving they were able to swing a hammer in those cramped conditions. One of the legs is exhibited in the Langton Matravers Museum. We happened to hit one of their lanes, walled up on each side with small rubble. The rest of their digging was more or less backfilled with underpicking shale, such that the supporting legs were difficult to see. Exploring their lane by crawling was made more difficult by the fact that over time the concentrated load on the lane walls had pressed them down into the shale floor, so that the middle of the floor of the lane had risen in a gentle arch. I have not seen the like, for in all the other veins a hard bed of stone is left as the floor. The iron tyred wheels of the standard quarr cart would soon cut into such a floor of shale. That is why Israel Bower at Oak Ridge used a cart supported on a pair of rollers rather than four wheels. Surely the Squibbs did the same?

Lying in that narrow, low lane with scarcely room to crawl on hands and knees, I found it hard to imagine getting out big blocks. A particular problem would have been how to get

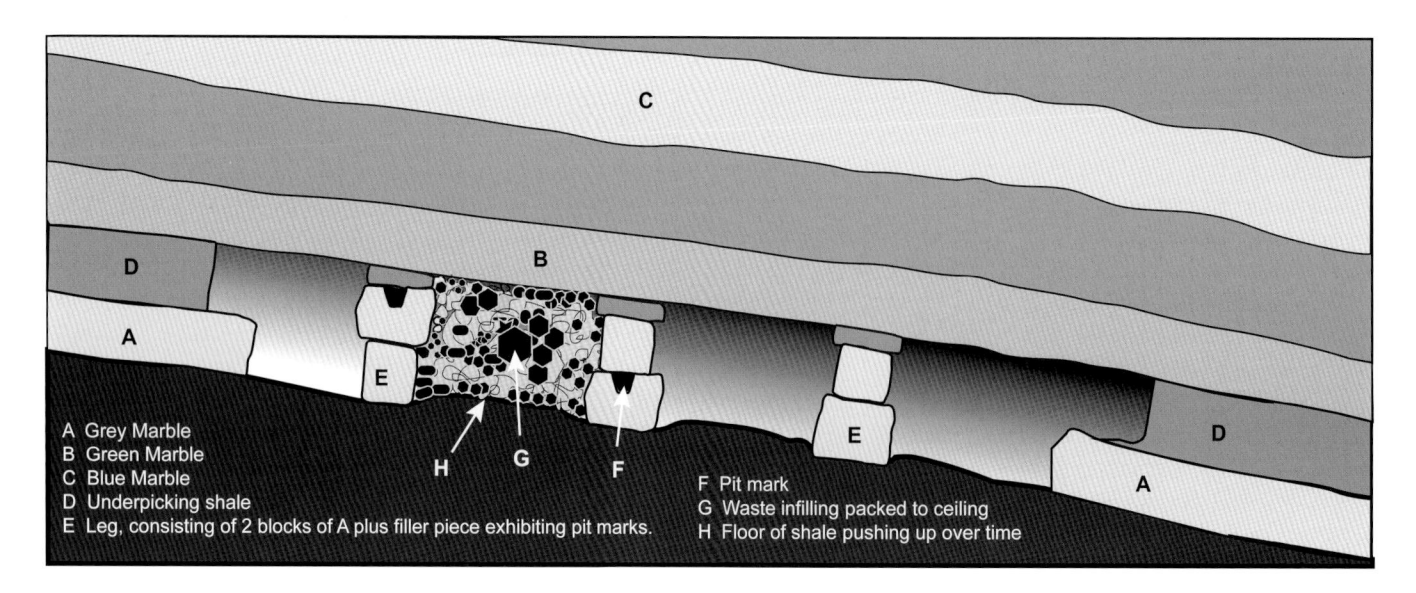

BELOW Woodyhyde. Section of underground working, Squibbs' quarry.

A Grey Marble
B Green Marble
C Blue Marble
D Underpicking shale
E Leg, consisting of 2 blocks of A plus filler piece exhibiting pit marks.
F Pit mark
G Waste infilling packed to ceiling
H Floor of shale pushing up over time

58 / PURBECK STONE

the blocks up onto the cart. In other veins at least the upper beds can be drawn and dropped on the cart before removal, but this certainly did not apply. They had to get the block up on to the cart that could hardly have been less than a foot high from the floor. When loaded, that only left a few inches of head room. It would seem they had to get a block of any size up by keeping it level before slipping the cart underneath. To have tipped it at an angle would have been impossible in such a low space. Was it the most difficult working quarry of all? What drove them was the relatively high price, as revealed by the Rev. Austen.[46.] His list of 1852 shows marble was worth two shillings per cubic foot, or roughly four times the price of other block, which was sold for six shillings per ton. To make another comparison, finished kerb was only worth about seven pence per foot cube, with all that meant in terms of extra hard work dressing it.

Latterly the Squibb family had a Freestone/Downs Vein quarry, which is still open, north of the Worth road, almost opposite the old approach road to Eastington Farm. They worked there in winter, fishing out of Chapmans Pool during the summer. It was said of one that he could spit and hit a fly. Now there is a talent! Much of the marble they supplied for the Temple Church was destroyed in the war, but some can be seen in its Round Church wall shafts. Other 19th century work of almost certain Woodyhyde provenance, much of it now in a poor state, remains. One certain piece is the font in Swanage Church, worked by John Haysom (then manager of Randell's), and polished by Nathanial Turner.[47.] Randell's were also doing fiddly bits for repairs at Salisbury around this time. One of the Phippards who appears in the photograph of Randell's banker (*see page 9*) was particularly good at this demanding work.

A plethora of shafts, string course, etc. dating from the 19th century restoration of St. Mary Undercroft in the Palace of Westminster, looks like Woodyhyde bottom bed. It is all of one bed, indicative of underground working. This contrasts with other 19th century marble shafts at Southwark Cathedral which are definitely cut from at least two, if not three, different beds. These cannot therefore have come from Woodyhyde, but almost certainly from Crack Lane or Oak Ridge. Another late 19th century project is architect George Street's Purbeck shafting in his Law Courts in the Strand, London. None are particularly long and there is little variation. Knowing of his use of Blashenwell marble in contemporary Kingston Church prompts the suspicion that the London marble was also from that source. Separation of Blashenwell upper blue bed from Woodyhyde bottom grey bed is difficult.

The flawed nature of the upper bed and the virtual absence of the green perhaps explains why the Woodyhyde area was not much dug during the medieval boom. One wonders what 19th century knowledge there was, and in particular how the Squibbs knew that weeks of unpaid work digging a shaft would be rewarded. Indeed, if it had not been done before, how did they know that it would even be possible to get block out by such means? Their sunken track remains, leading into the copse from its northern edge towards where the former shaft lies, now filled. Spaced across it are two mysterious pieces of marble, set up rather like a pair of crab stones, but too far apart. They also

Southwark Cathedral. Purbeck shafting in the nave, (1890-7). Note contrasting beds of Purbeck Marble, the upper Blue or Grey with oxidization indicating extremity of block. The lower one is Green bed: note unios.

lack collar board slots, but instead one possesses a horizontal drill hole, the other a vertical. One is about two feet six inches, the other three feet six inches high, and they can hardly be gate posts. For a time at least the Squibbs made use of the 360 degree Portsmouth Harbour crane, later set up on Randell's banker, but these stones would not seem to be connected to that. My father said that they hauled the blocks out to a banker somewhere near the route of the present Valley road. The pair would not seem to have a function in that part of the operation either. Less of a puzzle is the bank and ditch that curves around the top side of the copse. This must have been dug to shed surface water away from the open shaft.

The Renaissance had seen the passing of the Purbeck fashion. This may have coincided with the practical exhaustion of at least the best marble quarries. By the time of the 19th century revival what choice was there? My father, Thomas Bonfield and others would say that the best marble came from where it was wet. Perhaps such an idea was just a consolation as they struggled against flooding at Lynch; perhaps there is something in it. Certainly a trial hole I dug near Blashenwell in a dry area produced nothing but poor quality, small stuff, fit only for rubble. Some undug parts of the outcrop can perhaps be accounted for by reasons of this sort; restrictions imposed by owners are, in my opinion, less likely. When Henry III wanted marble for his abbey, or Bishop Poor for his cathedral, they surely got it.

In my opinion, based on some evidence but more on

surmise, it is likely that medieval activity had exhausted the relatively easy exposures from Peveril westwards to where Swanage has since grown up. Here the northern limit of the Burr syncline gives rise to the steep lower slope of the limestone ridge. For example, the High Street at the British Legion Club runs along the Burr, whilst a few yards to the north the marble outcrops under the old police station. Springs, each no doubt fault-related, punctuate this outcrop. One supplies the Mill Pond, another at Court Hill is piped away to the north before it surfaces. Another, at Boilwell, erupts almost on the shore, Was any of this stretch quarried? Pits on Newton knap are said to be old marble quarries. When the Steer Road estate was developed contractors hit the marble in service and foundation trenches. Some was used for the walls on the High Street at the eastern arm: not many council estates can boast marble garden walls. Recently service trenches cut in the western arm reached marble depth but did not fully penetrate it.

The 1920s development revealed a splendid fish or crocodile fossil in the marble layer, which extended beyond the confines of the trench. In spite of appeals, the Clerk of Works would not allow the trench to be widened out, so it was destroyed.[48.] It would seem this Herston stretch was not much dug. Westwards of the Cross there were undulations close by the road, indicative of quarrying, all since levelled out. On the approach to the new St Mark's Primary School, splendid oaks grow in hollows and on banks. These are surely medieval quarries. Westwards towards Oak Ridge, my father found a patch of blue or perhaps grey beds amongst earlier diggings, whilst Phil Keates, trying a few years later further east, found a dense green bed, rich in unios.

At Oak Ridge there are big holes, evidence of much activity. Some at least is 19th century, for Isaac Bower, his son John Ivamy Bower, and Israel Bower were working here underground. Strahan mentions this quarry in 1898: 'The pit referred to by Mr. Woodward as being open in 1884 lies 150 yards north of the farm now known as Coombe, 1/2 mile east of Langton'.[49.] Presumably this Oak Ridge marble went for ecclesiastical use. But my father had not heard it talked of in connection with any particular project. This may just serve to point up weaknesses in oral tradition. He knew of his grandfather working on the rebuilding of the Palace of Westminster, but I do not remember him talking about the use of much Purbeck there, when in fact there is a lot. Israel utilised some of the small blocks for pitchers and kerb, some of which, still in good condition, served in Langton High Street before the road authority replaced them with concrete. Close by the main Valley road, in the wood west of Piggery Lane, there are holes which must again surely be medieval marble quarries. Continuing westwards there is little evidence before Crack Lane is reached. One wonders why? I suspect it is more to do with geological rather than ownership considerations.

About 1890 Walter or William Brown was digging marble east of the lane, in Putlake meadow at about the level of the so-called marble quarry entrance gate. Flinger Bower, when a boy, had the job of digging a trench to drain the quarry! This Brown family had cliff quarries at Sheepsleights, East Winspit and Halsewell, as well as a quarry in Captains (Capstan) field, where they employed several men. They did a lot of work for the Duke of Norfolk at Arundel, and the Putlake meadow marble went for his new chapel there around 1890. My father mentioned that Browns supplied Rattee and Kett of Cambridge who worked the marble for the chapel. However, the Bankes Estate papers reveal that Rattee and Kett also came to an agreement with that estate to quarry marble on Wilkswood farm in 1898. They paid for 2,798 cubic feet at one shilling per foot royalty.[50.] The Browns surely organised things in Purbeck for the Cambridge firm. However Putlake meadow is not Wilkswood land; if father's account is correct they must have had an agreement with the Encombe Estate as well. Rattie and Kett worked the marble to the same exacting standards of contemporary Kingston Church, Dorset. Unlike Kingston, this Arundel marble shows variety, as it is of more than one bed.

For some reason, possibly flooding, part at least of the Putlake meadow had been left by the medieval quarriers, but from here westwards there remains evidence of massive exploitation over a full mile. A small part of this is also late 19th century, for prominent stone merchant Henry Weeks Burt employed men, including Fred Audley, digging not far west of the lane. This may well have been for the Duke of Norfolk, but possibly other work as well. My father knew of this thanks to a chance remark made by Fred, but he had little idea of how much was done or for how long. Activities were concentrated in October, which on the face of it is odd, for such a late date brings the risk of frost damage. Presumably the more important consideration was that this is when the water table is at its lowest. It was some of this marble, dug by 'Grocer' Burt, as H.W. was known, that remained in the depot into the 1920s. Grandfather used it for work at Salisbury, supplying the Clerk of Works, Mr. Messenger, with small moulded pieces, worked in sand boxes by Burt and George Harden, Bill Chaffey Bower, and Jack Edmunds. Chaffey was well named, hiding Jack's piece only for him to find it in his own tool box, etc.

One of the jobs my father worked on in the 1930s was paving

Painted Hall, Greenwich, interior showing paving.

60 / PURBECK STONE

LEFT AND BELOW LEFT West Lynch, Dorset. Quarrying for the Painted Hall. Greenwich, c. 1938. Note crane and pump.
Left to right in the lower photograph are Harry Prior, R. Bartlett, probably Jimmy Ivamy Bower. Note the contrast between the conditions in the quarry and the final results of the work in the photograph on the opposite page of the paving in place.

for the Painted Hall, Greenwich, taken from West Lynch. The original floor is Sussex or Kentish marble; presumably, with those being unavailable, Purbeck was the nearest match for replacement of stones damaged by damp or salts around the periphery. This cutting was done in Haysom and Sons' yard, the depot, King's Road, Swanage. An exceptionally large block was kept back for something special. The war intervened and the yard was sold to the Council. Some stock, including this big block, was taken to Lander's quarry. After the war George Hancock bought it to supply a London firm carrying out repairs to the splendid canopied tomb of John Croke (1477), shattered by the bombing of All Hallows by the Tower. Prior to despatch to London, Hancock's got Bob Harris to cut it on his framesaw at Winspit. One wonders whether any medieval block led quite such a convoluted 'gothic' career.

BELOW London, All Hallows by the Tower. Croke tomb, 1477.

MARBLE / 61

THE EXTENT AND NATURE OF MEDIEVAL QUARRIES IN PURBECK

For a full mile westwards from the bottom of Crack Lane, mounds and hollows remain. The medieval quarriers took out from the surface outcrops northwards to the stream and sometimes west of the farm, even beyond it, which would have made progress difficult but not clearly not impossible. To the north of the streamline the land rapidly rises at the same time as the veins of marble dip deeper. They are there, of course, but buried under a crippling amount of overburden. When the stream was not the limiting factor, the exposure of the Quarr medieval quarry phase suggests that they stopped at about fourteen feet depth of overburden. Much of the confusion of bumps and dips is now clothed in splendid oaks. It is hard to imagine what a transformed scene it was seven or eight hundred years ago.

East of Wilkswood farm the quarried area is more or less defined by the stream to the north and the edge of the wood to the south. Within this wood north of the ruined brick water treatment lagoon, close by the stream, springs that rise after heavy rain break out of quarried waste. Here the north to south extent of disturbance runs to about 300 feet. Nearer the farm it is reduced to about 230 feet. West of the farm the stream runs through a series of bowl-shaped old workings again extending over a width of about 300 feet. As the stream seldom dries it is hard to see how they coped with the water. Further west, near the boundary with Quarr, this quarried strip again reduces to nearer 200 feet.

Wherever exposures have been made by winter torrents, by the up-rooting of big trees by gales or by diggings in the 1950s, the evidence is of disturbance. In the case of clay, the difference between virgin and dug is not easy to tell, especially where it has been redeposited by water, such as we found at Quarr, but the manmade spalls and scars are obvious. Difficulties caused by faults, flooding, etc. may have meant that undug patches have been left, not to mention the 'hundred foot rule': the measurements are extremely crude. However, a likely estimate is that an area of rock about 200 feet wide by one mile long has been taken. At Quarr, which is probably typical of this stretch of the outcrop between Crack and Dunshay lanes, the three main beds add up to over six feet total thickness. On this basis approximately 633,600 tons has gone.

Recent transcripts of Langton Wallis Manorial Court records reveal quarrying still going on at Wilkswood Priory during the 15th century, 200 years after the heyday.[51] Some entries may refer to digging Burr, but most relate to marble. In February 1419 one 'quarera'(quarry) called Hykerell was 'sold' to John Lyecchet for the following year for 13s. 4d. In April follows a similar year-long agreement with Thomas Reede of 'Corff', also for the same sum for Hykerell. These sums are what we would now call royalties. Years before, in 1258, £35 was paid by Nicholas Red and his fellows, 'surveyors for purchasing the king's marble in Purbeck for the king's works at Westminster'. These two men, Reede and Red, were probably of the same family and latterly were paying the lord the equivalent of over a month's artisan's wages for the freedom to work the quarry for a year. It must have been difficult to anticipate accurately how much they would get out in the time allowed, but it seems they had to. There were other problems: once digging was discovered in the prior's garden a fine of 3d was imposed.

In October 1479 the Langton Wallis court granted 'John Russe and Stephen Atkyn the rights to quarry Marble in the north part of the Prior of Wilkswood's lands for a year from Christmas, for themselves and six other men, for a rent of 40s.' Eighty six years earlier another John Russe had been supplying marble to Westminster Abbey; the same name appears, working with Richard Knappe also supplying to Westminster, in 1413. The Fabric Rolls specifically refer to '24 small pieces for the nave.' Surely in the 1479 agreement we see the provision for the supply of the last Westminster pillars for a building that had involved two or more generations of the Russe family. The last part was certainly dug at Wilkswood and probably all of it from its 13th century commencement. John Russe continued digging in 1488, for he paid, with Stephen Atkyn, for a 'large quarry called Brigge for themselves plus ten men to work for Marble, £2 13 4'. Then he paid £3 for himself plus three men for the next year. Two years later he again paid £3 for 'a quarry on the land of the prior of Wilcheswode to be worked by him plus three men', at the same time as he and Stephen Atkyn plus 6 men paid £2 for 'a small quarry at the south of the Prior's meadow.'

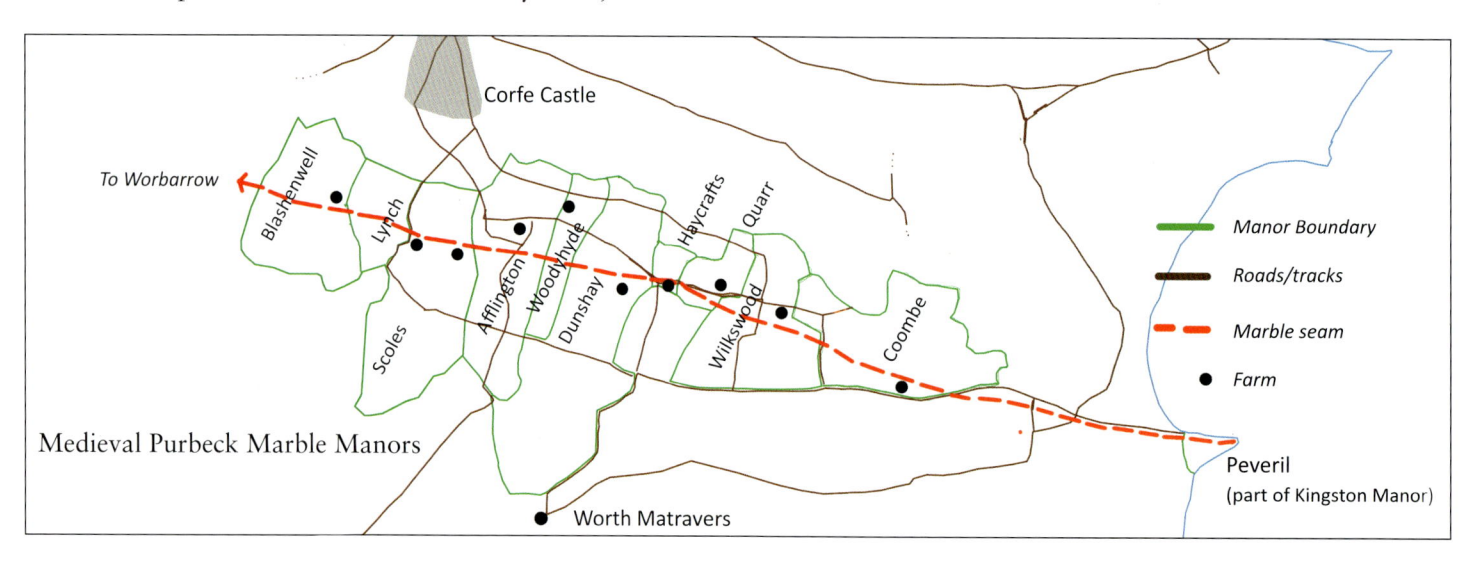

Medieval Purbeck Marble Manors

Elsewhere in 1491 John Benvyle and John Baker paid for quarrying in the 'lord's coppice' for the Michaelmas to Christmas period: 6s 8d, Benvyle 7s – a curious difference. In considering relative money values for the period, a tiler working on the priory hall that same year received 5d a day, whilst his labourer got 3d. The season was late, which brings the risk of frost damage to freshly dug stone, but the over-riding consideration may relate to the low water table. However this thought may be quite irrelevant, for one of the last entries includes '1491-92. One marble quarry of Priory of Wilkswood held by John Russe for one year and for extraction of stone called marble from Easter to Michaelmas £2 6 8.'

In summary, in the late 1400s Marble quarrying was still going on at Wilkswood probably with five or so separate holes: one in the 'lord's coppice'; one with the name 'Brigge' meaning bridge which suggests a location close to the stream west of the farm; another was 'Depe Quarre', a clue to its location being that it was adjacent to the Close; another 'south of the Prior's meadow'; plus the mysterious 'Hykerell'. Since writing this I have spotted amongst Westminster Stores of about this same period, 'bykerell with hawk'. The suspicion arises that modern transcribers mistook medieval 'B' for 'H'. The hawk is the horizontal timber supported on an upright 'bykerel' (post) which together formed some sort of medieval crane. There must be a strong possibility that there were other marble quarries active in the period on other manors, but records are unavailable or lost.

The grant made by Alice de Brewer identifies Dunshay as being the source of most, perhaps all, of the marble in Salisbury Cathedral. In my opinion what we see in Canterbury is from Swanage, so three of the major medieval projects can be linked to a source. Experience of the nature of the marble gained by digging at Quarr, which is sandwiched between Dunshay and Wilkswood, and comparing it with what we see in Westminster and Salisbury, confirms the documentary evidence. Canterbury stands out as being significantly different, particularly on the evidence of its abundant lists. The grant to Russe and Atkyn is a tantalising glimpse of how things were organised. It would seem that above them came the master in charge at Westminster, the unknown successor to that towering figure, Henry Yevele. Were they also marblers supervising others or the entire work force? Does the series of holes with waste piles we see left in the woods reflect this organisation as much as it does the geology and technology? Can we see the hundred foot rule being applied?

LEFT Salisbury Cathedral. Purbeck Marble shafting in clerestory.

CENTRE Canterbury Cathedral. Purbeck shafting in north ambulatory of Trinity Chapel, late 12th Century.

RIGHT Canterbury Cathedral. Purbeck shafting; note calcite lists, which show that the Marble comes from Peveril Point (Swanage) region.

In 1484 John Russe senior was again before the court. He with 'William Boyeler and other labourers of the lord are presented for cutting down the lord's wood and transporting it to Corfe'. They were each fined 13s 4d. Perhaps this was to do with getting the marble out. Old oak trees now clothe the abandoned workings and I have rather assumed that the wood grew up, perhaps accelerated by deliberate planting, on land left so uneven as to be of no other use, but that prior to the medieval quarry it had been cleared of trees. However,

West Lynch, Dorset. Marble quarrying, c.1950. At left, Edward Bartlett, centre, Thomas Bonfield. Note minor fault immediately behind him to the right.

ecologists point out the presence of rare lichens that are slow to colonise, the suspicion being that they may indicate that trees were there supporting them before the growth of the post-quarry wood. These manorial records tellingly reveal that coppiced woodland was established by that time. One wonders just how old are the most ancient ash mocks that continue to grow to this day; from examples cited by Rackham some could date from then.[52.]

An early gift of land in Worth to Wilkswood Priory mentions marble quarrying. The surviving deed would appear to be a 13th century copy of a 12th century original, and relates to Quarr or Dunshay, or possibly both. It indicates quarrying going on there before the big Salisbury project of 1220.[53.] The question arises: was marble taken westwards towards Corfe or eastwards to Swanage? The abundant evidence of trackways crossing Corfe Common suggest the former, as do tracks within the quarried area as far east as Wilkswood. Westwards from that farm a collapsed wall winds through the wood close by the stream. It consists mostly of marble waste rubble, plus some Burr, and it weaves along, more or less level, through the confusion of hollows and banks. Its builders would appear to have taken advantage of the almost level contour provided by an abandoned track and the plethora of waste rubble left lying about in the deserted quarries. This wall stops short of the manorial boundary with Quarr, but the 'track' would appear to continue towards it. It is but a short distance to Haycrafts, where worked marble pieces, including a splendid 13th century column base were found, and from there it is an easy way onwards to Corfe. Other tracks ascending Lanchard Hill out of the quarries similarly head westwards, surely leading to Ower via Corfe.

The north to south extent of much of this old quarry evidence would suggest a geological structure such as the folds at Peveril and Woodyhyde, rather than one simple sloping shelf. This could mean saucer-like forms, which tend to be productive of big blocks. The number of long marble shafts in monuments such as Salisbury is impressive. It is clear that they were not finding just a few long stones, but block after block of big ones, at least of the lower green and grey beds. The upper blue bed is consistently more broken. Hence, in Salisbury where we know the marble came from Dunshay, the load-bearing drums stacked up in bed are in the main of this upper blue bed, whilst the long shafts are mostly of the grey. In my opinion this differentiation in usage is from purely practical considerations, not aesthetic. Some, but fewer, are of the green bed, perhaps because it is harder to work than the grey. This green bed tends to oxidise and become reddish in a way the grey does not. It almost invariably contains some unios, as can the upper blue bed, though the bottom grey bed does not (at least, not from Quarr, but I suspect it does elsewhere). One of these green shafts in Salisbury, at the northwest crossing pier, contrasts with its fellows sufficiently to have aroused suspicion that it is of later date.[54.]

Dunshay, with its outcrop-related spring and pond, has medieval diggings close by the house. These continue westwards towards Woodyhyde before becoming intermittent. Further west there seems little evidence of exploitation, but this apparent lack could be misleading, for Kingston Church was quarried at Blashenwell: the evidence is not obvious. At Lynch the Temple Church dig from about 1950 has left little more than a low mound. There may well be other such dug areas, since backfilled in such a way as to be undetectable. In the 1930s my father reopened Blashenwell, revealing the steps, cut in the overlying shale, that lead down to the working of fifty years before. It was difficult to pursue, and he obtained permission to work over the wall in West Lynch to get paving for the Painted Hall at Greenwich. He continued after the war at Lynch, quarrying marble particularly for the Temple Church. They only dug the one blue bed. I asked him if he was sure there was none below. He said they dug into the floor, which was difficult because of the water, and drove a bar down further, hitting nothing solid. I suspect that lower beds are present, but well separated. The next bed down is a thick green layer at Quarr, but much reduced at Woodyhyde and could be quite absent at Lynch. Perhaps the bottom grey bed also thins out westwards in the same way. What is evident is the very different section at

Worbarrow, where two upper beds are separated from a group of lower beds by about ten feet of shale.

In the late 19th century, Henry Lander quarried marble at Orchard. Strahan wrote: 'S.W. of Orchard the rock is being quarried for use in the Cement Works at Newfoundout, at Orchard the long line of marble quarries ceases.' Exeter Cathedral pillars contain marble with stromatolite. This distinctive rock only occurs in Lulworth Cove and Mupe, but not further east. Both in the medieval period lay beyond the bounds of Purbeck. I remember first noticing this very different rock and concluding that William Canon was questing widely to find his marble. My father cautiously remarked that it could be repairs where spalling has occurred. It seems he was right, for in every case these stones are quite small and surely a 19th century intervention. The same distinctive marble occurs as paving in Salisbury Cathedral, some of it cut across the bed, so definitely sawn and virtually certain to be 19th century. Where this bed rises out of the shore at Mupe it would appear to have been dug away. However, the acute angle of dip, as at Lulworth, would preclude any substantial development. In 1826 James Marsh of Swanage and Thomas Lander agreed a 25 year lease to quarry at Mupe. Obviously a substantial area of Portland beds has been quarried away, probably by them, but it would seem likely that they were active on other beds including the marble, although the evidence is less obvious.

INDUSTRIAL ARCHAEOLOGY

Digging in the manor of Quarr in 1994 and again in 2004 we revealed old back-filled workings and a face of *in situ* marble which the medieval marblers had abruptly left years before. Sadly we found nothing to give an absolutely firm date, but what clues we had – maps, the odd oyster shell, lack of oral tradition, etc. – suggest early. In particular, the discovery of several blocks cut to tapered coffin-like shapes, which are typical of 13th century work, lay mysteriously abandoned. The work appears to have suddenly been stopped, with some pieces halted in the process of being split. The fashion for tapered tombs gives way to rectangular in the early 14th century. It would therefore seem that these stones are pre-Black Death, and possibly coincident with the Great Famine of 1315-17. Ideally it would have been best if we could have dug away the old waste first and so revealed the medieval quarry face before disturbing it, but this was not possible, for to do so would have threatened the stability of adjacent land in separate ownership, including sizable trees and a bridleway. The slope of the hill and the dip of the rock was against us. To prevent a potentially serious landslip we had to dig a small patch of old back filling together with some new marble before quickly back-filling behind us so as to buttress up the threatened area before progressing to a second patch, and so on.

This had been difficult in 1994 when we found the rock to be dipping to a gradient of about 1 in 5, but it became more of a problem as our advance eastwards revealed the rate of dip increasing to 1 in 3 at the same time as the edge of the old workings converged on the boundary hedge. Though able to expose this old heading down to the depth of the blue bed, and

From Quarr Farm, Harman's Cross. Green unio Marble from medieval quarry: the upper half split to a tapered shape and slightly dislocated. An additional, incomplete row of wedge pits forming a second tapered shape with modern(ish) wedges inserted at centre. The severed cut (left) would appear to lack a pit at the far end, which has resulted in a bad break at that point. At far end of slab, a hammer with punches of various lengths such as was used for cutting the pits. In foreground two blocks worked from the rough by Brian Bugler to establish approximate medieval man hours required for such work. Both blocks freshly quarried; at right, plain Burr quoin which took two and a half hours, at left section of string course, approx. five hours. Note missing corners where they are not required; a characteristic of much medieval work, but which many modern masons cannot understand.

thereby see the interesting configuration of a surely medieval quarry face, it was not possible to get more than glimpses of short stretches of the *in situ* green bed below; the lowermost grey proved quite impossible to see clearly. This had mostly to be left. Exposing the old blue bed configuration before extraction revealed a large block cut by means of a splendid long continuous pit. Both bits were still left in place and there was a curious loop in the quarry face configuration. This we called 'the pond', as it lay on the same spot where a pond is shown on the first Ordnance Survey map. However the pond was filled in about forty years ago as part of a general levelling at that time, when old waste piles were bulldozed into old hollows, which has rather muddied the archaeological waters. Former quarry hollows are now occupied by medieval waste put there in the 20th century. It remains a considerable puzzle.

We found the virgin shale overlying the marble to be dry and crumbly, in marked contrast to the old backfilling which was waterlogged, thereby well lubricated and prone to slippage. This was particularly true of the 'pond', where the water was bayed back against the quarry face. By digging away in stages on the down dip side we were able to release it down to a sump from which it could be pumped away. It ran for over a month of fine weather, but was showing signs of lessening before we finished digging and began to backfill properly. At the blue bed level the 'pond' was an indentation of about ten feet by ten feet in the heading that ran from about east-south-east to west-

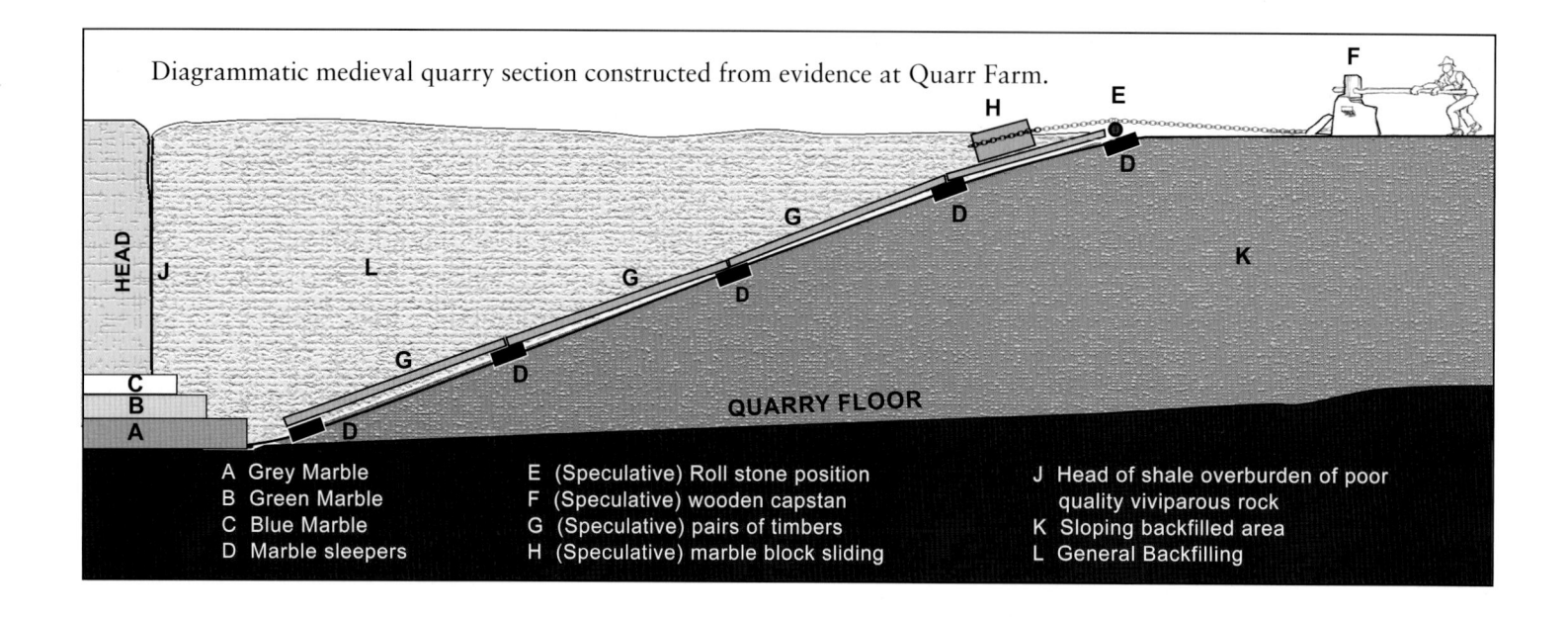

Diagrammatic medieval quarry section constructed from evidence at Quarr Farm.

A Grey Marble
B Green Marble
C Blue Marble
D Marble sleepers
E (Speculative) Roll stone position
F (Speculative) wooden capstan
G (Speculative) pairs of timbers
H (Speculative) marble block sliding
J Head of shale overburden of poor quality viviparous rock
K Sloping backfilled area
L General Backfilling

north-west along the flank of the hill. Its open side faced about west-south-west. At the next layer below the blue there was no indentation, but a sinking. They had broken down through the green, leaving *in situ* rock all around them, as they had also done further down in the next layer, the grey. There must have been a powerful reason for doing this. To break down through a layer is much more difficult than following it once an edge has been created. Following the direction of the open side away to the west-south-west, we found it was flanked by a salient of *in situ* green bed only about one block wide that had surely been left to keep backfilling in place, so it seems we were looking at work of different periods.

On the west-south-west alignment, within the back-filled jumble of shale mixed with small spalls of marble, we found five foot long slabs of marble that had certainly been set in place rather than dumped. They had been positioned square across a gentle gradient at intervals of about 15 feet, the furthest being a pair, one placed on top of the other, almost at surface level. The lowermost had spalls jammed under a corner, obviously in an attempt to get it set at the right angle. The straight alignment and regular spacing suggested that they had served as sleepers supporting timbers forming a slide, up which marble from the 'pond' cutting could have been drawn by a capstan. They bore no evidence of abrasion nor how timbers may have been fixed, nor indeed of any timbers (we did find odd bits of carbonised broken branches within the old waste), but perhaps that should not be expected. The whole arrangement could have been moved forward as the quarry progressed. On such a move the sleepers, perhaps not worth the struggle to retrieve, got left behind before being buried by yet more waste.

In the recent past the steeply sloping side to a shaft was called the slide, but carts did not slide up it, they rolled on wheels. The Quarr Farm marble evidence suggests an earlier development, when the blocks were literally slid along, and from which the name has perhaps derived. Simple capstans are capable of hauling heavy loads, and some medieval slabs weigh as much as three tons, but evidence that the biggest raw blocks were being reduced by splitting with wedges whilst still in situ was provided by the fine block of blue, weighing about 5.8 tonnes, already mentioned, and another of green, both cut to produce pieces of coffin size and shape.

In considering the configuration of the 'pond' it is of course difficult to drive forward on a narrow face, especially when big blocks are encountered. However, once this first difficult breach has been made, marble lying up the dip slope alongside it can easily be loosened and slid into the cut, using bars alone. A chain can be attached and the block hauled away. Such a slide could go on serving a fair sized patch without alteration. This is how some underground runners were worked in the recent past.

The dug area at Quarr held enigmas. A number of quite large blocks, too big to be rejects, lay jumbled at various angles in the top few feet of the old backfilling, some only just beneath what had been a soil level before the 20th century bulldozing. Associated with these blocks were a noticeable number of small marble scars, indicative of some finer dressing having being done. These were as fresh as when made, but under the former soil level a thin scatter had decayed down to individual fossil snails, telling of lengthy exposure at the surface before subsequent burial.

When active, the 'pond' would have been very confined: about 12 feet across, enclosed on three sides with walls rising almost vertically to the grass 20 to 30 feet above. The southern side, because of the dip, would have been particularly dangerous for the adhesion between alternating layers of shale and Marble is poor, especially when lubricated by water. With their feet stuck in clay and water, their greasy tool handles slipping out of their grasp, was it in such a death trap that Walter Le Vel and Hugh Le Mochele died, on this manor, in 1268?[55.] The backfilled waste consisted mostly of shale mixed with spalls of marble, some exhibiting conchoidal fracture surfaces from heavy hammer blows. A few exhibited pit marks showing they had been cut off with wedges. The first ten feet or so of shale under the surface is oxidized and brown, below that it becomes blue. We found both sorts to be mixed in an apparently haphazard way in the backfilling. It tells us they were digging at high and low levels more or less at the same time. Some of these lenses sloped steeply, showing that they accumulated sideways. An exception to this apparent chaos was a thin layer, only a few inches thick, of blue shale lying almost flat over several square yards a few feet below the present surface. It had been surely put there in a deliberate way rather than just tipped. One day a fall of rain stopped the wheeled dumper getting up the clayey ramp to our waste dump and we found that spreading a few bucketsful of freshly dug crumbly blue shale provided a good grip surface which allowed work to carry on. Perhaps they had done something similar 750 years ago.

The medieval marblers extracted the shallow marble more or less continuously along the outcrop line across the manors of Langton Wallis, Quarr and Dunshay. Just how far into the *deep* they pushed may have been controlled by various factors. A dip of 1 in 3, perhaps getting even steeper, could be why they left off relatively early, leaving us to find shallow marble years later. Another factor could be size, which we found varied in short distances without obvious reason; and another, so far as the blue is concerned, is that it is current bedded. The result is that again in a short distance the blocks can be solid or subdivided by several weak beds. If the requirement was for a layer thick enough for, say, a font, then the 'beddy stuff' would be no good, but if, say, string course was the requirement, then the presence of beds could have been a benefit, even a necessity, with the tools they had available. As mentioned, the archaeology of the area we were able to dig at Quarr had already been confused by 20th century levelling works. To the east, old workings continue to slumber since they were abandoned. Archaeological investigation would no doubt be informative. What we can be sure of is that there are extensive concealed medieval quarry faces. I would particularly encourage a look at a Wilkswood site. About 80 yards west of the holly-filled track cutting mentioned on page 232 there is a much smaller cutting on Lanchard Hill, a ridge north of Wilkswood. Its brow along this section is steep, below it the flooded diggings are big. I proffer the thought that this cutting marks a gibbet position; where the cut terminates marks the point at which the blocks became airborne.

How knowledge was lost is nicely illustrated by John Aubrey, writing in the late 17th century:

> Tis strange to see how error hath crept in upon the people, who believe that the pillars of this church [Salisbury Cathedral] were cast, forsooth, as chandlers make candles; and the like is reported of the pillars of the Temple church; they are all real marble, and shew the grain of the Sussex marble (see the little cockles) from whence they were brought. This quarry hath been closed up and forgot time out of mind and the last year 1680, it was accidentally discovered by felling of an old oake, and it now serves London.[56.]

What comes up on root masses torn out of the ground as great trees blow over can be archaeologically revealing. Several recent storm victims growing on old marble workings in Purbeck have revealed waste rubble, scars and oyster shells. Aubrey was on the right lines with the cockles but his

Quarr Farm 2004. Medieval quarry face. Dr John Beavis stands astride severed block as we found it. The upper Blue Bed behind John's feet had been removed.

Quarr Farm. Same view, slightly later, looking south east. Medieval quarry face behind author with backfilled area to the right. The loose block at lower right is a 'sleeper' replaced in its approximately original position.

informant, a stone cutter, was wrong on the location. Oysters discarded in the Wilkswood workings tell us, I guess, of the carters bringing them back from their deliveries to Ower. We found lots of them in Norman and 15th century masonry at Chichester Cathedral. In the latter they were used as wedges within the bed joint mortar serving to keep the stone in position as the slow-setting lime went off. Medieval Burr masonry ruins at East Stoke reveal the same usage as well as pieces of slate used for the same purpose. This is probably from Cornwall and must tell of a traffic in the finished roof slates rather than mere broken bits. More puzzling is a slate lacing course within the rubble of the defences west of the outer gatehouse at Corfe Castle (c.1250).

THREE
Inland Quarrying

BURR

Burr was the uppermost of the three inland building stone beds, and was the medieval building stone *par excellence*. However, as a mere building stone it generally did not travel far, though there is some in the 14th century nave at Exeter Cathedral[1.] and in the Tower of London. Its main use was in Purbeck churches, some manor houses and in the castle at Corfe. The use of Burr continued for churches during the 14th and 15th centuries and for additions to local manor houses such as Barnston and Tyneham.

All three Wareham churches, and elements of Wimborne Minster are also examples, as, in my opinion, is some work at Christchurch Priory and Boldre. But Christchurch presents the difficulty of separating Burr from some of the Isle of Wight stones, which it also certainly contains and which look similar. This eastward region of Christchurch, Romsey Abbey, Winchester *et al* lies in the domain of Isle of Wight stone rather than that of Purbeck Burr. Having said that, medieval builders had a genius for mixing materials. Wimborne Minster lies more in the Purbeck orbit than Christchurch Priory but also contains Isle of Wight stone.

The medieval Burr list includes all the old Purbeck churches, including bits incorporated in 19th century rebuilds at Kingston, Langton, Corfe and Swanage. At Langton there are just a few pieces put out of general view around the furnace room door, as well as the surviving medieval tower. Kingston's old church has an early Norman doorway arch incorporated in the external, west wall enriched with diapers, not dissimilar to some on Marble fonts of the time. At Swanage Burr appears in the east end lancets and quoins to the south transept buttresses. One wonders to what extent they were reworked. Similarly, in Corfe I suspect that all the Burr in the lancets and elsewhere is medieval, much of it retooled, but probably without significant alteration of the original shape. In the case of the north porch they took it down, rechiselled it, and put it back up: an extreme example of the 19th century improving mindset.[2.]

With reference to Studland, my father talked of his father quoting an architect as saying: 'lay not a tool to the fabric'. I guess this was a member of the newly formed Society for the Protection of Ancient Buildings, who were consulted before the work of 1880 began – rather than Crickmay, the architect on the spot. Crickmay was also responsible for Langton, where if his record there is anything to go by, he was an 'improver'. Perhaps if there had been more money floating around Studland would have had the full treatment, but luckily attitudes changed before it happened. That the medieval church at Poole was also of Burr is suggested by bits in the adjacent prison of 1820, built two years after the old church was demolished.

To the west there is some Burr in Winfrith, East Lulworth (where internal tower arch jambs of Burr bear mason's marks), Wool and Bindon Abbey, but it seems not to have got much further. West of Purbeck there is a problem of separation of some Ridgeway beds from Purbeck proper. Athelhampton contains a sort of Portesham stone that is worryingly similar to typical Burr. Piddletrenthide's splendid 15th century tower is said to be Purbeck. It is of a sort, but from the Ridgeway Beds, not from Purbeck itself. Like Wolfeton House, Charminster, it provides evidence of medieval activity in that area. In many of

Langton Matravers, St George. Medieval tower of Burr.

these examples the Burr is combined with other material such as Carr stone from the heaths. Wimborne Minster's 12th century tower is particularly notable. The combination produces a spotty effect, not admired by Pevsner.[3] It must tell of stone being drawn from the different quarries and incorporated without much discrimination. It was probably whitewashed, so the difference in colours did not matter. The remnants of Bindon Abbey include exquisite Burr voussoirs with deeply cut mouldings characteristic of the 13th century.

Northwest Dorset and Somerset beyond is the realm of Ham stone. That Ham appears in the tower of St. Mary's, Wareham (c.1500), must tell us something about Purbeck trade of that time. Some of the admixtures are puzzling. What explains Tarrant Crawford's apparently 15th century porch dressings containing Greensand, Heath stone, plus one piece each of Portland, Ham stone and Purbeck Burr? It would perhaps be more understandable if it was post-Dissolution work. The archaeology of such buildings is a great challenge. Another example of mixed use of stone is Pond's store shed, called a 'smithy' in RCHM's report, at St John's Hill, Wareham.[4] Its blocked two-light windows have hollow chamfered Cliff stone mullions and jambs typical of the late 16th century. A raking list is consistent with St. Aldhelm's Head being the source. The mullions and jambs rest on a Burr cill and support lintels that are not Purbeck of any sort, that in turn carry a label course that looks more like Portland than Cliff stone. The adjacent door of c.1500 is entirely Burr. Is the window a few decades later?

Wimborne Minster. Central tower; mix of Burr and Carr/Heath stone.

Wareham. Burr doorway of Pond's store shed.

INLAND QUARRYING / 69

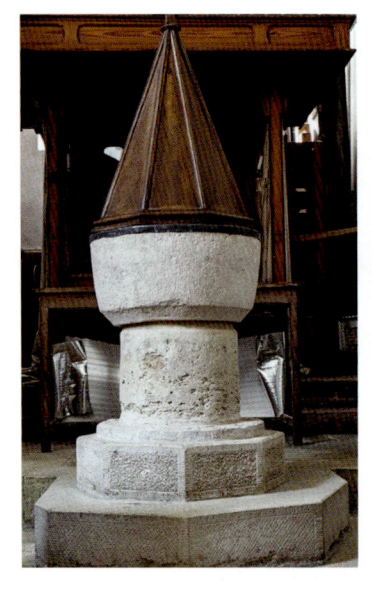

LEFT Steeple, St Michael and All Angels. Burr font.

RIGHT Studland, St Nicholas. Burr font.

The rubble around includes sea-worn marble, one piece with piddock holes, so a Peveril Point source is certain. However, the rubble also includes Cinder and Vie bed, such that does not occur in the shore, but does around Kingston.

Other churches in Dorset that contain Burr include West Almer, Tarrant Monkton and Winterborne Tomson, whilst recent archaeological finds show that Blandford's destroyed medieval church also included some.[5] Bere Regis's splendid 16th century tower is a strict arrangement of Ham plus Ridgeway Purbeck beds plus flint, but earlier work, much complicated by alterations, includes quite a lot of Burr, in particular the sill of a lost lancet, 14th century window tracery, and the mutilated ogee canopy of the Turberville wall recess tomb. Its tomb slab is Marble; the whole is surely all an example of the 14th century practice which uses Burr and Marble together.

Burr also occurs as coffin lids such as the smaller of the two in the Worth Matravers church sanctuary, but the shape of the natural blocks would have mitigated against such use and, relative to Marble lids, the number of Burr examples are few. There are also some fonts such as that at Cranborne, and oddities including Corfe Mullen's old churchyard cross where Burr is combined with Heath stone. Of the fonts, the plain circular bowls at Steeple and Studland, both of high quality, are apparently early 12th and 13th century respectively.[6] However, some authorities claim that they are pre-Conquest. Burr tends to come out of the ground in small pieces. These font bowls are relatively big stones. They would have been hard to obtain unless other work using smaller material was generating a large quantity of excavation, which would have led to the production of occasional larger blocks. Certainly this was happening after the Conquest, with big projects such as Corfe Castle taking up the small stuff for ashlar and rubble. Most of the Burr in the rest of the Studland fabric is readily recognizable but not all: the 13th century east window is worryingly atypical. The extraordinary nave north door is also atypical, both in form and the appearance of the stone. The suspicion is prompted that this may not be burr at all, but Isle of Wight stone, and possibly therefore of a Pre-Conquest date.

In describing his 1880s repair work the builder W. M. Hardy reports something startling:

'The groins are of Purbeck Burr and soft enough to be carved with a knife, wondrously light for such architecture being porous the Burr is unfitted for facing. The stone can be obtained only from rocks which appear at low tide 30 yards east of the stone quay at Swanage. There are no other arches in the neighbourhood turned with this stone.'[7]

What Hardy is describing seems to be the vault infill, rather than the rib, and his observations of the properties of the stone hardly fits typical Burr. But is he describing Tufa? This stone results from the evaporation of water. The minerals build up in the open air at the same time as plant growth, resulting in a distinctive porous lightweight rock. There are several examples of its use by medieval builders, notably for the Worcester Cathedral vaults where they sourced it from spring deposits in the Malvern Hills. In Purbeck, streams spilling over the sea cliffs are leaving accumulations now. The mineral-rich stream rising out of the Burr at Blashenwell has left Tufa which has yielded mezolithic flints. It would seem that the Boil Well spring, close to the stone quay and similarly emerging from the Burr, has also left Tufa accumulations. These have subsequently been drowned by rising sea levels and are only visible at low spring tides. They offer incontrovertible evidence of sea level rise in Swanage Bay since the Ice Age. One wonders how extensive the Tufa bed was before exploitation or erosion by wave action

Studland, St Nicholas. Nave north door.

Lander's quarry, Tufa.

Worth Matravers, St Nicholas. Defaced 12th century tympanum in porch.

Bloxworth, St Andrew. Font. Note Fleur de Lys of the savage family.

began. Bones of Ice Age fauna were found in the course of digging the Wessex Water tunnel in the late 1990s immediately beneath where the spring currently emerges. How far away was the sea when mammoths drank there?

How did 'old W. M.', as my father referred to him, know the medieval story? Of course sourcing stone from the shore is not unusual; quite the opposite: it was the norm. A lot of Studland's medieval rubble is obviously sea-worn; the southern side of Swanage Bay to Peveril Point certainly the source. I guess that in grabbing any stone that came easily to hand, the medieval builders hit on the soft Tufa and used it selectively for the vaulting. It is difficult to prove the point, for the vaulting web compartments ('groins') are hidden by whitewash. As for the ribs they appear to be typical Burr and therefore all of a piece with the rest of the Studland fabric and indeed with Worth, particularly the two chancel arches. Wherever that quarry or quarries were, they were certainly not in Swanage.

It is perhaps surprising to realise that most of the 12th century dressings of Worth Matravers church and the chapel at St. Aldhelm's Head are of Burr, especially as for the latter Cliff Freestone would have been available from close at hand. What is more surprising about the chapel is that three of the internal responds, part of the central capital and at least two of the external corbels – all original it seems – are Ham stone from Somerset. It is not unusual to find in medieval work stones from different sources integrated in an apparently piecemeal way. Indeed in parts of Dorset it is almost the norm. But to find Ham stone at the Head is surprising, especially if the building is of the date it appears to be.

We can, I suggest, envisage a hive of medieval activity along the Burr/Marble outcrop (the two lie close together) which runs along the lower northern flank of the Limestone ridge. It was particularly busy perhaps from Crack Lane westwards to beyond Dunshay. But that is not the whole story. Renovation of Worth's western churchyard wall in 2013 revealed pieces of worked masonry.[8.] Some are certainly Burr, but one chamfered piece is soft Thornback such as occurs in a restricted area east of Worth. It is probably a piece of plinth course or water table from the medieval church. The defaced 12th century tympanum in the church porch is another example of this distinctive Thornback; the fact that it is jointed indicates that large blocks were not readily available. Brian Bugler's and Andy Webster's detective work has led to the discovery of other examples at St. Aldhelm's Chapel, and at the Gloriette at Corfe Castle; all late 12th – early 13th century. The key to this discovery is that the Middle Purbeck fossil Ostrocods are different from the Upper Purbeck.

Burr's usage declined as the use of Cliff stone increased. Mortons House, Corfe, and Barnston Manor have fireplaces of c.1600 that combine Cliff stone lintels with Burr jambs, whilst the external dressings are Cliff stone with Burr ashlar, reflecting this transition. The two Wareham fonts – in St. Martin's (1607) and Holy Trinity (1620, since removed to Wareham St. Mary's, but not to be confused with the lead font) are of Burr. Wool has an earlier perpendicular example, unusually engaged with the adjacent pier which is also Burr; it seems to be an example of a font being worked on site. Another Burr font, redundant and loose, lies in Wareham St Mary's. It is crudely worked, roughly oval, with a shallow bowl only about four inches deep. The suggestion has been made that it has been reduced in depth. Is it not pre-Conquest, from a time when adult initiates stood in the font?

As well as at Steeple and Studland, plain round Burr bowls occur at Kimmeridge and Bloxworth, and there is another similar one at Melcombe Horsey. The RCHM and Pevsner both say Bloxworth's is 13th century, but it bears the *fleur de lys* of the Savage family, who acquired the estate at the Dissolution. Is it

INLAND QUARRYING / 71

ABOVE Wool, Church of the Holy Rood. Burr font.

ABOVE RIGHT Wareham, South Street. Manor house with Cliff stone façade and Burr plinth.

not an earlier font reworked? Not far up the road Sturminster Marshall has another Burr oddity, surely also the result of reworking, perhaps by the same hand as Bloxworth. One guide says it is modern, another 16th century. It has clasp holes, so can hardly be modern, but is definitely Burr. Bloxworth church itself is puzzling, with an obvious 13th century Burr lancet reset in the south side, plus Burr ashlar together with a weird window of round headed lights. It seems this rebuilding is late 17th century work. If so the suspicion is prompted that Corfe Castle was the source of this substantial amount of ashlar. Such stone was certainly being taken in 1661 to nearby Charborough House by Sir Walter Erle, commander of Corfe Castle's besiegers. Another difficult Burr font is at Durweston, where an octagonal top, exhibiting a nice vertebrate fossil, sits on an ill-fitting standard square Marble base. The RCHM says 'reworked but possibly original'. It is surely medieval but never of a piece with the base. Cranborne is perhaps easier to date: octagonal with two pointed blank arches per side, like so many Marble examples of the 13th century.

Corfe Town House is late 18th century, but the mere fact of it being Burr of that date is odd. Is it medieval castle ashlar reworked before re-use? Certainly such stone that has not been re-worked can be seen in post-Civil War buildings such as Tudor Cottage, Corfe, and Scotland Farm (1665).

The early 18th century Cliff stone façade of the Manor House, South Street, Wareham, rests on a Burr sub plinth. At Smedmore the south façade of about the same date has splendid Portland Whitbed dressings combined with rubble which is mainly Purbeck, also on a Burr plinth. Informatively, the Burr is carried to the full height on the rear and end elevations of the western extension to the house that followed later that century, whilst the main northwestern facing façade is Portland with,

almost certainly, some Cliff stone. This is a good example of how the fine grained white Freestone was the preferred smart material in the 18th century; Burr being left for less important elevations. Perhaps the castle ruins provided the Burr, but the old quarries now hidden by trees either side of Devil's Staircase are probably where the Clavells had it dug.

Burr was revived again in the 19th century for renovations at Christchurch Priory, dressings for the new church at St Mark's, Herston, and the entire external shell of Kingston new church. The latter was dug at Blashenwell, St Mark's near the site of that church, which allows for comparisons to be made between these different sources, four miles apart. Bristow, (1884), mentioned it being used in the restoration of Wimborne Minster by Wyatt in 1857.[9] Kingston church's designer, George Street, is said to have praised the stone in glowing terms. Was he influenced in his choice by Wyatt's earlier use? Wyatt was also let loose on Christchurch Priory where his work also includes Burr. The difficulty with men such as Wyatt and their impact on these medieval buildings is to distinguish how much stone was reworked as against that supplied new at the time.

OTHER BEDS

Further to the south other beds with the quite different property of readily splitting, were being exploited in the Middle Ages for roofing tile. This stone was quarried all the way from Gallows Gore to the south of Swanage. Soon after, men were also getting other types of stone from that most convenient of all quarries: the sea cliffs, particularly the St. Aldhelm's Head undercliff, Peveril Point and Durlston Bay.

CORFE CASTLE

Corfe Castle's two inner wards of 1086 are of rubble, most of it Burr, some of it in quite large pieces, 24 x 14 inches being amongst the largest. There is also a small amount of Marble, Vie

Bed and Cinder. The herringbone work of the coeval Old Hall is different. Argument about the date of this work continues; some authorities insisting that it is pre-Conquest. It consists of flat bedded rubble, mostly of a fairly consistent size, around 8 inches long by 1½ inches thick. The thinnest go down to about 1 inch, the thickest up to 4. This thickest stone is telling, for whilst most of the rest are fairly bland, suggesting Downs Vein, this one has a flint. It is part of the Flint bed that lies beneath the New Vein. This stone and the rest of this rubble, including the inner ward, surely came from the hill around Kingston where these beds outcrop. At the same time the beautifully integrated window jambs are of Burr, from a nearer source; the lower slope of Kingston Hill at about the level of East Lynch farm house. The rubble could have been field picked. Cinder is not normally used much, as it has a clay matrix that 'rots', but it does contain a few inches of almost pure oyster shell sediment that endures relatively well and which appears in field walls as a result of picking the ground clear of stones turned up by the plough, particularly in the Kingston / Gallows Gore area.

The impressive keep of 1100-1105 is all Burr ashlar. King John's work, following a hundred years later, is mostly Burr dressings, but also includes Thornback. This c.1200 work also includes beautifully fitted rubble, much of it again Burr, but almost one eighth Marble which looks so brown as to suggest heath stone, of which there are just a few pieces. This Marble rubble is surely a semi-by-product of the trade in monuments and architectural components which was growing at that time. But it is not all Marble for we find, as in 1086, other beds: Vie Bed, some Cinder and a little of Flint Bed.

There was a quarrel in 1278 when William Clavill of Holme objected to the taking of stone from Holme by Elyas de Rabayne, constable of the castle.[10.] Other Clavills had quarries at Quarr. Holme is a possible source of Heath, sometimes called Carr stone and rock of that sort does appear in castle work. Some sandstone ashlar west of the Gate House is of about the right date, circa 1285. But why bring stone three or more miles when alternatives were available at less than half that distance? Was there a hiatus in the supply of Burr? The mystery is compounded by negligible evidence of quarrying at Holme, but shallow medieval quarries may be overlooked, or obliterated over time.

The building accounts for Corfe Castle contain much informative detail of how things were done in the 13th

Corfe Castle. Staircase west of gatehouse; Burr ashlar incorporating blocks of Heath stone (the dark element).

century.[11.] Lawrence Cok, William Burleys, John Lenard, Robert of Rodlyngton, Gilbert Tully, John Leking, John Champion, John Le Mere, Peter the Chaplain and Thomas Cusyn were providing cartloads of 'coarse stone', that is the rough stuff forming the core of the massive walls; but possibly facing rubble work as well. Almost all of this core stone is Chalk with some Flint. Consolidation and repairs to the ruin have gradually introduced a lot of other sorts of rubble, but where identification of the original is safe, it is almost all Chalk. The early development of the fortress may have involved slight modification of the natural contours of the hill, in which case Chalk rubble would have been there for the taking, but by the 13th century they were bringing it from elsewhere. These men had carts it seems, and were perhaps farmer-haulage contractors rather than quarriers. In the 18th century farmers certainly provided the haulage of stone from the quarries, perhaps with small hand carts, an arrangement which only ended in the mid-19th century, when the stone merchants equipped themselves with horses and wagons.

Corfe Castle village. Re-used Burr from the castle, showing Beaufort portcullis. The Beauforts held the castle during the period of the Wars of the Roses.

Cusyn was also providing 'Freestones' in 1280. This is not the bed that is now known as Freestone, but surely Burr. Four large 'freestones' were bought for corbels. It would seem that the term was used for readily-workable stone cut to a semi-dressed state at the quarry with further refinements done on site. They were being brought from 'the vill', which suggests the town, but means in fact the quarries within the parish. Philip Scroylle provided fifty freestones for three shillings plus carriage to the castle at four pence. Walter Mogga, Richard Marsh and Ralf Totewys were paid for hewing stones. Next year Phillip Scroylle was paid for trimming stones. (Scholars tell me that understanding what is meant in medieval Latin texts is a challenge: the original accountant may or may not have been making a real distinction between hewing, trimming, etc.) Two quarries of Burr are suggested, supplying it in a semi-dressed form, with men at the castle doing the fine dressing, others laying, making mortar, etc. P. Scroylle provides a lintel for over a window for 4d. Is this Marble? Burr for the most part occurs in small blocks. The interior arrow slit splays are corbelled inwards before a longish lintel closes them over. A number of these are Marble for purely practical reasons. Of course there are exceptions: Corfe church gargoyles (about five feet six inches) are quite long, whilst Smedmore House has four window jambs six feet six inches long. At risk of labouring this point these long stones have been selected from a general run of blocks that are smaller and only became available because other work was absorbing the more common small stuff. I remember my father, commenting on a fine big Portland ledger in Thomas Bonfield's presence: Tom said 'You don't know how much they had to turn to find 'im'.[12.] Interestingly Swanage, Herston and Acton, all have 'Fields', all much quarried. Were they in the more distant past, the 'vills' of those settlements? A much-altered house on Langton Matravers High Street was formally Hall's Vill, probably pertaining to the land now called Tom's Field, and deriving from the prominent 17th century stone merchant, James Hall.

In October 1285 Edward Brandon was paid 18d. for 500 stones for roofing. He was surely digging Downs Vein, but where exactly? Thomas Cusyn, the rough stone supplier, got 12d. for the carriage. Above Scowles Manor, where the Downs Vein outcrops, it has been taken. Cinder, showing in a ditch, lies almost parallel to the northward dip. It indicates the missing layer of Downs Vein was shallow and diggable over a fair area. This field and others nearby could well have been highly productive of tile.

EXETER CATHEDRAL

The main fabric of Exeter Cathedral consists of Salcombe and Beer stones, both fairly local. Inside, some of the most demanding elements are Portland, and the columns are Purbeck Marble. These were being supplied by William Canon of Corfe finished, rather than in rough form.[13.] There is also Burr in the external work, in the splayed buttress at the northeast corner of the choir. The easternmost north chapel also has lower stage weatherings of Burr, and there are more elements, all perfectly integrated in a somewhat piecemeal way with the local stones, so surely worked on site. Perhaps this Burr is that listed as loads in the Fabric accounts for Michaelmas 1310: 'For carrying one load of Corfe stone from Topsham to Exeter 66s. 8d.' (Topsham is at the head of the Exe estuary). And again 1312: 'For discharging one boatload of stone from Corfe at Topsham 12d.' It is a pity that the accounts only seem to record this relatively minor part of the transaction. Seven years before, Master Roger was paid to buy stones at Corfe 'going and returning'. Was this actually just stone or, what seems more likely, Marble? A similar question mark hangs over the record of a Winchester Castle stonecutter being paid 2s. in 1221 for 'going to the quarry at Corfe'. Was he organising the supply of Burr or Marble?[14.] Generally the references in the accounts to Purbeck use the term Marble or Marblestone, so when the accountant uses the term stone he may have been precise. In the following year, 1311 Master William De Schoverwille, mason, 'coming from Salisbury to visit the new work' (at Exeter), was paid 20s. Is he the 'viewer' as is the term used in the Corfe Castle building accounts for the overseer. Surely this is the same name as Scroylle of the Corfe Accounts and of Scowles, the manor straddling both Burr and Marble outcrops. The word 'scowles' is applied to land which has been mined for iron ore in the Forest of Dean. William was caught by the tax of 1332, paying 2s. in the manor of Alfryngton, which is next door to modern day Scoles Manor.[15, 16.]

THE TOWER OF LONDON

The Cradle Tower of 1348 within the Tower of London complex has Burr elements, including buttresses on the north side, quoins and internal angles at the lower stage, plus two sections of chamfered plinth; also some stones of what looks like East Winspit Blue Bits. This work appear to be original, as it has later Portland piecings let into it. Salzman says: 'among the stones belonging to the works of London Bridge in 1350 there are 18 great stones of Bere, weighing 18 tons, value 6s 8d the ton.' As these are relatively large stones, it is probably a safe assumption that these are from Beer, in Devon. However, he continues: 'For the Tower in 1361, Bere stone was brought at 8s 6d the ton 'including freight from the castle at Corfe'.'[17.] Salzman suggests that this may be stone from Bere Regis, near Corfe, but this makes no geological sense. There seems to be no apparent logic in the freight coming from the castle at Corfe if this is Beer stone, which prompts the suspicion that it may be Purbeck Burr. He also mentions 'hard Freestone of Corfe', nine shiploads costing £48 11s 6d being brought for the tower in 1278.[18.] Burr is not usually 'hard'. Is this the Blue Bits from Winspit?

Dr Tim Palmer informs me of Purbeck and Portland (Cliffstone?) in 13th century work in a not easily-visited curtain wall near the chapel in the tower, normally closed to visitors.

PAVING

Shallow Downs Vein is often productive of thin stuff suitable for roof tile. However, as the layer dips deeper and the overburden increases the vein becomes more solid, with fewer

Tower of London. Cradle Tower, 1348, with Burr quoins and chamfered plinth.

free partings. Thin tile gives way to paving thicknesses, but the same quarry is often productive of both. One such in Langton Wallis is referred to in a court record of 1425.[19.]

Therefore surviving Downs Vein paving of 14th or 15th century date is perhaps to be expected, but there does not seem to be much. The late 15th century hall, porch and oriel at Athelhampton have apparently contemporary floors. These are of Downs Vein, more similar in character to what we find at Gallows Gore than around Acton or other current quarries, which suggests a source at Gallows Gore or possibly westwards.

Other floors of great interest survive in Westminster Abbey. In addition to the splendid 13th century Cosmati pavement (*see following page*) there are other areas of Marble, also surely medieval. In the eastern part of the nave north aisle there is an area of mostly Downs Vein, which is also probably medieval, perhaps contemporary with, or soon after, the completion date of the building around it. This area has alas been much altered by the insertion of ledgers and the 19th century heating system. West of it, the whole nave plus aisles are all of a piece, done between 1507 and 1517.[20.] There are areas of repairs using stones I cannot recognise, plus Portland and Purbeck, including Cliff Stone, but the mass of this floor would seem to be original, and of Purbeck stone rather than Marble. Much of it is Downs Vein of a Gallows Gore / Kingston type, but there

INLAND QUARRYING / 75

Westminster Abbey. Part of the Cosmati pavement.

are other beds also, including Vie bed, Laining Vein and almost certainly Roach plus New Vein White Bit.

Around Spyway some beds in the Laining Vein are dominated by the same snail species characteristic of Marble and this is just what we see in some of these pavings. These may have been quarried from various locations, but the diagnostic snail occurs in abundance in the Spyway district. Remnants of squared paving, broken in manufacture, can be found in field walls in that area. The location of the Tudor Vie Bed quarry is more open to question. It could be anywhere along the outcrop which runs in a narrow ribbon from Durlston westwards along the top of the Wares to East Man before it turns inland to Gallows Gore, then resumes westwards to Kingston. It disappears somewhere before Worbarrow.

In digging any quantity for such paving the occasional

RIGHT Dunshay Manor, Harman's Cross. John Dolling's porch, 1642, raised in 1906.

BELOW Church Knowle, St Peter. Downs Vein altar.

larger block is likely to be found. There are at least two pre-Reformation Downs Vein altars that may be 'spin offs' from this tile/paving trade, one at Church Knowle and one at Arne. There are also several 16th century ledgers, discussed below. A few big ledger slabs were taken from the cliffs, but apart from this coastal activity, the pattern in about 1500 seems to have been a declining Marble trade, some small-scale Burr exploitation, some Downs Vein and a small amount of New Vein and Laining Vein, particularly from shallow workings productive of roof tile.

OTHER USES OF 'INLAND' STONE

In some instances Burr and Cliff Stone were combined in use, notably several fireplaces with Burr jambs and Cliff Stone lintels. Perhaps the Burr was becoming difficult to get; apart from a few exceptions, its usage tailed off in the early 17th century. Pinholey Inland Freestone is difficult to differentiate from some Burr. The Dunshay (1642) and Scoles Manor porches, as well as window jambs in Corfe Town Hall, could be either.

In the 16th century other Purbeck beds, some difficult to identify, began to appear as ledgers. Most are probably Laining Vein. Examples include one with a black letter peripheral inscription in Bovey Tracey, Devon, Orford, Suffolk (1580) and Cerne Abbas (1612). Tudor strengthening of the medieval Castle Cornet commanding St Peter Port, Guernsey includes an entrance arch of Purbeck stone. Some of this, possibly Durlston Bay Downs Vein, remains in good condition, but much has eroded badly. Evidence of digging this Laining Vein outcrop occurs at Southard, Court Cowlease, Belle Vue, Greyseed, Gully, Leeson and westwards.

Downs Vein continuation is evident in a slab bearing a peripheral inscription of 1584 at Sandwich, Kent. However, it is in the next century when the real diversification begins. Thornback of an Acton type appears as ledgers from 1632. No.22, West Street, Corfe has Thornback or Wetsun bed

ABOVE Castle Cornet, Guernsey. Purbeck Stone arch; Tudor period.

BELOW LEFT Corfe Castle village. 22 West Street.

BELOW RIGHT Steeple, St Michael and All Angels. Lawrence family coat of arms in outside wall of north transept.

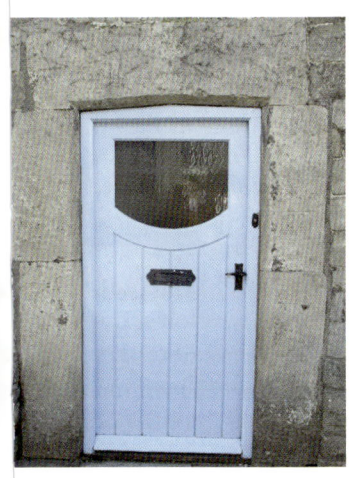

Corfe Castle village. Uvedale's house.

dressings of the same sort, as well as Cliff Stone. RCHM says 'late 17th century'.[21.] The 1616 Lawrence coat of arms outside the north extension to Steeple church is similar and could well be from Acton. Interestingly, the other Lawrence Arms in the porch, undated but certainly older, is of different stuff, either Portland or Cliff. As remarked, Uvedales at Corfe has Cliff stone elements in its mullion windows, but also what looks like original Thornback too. No. 22 West Street, Corfe is interesting to compare with No. 23, which the Royal Commission says is 'late 16th or early 17th century'.[22.] Its door jambs and four-centred arch are mostly Marble, which would therefore suggest an earlier date, if only by a decade or so.

Ledgers serve as conveniently dated stones to chart these developments. Many, beginning in 1655, are Grub of the Swanage type; next comes the first Brassy bed in 1698; finally the first Cap 1718. The Brassy bed is much like what we quarry currently at Belle Vue, and is almost certainly from the Swanage region, as is the Cap. By 1650 inland quarrying activity extended around Gallows Gore, Acton and eastwards along the limestone ridge to the south of Swanage.

Clerk in Holy Orders William Rose's will of 1690 left to his son Thomas to 'all the quarring' and 10 sheep light [sheep walk or pasture] to pasture in Sandwich South Field and Hancombe [Hawcombe?] bought of Samuel Tarry, senior. Stone that shall be dug in the second piece of ground west of the drove in Sandwich North Field in the lower part where John Melmouth has a quarr'.[23.] This location is due south of the Swanage Cottage Hospital. Close by in Townsend, preparations to build a house in 1982 revealed a back-filled Laining Vein quarry, the floor of which was a mass of dinosaur footprints. Some of these were removed to Dorset County Museum. No doubt similar shallow ridden holes, long forgotten, extended across William Rose's land to the east. Swanage South Field and Hawcombe can still be readily identified. Holes and waste piles tell of much activity, particularly around the top of the combe. Some work was clearly going on here in the late 17th century. One wonders from just how much earlier?

What makes understanding old quarry evidence difficult in Purbeck is that different veins have been dug at the same location over a period of hundreds of years. Beneath what may well be 17th century Laining Vein surface workings, as many as three other separate veins may well have been taken over the next two hundred years or so. Nor, necessarily, was this done in descending order. It is certainly true that in Langton and Worth a great deal of Downs Vein was dug underground before the Freestone above, first quarried in significant quantities in the 19th century. Counter-intuitively, the lower layer was taken first. It is probably true to say that all the existing Freestone

INLAND QUARRYING / 77

to rescue a dog that had got stuck. He was amazed by how flimsy the ' legs' were: 'just a few wall stones coggled up one top tuther', and the sight of the thorn bush roots coming down from the ceiling. Was Roy in a 17th century working?

This deposition record was a lucky find. It is perhaps not unreasonable to infer from it that underground work was fairly extensive by the middle of the 17th century. Dennis Smale has suggested that mining in England followed the arrival of German engineers in the 16th century.[28] For what it is worth, a Marble quarry face of almost certain 13th century date revealed at Quarr was stepped, with no suggestion of an underground method. However, the Downs Vein lends itself to underground working better than the Marble. Whatever the date of the commencement of underground working, it is clearly well established by 1774 for Hutchins to be able to say: 'The Quarries lie on the south side of the town, sometimes 3 or 4, one under another.' Seventy odd years would hardly seem sufficient time for such a full development.

All through the 17th century paving was the staple, and men sought beds that would split out flat. Quarries developed on quite a scale and the traffic, particularly to London, was considerable. The measurement of paving was by superficial feet, not cubic feet, which is often not made clear in old records, such as the following Old Bailey Indictments: '1694 Thomas Lambeth was indicted for stealing 114 ft of Purbeck stone value 25s the goods of Thomas Raper, he denied the whole matter, saying he was to pave a kitchen of a gentle woman that was evidence against him...'

This paving trade continued in the 18th century, together with a call for more solid beds suitable for harbour works, fortifications and genteel manor houses. Some manorial maps showing quarries survive, as well as records of royalty payments. There are also wills and inventories of quarriers which begin in the 17th century, but sadly almost no documents of that century specific to the Company of Marblers.

The Court Baron held at Downshay Manor at Worth in 1708 records:

'Item We present Lewis Gover, Nicholas and John Harden, Richard Haskell, Robert Seamore for digging up and spoiling the herbage and grass in Gallis Gore Common'.[29] They were either 'ridding' Downs Vein or breaking open shafts and thereby spoiling the Common pasture. Perhaps they were stopped, for in 1725 Richard Haskell was working on the nearby Bankes Estate.

RECORDING AND ROYALTIES

In 1724 John Bankes, in getting to grips with his inheritance, spelt out his terms: 'The tenant has liberty to open quarries of stone allowing me 100 ft of paving out of every 2000 and 1 tunn out of 20 of Freestone [Cliff stone is meant here] and one tunn of healing stone out of 4'.[30] His agent, Mr. Guy, recorded his 'Lord's rent out of Purbeck' in an account book covering the years 1691-1740. It was not until 1706 that a specific reference to stone appeared, but it is probably wrong to conclude that stone was not being dug in previous years on the Estate.

The 1706 entry recorded: 'received of William Costfield for stone £1 5s.' This was for 5,000 square feet of paving (about 100 tons). It was another 12 years before another Costfield paid, this time Thomas, for a similar amount. Their tenancy included parcels of land at Batcher's Nap, a field northeast of Blacklands and two small fields west of the Acton approach road, all possible sources of paving, with perhaps the field near Blacklands being the most likely. Sadly, the cottage at the top of Langton formally called Coastfield's has had its name changed.

The next payment to the squire for stone after 1706 was made by farmer John Brown of Eastington. In 1713 he paid £16 10s, the next year about half that amount, which suggests that the larger sum was for two years. This translates as about 700 tons per year. Farmer Brown was collecting dues from quarries active on Eastington and Langton Wallis. The arrangement of farmers, or men outside of the stone trade, collecting the dues remained the custom on the estate until the final years of Bankes family ownership in the late 20th century. The last was Thomas Lovell of Wilkswood Farm, followed by his son David, who gave up farming to concentrate on quarrying.

In 1717 Alexander Corbin paid for 3,800 foot of stone dug out of 'Havilands ground in Purbeck' at 9d per hundred. Havilands or Wilkswood Farm then included a block of fields in eastern Langton Wallis, lying both north and south of the Priest's Way.[31] In 1722 600ft of 'rough stone' was dug in Wilkswood ground, probably for paving. The fields in question south of the Priest's Way show evidence of quarrying, in spite of some old workings being obliterated in my lifetime.

Alexander Corbin agreed the Joint Stock Company formation in 1698. In the 1720s he was continuing to pay dues for paving dug on Eastington or Langton Wallis as well as renting a house and land at Studland, where he was also paying dues for heath stone ashlar. Firstly he paid 1s for every hundred foot, increasing to 2s per hundred, with a single payment for no less than 2,700 foot superficial, a considerable amount. One wonders where the quarry was, how neatly squared up he made the ashlar, and where it went. Woodhouse Hill is perhaps the most likely location for the quarry, where later in the 19th century the Duke of Hamilton sourced the colonnade for his lodge, later the Knoll House Hotel. It seems Alexander was living at Studland at the same time as he was working quarries in Langton Wallis and/or Eastington. He probably employed others, but no doubt often travelled between the various quarries.

Just how far was the maximum distance for a man to walk and do a day's physical work? For a while William Bower, whilst living at Winspit, worked at the Currendon Pit, where chalk was dug for the military during the First World War. The straight line distance for both Corbin and Bower to walk was similarly about four miles. More recently Thomas Bonfield and Rippy Norman worked at St. Aldhelm's Head whilst living at Gully and Herston respectively, which meant a cliff walk almost as long. As masonry yards developed on Portland during the later 19th century quite a few Purbeck men took jobs there. Some, in lodgings, would occasionally walk the distance home and back over a Bank Holiday weekend, avoiding part of the tiring coastal switchback by keeping inland of Bindon Hill.

Ralph Treswell's map of Langton Wallis and Eastington, 1585-6. The map has East at the top. The 'ground' where Alexander Corbin was working is on the east side of Langton Wallis, marked with an 'H'. 'Highlands', mentioned below, can be seen south and west of Acton. (Dorset History Centre D-RWR/E15-16)

Albert Harding of Langton and Horace Norman of Swanage were two who did this, but of course it was occasional, and not part of a regular routine. Horace was used to walking. Lodging at 'Top Hill' on Portland he used to play his violin in the silent cinema 'Under Hill'. After retiring to Swanage he amused himself by carving stone in his family quarr house at Herston Field. A fireplace in Magnolia House, Swanage, is an example of his work.[32]

Royalty rates on the Bankes Estate can identify types of stone, but increases made during the 18th century make comparisons of output difficult. 6d per 100 ft of paving (this is of course superficial not cubic feet) charged in 1706 became 8d and then 1s by 1722. The establishment of the Joint Stock Company in 1698 shows the price for common paving 'at the waterside' (Swanage) to have been 16s per 100 foot.[33] Getting it to London doubled this to 34s. per hundred, roughly 4d per foot. In 1758 James Keats, father and son, supplied and laid 484 foot at Turner's Puddle for 4½d per foot. The client farmer was meeting certainly half if not all the haulage cost.[34]

These prices do not sit well with the apparent cost of a substantial 18th century floor: the cloister at Norwich Cathedral, where between 1758 and 1759 5,794 square feet was laid for a halfpenny per foot. Such a low price must tell us that this was for the fitting and laying alone, and not the full cost, which some who have read the surviving accounts suggest.[35] This floor consists of courses running lengthways, with the widest in the centre (about 3 foot), diminishing to narrowest at the margins, almost a standard 18th century way of doing things; the Corn Exchange, Blandford, is similar. To achieve this from random sizes, which I suspect was the way it was dispatched from Purbeck, would have required some reworking of the joints.

Other tenants digging stone as well as Costfield were Edward Hancock in Havilands ground and William King, who held Captaines (now Capstan) Field and another northwest of Seaspray. However, the big player was farmer Brown of Eastington, whose returns were regular. He was collecting from several quarriers, to a total tune of about £10 per annum.

INLAND QUARRYING / 81

The proliferation of quarries there is revealed in detail by his successor, Farmer Edward Dampier. He wrote 'An Account of stone dug by the several Quarriers who work on Eastington and Langton Farms as entries in a book kept for the purpose, beginning at Lady Day 1725.' It records the production of paving in quantity by all of them, plus tombstones and step by some. Over a year or two 32 quarrymen are named (three of whom were also merchants), seven sets of them in partnerships, so 24 active, supplying 13 merchants: a recipe for low prices if ever there was one. The book continued:

> 'The names of the quarriers ye dig stone on Eastington and Langton Farms: 1726
>
> In the Cowlease
> Peter Corbin, one quarry
> William Corbin, one quarry
> Edward Haskol & John Bower, one quarry
> Tom Bower, one quarry
> John Summers & Tho. Webber, one quarry
> Giles Speare, one quarry
> James Hall, one quarry
>
> Rich. Haskel, one quarry in Highlands
>
> In the Arable
> Timothy Chinchen, one quarry
> Wm. Chinchen, one quarry
>
> In the Meadow
> Rich. & John Keate, one quarry
> James Keate, one quarry

In the 18th century Easington Cowlease was big, taking in fields known more recently as Nunbarrow or Quarry Close. From south to north it stretched from the farm to Dinney; from west to east from the boundary with Worth (Letterbox Gate) to the original farm access road, now the track to Keates Quarry. Highlands lay to the south and west of Acton. The meadow is surely what is now called Broad Mead. Both Freestone and Downs Vein run out of the ground there and at Cowlease, but Highlands is generally deeper, which suggests underground working there, if not in all three.

Almost contemporaneously the same compiler added more names: Will Bower, Thomas Corben, John Barnes, with John Cull in partnership with Edward Hancock and John Chinchen with Peter Phippard. John Bower left Edward Haskol and worked alone whilst Thomas Lander joined up with Edward. That the list may not be entire or that men were often coming and going is hinted at in a note of 1728: 'John Benfield [who otherwise does not appear] says had 2 ton of Healing Stone of him for late Bowles house in Corfe, but a ton and a half, for one load.' The measurement of random roof tile presented a difficulty then as now, and a recipe for argument.

Alexander Corbin was still going in 1730, with seemingly two paving quarries, for he paid on 5,900 square feet dug in Eastington and Langton farms. Three years later the annual total for all the quarries on the two Bankes properties was 41,850 square feet which brought in £20 18s 6d to the estate, the equivalent of about forty weeks' wages for a quarrier. During the next few years Edward Dampier continued to record the annual paving incomes, which ranged from an exceptionally low £13 8s in 1734 to £27 5s in 1739. I doubt whether any

Langton Matravers Museum. Thornback sink.

other estate received so much, for though the concentration of quarries in the Swanage District may have been greater, no individual estate was so big.

What were the quarriers doing with the stuff that was small but too thick for paving? Were they making pitchers perhaps? If so, the landlord was not demanding a royalty. Farmer Edward Dampier's list is simply paving output, the tombstones added in later, which begs the question as to whether the estate was getting a royalty on everything produced.

During the second half of the 18th century the production of thin stuff like paving and channel continued to dominate the Bankes Estate output from over a dozen quarries. In the main they were obviously digging Downs Vein, but in 1772 Thomas Bower included step and troughs in his output from Purbecks field (sometimes called Judas). This tells of him definitely working a Freestone quarry there. Most 'hollow' work that survives is of Cliff Stone, but there are examples of Thornback and Inland Freestone. In parts of Highlands the Thornback is hard and thin, so not useful for troughs, but north of Acton it thickens sufficiently to make one.

Perhaps the estate took all the field wallstones they wanted too, for this category doesn't appear in the royalty lists. There is evidence of 're-setting' and new building of field walls at that time. Most of the 18th century vernacular cottages in Langton, Worth and Corfe are of Downs Vein. Jasper Cottage, circa 1600, is perhaps the oldest in Langton.[36.] It consists of thin Downs Vein rubble with some quoins of re-used Burr dressings, the latter presumably taken from the dissolved Wilkswood Priory nearby, the former from quarries active at the time. Worth has exceptions to the Downs Vein norm: Rose Cottage and No.2 London Row are mostly of New Vein and Cap, which suggest Long Ledge, East Man or Newfoundland (a field at the eastern edge of the village), as the probable source. Where current quarrying has broken into 19th century ridden holes, tons of good wall stones are sometimes found discarded. The 'old hands' would not have done that if they could have readily sold them.

Dampier's list of quarries appear to be comprehensive, but he makes no mention of the cliff quarries. They may have been active but treated separately, for in another document dealing with a wide range of estate matters appears: 'Chinchen and

Phippard account for blockstone'. Blockstone almost certainly tells of these men working at the cliff, but it just could be Freestone from their inland quarry. Though Dampier has not included it, perhaps Mr Bankes' steward had got wind of it and put it on his list of matters to deal with. These are surely the John Chinchen and Peter Phippard who, between June and November 1727 supplied 5,659 ½ foot to merchants Melmouth and Chapman. This, of course, is paving, so they definitely had inland quarries as well. Considering the possibility that Chinchen and Phippard were quarrying Inland Freestone, my great-grandfather remembered when the first Langton Freestone started to be brought to Swanage.[37.]

Of course that was an over-simplification. There are examples of earlier use, notably Durnford Manor, but by and large it does not figure much before the time he was recalling, around 1860. All the scatter of underground shafts around Acton that remained open into the 1950s were sunk into the Freestone. Many, if not all, had earlier Downs Vein workings beneath them, some known about, some forgotten. Charles Sheffield Harris told me that they got in underground in their Freestone working one morning to find that the legs were not touching the ceiling. Their floor was going down! In a short while it all collapsed, producing a hollow still evident in the field. The Bankes and Calcraft papers provide much information about such quarrying activity, as indeed do the Serrell papers for the 19th century. It is a pity that similar records do not seem to have survived for manors further east.

Evidence that thicker beds, too thick to make paving, were being used at the time, is provided by the use of Purbeck in the London bridges. I suspect some references to Portland just could mean Purbeck Cliff stone. Surviving work at Chertsey certainly includes both Purbeck Cliff stone and Portland. Westminster Bridge, since replaced, was built between 1740-45. It soon began to sink. By 1748 this required 'the dismantling of the Purbeck stone counter arches', then later 'the taking down of the damaged Portland stone arches'.[38.]

William Melmoth's wonderfully detailed inventory of 1689 is illuminating.[39.] It was witnessed by Joseph Hort and Anthony Serrell, who, with William were also signatories to the 1651 'Articles of agreement' for the Company of Marblers. It itemises his possessions in more detail than any other such inventory. It includes, at the quarr, '10 Resonable tombstones' [his fellow marblers' informed assessment of his stock is evident here] and round gutter and step. At the sea shore he left £15 worth of tombstones and other small stones listed as one item (are tombstone large ledgers, small stones perhaps headstones?), plus more gutter and step. Planks and wheelbarrows suggest a surface ridden hole; running a laden iron-tyred barrow over soft ground calls for planks. Four, as listed, or even fewer, would provide a runway of sufficient length to get the muck far enough away from the active face, so as not to encumber. I bet he did not wheel it further than necessary. According to Billy Winspit, 'Pushing a loaded barrow uphill is the one job in this life no man can fiddle'. If he had had a capstan would not the compiler have listed it, given that he saw fit to include the timber of the quarr house, surely no more valuable than a capstan complete with chain?

Use of the term 'resonable' suggests that the compiler had a problem. I think it was about size rather than quality. A stone eight feet long would have been more than reasonable, one at five feet perhaps less. A random sample of the lengths of Grub ledgers in Winchester Cathedral ranges from 8 foot to under 6. Was coffin length the minimum requirement, and anything more than this a bonus? The average headstone of that time is somewhat smaller, so perhaps less 'resonable' stones were used for them. These 'resonable' stones average out at ten shillings each, more than a week's wages.

A number of Grub headstones from the late 17th century remain. One wonders how finished they were at the quarry. Presumably they were worked square and tooled over to a fair front face. Was this then rubbed smooth and the top shaped before dispatch, or was that done by the letter cutter at the receiving end? For what it is worth, a number of c. 1700 Purbeck headstones are of the same shape with a round top between square shoulders. It may suggest cutting of the shape at source. Lulworth has one, Shapwick three, all certainly Purbeck of some sort, one of them definitely Swanage Grub. Castle Cornet, Guernsey, contains Swanage Freestone ashlar in the ammunition magazines, built round about this time; a relatively early date for that particular bed.

Another absentee in the Melmoth inventory is the cart, unless it is included in the quarry tools, which seems unlikely. Both capstan and cart are essential for underground work, but possibly not for surface working. This would appear to be the inventory of a man occupying a shallow Freestone quarry south of Swanage at a time when we know a lot of Grub ledgers were being dug. The fact that the Grub series of tombstones ends early in the 18th century, but that production of such monuments from other Purbeck beds continued, suggests that this particular resource was exhausted, not that demand had ceased. Does it tell us that they were beginning to follow the deepening beds underground, a development which would have meant that the Grub, the uppermost bed in a Freestone quarry, had to be left in situ to serve as the ceiling, hence no undergrounds produced it? Supporting evidence for this shift, broadly from south to north, may be seen in a map of the manor of Eightholds, Swanage, of 1806. This shows eight men occupying quarries between roughly the east-west lines of present day Queens Road to the north, Bon Accord to the south, all surely underground. To the south of modern Bon Accord, or thereabouts, the next field is marked as 'quarries and pasture', but without occupiers, so where the Grub would have shoaled out to the surface was already abandoned by 1806.

This pattern, as far as inland quarrying is concerned, was probably the same on other Swanage manors. Early, that is 17th century or earlier, activity was largely on the shallow southern outcrop, and shafts were sunk progressively northwards and deeper. However, though the Melmoth inventory, the earliest and most detailed, may point to surface quarrying, it may be misleading. Is it possible William was using a capstan belonging to others? Next in date, Hugh Hort's inventory of 1693 lists two quarry 'barres' and a kevill valued at 15s; this equates to William's quarry tools valued at £2. Again there is no mention of a capstan. But in Alexander Melmouth's list of 1703 his quarry tools were valued at £7 15s.[40] Given that he was working at Tilly Whim, where a gibbet would be an essential, it would seem that 'quarry tools' was a catch-all term which included the crane. Oh that those compilers had given more attention to detail!

Beginning in January 1776 John Lampard took on the task of recording 'money received of the quarries on Eastington and Langton Wallis farms'.

> 'Titus Corben pays for the ground of 400 ft of paving dug in Akin Lane at 1 shilling per 100 square foot.' [Treswell's map shows two small enclosures on the west side of the Acton approach road. This must be where Titus was working. The 't' in Acton tends to be dropped in local dialect pronunciation.]
> 'John Bower, 640 ft paving
>   203 ft of step dug in Cowlease
> John Pyke, 2050 ft paving in Cowlease
> Mr. Titus Chinchen, 4948 ft of paving dug by Peter Bower in Cowlease [note his title]
> Peter Bower, 1550 ft dug in Cowlease
> William Chinchen, [no site given]
> James Barnes & Joseph Curtis, 750 ft in Cowlease
> Titus Corben, Akin Lane 400 ft
> Titus Corben, 207 ft and 272 ft chanel
> John Pike, Cowlease 2550
> William Bower, Cowlease 2100
> Titus Corben & James Barnes, Akin Lane 1000
> Joseph Curtis, 3050 in Cowlease
> Titus Corben, Akin Lane 4000
>   Akin Lane and Esay 2284 ft
> Harry Bower, Esay 2000 paving, 150 step +150 Chanel
> Titus Corben, Akin Lane and Esay 3000 ft
> John Pike, Cowlease 4650 ft '

This seems to be a record of work over a considerable period, possibly more than two years. Five quarries continue in Cowlease. They seem to have finished in Highland but are at work in pastures new north of Acton. Again there is no mention of healing stones nor of tombstones, which is puzzling. The total number of quarries working inland on the estate had reduced to a mere seven.

Five years later, in 1781:

> 'James Hayward is in Titus Corben's Akin Lane quarr making 503 ft paving.
> Also William Bower, son of Charles of Worth, is in Titus Corben's Akin Lane quarr 600 ft
> Titus Corben, 559 ft also Akin Lane
> Edward Barnes, 1400 ft in Cowlease
> Peter Bower, 1500 ft in Cowlease
> Titus Corben, 5225 ft + 285 ft chanel Akin Lane
> John Bridle, 1000 in Esay
> Peter Bower, 1100 in the new place in Cowlease
> John Pike, 2950 in Cowlease
> Harry Bower, 600 paving, 573 of step and chanel in Esay
> Peter Bower, 700 paving dug in Nun Barrs in Cowlease. [this area, recently called Quarry Close, now lies north of the Worth road].
> Titus Chinchen, 1022 from Broad Meadow
> John Pike, 1700 ft part in Cowlease, part in Akin Meadow
> John Bower, 1350 ft landed in Mr. Heart's Meadow [41]
> Edwin Barnes, 2059 ft dug in Cowlease
> John Bridle, 2000 ft dug in Esay,
> Peter Bower, 950 ft in Cowlease
> Titus Corben, 2000 ft Akin Lane, 1165 ft
> John Bridle, 4500 ft in Esay'

That same year to the west in Worth at least 17 quarries were active. Thomas Bower, Joseph Chinchin, William Turner and William Bower were obviously in the cliff, which means Winspit, and/or Rope Lake or the quarry where the water treatment works has been built. The rest were all supplying paving, with a small quantity of step. They were William Keats, John Keat, James Hayward of Langton, James Keats of Corfe, Samuel and Thomas Lander, Sam Dowland, John Pike, Robert Squibb, Robert Bonfield, Elias Bonfield (or Benfield) and Thomas Lander's son.

There were 11 inland quarries in total. Samuel Donne's map of 1772 shows the general distribution around that time.[42] There was at least one quarry on Long Ledge, on the east side of Winspit Bottom. Others were under and east of where Abbascombe houses have been built, another one field east from there, whilst the main concentration was around Gallows Gore. Two were just south of the turnpike road, west of the row of cottages. North of the turnpike road there were seven west of Haycrafts Lane, in what is now Landers quarry, with ten more scattered east of the lane from Ann's Field to Purbeck View Farm.

The Corfe census of 1796 lists eight quarriers, including two James Keats, at least one of whom was walking to Gallows Gore each day to work. The Corfe Parish stone account of 1800 reveals Samuel Keat inspecting paving in Bernboat (surely Burngate, which lies north of Worth gate), Woodclose (which lies west of Castle View cottages) and Hosey (surely Esay and Treswell's Hethershay, that lies east of the Acton approach road). Most, perhaps all, of those Corfe men were walking to Gallows Gore or Langton to work. It prompts the suspicion that quarries nearer to home had been worked out. Stone lying at any angle can be dug in a ridden hole, but underground working becomes impossible if the beds lie too steep. This daily tramp eastwards of the Corfe men suggests that along the Downs opposite Corfe the shallow stuff had been ridded, that there were difficulties in going underground, whilst from around Gallows Gore and eastwards the widening level plateau offered opportunities.

In 1825 the Bankes Estate drew up a complete list of all their Purbeck quarries including dates of leases and locations with comments. Twenty were inland. Edward Bower and Titus Corben were in Island (Highland). The comment was: 'Titus C. died without executing the lease. His father has worked it ever since. Question if Mr. Bankes will dispense with his having a lease (?)' George Benfield and James Hayward were in Little Cowlease. James' quarry was being worked by his son Charles, who served as Langton church warden and is commemorated by a tablet on the north wall of the church. James had moved from the Worth estate but it seems into a bad situation, for the report said: 'This quarry is a bad one. Taylor (?) says that Hayward cannot afford to pay for a lease'.

Joseph Chinchen's almost exhausted quarry in Cowlease was being worked by his son Charles. George and James Barnes and James Bower Junior were in Great Cowlease. Richard Bower and a Turner were in Judas (southeast of Court Pound).

ABOVE A detail from the north part of Worth Matravers Manor estate survey, by Samuel Donne, 1772. The map shows 'paviour quarries' in the Gallows Gore ('Callos Gore') area. The field numbered 258 may be 'Gallis Gore Common'. The wall being dug under in the 'Walter Corbin' extract above is probably the east wall of Denney field number 257; the field on the other side, marked 'Eastington Farm' formed part of the Bankes estate, now known as 'Broad Mead'. (Dorset History Centre D/BKL/E/A/3/1/1).

BELOW A detail from the Bankes Estate inland quarry record, November 1825. 'List of Quarries in the Isle of Purbeck belonging to Henry Bankes Esqre.' The list gives names of lessees, date the lease commenced, duration of lease, 'situation' of quarry, whether on Wilkswood or Eastington farm, 'by whom now worked', 'expiration of leases' and 'Observations'. (Dorset History Centre D/BKL/E/L/9/31).

INLAND QUARRYING / 85

Some men worked in partnership: Bower and Phippard, Bower and Sanders, and Richard Bower and Thomas Bridle, all in Burnbake (Burngate). Partners John and Charles Bower and William Bower were in East Hay, while Thomas, James and Edward Lander also shared a single quarry in Woodclose, with James Bower Senior in another there. It seems the Landers moved from the Worth estate as Hayward had done. Thomas Corben was in Long Mead (more often called Long Close), the comment being: 'This quarry is nearly worked out. Corben can barely maintain himself by working it'. William Brown junior was in Purbeck field (south of Court Pound). Albert Brown later foundered this quarry and left it.

James Squibb was in Broad Mead, with the comment: 'He has opened a pit in Little Cowlease but the stone is still taken out of Broadmead.' This shaft remains open just outside the southeast corner of Broad Mead, but the workings extend well under it. It was latterly worked by Nelson Burt's father. It is right in a joint which can be an advantage in sinking a shaft, for the step in the strata allows for easier penetration. I guess Squibbs knew about the alignment of the joint, from their earlier work in this field to the northwest. Away from all the others, partners Israel Bower and G. Bridle worked Verney field. There is a lot to be said for working in partnership as quite a lot of these men did, but of course it is worth remembering that apparent 'solo' operators may often have employed apprentices or others.

Continuing eastwards, a 1776 survey of Trenchard's estate in the manor of Langton Matravers shows 'quarries in work'.[43.] Three were in Main Hyde and Putlake; mounds and hollows remain there. The Post Office Bowers were among others who worked these quarries.[44.] Four more were in Strapps, Quarry Close and Inhooks; these three fields lie east of South Barn Road. Trenchard owned three more in Grayseed, all north of Priests Road (Way) and all surely shafts. There were probably more in the adjacent unsurveyed Archer Leeson estate, but records seem not to have survived.

Further east a 1798 diagrammatic map of Benlidge shows just two shafts, one of which, last worked by Lewis Tomes, remains open to this day.[45.] At this Swanage end of Purbeck the manors are small. They run in long north to south strips, some only one field wide, each with its quarries, but in contrast to the larger estates to the west, they changed ownership more frequently and there is a lack of surviving records.

An 1820 rate assessment provides an illuminating snapshot of all quarries active in Swanage parish at the time.[46.] Some men were operating more than one. An abridged list giving names and number of quarries follows:

Robert Stevens 2, Joseph Harden, George Harden, Jeremiah Warren, William Haysom senior, Titus Haysom, Thomas Benfield, John Harden 4 (1 in Durlston Bay), Messrs. Chinchen (1 in Benlidge), Thomas Randall, Matthew and James Benfield, George Pushman, William and George Butler, William Phippard, Timothy Collins, George Haysom, Richard Best, Robert Burt senior, Thomas Warren, Robert Norman, Martin Phippard, James Stickland, William Collins, James Warren, Abel Bonfield, George Chinchen, Joseph Collins, William Tombs, William and George Medway, Peter Phippard 2, Joseph Coleman and Moses Manwell, William Stickland 2, Thomas and Jon

Witchampton, Dorset, St Mary, 1832. Swanage Freestone combined with flint.

Stickland, Thomas and James Stickland, James Tombs, Sam Harding, James Haysom and Joseph Dowland, Joseph Collins, Jon Toop, Thomas Burt, George Hibbs, W. Melmoth and J. Coleman, Isaac Haysom, Jon Webber, Thomas Webber, Joseph Tombs, George Weeks, Joseph and Thomas Collins, J. and T. Collins with Mr. Marsh, Esther Haysom and P. Gover, Jas. and Robert Mowlam, Messers Manwell, Jon Short, William Cole, Peter and George Hancock, Jon Stickland, Henry Hibbs, Joseph Stickland, Jon King, Jon Ellery, Robert Chinchen and James Collins, Thomas Corben, Thomas and William Seymore, James and Henry Edmunds, John and R. Bower, J. Bonfield, Joseph Foot, Jon Keates, Anthony Saunders, Benjamin Bower, Jonathan Chinchen 2, William Brown, Charles Lander, Thomas Cross and Jas. Bower, William Phippard and J. Bower 2, Robert Seymour, Jon Clark, James Warren, Robert Haysom, Abraham Collins, Isaac Hatchard, Jon Cull, Charles Harden.

This gives a total of 91 quarries. So at the beginning of the 19th century the centre of gravity lies firmly in Swanage, as it probably had since about 1650. Paving may well have been their staple output, but they were, or had been, busy with other items. In particular, the Napoleonic forts around Portsmouth had been taking big quantities of ashlar. Fort Cumberland (1782-1812), is mostly Swanage Freestone; the square tower in Portsmouth dockyard was surfaced in 1827 with Cap. Newport Guildhall (1819) on the Isle of Wight, by Nash, Poole Church (1820), Witchampton Church (1832), are also Swanage Freestone. Much of this has weathered badly, especially in highly saturated environments like the face work to the forts, and particularly a flight of New Vein steps at Fort Cumberland.

In 1843 Colonel Cardew of the Royal Engineers, Portsmouth, wrote to the Inspector General of Fortifications:

'The result of many years' experience having sufficiently proved the want of durability of the Purbeck stone used in the

ABOVE Portsmouth, Fort Cumberland, 1782-1812. Badly laminating New Vein steps. Note flint nodules.

RIGHT Swanage, Newton Manor. East front of broached Freestone, late 1700s.

repair of the facing of the escarps, etc. exposed to the influence of the weather in the fortification at this station [...] I propose to try the effect of making these good by means of spalls and good mortar, with face of cement ½ to 1' thick'. He goes on to list the beds he would accept.[47.]

Though some Swanage Freestone and New Vein other than Vie Bed has failed in the forts, Swanage has an example of the Freestone lasting well. The east front of Newton Manor was re-faced by Captain Cockram in the late 1700s, perhaps on the proceeds of his privateering. The broaching of the Freestone shows a meticulous consistency throughout, the stones lasting well in the Swanage environment. Perhaps the stone was quarried on his estate. Much 18th and 19th century Purbeck was broached, and one wonders when that treatment started first. It would seem to be post medieval. Several old road bridges show a variety of surface finish. For example Totton Bridge, Southampton, is a mixture of unbroached Isle of Wight stone, perhaps medieval, with the western side built mostly of broached Purbeck, surely from a later widening.

A Serrell Estate rent book reveals that between 1832-1858 there were eight quarries on their Benlidge farm, paying dues half-yearly. The entries suggest that John King and John Bonfield were separate from the other group of Abraham, John and Isaac Collins, John Stickland, Samuel Phippard and Edward Brown. Edward was also paying the same estate for the Dancing Ledge quarry at that time. In the ensuing years some men came and went. John and Edmund Corben first appeared in 1836, paying £3 16s and 10d for a half year's dues. In 1838 they gave way to Mr Burt, with him paying their outstanding dues of £5 and 9d. Burt clearly had status: surely he was merchant Robert. In 1840 he paid £2 4s 6d 'by the hand of James Harris'. James was probably working the quarry on a day-to-day basis. Harris moved on: Burt later combined with Thomas Phippard. Seymour and Toms appeared as two Collinses dropped out. John King died, giving way to Joseph, presumably his son. Thomas Bonfield remarked that King's quarry, now filled in, lay close to Priests' road, east of the north-south Belle View footpath. It was one of the most extensive workings, Thomas said. When the quarry was given up, the Kings 'barred out the arch', which meant that shaft would fall in and no one else could gain access. By 1858 the list of quarrymen was Joseph King, Isaac Collins, Edward Brown, William Toms, Mr Burt and Joseph Bonfield. Joseph's quarry mouth was not on Belle Vue land, for he paid for 'stone drawn out on Mr Yeatman's land'.

In 1844 the Serrells purchased Court Farm, Swanage, consisting of 177 acres let to John Smith, containing 'numerous stone quarries'. This manor stretches from the stream to the cliffs and from about modern Cecil Road to the junction of modern-day Priest's Road with the High Street. The quarrymen in occupation in April 1848 were: William Collins, James Haysom, Robt. Moulam, Charles Moulam, Henry Moulam, Joseph Manwell, George Hibbs, Samuel Haysom, Isaac Collins, George Toms, Henry Pushman, Peter Gover, George Keats, William Keats, George Shott, Henry Chinchen, George Weeks, Phineas Turner, W Stickland, James Toms, Emanuel Turner, W Coleman, G Medway, Moses Manwell.

Over the next ten years most men persisted, but others came and went, such that, by 1857 the list was: George Harden, James Toms, W Collins, John Hibbs, S Medway, John Hancock, S Keats, S Shott, Peter Gover, John Collins, H Haysom, Joseph Manwell, S Hibbs, H Seymour'.

William Toms fell into arrears for quarries on both Belle Vue and Court farms. Andrew Corben paid dues for his quarry and also for stone dug in 'Herston Farm from under my land'. The writer of the rent book, possibly Serrell himself, clearly accepted the situation that Andrew was advancing underground from one estate to another. Andrew was not alone in this, for Henry Haysom, Joseph Bonfield and Joseph Cooper were all doing the same: they were paying half their dues to Mr Serrell and half to Mr Yeatman. Practicalities would have driven the direction of working. One wonders when the respective landowners got wind of just what was going on, but they did, and an understanding was reached. Thomas Bonfield remarked

INLAND QUARRYING / 87

how reluctant some men were in disclosing where they got to underground. Some fixed up doors to keep enquirers out.

He also remarked that on reopening one quarry his uncle Jo said to Sam Bonfield 'Which way we going?' 'Under Ma Serrell's' was the reply. This was probably a later Joseph, but surely the same scenario, and possibly the same quarry, adjacent to an estate boundary. Ma Serrell was Frances Serrell, the grand lady of Durnford Manor who inherited the estate on the death of her husband, Mr Sheffield Serrell in 1859.

The 19th century saw a decline in the number of Purbeck quarries from about 200 to 45. There were just two in Worth, 14 in Langton, 29 in Swanage, as listed by H. M. Inspector of Mines in 1896.[48] In 1877 the then Inspector, Dr. C. le Neve Foster, commented:

> The Purbeck stone is a new feature in my statistics. In spite of a great many difficulties, I believe I have at last attained a fairly correct statement of the total amount raised from mines. There are nearly a hundred stone-mines in the Swanage district, worked by one, two, or three men underground, who are in many cases the owners as well as the occupiers. Their work is often most irregular; if the men can find work as masons, they abandon their quarries for a time, and do not return to them till other work is slack. As the quarrymen of the Isle of Purbeck had never been troubled with Government forms till this year, I had considerable difficulty in getting returns from them. Endless mistakes were made, requiring investigation by correspondence, and I may safely say that the 92 stone mines near Swanage, employing only 264 persons, gave me more trouble than all the other mines of my district put together. No doubt I shall have very much less inconvenience in future years, as the men will soon get into the way of filling up the returns correctly. The following figures represent the number of tons raised during the year: Purbeck stone and marble, dressed, 11,816 tons 10 cwt. Purbeck stone, undressed, 1411 tons 10 cwt.[49]

Thomas Collins told me that up Belle Vue the inspector drew attention to the fact that the horse, standing on a scar bank, had little to eat: 'Not much feed for the horse, Mr. Tomes. 'No, but look at the view 'ee got.'

On the face of it, the mines inspectorate provides a comprehensive list of active quarries, but I suspect some were missed, for it was not necessarily a benefit to 'appear'. Also there are confusions. The 1896 list, for example begins with J. Balls at Blackland. This is corrected to J. Ball Bower in the subsequent list of 1908. Bower was such a common name in Langton and Worth, though not in Swanage, that branches of the family were known by other names that sometimes continued over generations. Some, such as 'Post Office' and 'Dressmaker', arose from other occupations, 'Sugar' from possession of a sweet shop. Some were based on talents: 'Singing Eddy' had a fine voice, heard not only in the Square and Compass but also in the London music halls; 'Fiddler' was accomplished on the violin. 'Flinger' got his name from throwing stones at birds out on the water whilst 'mucking about' at Seacombe with other youths. Some were probably just nicknames. Most were drawn from the distaff side. These include 'Brownsea', 'Coffin', 'Rabbit', 'Cake', 'Short', 'Ivamy', 'Chaffey', 'Thorn', 'Brown' and 'Smith'. Others were geographical: Billy 'Preston' had worked in quarrs in that area for years before returning

Swanage, Linden Road. 'Cardiff Work' stone dressings on Edwardian houses.

to Langton; Billy 'Winspit' lived at Winspit; others such as 'Razorback', 'Captain Whistler', and 'Trink', 'Frenchy', 'Tucker', 'Chucky' and 'Mouse' are more puzzling. 'Buff' presumably once grew a beard. Men of my father's generation would talk of Dick Gad (I am not sure of this root), Jim Cake *et al.*, without giving any indication that the proper name in question was Bower. There was not the same problem with less numerous families, but Joe Baker Corben tells of the same need for secondary names in that family also.

Not many quarries gained names other than that of the men who worked them. Two that did were 'Blowhole' and 'Mutton Hole'. The former, worked by George Norman, lay in the grounds of the Townsend Field Study centre: the latter developed into the Council tip, now closed. The listing of William Collins at 'Lanery Vein', is also odd, suggesting a mix-up with Laining Vein. His location was actually in Lanchard, Herston, where he was down in the Cap.

The Inspector's list is informative for it gives the numbers underground and on the surface, but like any Government statistics, should be taken with a good pinch of salt. Most men had to be flexible. Of course the two at Seacombe got together as occasion demanded. What the list demonstrates is that the average quarry consisted of three or four men working together, probably much as things had been since underground working began, if not earlier. Some men, like George Norman, worked alone, whilst the largest workforce was at George Burt's Cowlease quarry at Swanage, employing three underground and nine up top: this is 'Boss' Burt, not 'Sherriff' Burt, who was also a George. J. Brown in Langton was almost the same, with three underground and eight up top.

Perhaps surprisingly, self-employed quarrymen usually dug and cut up their own stone, rather than employ others at that end of the operation. They either then went on to work it to its finished form, or employed pieceworkers for the final stage.

Partners John Ivamy Bower and Charlie Harris did this in their Burngate quarry in the 1930s, where they employed Billy Preston Bower to do the final shaping, by the foot run. The logic was that they overcame the underground vagaries and did the important cutting stage where stone can be easily wasted, or not, but left the financially straightforward final dressing to others.

Staples like curbing went on being produced over lengthy periods: work was always variable. In 1896 Ambrose Bower Jr. had two men underground with four up top; twelve years later he had three underground only. This could be explained by on the one hand doing work like the Worth churchyard cross which called for skilled masons; whilst later supplying block to the Swanage merchants for their own projects.

Around this time the big player George Burt, amongst other jobs, was doing what was known as 'Cardiff work'. Edwardian housing in Swanage has dressings such as that at Linden Road, which would call for several banker hands. Burt's quarry is still open with a lot of stone taken, approximately the size of a football pitch, much of it down a runner and flooded in winter. All the stone was taken out up one little shaft. Albert Chinchen, who had worked for him, remarked 'We were right down in the wold' [old] – a remark informative of his mindset and perhaps that of preceding generations in general. A lot of footprint casts such as they encountered are nondescript and don't obviously add up to much, especially when revealed piecemeal. But in Boss's quarry a splendid trail of three-toed prints protrudes from the Roach ceiling. What did men like Albert in the past make of such finds and other fossils such as the fish? 'Noah's flood', my father said!

Around this time Brown's were doing a lot for the Duke of Norfolk at Arundel, which would have called for several men on the banker. One small building of their inland quarry remains in Captain's [Capstan] field by the approach road to Acton Field cottages. These quarrymen had masons doing quite fine work, but of course most of this sort was being done by the Swanage merchants, who do not appear in the statistics but who were dependent on these men for stone; they were no longer based on the shore but in and around the railway yard.

LAINING VEIN

Laining Vein is mostly thin bedded and therefore productive of roof tile, paving and ledger slabs. Some 16th and early 17th century ledgers are certainly made of it and they may well tell of a considerable level of exploitation at that time. Starting in the west, disturbance on its outcrop line is evident, both west and east of Haycrafts Lane. Around Spyway and eastwards there is evidence of much working. However, the field south of Leeson park also has wartime bomb craters, which may be confused with quarry workings.

In some areas, notably Spyway, part of the vein is dominated by the same fossil snail as is characteristic of Marble, and can cause confusion. Such stone occurs in late 18th century fortifications at Portsmouth, but it seems there is no medieval work. I suspect that this good quality bed does not run to big pieces and is therefore not to be expected as large ledgers, but other Laining Vein beds do. Much Laining Vein was dug in Inhooks at Gully. The fact that a manorial map of 1776, showing quarries 'in work' there, only shows quarries south of the Laining Vein outcrop suggests that they were dug and largely finished by that time. The next field eastwards is Greyseed. When an area close to the main road was levelled to provide for a farm shed in about 1980, back filled Laining Vein workings were revealed. Continuing eastward, the Laining Vein outcrop is marked by undulations and thicket – filled hollows across the entire spread of Benlidge.

Eric Benfield, discussing his father's quarry in Townsend, remarked that the old men had taken the 'Lannen' Vein long before and that knowledge of these activities was mostly lost.[50] Towards the western end of the Sunnydale dip there are quite extensive bumps and dips on the Laining Vein outcrop. Laining Vein Rag occurs here and in big sizes but it does not serve well. There are 18th century ledgers of it that literally sag as they slowly craze and break up. In the 1930s, Fred Bower was digging it underground in Court Cowlease, where he was selling a bed he called 'Black Bit' to my grandfather for sawing. I am not certain just which bed this was, as the name does not appear in the early lists of beds. In the 1970s Thomas Bonfield dug in Gully ground quite close to New Buildings, where he found a curious configuration of ridden and undug patches.

Above the Laining Vein lie Toadseye and other beds with which I am unfamiliar. They were exploited to some degree. This activity may have been restricted to quite shallow workings, for it make no sense to dig off a lot of overburden for a small thickness of stone. Phil Keates' maxim, referring to the days of pick and shovel, was that you could shift a foot of muck for a foot of stone so, going after the Freestone, six foot was about the maximum depth to rid off to get down to the Grubs. However Purbeck frequently surprises. A premium bed may have justified a different ratio. Astoundingly, underground workings in beds well above the Toadseye show in Durlston Bay cliffs.

THE TWENTIETH CENTURY

During the first part of the 20th century the number of quarries in Swanage gradually decreased; some as men gave up the trade, others as men moved west to Langton. This migration included George Harden and his brothers, George Hancock and his sons, Bill Keates, Jimmy and Albert Chinchin, William (Bubbles) Haysom, Alfred Norman, Bill Galley and more. The new arrivals were was not always welcomed by the 'Westerners', which sometimes led to fisticuffs. One remark my father made with regard to this shift was that these men could sell a good Langton Thornback in the rough state to the depot for sawn work for the same price as for worked up kerb, made out of Cap, Feather etc. that their Swanage quarries yielded, with all the extra labour that meant. Another reason for the migration was the acquisition of small parcels of stone-bearing freehold land, resulting from the dismemberment of the Worth Estate (1919); another was the policy of the Bankes Estate,

Verney, Herston. Bonfield's quarry. The cart (hidden by its load) about to go over the roll stone at the top of the slide; Thomas Bonfield, right, on steps. The horse can be seen at left, going round the capstan.

Acton. Dennis 'Short' Bower's quarry. Dennis stooping at right. Note roof of 83 Acton cottage.

which remained more conducive to quarrying than some others. In 1929 Bankes' steward, Thomas Lovell of Wilkswood Farm, mapped and numbered their quarries, including those at the cliff and Verney, plus a number that were dormant; he got to 61, almost all undergrounds. Extra to those were seven ridding holes in Longclose, numbered separately. The established undergrounds, by this date virtually all worked in the Freestone, were productive of relatively thick stuff such as the staple kerb. But a demand for garden stone, particularly crazy paving, drove the search for thin beds, which shallow surface ridding holes can best provide where the right layers come close to the surface. Longclose must have been a good prospect. My father remarked that for those men, used to making squared up paving, to dig a patch and sell it for crazy paving without working it to shape, was like ' being let out of school.' Another 'liberation' followed in the 1960s with the advent of the hydraulic splitter. Simply to pull a handle and split a stone in the desired way rather than have to skilfully cut wedge pits was almost beyond imagination.

By the time of the outbreak of the Second World War Ernie Burt's operations at Mutton Hole had developed into Swanage Quarries, owned by Exeter-based haulage contractor Mr. Crew. The Rag was being crushed for the war effort. Only one Swanage underground was left, producing I know not what. Two Dowland brothers continued working underground in what had been Charles Benfield's quarry in Court Cowlease. Brian Button, who as a boy helped the farmer there, told me of an occasion when, there being heavy rain, the loaded cart was stopped part way up the slide. He thought the donkey had been unhitched but left standing on the circle. Somehow, perhaps the pawl on the ratchet slipped, the spack whirled around, striking the poor beast in the head. The vet was called and he shot the unfortunate animal. This was almost the last underground working in Swanage parish, but not quite. Jim Norman said that when working at Mutton Hole in about 1951, when the weather came bad in the winter they would do some work underground in the workings developed by Ernie Burt. There was not an underground with a capstan, but the workings ran in underground on the level. It was the only Inland quarry like it in Purbeck. 'You could put a load on the cart [which ran on rails], give it a good kick, and it ran out into the daylight,' said Jim.[51.] This entrance lay more or less south of the modern complex of the Swanage Bay View Holiday Home Park.

After the war some of the Swanage men, including Jacky Collins, returned to restart work, but found the years of neglect had left the hauling gear damaged or missing, and that it was difficult to resume. In 1956 the property was acquired by the Council. Four men holding old redundant undergrounds were given notice to quit. William Dowland, Walter Brown, Harry Chinchen and Fred Meader appealed to the Ancient Order of Marblers for help. The wardens negotiated 'time to remove their shelters'. I guess they got a few pounds for the wall stones. Thomas Collins talked of a Meader sinking a shaft late in life, not a thing many old men did: perhaps it was Fred's father doing it to benefit him. In these later, derelict, years the old quarr houses close to Swanage had been a place where men gathered to play Crown and Anchor, an illegal gambling game. Some of the shafts served as air raid shelters for people living nearby. Sometime after the war Swanage Quarries ceased their opencast operation as well. After a few dormant years, in the early 1960s John Suttle revived Swanage quarrying, centered on Mutton Hole, which by this time had become the Swanage rubbish dump. Quarry holes in general were convenient places to get rid of rubbish, particularly those easy to get at. Some now contain rich bottle collections.

After war service, brothers Jack and Fred Norman returned to underground work for a while in what had been Alfred Benfield's quarr near Worth gate. Jack said the roll had not been set up properly. 'I seen our horse with his belly nigh on the ground struggling to get the cart over the roll. We put it right but never pulled out another load after that.'[52.] In the late 1940s bulldozers and draglines were beginning to be hired to strip off overburden, and the Normans moved to a ridden hole further west on the Worth road. Ernest and Doug Norman returned to their father's two quarries near Castle View but did not pursue either much.

Thomas Bonfield returned to underground work in both Burngate and Verney, where he and his son Harold, bucking the trend, actually sank a new shaft. I asked Harold how they kept the angle when sinking it. He said they were going nice and steady when he was called up to do National Service. His father then went steeper! It was there that a fresh young Mining Inspector produced a lengthy list of things that had to be done to comply with safety regulations. One was that the

South West of Acton. Les Lock's quarry. Note differences between cranes, particularly Les's neat anchoring stacks that prevent the crane from toppling.

Detail of Les Lock's ridden hole (front right in previous picture) with Charles Audley, and Sheppy Lock (brother) wielding bar. Note pile of walling stone, and also Roach crazy paving at upper left, stacked on edge to prevent breakage. Charley is standing on backfilled waste from an earlier underground working, probably 'Phae Brownsea Bower's.

INLAND QUARRYING / 91

Lander's Quarry, Gallows Gore. The modern face of inland quarrying.

lanes had to be widened such that a cart could pass anyone in the way. Given that Thomas was invariably either pulling or pushing the cart, he was not likely to be run over by it. It was a regulation that may make sense in a coal mine employing scores of men, but hardly Purbeck. In effect it was impossible to comply with. The inspector compiled a lengthy list of more requirements before exhorting Thomas to carry them out. He responded 'I'll do better than that', 'I'll gie thee the place and you can do what thou like wi'it'.

It wasn't quite the end of underground work on the Bankes Estate. Harold and Roger did some more, escaping the arctic

Worth Matravers, Easington Cowlease, Nelson Burt's quarry, early 1960s. Note built up fireplace in the background and gate piers in construction. Stone at left on ground exhibits a pit mark, therefore this was before Nelson acquired a guillotine.

months of January, February and March, 1963. Some while later Harold modified the shaft, mounting a diesel powered crane over it, and began underpicking using a compressed-air driven hammer, but found the tools kept breaking. He has since pursued open cast quarries. According to Harold's remarks in *Written in Stone* it was recent restrictions based on the ever-present bats that brought the final demise of the underground way of life.[53.]

Other men who carried on underground between the wars included brothers Jim and Albert Chinchin, who sank a shaft in Captain's Field close by Judas Gate, a quarry of particular geological interest in that a slab of their Roach, now in the Dorset County Museum, has impressions left by a Pterosaur. Albert went to Malvern with the Telecommunications and Radar Establishment, while in the postwar years Jim worked in Thomas Hancock's Swanage station yard. No sign of their Judas Gate shaft remains. In the inter-war years and early 1950s a number of men set up wooden Scotch derricks over their ridden holes. Most were concentrated on the Bankes Estate around Acton and along the Worth road. These quarrs were not productive of good waterworn rockery, which prompted George Lander to go for Burr southwest of Wilkswood Farm, where pieces of his crane still remain. His brother Hedley exploited the same bed at Primrose Hill Farm, whilst the Co-op went for similarly weathered Rag where it is close to the surface inland from White Ware. Dorothy Gardiner encountered Hedley, identified by her as 'Warden of the Ancient Order', and recorded that he was supplying rockery to Southend, Essex.[54.]

The Marblers, as an organisation, pressed the Bankes Estate to grant more land for quarrying. The upshot was the development of several quarries in Queensground in the 1950s. This area did not have any particular geological merit, but was chosen simply because from the farmer's point of view it was of lesser value, being far from the farm at Eastington. Perhaps in that decision we can see the marginalisation of the stone industry.

FOUR
Peveril Point & Durlston Bay

There is difficulty in separating the rotund forms produced by subaerial weathering from those produced by the action of the sea. In my opinion the rounded shape of some of the 11th century rubble in Corfe Castle, suggestive of sea action, is in fact simply stones dug from just beneath the surface. What puts shoreline stones beyond doubt is the evidence left by marine borers such as gribbles and piddocks.

In the days when the easiest way to move heavy loads was by water, the environs of Peveril were obviously the nearest source of rubble stone for Wareham and Poole – even Christchurch. Evidence that this traffic went on for years is provided by the 12th century Constable's Lodge near Christchurch Priory, now a ruin. This building has a lot of sea-worn rubble, much of it Marble, some with piddock holes. There is more sea-worn rubble at St. Martin's Church, Wareham, probably dating from the 11th and 12th centuries, but the possibility of later insertions cannot be ruled out. The same can be said of Studland and Arne churches, where sea worn rubble crops up in several areas. Later 14th century rubble beneath the east window at St. Mary's, Wareham, has at least one piece of Marble with a piddock still remaining in its selfmade tomb. There is more in Holy Trinity, and in the walls of Pound Lane, whilst the 17th century Priory wall adjacent to St. Mary's has a lot. Poole has further examples. They include: in Market Street No. 6, Byngley House, the flanking wall of No. 14, and the Almshouses. The 15th century Town Cellars have old worn Marble mixed with, amongst other stuff, Heath Stone and exotic Granite that surely arrived as ballast. Scaplens Court also has seaworn Marble, as have several rear walls to buildings in Church Street. Some of this is Flint Bed, with its characteristic nodules. East Lulworth's splendid 15th century tower also has sea-worn rubble, surely taken from the nearby cove. This all adds up to a considerable medieval traffic in rubble taken from the Swanage shore. What must be certain is that they were shipping more valuable items from there as well.

An undated letter tells of 17th century quarrying at Peveril.

TOP RIGHT Corfe Castle. Subaerial weathering in 13th century rubble wall.

CENTRE RIGHT Seaworn stone piece of yellow bed from Kimmeridge exhibiting piddock and gribble boring.

RIGHT Cross section of Marble section from Peveril Point showing gribble and piddock holes. Note daisy for scale.

PEVERIL POINT & DURLSTON BAY / 93

ABOVE Durlston Bay. Drawing by Thomas Webster, 1812, published in H. C. Englefield's *The Isle of Wight* (1816).

BELOW Durlston Bay, 2020: approximately the same view as that drawn by Webster in 1812.

It was written by Anthony Dennet of Langton to his brother-in-law, Mr. William Pitt, at St. Stephen's Westminster, sometime before 1636, for William died that year:

> 'I have sent you a note enclosed of your gutter and channel stone I sent you herein inclosed. And so concerning your land called Peverell, the stone that your tenant Hayward doth sell are stones that are taken out of the Clyffe and not out of the Quarre (he hath a Quarre in Peverell besides: all the wallestones they buylde withall in Poole they have for the most parte thence which he doth sell for *vj*d a boate loade the boate carrying not above *V* tonnes he doth sell thence out of the same clyffe marble and paving stones he hath *ij*s the hundred for every hundred of pavinge and as I can learne be hath *j*d ob. for every foote of marble and all this cannot be lesse worth than *iiij* li. per annum when yt is lest, and many yeres when byyldinge goeth forth in Poole or any other place nere more. I give you intelligence thereof so much the more because I did understand that Hayward was to buy a further estate of the same Peverell.'[1]

Treswell's map of 1584 shows Robert and John Hayward with John Burgess at 'Owre'. Perhaps that was where they were based and kept their boats.

Recently the Purbeck paving and pitchers and flint cobbles of the school yard at Eton, laid between 1706 and 1716, were renovated. On being lifted it became apparent that some of the pitchers had been made from large sea-worn pebbles that had been cracked in half. The straight broken surface had been presented as the face, leaving the tell tale rounded side hidden below ground. These stones had certainly been taken from the shore.

Contrary to Robinson's remarks that 'there are no particular traces of any large quantity of stone having been removed from Durlston Bay itself', a great deal was dug here, although the tendency for slippage and for trees and bushes to grow up obscures the evidence.[2] The bay as we see it now has been, to a degree, modified by quarrying, but unlike the Portland Bed cliffs west of Durlston Head, which are eroding slowly, the sea is making relatively rapid inroads into Durlston Bay. This would have been accelerated by the removal of stone from the shore. The bay was an obvious source, nature providing loose, ready dug stone, lying there for the taking. Its removal triggered more slippage. The useless clays and shales were washed away in storms, leaving more stone ready to be exploited. As the readily available stuff was consumed, the quarriers pushed in underground. However, unlike the cliff stone undergrounds, these were relatively unstable; a tendency the quarrymen took advantage of.

Webster describes a 'tunnel and collapse' system of working at Durlston which he saw in 1812: 'The mode of quarrying this stone is here represented; this is by making excavations and inserting slight props; in the course of time, these props giving way, a part of the cliff falls down, and the fragments are worked by the masons into the forms proper for several purposes.' However relying on 'slight props' giving way was not the whole story. I have been astonished to find a piece of Freestone spilling down from above the easternmost Cinder reef which exhibits a drill hole. The hole is about ten inches deep, one and a quarter inches diameter, and knocked in at a sloping angle. It is just like the abundant cliff quarry drill holes which are sure evidence of the use of explosives, but why resort to gunpowder in these Durlston Bay inland beds?

GEOLOGY

Both Peveril ledges, pointing towards the Isle of Wight, are formed by the two edges of a hollow fold of Burr. The layer once carried on northwards in an acute arch downturning so sharply as to be almost vertical at sea level. This anticline has eroded away but stumps of the vertical limb form a reef, visible at low tide, running eastwards, parallel to the main north ledge. The modern sewer pipe lies between them. The Marble approximately ten feet above would have followed the same configuration, but has washed away. The Burr, much fractured but tight-jointed and relatively massive at ten feet thick, goes on stubbornly resisting the sea. Within its protecting hollow lies a remnant dish of Marble. Several beds of it are exposed in the low cliff above, from which good blocks are falling onto the shore. I suspect that this exposure is relatively recent, for close by there is evidence of quarrying. Those men would have surely taken blocks such as these now visible had they had been easy to get at then. Evidence of quarrying of Marble is indicated by back filling, revealed by recent minor falls from the cliff top on the south side of the Point. This waste largely consists of shale, but includes spalls, scars and larger pieces of Marble, some bearing tool marks, much like medieval back filling recently revealed further west at Quarr. One roughed-out lump could well have been intended to make a small capital. The dug area would have extended approximately from the helicopter landing pad, or due south of the easternmost house, westwards to due south of the row of cottages east of the Lifeboat Station; more or less to the break in the cliff line.

Peveril's horribly complicated folding must have provided obstacles for the quarriers, and perhaps prevented extraction in some places. The challenge this complexity presents is illustrated by the fact that, in my opinion, the full annotated section shows the same Marble bed twice.[3.] *The Hatcher Review* is in error for this reason.[4.]

No doubt it was easiest to begin quarrying on the Swanage Bay side of the Point rather than where we can see the obvious evidence now exposed on the brow of the cliff. It is probable therefore that the Marble has been taken from under the coastguard lookout and the easternmost houses westwards to

Swanage, Peveril ledges, looking east. The two ledges are formed by a syncline of the Burr. The Marble lies in the trough between them.

Swanage Bay, Slippery Ledge. Upper surface of Burr with steps cut into it for the Grosvenor Hotel, now destroyed.

the boat park. Above this park Burr forms the brow of the cliff. From this brow the downs slope northwards, plain and undisturbed. This evenness must reflect the twelve foot or so of shales and useless stone beds that lie between the Burr and the Marble, but from just south of the road the slope steepens, and the surface becomes more undulating. This is about where the Marble should outcrop and suggests its removal down to the water. It may not all be the work of man. It is possible that as the sea ate into the bay these sloping layers of shale, greasy when wet, tended to slide down into the shore, a process that may have made the Marble even easier to get at. There is little adhesion between alternating layers of clay and limestone when wet. Where they slope, as the Marble does for the entire length of the Purbeck outcrop, any breach on the downside can destabilise the mass upslope, as I have learnt to my cost when trying to dig it.

The extent to which Buck Shore's Slippery Ledge (which is the top surface of the Burr) extends up out of the shore suggests there was once more Marble there. Its 'roots' are revealed at low water spring tides. From here to the stream the shore has been much modified. Buck Shore has grown since the pier was

PEVERIL POINT & DURLSTON BAY / 95

Swanage, Mill Pond.

built; the pier's masonry acting as a groyne, trapping the drift of material coming from the southeast. Eastwards, Slippery Ledge slopes more or less at the same angle as the Downs, until it disappears from view under the masonry of the Grove.

However this even angle does not continue. Near the Wellington clock tower the same layer rears out at a very different angle. Close by, only exposed at low water, lie *in situ* reefs of both bottom and green Marble beds, gently shelving east. They link to the intertidal rocks called the Bury. It is open to question how natural that patch of rocks is; most are dislocated. Why is there no blue reef where the other two beds yet remain? Surely this is evidence of quarrying, not just down to average water level, but to as far as they could get without diving.

Springs break out along the Burr outcrop and serve to indicate its route; Boil Well on Monkey Beach is the easternmost, continuing westward, Spring Hill, now hidden away, the Mill Pond and Court Hill, also now hidden. It is probable that the Marble lay close by the water's edge, even as far west as about Cliff Place, and that the medieval tomb makers and builders, even their Roman predecessors or indeed Saint Edward's executors, quarried it away. What a quarry: a sheltered shore and Marble so close. Marble from this eastern end of the outcrop is characterised by having more thick 'lists' than that from further west, just like the 12th century work in Canterbury Cathedral. Knowledge of early quarrying lasted until the time of Hutchins' first edition in 1774, for he mentions: 'Stone called Purbeck marble dug near the fort' (Peveril Point).

The present stone quay is surely Leland's 'peere'.[5] What is not in doubt is that additions were made to it several times, the last campaign being quarrier Strickland's addition of the parapet wall, probably paid for by Mr. Morton Pitt. Quarrels over ownership led to riots. A conveyance of 1837, between James Marsh and Mr. Morton Pitt refers to two quays: 'little,' and 'King's'. Chris Kaye, in researching this part of Swanage, concludes that the present quay is 'little', and that 'King's' was situated about opposite Burt's Lane. The family of King figures in the stone trade, but it is possible that the name derives from Crown usage, and that this pier was originally of medieval date, and linked to the Marble trade.[6]

Returning to the Durlston Bay side of Peveril and leaving behind the evidence of Marble quarrying close to the Point. The Burr ascends the cliff westwards to opposite the boat park. There is no evidence of quarrying in this section, Swanage Burr being poor compared with that lying further west, but at about this point a fault throws down about six feet to the northwest. The Rag forms the first big ledge west of Peveril and quarry evidence starts. Where it rises westwards out of the shore it forms a sloping platform about 100 feet by 20 feet wide. Here the Laining Vein has been dug out. High above the western end of this shelf, where the Cinder emerges from the water below, beds above the Toads Eye have been dug out by driving under the ground into the cliff face. These workings, inaccessible now, are not obvious, for they have been back-filled, and there are no conspicuous voids. However, tell-tale supporting legs remain: this could be the one and only such underground working at that particular level. The Laining Vein may have been particularly good in this area. Until swept away in a 2014 storm two big slabs of it lay on the shore.

It is difficult to fit the names given in the old lists to these layers above the Laining Vein. Clement's 173 is the same as Ensom's 166, and is probably Bonfield's Blue Bed, but just possibly his Step Bed. This bed is of good quality and exhibits footprint casts on its underside at both Peveril and Worbarrow; how many prints are there in between? There is a slab of it containing rivets in a Suffolk church that must be medieval, plus several pavings in the 18th century cloister floor in Norwich Cathedral. The bay is perhaps the most likely source for the Norwich stones, for the good bed in question is isolated within useless beds which would preclude quarrying to any great extent away from the coast. However, it was quarried to a degree inland, certainly just south of the 'Welcome to Swanage' sign on the A351, but I guess to no significant depths. More puzzling are the high level undergrounds mentioned above, for where these beds are accessible on the shore they do not look much good. They are around Clement's 180, probably what Bonfield calls 'Lepers', and not to be confused with the Leper that rests on top of the Downs Vein.

Westwards from where the Cinder rises out of the shore, the Downs Vein has been taken for about one hundred yards. A shelf, extending for part of this distance, marks where the Laining Vein was taken. Now blocked off by slips from the eastern shelf, it is likely that at the time of working they were linked, so it would have been easy to run a loaded cart eastwards down the slope to the shore and loading place, at its maximum a distance of about one hundred yards. That they were working the stone to finished shapes up on the shelf rather than down on the shore is betrayed by scars and spalls spilling down from the high western end. West of a small fault that throws down about two feet on the western side, some collapsing of the Cinder would suggest removal of the New Vein for perhaps fifty feet, but this is uncertain, much of it obscured by falls. The Cap is of poor quality and left, as is the Feather, which contrasts with the repeat exposure south of the Zigzag path, where the latter was valued and indeed gave its name to the quarry.

Undug Downs Vein appears in the vertical cliff face about one hundred and fifty yards or more east of the modern sea defence, but only continues about fifty yards westwards before it again has been taken. This approximates to where Strahan indicates Butler's Old Quarry.[7] Evidence of removal continues westwards and upwards until the Vein disappears into the vegetation towards the cliff top, near the sea defence. Here the digging is clearly back-filled with waste, not just the result of slumps. Here also the Cinder sags, betraying the taking of the New Vein.

FOSSIL HUNTERS

W. R. Brodie's important find of the first mammalian jaw bone in 1854 led to further exploration.[8] Towards this western end of the Downs a substantial cutting, now bisected by a causeway supporting the cliff path, is probably nothing to do with quarrying, but 'Beccles Pit'. Samuel Husbands Beccles was gentleman fossil hunter.[9] In 1857 one item of his expenditure was £200 for a team of workmen to excavate 3000 tons. An account of his amazing project was given by Charles Kingsley of *The Water Babies* fame, published in *The Illustrated London News* in December 1857. This was fortunate as Beccles failed to publish his findings, although according to Kingsley he intended to do so in the transactions of the Geological Society (as it then was). Kingsley wrote: 'Before he could lay it bare [the fossil bed] he had to remove a superincumbent load of fifty-two feet thick and laid bare an area of nearly seven thousand square feet (the largest cutting ever made for purely scientific purposes), and, even more difficult, he educated the more intelligent of his Swanage workmen into trusty and observant fossil hunters.'[10]

Illustrated London News, 26 December 1857. 'Scene of the Geological Discoveries at Durlston Bay near Swanage, Dorset'.

Setting aside the last remark, fifty-two feet is a great depth to strip from the surface, though driving in from the open cliff would have made the enterprise slightly easier. An impressive amount of waste would have been created down on the shore, all carried away by the sea years ago. Probably what good stone came out would have been sold to the merchants. Sadly nothing much can now be seen. Is it that the owner at that time, the Earl of Eldon, required a sloped restoration or is it the result of subsequent tipping of waste, which the Coast Path 'causeway' certainly is? That has been built up within living memory.[11]

The excavation extends to the west across the manorial boundary wall where other humps and hollows are unquestionably the result of quarrying.[12] The fossil-bearing bed was deeply buried on the Peveril Estate. Even where shallowest in the extreme west corner of the Downs it was fifty feet or so. The situation on Filliter's Sentry Estate to the west, soon to be acquired by George Burt, was worse. Within yards of the boundary which curiously breaks the normal east/west alignment before it reaches the cliff edge, lies the big Durlston Bay fault. In these circumstances, Beccles probably started by doing the straightforward thing: attacking the cliff where the fossil bed could be seen. The fossils lying in a discontinuous pocket led him into the cliff on a narrow rather than broad front. His finds, hundreds of reptiles plus fourteen species of mammal, remain among Purbeck's most exciting fossil finds.

The Beccles episode, massive as it was, was not the end of big-scale fossil hunting. Twenty-two years later, in 1880, Mr Henry Willett repeated the experiment. With Lord Eldon's permission he employed quarrymen for some weeks to 'scarp the cliff' for forty feet down from the top until an area ten feet by ten feet of the critical layer was laid bare. However, despite careful examination, in contrast to Beccles, he found very little.[13]

PEVERIL POINT & DURLSTON BAY / 97

QUARRY EVIDENCE IN THE LANDSCAPE

Where the eastern Cinder ledge rises from the shore a shelf between 20 and 30 feet wide has been developed, with a lot of Downs Vein exposed, some of it loose. This can only have happened since quarrying was given up here, for it was one of the most sought after beds. Amongst the flow of clays and stones from higher levels there are spalls of another good quality bed from above the Laining Vein, telling of workings at those higher levels as well. The landslip of the winter of 2000 immediately west of the Zigzag path has brought thousands of tons of clays and Burr plus a few pieces of Marble down from the cliff top level to the shore, completely obscuring lower levels. If a similar flow were to smother Tilly Whim there would not be much quarry evidence left to see. So it is with the quarries that extended westwards from this recent slip. The old hands took the Downs Vein for 150 yards or more from where the Cinder emerges above water level, this being Strahan's 'Feather Hole' quarry, but the resulting shelf has been buried, and it is easy to overlook the evidence. The shelving, easternmost part of Swanage quay mostly consists of Feather bed similar to the Feather from this location. This landing includes a continuous step running down the slope which was presumably intended to facilitate a dry foot when stepping out of a dinghy. This suggests gentrification of the quay, probably during the W. Morton Pitt period (1820s).

What is striking is the absence of Downs Vein showing above this western Cinder shelf, or lying on the shore; it has clearly been taken here. In places back filling of quarry waste, some containing scars, is evident, rather than natural slippage. This rests on the Cinder shelf. Minor falls over 2009-10 revealed a 'leg' including a stone with a nice pit mark built at the New Vein/Feather level. This old underground working was not obvious in that there is no open void, only back filling. However, storms in 2014 have reopened it. The triangular shape of the underground void is produced by constraints imposed by a big fault to the east and a lesser to the northwest.

To the south, the Cinder has sagged. Underground ceilings, if tight jointed, tend to hold up, so long as 'the pinch' is retained but cannot be if a cliff such as this is penetrated on a wide front. This stretch of Cinder has moved outwards a bit, sinking down as far as the back filling allows. The higher beds are obscured along this stretch, but evidence of them having been worked occurs in the form of scars spilling down in some of the slips.

More or less midway between the Zigzag path and the castle lies a massive fall, referred to by my grandfather as 'the founder', which destroyed Sheriff Burt's road. Because its eastern side in particular consists of clean stone rather than the usual stone/clay mix, the suggestion has been made that it is a product of quarrying. In my opinion it is natural, and the mass is Rag. It is marked at its eastern end by a particularly big Cinder of approximately 150 tons, with the lowermost part of the Downs Vein adhering to it, lying on the shore. Towards the southern end of 'the founder' a concentration of waste scars, including offcuts bearing pit marks, have almost reached the shore. They tell of a workplace that, before its slide to the sea, was about half way up the cliff. From here to Durlston Head evidence of quarrying is difficult to see because of all the slips and vegetation, but north of the castle and linked to it by a bridge, is an exposure of Rag, mostly, if not entirely, the result of digging rubble for the park walls, etc. It is exceptionally thick, about twenty feet, as against about two feet at the north end of the bay. This Rag lies more or less flat, but only yards away, south of the bridge, the Roach is plunging north at an acute angle. The castle is perched perilously close to a fault, which is revealed best by the Portland beds where they suddenly plunge below sea level north of the headland.

HISTORICAL RECORDS

Evidence of 18th century quarrying appears in an agreement of 1774. George Pitt (Senior and Junior) leased land with the quarrying rights at Peveril to John Chapman, Rector of Silton (son of stonemerchant John). The parcel of land included a former withy bed, summer house and quarry 'in possession of Stone Merchant John Melmouth aged about 40.' Also in the will of Samuel Warren of Sandwich, marbler 1779: 'and whereas my late father John Warren deceased was in his life time legally possessed of a valuable stone quarry situated lying and being in a Bay called Durlston Bay hereby give demise and bequeath all such my said fourth or quarter part of all and singular the said stone quarry and premises unto my said daughter (a minor)'. Ramsgate Harbour Accounts for 1767 include payments to Hannah Warren for 'Lyme stone'. Downs Vein, which crops out in the Bay, makes good lime. Hannah, widow of stone merchant Francis, died that year. It seems there were two concurrent Warren Durlston Bay quarries. It is just possible that 'Lyme' means 'Lyme Regis', which is productive of stone for cement, but it seems unlikely in this case.

John Harden, stone merchant, included in his will of 1789: 'bequith to my 2 sons Joseph and Richard Harden the South quarry in Durlston Bay and the quarry in Court Ground [Carrants Court Estate].' 'One full moiety or half part of that quarry called the cinder' was bequeathed to another son, Samuel. John had been involved with Howard Serrell, 'Gent, at Swanwich' who included in his will of 1767: 'John Harden be permitted to work my quarr in Durlston Bay for the space of one year after my decease and no longer on the same terms as present'. Ramsgate accounts include for October 1760 'for Hon. Serrell draft to John Harden £100'.

Large quantities of stone were being sent to Portsmouth for defensive works. J. Phipps, Commanding Engineer in 1786 at Fort Cumberland, wrote to the Swanage merchants: 'For the supply of Purbeck Cordon Stone from any of the 4 following Veins or Beds and no other will be permitted to be received: Thornback, Freestone, Downs Vein and Five Bed'. Cordon is a projecting course, about ten inches thick, semi-circular in section. To learn of Downs Vein being used for such work came as a surprise to me, brought up with the knowledge that Downs Vein splits into thin beds. But the western Durlston Bay Downs Vein does not split: the top twelve inches or so is solid.

This part of the Bay was surely the source of the Downs Vein we see in solid form in that fort and elsewhere in Portsmouth, such as on Grand Parade. Four years before, 2,000 tons of best Purbeck plus 12,000 tons of backing, had been ordered for the fort.

These quarries were active in 1812 when Thomas Webster visited. One of his drawings shows an underground with 'founder', another a burning kiln on the shore. This could be the burning of gypsum rather than limestone.

After W. Morton Pitt's death in 1836, the Peveril estate was sold to Mr. Daniel Alexander. He imposed licences on the men active in his part of Durlston Bay at that time. They were Thomas Benfield, William Butler and Francis Haysom. Francis was descended from William, Christopher's half brother. Christopher had been killed in an accident at the Point. The Rev. T. O. Bartlett included the following in his diary: '31 March, 1823. This day Christopher Haysom, an old man, fell over the clift near the fort 30 or 40 feet high and was so much injured that he died the next morning.' Christopher had married Kate Warren, whose family, as already mentioned, had earlier had quarries in the bay. Whether his death was work related or not is unclear, but a few years later John Harden's certainly was: '17 August 1832. This morning J. H. aged 54 was killed by the falling of his quarry in Durlston Bay'. Latterly Francis had another quarry immediately southeast of the position of the present Cottage Hospital in Queens Road, but he was still in occupation in the bay in 1845, for in that year Thomas Benfield was let a quarry 'lying next east to the quarry now let to Francis Haysom and being the same quarry as was formerly occupied by the father of John Harden'. An accompanying map shows George Butler towards the west corner of the Downs (the western extremity of the Peveril Estate), Benfield to the east.[14] A clue to Francis's quarry's location might be that he was required to pay a royalty on gypsum as well as stone, which would put it to the west; gypsum appears in the cliff not far east of the disfiguring 'defence' armouring. Latterly, lifeboat coxswain Bobby Brown reckoned Butlers were further east, more or less due south of the lifeboat station. In 1810 Francis, aged 19 and master of the fishing smack, the *Hart* had been granted a certificate which exempted him from being press-ganged into the Navy; as a fisherman, he was in a 'reserved occupation'. His quarryman-fisherman uncle, John, pronounced 'Jan' in the dialect, had fought the press gang. One of his boys had been caught and was being held in the boat whilst the main body of naval men went off to catch another. Jan managed to overpower the guard and the boy ran off. John Mowlem recalled later in life that he once evaded the press gang by running all the way to Knitson Farm, where he was hidden away under sacks.[15]

In 1887 James Butler sold his rights to Frank Burt of Burt and Burt, who had already taken over Thomas Benfield's quarry in 1877. By this time the Peveril Estate had been bought by Lord Eldon, who did not want further quarrying. Burts, who had invested in a 'lighter' to carry the stone away, insisted they had the right to continue. In 1889 Lord Eldon paid £20 to settle the matter. Papers relating to this dispute reveal that by this time Haysom's quarry had been abandoned for at least 20 years. James Butler's, which he had inherited from his father George, he in turn from his brother William, 'was midway in a 120 ft high rugged cliff most dangerous of access about 120 yards east of western boundary of the estate', that is towards the southwest corner of the Downs. Thomas Benfield's was 'bounded on the west by Butler's, on the east by the steps at the fort.' Activity on the Sentry Estate ended with Sheriff George Burt's 'parkification', if not before. There must have been a certain piquancy in the situation with his cousins trying to continue quarrying Lord Eldon's land while he gentrified his estate next door.

So finally ended Durlston Bay quarrying. It was part of a process. As Swanage was growing southwards, manor by manor the quarrymen were forced out. For these two easternmost estates, Sentry and Peveril, evidence suggests work had started in the early medieval period from about 1160; following a probable break, there had been more or less continuous activity there from the reign of Elizabeth I right up to 1889.

Lime burning in Durlston Bay. A detail from a drawing by Thomas Webster, 1812, published in H.C. Englefield, *The Isle of Wight* (1816).

FIVE
Cliff Stone

INTRODUCTION

The Portland Group of rocks, best known from the Isle of Portland, are also exposed in Purbeck. They form sheer sea-cut cliffs from Durlston Head in the east to St. Aldhelm's Head in the west. It is along this 4½ mile stretch of coast that quarrying developed. As at Portland, only the topmost beds yield useful Freestones. Along this Durlston to St. Aldhelm's stretch, apart from a narrow coastal fringe, the Portland Beds are overlaid by the Purbeck beds, so the exposure is narrow. However, inland from St. Aldhelm's Head they appear at the surface as far north as Coombe Bottom. Westwards from Chapman's Pool they form a scarp extending to Swyre Head, Smedmore Hill and Tyneham Cap. Here the sea again reaches the scarp, producing Gad Cliff before, at Worbarrow Tout, both Portland and Purbeck beds plunge below sea level. West of St. Aldhelm's Head the Freestone beds are thin or absent, and quarrying for masonry has been insignificant. For obvious reasons these beds are called Cliff stone and that term is used throughout this text rather than the clumsy Purbeck Portland. Portland only means stone from the Isle of Portland.

In late Jurassic times a regressing sea covered the area of what is now South Dorset with beds of limestone deposited in conditions much as currently prevail in the Bahamas. In shallow water, oolites proliferate so as to dominate the accumulating sediments that storms build into dune-like structures, interspersed with fixed reefs built of big shells, just like late Jurassic Portland. Where the water begins to deepen and the oolites fade out, shell sands dominate, as in late Jurassic Purbeck. Though not totally absent, particularly in the west, the relative lack of oolite from the cliff Freestones is therefore useful when attempting to make separation between stones from the two localities.[1] Equivalent beds in the Dorset Ridgeway differ more. They tell of a more lagoonal environment, and are less of a problem to tell apart.[2]

It is relatively easy to differentiate between the various Portlandian shelly beds; layers accumulating at the same time in Purbeck and Portland are similarly built of big shells. However, the admixture of species can be different, some which are abundant in one locality being entirely missing in the other, 17 miles away. Purbeck Spangle and Blue Bit have no suet-like blobs formed by calcareous algae such as some Portland Roach exhibits. The twisted gastropod called 'the screw' by the quarrymen is abundant in Portland Roach, but almost entirely absent from its Purbeck equivalents which are generally harder. Trigonia, abundant in Spangle, built its shell of Aragonite, which has since been dissolved out, leaving cavities filled or partly filled by crystalline calcite, which looks different from any of the Roach that comes out of Portland. The oft-repeated claim that the St George's Church, Reforne, is built of Roach is refuted by some, who say that it is in fact of shelly Whitbed, the product of a localised patch reef. Such reefs seem not to occur in the Purbeck cliff Freestone beds, formed at the same time as the Portland Whitbed, but two do so higher in the succession at the Titanites level. One occurs at East, but not West Winspit, the other at Tilly Whim. Both give rise to a coarse, distinctive shelly rock. Each reef differs, so East Winspit Blue Bits can be recognised in parts of Margate sea wall and some farm rollers and gateposts. I have not spotted the Tilly Whim equivalent in any masonry. Great boulders of it lie collapsed in the quarry and though unattractive for masonry, nevertheless it must have been used to some extent. You can see where the reef ends just to the west end of the Ragged Rocks; it is not visible at the next quarry, Chilmark.

The greater difficulty is to distinguish the Freestone beds: Portland base bed compared with Bottom Freestone; Whitbed with Pond Freestone, especially when they are patinated, as in old masonry. But another difference between the two locations is that whilst tectonic movements have left Portland relatively unscathed, just sloping gently to the south, Purbeck has been

Langton Matravers, Museum. The larger roller (agricultural) is East Winspit patch reef stone. The small hand roller (domestic) is of indeterminate Cliff Freestone.

positively tortured. All this stress has left evidence in the rock that, although not unique to Purbeck, is characteristic of it. Calcite veins, common in many stones, including Bath and Chilmark, are a feature of Purbeck, much less so Portland. Usually called 'lists' by the Purbeck quarrymen, less often 'lakes' or 'glares', they can show up strongly, especially if pure white in one of the dark beds, as the last name suggests. At Haysom's St. Aldhelm's quarry they are vertical, parallel, and run a few degrees off true north, which is in marked contrast to what happens in other inland beds, where they can run in all directions. In some layers they cross one another. Such crossing can display lateral displacement, telling of fracturing, followed by cementation going on more than once. At St. Aldhelm's quarry they can be as wide as one eighth of an inch or thin to disappearing. Generally they are several feet apart, but at some other cliff quarries there are more of them, whilst at Seacombe, at least in the Bottom Freestone, there are far fewer. Their near north-south direction at the Head is a little off square to the run of the main joints, so masonry cut from a block from there typically displays a list running across slightly off square in one plane, square in the other. This is exactly such as we see in the splendid 18th century pilasters at Encombe House. In the natural sea cliffs at Crab Hole and in West Winspit quarry, surfaces exposed by the fracturing of lists are visible at the Pond Freestone level, the calcite content of the list becoming the face of the cliff. Some are conchoidal; some of these centre on particularly big flints which lie beneath.

Another phenomenon which can help differentiation is the formation of stylolitic planes caused by pressure solution. They occur in Cliff stone, but not, it seems, in Portland. Some, called blacks, can be little more than a dark line running more or less level, such as to suggest a bedding plane. Good examples are some pavings of unknown date in Westminster Abbey

Purbeck coast, Seacombe to Anvil Point. The dark cave in the distance is Blacker's Hole. The rock in the foreground is Watch Rock, separating William's and Michael's coves. The Seacombe quarry loading rock is centre foreground just above water level and the flat grassy surface above is the floor of Seacombe quarry.

and a few 18th century ledgers in Chichester Cathedral. In addition they tell of the fact that the stone has been cut across the bedding plane. Others in the Freestone run parallel to the main joints, but sheer up at an angle. Where these are weak the stone can be split off along them, which reveals a curious uneven surface typical of stylolite. They were called 'slivers', produce undesirable block shape and were, as my father put it, 'an infernal nuisance'. The lower part of the Blue Bit at the Head can also be split along such a distinctive horizontal bed, hence its name, 'crinkly'.

Other helpful fossils are serpulid worms of more than one species. They can be so abundant as to be a rock builder and are common in the Cherty series of both Purbeck and Portland. At the Head they are rare in both Freestones, common in the Spangle and Blue Bits, sometimes clustering on ammonites or other large shells. In other cliff quarries, notably Seacombe, they are more common in the Freestone. The white species is particularly visible in dark blue hearted Blue Bits. Without them I would have overlooked the memorial in Ely Cathedral to Bishop Goodrich, who died in 1554. His slab also contains an oyster, more resistant to wear than the matrix, so it now stands proud. In the Blue Bit at the Head these hard shells form a continuous layer within the bed. They are sufficiently smooth and close together to cause a weakness such that it can be split at that level. Hence its name, 'oyster bed'. At East Winspit they thicken up to form a very different mass. Two more single-shell-thickness oyster rich horizons also occur in the Spangle.

Rempstone Hall. Part of broken, unfinished font, probably originally from Winspit.

The vertical cliffs running between the two headlands of St. Aldhelm's and Durlston are cut by three valleys, Hawcombe, Seacombe and Winspit, which would have afforded the most accessible stone. It is probably a safe assumption that the first quarrying began at these sites, and at St. Aldhelm's Head, where the good upper beds would have been lying loose in the tumbled undercliff, and where, at the cliff top, they are relatively easy to reach by horse and cart. At the other end of the accessibility scale are Halsewell and Reforn, where work must have started by men digging away on the brow of a vertical cliff. Unlike the Purbeck stone and Marble quarries inland, where it is now often difficult to tell where former working existed, cliff quarrying has left near permanent scars which tend to distort our impressions of its scale in relation to the rest of the trade. With insignificant exceptions it is possible to see every quarry much as it was when abandoned.

Hutchins, quoting 'Smeaton's Eddystone' says:

'The quarries situated at or near the high land about three miles from Swanwich called St. Alban's Head, afford a species of stone in blocks, much of the nature and colour of Portland, which is called Purbeck Portland. The strata of merchantable stone lie here in the upper part of the cliffs as they do at Portland, but having more cover they are in some measure worked under ground. [No underground work was ever done at the Head itself; he is bringing Winspit, or other quarries to the east into the picture]. This stone is of the like nature, and puts on so much the appearance of the Portland that it is often used in lieu of it. It is, however, inferior in colour, harder in work, and, according to the information I then got, not in general so durable. But what seemed to me likely for ever to prohibit this field of stone from coming into competition with Portland is that, as it cannot bear the expense of land carriage down to Swanage to be shipped, the workmen are obliged to let it down with ropes from the place where it is wrought, to the surface of the sea, either into vessels lying at the foot of the cliffs, where there is deep water, or where there is a dry strand at low water; but, there being but little shelter from the winds and seas, this can only be done in very moderate weather, and particular winds; wherefore the shipping it there must necessarily be somewhat precarious.'[3.]

What seems to be clear is that, from the evidence of surviving monuments, exploitation of the cliff remained at a low level until the 16th century. It therefore mirrors developments at Portland, where relatively low levels of medieval quarrying activity became greatly expanded by about 1700.

Commencing in the mid-12th century, large quantities of Marble fonts were made, based on a Tournai pattern. There are also rare Cliff stone examples: one survives in Morden, another at Tarrant Monkton. Yet another has recently been discovered, broken and incorporated in 18th century work, at Rempstone Hall. What pieces of a 12th century font are doing in the rubble of an 18th century manor house is a mystery. It may be linked to the Rempstone Calcrafts' acquisition of Worth with its Winspit quarries in the 1770s: if this is so, it suggests that the Winspit quarries may have been in use during the medieval period. What is left of the 'Rempstone' font shows it to be square with four round-headed incised arches per side and with the usual round interior bowl, just like the one at Tarrant Monkton and many Marble examples that survive. The top surface has been left off the punch so it is unfinished. There is something odd about this work sequence. I would have expected the top to be finished before the incised blank arches or indeed the bowl. But perhaps this expectation is a failure to get inside the 12th century stone cutter's mind. My father's age-old admonishment was: 'get rid of your waste first'. It is no good to spend a lot of time refining the outer shape only to spoil the job by reverting to heavy work later, such as punching out the bowl, which causes it to break. What the uneven top surface does tell us is that the cutter could not have used a sinking square, which is a great aid to accuracy in cutting out the bowl. Given that the tool incorporates a screw thread, I guess it was yet to be invented. The medieval stone-cutter had to be more reliant on the eye than his successors, which contributes to subtle differences between the work of then and now; contrast the machine-like exactitude of Kingston's 19th

Morden, St Mary. Pond Freestone font, previously square, showing traces of blank arch enrichment.

Worth Matravers, St Nicholas. 15th century Cliff stone coffin lid, uniquely twisted.

century font with 15th century Worth's.

That Morden's octagonal font was once square is not immediately obvious. However four opposing sides show traces of blank arch sinkings. Its reworker cut off the corners before going on to chisel away the arches down to the depth of their shallow sinkings on what was left of the remaining four sides. In attacking the narrow raised strips between the arches he has accidentally allowed plucks that have carried below the desired face depth. This would tend to happen if not carefully avoided. A little more care, a few more minutes' work, and all the old surfaces would have gone without trace. As so often, it is the 'cowboy' craftsman who gives the game away. The Morden bowl but exhibits a bold white list at an odd angle which shows it not to be in bed, for in the quarry such lists are vertical. Tapped by the knuckle it rings, and I venture that it is Pond Freestone from the St. Aldhelm's Head undercliff. Identifying stones by comparing different sounds produced is a so-far unexplored area of research. My father said of Teddy Corben, that though he was deaf, he could still tell if a stone was sound or not by its ring.

Cliff stone was used in other medieval ecclesiastical contexts. Just one of the five 13th century lancets by the pulpit in Worth Matravers church is of Cliff Freestone.[4] One of its external jambs exhibits two pit marks! Worth also has an unusual Cliff stone coffin lid, the incised cross possessing seven rather than the usual three arms, each with a trefoil terminal.

Similar medieval lids of Marble, but with raised crosses, remain at Kimmeridge and Wimborne Minster. There is an excavated 15th century Cliff stone coffin, complete with lid bearing a raised cross, in Worth Matravers churchyard, which is probaly later than most, perhaps all, of the Marble examples. It is doubly unique in that I know of no other like it made of Cliff stone or worked with such a twist to it. It is a rudiment of good masonry practice to first take the surface of any work piece 'out of winding' by means of boning blocks and straight edges. The man who fashioned this coffin lid failed to do this. Marble examples of similar lids bearing raised crosses on stepped calvaries are commonly distributed across England. None that I have seen are twisted in this way, nor are there any others of Cliff stone surviving of this design.

It seems clear that the Marble was more prized and was taken long distances, whereas the local Freestone remained much more 'down market', fit only for local consumption, especially if of defective workmanship. That this may have been the case is also suggested by a collection of somewhat similar Portland examples discovered during archaeological excavations at St. Andrew's, Portland.[5] With regard to the choice of material, whereas Marble is much harder to work, and the cutting out of the interior of a coffin represents much labour, the Marble has the advantage of coming out of the ground in much better shapes. In particular, nature supplies beautiful flat slabs of it, ideal for coffin lids. By contrast the Cliff stone beds tend to provide uglier shapes, a disadvantage only partly redressed by the stone's easier working properties.

However, one bed that does occur in the cliff, 'with shape to it' (to use a quarryman's term) is the Blue Bit which, particularly at St. Aldhelm's Head, comes out big with a good flat bed and of a convenient thickness, about nine inches. Christchurch Priory has a unique assembly of six or more such slabs, some mutilated and bearing post-medieval inscriptions, but three certainly of the 14th century. Such blocks would have occurred naturally in the St. Aldhelm's Head undercliff, and I suspect this to be their source. The apparent absence, at least of datable Blue Bit slabs elsewhere, makes the medieval Christchurch assembly of particular interest. There are numerous examples of Marble brass indent slabs from this period distributed generally, because the London workshops, which dominated, were setting their brasses in Purbeck Marble; however, there seem to be no other Blue Bit examples. However what looks like original work in the Cradle Tower (1348) within the Tower of London contains East Winspit Blue Bit.

The next apparent usage of Cliff stone is again local: the fonts at Worth Matravers and Arne. Astonishingly, the RCHM suggest the Worth Matravers example is early 19th century, that at Arne 14th century. To my eye, they are of the same

BELOW LEFT Worth Matravers, St Nicholas. 14th century Cliff stone font.

BELOW RIGHT Arne, St Nicholas. 14th century Cliff stone font.

Worth Matravers, St Nicholas. Fragment of Cliff stone canopy head, late 14th century, in east wall of south porch.

Corfe Castle, St Edward. Cliff stone niche flanking west door of Burr tower.

Corfe Castle, Uvedale's house. Cliff stone mullion window.

workshop, if not by the same hand. There is a close similarity in the mouldings and blank tracery, both have a 'softness' in their working, an unevenness in the sinkings, etc. that give them, in my opinion, a medieval feel. This is in marked contrast to the 19th century examples at Kingston and St. Aldhelm's chapel, with their exact execution. Worth Matravers church also contains, reset on the east wall of the south porch, a fragment of a Cliff stone canopy head which has on its underside ribbed vaulting of the late 14th century.[6.]

The 15th century tower of Corfe church is of Burr, but the two niches flanking the west door lintels are Cliff stone. The builder obviously knew about the relatively easy working properties of Cliff stone and obtained two pieces just for this, the most demanding element. From after the Conquest right through the medieval period the stone used in local churches and, *par excellence*, Corfe Castle itself, was the Burr.

By 1600 it is clear that cliff quarrying activity was increasing, almost all for local use. In Corfe, Uvedale's House has Cliff stone included in its mullion windows, 1575 (the label stops bear I. V., for John Uvedale). A similar window has been reset in Box Cottage, Coombe, Langton Matravers. Jim Puckett, a descendant of Israel Bower who lived there, said it came from Corfe. Other mullion windows of Cliff stone remain in Corfe cottages at 51 West Street and numbers 31, 98 and 101 East Street. Another with similar profile has been reset at Afflington, whilst Court Farm House in Swanage has bits of similar windows incorporated into its rebuilding. Dunshay Manor has similar Cliff stone windows, the label stops

Corfe Castle, National Trust shop. Cliff stone fireplace re-used as internal doorway.

104 / PURBECK STONE

bearing E.D. for Elizabeth Dolling, the wife of Christopher, who purchased the Manor in 1561. These windows predate the work of her son John Dolling, who extended the house using Burr in 1642. A mutilated male figure of Cliff stone is possibly him.

It seems that conservative-minded stone cutters stuck to their patterns over decades, so some examples may be later. In the 1600s, hollow chamfers often gave way to ovalos, which are a clue to a later date. Mortons House, Corfe Castle (c. 1600), has mullions which are of Cliff stone, as are the central porch door arch and the remarkable ornate fireplace in the master bedroom. The wide, debased, four-centred arched fireplaces at Mortons House have long lintels that are cliff Blue Bit (one of these heads is seven feet nine inches long) whilst the jambs are Burr. A similar fireplace, also of Cliff stone, now reset as an internal doorway, remains in the National Trust shop, Corfe, whilst another has been recently revealed at West Wood Farm, north of Harman's Cross. The combination of Burr and Blue Bit in Mortons House and Barnston is interesting as, apart from 19th century revivals, it is towards the end of Burr usage. Burr block tends to be short, whereas Blue Bit comes out in long lengths. Hence that aspect of the combination was surely practical, not aesthetic. In my opinion the suspicion that the different stones suggest different dates is not well founded. Mortons House exhibits a rare mason's mark outside on the right hand flanking wall of the central porch, presumably that of the master (*see page 277*). With these properties mentioned above we can recognise the dwindling end of Burr usage and the beginning of large scale activity at the cliff. Major developments of those quarries occurred when the Uvedale estate was inherited by the Okedens or Okendens, and particularly at the time of the second William in the early 18th century.

However, production for local needs is not the whole story, as is revealed by the survival of a remarkable Blue Bit ledger slab dated 1607 in the north choir aisle at Exeter Cathedral. It is large – ten feet by three feet six inches and commemorates four members of the Heliar family. This fine slab is of Blue Bit such as occurs at St. Aldhelm's Head. Recently two more large Blue Bit ledgers, close in date, have been identified at Ottery St. Mary, Devon and Ely Cathedral. In my opinion all three are from the St. Aldhelm's undercliff.

The fireplaces of Barnston, Mortons House, the National Trust shop at Corfe, etc. tell us that someone was working Cliff Freestone at the time of the Heliar slab. The source was either the quarry on the point of St. Aldhelm's Head or, much less likely, the quarry latterly known as St. Aldhelm's quarry. It was surely easier to obtain stone for use in Corfe from these cliff top quarries rather than retrieve it from the undercliff. Slabs of this Heliar size do occur in these quarries, but not that frequently. However, if other work such as the fireplaces was absorbing the long but narrow blocks which these quarries yield most of, it is possible that on finding a good wide stone, they reserved it for a ledger, which would have carried a premium price. Quarr farm house has mullion windows similar in section to the Corfe examples but they may be later, suggesting a certain stylistic conservatism, as the remarkable Cliff stone fireplace is dated 1651. This was the year, the Civil War over and a Republic established, that the Company of Marblers and Stonecutters reiterated their rules or '10 Articles of Agreement'. One of the signatories must surely be the stonecutter who produced the fireplace.

The work was therefore relatively new when Celia Fiennes, cousin of the resident Colliers, visited in about 1685. This, together with her visit to Seacombe may have prompted her to observe:

'there are many quarys in these hills of that which is called the free stone, from whence they digg it [...] At a place called Sea Cume the rocks are so craggy and the creekes of land so many that the sea is very turbulent, there I pick'd shells and it being a spring-tide I saw the sea beat upon the rockes at least 20 yards with such a foame or froth, and at another place the rockes had so large a cavity and hollow that when the sea flowed in it runne almost round, and sounded like some hall or high arch'.[7]

She omits to mention the paving trade, which was surely greater and which is what drew Daniel Defoe's attention forty years later.[8]

The 18th century witnessed the building of a whole crop of local manor houses, using what had become highly fashionable Cliff Freestone ashlar. Among these is the Manor House, Swanage, built by John Chapman (pre 1721), where he used Cliff stone in the central pediment and in the columns of the cellar carrying the brick vault. Another is the Manor House, Wareham (1712), which is particularly fine work, closely jointed with the detail over the door well preserved, the enriched lintel resting on impressive eight feet long jamb stones flanked by ashlar still bearing fine measured tooling marks. Yet another was Durnford Manor, Langton Matravers, built by Samuel Serrell of Combe Keynes in 1725, using a combination of inland Freestone ashlar and Cliff stone for the moulded window casements, the central pediment, the pair of gate piers, etc. It was rebuilt using the original stone in the 1950s. It is perhaps a safe conjecture that this stone was dug on Serrell's manor at Dancing Ledge. An enigmatic survival, possibly from Durnford, now serves as a fireplace lintel in a cottage in Worth parish which was built by a Langton quarrier about 1810. Combined with rubble, the long, finely cut architrave complete with return ends, a delicate bead and engaged convex frieze, suggest that the piece was formally an internal doorway lintel. The section is characteristic of the Wren/Hooke generation of architects. At Creech Grange, some if not all of the dressings on both the south front (1738-41) and the eastern elevation (mid-19th century), are of Cliff stone rather than Portland. A particularly informative quoin near the main door contains large coarse shells plus stylolite unlike any examples we find at St. Aldhelm's. It must have been sourced at Winspit or eastwards. Interesting corduroy tooling on the 18th century front includes Burr ashlar, some with unusual hard bars, possibly reworked from the earlier house.

Of the vernacular, Virginia Cottage, Swanage, sadly demolished by Swanage Council in the progressive 1960s, was unique in being built of Cliff stone ashlar. This was the only cottage of its sort in Swanage, almost certainly of Tilly Whim stone and, I suspect, early 18th century or before.

Encombe House. A view from the south across the lake.

Encombe House. Stable block.

Encombe House, built between 1734 and 1770, is another Cliff stone example: the stables were added in the early 19th century. This stable block exhibits a mixture of Cliff stone beds, unlike the 18th century work of the house proper, which is mostly of Pond Freestone. The RCHM suggest that the Rock Bridge was perhaps built by John, Earl of Eldon (1838-54), at the same time as he improved the park, extending the lake. However, this rock bridge is formed of blocks of Spangle, which would have been a by-product of digging the Pond Freestone for the house, suggesting that bridge and house may be contemporary. This Encombe ashlar and in particular the splendid pilasters of the south elevation are almost certainly Pond Freestone, from the quarry on the end of St. Aldhelm's Head.

BELOW Encombe House. Pilasters of south elevation.

BELOW Encombe House. Rock Bridge.

106 / PURBECK STONE

Langton Matravers. Durnford House, Cliff stone gate piers.

Dunshay Manor, Worth Matravers. Gate piers with obelisk-like finials.

Smedmore is more difficult to be sure about. The early 18th century elevation has splendid Portland Whitbed jambs combined with mostly Purbeck rubble on a Burr plinth. But the later northwestern façade of 1761 consists mostly of Portland with some Cliff stone. Encrusting lichen obscures most surfaces but a number of stones clearly display lists typical of Cliff and one piece has stylolite, again typical of Cliff stone, but not of Portland.

Imposing gate piers became fashionable. Lynch Farm has moulded caps surmounted by balls on brick piers. Mortons House has similar caps but with finials, also on brick piers, recently moved. Durnford has similar caps but on massive single stone panelled piers (but now lacking balls or finials). Grandest of all are those at Dunshay, where panelled single stone piers, as at Durnford, carry enormous obelisk-like finials. They are similar to those that enrich the Wareham Manor door jambs, so may be of that date. The pair of finials on the lesser pair of posts are replacements made by Mack Rose in 1926, using inland Freestone. The big pair were refixed after one had fallen, by Ambrose Bower in 1908, at the same time as he provided the masonry for the north wing for Captain Marston. Ambrose re-erected the left hand grand pier. The moulded necking stone was worked for him by Gilbert Edmunds; it is of inland Freestone from Ambrose's quarry in Burngate. The splendid original stones are either Cliff or possibly Portland. Tyneham also had a pair, of which only one remains. It is certainly Portland.

In addition to these manor houses, substantial as the output must have been to provide for them, there were other developments, in particular the great works in which two William Okedens, father and son, played a key role. The finely wrought weir on the Corfe river bears 'N.B. W.O. 1711' in beautiful raised lettering, W.O. surely stands for William Okeden (Snr), the engineer/landowner. It is of Cliff stone, many of the closely fitted blocks exhibiting mason's marks on the face. These are fixing marks and inform us that it was made in the quarry before assembly on site. A much larger Okeden project followed.

In July 1749, after a meeting at Lloyds Coffee House, London, Trustees advertised for engineers to deliver plans for the erection of two piers to improve the harbour at Ramsgate, finally awarding the contract to William Okeden (Jnr, 1703-53).[9] So began what was to prove perhaps the largest single work carried out using Purbeck stone, most of it Cliff. Soon there were controversies, and problems with silting, and Okeden was ultimately replaced. It seems that the difficulties that arose with his Ramsgate contract may have ruined him: Hutchins states that Rollington Farm, which had come from the Uvedales to the descendants of the Okedens of Moor Critchel, was 'sold by a decree in Chancery, with other estates of that family in this island, late William Okeden, esq.[sic]' to John Calcraft in 1757.[10]

Between 1750 and 1752, the Ramsgate Harbour Trustees employed '50 sail' in transporting 15,000 tons of stone. There was a hiatus before another 94,000 tons were shipped between 1764 and 1771, some used in building houses in the rapidly expanding town. John Smeaton took over the contract in 1774. In 1776 the first 'Foreman of Stone Works' Thomas Preston died and Henry Cull, surely a Purbeck man, became foreman. In June 1788 difficulty in retrieving a block from the water prompted Cull to suggest using a diving bell. Smeaton had one made. Several aspects of the engineering were pioneering. In 1792 Smeaton resigned, by which time the Harbour, to all intents and purposes, was finished. Samuel Wyatt succeeded him, and Henry Cull was made his resident deputy. Wyatt

Scotland Farm, weir on the Corfe River. (William Okedon Snr 1662-1718).

CLIFF STONE / 107

Between 1760 and 1815 large quantities of Purbeck stone were shipped to Ramsgate (above) and Margate (below) for the building of their harbours.

designed the lighthouse for the West Pier Head, one of the first with a flashing light. Wyatt died and was replaced by John Rennie in 1807; he began to use Dundee stone for steps. By 1819 the total works had cost £1,700,000. Rennie was succeeded by his son, Sir John, knighted for his work on London Bridge, who completed Ramsgate's 'great entrance' with 30,000 cubic feet of Cornish granite. So we can see that the last stages of the work were completed using other materials. Granite is, of course, superior for this sort of engineering, but when we look at the harbour now, much of the Cliff stone element (mostly Spangle and Blue Bit) at least low in the wall where regularly swept by the sea, is as good as when it was built. In the upper work, paradoxically, for it would seem to be a more benign situation, some has been frost damaged. The relative absence of Cliff Freestone is significant in that engineering of this sort offered a way of using the coarse textured, shelly beds whilst reserving the finer grained material for other work.

After Okeden's departure, Thomas Preston had made a report to the trustees:

> 'The property and estate of the island belongs to a clergyman Mr. Serrel and others, but all the men who have served their time in the island become free, and have the right to work the quarries. Those workmen are dependent from time to time for supplies on others which are called Merchants and must also be Freemen. The names of the merchants are Timothy Chenchin, Howard Serrel, William Chenchin, Henry Vye, John Pushman, Francis Warren, John Melmer, William Melmer, John Cole, John Collins, John Harding, John Marsh and Matthew Benvil, and these are the persons most proper to treat or make contract with'.

Preston singles out 'Mr. Serrel' as the major Purbeck landlord, which he was not. Does it suggest Serrell's quarry at Dancing Ledge, as the main source? It may have been, but others, certainly Winspit, were also supplying the project. East Winspit Blue Bit is distinctive. It is also recognisable mixed with other Cliff stone in Margate Pier that more or less followed Ramsgate in 1810-1815. Calcraft and Bankes Estate Records include accounts of the supply of stone for Ramsgate from their cliff quarries but other Purbeck suppliers' names crop up in the copious records preserved at Kew. The location of their quarries is less sure. Francis Warren's was almost certainly Durlston Bay but where was Sarah Vye's? Was it Blackers Hole? The Kew records reveal the competitive struggle waged between these various merchants.

Other important products of these quarries at that time were

108 / Purbeck Stone

Rempstone, Dorset. One of a set of staddle stones under a granary to keep out rats and mice.

stones that combine beauty with utility: gate posts, farm rollers, staddle stones, troughs and sinks. When these first began to be made is obscure, but in the case of troughs, probably in the Middle Ages. Though shallow examples made of other Purbeck stone survive, most of the deep examples are of Cliff stone. This hollow work was sold according to capacity, which was measured in pecks. This measurement was cut on the back. Such marks therefore are not the personal mark of the stonecutter, but simply a measurement. As with the marks found on paving, they followed a Roman system including ½. For speed of cutting, cursive shapes were avoided, the width of the straight strokes being the width of the chisel used. The Tithe Barn, Swanage, has a salting trough, pitted on the inside from the brine, which contains 4.3 cubic feet, which calculate roughly as 15 pecks. The mark on the back is x IIII These marks can be confusing, as they can be read right to left, or left to right, or, indeed, any way up or down. Sadly many of these old troughs and sinks have been filled with earth for flower planting. If this is not sufficiently free draining, saturation puts them at risk from frost. An early reference to the production of troughs comes in the inventory of John Cook, 'marbeller' of Sandwich, 1699, which includes 'two trows worth 13s. 0d.' This represents more than a week's wages for two stones! They must have been big.

The building of granaries on rat and mouse proof staddles was established by the end of the 16th century or perhaps earlier. By the 18th century the cliff quarries were producing large numbers, beautifully made, neat beyond practical requirement it seems to me. Two agricultural reports are informative. In 1813 Charles Vancouver wrote, in his report to the Board of Agriculture for Hampshire: 'A very excellent practice seems to be fast gaining ground in many parts of the County, of building wheat barns, as well as corn stacks in general, upon stone stands or staddles, the stones, or legs and caps (as they are usually called) are supplied from the quarries of Purbeck and Portland, and cost at the sea ports or wharves at the head of the Marine Navigation, about 7s. per pair.' Claridge, in 1793, says, 'The feet and caps for rick staddles are worth about 3/6d or a set of 9 delivered at Sandwich of the best sort, at 36s. per set; but there is an inferior sort not tooled which is worth only a guinea a set.'[11.] The Rev Austin's list of quarry products (1852) prices them differently, however retaining the price distinction between square and round 'legs': round 4/- per pair, square 3/- per pair (pair is cap plus support).

I have seen examples of 18th or 19th century granaries on Cliff stone staddles as far east as Kent. Woodbridge, Suffolk, has some outside the churchyard (perhaps Suffolk was far as they originally got on vessels going east-about). Staddles have become collectable and I guess are now moving around more.

Other Cliff stone work of this period appears in Chertsey Bridge (1785). The main structure, recently extensively restored, is of Purbeck stone, but the double faced ashlar blocks of the

Chertsey Bridge, Surrey (1785). Designed by James Payne, the lower courses Inland Purbeck beds, uppermost solid parapet is Cliff stone.

Corfe Castle village. 'Jutty' at Cleall's Stores. One of the columns was damaged in the 1960s, Jack Norman working its replacement by hand.

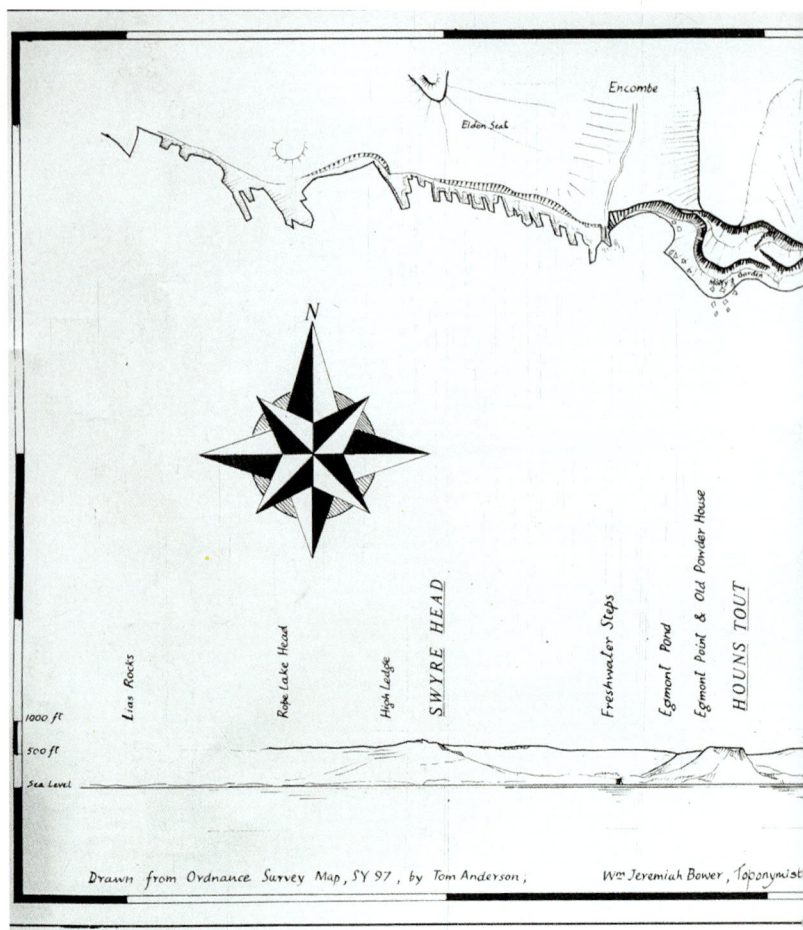

A map showing the cliff quarries. The information was provided by Billy Winspit, drawn in 1962 by Tom Anderson, and sold in aid of the RNLI. Author's revisions in pencil.

parapet are Cliff stone, restored and altered with Portland. The old bridge over the Frome at Wareham also had Cliff stone 18th century copings, the bridge itself being much older but widened in 1775. When it was demolished, Mr. Sturdy acquired the stones and incorporated them into Trigon House. Other 18th century London bridges certainly had a Purbeck element which may have been part or entirely Cliff stone. The first, Westminster, built between 1740 and 1745, experienced the problem of the central piers settling into the river bed before completion. This called for the 'dismantling of the Purbeck stone counter arches' whilst the engineer later reported the 'taking down of the damaged Portland stone arches'. Perhaps they were one and the same. The whole structure was replaced after about a hundred years.[12]

In the 18th century 'jutties', supported on columns and projecting over the pavement, were added to some houses in Corfe and Swanage. All the Swanage examples have gone, but some survive in Corfe. The Greyhound pair, one of which is bricked in, are supported on Cliff columns and bear the inscription 'I C 1733'. This might suggest John Calcraft, with his Greyhound crest, but the date is too early. One of the Cleall's Stores' columns suffered damage in the 1960s: Jack Norman turned down my offer of the use of the lathe and worked the Pond Freestone replacement by hand. They were lions in those days! Also in Corfe, the Town Hall was altered in the 18th century, Cliff stone being incorporated in the new windows.

18th century ecclesiastical work includes what is almost certainly Cliff Freestone in major alterations on the two churches of Winterborne Stickland (1716), and Charlton Marshall (1713). The similarities between the treatment of the round-headed windows and the baluster fonts would suggest the same designer. Stickland's has a pronounced list, and looks like St. Aldhelm's Head Pond Freestone. I am more doubtful about Charlton Marshall and its remarkable internal columns, forming the northern arcade. Each is over seven feet high, bearing moulded capitals and round arches. The stone is very bland, but exhibits lists, and I suspect is also of St. Aldhelm's Head provenance. Since writing this Mark Churchill has pointed out that the churchwarden's accounts do indeed record the purchase of Purbeck stone pillars. One entry is for their transport from Wareham. Each weighs 1½ tons or so and they are 'clean all around'. This is a demanding category of masonry. I suspect they were wrought to a final finish on site.

The wreck of a stone vessel lying on the Hook sands off Poole Harbour, known to divers as the 'antler wreck' due to the presence of many deer antlers on board, has Purbeck paving stacked on edge on top of solid Cliff stone steps lying in the bilge. This may well be the vessel lost, according to Hutchins,

110 / PURBECK STONE

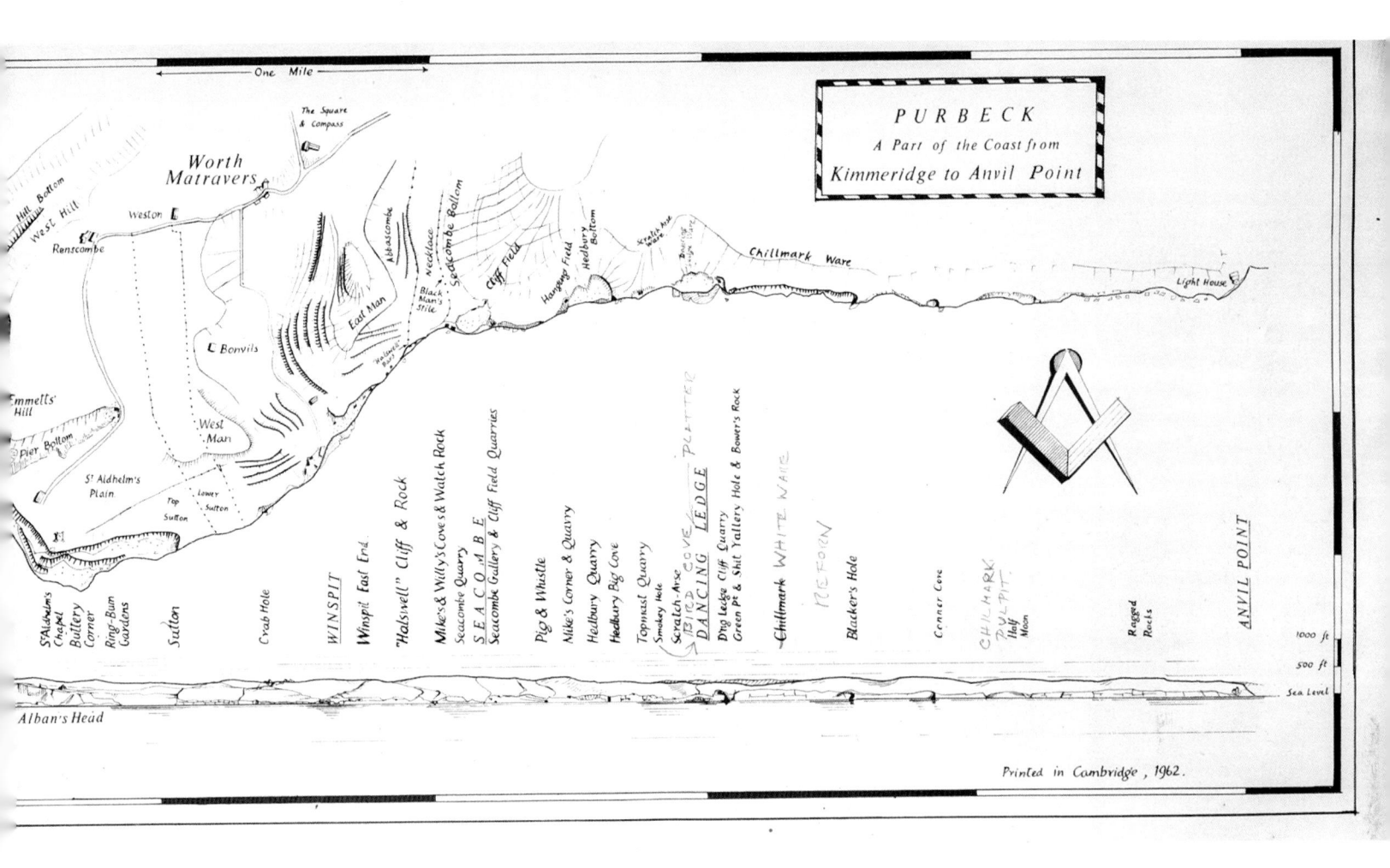

*PURBECK
A Part of the Coast from
Kimmeridge to Anvil Point*

Printed in Cambridge, 1962.

in about 1790.

Estate papers for Worth Matravers, Eastington and Langton Wallis shed more light on developments in the 18th and 19th century and are referred to in the following individual quarry accounts. In a nutshell, Purbeck Cliff stone beds are far too fractured, so scarcely compare with what can be obtained from Portland. Portland's dominance can be seen in George Burt's use of it for his globe and the most demanding elements of his castle, such as the cornice, and similarly, right in the heart of Purbeck, Langton Matravers church's internal pillars, etc., not to mention the plethora of its 19th century headstones.

THE CLIFF QUARRIES

An Ordnance survey map of 1902 that was formally in the Depot Office at Swanage shows annotations in pencil relating to the cliff quarries between Dancing Ledge and Winspit. The writing is probably that of one of the Burts, and was done before 1927 when 'Squire Marsden' [sic] died. The Western part of Dancing Ledge quarry is identified as 'St Thomas Ware'. This clearly refers to the ware that extends between western Dancing Ledge and eastern Hedbury, owned at that time by brothers Jack and Thomas Stevens, tenants of Eastington farm and rival stone merchants. Is it conceivable that the name now applied to the quarry between these two major quarries, 'Scratch ass' is a corruption of 'St Thomas, as 'Necklace', west of Seacombe is of 'St Nicholas'? Captain Serrell Rogers had inherited the Durnford Estate from Mrs Serrell in 1889, and leased part of it to Thomas Pellatt in 1893, the date of the founding of Durnford School; Rogers is therefore listed here as the landowner, although Pellatt and his school were using the ledge by the date of the map.

The 'Depot map' is clearly Burt assessing the economic potential and the current ownership of the various quarries along this part of the coast in the new era of the railway. At the time he was looking for sources of Cliff rather than Inland stone. He records the strange situation at East Hedbury, where there was no way out by land other than over the neighbouring landlord's farm tracks: permission might be withheld. If a quarry was marked 'Water only', this meant that loads had to be taken away by sea, with all the problems of inclement weather, and involving the use of cranes and associated technology.

The list that follows describe the quarries in order from east to west. The names are as drawn from the Billy Winspit map (*illustrated above*), but with revisions.

CLIFF STONE / 111

TILLY WHIM / HAWCOMBE

These two quarries adjoin, but at the time of operation were owned by different proprietors, which is reflected in their configuration. The wall that ascends the ware close by the measured mile posts east of the lighthouse is the boundary between them, with Hawcombe quarry to the west, within the manor of Swanage, Tilly Whim to the east, within the manor of Eightholds. Hawcombe is, of course, the valley, and a name that has largely gone out of use. George Burt had the name 'Tilly Whim' cut at the Hawcombe end of the combined quarry. The valley is now usually called the Gully, and 'Light House' now serves to identify the general area. My father said Jessie Lander was one of the last to use the old name whilst describing his times fishing out of Chapman's Pool. He said they worked as far east as Hawcombe and a patch of ground called Fredreco. That the two quarries could have been operated separately is shown by each having a crane position. There would have been no way in and out of Tilly Whim proper even for the men themselves other than through Hawcombe, but that would not have been an issue as it was common land.

Brannon writes: 'The name Tilly Whim is said to have been given to the place in derision, on account of the increasing hardness of the stone here. For this reason, the speculator, a man of the name of Tilly, not being considered wise either by workmen or merchants, gained for his quarry the soubriquet of Tilly's Whim'.[13] It is unlikely that the stone became increasingly hard but, as with all cliff quarries, it would certainly have got more tightly jointed and difficult to get out the deeper into the cliff they drove. Tillys certainly were a Purbeck family; a John of Corfe made a will in 1633, a William was living at Tyneham in 1641, and a John in Langton. Before that, but with no apparent Purbeck connection other than stone craft, John Tyllie and quarrymen of Kent in 1442 undertook the supply of stone for Eton College. Forty years later another John was working as a mason in Suffolk.[14] Gilbert Tully was one of several men supplying stone to Corfe Castle in the 13th century. Tilly Whim was not his source but he could have been one of the same family. No Tillys appear in either the Articles of Agreement 1651 or the Joint Stock Company list 1698. If they had been quarrymen in Purbeck it seems to have been before 1651. In the recent past a Swanage quarryman, Thomas Phippard, was always known as Tommy Tilly. There is a masonry firm of Tilly in Brighton, which removed from London three generations ago. Perhaps Purbeck was the provenance of these London Tillys. It is curious that at the northern extremity of the manor of Eightholds in which the quarry lies, is Tilly Mead, situated between the stream and the High Street. It is now cut by King's Road East. Robinson suggests that 'Whim', rather than meaning a folly, derives from a type of crane. My father related that all that generation who worked the cliff last, simply called the cranes gibbets. It is possible that the term Whim was applied to the winding part of these antique machines. However, not according to W. M. Hardy, author of *Old Swanage of Purbeck Past and Present*, for he says: 'they lowered the stone over the cliff into boats with a machine called a jenny, a gibbet, and a strong rope around the jenny over the gibbet'.[15]

The earliest use of the name Tilly Whim seems to be in the inventory of Alexander Melmouth, Marbler of Swanage, who died in 1703. He was a member of the Joint Stock Company and had more than one quarry, for it includes:

Stones and labour at quarr £7/10/00
and Stones and labour at Tilly Whim £20
Stones by waters side £16
Quarr tools £7/15/ [16]

'Stones by waters side' would have been on the bankers, which suggests he was a merchant, or was taking Tilly Whim stone around to Swanage for secondary shipment. This was done to a degree in the working of other cliff quarries later. He retained the old title of Marbler and the compilers used the interesting term 'labour', which is discussed elsewhere.

In the early 19th century a major dispute erupted, involving all the quarries on this manor. The upshot was that William Taunton of the Middle Temple leased the quarry to four men. He imposed detailed conditions (see below), which perhaps can be seen as signalling a new age in Purbeck. But it was almost academic, for it was not worked for much longer; the configuration that remains is a product of the 18th century and earlier, plus a small amount of early 19th century work.

'Lease of Tilly Whim 1805 between William Leonard Thomas Pyle Taunton of the Middle Temple, Esquire and Henry Gillingham the elder of Swanage, Stone Merchant, Samuel Marsh, Peter Marsh, Thomas Randle (all stone merchants of Swanage) demised to Gillingham and Co. all these 2 several ancient stone quarries or pieces of land immemorially used as stone quarries called TILLEY WHIM one was formerly occupied by Edward Hancock and afterwards by William Cole but now of late of the said Peter Marsh, and the other which was formerly in the occupation of Thomas Hancock and afterwards of the said Henry Gillingham, bounded on the west by a quarry and land of H. Dampier Esquire, term of 16 years payments to be made 4 times during the year:6/d per ton block, 3/d per ton pitchers, 1/d backing. Paving 2/s per 100 sq. ft. . . . other items . . . discharge rates and taxes . . . keep an account book to include nature, quality, persons to whom supplied . . . thrown over the cliff all useless and unsaleable stone, earth etc. . . . peacefully and quietly quit and yield up the said demised premises (at expiration of term) . . . . leave standing a sufficient number of pillars . . . pay at least £8. 0 every 2 years. . . . as soon as the Exeter Dean and Chapter shall grant a new lease of the Manor of Swanage to W.L.T.P. Taunton
Signed and sealed by Taunton, Henry Gillingham, Peter Marsh and Thomas Randall.'[17]

We learn from this lease that some time earlier the quarry had been worked in two parts, one by Edward Hancock and William Cole, the other by Thomas Hancock. Edward and William both signed the Joint Stock Company agreement of 1698, so their working must have ceased by 1750 at the latest, by which time age would have overtaken them. William's father, another Edward, had willed a quarry to him in 1714, but this would seem not to be Tilly Whim:

'1714 the WILL of Edward Cole of Langton Marbler. I give unto my wife Sarah which will be if please god the sum of one pound and also I give to my son William Coles children one shilling a piece. Allso I do make my son William sole executor of this my last will and testament and also the quarr after which he hath now broke up after my decease paying nothing for the ground of it to her except the Lord. If I should happen to die before her and

to have the privilege to carry the stone out of the ground as he has occasion .....
(Signed Edward Cole)
Witnessed: John Cull, John Peverill, the mark of Edward Hancock.'

Hawcombe and Tilly Whim quarries from the sea. Note underground workings at left, and collapsed founder below pylons. The pylons up the slope, together with another pair to the west, define a nautical mile.

This is almost certainly a different inland quarry which would fit the known later 19th century pattern of men working inland and cliff quarries alternately as demand or weather allowed. In 1718 Edward Hancock was paying rent 'for late widow Hancocks Tenannt in Langton Wallis' and, it seems, digging stone there, but the rent returns are not entirely clear. However about ten years later he and John Cull (Cull / Cole being one and the same family) were definitely working a quarry together on Eastington or Langton Wallis.[18.]

C. E. Robinson gives an account of the last days of the quarry, which would suggest that these men had given up by 1812. He quotes a letter from the lord of the manor which includes the following:

'There is so much room in this quarry for any assignable number of men to work, and so great a facility, in summer, of shipping the goods, letting them down at once by a crane into the vessel, that men of industry and enterprise ought to command almost the whole market for the species of articles which this quarry produces, and to supply it from this spot only [...] The sort of goods which this quarry yields are of what is called the Portland Purbeck, a sort of freestone, much like the Portland, only harder, and much used for building in bridges, harbours, fortification walls, troughs, columns, rollers, staddle stones, etc.'[19.]

Robinson continues:

'The real reason for the final abandonment of Tilly Whim was not, as will be seen, the "increasing hardness of the stonen," which, on the contrary, was a quality for which it was valued, but the increasing slackness of the demand. In the two years ending Ladyday 1812 there was only occasion to ship away 110 tons of pitchers, and after that date the quarry ceased to be worked altogether [...] At the close of the great European war, which occurred about this time, the sudden cessation of all public expenditure on fortifications, and the absolute necessity for general retrenchment, threw out of work the great majority of the Swanage quarriers, and caused the desertion of a large number of quarries. So many persons came on the parish that in 1813 the poor-rates amounted to no less than thirteen shillings and fourpence in the pound, as evidenced by the farm accounts of Eightholds for that year! And it is still told that men would leave their work at noontide when the rest for lunch was taken, and walk away separately for a few minutes, each out of pride endeavouring to conceal the unpalatable fact that he had not even a crust of bread to eat. When, years afterwards, the demand again grew brisk, it was found that so many of the quarrymen had been forced to seek work elsewhere in that trying time, that there were not enough to re-occupy all the old quarries, and so the workings at a distance from the town, near the sea, have never been resumed.'

The boom days were over. Between 1825 and 1836s William Morton Pitt owned the manor house and estate of Swanage. In that time he added masonry to the ancient quay, Leyland's pier, which included the steps on the west side and the parapet wall. This parapet is Cliff stone surely from Tilly Whim or Hawcombe. It was perhaps this work of his philanthropic predecessor that led Mr. Daniel Alexander, the next owner, to believe he had ownership of the foreshore, including the quay. His attempt to control it led to a riot. In the ensuing controversy affidavits were sworn by local men, including William Stickland, who said he had built much of the present quay for Mr. Pitt on top of the older structure that Swanage men had set up years before in a joint effort, no fees or tolls ever having been paid.

CLIFF STONE / 113

'Tilly Whim' by Thomas Webster, published in H C Englefield's *The Isle of Wight* (1816).

Tilly Whim. Thomas Webster's sketch of east end of the quarry showing gibbet with a two-wheeled jenny. In Hutchins' *History of Dorset*, extra illustrated edition.

According to W. M. Hardy, John Mowlem, together with his father and brothers, were the last gang to work at Tilly Whim.

There is a sequel. At the time when Trinity House were deliberating on the best location for a lighthouse, finally built in 1881 at Anvil Point, John Haysom was manager of Thomas Randell Junior's business. With the prospect of compensation in mind, Randell, a lawyer, directed him to send men to work at Tilly Whim. They did not do much, and nothing came of it. When George Burt acquired it he sank the access shaft, one reason being that he did not own the western part which controlled access. During the entire time of operation the only way in was a footpath from Hawcombe, so no stone got taken away inland from either quarry.

In the early 19th century the manor to the west of Eight Holes was held by Mr. Dampier.[20] The ware, including Hawcombe quarry, was part of the common land. No written records seem to survive of this quarry, but Thomas Webster drew it in 1814, just about the time it seems Tilly Whim was abandoned. His view shows a man operating a capstan pulling up a long timber from the loading rock. Whether this tells us that the quarry was operational or not is uncertain, as it is just possible that Hawcombe was being used as a loading place for stone dug from quarries up the ware at that time. W. M. Hardy says: 'Thousands of tons of stones were shipped at Tilly Whim, and a quantity was brought down the valley and shipped off at this place'. The way down to the water at the bottom of Hawcombe now consists of a series of steps which are man-made, for at the Puffin bed level there are two fifteen inch deep drill holes that tell of the use of gunpowder. Continuing downwards, more 'steps' exhibit vertical wedge pit marks. The lesser degree of weathering at the northern part of the eastern cliff wall suggests a removal of rock. This is about 30 feet north to south at base loading rock level. Whenever this was done, it seems it was after the introduction of gunpowder. The blasting suggests removal for the sake of it; the wedge pits, use of the stone which, unlike these beds further west, is relatively flint free. What must be certain is that this modification was not done for access of the men. It was either for the operation of the cliff quarry, or more likely for the traffic coming down the combe.

Webster's view in Englefield shows the configuration of the quarry much as it remains now.[21] However, aspects of his figures and machinery are worrying. The figures stand where the ledge is too narrow and the capstan is being operated in the 'wrong' direction, the strain lying in the same alignment as the collar board, rather than square to it, which does not make sense. Presumably he made sketches at the quarry which he worked on in more detail in his studio before handing over to his engraver, who completed the work and got the capstan wrong. Alternative sketches of the same view, plus another of the eastern part of the quarry, unsigned but almost certainly also by Webster, have been incorporated within a unique volume of Hutchins' second edition.[22] The eastern view shows a jenny mounted where a pair of holes remain, but where the kingpost hole has since fallen away. It is unlike the known Hedbury machines in being possessed of two rather than one wheel. It stands alone in being the only representation of such a machine in Purbeck. The extra wheel would have allowed for more muscle power to be applied than with the single type. Below this position the water runs in in a narrow cleft that yet retains a tying on arch on one side.

Most of the stone coming down the valley could have been man-handled, but the loading rock bears four puzzling holes for timbers cut in vertical surfaces, plus a gibbet position. It was less than ideal in that a low, five foot wide shelf of rock would have kept the boats away. The jib must have had a reach of more than that to cope, or, which seems highly unlikely, they could have only loaded at high water springs which would have meant the men on the winding gear getting wet, if not swept away. This Hawcombe gibbet is an enigma. The king post hole is typical at about 18 inches by 18 inches by 18 inches deep, the pair of jenny holes at about 12 inches by 15 inches lie set back about 11 feet, well out of square with the ledge to provide room for stones being dropped from above behind it, or for stone coming down the valley. Behind them a leaded pin close to the cliff obviously secured the usual brace that prevented the whole thing when under load tipping into the water. If this machine was to do with traffic coming down the combe as well as the cliff quarry, it shows that heavy stones such as ledgers could have been handled there, but beyond the evidence of the manmade steps there seems not to be any other modifications of the descent from the valley floor. Perhaps it tells us of the stones being manhandled step by step all the way!

What is certain is that the low loading rock and quarry edge crane positions relate to each other. Presumably the pair of holes, set about a foot apart and cut into the vertical wall, provided for horizontal timbers that, at about 20 feet long, would have made it easier to manhandle stones across the uneven ledge to the seaward crane – shades of W. M. Hardy's 'stage' used in Durlston Bay. They could very well be the long spars that appear in Webster's view. Even on the highest tide there would hardly have been sufficient water for the boat to get close alongside above the low level ledge. It would seem that at all states of tide the boat would have needed fending off. The hole cut in the vertical face just by the king post with its companion about ten feet to the north must be to do with this. What is not evident is how they secured whatever this timber arrangement was, but tying on holes are also lacking and there must have been some. Survival of such would seem to be almost a matter of chance. There could hardly be a more exposed place than the southwest point of Dancing Ledge, where one yet remains, battered by innumerable waves.

Scars now cover the floor where Webster shows a capstan, but to the southwest, where he shows a post secured by block and tackle, there remains a puzzling assembly of socket holes. They lie adjacent to a seven foot wide ramp and cutting, sunk into the floor to a depth of about two feet, that widens out at the cliff edge immediately above the gibbet position on the loading rock below. What remains at quarry level includes an iron pin set about central to the sunk area, a seating for a horizontal timber, an anchoring arch and sockets that held sloped rather than vertical timber. What seems to be lacking is a king post hole sunk out on the edge. This may have since fallen away, but the appearance of the cliff does not suggest post operational falls. It is all rather odd, especially the cutting into the floor, which does not have an equivalent in any quarry to the west.

From an operational point of view, where the quarry floor is exposed it looks horribly uneven. This is particularly evident where the two quarries meet. Horizontally cut deep wedge pits show what a struggle they had forcing the blocks up off the floor. The openings that face west have floors of fine scars, so that is where the finer dressing was done. Further in, rough spalls remain. There are drill holes mostly high in the Underpicking Cap but, oddly, one or two also low in the Freestone. One shows a diameter of about 1½ inches, cut to about 18 inches deep, which is typical. One remaining visible in the ceiling is atypically high! By one of the western entrances there is a remarkable row of 16 wedge pits cut vertically over eight feet or more, perhaps the greatest number effecting a single cut in Purbeck! They are all about four inches deep, three inches or so wide, leaving only two or three inches between each. My father remarked regarding this sort of thing that it seemed to him that it would almost have been as easy to cut a continuous droke rather than all those individual slots, yet they did not. One is inclined to think that this cut, being near the entrance, was effected relatively early in the life of this underground, but that is not certain.

Before leaving Hawcombe, it is curious that no quarrying was attempted on the west side where the lighthouse now stands. During its abandoned years it was very much a place to muck about. It has a lot of graffiti, and crude attempts at carved busts on projecting corners, all of it post operational, it would seem. Some of it is quite neatly cut in some instances, no doubt by quarry boys. Early examples are 'MANWELL 1862', 'A VYE 1876'. Other Swanage worthies include the photographer William Powell. A nice gaff rigged schooner could be from the working years. 'J. PIPER GREENWICH 1881' was a boat builder involved in the timber work for the second pier. His yard on the Thames lay alongside Mowlem's.

CHILMARK QUARRY

There is some confusion over this name. Sam Bower, Nelson Burt and others said Chilmark quarry was 'up the Ware between Dancing Ledge and Hedbury'. Billy Winspit put it at the place most people call White Ware. Such inconsistency points up the uncertainty that surrounds the location of some of the more obscure quarries. Alan Lander said that his father, Sidney, who fished off this coast all his life and knew it as well as anyone, called this part Top Mast, because that bit of the *Alexandrova*, wrecked in a hurricane in 1882, was left lying on the grass there, all the rest of her going to smithereens and drifting away eastwards. Billy Winspit puts his 'Top Mast' as the small quarry high on the east side of the cove at the east end of Hedbury. He provided the information for the Anderson Map of 1962, which has been much reproduced. One or two names are in the wrong place, but as Dr. Anderson remarked, it would have been a miracle for it to be entirely accurate considering how much whisky was drunk by the toponymist during its preparation (*see pages 110/111*).

My father was quite insistent that Chilmark referred to the cliff quarry 'west of pulpit'. It was worked last, he said his father told him, by Henry Lander., who died in 1879 aged 79. During his life Henry had a number of quarries, including a Marble quarry at Orchard and a paviour quarry somewhere near Preston, on the Ridgeway. I suspect Henry quarried little if any Cliff stone but used it as a shipping place. What must be Henry's slide is indicated by broken crab stones still standing at the top. They are of White Bit, so not from this quarry. Nearby in the field is a small loading banker with a walled up track leading eastwards from it. The bottom end of the slide is also built up, so it was obviously made after that part of the quarry had been cut out.

The Ware inland from Chilmark is confused by natural land slips that have brought blocks of land, including useful beds, lower than where they 'belong'. A particularly prominent outcrop of Rag only 100 feet above the cliff top marks this place. These slipped masses were worked on a considerable scale, but there was no working immediately above, for the good beds are absent there. The question remains: was the capstan used for drawing stone up from this cliff quarry, or for lowering stone away from those quarries in the ware only? It would seem to be too perilously close to the edge to be used for bringing stones up, but possible alright for lowering loads down. About half way down the steep cliff slope an almost hidden stone exhibits a groove, as does the *in situ* Blue Bit at the quarry proper. Below this a heap of small debris is consistent with the cut made into the brow necessary for the haulway to the capstan. It is likely that these grooves held wooden sleepers that in turn supported lengths of railway line that formed the slide, rather than timbers or stone. Lengths of heavy duty figure of eight section rail laid flat form just such a slide in the northernmost Edmunds shaft in Burngate, Acton. It would have been quick to assemble, suited to a conventional non-flanged wheeled cart, which it would have kept safely restrained.

The last surviving gibbet king post in Purbeck remained here, at the eastern end, until about 1960. Below it, on the loading rock, which is in this case is the Puffin bed, there are socket holes for a gibbet, together with the iron bearing for the gudgeon pin, so well fixed on that centuries of being swept by the sea in heavy weather has not moved it. At the upper gibbet position three sets of grooves show where timbers spanned a perilous gap. The Spangle level has a number of drill holes, all showing gunpowder effects. A nice series of big six inch deep pits has resulted in a cut that spurred out badly. Perhaps that was the day, some time in the 18th century, when they decided to pack it in.

Henry Lander's wife was Keziah. Her headstone stands in

Chilmark quarry, looking vertically down on to the loading rock. King post hole at upper right, for the gibbet at the water's edge. The two smaller holes on the right side of the central rock held the jenny (winding gear). The boat would have lain alongside, on the right hand side of the picture.

Chilmark quarry. Broached Five Bit kerbs.

Langton Matravers churchyard. It is of Cliff stone, the back a beautiful example of fine broach work. It is tempting to think that this slab was obtained from this quarry, but probably wrong. Some worked kerbs and a broken sink remain at Chilmark. Some of these kerbs are broached and of Five Bit, which must therefore have been brought down from the Ware above. They are therefore certain evidence of this place being used to ship away stone from other quarries, surely worked by Henry. The logistics must have been finely balanced. Was it to be a short haul to this highly exposed shipping place, or a longer overland haul to the relative security of Swanage Bay? I suggest that this quarry is largely pre-19th century, but was re-activated as a shipping place before the arrival of the Swanage branch line in 1885.

BLACKERS HOLE

There may be no documentary evidence of the working of this quarry (see Hawcombe above). The access is a steep descent, and it is certain that no stone was taken away inland from this one. It has been worked for the full height, indeed even below the Under Freestone for quite a large area. Below, at the eastern end, there is a trackway with a gauge of about two and a half to three feet, ending at the water's edge. Adjacent are four jenny holes arranged in a square ten feet back from the water's edge, and a crane anchoring rather than a mooring arch, but no king post hole, showing that the rock has gone. Cut across a low step in the Puffin bed the track is similar to tracks on Dancing Ledge, but, at about fifty feet, much shorter. The quarry face is overhung; in the 1960s a Buddhist built a cell and cut a petroglyph here. Nearby is a hole to catch water under a drip. This was present before the aesthete, and probably dates from the working of the quarry. Perhaps they used the water for drinking, or maybe just for wetting their sharpening stone. W. Diffey left his name in 1928, but other marks could be contemporary with the quarr. The quarry has altered the configuration of the cliff considerably. Looking at it now one wonders how they ever got started. It would seems they had to begin by attacking a vertical cliff. Perhaps there was a stage when it was easier to get the gibbets and carts down which subsequent development has made more difficult.

But these would have been required from early on, so perhaps they brought them around by sea. A small fall in 2003 threatens to make the top part of the descent yet narrower. Otherwise I guess it remains much as when the place was last worked.

REFORM OR REFORN

This lost name appeared on a list of Cliff quarries formally in the possession of Frank Ball of Langton. The quarry was worked mostly to the Pond Freestone level only, but a small part at the east end is sunk deeper to the Bottom Freestone. A collection of enigmatic Arabic numerals, which are unusual, including + signs, occur about midway along the quarry face; also carvings of a couple of gaff cutters and possibly initials. There is a talus of large boulders beneath the entire length of this quarry, so it is hard to see how the quarrymen got a boat in. They surely blew them up where it mattered. They certainly had to lower the stones in one go from what was probably the highest crane position along the entire cliff. To the east, slippage of the lower Purbeck beds, which forced a major re-routing of the cliff top fence in 1957, has spilt into the eastern end of this quarry, covering the finished work. A subsequent small fall during the winter of 2004 has revealed some of it again.

WHITE WARE

This quarry was worked in two levels, the Pond and the Bottom Freestone, without any suggestion of attempting to push in underground; it is therefore atypical on these two counts. A natural defile in the cliff allows access at the west end, so it would have been easy to get started here and, in theory at least, stone could have been taken away inland. Below this defile pit marks tell of modifications being made down to well below the quarry level, below the Puffin bed in fact. That some have been cut, but without the blocks then being split away, suggests a sudden cessation of work.

The modifications below the Bottom Freestone level may not be quarry related. As with Reform, big boulders make it impossible to get a boat in anywhere now, but obviously there was once a gap. The vegetated floors hide what crane positions may exist. There is no apparent track out of the upper Pond Freestone level. There is one out of the lower, but at its western accessible end the bottom Freestone has been left *in situ*, whilst further east they took it. This strongly suggests that the crane position lay to the east. If that was the case and the Pond Freestone was dispatched in the same direction, why not work the place in the same way as most of the other quarries – that is take it all in one go by undermining the Underpicking Cap? It may indicate that the Pond Freestone shelf was cut first and then the lower one later. The gradation of the floor step and the track running inland suggest that stone from quarries up the ware may well have been brought by cart and shipped here. A tip of waste adjacent to and probably produced by cutting the upper entrance is, I suspect, post-operational. There are a few pit marks, a nice carving of an engraved vessel towing a dinghy or stone boat and 'R.D.M. Oxford'; the latter hardly quarry related, but perhaps one of the gentry who frequented this place about 1900.

The narrow ledge configuration bears similarities to St. Aldhelm's Head. Its easternmost limit coincides with the wall which in earlier times may have been a manorial boundary, which suggests that the extent of working in that direction was to do with separation of ownership at the time of working, rather than being reflective of the geology. This quarry does not appear on a survey of 1776 along with other quarries in work on that manor; in my opinion it is probably earlier. However, this may be incorrect: stone merchant James Chinchen's multiple possessions, listed in his will of 1827, include an interest in Putlake Farm. It seems that each landlord in this stretch of the coast had his own cliff quarry: Durnford had Dancing Ledge; Putlake this one, Leeson had Reform and Blackers Hole and Chilmark was on the Benledge estate. Each landowner was getting in on the Cliff stone act with the quarriers surmounting the topographic difficulties, White Ware being surely one of the most challenging.

DANCING LEDGE

The main part lies in the manor of Durnford, Langton Matravers, but to the west it extends into Langton Wallis, which Treswell's map shows was held Richard Edburey as part of his tenement in 1585; Sir Ralph Bankes sold it off in 1665. By 1775, which was a time of quarry activity, this western end of the quarry was part of the freehold of Mr. Willis Hart, and it remained in separate ownership, which may be relevant to its development. The fact that the eastern part has been pushed deeper into the hill than the west could be to do with matters of ownership or it could be to do with the periglacial head which smothers the area west of the way down.

The broad ledge below the quarry is natural. It is at the level of the Puffin bed, which for much of the cliff lies about half way up, but here slopes to below water level. This thin double layer in the Cherty series is relatively soft and weathers out, allowing the beds above to drop. It may be only a few inches, but this dislocation allows for loosening and advance by the sea. The tendency for a ledge to form at other places where the Puffin bed also descends to the water line is evident, but nowhere else matches its wide expanse here. The stubborn resistance of the ledge below, rather than the beds above, is partly because the blocks below the Puffin bed level are so large. For example, the block forming the seaward side of the swimming pool is roughly 22 feet by 120 feet by 6 feet thick, which makes it more than 1,000 tons; it is a tight fit with its neighbours, some of which are yet larger. Only Gad Cliff is productive of such massive lumps, but they scarcely compare in size on plan. It is just that there the lower cherty series are more strongly cemented vertically than in eastern Purbeck, so the great boulders that fall to the shore there are thicker. To the east of the pool the surface is uniquely sculpted by the scouring action of the small stones falling from above.

The access down into the quarry is sloping and could well

ABOVE Dancing Ledge. The first of four remarkable 1910 photographs taken using glass negatives show stone being lowered from a cliff quarry. A crane is being used at the final stage of the haul. Note use of nips and rollers.

RIGHT Stacking block preparatory to shipping. Note rollers.

BELOW Tug waiting off while 'lighter' is being loaded. The extra rope attached to the jib was for pulling it back if and when the load hook was out of reach. For some reason, the crane platform is raised above the quarry floor.

once have been a slide, which would have allowed for stone to be drawn up to the top and so away inland. Such a slide remains at West Hedbury, where the capstan position is still indicated by a roll stone. Dancing Ledge could have been similar, but the area where such a roller would have been set has eroded away enormously in the last 50 years.

Around 1910 Thomas Webber was in possession, but he seems to have done little work there before the involvement of Henry Weeks Burt of Burt and Burt, the principal Swanage merchants at that time. Burt and Burt wanted stone of a Portland type for work on the terrace at Luton Hoo House, Bedfordshire. Henry came to some arrangement with Webber, and had a Scotch derrick type of crane, the first of its kind in Purbeck, taken down the Ware to Dancing Ledge. It was set up on the quarry edge close to where two squared up blocks remain, and where deep water at the foot allowed for easy loading straight into a boat, by this time a tug-towed barge. Other than the crane they had little equipment. Sam Short Bower, who was there as a youth, helped his father Thomas Short, Captain Whistler Bower and others in digging the blocks underground and rolling them out to the crane on wooden rollers. The roughly-squared blocks were lowered into the barge, towed to Poole, craned up onto the quay, put into trucks and taken by rail around to Burt and Burt's depot in Swanage; there was no crane on Swanage pier at this time. There the blocks was worked before final dispatch to Luton Hoo. It seems they did not supply much stone for the project, in that when I looked at it, the entire terrace with balustrade appeared to me to be Portland. This work in Swanage resulted in offcuts which were being used when my father started work just after the First World War broke out. In 1955 Lady Savage had the date of the rebuilding of Durnford cut by my father in an original stone. He found the piece to be just like bits he had been familiar with, left over from the Luton Hoo job.

Glass photographic negatives, recently discovered far from Purbeck but recognised for what they are by the late Michael Norman, show the operation of about 1910 in progress. They confirm Sam Bower's comment about the lack of a cart. Perhaps because of the confines of the narrow shelf, and the need to get the area covered by the two supporting timbers level, they brought the crane base up several feet with hardcore.

118 / PURBECK STONE

With a purchase by means of nips it is shown drawing a block to within its scope, assisted by wooden rollers of about the girth of telephone poles. Sam Short's memory had served him right! On the face of it, to manoeuvre blocks all the way out from underground to the crane position by employing bars and rollers alone seems bizarre. Yet without cranage at the face it would have been difficult to get big blocks on to a cart there. The glass plates prove that heavy blocks were moved some distance without a cart. I suspect similar things were done at other quarries. In particular Ambrose Bower's handling of his massive sink at Seacombe comes to mind. I guess he managed to get it free off its bed with wedges, levered it up enough with bars to get rollers underneath it and then barred it along out into the light, as Captain Whistler did with the Luton Hoo blocks.

Luton Hoo was not quite the last chapter, in that when the Dorset Quarry Co. acquired the contract in the 1920s for the Training Bank beyond the mouth of Poole Harbour, they mostly used rock from Seacombe. However, a small quantity came from Dancing Ledge. Jim Ivamy Bower was one who assisted. They were mostly working at other quarries, so when Walter Masters in his tug, the *Gamecock*, was making across Swanage Bay towards Dancing Ledge, he would toot his whistle. It gave the men sufficient time to get to the ledge by the time he arrived, where they rolled the lumps over the cliff down into the barge, for by this time Henry Burt had removed the crane to his Swanage depot. This removal caused a row. In the absence of her husband, Mrs Webber tried to prevent its progress as the team of horses passed over the top of Steppes Hill on the way to Swanage. Subsequently this crane was taken to St. Aldhelm's quarry, where we continued to call it the Dancing Ledge crane. I am embarrassed to admit scrapping it. It was a good crane to use, the mechanism more user friendly than the bigger version that remains set up.

The quarry as we see it now is surely a product of some 19th century work, a lot of 18th century, plus possibly some earlier. 20th century episodes were of course relatively insignificant, barely having any effect on the general configuration; the last probably only consisted of taking away stone from Grocer Burt's crane base, which had been left in exactly the best position and which has entirely gone.

As I said earlier, Serrell's Estate, which included Dancing Ledge, could have been a major source of stone for the 18th century work at Ramsgate.[23.] In 1762 James Thickes was killed at Dancing Ledge quarry almost certainly whilst on Ramsgate work. He had married Rachel, daughter of Thomas Bower of Langton, in 1731. He, or his father, also James, cut his name in St. Aldhelm's chapel in 1729. A Serrell Estate rent book covering the years from 1832 to 1858 include dues paid for that period for Dancing Ledge quarry by Edward Brown of Herston.

Stone in mid-air. It is being lowered into the 'lighter'. This is the only 20th century image of stone being lowered over the cliff.

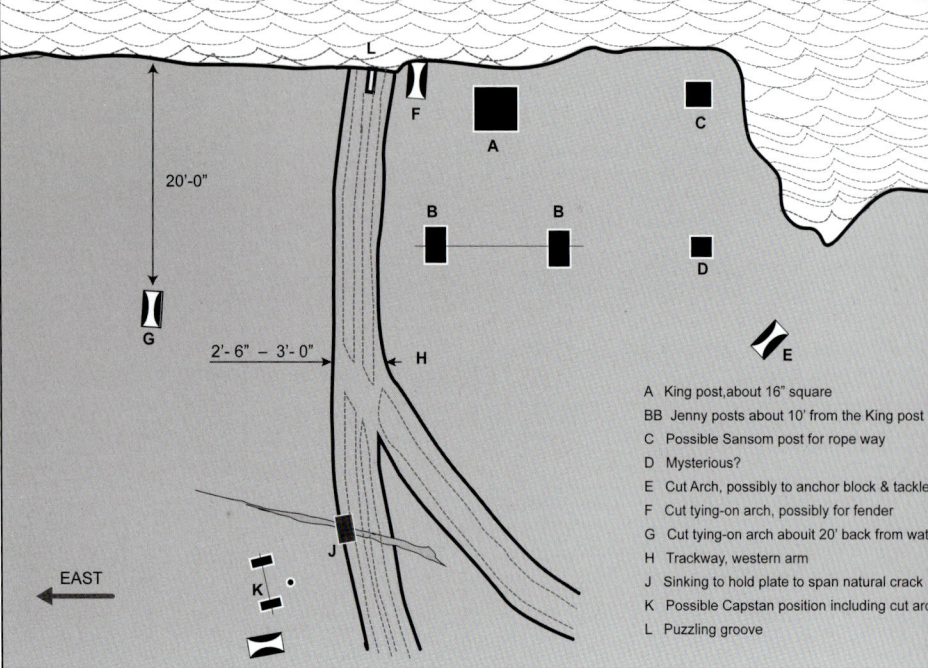

Dancing Ledge trackway from above.   Dancing Ledge. Southwest extremity of the natural ledge at water level.

Key to diagram:
A King post, about 16" square
BB Jenny posts about 10' from the King post
C Possible Sansom post for rope way
D Mysterious?
E Cut Arch, possibly to anchor block & tackle
F Cut tying-on arch, possibly for fender
G Cut tying-on arch abouit 20' back from wate
H Trackway, western arm
J Sinking to hold plate to span natural crack
K Possible Capstan position including cut arc
L Puzzling groove

Geologist G. F. Harris, came to Purbeck in 1893 and described its quarries. He visited Dancing Ledge when things were at a low ebb. He descended to James Webber's quarry and reported that: 'a boy prowling about told me that it was some months since any stone was raised, but that 2 or 3 men used to be employed [...] Old fashioned wooden cranes – old and rusty here.'[24]

Dancing Ledge exhibits the longest trackway up cliff. It extends from the loading position on the point of the ledge, where there are gibbet holes, northwards across the ledge, where it divides before both tracks end some way short of the present quarry edge. This is indication that much has fallen away along this central part of the quarry edge, as it continues to do. This gap is about 18 feet at the western branch but is as much as 40 feet, including the depth of the cave, at the east. The gibbet that dropped stone down to those trackways had limited reach, only about six feet, so it is clear that a lot of quarry floor has gone since the tracks were last used. The rate of attrition of this part of the quarry edge is quite rapid, quite a lot falling in my lifetime. Erosion at the seaward edge is insignificant, so the ledge, which is natural, in spite of what several authors claim, continues to widen. Its pillowy surface would have been difficult to drag a cart over without modification so they must have punched off the worst bumps.

The eastern branch is the deepest and straightest, consistent with it being developed first and carrying the greater traffic. It has the larger catchment area, for there was no other crane position further east, whilst to the west there were several. The gauge of about 2½ feet tells of the use of the horn or similar cart, but the eastern branch also has a third intermediate groove consistent with the width of a typical inland quarr cart. Where it crosses joints, they cut sinkings to accommodate iron or possibly board bridge plates, clear evidence of the use of wheeled carts rather than sledges. As with the other trackways at Blackers Hole and Winspit the gentle slope towards the water would have aided getting the loaded carts in that direction.

At its extreme west end the ledge drops to a lower level, Fisherman's Rock, where there are three holes marking another gibbet position, plus tying on holes. What was the point of this low position, when close by a boat could go in right under a position where a crane could be left set up in all weathers? It must tell us that it was easier, surely safer, to operate with the crane near to the level of the boats rather than where it was mounted much higher. This must have outweighed the disadvantage of additional handling and the need to set up and then take away the lower crane each time. As with the loading position at the end of the trackway, a rough sea would have wrecked any crane left in place.

Further across the gap to the west, Flat Rock also has more timber holes at its south-eastern extremity. The seaward side of the king post hole has gone, but its associated pair of jenny holes remain obvious, also a tying on arch to the north. Set back away from the water a pair of mysterious holes indicate some sort of timber arrangement, surely to do with loading, but their function is not obvious. As with the other low level crane position across the cove, this one must tell of the advantage of setting up a crane low down, even when the option of doing so higher and therefore clear of the reach of the sea, existed close by. Dancing Ledge demonstrates better than anywhere else that, at least in certain conditions and where they had a choice, it made sense to set up a second crane close by the water, even though it meant extra handling stages and an additional machine. There are more gibbet holes up on the quarry floor at this west end, and a photograph of 1902 shows a gibbet still in position over the water gap. Its king post socket has a stone fitted in flush.

At the extreme west end a small patch of Underpicking Cap has been taken, but not the Bottom Freestone beneath it, which is unusual. Above, a higher shelf has been cut at the Pond Freestone level, which may well pre-date the lower work. Here an attempt to cut a block vertically with five pits has gone badly, the break spurring out. Above, 'C.E.B. 18??' may be quarry-related. Underground, now blocked off, are superb examples of the art of cutting pits, eloquent testimony to the tightness of the block and the skill of the quarrymen. These pits could have been cut by Captain Whistler Bower during the Luton Hoo episode. He was an accomplished cliff quarry man, working for years at Seacombe for Ambrose Bower. At the time of building the Lodge at Studland for the Duke of Hamilton, now the Knoll House Hotel, the sandstone for the colonnade was being dug at Woodhouse Hill (this quarry can still be seen hidden in the fir trees), and proving difficult; the men were having trouble getting out the closely jointed block. William Haysom, one of the masons, suggested they got Captain Whistler, who succeeded.

In addition to the normal gibbet holes, Dancing Ledge bears evidence of other wood fixtures. On the quarry edge above and a little west from the swimming pool is a strong mooring hole and iron ring plus lesser holes for timbers. Dead in line with it and the gibbet position out on the southwest point there is a cluster of square sinkings, some of them inclined to take braces that indicate the direction of strain being towards the gibbet. This alignment can hardly be a coincidence. Forward of this cluster, heavy duty mooring holes provided anchor points for guy ropes. Obviously some sort of wooden structure was mounted there. It tells of a heavy warp that was strained across the ledge between the gibbet and mooring hole, with a 'pylon' breaking this long span in two, one of about 70 feet, the other about a 100. It seems a breeches-buoy type arrangement conveyed smaller stones from the eastern end of the quarr out to the boats more speedily than by cartage. Is it possible? For what it is worth, exceptionally heavy spray in February 1977 washed out scars forming the quarry floor, exposing worked pitchers left not far west of the swimming pool, proof of the production of this sort of small stuff, and of it being stacked near this ropeway position. Close by the trackway a pair of holes for timbers, plus a small one in the right position for a bearing, tell of a capstan position. The adjacent ledge towards the sea is flatter than average but the direction seems wrong, for the best place to pull up a boat lies further east. Dancing Ledge has its enigmas.

The 'pylon' begs the question as to whether or not it was possible for a suspended load to pass under a fixed support. Suitable pulleys may have worked effectively and provided a solution on a hard steel wire, but hardly on fibre, which would tend to squash. The first English wrought iron wire ropes were being experimented with for ships' rigging in the 1830s. Perhaps the Dancing Ledge arrangement is of that technology. '1853' has been boldly cut with a hammer and punch close by the landward end fixing point. Perhaps that was the year they rigged it up. However, if the arrangement is of a pre wire rope date, could the set up still make sense? Winspit almost certainly had a similar breeches-buoy type rope arrangement,

Dancing Ledge. Anchor point for breeches-buoy apparatus.

probably first operational in the late 1820s. The holes in the ledge suggest that they set the pylon up, then did it again on a slightly different alignment, Perhaps the basic arrangement was no more than that simple goal post-like set up, wide enough at four feet for a load to swing through. However, there are additional more puzzling holes for timbers lying in the quarry direction but not the other. Perhaps they provided for a platform which allowed for the load to be grounded and the weight transferred from one side of the cable support to the other, and which may therefore tell of a fibre rope date.

However it worked, speed was of the essence. Stone could not have been accumulated for any length of time by the water in advance of the vessel's arrival. When she did appear they had to move fast. The goal post assembly lies someway up the ledge and could have been left in place for weeks at a time. Nevertheless in heavy weather the entire ledge is swept and they would have had to dismantle and move it up into the safety

Dancing Ledge. Early 20th century photograph of 'boat ladder' for fishing boat, showing how boats could be moved safely up and down the cliff. The metal anchor points for the rails can still be seen.

CLIFF STONE / 121

of the quarry or lose it. I guess the best way to rig up would have been to attach the hawser first on the seaward Samson post. Next it would have been brought to and over the 'goal', then to the quarry; pulled as tight as possible by hand before tensioning by block and tackle at the anchor point.

Thomas Pellatt commissioned the cutting of the swimming pool for his school boys. It is said that it was done under the supervision of James or Timothy Brown. Since it was made around 1910 it has several times filled with boulders that have washed eastwards from falls further up the ledge to the west. The detached rock towards the west end of the ledge bears two iron pins which secured a diving board, also for the boys' use. The sloped access way down to the ledge, the lower part of which was swept away in the 1950s leaving it difficult to use, may have also been modified by Pellatt, but is probably in the main older. The shelf to the east cut below the quarry floor proper may have provided approach for stones to the ropeway. But, though of poor quality, these beds may have been usable for low grade work such as harbour wall backing so could have been dug for their own worth. Dancing Ledge has more of this low grade stuff taken from the Upper Cherty series than any other cliff quarry. A pair of iron pins set in concrete above and a plethora of iron pins let in lead in the ledge below the sloped access are probably post-operational, and to do with fishing boats rather than the quarry; similarly the seaward facing boat shed (about seven feet by twenty internal) with its fillet of cement remaining in the door jamb. Herbert Hooper, one of the wartime coast watchers, was about the last to keep a dinghy here until someone sat on it, forcing a sharp stone through its bottom.

PLATTER

This is a small cutting on the projecting corner west of Dancing Ledge. Not much work was done here, but mooring holes and a square sinking show the quarriers got as far as setting up a gibbet. Does the name possibly derive from Platner/Platna/Flatner, meaning some type of flat stone used for paving?

ST THOMAS / SCRATCH ASS

There is no loading rock below this quarry, so it was a single, quite high, drop from the gibbet to the boat. Its position is marked by a king post hole torn out on the seaward side. Close by, a small underground tucked away from the southwesterlies was surely a place to work the stone. The quarried area is pushed a fair way into the Ware, but a big part of this working is blocked with a founder that somehow looks wrong. Was it not planned? That it possibly was not, is indicated by the fact that Charley Harris said two men were killed here.

Across the cove to the east guillemots once laid their eggs in a deeply recessed ledge. When we first explored it by climbing up from a boat I was astonished to find a rusted iron pin fixed towards the back of the recess. It is puzzling to see what use it had, the ascent above being difficult. Perhaps it was to do with raiding the sea birds eggs for food, which surely went on along this part of the coast. Perhaps it was to do with smuggling.

The deeply recessed ledge would have been a good hiding place, but getting stuff to it and away again in the dark would have been a challenge. However the quarry gibbet stood only yards away. Billy Winspit said that one morning the revenue officer was found bound, gagged and tied to a heavy quarry bar somewhere near here.

TOP MAST

Even though not much stone has been dug here, the quarrymen pushed in underground. As with Scratch Ass, there is no lower level loading rock, so the stone was lowered directly to the boat.

HEDBURY

In general, a quarry was simply known by the name of the man who worked it and therefore over time was subject to change, but in this case a family name has stuck. Richard Edburey was a tenant in Langton Wallis in 1585. Treswell's map shows Edburey holding several scattered fields including that on the cliff at the eastern extremity of the manor, which is not quite where this quarry lies. Treswell shows Walter, John and Richard Tomes holding that part of the manor.[25.] The Worth Court Leet book of 1613 records a Robert Idbry and, though none appear on the 1651 articles, a Thomas Tidbury, who may or may not be of the same family, made his mark on the Joint Stock Company agreement of 1698. Perhaps he had taken over this quarry that has gone on bearing his name, or one like it, from the Tomes family by this date. With regard to the later spelling of the name, ignoring the T variant, Lilian Bond has pointed out that in the local dialect initial Hs were dropped, but added to words beginning with vowels!

Hedbury lies in Langton Wallis, the court records of which include several references to the quarrying of roof tile and Marble during the 15th century. It would seem that almost no other categories of stone were being taken throughout that century from the manor and that therefore this quarry, that yields Cliff stone, had yet to start.

In 1720 Mr. Bankes was after a Peter Tidbury: 'for a hogshead of wreaked wine that came ashore in Purbeck and which he had fraudulently converted to his own use £8-19-0.' Poor Peter; the squire owned almost everything, including what was washed up by the sea. Another similar case followed a few years later: 'Edward Bower of Blacklands took up a mast on ye shore and converted it to his own use in repairing his house with it'. Edward could not even lug a spar up from Seacombe or wherever he found it without Mr. Bankes getting wind of it.

Woodward's map of 1775 shows the quarry already in two parts by that date. In my opinion this is the central and eastern part of the quarry as we still see it and does not include the western part, linked only underground, which therefore developed later. A dividing strip of undug stone remains as Woodward showed it. It possibly tells of the relatively poor quality of the stone beneath, or it just could indicate the application of the 100 foot rule. But in my opinion a more likely reason this tongue remains is that it has a covering of periglacial head that did not extend to either side, east or west. What is more puzzling about it is that it supports a waste pile of shrimp, which makes no obvious sense. The normal working practice, which is clearly reflected in the rest of the quarry, was to undermine before bringing down all the superincumbent beds to the quarry floor. Why was this tip put on top of the field? It just could reflect a problem of congestion. To the north of it a walled up track leads at a gentle angle down into the working at its northern extremity. To remove the shrimp rubbish from here meant a long haul out to the quarry edge. There was nowhere else to get rid of it easily within the quarry, so the choice was either to do that or a shorter but uphill haul on to ground they were not going to dig. The tip configuration suggests the use of the horn cart. They pulled it up the slope to the top before pushing it out on to the tip, starting at the far south end.

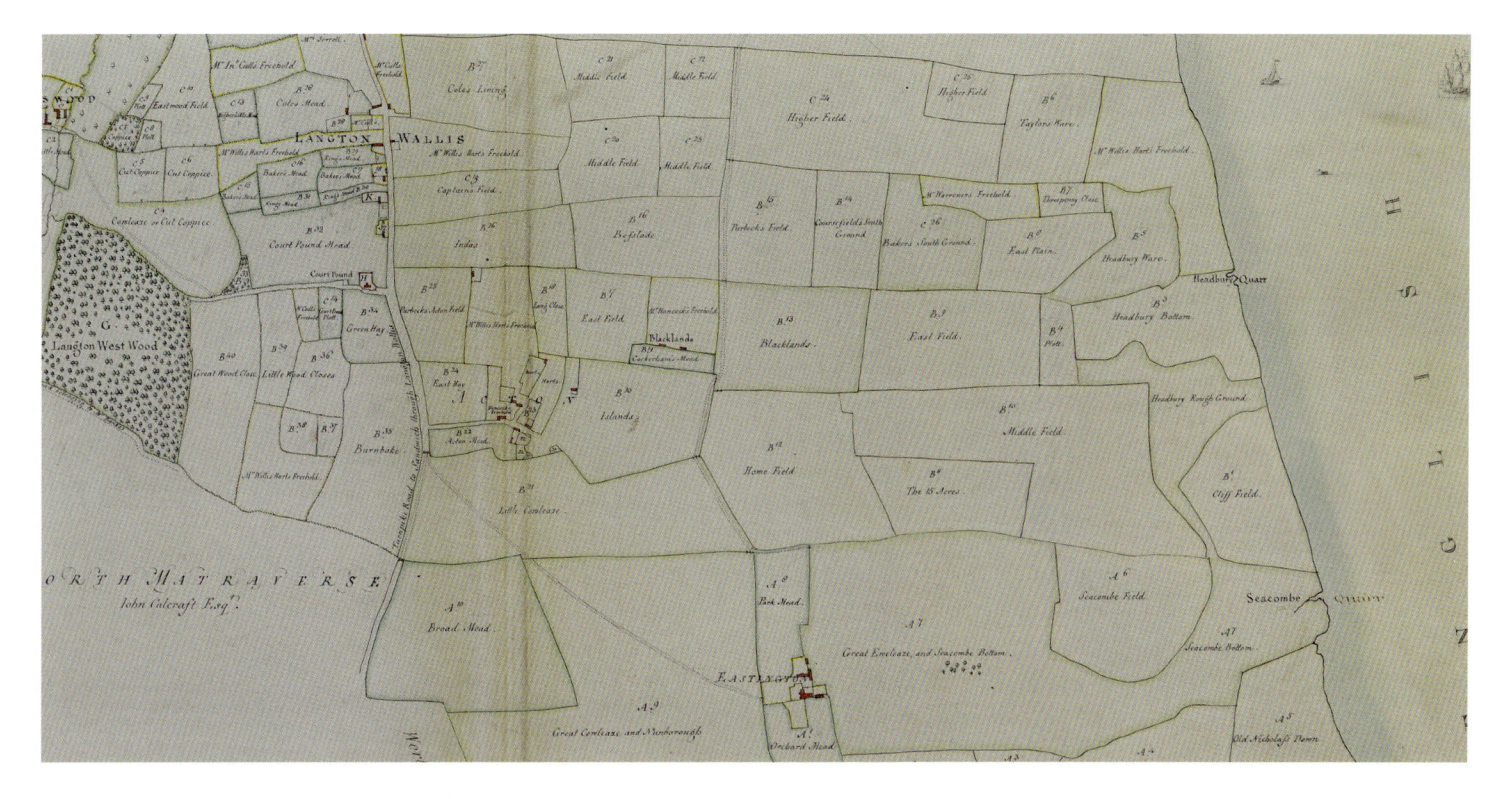

At the same time as Woodward was drawing his map, Titus Chinchen was quarrying paving at Akin (revealing how they pronounced Acton) Lane. The accounts also record him paying royalties for '40 tun Ashler at Idberry'.[26] Similarly, Timothy Phippard was producing paving from Broad Mead at the same time as '53 tun of Idberry Ashlar'. The next year John Lampard, Bankes' Eastington Farm tenant and acting as Bankes' steward, included in his list of money received from the quarriers: 'Mr. Phippard and Mr. Joseph Chinchen and Moses Bower for grant of stone dug at Idberry £5-7-10d.' Working of a cliff and an inland quarry in tandem remained common practice. Jack Edmunds, describing his experiences 130 years later, said they would pack up 'up cliff' and go inland underground for the winter.

In 1781, whilst Titus Chinchen continued to pay dues for 'Idberry', Joseph Chinchen was paying dues for the west part. This just could be the beginning of work at what we now see as the extreme western part of the quarry. The gibbet that served it was fixed someway to the east along what remains as

Part of Woodward's map of Bankes Estate lands at Langton Wallis and Eastington showing Hedbury and Seacombe quarries, 1775 (Dorset History Centre D-BKL/E/A/1/13).

a relatively narrow quarry shelf. The configuration of the cliff at water level would have dictated where the boats could best get in and the crane be mounted. To have got it operational at an early stage would have been essential and would have called for a start to be made on a vertical cliff. Close to the crane position they pushed in underground, perhaps in order to leave somewhere dry to work in, avoiding the need to build sheds. The floors consist of a lot of small scars telling of fine dressing being done there. Behind it in the underground there are roughed out blocks of Front still left, according to Billy Winspit, from the Ramsgate job, plus a lot of rough spalls. In the northeast corner they broke through only at the Underpicking Cap level to an underground extension of the main eastern part of the quarry.

The spalls in one place, dust in another, tell of their methods. The blocks were loosened, cut out and roughly dressed before being taken out to near the crane to be finished, this final shaping being productive of the finer waste. However, it is worth bearing in mind that before mechanisation they did not want big blocks for much of their work. To render items such as staddles from large, solid block, such as typifies Portland, was probably more work than to do so from sources such as Hedbury. However the quarry varies in this regard: parts of it did yield relatively large, sound blocks. Where they pushed in furthest underground, below the hollow of Hedbury Bottom, flow stone is forming over fine big *in situ* blocks, some showing split surfaces exhibiting pit marks.

By the early 19th century the quarry was still in the possession of Joseph Chinchen, and Henry Bower appears in the estate records. He was surely a relative, having married

CLIFF STONE / 123

Elizabeth Chinchen, daughter of Titus, in Langton in 1777. Henry's will tells us of his having had other quarry interests in Worth and Swanage:

> 'This is the last will and testament of me Henry Bower of the parish of Langton Matravers in the Isle of Purbeck, 1814 as follows that is to say, First I give and devise unto my son Isaac all my right title estate and interest of in and to all these my 2 stone quarries now or late in my occupation respectively called or known by the names of Seacombe and Idbury situate at cliff within the parish . . . that other stone quarry now or late in the occupation of myself and Robert Stephens and situate in a certain field called Swanage field . . . . that other stone quarry now or late in the occupation of myself and of Samuel Marsh situate at Herston in a field there called Lanchards . . . also with all and singular my tackle, quarrying tools and implements at or in the aforesaid quarries .'

Informative returns survive from both men. They provide a real window into the past, even telling us which days were calm! What a loss it is that no account books and hardly any contracts or other papers of these 18th and 19th century quarrymen and merchants have survived. However, thanks to landlords keeping at least some records of royalty payments, we have the following. The sum given in these records is the royalty, not the cost of the stone, which usually was approximately thirty times greater, though this percentage was variable.

Either Chinchen or Bower wrote in his own hand (as opposed to the steward):

> 'Edbury Quarry from Xmas 1807 to ditto 1808
> 366 ton Ashlar at 6d per ton   1 - 3 - 0d
> 16 sets of staddles at 1/-   16 – 0d
> 32 Peck sinks, 1/- per 30 pecks   1 - 1d
> 10 foot rolors, 1/- per 20 ft   6d
> 80 'steps', 2/- per 100 ft   1 - 8d
> 15 peck troughs, 1/- per 30 ditto 6d'

He makes a distinction between troughs and sinks. The troughs may refer to what Billy Winspit called D trows (after their shape), used for feed in stables. This would appear to be East or Central Idbry, for in the same year he makes out a separate return for West Idbry:

> 'Henry Bower Due to Henry Banks Esq. (of Kingston Lacey Hall) for grant of stone shipped from the West part of Idbry from Xmas 1807 to ditto 1808
> 105 tons Front stones - 6d   £2 - 12 – 6 [this would be harbour wall work]
> 8 sets Rick stones, 1/-   8 - 0d
> 70 pk Sinks, 1/- for 30 pk   2 - 4d
> 2 ton Rollers, 1/s   2 - 0d.
> 40 pk Troughs   1 - 4d.
> Paid March 8 / 1809   £3 - 6 - 2d.
> Joseph Chinchen due to Henry Banks Esq for grant of stone ship from Edbury quarry from Xmas 1807 to Xmas 1808
> 366 tons ashlar, 6 per ton   9 - 3 - 0
> 16 setts Rick stone   16 - 0
> 32 peck sinks   1 - 1
> 10 Foot Roler   6
> 80 Foot Step   1 - 8
> 15 Peck troughs   6'

Joseph provides more detail the following year, despatching boats to Swanage on four dates in July, the first carrying five sets of rick stones plus half a ton of Roles (Rollers), the second carrying four sets of Rick Stones and the third carrying three sets of Rick Stones plus three quarters of a ton of 'Roles'. A 'set' is 9 staddles, as required by a typical granary, rather than just a single leg and cap. Brian Bugler has calculated, based on a leg 20 inch high, that a set of 9 weighs approximately 1¼ tons. It would therefore seem that the squire's boat, kept at Hedbury, could carry at least 6¾ tons of stone.[27] This gives us some indication of the usual capacity of boats that sometimes shuttled loads out to waiting vessels but also, as in this instance, took them all the way around to the Swanage bankers.

They also loaded larger vessels. April 11 1809 was a fine day, and a busy one, for they had two arrive, the *Unity* and the *Two Friends*, both taking on Front [harbour wall], four and fifteen tons respectively. The *Unity* was lost later in the devastating storm of 1824 that damaged Lyme Regis Cobb. 'The *Unity*, a London trader ready for sea, was driven with her crew to Charmouth beach; the crew were lashed in the shrouds, and were saved at low water'.[28]

These returns are all in the same hand, presumably Joseph's. He and Henry obviously closely co-operated, indeed at Seacombe they were in partnership. In 1809 Joseph agreed a new seven year lease which spelled out the terms: 'on Mr. Bankes part of West Idbry quarry'. This is a somewhat confusing title, as Bankes owned all of West Hedbury but not the eastern end of the main eastern quarry, which must already by this time have extended into the neighbouring Hart Estate.

By 1825 Isaac Bower had taken over the east part, whilst Joseph Chinchen held the western, together with Charles Chinchen. At the same time Charles and Isaac also held 'Seekham', as it was then written. The compiler of a systematic list of estate quarries in that year adds a comment: 'New leases for these quarries are sent herewith at an increase of 1/4th on the present rents for 2 years. This is the only instance of a ground rent being increased except in a cliff quarry belonging to Mr. Dampier, and then the increase continued only during the time the quarry men were working stones for building a church.'

In 1840 it seems that these quarries were vacant, for the Bankes Estate advertised them:-

> East and West Idbury and Seacombe Stone Quarries Isle of Purbeck
>
> To Be Let, On Lease For Seven, Fourteen or Twentyone Years Three Quarries Of Purbeck Portland Stone, Situate in the Cliffs of the Southern Coast of the Island of Purbeck, capable of supplying stone of considerable dimensions and in great abundance, and well situated for shipment to London, and other places in the south of England.
>
> The quality and durability of this stone, as well as the cost at which it can be produced, and other particulars of information, are specified in the 'Report on the selection of Stone for the new Houses of Parliament' to which the attention of the Architects, Builders and Contractors is particularly directed, and any further information may be obtained on application to Mr. T. G. Robson, Land Agent, Kingston Lacey, near Wimborne.[29]

Towards the end of the century 'Idbry' was divided into three: Edmunds at the extreme east end, the Landers in the central part and Michael Bower at the west. Just where the divisions were made, particularly in the main eastern part, is unclear but probably of little importance at that time when the operators, Thomas Chinchen Lander and Charles Edmunds, were linked by marriage, Charles having married Thomas's daughter. Luckily, Michael Bower's gibbet and jenny were photographed by Pouncy about 1885. They are not reeved ready to work and it would seem the quarry had been abandoned for a while, as indeed the whole of Hedbury certainly was by 1893 when G. F. Harris visited it. As these machines rotted away, the last timber to go was the fixed king post. This one lasted into the 1930s, for Phil Bower said he used it then for tying on his conger trots (lines). Pouncy's would seem to be the only photograph taken of one of these cranes while still in more or less working condition. It shows Michael was able to operate the winding gear sheltered from the rain. Since then the slab above, supported by a rather precarious looking leg, has fallen. Some bits of the machine remained trapped under it until recently. A roll stone at the top of a slide at West Hedbury tells of a capstan position and that therefore stone could have been taken away inland. But Harold Bonfield points out that it, being small, would only have carried quite light gear. The comment in the depot map is 'Water only'.

Miss J. Coulson and Thomas Webster both illustrate similar gibbets, but the most detailed view is by the artist Henry T. Wells, RA. It is a splendid work, full of men and activity, and though there are a few inconsistencies, such as the outline of the hill and the fact the machine has been turned around, it can be safely identified as the main part of Hedbury. He exhibited it as 'Quarrymen of Purbeck' in 1885 and one wonders, at 7ft x 4ft 8in., how much studio time it took (*see following page*). Between 1880 and 1881 this part of the quarry was held by Thomas and James Lander. The central figure is surely Thomas and the boys his sons Albert and Thomas, both of whom gave up quarrying to become bakers, one in Langton and the other in Swanage. Ralph Bower, who drove a delivery van for Thomas, retired in about 1956 after working for my father polishing much of the Temple Church Marble. He was shown a rather small reproduction of the painting and was able to identify other men, but sadly this was not recorded. It would have added even more to the work of this accomplished portrait artist. The whereabouts of the original was not then known in Purbeck, only coming to light after it was chosen, not wholly appropriately, for the cover of a new edition of Thomas Hardy's novel *The Well-Beloved*, which is based on Portland.

Wells' daughter married the son of George Street, the architect for Kingston Church. Is it too fanciful to think of these parents-in-law visiting Purbeck in connection with that church, built between 1873 and 1880, of them walking the cliffs and the scene catching Henry's eye? In 1874 my grandfather began work as an 11-year-old for his father on Thomas Randell's banker in Swanage. He would be sometimes sent with messages to Hedbury. An old man, 'Uncle Allan' Bower, would brew him a 'shard of tea' before he had to set off back along the cliff to Swanage. Bower must surely be one of the group. A likely identification of the bearded figure pausing the mallet at right of the picture is Ambrose Lander, brother of Thomas.[30.] In 1883 Wells had exhibited another work at

West Hedbury. Michael Bower's gibbet, c.1885.

West Hedbury quarry. Roll stone for small capstan. The distinctive cross shape accommodated the roller wheel and its supporting axle. The groove at the top shows where the chain has bitten into the stone.

CLIFF STONE / 125

'Quarrymen of Purbeck' (1885) by Henry Tanworth Wells, RA, (1828-1903). Guildhall Art Gallery, London. Oil on canvas. Note men on the jenny, right of centre; the man on the gibbet is pushing the rotating arm, holding the rope for control. On top of the king post of the gibbet, the load rope can be seen passing through the direction changer. The boy at centre is putting a sling chain around the dressed stone on the quarr cart ready for lifting by the gibbet. The man in the dark hat at right is hewing the centre out of a sink.

the Academy entitled 'Quarry on the Hill'. It could well have been another Purbeck scene, but sadly the painting's location is unknown. It was probably destroyed in the London blitz.

As well as the eastern extremity of Hedbury, the Edmunds family worked West Winspit. They provided stone from both these quarries plus a relatively small amount of Inland Freestone, presumably from their quarry in Burngate, for the last project to be taken away by sea. This was the 'Uplyme job', an extensive house at Rousden built for Sir Henry Peek, Bart. MP, between 1874 and 1878, latterly All Hallows School, and now private accommodation. Much of the stone was worked on site where Charles Edmunds was in charge. This big Uplyme job was going on at the same time as Kingston church, and quite a few men would switch from one to the other. Several marriage unions resulted from Purbeck people going to Uplyme, notably Charles' daughter, Jane who married a stonemason from there, Henry Rose.

Wells' painting shows a stock in trade sink being worked whilst what looks like a piece of twice-weathered coping is being slung, another lowered and a third being hoisted into the gaff rigged ketch typical of that generation of vessels, surely on its way to Uplyme. The work is a considered compilation showing the loading progression, rather than a snapshot. Its value in terms of cliff quarrying history can hardly be over emphasised.

By 1900 the market for staddles, rollers and hollow work, the stock-in-trade of these quarries, had collapsed. The Durnford School boys chucked sinks and troughs into the sea, whilst the unsold stock in the depot was finally sold at a knock down price to a landscape gardener who took more than one truck load. The arrival of the railway branch line was another nail in the coffin of these quarries lacking easy land access. Hedbury became dormant. Before the gibbet arm decayed away its gudgeon pin rusted solid to its bearing, where it remains sticking up as a spike to this day. When working, the crane dropped the stone to a lower loading rock where it was picked up again to be swung into the boat. This lower rock, actually the Puffin Bed level, has holes where successive cranes were set up. On the west side of the cave underneath this ledge, close to water level, a mooring bollard remains, cut out of the solid rock. To the east, up on the loading rock level, an arch shows where the stern line was secured. Michael Bower's gibbet to the west lacks surviving mooring holes close below, but one does remain yards away in a position where it is easy to scramble out of a boat.

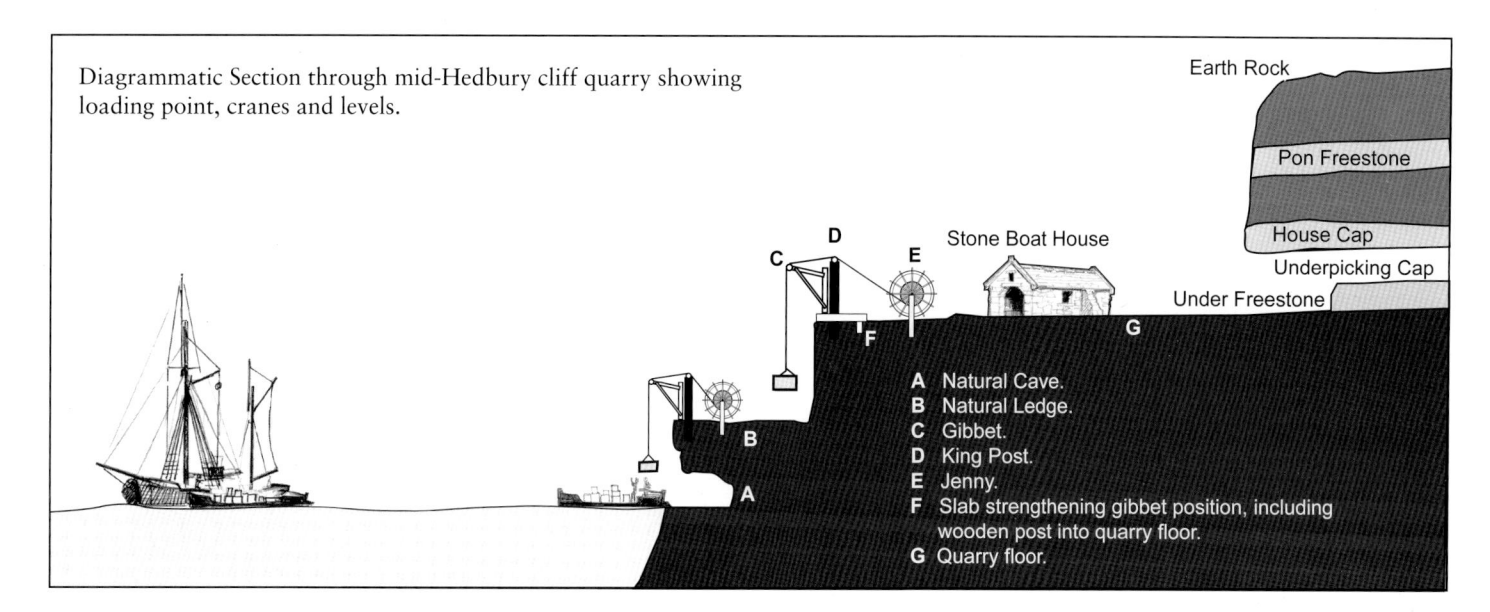

Diagrammatic Section through mid-Hedbury cliff quarry showing loading point, cranes and levels.

A Natural Cave.
B Natural Ledge.
C Gibbet.
D King Post.
E Jenny.
F Slab strengthening gibbet position, including wooden post into quarry floor.
G Quarry floor.

Earth Rock
Pon Freestone
House Cap
Underpicking Cap
Under Freestone

Fortunately this loading rock, one of the richest in terms of its archaeology (especially the survival of the bearing), still remains as it was. The lower crane, mounted on its shelf of Puffin bed over a cave, was safely out of reach of the sea except in really bad conditions. The king post hole plus bearing is obvious, as are the pair of holes about four feet apart, cut to take the winding gear, which was set back ten feet or so from the king post. The beauty of cutting fixing positions into hard rock is that they can go on serving for years, so long as the technology remains static. Generations of cranes may have been set up in the same holes.

Pushing in underground sometimes provided places well enough lit to work in but yet out of the wind and rain. However in some cliff quarries they also built sheds. Typically they are small and face away from the southwest, as the cluster here does. But one close by the gibbet was used for storing a stone boat, from where it would have been launched whilst there were functional cranes. 'A L' cut into one of its stones could be Ambrose Lander. This well-built shed complete with date stone, a stone tile roof, even a fireplace and a corbelled south door, survived into the early 1900s. Behind it a gap in the waste piles leads to a small underground that faces east. It is surely a workplace, comfortable in any weather. One wonders how many generations may have fashioned staddles and sinks within its shelter. One man has left 'T. E.' Is this Thomas Edmunds, 1802-1889? The Underpicking Cap exhibits pit rather than drill marks, which may suggest a pre-gunpowder date, but on the other hand the blocks are small and loose, so perhaps there was no need of it. It remains unique along cliff in being muddy, for periglacial head is finding its way down the joints from close overhead.

The final years were somewhat bizarre. Reg Bower, nicknamed Pickles and foreman at the Acton Co-op, had inherited Michael Bower's west end part. He and Jack Edmunds, who had similarly inherited the extreme east end, agreed to sub-let to

Hedbury boat shed, c.1910.

Hedbury from the north, showing boat shed and gibbet for lowering boat and stone down the cliff, c.1910.

CLIFF STONE / 127

Ernest Burt, who came to similar arrangements with the other cliff quarries at West Winspit and Seacombe. Burt sub-let to his own Swanage Portland Stone Co., who shared Weymouth offices with William David. His Dorset Quarry Co., launched in 1922, took over these leases as well as the Lander brothers' main part of Hedbury. These arrangements, agreed between the quarrymen, were of doubtful legality. Bankes' agent, Mr. Lodder, observed in a letter about the subsequent winding up of the Dorset Quarry Co. that he did not recognise them.

This complexity is illustrated by what happened at West Hedbury in 1919 when Reginald Michael Bower granted a lease to Ernest Burt: 'for a term of 21 years for a fixed rent of £7 10s p.a. and a royalty of 8d per ton. Burt assigned this lease to the Swanage and Portland Stone Co. and this Co. assigned to William David who in turn assigned to Dorset Quarry Co.'[31.]

Jack Edmunds came to a similar arrangement with the eastern part of the quarry, adding further to the complexity was the fact that some of Jack's part was separate from all the rest, by this time lying within the Durnford Estate. There was no possibility of a road out other than by going over Bankes' land. Hence, in a 1921 systematic list of all that estate's quarries, appears 'J. Edmunds Cliff Headbury half dues payable to Bankes Estate for privilege of carting stone across Eastington farm land'. Jack never made use of this doubtful privilege; to have constructed such a road would have been a big job. The quarry configuration as we see it now gives no hint of this separation of land ownership, which had existed since 1665 when Sir Ralph Bankes sold off the adjacent 'Edburie' tenement, including two small parcels where Acton has been subsequently built. Presumably he needed cash to build Kingston Lacy Hall.

Woodward's map of 1775 shows the then quarry limit coinciding with the boundary of Mr Willis Hart's freehold.[32.] The subsequent encroachment into Hart's land has occurred since. In 1760 Sir John Willis Hart was subpoenaed to appear as a witness in a row between a certain Carter and Timothy Edmunds, who was charged with trespass. The location is uncertain, but possibly Hedbury. Timothy was surely a quarryman. Was he pushing eastwards beyond Bankes' ownership into Hart's acquisition? Subsequent progress in that direction is probably to do with Charles Chinchen, who was both working Bankes' part of the quarry and farming Hart's various Langton properties around about the 1840s. He could easily have agreed terms with Hart, but it would probably have depended on the use of Bankes' loading rock. I wonder if Bankes knew? In effect, as the resulting bluff testifies, they pushed further into the slope of the ware relative to the overlying Purbeck beds than any other quarry.

The possible use of Bankes' loading rock to convey stone from another owner's quarry is guess work, and there is a modicum of evidence against it. The furthest eastern part includes a small shed ruin which faces eastwards away from the worst gales. In that direction a track skirts the landward side of a founder walled up with spalls. They did not do all that work for fun. It suggests access to a crane position right at the extreme end of the quarry that has since fallen away. Below this hypothetical position there are two holes low by the water that possibly once held gibbet timbers.

The position of the surviving quarry edge gibbet with its rusted on gudgeon pin is instructive as to how critical the location had to be. The king post hole is cut through a slab of Blue Bit which has been placed over the hole in the quarry floor, obviously to help strengthen it. Surely the rock around the timber was not holding well, but they could not move the crane far and still keep it in the best place to supply the boats. It was already a second try, for close by what must be an earlier king post position has been torn out on the seaward side. Imagine that happening with a heavy stone hanging out in space, with men and boats below! A pair of holes plugged with worked stones show the alignment of the jenny with the first king post position. A second, lesser hole piercing the Blue Bit strengthening piece was, I guess, to take another timber that acted as a dowel, sunk into a firmer area of floor. Within the arc of the gibbet the cliff below has been built up with blocks, obviously to make it easier to get the load better within reach prior to lifting. The top courses are now missing. Here the quarry floor is smoother than usual, the product of the scraping iron keel of the boat which was kept in the boat shed close by, as much as iron tyres, I suspect. This position, key to the working of this quarry over centuries, is under threat. Summer 2007 saw rock falls immediately adjacent to the walled up section, as did the violent storms of February 2014.

In the inter war years John Edmunds, known as Jack, worked on the banker in the Swanage depot, but continued to pay a nominal royalty to keep his interest in this quarry, as did his son and grandson after him. Whilst working fiddly bits of Marble for repairs at Salisbury Cathedral with Bill Chaffey Bower, he would yarn about the old quarry. He told my father of the use of the horn cart, the occasion when 'the old hands' put a broken bar in the cannon and fired it at a French privateer.

CLIFF FIELDS

There are three diggings into this part of the cliff between West Hedbury and Gallery. Two of them are small; these were perhaps just explorations to find out what the stone was like. However the easternmost has been opened out a fair amount. One of the larger faults lies between it and West Hedbury. This was a mark for the fishermen before the advent of noisy motors, for in certain conditions a blow hole can make a noise; hence its name 'Pig's head in the gate'. A length of chain that once helped secure the gibbet remains more or less central to the main working. However, this crane position could only have been used at high tide, for a shelf of rock forms an obstacle at low water. Along a narrow extension to the west, across a minor joint, stones fixed at the quarry edge and holes cut in a projecting block of Puffin bed below tell of another gibbet position. An episode of 'Some Mothers Do Have 'Em', which involved the suspension of a car, was filmed here.

The same men who were working Hedbury and Seacombe were here in the early 19th century. The royalty record of what Joseph Chinchen and Henry Bower dispatched between Christmas 1807 and Christmas 1808 has been kept:

7 setts of staddle stones at 1/s
15 peck of sinks at 1/s per 30 peck
+21 peck of troughs.

This quarr can perhaps be seen as an extension of West Hedbury. The fault which brings the useful beds relatively low in the cliff between the two quarries, which made the stone difficult to get at, was an obstacle the quarrymen avoided. The annotated map from Burt and Burt's office shows 'J. Curtis (Banks) load water only (suitable for small stone)'. One of the Curtis family was working in Webber and Corben's London yard when my father spent a few months there in about 1920.

In the 1780s a Joseph Curtis was in partnership with James Barnes in a quarry on the Worth Estate. The location is not given, but they were making Dover Front. It was therefore surely a cliff quarry, almost certainly West Winspit, where we know the Barnes continued later. By 1811 Curtis was in possession of a paving quarry on the neighbouring Bankes Estate in Little Cowlease. It was the norm for men to work quarries in tandem, so it is more than likely that he was working a cliff quarry at the same time, probably this one.

GALLERY / GARLEY

The quarry on the east side of Seacombe Bottom is now usually called 'Gallery'; the Burt and Burt map shows it as 'Galance'. However Bankes Estate records of 1922 put 'Garley' further east, at the same place as the annotated map calls 'Cliff Fields'. The estate records show that Charles Coleman had been in occupation of the one close by Seacombe, Henry Corbin of Portsmouth holding 'Garleys' to the east. One wonders which map is wrong. George Lander told me of another, less bandied about name, for the eastern one, which he called Bullock Hole, due to men driving a bullock over here and butchering it up. Before the invention of barbed wire, the cliff in general was not fenced, but the path was marked with white stones to aid the Revenue men on a dark night.

Whatever they called it, holes show where a gibbet/garly, was mounted at the west end of the quarry where the floor has moved out before stabilising again. The movement has created a split which gave access down to the loading road, but big rocks have recently fallen, making it much more difficult to get down to the where there are holes marking another gibbet position. The rocks that recently fell now lie in the water blocking what would have been the dock.

When Harris visited in 1893 it was derelict; one wonders for how long.[33.] Who were A.B. and W.B. who cut the date 1879 on the westernmost of two composite legs supporting the underground? These include bits of finished broached work jammed under the ceiling. Both legs have been tightened by bits of wood, some of it looking like wreck timbers (the *Halsewell* perhaps?). To the west of the underground the face has been cut back in steps with a lot of small stuff lying below, which is odd; it is possibly from the 1920s. This stepping provides access, especially now after the heap of wartime wire that was thrown over here has rusted away. In the original, working access was from the east end. There are holes cut on the low level loading rock which are not to do with the working of the quarry, but for tying on lobster pots or conger trots, for this place was reasonably easy of access, without being as public as Seacombe, with what that means in terms of interference. From a quarry perspective it must be instructive that while Winspit was quarried extensively on both sides of the valley, Seacombe is much more lopsided with little work done on this east side compared with the west.

SEACOMBE

The early Bankes Estate rent books cover the years between 1691 and 1740.[34.] They appear to make no mention of quarrying at Seacombe, though it was probably going on there at the time. A single reference in a parallel volume comes in 1724, when Peter Phippard was working in partnership with John Chinchin in a paving quarry on the same estate. By 1772 William Chinchen was in possession, and John Lampard, compiling the income from the quarries, makes a distinction between him, together with Titus Chinchen of Idberry, by referring to them alone as 'Mr'. They had rank in the eyes of the landlord which the other quarrymen lacked. In a systematic list, John records only that William and Titus were paying for 'ground of stone', but adds the detail in a footnote: 'Note the stone paid for Seacombe Quarry [...] is as follows: 418 tuns of ashlar or front at 6d. per tun, 181 tuns of backing at 3d. per tun. [This is harbour work, backing being rough hard core such as is used to fill up behind the dressed front work.] 7 setts of legs and caps and 1 tun of rollers'. The total income is the highest for any quarry on the list, followed by the other two cliff quarries at 'Idberry', all three substantially more than the most lucrative inland quarry. The Estate records may be rather scanty, but the output was either at high level during the 18th century, or operations had been going on over a longer period, for Samuel Grimm's inkwash views, made about 1790, show the open western shelf, with underground workings extending from it, cut away more or less as we see it now (*see following page*).[35.]

A surprising entry appears in 1781: 'Received of Will. Stevens for the ground of 163 ton of pebbles shipped at Seacombe by himself and Mr. George Bonfield at 6d per tun'.

West of Seacombe lie two coves separated by the solitary Watch rock. Pebbles accumulate in the back of both. There is a similar small amount in the back of a similar cove west of Winspit at Crab Hole. These coves are the only such sources of pebbles between Durlston Head and Pier Bottom, and on the face of it not obvious places to find such material. Durlston Bay pebbles were used for pitchers in the early 18th century. Perhaps by 1781 this supply was exhausted and they were questing further afield. If there was a requirement to crack the pebbles, as they did the Durlston stones which were used in the school yard at Eton in about 1710, the Seacombe pebbles would have been more difficult in that they consist of both stone and chert. These coves bear the names William and Michael. Is 'William' William Stevens? Since he loaded his stone, there has been a big change. On March 19, 1992, the roof of the western ('William') cove fell in. Landing on it a couple of months later I 'guesstimated' the fallen debris to be in the region of 10,000

ABOVE West Seacombe. Ink wash on paper, Samuel Grimm, c. 1790. (British Library, MS15537, f.157)

RIGHT Seacombe quarry. Ink wash on paper, Samuel Grimm, c.1790. (British Library, MS15537, f.158) (both are mislabelled as Peveril Point).

tons. The sea then moved much of it eastwards, tumbling it over the Watch rock ledge so that the depth of water by the loading rock was reduced. Subsequent wave action has recently returned the water to its original depth.

Evidence of the taking of pebbles from other Purbeck coves is suggested by the Woodward 1775 map of Studland, which shows Fairy Quarry not far north of 'Bollard Green' [Head]. There is a shallow cave at the foot of the cliff where pebbles accumulate. Parson's Barn is another cave further east, between the Wedge and the Pinnacle, and its pebbles, of a small regular size, were taken by builders for pebble dash during the interwar years and possibly before. Even after the war, when the need for repairs arose, fisherman Bobby Brown would get more for Hardys, the Swanage builders. This cave also collapsed some time in the 1960s, and now lies open to the sky, but its beach of evenly sized pebbles remains, as does an engraving of a sailing vessel, similar to the cliff quarry examples.

The configuration of Seacombe presents a difficulty. The loading rock is perhaps the best one along the cliff, comparing favourably with a man-made wharf, but it lies the full extent of the quarry westwards away from the valley where it is perhaps reasonable to suspect the initial breach would have been made. The road entrance is puzzling in that it goes over a hump and then across a patch of *in situ* Bottom Freestone. Why not take it, this good stone, after doing all the work of uncovering it? It would seem to be a way of getting a gentle gradient road into a pre-existing quarry with the least amount of work, and could well be late 19th century and not earlier. If the early progression was from the valley end, how did they load stone away by water before the quarry shelf was cut westwards to above the loading rock below? They must have managed as best they could.

About half way along at the foot of the cliff there are a couple of rows of wedge pits left without the stone being split away, which possibly tell of a significant amount of removal. Setting off the surviving wedge pits which can still be seen, cut in two directions, would produce a rectangular block about six feet by two feet by one foot. Did the quarrier cut the pits but then leave the piece for setting off when the weather was good and boat transport could arrive? The piece would then be quickly split and manhandled into a boat, thereby avoiding leaving it in a vulnerable position subject to sea damage. What is certain is that it was not, as elsewhere, simply dug to make the cliff configuration better for loading, but for its own sake. The men must have managed to get stone from this area into the boats without a crane, which suggests use of a 'ladder' or 'inclined portable stage' as W. M. Hardy puts it in his account of stone loading at Durlston Bay.[36]

However, the overwhelming pre-railway output of this quarry went to a single crane position at the west end. Below it on the sea-washed and uneven loading rock, sinkings for timbers show where a cart track of approximately two foot gauge, of timber or iron rails, ran out to the water's edge. On its seaward side a jenny position remains. It would have needed uprights of unequal length, and a king post hole, complete with the usual arch cut in the rock to take a chain that resisted the tendency for the gibbet to topple over. Another exceptionally big king post hole has been cut in an elevated part of the ledge to the north. It lacks any associated jenny holes almost certainly because they have been cut away to better to accommodate a derrick set up in the 1920s by the Dorset Quarry Co. to load the blocks for the Poole Harbour Training Bank. Sinkings for timbers to support some sort of trackway run from the foot of the cliff the short distance to the gibbets. Drill holes with shatterings show where explosives were used to cut the cliff back where the trackway commences. This is surely pre-1920s, when the gibbet above had a short reach. The dock itself is now partially blocked by a large fall which happened in about 1980.

Pushing into the hillside, the block becomes increasingly tight and difficult to get out, but parallel to the valley, as with the cliff face, it is somewhat looser and more diggable. Hence they followed the valley inland, keeping to Jack Edmund's dictum, 'between the deep and the shoal'. The old quarry therefore consisted of an open cliff edge platform and an underground, open only at the seaward end, extending inland a considerable distance. This underground did not approach the valley side too closely, as there the ceiling became too bad to support itself; Billy Winspit called this condition 'peabodied'. He also referred to there being a 'bar', which specifically describes the major fault that lies west of the main quarry, creating an obstacle to progress in that direction. Billy said that the stone there was 'all sodered together'. He was referring to calcium carbonate deposits which fill the joints and therefore bond the rock. It has been illuminating to read many years later of the building of Chantmarle Manor (1612-1623). Sir John Strode's accounts include 'Freestone walls made of great rock stones, sodered with new burned lime.'[37.]

What was once the main entrance to the old working can be identified by initials and the date 1923 cut close by. Returning to its earlier history, more detailed royalty payment records continue in the early 19th century – as here for 1809: compiled by the same men who were working Hedbury at the same time:

'Chinchen & Bower due to Henry Banks Esq. for ground of stone shipped from Seacombe Quarry, 1809.
May 11   By the Resolution Capt. Corbin
620 feet long ashlar   2/s   12 - 4d.
May 18   By boat 285 pk. sinks 1/s. per 30 pks   9 - 6d.' [This means by small stone boat to Swanage rather than a large vessel.]

By 1825 Joseph was in partnership with Isaac Bower, Henry's son.

The continuation of working is shown by the use of Seacombe stone for the Encombe obelisk erected in 1835. Blown down by the storm of January 1990, it has been re-built after frost-damaged parts of the plinth were renewed. Frost vulnerability is a Seacombe Bottom Freestone characteristic. Kingston cottages of about 1840 have Cliff stone paving and dressings which match the obelisk stone and are almost certainly from the same source, somewhat surprising on the face of it, as Encombe Estate had its own Cliff quarries. Perhaps they were dormant at this time. Wimborne Minster has 19th century 8 ft 6 inch longsteps leading up into the chancel that are Cliff rather than Portland. They look like Seacombe Freestone, with rather coarse shell, blacks and serpulid worm clusters, and are the work of Benjamin Wyatt (1857), or Pearson (1891): I suspect the former. Westminster Abbey nave floor, of regular twelve inch squares, contains some that are of the same coarse Cliff Freestone. They can hardly be original. The suspicion arises that they are also the work of Benjamin Wyatt, who succeeded his better-known father, James, as Abbey surveyor. A 19th century notebook refers to the use of Seacombe stone for a 'lighthouse now building on the Isle of Wight'.[38.] Concealed by coats of whitewash, broached ashlar remains discernible at St. Catherine's, built between 1838-40. The Needles tower of 1859 is of granite, so it must be that St. Catherine's is where the Seacombe stone went.

In 1840 this quarry was advertised at the same time as Hedbury. Jeremiah Bower, whose son Ambrose and grandson William Jeremiah (Billy Winspit) worked it in turn until about 1930, continued from about that date. He may have taken occupation following the advertisement. However a clue that Jeremiah was in occupation before appears in the Worth Estate

Encombe Estate. Obelisk, originally built of Seacombe stone in 1835 by Lord Eldon in memory of his brother. It was demolished by a storm in January 1990 and repaired incorporating other stones.

rents for 1827. In that year he paid boat money to the Calcraft Estate, but no stone dues. He was using the Calcraft Estate boat but not digging their stone it seems, which surely puts him in Seacombe. His father was Thomas, who during the early part of the 19th century was paying both stone dues and boat money to Squire Calcraft. Thomas's output included sinks and rick stones, so he was certainly working Winspit rather than an inland quarry. Latterly Thomas was in partnership with, variously, George and Sam Dowland; perhaps there was a parting of the ways between father and son.

In 1871 Ambrose dispatched a particularly large trough to the North Woolwich Galvanising Works. At eight feet by four feet by four feet it must rank amongst the biggest worked stones sent out of Purbeck, and he got it out from underground without a crane! Squared up before being hollowed out, it would have weighed about ten tons. Ambrose had more of a connection with Woolwich than just the supply of this stone. He worked there for a while and met his wife there. Ted Pushman, son of the postmaster, had a recollection of Mrs Bower. Chatting in the

Seacombe Quarry. J. Colson. Feb 26 1879. It would appear that the machine is out of proportion to the figures. The socket hole can still be found.

shop, she mentioned that that morning she had swum around to Seacombe with Ambrose's lunch. They were living in Winspit Cottage! One wonders how the exceptionally heavy sink was transported to London. A painting by a Miss Colson of 1879 shows a massive gibbet mounted on the loading rock which dwarfs the figures alongside. It was possibly capable of such a weight, whatever that was after hollowing out, depending on how thick he left the walls and bottom, but I doubt it. Ambrose may well have cut away six tons or more. This was not long before the opening of the Swanage railway branch but after completion of the London to Dorchester line. Perhaps Ambrose had this exceptional stone hauled to Wareham, whence it went to London by rail rather than by sea.

In 1893 the geologist G. F. Harris was most impressed by Seacombe. He found Ambrose Bower working alone making a pig trough. Ambrose said he normally employed seven men:

> 'It is evident, from the appearance of the place, that when trade is brisk he has assistance. This quarry has been opened a very long time. Bower has had it in his family for over 100 years. The working is partly open, partly underground. The quarry included an underground gallery. The custom was to blast off the cap, four to six feet thick; this was used to build sea walls. Beneath was an eight foot depth of building stone. Enormous blocks, which had to be cut out, were sometimes sent to London [...] The stone looked uniform in grain and tint. When one remembers that sea carriage is within a few yards, I must say I cannot understand why these quarries are not opened up more extensively. Bower, who seemed a hard working man ... old me he wanted more capital. The stone not only goes by ship alongside but is also sent by road to Swanage and elsewhere. Mr. Bower said the reason the stone was so little known was because the high Purbeck ridge between his quarry and Swanage was a fearful precipitous road for horses to drag the stone up and raised the expense considerably.'[39.]

Around the turn of the century Burt and Burt, the principal Swanage merchants, would buy block from Ambrose. We see an example in the long lintels of 'Cragside' on Spring Hill, Swanage. Burts had their own teams of horses. They would send three carters with three wagons, a brace of horses on each. The first wagon would be loaded, all six horses hitched on in order to pull it up to Eastington. The horses were unhitched, taken back down to the quarr where the second wagon had been loaded, attached and up to the farm again. When all three loaded wagons had been pulled up to the farm the team was again separated into pairs, and so to Swanage. Three men, six horses, made a long hard day's work to get about six tons to Swanage. A photograph in *Langton Matravers in Photographs, 1850-1900*, shows this trio of wagons. The procedure is illustrated in some of the 1910 collection of glass negatives. They include one showing seven horses attached to a loaded

132 / PURBECK STONE

wagon at on the way up from Seacombe. The negatives reveal how they managed loading in those pre-derrick crane first years of the 20th century at Seacombe. The scappled blocks were brought out from underground on a low cart of rather wider gauge than the standard inland cart. It was pulled up on to a banker that lay far enough outside the underground entrance to provide a gentle incline, but which has since been cleared away. The block was barred off the cart onto a pair of timbers to reduce impact, on the edge of the banker. Burt and Burt's wagon was brought alongside and the stone barred across on to it, all on a level. At the Swanage Kings Road depot they surely had a similar banker to receive the stones. In this age of forklifts, etc., it is hard to imagine what was done with bars alone before the 20th century. Legs coggled up in the wide part of East Winspit are perhaps the heaviest blocks moved in this way left for us to see.

One wonders how many it took to get Ambrose's great trough up the hill if that is the way it went. That greater loads than normal could be tackled, is demonstrated by the fact that in the course of constructing the Wareham to Swanage railway, the line was advanced from both ends. As the track lengthened, a locomotive was brought in to Swanage to help with construction. The only way was along the turnpike road, which meant pulling the Beattie 2-4-0WT Well Tank engine up Kingston Hill using horse power! William Bradford told me that his grandfather William, who worked as a carter for Henry Weeks Burt, got involved. The team of 24 was 'stooded' but he got them going again. So far as completing the journey down to the depot was concerned the only significant obstacle was the steep ascent of Steps Hill. Burts sometimes left a horse by the Putlake elm tree and it was added to the team just for that short haul. Thomas Collins, a Bradford relative, told of Bill being sent up to collect a load from Sunshine Norman's quarr at Castle View; Sunshine had married a Burt. Seeing the banker empty he enquired as to where the stone to be collected was. 'Down there,' Sunshine pointed down the mouth!

Sometime around 1920 Burt and Burt, by then controlled by Ernest Burt, amalgamated with others to form the Purbeck Stone and General Trading Co. Ernest bought out Jack Edmunds' interest in West Winspit and sent men to work there towards the west end. He then came to a business arrangement with a Mr. William David. David supplied a big derrick crane which carter Bradford dragged down to Winspit via Weston

ABOVE Between Seacombe and Eastington Farm. Team of horses going up the valley, 1910.

BELOW Seacombe. Barring the block off the cart onto timbers at left on the edge of the loading banker, 1910.

BELOW Seacombe. Burt and Burt's wagon beside the loading banker, 1910.

CLIFF STONE / 133

Dorset Quarry Co. Wareham Yard, about 1927. The men are standing in front of two frame saws and a Coulter planer (L-R). The blades on the frame saw in the centre are right down, whereas with the partly-visible one to the left, the blades are lifted a foot or two. The two frame saw operators are holding the long-handled shovels used to apply the sand. Front Row L-R: Martin Brown (Manager),?, Arthur Corben (Blacksmith), John Brown (brother of Robert, Swanage Lifeboat Cox), Ernest Edmunds?, Reuben Short Bower, 7 unknowns, Jimmy Chinchen, 2 unknown, David Coleman, Thomas Benfield. Back Row in Planer gap, L-R: Albert Haysom,?, Levi Bower, Percy Turner. Foreground rails carried the travelling crane to pick up blocks to load machines.

and Rope Lake. They set it up on the cliff top above the western quarry. But disagreement with the new landowner, Walter John Strange, followed. In the meantime David had entertained Billy Winspit to a slap-up dinner and got him to sign over his interest in Seacombe. As George 'Buff' Bower, William's cousin, put it:- 'Will signed away his birthright for a mess of pottage'. David wanted to use the new crane at Seacombe, but Mr Strange would not let him take it away over his land. So they lowered it over the cliff and floated it to Seacombe.

So began the final, literally explosive, chapter in the story of this quarry. William David had founded the business of David and Co., Forest of Dean Stone Quarry Owners, sometime around 1890. He had other business interests before becoming General Manager of the Bath Stone Firms Ltd., 1898-1903, and later Managing Director of Bath and Dorset Quarries Ltd. In 1922 he founded the Dorset Quarry Co. Ltd. Men were brought in from both Bath and the Forest of Dean, cranes installed and a masonry yard established by Wareham Station, where houses were built for some of the key employees. Machines included two new frame saws, a planer and a lathe. David also re-opened Crack Lane quarry at Langton. He occupied an office upstairs at the Trocadero, Swanage, and contributed articles to *John Bull* magazine. He appointed John Brown as stone yard foreman and his brother Martin as quarry manager, both Forest of Dean men. Billy Winspit was retained as quarry foreman as part of the deal. They upgraded the track up to the farm and began work at the seaward end of the platform, opening out the quarry further. Leslie Ward's watercolour opposite shows this stage of the work. Billy Winspit, or Brown or David realised that, with the advantage of steam cranes, they could exploit the shallow block left between the old underground and the valley. So they mounted cranes along the top of the quarry, and tore the side out. Having opened it out in this way, they installed underground cranes of the Bath type, attacking the old heading both west and north. For some reason they also jumped further northwards along the flank of the valley, and sank another hole from the top. The massive joint or fault at the western end barred much progress there, so they again jumped across it and sank another hole almost at the boundary with the Worth (Rempstone) Estate, just on the landward side of the coast path. The key to all this was, of course, the power provided by steam.

Indeed, this was the steam age as far as quarry operations in Purbeck were concerned. It lasted eight years. A record of these cranes remains in a number of photographs, particularly those taken by the British Geological Survey, whose work in Dorset coincided with the Dorset Quarry Co. Further evidence can be seen in concrete foundations, fixing pins and ash from the boilers. Blocks left hoisted out of the quarry and several conical waste tips, only achievable with cranes possessive of a long reach, bear further witness. These blocks bear 'nip holes', which firmly date them, as does the odd discarded block half way up the track. Unfortunately no-one seems to have taken a photograph of the underground cranes, an innovation in Purbeck, though evidence of them remains in circular holes cut in the underground ceiling, which held the centre pin. Each

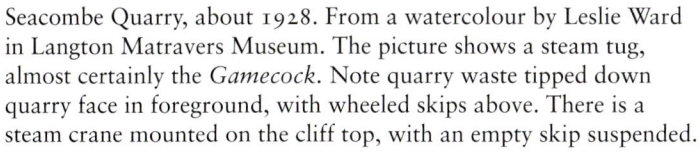

Seacombe Quarry, about 1928. From a watercolour by Leslie Ward in Langton Matravers Museum. The picture shows a steam tug, almost certainly the *Gamecock*. Note quarry waste tipped down quarry face in foreground, with wheeled skips above. There is a steam crane mounted on the cliff top, with an empty skip suspended.

Seacombe quarry, 1920s. Front Row L-R starting with man immediately behind block at left. Arthur Gad Bower, Michael Bower, Miller Lander, 6 unknown, Sid Lander (standing on block), Edwin ('Britches') Corben (holding pickaxe), 2 unknown, Jack Corben, Billy Winspit, Martin Brown, Manager, with collar and tie. Back Row, L-R, starting with unknown man with folded arms, 'Buff' (George) Bower, Victor Bower (holding biddle), Albert Sheppard, Harry Smith at back, 2 unknown, Ambrose Bower, with light clothing and broad-brimmed hat. The crane is of the type more usually mounted within the underground working, in which case the long horizontal timber is an adaptation to being mounted outside.

'Dorset Quarrymen' by Alfred Palmer (Dorset County Museum).

one of these holes is accompanied by a Lewis slot. This was for a fixing used in pulling the crane up into position. Alfred Palmer painted some of this activity. One of his works, now in the County Museum, shows men heaving at a rough block. Tom Short's son Victor, a man of fine physique, posed for him in his studio, which prompted ribaldry. One of the figures is shown levering with a pickaxe, which, if John Brown had seen it happen, would probably have got him the sack. John Brown was a martinet, as was his brother Martin, who ran the Wareham yard, and they drove the men hard. There were injuries and at least two deaths. Times were difficult in the 1920s, and the firm were in close competition with Portland.

CLIFF STONE / 135

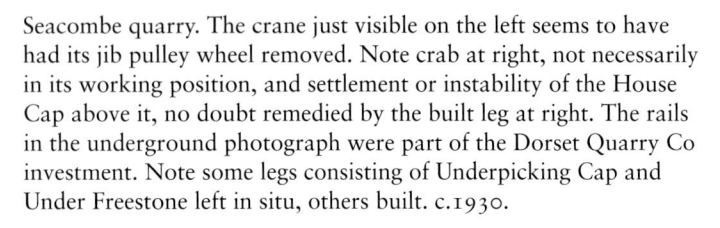

Seacombe quarry. The crane just visible on the left seems to have had its jib pulley wheel removed. Note crab at right, not necessarily in its working position, and settlement or instability of the House Cap above it, no doubt remedied by the built leg at right. The rails in the underground photograph were part of the Dorset Quarry Co investment. Note some legs consisting of Underpicking Cap and Under Freestone left in situ, others built. c.1930.

It must have been galling for the Portland people to see them do Weymouth Bridge. My uncle Albert, who worked in their Wareham yard, particularly mentioned a big classical facade for the Westminster Bank in Kettering, complete with fluted columns. Other projects listed in the Bankes Estate archives include Newton Abbot Station, the Vaudeville Theatre in the Strand, 56 Fleet Street, and Barclays Bank at Weymouth. To this list can be added the King George pub in Poole. One wonders why the enterprise failed. Thomas Bonfield remarked that one problem that may have had a big influence on the viability was that as the working was pushed deep into the hillside they found the blocks to have blue hearts.

A non-masonry job was the Training Bank outside Poole Harbour. It was in connection with this that they set up a small derrick down on the loading rock, from where rough blocks were conveyed in steel lighters towed by Walter Masters' tug, the *Gamecock*. Bobby Brown, later cox of Swanage lifeboat, assisted. He explained that, lacking cranage on the lighter and not being able to get stones weighing a few tons up out of the hold, they kept them at deck level. On arrival they would bar them to the side, making the lighter heel so the stones slid off more easily! There may have been more than one type of barge, for Harold Bonfield told me that Bert Alben told him that the men had to tie themselves on before discharging the load by opening doors in the bottom, for it leapt so violently.

Stories about Seacombe are legion. They tipped waste, which threatened to block access, down onto the rocks until stopped by the coastguard (*see watercolour on previous page*). Bert Wingate, a carpenter working for Oliver Marsh of Langton, was fixing a wood cabin to one of the cranes when there was a warning shout – the jib crashed down, splintering to bits. The steam lorry drivers, competing to get the first load in the morning, would arrive in the winter before daybreak. The crane driver, high above, could see little of what was going on, so the man below held a lamp inside his coat, one flash meant tighten up, two flashes jib out, and so on. One man bought a brand new lorry on the strength of getting the haulage work. Only days later the company went bust. He went to the quarry, started the lorry, left it in gear and jumped out, hoping to claim insurance. It tumbled over the cliff, where bits remain. On later examination of the policy he realised that it was uninsured off the road.[40]

David attracted investors, mostly from Bath, by showing them photographs of the cliff, making out it was all good stone.[41] Uncle Albert was working as a banker mason in Wareham when David came around the yard with several investors. One, a retired clergyman, warmly congratulated him on providing men with jobs. The firm went broke only weeks later. Swanage boys Billy Hancock and Thomas Collins were apprentices at the Co-op at that time.[42] Both got disgruntled as they reckoned Reggy Pickles Bower, the foreman, was giving Langton boys the best jobs. Both went to Wareham to see about a start with the Dorset Quarry Co. Martin Brown's upstairs office door was ajar. They tentatively entered. He wheeled round with 'Don't you boys know how to knock?' They fled back to Reggy Pickles. Pat Brown used to dive under water to secure a chain around blocks that fell from the crane and threatened to block the dock. Fred Stockton was killed by falling material and George Miller also killed while working at the quarry. Harry Bridle and Percy Aust fell together at the west end whilst barring over Shrimp during frosty weather. Bridle lay on the quarry floor, but Aust went on down to the loading rock. Pat Brown scrambled down the ladder (the fixing bolts remain) and was the first to reach him. Percy, with much of his scalp missing and broken limbs, was conscious, and 'not repeating the same swear words twice'.[43] He recovered and visited Worth Matravers on holiday many years later. The receiver was called in in 1931. Billy Winspit was left without a quarry. In the meantime David had obtained permission to quarry on the Encombe Estate at St. Aldhelm's Head.

It must have been obvious to Billy, as it had been to his father before him, that the quarry needed a lot of capital that he did not have. Mr. David offered a possible solution, but when his company failed William was left without a quarry or a job. David lamented: 'Bower, you have ruined me'. So he obviously attached blame to Billy. He did not employ him in his subsequent attempt to open up the three St. Aldhelm's Head quarrs on the Encombe Estate. My father remarked that men at the time were surprised that, after the Worth and Bankes Estate experiences, Sir Ernest Scott gave David permission, especially as no local quarrymen had been allowed there since the building of Kingston church. These quarries also failed after a few years. My father took Billy on as foreman. By the early 1950s he was semi-retired, but he continued to dress the tools in the blacksmith's shop. One day, it being bitterly cold, which is less than ideal for such work, he turned up. Father said he did not know what there was to do on such a day, and Billy walked back home, never to return. Some years later I got him to dress our tools again, carrying them after work to his cottage, where he maintained a forge and sometimes spent time carving stone, particularly cats. He and his wife were always welcoming, and a cup of tea off the range, laced with whisky on a cold winter's evening, was a fortification for the rest of the walk to Langton. In enquiring about the merits and demerits of various cliff quarries, he said with regards to all of them: 'You just as well go out to edge of clift and start chucking your money over'. I regret not persuading him to walk to Seacombe to look at it with him. He once pointed out a particularly large tipped block at Halsewell, on which he said some survivors of the wreck had gathered.

At the seaward entrance to the underground, now partially blocked by falls, there are seatings cut to accommodate a heavy horizontal timber. This was to give support for the underground type of crane which had been installed in the open by the Dorset Quarry Co. This was at the same time when several derrick cranes of a more advanced sort than the old gibbet, both hand and steam driven, were also set up in the open. Close by, a series of initials with MAR 23 1923, are clearly from men working there. Amongst the quarry names, W. J. B. is obviously William Jeremiah Bower, who had inherited the quarry and come to an arrangement with Mr. David's new company the year before. The others are not so immediately obvious. They are J.S., W.C.W., A.C., A.F.R., E.W.B., F.W. and, to the right, F.W., T.S. and possibly A.D. Billy's older half brother, Ambrose junior, worked several inland quarries around Acton, but not Seacombe, it seems.

Other Seacombe graffiti are not related to the quarry. To the west FRED 1.7.1.6 STEF, EDDY, LES, BANGER, STEW, PETER, are probably troops of the 1939-45 war. Outside the quarry, on the valley floor, brick footings remain from a wartime building. The soldiers had their cookhouse in the underground entrance. One, on washing up detail, in throwing the dirty water away over the cliff, let his billy can fall. The sergeant told him to go and retrieve it. He was never seen again.[44]

As remarked, the original underground had only one mouth

Billy Winspit at home, 1950s, and his cottage in 1973, from estate agents' sale particulars.

at the seaward end. It ran northwards parallel with the valley, perhaps nearly as far as it goes now. Obviously there was a chronological progression, but this first configuration has been much altered by the 1920s Dorset Quarry Co. episode, when they had gangs breaking down from the surface along the flank of the valley and others at various points underground driving westwards into the hillside. The underground area so left is now wider and open on the valley side in many places, when before it was narrow and enclosed, and therefore dark. There

CLIFF STONE / 137

Seacombe quarry, 1920s. Block being squared up prior to dispatch to Wareham. L-R, Billy Winspit, Jack Corben, Buff Bower.

are many superb examples of pits, some not even set off. One wonders why they were never split, having done all that work. There is much evidence of the use of drills at the Underpicking Cap level, and judging by the extent of radiating shattering from some such drill holes, the setting of big charges. It is probably safe to say the big charges are all Dorset Quarry Co., whilst the smaller may be earlier. It is perhaps significant that at the entrance the Underpicking Cap exhibits pit rather than drill marks, which may tell of a pre-explosive date. There are at least seven round ceiling holes, each with an associated Lewis slot, which tell of crane positions but not the number of cranes. These are all from the Dorset Quarry Co. period rather than earlier. At least one of these holes was made by first drilling a cluster of small holes before tidying up the resultant cusps with a punch. It is not an easy job forcing a hand-held pneumatic drill into a roof over one's head. Nor indeed was the cutting of the Lewis hole close by, which was necessary to get a fix, in order to pull the crane up into position. These cranes could pull a loosened block across the quarry floor some distance before lifting it clear to a sufficient height to get it onto a cart.

A clue to how these cranes could pull over quite long distances is provided. To the south-southwest of a pillar marked 'No1 Works' in tar, there is a crane position. In the opposite direction the corner of a pillar has striations sawn by the crane wire or chain rubbing hard against it. About thirteen yards north of the tarred pillar there is another crane position. In a nearby leg there is a Lewis hole which would have supported a pulley block which would have allowed for a change in direction of pull. This could relate to the external cranes mounted close by above as much as to the internal arrangement, for the blocks were taken out into the open and lifted away by the big steam cranes. Outside, where the Under Freestone has been left in situ to the east, another Lewis slot remains cut in a vertical face. Near the double Lewis hole crane position there is an extraordinary, enigmatic leg. It consists of a single lump of *in situ* Underpicking Cap resting on several small, built up blocks. How can this be, when the normal way of working was first to cut or blast away the Underpicking Cap before then lifting the Freestone?

Another leg close by has E.R., F.G AUG 21 1908 and J.T. cut with a punch: it is unlikely that these are quarrymen's names. A few years after that time my father's older brother Albert found where Ambrose had hidden his gunpowder up on a dry ledge. Albert and his mate, an apprentice plumber, pinched some, put it in two iron water pipes and set them off one night up on Peveril Downs. The bangs mustered the lifeboat crew. Grandfather was secretary of the Swanage R.N.L.I. at the time. It was not well received.

All the dirt now on the quarry floor was brought in by cows over a period of fifty years or so from when the quarry was abandoned, until it was fenced off after its acquisition by the National Trust in 1981. The sudden collapse of, and abandonment by the Dorset Quarry Co. left the quarry choked with hard core. Much of this was cleared away for military purposes during the 1939-45 war. Charles Burt supervised the loading of American lorries by hand, some being driven in underground. The other Dorset Quarry Co. operation at Crack Lane was also taken on by Burts, who used it as a storage yard and waste dump, as much as a source of stone. With several others, Mr. Bankes owned shares in the company. He had 4,400 against Billy Winspit's 200.

As a result of this close, indeed unique, interest in one of his quarries, the Bankes Estate papers include a lot of related documents. In a letter of July, 1924 William David optimistically said: 'We have an unlimited supply of the same stone (Portland) but on the mainland'.[45.] He mentions the Poole Harbour contract for 60,000 tons of waste over two years. Not all of this low grade rock went all the way by sea. When the weather was too bad for loading at Seacombe, some was taken by steam lorry to Norden, where it was transferred to the clay railway that ran to Goathorn Pier. From there a lighter took it out through the harbour mouth to its destination, the Training Bank. David reported to the same prospective investor that he foresaw an output of 10,000 to 20,000 tons *per annum* and the purchase of £10,000 of machinery, especially steam or electric cranes. He did install one of those at his other Purbeck quarry at Crack Lane, Langton, where the remaining conical waste pile is testament to the one and only electrically driven derrick set up in Purbeck. He also anticipated the setting up of a modern stone mill for another £10,000, with a second mill in London. In fact, the next year a mill was installed by Wareham station, and a big crane for handling block only, at Swanage station; also a loading ramp for the lorries to tip directly into trucks. The Ferry road must have been a tonic, absorbing 14,000 tons of small waste during the building process; the Swanage to Corfe road took another 6,000 tons. This helped to uncover block which was then cut up in the Wareham yard for several masonry projects. However the finances were not good. In 1926 David was pleading for more investment. Walter Bryant, a Bristol quarry operator, joined the board, and David went the following year. The receivers were called in, failed to dispose of the Dorset Quarry Co. as a business, and handed back the property to the estate in 1932. A list of equipment left lying about was drawn up. It included a fifteen ton steam crane at what the receivers called the north borehole; a 3 ton crane with two scoops (skips) at the loading yard near the above; a skip at the west borehole with trolley rails; a 75 horse power engine with two air compressors; blacksmith's anvil, block, saw, sheds, tanks, trolley rails in the open quarry; four hand cranes underground with trolleys and rails; a three ton hand crane, a 5 ton steam crane with trolley, and more scoops and a set of dogs with chain (lifting nips) at the eastern end. One of the timbers of the hand crane was bought by Hilda Spencer Watson, who used it in the roof of her new workshop at Dunshay, where it remains. The Estate entered into correspondence with Dr. C. Ruzicka, who had married Billy Winspit's sister, but his attempt to form a consortium to buy the quarry broke down and nothing came of it.

During 1929-30 Haysom and Sons supplied a mix of Purbeck for St. Francis, Charminster Road, Bournemouth, prepared in their Kings Road Depot. Some of the more demanding elements, like the carved tympanum, are Portland. However two altars look like Seacombe Freestone, for they exhibit typical serpulid worms, stylite, etc. and are certainly not Portland. One 10 ft by 3 ft 2 inches is particularly splendid. It is the maximum length their frame saw could have cut. I guess they must have bought the block from the Dorset Quarry Co. My father did not especially mention these stones, and I did not see them before he had died. However, he did talk of the architect Harold Gibbon's Arts and Crafts approach, and that Harry Tomes assisted the tympanum carver, Mr. Fraser.

HALSEWELL

The Worth Estate papers in the Rempstone collection include:

Wareham 5 July 1786
'Dear Sir, Titus Chinchen has applied for leave to open a quarry in the cliff on the east part of Windsprit quarry, where he thinks and hopes he shall be able to make and vend a large quantity of stone, Pray may he have liberty or not?
I am Dear Sir
Your most obediant servant
Thomas Bartlet.'

This could refer to East Winspit or, more probably, the separate quarry to the east that has become known as 'Halsewell' from the wreck of the East Indiaman of that name that occurred earlier that very same year. By the late 1800s James A. Brown was in possession. He suffered an accident there whilst trying to blow up rocks at the foot of the cliff to improve the loading. He had drilled a hole and set a charge of gunpowder, lit the fuse and rowed away in a dinghy. It failed to go off, and as the hour was late and the tide rising, he left it until next day. On returning, he was reaming out the hole with a drill in order to set a second charge when the first went off, blinding him in one eye.

As with other cliff quarries, over time the unstable upper face has fallen to the floor, obscuring it and tending to block off the underground. The gibbet position has possibly gone.

Halsewell quarry. Sailing vessels engraved within quarry. 'AB' may be Albert Brown. The smaller vessel is a sloop.

Exceptionally violent storms during February 2014 caused the fall of a pair of big boulders into the water at the base of the cliff. They lie at a similarly-inclined angle to the sea as another big one not far away on which desperate survivors from the wreck of the *Halsewell* clambered in 1786. Remaining at the quarry are a few lengths of finished broached kerbing and chiselled gutter sole.

WINSPIT

Reference to Winspit occurs in an early license agreed with a mysterious Benjamin Bersone; it tells of a pre-existing quarry, and that agreements were being entered into that were time-limited, and therefore, it seems to me, in breach of Article 1 in the 1651 agreement (see 'Trade Organisations'). Note the different spellings on the same document:

'Lease for 7 years from 25th March 1719 of Winsprit.
Having taken a lease of Robert Pikes Esq. of a Certain Quarry called Winchpitt Quarry, and the Cliffs thereto adjoining for seven years from 25th March 1719. I do hereby Bind and Engage myself any Excutor Adminiss and Assignes in case I do not perform the Covenant of the said lease for the space of 3 years from the Date thereof to pay unto the said Robert Pikes the full sum of Ten Pounds.
Written by hand and sealed.
Benjamin Bersone
Witnessed by Henry and Abraham Paulet.' [46.]

A Henry Paulet also witnessed the death of James Meader of Herston in 1760, run over by a wagon drawn by six horses. This may not have been a stone wagon, and had an exceptional number of horses, but the other witness was stone merchant Thomas Pushman.[47.]

In 1759 Thomas Dowland was drowned in a small boat 'By accident overset' when with two others in a 'creek or bay of the sea in Worth Matravers. The sworn witnesses included Will and Titus Chenchen, both independently supplying the big

140 / PURBECK STONE

OPPOSITE PAGE South part of Worth Matravers Manor estate survey, by Samuel Donne, 1772. Several quarries are marked: those at top right are in the area of the present Abbascombe cottages, while others can be seen around Winspit. (Dorset History Centre D/RWR/E16.14)

Ramsgate harbour project at the time. The other 'good and lawful men of Worth and Langton' who also sign the inquisition are John Cox, James Turner, Sam Bower, Sam Phippard, Robert Bower and Rose-Smith. Thomas Vye, Tucker Bower and Peter Bower made their marks rather than signed. So it seems about three quarters of them could at least write their names. Most, but not all, were quarrymen; Rose-Smith, for example, was a blacksmith. Little did they know, but two of them were to meet a similar fate six years later. In October 1765 the Worth church registers record death by drowning of three men at Winspit. They were all related: Sam Phippard, Tim Phippard and Sam Bower. It must be a reasonable suspicion that both accidents occurred during the loading of stone.

Winspit remained a notoriously difficult place, at least on the west side. Sam Bower had married May Lander four years before, Samuel Phippard married Jane Bower just two years earlier, both at Langton. It seems they were probably young men in their twenties. I suspect these tragedies tell of the dilemmas faced by men all along the cliffs. In a gale there was no question of loading a boat; in a calm it was a fairly easy procedure, but what of all those in between days? The vessel had arrived, her master was under pressure not to lose a day, you needed the money . . .

In 1771 the manor of Worth was sold. A controversy arose about the ownership of stone being dug at Winspit. Were royalties due to the outgoing Pike or the new owner, John Calcraft?

Rempstone Hall 10 June 1771
My Dear Sir

Notwithstanding Mr. Pykes promis to produce me all the grants he hase made or agreed to make, in a few days from our last meetings, he hase not as yet produced them, neither will he com near where I am. I called at his house this morning but he is not to be found, his wife says that she hase some reason to think he is intended to set of for London within a day of two in order to compleat the sale of the estate with Mr Calcraft and I know he is very closely prest for money which he must pay or keep out of the way for the present. I shall be glad you will give me a hint of the time you think Mr Calcraft is to enter on the manor of Worth, on account there is some dispute amongst the people who are now shipping off stones from the quarry. The afaire is that they have agreed sale of stone ready to go to Ramsgate peare and a vesel or two were ordered to load it off and attended acordingly but after taking in part of their loading the master was deluded by people of other quarries to refuse taking in their stone, and remove to other quarries to finish their loading, by which both the lord and the workmen are suferers and will both loose many pounds by not getting rid of the stone in order to make room to work more, and which is not custom to be done.
Now in this affair if the profits of the stone belong to Mr Calcraft its right for me to Demand the stone to be taken away in proper time but if Mr Pykes is to have the profits, then for me to say nothing for the present. I apprehend if the cleft quarreys are not hindered they will bring in more this summer than they have for several years past. I doubt not but you will understand me in the above.
I am Dear Sir Your Humble Svt,
Bishop.'[48]

Returns for stone dug on the Manor of Worth exist for most of the years between 1780 and 1828. They only list names, without locations, and the main output was paving. These are clearly the paviour quarries that appear on the survey of Worth manor commissioned by Squire Calcraft in 1772, clustered around Gallows Gore, together with two just south of the Worth road, near Abbascombe, and one out on Long Ledge, East Man. The same map shows quarries of Freestone at both West and East Winspit and, remarkably, further up Winspit Bottom at Rope Lake and at the corner now occupied by the waterworks, all worked in the Portland beds. To claim, as has been written in a local guidebook, that the waterworks quarry supplied rubble stone for the local cottages in Worth is nonsense; there were closer quarries at the top of the hill.

The 1780-81 accounts include Thomas Bower, then certainly working two quarries, one of them at cliff producing the block and cornice etc., the other inland, producing only paving.

In the same year Joseph Chinchen, who was also active at Hedbury and Seacombe, produced from Winspit 38 tons for Portsmouth, 40 tons backing (rough hardcore also probably for Portsmouth) and three tons of Ramsgate block as well as paving. There is a clear pattern with these Cliff stone quarriers: they were working inland quarries in tandem.

Worth records, full of detail, continue. Between Lady Day 1789, and Lady Day 1790, they show Sam Keats, Thomas Bower, George Butler, Samuel Lander, Robert Squibb, and John Bower's son all working inland paving quarries, whilst Joseph Chinchen, William Bower junior, William Bower and sons and William Brown were active in the cliff. William Cole was owing his dues, also from a cliff quarry it seems, for he appeared back on the lists working one two years later. They were making Front for Ramsgate, London and Portsmouth, paying the estate 6d per ton royalty. It is perhaps surprising that squared walling such as this was not sold by a face measurement rather than by weight, but to have done so would not have allowed for wide variations in depth on bed which that sort of construction called for. The temptation would have been not to include deeper bonders if you were not getting any more money for them by doing so. It is surprising to read of some of the backing being 'scappled', which tells of a degree of dressing. This attracted royalty of 3d per ton, the rough only 2d.

Some entries at that same rate are for 'front ashlar', which probably means the same thing as Front, but 'ashlar' alone is clearly something different, for they sold it by the foot paying 2s per 50 foot to the estate rather than by weight measurement. There are of course degrees of refinement in masonry. Harbour work is quite rough with the face left off the punch and the joints not particularly neat, whilst some contemporary Portland ashlar, such as the Shire Hall, Dorchester (1797), is so accurately worked that a knife can scarcely be slipped between the joints. Margate and Ramsgate harbour work consists almost entirely of the tough coarse beds, Spangle and Blue Bits, some definitely of East Winspit Blue Bit, for it is distinctive and sold by the ton, whereas the 150 ft. of ashlar sent out by Joseph Chinchen in 1789/90 was almost certainly of Freestone, and surely more finely dressed.

The scale of the Ramsgate job can hardly be exaggerated. Between 1760 and 1767 the lion's share of the work was going to James, William and Titus Chinchen, all in receipt of separate stage payments, usually of £100 lots. In 1765-6 they sent 12,324 tons, next year 14,578 tons. As well as inland quarries they were operating parts at least of Winspit, Seacombe and Hedbury, and possibly more on the cliff on estates where records do not survive. Titus Chinchen built the earliest part of Arundel Terrace, Langton, which has beautifully cut dressings of Cliff stone. These could be from Winspit, or possibly Hedbury, which he also held.

Rollers were sometimes measured by the foot, more often by weight, which begs the question of whether the quarriers resorted to Pythagoras! In 1790 William Brown sent off 181 foot of garden rollers from East Winspit, paying 11d. They were obviously fairly small, one such in my possession is two feet long, about 12 inches in diameter. Farm rollers, on the other hand, were much bigger. One of East Winspit Blue bit, once belonging to Eastington Farm and now serving as a seat outside Langton Martravers Museum, is over 6 feet long. Another survivor just like it in Langton is about 7 feet long, with a girth of 20 inches. In 1793 William dispatched one ton of 6 foot roller, the agricultural sort, paying 1s 3d royalty to the squire. The inclusion of a six foot length specification is unusual, but perhaps provides a clue that it was a minimum agricultural requirement and that all the roller per ton entries tell of such large stones.

Block value varies according to size. A letter of 1718 describes the system then operating in Portland, where they applied no less than seven different rates per ton. At the cheap, small end of the scale was 'casual block and Ashlen stone, 5/s per ton, 6/s 2d per tun for 3 tun stone' at the other '7 or 8 tun stone 14/s 2d per tun'. The big stuff was worth almost three times the small.[49.] Purbeck had fewer categories, cutting off at a much lower weight. Even if the quarries did produce the occasional big block, they were forced to cut it up in order to handle it. No cliff quarry gibbet was capable of handling the big weights such as at the top of the Portland scale, nor could they have hoisted them out of the boats and into the vessels. We are left guessing the size of the biggest stones they could manage.

Clearly the entries reveal a distinction being made between ashlar block and block, but it is not always easy to know what is meant. The term 'block' could also refer to small stuff, even indeed to a category of smaller stone than ashlar block. Thomas Bower was clearly dividing his time between an inland paving quarry and another, almost certainly in the cliff, where he dug a small amount of block which was attracting a low royalty value, 3d. per ton, no more than backing. William Corbin was producing the same relatively small amount of low value stone and it seems nothing else.

The big players, Joseph Chinchen, William Brown and William Bower were also producing items more often associated with the inland quarries, step and channel. They were of course opportunists. If a stone leant itself to a particular application they made the most of it. As a result of that sort of approach one can even sometimes find examples of cliff stone paving, but it is rare. The lion's share of their work consisted of harbour wall plus staddles and hollow work, some of which may have gone in a semi-dressed state, as a letter written by Nat and James Chinchen to do with supply of stone for a prison a few years before illustrates:

'To James Paine, Architect, respecting the stonework
Swanage 29th March, 1787
Sir,
We have favor of the 23rd Inst. Concerning the New Bridewell for the County of Middlesex and should be happy to supply you with what Stone may be wanted for that Building provided it does not exceed our Scantlings. The shafts of the Piers we cannot get in one stone our Blocks seldom running large enough, and as to the Cornices and other fine mouldings would by no means recommend you to have workd here being attended with many disadvantages, not only in the danger of breaking the edges &c. but we are of opinion the mouldings could be run cheaper in London, our people here not being much accustomed to any but plain work; we can work it to the size and cut it to the Angles so that you will have nothing to do but run the mouldings, which is the usual manner of sending it from here all the other Articles we can send compleat for seting delivered in the River Thames for the following prices.

Purbeck Portland Stone in Facias Plinths Chain   s. d
Bondstones Imposts & Aubes per foot Cube   1 .. 9½
Landings at per foot Supl. toold on one side   2 .. 0
Cornices at per foot Cube wrought as
mentioned above   1 ..10
Blocking Course at per foot Superficial   1 .. 3

We hope what we have said will meet your approbation but should any further information be wanting beg you will give us a line as one of us shall be in Town when we will take the liberty of waiting on you.
    We are Sir with respects
    Your most obedient Servts
    Nat & Jas. Chinchen'[50.]

Another informative entry in the Calcraft Worth Estate papers is that of William Brown, making 202 ft of headstones in 1792. Those must have been hand sawn!

Royalty payments for Winspit continue for the first quarter of the 19th century, but sadly do not include details of output.

Record of Worth estate stone dues 1792 showing William Brown's 'Head Stones'. (Dorset History Centre, Calcraft papers, D/RWR E11.1)

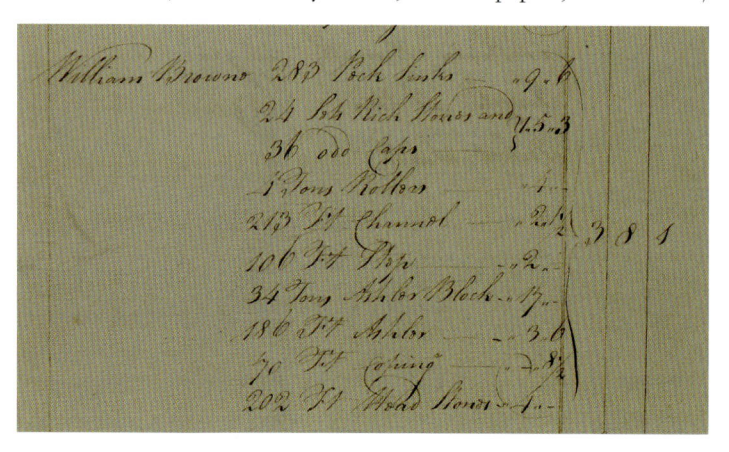

In 1825 a new category of payment, Winspit boat money, began. It informs of stone being dispatched from there by more men than just those working the cliff close by, and that they were using the squire's boat. Those not paying for the boat but only for stone include John Corben. The John Corbens, father and son, built the row of cottages at Gallows Gore on the Turnpike road, and worked the quarry on the opposite side of the road; John Corben Junior's wife Ann's name is retained in the field name. The Corbens surely sent their stone to Swanage by the Turnpike road.

Other quarriers working the Worth Estate and only paying for stone include James Thicks, Sam and William Bower and John Lander, which must locate their quarries away from the immediate coast. Those certainly operating Winspit include the William Browns Senior and Junior, who have the biggest annual output of any Worth Estate quarry, paying £11, plus £1 19 2d boat money. Next came F. Bowland – a name that only crops up once and is surely an error: Dowland is meant, working partner with Sam Dowland, who paid £10 6s 4d plus 5s 10d boat money. This is proportionately a significantly small amount of boat money, which suggests the quarriers were dispatching some stone by road, some by sea. This points to a quarry location at a finely balanced distance from Winspit; perhaps under and/or east of where Abbascombe cottages have been built. Uncle and nephew James and Charles Chinchen were certainly working Winspit but not paying boat dues, no doubt because they had their own boat, which they kept at Hedbury. This could be true of others who were not obviously shipping away stone at all according to the estate boat receipts, but in fact were doing so by using other peoples' boats. Perhaps this is what Robert Barnes was doing too, though we have no direct evidence of him at Winspit; however George of that family held part of West Winspit later.

Nearing the end of his apprenticeship around 1830, the autobiographer James Corben spent a few months working at Winspit. In part at least it was to do with the building of a Baptist chapel in Langton, the date stone of which is of Cliff stone, and is now in the parish museum. James records that sometimes his uncle John left him working alone, which surely provided a respite from a harsh taskmaster, but brought another difficulty. The local boys picked on him, so he had to fight them. Being born in Portsmouth made him, in their eyes, an outsider, even though all his close relations were of Purbeck quarry stock, including his aunt who was born Elizabeth Chinchen. Other than the date stone, little else of the former chapel, No. 30 High Street, is from the cliff, which conforms with the way other chapels were done near that time. Both Langton's and Worth's Wesleyan chapels are built of other beds, but with Cliff date stones. What is now the Langton Village Hall has its date stone, 1845, with extra fiddly bits: the ventilator, cherub, and probably the gable cross, also of Cliff stone. James's stint at Winspit was surely under the Chinchen banner so to speak, but by about this time the family seemed to drop out of cliff quarry operation.

The west side had been occupied by George Barnes, but he was gone by 1883, for in that year it was let to brothers Charles and George Edmunds of Langton. This date is somewhat odd

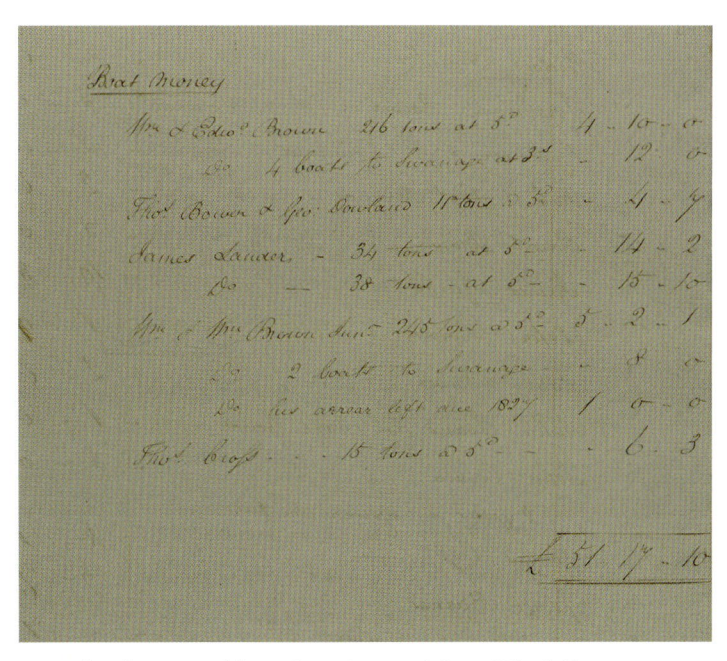

Records of stone and boat dues, (1827-8) from Worth Estate. (Dorset History Centre, Calcraft papers, D/RWR E12.1)

in that my father said the Edmunds had supplied the stone for the Uplyme job from their Hedbury and Winspit quarries, but it was finished before 1883. Perhaps they had had some arrangement with Barnes. An earlier generation of Barnes had married into the Chinchen family. It seems likely that the Chinchens had held the west side as at one time they certainly had the east. During the 18th century they were working Hedbury, Seacombe and Winspit and possibly other quarries. By the end of that century the Browns held the east side, while John Turner held the quarry called Port Arthur at the end of the cottage garden, now screened off with iron grilles to protect hibernating bats.

The Edmunds did little after the Uplyme job, which was finished by 1878. The biggest merchants in Swanage, Burt and Burt, who were buying cliff stone block about this time from Ambrose Bower at Seacombe and who had had a go at Dancing Ledge, became involved; Jack Edmunds relinquished his interest. After the 1914–18 war company promoter William David appeared on the Purbeck scene and became involved with Burt and Burt, by this time managed by Ernest Burt. Under the name of the Purbeck Stone Co., they made improvements to the road, in particular at 'the bridge' which is where the road crosses the Rope Lake hollow. A sale brochure of 1919 for Worth Matravers which includes Weston Farm in whose lands West Winspit quarry lay, refers to this road improvement as being beneficial for the quarry royalties which might accrue to the potential purchaser of the lot. The royalty rate for the stone was 4d per ton.[51.] Burt and Burt became the Purbeck Stone and General Trading Company and David took over control of the quarry. He mounted a big crane up in the field above the west side. The workforce included Billy Winspit, Levi Bower, Charles (Sheffy) Harris and John Ivamy Bower: these last two were relatives, who more often worked at their own quarry in Burngate. They widened the seaward open side at West Winspit and did a small amount underground towards the west end.

1930s L-R: Michael Bower, Jesse Lander, Billy Winspit Bower, Fred 'Darky' Bonfield, Buff Bower. Possibly at East Winspit, or more likely St. Aldhelm's Head.

Some block was taken to Swanage. It was used for the panels in the War Memorial and for 2, Sanctuary Chambers, Great Smith St., London. Arthur Collins, manager of P.S.G.T.C in 1924, cites this job in a Dorset Quarry Co. prospectus as an endorsement of how good Purbeck Portland is and how difficult it is to distinguish from Portland. Part of this London façade remains, including a long lintel enriched with sunk tracery panels. It was long enough for Arthur Harding, assisted by my father, to work on it at the same time. Looking at it now I wonder which one did which end.[52.]

I am not sure quite how it 'fits in' but before the war Arthur Collins' father Billy had supplied the Walter Bankes (1904) memorial cross at Pamphill. Collins' yard was off Kings Road, Swanage. Perhaps he temporarily employed men to obtain such 'one-off' stones at the west side of Winspit, which his son certainly made a claim on later, or perhaps he got the block from the Turners or Browns to the east. Samuel Tomes worked the cross before Mr. Shepherd executed the carving: he also carved the Clifton arcade in Swanage High Street near the library. It seems odd that the Seacombe-owning squire is commemorated in stone dug on a neighbouring estate, but we perhaps should not be surprised. Barry's 1835-46 alterations of Kingston Lacy Hall include Portland Whitbed, not stone from Bankes's own cliff quarries. As far as I can see, just a few paving stones in what is now the gift shop are the only pre-20th century pieces of Cliff stone at Kingston Lacy. Since acquisition by the Trust, St. Aldhelm's quarry made turned Freestone balusters, now painted.

The Bere Regis war memorial cross is another of West Winspit Freestone, but not the die which grandfather had to go to Portland for because of its size. He chose a block from Shepherd's Dinner Quarry. My father cut the names. Two men died of wounds after the cross had been fixed, necessitating additions. Father took the train to Wareham, rode his bicycle to Bere Regis, cut the additional names *in situ*, then went home the same way. The Briantspuddle war memorial cross is another from Winspit. It was worked in Kingston-on-Thames, before Eric Gill carved the figures at Ditchling, Sussex.[53.] The shafts are not Purbeck but Petworth Marble, surely explained by Gill living near there. The Second World War names were carved by Walter Haysom, and possibly the First World War names too. Eventually West Winspit was left dormant. It was not until another war started that it was reactivated.

Sometime in the late 1800s Albert Brown revived East Winspit, between Folly Corner and Port Arthur, for a consortium of London Masonry Companies. They were listed as the Purbeck Portland Stone Company Ltd. [as an alternative to Portland] at Tothill St., Westminster, in the Mines Inspectorate report of 1908. Hubert Lander and others worked for Brown there for a short while, but little was done. Some while later, another of the family, Walter Brown, by this time working as a mason in London, tried to keep his claim on the quarr, but encountered difficulties with the new landowner, Mr Strange. In about 1932 my father, with Brown's agreement, reopened the east part between Folly Corner and Church. This was when the photographs were taken of William Bower (Billy Winspit), Michael Bower and Jesse Lander, that appear in the original version of Eric Benfield's *Purbeck Shop*. One of these shows Jesse cleaving a block. There is an amusing account relating to Michael: walking up Langton High Street, somewhat the worse for drink, he encountered the Rector. 'Drunk again, Michael?'

West Winspit quarry, external buildings. Main building, frame saw; note water tank mounted above the saw.

'Ah, an' zu be I' he responded.[54.]

During these inter-war years not much was done at the quarry face, for the men were mostly going through the founder that blocked the part of the quarry called Church. However there are pit marks that yet retain a rusty mark from wedges being driven, which must be their work. I regret never looking at it with my father. A demand for broken rock arose with the threat of war. Hard core was sent to Blandford Camp and Stoney Cross airfield in the New Forest. Jews escaping from Germany and Austria were being directed by the government to assist the military effort, and some came to work at Winspit. One, unable to speak English, was known simply as 'Vienna', from his home.

With the wartime emergency, Robert Harris reopened the west side. His men cleared away tons and tons of foundered waste that choked the old quarry, much of it going to Blandford Camp. There was a shortage of lorries, but when the Americans arrived this changed. One morning the queue of vehicles for loading by hand stretched from the quarry 'half way back to Worth'.[55.] During the war, my father decided to give up on East Winspit and concentrate at St. Aldhelm's Head.

The old West Winspit quarry was somewhat similar to Seacombe in that it followed close along the cliff to the west and close to the valley to the north, the focus being the narrow entrance in the southeast corner which led out to the gibbet position. A few blocks built up on the quarry edge show where this was. Below on the sea-washed ledge trackways lead away

West Winspit quarry, aerial view. The last founder (top left) Road out to gibbet position bottom right of centre. Machine sheds and blacksmith's shop and ramps all from Bob Harris's Purbeck Quarry Co. post Second World War.

from it out to gibbet positions at the water's edge, variously used according to tide. The main western quarry was modified by Bob Harris during the course of his fifteen years or so of occupation, but one wonders by how much. The extension to the north, close by the valley where what remains of the underground is sagging, is in the main earlier, but as well as pit marks there are plug and feather drill holes which are certainly his work. The hanging underground cut in at the Pond Freestone and Spangle level is curious. Presumably it was driven in at an early date straight from the hill side. Later they ran underneath in the Under Freestone, collapsing and obliterating what was overhead, including most but not all of this working. How early was the commencement of this sequence? At least 17th century, I guess. The 'normal' way of advance at the Bottom Freestone level is to penetrate by first loosening the Under Picking Cap with gunpowder before then lifting the block. They did something different here. Billy Winspit said that they cut their way in using wedges only. Bob Harris broke a second entrance in further north and, after the war, cut away part of the quarry floor to facilitate loading crushed stone. This cutting bisects the narrow cliff edge track, which would have formerly been used to bring stone from the west end around

Winspit quarry. Press photo of Bishop's visit, July 1950. L-R: The Rural Dean, Sam Dowland, Jack Corben, in front of the Rector of Worth? Flinger Bower, Nelson Burt, Alfred Meader,? Wright, 'Taffy' Davis,? Burt, Fred Wellman, the Bishop, Robert Harris, Clergy?, Jimmy Ivamy Bower, *Western Gazette* journalist?Brown.

to the gibbet. Bob, trading as the Purbeck Quarry Co., opened up the quarry with surface cranes and pushed underground, leaving the spacious chamber we now see where he used a Bath type underground crane, perhaps one from Seacombe. The crane could rotate through 360° and pull a loosened block towards it before lifting it clear of the floor sufficiently to get it onto a cart. This ran on rails out to the crane that stood in the open and which served the various machines in the sheds that yet remain. He installed a sand frame saw, a circular saw and blacksmith's shop. The mason's shop was against the east side, with the explosives magazine on the bank above.

Work done by Bob using Winspit stone remains in the coping of the new Wool road bridge, dressings at Days Home, Swanage, and Studland church hall. The list also includes the Langton war memorial, the stone being given by Bob and lettered by Harry Burt of Vokes and Beck of Winchester, a firm Bob supplied with monumental slabs. Bob had other interests, including building and fishing, and he let the quarry run down, finally pulling out about 1957. A few years before this the Bishop of Salisbury, in a 'walkabout' of his diocese, visited Purbeck, and was photographed at Winspit with Bob Harris and the men working for him at that time.

Further to the west, when he left the quarry Bob blew out the supports, leaving a collapsed founder that is still there; the last one of many. In the underground immediately east of it a horizontal row of plug and feather holes has failed to split the block off in the desired way. In this part of the quarry they had blocks that glowed in the dark, an effect caused by some sort of bacteria. [56.]

Up the track, opposite the cottage, is an underground quarry. Billy Winspit called it the Fernery and said the stone was 'all to fritters'. The underground forms a blunt L shape, with the entrance at the bottom of the heel. It goes in about thirty yards with a lot of spalls left against the wall that lies in the direction of the main quarry. So they had no intention of working that way. The extension in the opposite direction, parallel with the valley to north, complies with the 'keep between the deep

and the shoal' maxim. The main western quarry was also left congested by spalls before wartime and the subsequent clearance there. The Fernery spalls contain bits of sink, broken in manufacture, as well as fine scars. Curiously there is not an obvious waste tip opposite this entrance. It would seem they took the waste some way towards the sea before getting rid of it into the stream defile. A few rock faced dubbers near the entrance look modern. They could tell of Billy Winspit making some beer money. Arthur Collins laid claim to this quarry in the 1920s, but did not pursue it, reaching an agreement instead to dig New Vein near Compact Farm.

Further inland a head of Shrimp and Earth Rock still shows at Rope Lake. It has been partly back filled, for bits of Pond Freestone lying about show that it had once been deeper. Samuel Donne's survey commissioned by John Calcraft shows this to have been dug before 1772, one wonders with what logic. Even if the Shrimp was made use of, for lime or the field walls perhaps, the cost of getting the Freestone would surely have been far greater than for the quarries driven into the cliffs not far away?

Port Arthur (the name was written up in tar and was perhaps a joke, applied at the time when Amos Bower lived rough there; Port Arthur was a notoriously harsh penal settlement in Australia) was last worked by John Turner of Worth, of the family who also kept the shop. Some of the stone of the rebuilt 'County bridge' by the Mowlem at Swanage in 1910 is from there. It was worked in Stevens' stone yard in Swanage, where my uncle Harold, as a school leaver, was shown how to do broach work by one of the older masons. The Turners shaped some of the headstones in Worth churchyard in a distinctive style. They are of Cliff stone, so certainly from Port Arthur, as also is the Palgrave cross on Church Hill, Swanage, worked by Samuel Tomes whilst he was employed by Billy Collins, Arthur's father.

According to the Mines Inspectorate, 'W. and J. Turner' were in occupation at Port Arthur in 1896, with two working underground and one above. William and John ceased working there sometime during or just after the First World War. Clearly the scale of working and the filling in of the stream bed by waste from here before Brannon's visit etc. all tell of substantial earlier work. A photo from the latter part of the 19th century shows it in operation. Rubble is thrown on either side of the entrance, right to the top. This is the clue that rather than drive in horizontally down at the Bottom Freestone level, they started clearing the overburden up on the hill slope above the point where it would be safe to commence driving underground when the unsupportable upper layers had been removed. That point in the hillside is where the rock is no longer peabodied as it is sufficiently large; therefore it can be used as a ceiling.

The workings at Port Arthur were pushed into the hill about 25 yards, with a small extension to the north and a much larger to the south. The stone from the southernmost part of the underground must surely have been taken out in the now-blocked seaward direction as lots of spalls, a configuration of built legs and even in one place the lower part of the Freestone left down, would have prohibited egress from the remaining entrance. The eastern wall of this remaining southern underground void consists of a collapsed mass including big blocks of Blue bit that have come down 25 feet or so. Within the chamber, towards the seaward end, big blocks of House Cap that would have formed the ceiling have dropped to the floor. Nearer the present entrance some have partially dropped before being caught up with legs. The spacing of these remedial supports would have precluded advance in that direction. They tell of attempts to keep the ceiling up whilst conversely the collapsed founder must surely be deliberate. It is difficult to see the logic and one wonders what was the sequence of work.

The cliff edge quarry, now open to the sky but originally worked by progressively undermining before foundering, was driven inland close by the valley as well as along the open cliff. Standing on the top of 'Turner's garden' the walled slope between the Port Arthur entrance and the sea, one is standing on the hidden chamber. It would seem the intention was to bring the whole mass down, but part stayed up, maintaining a void. Had they gone on and worked their way through the fallen mass as normal they would have in due course got back to the Bottom Freestone again, but for some reason they left it and broke in the present entrance further up the valley. Perhaps the logic was that to clear the founder and continue to push the quarry from the seaward end meant a lot of work unproductive of what they wanted most, the Bottom Freestone. Another possible explanation is that the two quarries were operated by rivals; that we see in these separate entrances the hundred foot rule in operation.

There is a common tendency for cliff quarry founders to be incomplete, leaving voids behind the collapsed stuff. West Hedbury remains like this. In West Winspit Bob Harris cleared away such a founder, reopening a chamber the bats had been managing to get into, for their droppings were so thick on the floor that Billy Winspit took them away by the wheelbarrow-full for his garden. Joe Guy lived in another dry part. He walled in a barrel lacking its bottom which served as his entrance. To the west of the founder the underground with its built legs is pre-Harris, as is the narrow cliff edge shelf that extends yet

Port Arthur quarry, East Winspit. Note spaced stones towards top right defining the coastguard coastal path.

further to the west. However, in the quest for hard core left in the old working, Bob's men worked in that area. Fred Wellman said that they backed the lorry along where it is so narrow that driver Darky (Fred) Bonfield could not get out of the cab without falling into the sea. A disadvantage in pushing this far west is that the configuration of the rock at the foot of the cliff makes loading difficult. In the days of sail, finished work ready for dispatch had to be taken east to where, marked still by built-up stones, a gibbet was mounted. Bob subsequently cut away part of this cliff edge route. At sea level beneath the gibbet, a two foot six inch to two foot nine inch span trackway, about the same gauge as Dancing Ledge, runs southwest across the sea-washed ledge, which is only fully exposed on low spring tides. Sinkings show where timbers spanned the wide joints. At the landward end the track apparently stops short by 40 feet or so of the quarry edge crane. It suggests that the carts could be manoeuvred over a fairly rough surface or that they chucked down a few scars to fill in some of the worst holes. Whilst working this far up the ledge such scars would have remained between gales. The gap certainly does not tell of the crane having a long reach, indeed I suspect they have cut in at the cliff foot to get the cart nice and close. In my opinion, whilst the gap at Dancing Ledge tells of retreat of the quarry edge, here it tells not of that but of manoeuvring the cart about without a prescribed path. The loading rock surfaces are different. Winspit is relatively flat limpet rock, whilst the Puffin bed surface at Dancing Ledge is more pillowy and uneven and was sometimes called Pricklebed.

To the east, another track leads out to a confusion of holes on the western side of the dock, although the king post hole is clear at 15 inches square. Like Dancing Ledge, a smaller cart with a gauge of only about 15 inches to 18 inches ran on the same line as the bigger, but its track veers. For a part it combines with the left hand, wider gauge, before changing to

CLIFF STONE / 147

Winspit. Early 20th century postcard of fishing boats drawn up. A gibbet combined with a capstan was formerly mounted on the shelf, centre top, where timber slots remain to this day.

the right, obviously in an attempt to avoid the worst holes. At the head of the dock a clear isosceles triangle of holes marks another crane position. This shows that they had low and high tide berths, the range being about six feet on springs, but the latter would be inoperable now as it has become choked with big boulders. The sea is bringing these across the ledge from falls occurring towards the southwest. When Billy kept his fishing boat here he resorted to blowing up such offending rocks with gunpowder. Perhaps that sort of thing was being done from an early date. What is odd is that there seems not to be a link between these gibbet positions and the trackways, nor the quarry edge crane position, the position of which is still shown by built up dressed blocks. The dock's rectangular form has prompted claims that it has been man-made. The probability that this is the case is increased by the fact that over at least 60 years or so it has become filled with boulders. Of possible relevance in this consideration is that Dancing Ledge swimming pool, now about 100 years old, has required four emptyings of boulders since the war.

To the southeast of what the bathers call Cheese Rock, a flat ledge about half way down has an interesting configuration of holes that suggest they could have alternatively combined a jenny or a capstan with the same gibbet. What is almost certainly a capstan position has a pair of holes for vertical supports plus braces plus a hole that must have held the bearing. Close by there appears to be scuffing from iron tyres, but a big loose block and a gap in the ledge now interrupt the capstan circle.

Continuing eastwards there are more gibbet positions on the quarry edge, which is loosening and becoming precarious. Below, more holes mark where the standard gibbets were temporarily set up near water level. One of these has a short trackway, now not easy to discern, that has a central section that slopes steeply seaward. Perhaps for this reason there are holes at the water's edge; I guess they put in posts as an insurance against the loaded cart taking charge and shooting over the edge. The eastern end of the quarry consists of a narrow shelf with small undergrounds driven in at almost regular intervals. To the west the shelf widens, but near the seaward edge small spaced patches of *in situ* Bottom Freestone are perhaps ghosts of a similar configuration that still remains to the east. They suggest an early narrow development altered in the west by later widening. One of these *in situ* patches was once higher and provided a fishing mark called the 'Cobbler' until blown up by the Americans. Part of this remains, with evidence in the form of fine scars and engraved sailing vessels, indicative of its once being a place where dressing was done.

The big heap of waste obstructing access to much of the face where the quarry is wide, suggests a final lateral progression rather than square attack in from the cliff. This relatively wide working ends at the east at Church where they were working in the 1930s, mostly clearing away discarded waste. Its structure is quite amazing, a single leg built on a mass that has collapsed down and northwards a few feet, holding up the Spangle and all else above.

Presumably this work at the Pond Freestone level was early. Fine scars around the leg, now perched in an apparently nonsensical place, are the result of final dressing going on there. The open underground was clearly being used as a shelter. Later, men driving in from the west undermined it at the Bottom bed level. They foundered it, but the Spangle held up. This was a benefit, for it was keeping up all the worthless Shrimp, which otherwise would have had to be shifted. Things looked precarious, hence construction of the leg. However this conjecture may be quite wrong. My father discussed this puzzle with Buff Bower, Jesse Lander *et al.* when they were working close by before the war. They all scratched their heads. One suggestion made was that the 'old hands' could have gone into the Under Freestone first and it sagged, which allowed for easier drawing of the Pond Freestone, but there is not much logic to it. Another puzzle is that if the Pond Freestone dig came first, how did they get it into a boat, for the cliff would have sloped outwards before the vertical drop to the water. This would have made it impossible to mount a crane, even if there had been clear water at the foot of the cliff, which there is not.

CRAB HOLE

This is a relatively small working at the Pond Freestone level only, on the east side of the cave of that name. Blocks of Puffin bed extending below lack any evidence of crane positions, which suggests quite a lot of quarry floor may have fallen away.

ST ALBAN'S OR ST ALDHELM'S HEAD

Perhaps because it is easier to pronounce, the 'D' in the name sometimes becomes 'B', a confusion that has gone on at least since the 16th century. A map of 1539 shows it as Sent Albanys, but John Leland, writing at the same time, uses St. Aldelmes; a letter of ten years later, referring to the quarrying of touchstone and alabaster to the west, refers to it as Sayntt Aldomis. Treswell, in 1586, used St. Aldams; Coker in the 1620s St. Aldene's; Isaac Taylor in 1765 St. Aldans; influentially the chart maker Mackenzie in 1787 uses St. Alban's, and so navigators and therefore the coastguards have since.[57] Most real locals use the 'B' variant or simply 'the Head', which from a Worth or even Langton perspective is hardly likely to cause confusion with anywhere else.

In the main, this quarry was worked at the Pond Freestone level only, the Bottom Freestone being thin and not worth taking. However, in some areas the next layer down, the Listy bed, has also been taken. The logic is hard to see, for it is thin, small, contains flints, and to get at it meant removal of the Flint proper. Why was it done? The quarry was worked in a narrow strip along the comparatively-loose cliff edge, to the west of the pillar known as Man's Head, which displays pit marks on its landward side. Opposite there is H T and J D, with '1736' carved twice, so this shelf had already been cut away by then. Amongst the names which appear on the Joint Stock Company's agreement of 1698 are two John Dollings and a John Dowland. Could this be one of them? Mostly the Pond Freestone is hidden by fallen Shrimp, or at this point concrete debris from the war time buildings. It is ironic that this wartime debris was pushed over the cliff by a German bulldozer driver. Karl sustained an injury that put him in the Channel Island garrison rather than the Eastern front with the rest of his unit, most of whom were killed.

Quarrying in Purbeck has been destructive of interesting archaeology, not only at the Head. Digging southeast of Letterbox Gate, Bob Harris came across lots of pottery, coal money and tesserae. He seemed to have a knack, for he found more pottery on the west side of Badgers Nap.[58] Bernard Calkin talked of skulls flying through the air when they blasted at Mutton Hole. At Sheepsleights, he showed me grain preserved by having been burnt in pits which were later destroyed by modern working. The find mentioned by Hutchins at the Head must have been one of the most remarkable: 'a little south of the chapel, on digging stone, was found a square hole ten feet deep, in which were many human bones.'[59]

William Burgess's survey map of Renscombe (1737), shows a 'stone pitt' at St. Aldhelm's Head.[60] Elizabethan Cliff stone items in Corfe are probably from this cliff top quarry; also mullion

Encombe House, Kingston. Matching St. Aldhelm's Head Pond Freestone pillars at south door, mid 18th century.

windows in several cottages, fireplace lintels in Mortons House, the castle, etc. This early working, is what we see remaining as the relatively narrow western half of the quarry. But the Victorians, and to a lesser extent William David, widened the eastern end which now contains the ruinous wartime buildings.

Similarities make it virtually certain that the stone for Encombe House, built between 1734 and 1770, was dug at the Head. The splendid pair of 8 ft 6 inch high pilasters that flank the south door display matching lists which tell of their having been cut from a single block. The lists show that prior to cutting one stone lay above the other within the raw block, which could hardly have been less than four tons in weight. At four to five feet in thickness, the Pond Freestone is more than sufficient for this. The 18th century external masonry of Encombe's southern elevation seems to be all Pond Freestone and tooled, except the pilasters, which are worked to an entasis and rubbed. Within the house the staircases are also mostly of Pond Freestone, but they include Spangle and Blue Bit as well, both also similar in character to material from St. Aldhelm's Head.[61] Spangle generally does not run to long lengths, but at this quarry the Blue Bit does. When wide enough such large stones take on a value as ledgers. A number of these of 18th century date and matching the Blue Bit steps are scattered across the South of England.

The Poor Account Book of Worth recorded in 1820: 'Paid James Squibb for going to St. Albuns to take an account of

Kingston Church. Pond Freestone capital on Marble pillar, 1873-80.

William Haskells stone 2/6d'. There were other regular payments to Haskell's children. Four years before there was a payment to T. Smith (blacksmith) for dressing Haskell's tools. Whatever William was doing, it may have been here or in what is now Haysoms. Quarry activity may have been at a low ebb, but other things were happening. In 1827 the Rector of Swanage, the Revd. Thomas Oldfeld Bartlett, noted in his journal for 20 September:

> 'A severe fight took place last night at 9 o'clock on St Alban's plain between the Swanage Preventive Men, eleven in number, and, it is supposed, more than one hundred smugglers. All the Preventive men were more or less hurt. Lt Holman lost some teeth as well as bruising about the face. It is thought that some of the smugglers must have been killed.'

Between 1873 and 1880 the Earl of Eldon built the new church at Kingston (*see page 11*). George Street, the architect, employed a foreman of masons, Mr. Elder, who was not a Purbeck man. Burr and Marble from Blashenwell were used; Marble for all the internal columns; Burr for the external work. However, inside, most of the demanding elements such as the capitals are Pond Freestone from the Head. The font is also of Pond Freestone, worked by Isaac Bower. It is a second attempt, the first having been rejected by Mr. Elder after several weeks' work. My father said of Elder that when he walked by the bankers each man would doff his cap. The font in the chapel at the Head is of a similar perfectionist stamp, dating from the same time.

There was a period of dormancy at the quarry after this. In about 1931, William David, emerging from the collapse of the Dorset Quarry Co. on the Bankes Estate, obtained permission from Sir Ernest Scott to reopen the quarry at the Head, the quarry at the top of Pier Bottom, now known as St. Aldhelm's quarry or Haysoms, and another southwest from Scripture Gate, now entirely filled in. Amongst others who worked at the Head for William David for about the eighteen months it lasted, were Jim and Jesse Lander, Bob Turner, Jack (nicknamed 'Rippy') Norman, Bertie Sheppard and Thomas Bonfield, who walked daily from Gully. Bertie was one of the Bath contingent who had moved to Purbeck with David. Billy Winspit Bower was notably absent. The group had a wooden hand derrick crane, and dug off the Shrimp, the Blue Bit and Spangle, tipping all of it over the cliff, in order to get the Pond Freestone underneath. They made, or at least added to, the tip on the cliff top to the southeast and part of the tip that smothers the west end of Ringbum Gardens.

The tips to the west are older and are interesting in that only here at the Head, due to the natural undercliff, do such tips remain. They are time capsules with the earliest work now deeply buried. At all the other cliff quarries this waste went into the sea. David's waste Spangles can be distinguished by nip holes which show that they were lifted by crane. They would loosen the block with wedges and bars, then get a nip attached to the crane under it and heave it up. It was in this way that Percy Wallace lost two fingers. They had one end of a block heaved up a few inches as Percy was passing. 'Chuck a spall under it'. Percy mis-threw one, tried to retrieve it as at that moment the nip let go and the block dropped. Percy wrapped the stumps in a rag, walked into Worth alone and took the next bus to the Swanage surgery. After some weeks he went back to work; they had set charges but failed to count the bangs. He was moving forwards as a delayed one went off, a fragment lodging in his eyeball.

To the west of the look-out there is a small cliff top cutting now partly obscured by debris tipped there from the wartime radar buildings. There are pit marks, so it is a quarry. Stone from here could only have been cast down to the undercliff below before being worked, which begs the question of to what extent the larger quarry was worked in that way. We possibly see in this the hundred foot rule being applied, that a rival saw the quarry flourishing and got going as close as possible, but did not pursue it for long. Can we also see the hundred foot rule in the shape of the main quarry? Perhaps a rival got going on the vertical cliff more than a hundred feet west of the first man, who was not allowed to stop him. Perhaps the new man had no other way out but to cast his stone down to be worked below. Perhaps, over time, the two separate quarries met at Man's Head rock? But enough guesswork. About 200 feet east of Man's Head and well below, the natural landslip mass shows a nice Pond Freestone exposure. Lo and behold, there are pit marks! To drive those wedges meant standing on a perilous ledge. There is no question of stone being hauled up from such eyries. The stone was loosened and then let fall.

Much of the early quarrying on Portland was on the northeastern cliffs, which are of about the same height as St. Aldhelm's Head and which similarly consist of a vertical upper wall of limestone resting on a steep slope of soft Kimmeridge Clay, extending to a flattened boulder-strewn undercliff. Workings at Portland are more extensive than at St. Aldhelm's Head, but the parallels are obvious. By 1765 the Portlanders had stone piers equipped with cranes. It is virtually certain that nothing like this was ever attempted under the Head other than one step removed at Pier Bottom. Stone from Haysom's quarry was taken that way, and possibly from this quarry as well. There is a possible route northwards across the plain to the nameless Pier-Bottom-side valley, and thence to the pier. The undercliff below the western end of the quarry shows evidence of much work. There are areas of spalls and scars, and part-worked legs and caps, troughs and architectural components.

St. Aldhelm's undercliff. Pond Freestone ball.

This was where stones cast down from above were shaped. Additionally, good stone found lying in the general undercliff was dressed on the spot. There would have been a lot of good Freestone and Blue Bits lying about naturally, and when we look at the undercliff now there is a general dearth. However, a few splendid blocks remain; one particularly fine piece of Pond Freestone lies at the western end of the working area. It seems there were times at least when waste was being tipped over at various points, whilst the good stuff was being cast down to the working area. Close by the foot of the western tip are two big Pond Freestone balls beautifully worked to a punched finish, one 28 inch diameter, the other 34 inch, so not a pair. Their position would suggest that someone rolled them from the top.

Billy Winspit told me of lengths of 'columns', but it has taken me forty years to find one. It lies in the old tip such as to suggest that it was rolled over the cliff before that part of the working ceased, for more waste material has accumulated around it. At about 33 inch diameter and 30 inches high, the curved surface has been left off the punch, whilst the only visible flat surface is a nice straight cut which bears surprising pit marks. They show that it must have been split after the round was effected, which seems odd. Perhaps it had also been intended to be a ball. One way to make them is first to work a cylinder. It would seem the block had been big enough to make a pair and that they first worked the cylinder shape before cutting it in half. I dare say most masons, faced with making a ball now by hand, would first saw out the containing cube, then work the equator in four stages using a reverse quadrant, before applying the quadrant repeatedly between equator and poles. But the initial cutting of a cube by hand would have been time-consuming and only productive of six useful points. My father remarked on the way the 'old hands' worked staddle legs. Those broken in manufacture show they roughed them out to a taper at an early stage. But having done that, how are the flat top and bottom surfaces obtained, square to the central axis? By eye alone?

As previously remarked, much of Encombe House is St. Aldhelm's Head stone. Would it have made sense to ship it to Freshwater and pull it up the cliff, or was it taken all the way by cart? Considering the latter alternative, is it possible that the carriageway route through Houns Tout half cliff was made then? William Bower told me that his grandfather Jeremiah remembered seeing boats being loaded at the point of the Head. There seems to be no trackway of any sort from the working area below the look-out to the shore. How did they get it away? The sea is making inroads into the undercliff, so the actual shore is altering. A step in the area of spalls demonstrates slippage of a mass towards the water, but the broad area towards the point appears stable. Judging from the projection of the chert nodules, these rocks have been exposed for a long time; hundreds, perhaps thousands, of years. Other evidence of the age of this cliff, that is the general form of the undercliff, including the slipped masses of Ringbum Gardens and Molly's Ground, is provided by the extreme weathering of the Puffin bed, an undercutting that must represent centuries of exposure.

In the undercliff, near, but not part of the quarry waste tips, lies a splendid loose Blue Bit. It is in two beds, each about twelve inches thick, and measures about nine feet by five feet. Though it is difficult to see how it was done, in my opinion there must have been more of these that have been taken away by sea for the Christchurch, Exeter and Ely slabs discussed earlier. It is so lucky that this one rough block was left, providing proof that such splendid slabs occur here.

Yet another undercliff block, of perhaps even greater interest, lies west of Man's Head, almost beneath the walled up gap and just off the seaward edge of the flattish area. It is of one of the beds beneath the Pond Freestone, lying on edge, about 3 feet thick and 11 feet long. An attempt has been made to split it but it broke and has been abandoned. What makes it unique is that the cutter did not attempt a series of pits, examples of which are common over much of the undercliff, but cut one long continuous shallow droke, much as used to be done on Portland until recently. I suspect this cut was made 'Portland fashion' by use of a kibble rather than a hammer and punch and that this work is more likely, therefore, to be of late medieval or perhaps 17th century date. Blocks bearing normal pit marks occur over a wide area and pose the question of how the worked stone was moved to the boats across this jumbled terrain. The sheer size of some of the obstacles, the biggest boulders being about 100 tons would have made any modifications difficult and there is no obvious evidence of a track. I guess one or two long planks would make it possible to tumble staddle stones and the like to the shore and into a boat, much as we know things were done in Durlston Bay. Such a flexible arrangement would not have been confined to one part of the shore. However, large slabs such as the ledgers at three tons or so must have been a challenge; but they were premium stones and no doubt commanded a good price. Also, of course, there were no digging costs.

From a shipping point of view the small bay at the tip of the Head is more or less screened by a scatter of outlying rocks, at least at low tide. The slight bight to the west is also similarly screened but west of that the approach is open. During the ebb the water here is slack, though the race tears by not far off. In one place a particularly massive boulder may have provided a place to get a boat alongside, but there is no firm evidence in

St. Aldhelm's Chapel. Drawings by Thomas Webster, published in H. C. Englefield's *The Isle of Wight* (1816). The interior view shows the chapel in use for storing fishing gear.

the form of crane timber socket holes. However survival of such for any length of time is hardly to be expected on this extremely exposed shore of loose blocks rather than solid cliff. What is telling are Pond Freestone blocks bearing pit marks, low in the shore, well west of the Coastguard lookout.

The chapel was almost ruinous until repaired, first by William Morton Pitt some time before 1807 and then again in 1873/4 by Lord Eldon.[62] I suspect the graffiti is largely the work of quarriers, perhaps using it as a refuge during rain. Webster drew it in its neglected state, when it was used to store fishing gear.[63] The central pillar has on the south side of the capital: ' J Thickes 1729'. A James Thickes, Marbler and Joint Stock Company member, leased a meadow at Blacklands in 1711, and John, Marbler or shoemaker of Langton, made a will in 1764. One of these is likely to be the name in the chapel. This Nonconformist family continued quarrying at least until 1826, when another James was paying dues on the Worth Estate. Yet another John figured in the early days of Methodism on Portland. He walked there to preach before Portland was connected by the bridge at Smallmouth, perhaps at the Ranters Chapel that yet remains. A contemporary account records:

'One Saturday morning in the year 1806, Mr. John Thicks set out from Langton in the Island of Purbeck to walk to Portland, a distance of about twenty five miles. Nothing very great about that you may say – but wait. It was mid winter, and there had been a very heavy fall of snow, the roads were almost impassable, the drifts billowing over the hedges and blotting out the paths. A sharp icy wind whetted into bitter keenness by its journey across the sea, cut into his eyes, but he struggled on, often losing the way, but never daunted. At last, hungry and frozen, he arrived at the home of a friend of his in Weymouth. After a warm and a drink, he refused food, having rested he again set out through the snow for the Ferry to take him across 'Smallmouth' to Portland. But not withstanding his loudest hallooing the little boat persisted in staying on the opposite side until the leisurely pilot, who no doubt didn't like leaving the warmth of his fire, saw fit to appear. Such were the trials and tribulations of all travellers that crossed the scene in those far off days.'[64]

I guess John was happy to get home to his ancient cottage in Langton, just east of where the Methodist chapel was subsequently built. Luckily, a photograph was taken of the cottage before its demolition.[65]

ST ALDHELM'S QUARRY (HAYSOMS)

The quarry appears as a 'stone pitt' on William Burgess's 1737 map of Renscombe. The survey was commissioned by George Cary, Esq. when he acquired the manor.[66] Hutchins disagrees with the date, giving the acquisition by Cary as 1763. On this map the valley, now known as Pier Bottom, appears as 'Coome Bottom', which suggests a pre-pier date for the survey. Until recently, squared up Front stones could be seen lying on the bank above the shore, close by the site of the pier. Billy Winspit told me they were left over from the Ramsgate job, a remarkable piece of oral history, given that that this was complete by 1800. So the pier must have been built to ship the stone for this work sometime in the second half of the 18th century. Cary's tenant for this period was George Cull, who held both the farm lease and 'the quarries thereon' before he died in 1772. However, the pier was not only used for Ramsgate.

The storm surge of January 1986, that moved this shore about a great deal, revealed a staddle cap 200 yards to the north (the longshore drift is to the north) and recent erosion of the shale bank has produced a roller and a staddle legs, all standard Cliff Stone fare. Erosion has recently brought several Ramsgate blocks down into the shore. One bears the mark IV which is probably 5½ cube feet, another IIII, which is certainly 4½ cube feet. The Portland system was the same. A block now exhibited in St Paul's Cathedral is of this same size and bears

152 / PURBECK STONE

the same mark.

Recently the sea has made great inroads. A particularly big rock, known as 'Chance it', that formerly gave a slight measure of protection, has more or less gone. It seems amazing that men attempted the solid masonry structure of the pier here, but they did, as proved by all the remnants, scattered along 100 yards of shore. There are 55 or more, virtually all Spangle or Blue Bit, which shows that they were brought there, the biggest at 5 ft by 2 ft 6 inches by 1 ft 9 inches. The two foot thickness is more or less the bed height of Spangle at St. Aldhelm's quarry. The stones are squared up and exhibit pins run in with lead and sockets for wood or stone dowels averaging twelve inches by ten inches by six inches deep, which would have served to lock the pier structure together. I suspect the sockets with dowels were on top, the pins on the underside, protruding down into the rocks of the shore. But how did they do it? Looking at the confusion now it is hard to see how one would start to build such masonry on the rough natural shoreline rocks. A large 4 ft 6 inch Blue Bit has an 18 inch socket cut right through it.

The pier's construction must represent a lot of unprofitable work, and perhaps reflects a buoyant time when there was ample work for the cliff quarries. Along the bottom of the northern flank of Pier Bottom, from about the small side valley to the cliff, there is a ridge. Landslips in the 1980s revealed that at least at its seaward end it is pitched with stone! It is surely the track leading to the pier. The Isaac Taylor map of 1765 shows it continue in a hairpin bend down to the shore, presumably metalled all the way, which seems hardly credible now. However, they could have taken the shortcut of tumbling stones down the soft shale undercliff. Billy Winspit said of loading small stones like pitchers at Seacombe, that they did not laboriously lower all that category of work down by crane, but that they would have a clear out of scars, throwing them

Pier Bottom, Worth Matravers. Relic of pier. Note binoculars to give scale.

down to the loading rock to first form a soft bed, then chuck the pitchers on to it.

Soon after the 1980s slippages a squared piece of Marble, bearing punch marks, appeared in this rapidly eroding shore, then another. The nearest source of Marble is Dunshay. What does it mean? It seems the pier was built and destroyed in the 18th century or soon after, a time when not much Marble was being dug. Another puzzle is a slab of Swanage Grub revealed in 2014. The latter was much quarried during the late 17th century, virtually not at all before that, and not much

'Quarry at St. Aldhelm's Head' [Haysoms], c. 1930, Gerald Gardiner (b.1902). Oil on canvas. Looking north; note telephone wires and poles, and Worth Matravers church. This is the earliest representation of the quarry.

afterwards. The date of the pier's demise is elusive. However, an advertisement for the sale of Renscombe in 1810 may refer to it still being functional then:

'The valuable Purbeck stone quarries [this is misleading, either this and/or the cliff quarry at the end of the Head, both of Portland beds, are meant] belonging to it, which is bounded by the sea, may be made extremely advantageous, from the facility of shipping stone to be excavated therefrom, which is of a very superior quality'.[67] Perhaps it was the devastating storm of November 1824, that dumped seaweed outside the door of the Anchor Inn at Swanage, that demolished the pier.

When my father took over St. Aldhelm's quarry in about 1934, Jesse Lander referred to it as 'somebody [maybe George] House quarr' (sadly I have forgotten the Christian name). This family seems to have no other certain connection with the stone trade, but the name appears in the 18th century Swanage church registers, and the Churchwardens' accounts for Worth record a payment in 1801 to George House for repairing seats in the church. Before 1934 an area of Shrimp and Blue bits had been dug and not much else, and there was a lime kiln. Maybe the House family operated it. Shrimp can be burnt for lime, but is not particularly good. Geoff Hooper, who worked on the kiln at Sheepsleights, said it tended to explode. Perhaps the primary requirement was agricultural. William David briefly held the

LEFT Ralph Bower and the author dressing dubbers from offcuts, c.1952.

BELOW Wedge-cut Pond Freestone block (destined for Portsmouth Cathedral) suspended in nips, being pushed by Tom Bonfield. Late 1930s.

154 / PURBECK STONE

quarry before 1934, employing fisherman Frank Lander, Mont Hooper and others to sink a test hole to the Bottom Freestone to assess the stone's quality. Presumably these men did this when the weather was inclement for fishing. When David's enterprises failed, the estate agreed the transfer of permission at this quarry to my father. The wooden hand crane was left by David. My father opted to continue here rather than out at the end of the Head because of its easier road accessibility. Billy Winspit, who had been the foreman at Seacombe with David, and who had become jobless and quarryless when it closed, was taken on as foreman. The block stone for masonry was taken to the Swanage Court Hill depot.

The depot was wound up and sold to the Council, and after the war my father continued masonry work and installed

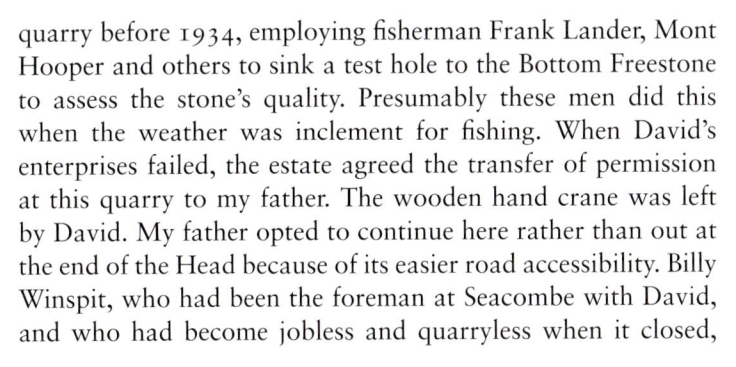

ABOVE Langton Matravers, old cemetery. Keeper Murray's headstone.

LEFT Swanage, All Saints. Pond Freestone east window, designed by Robert Potter, 1956-7.

Pond Freestone block at St. Aldhelm's quarry, loosened by David Sole and Clarence Riman, c. 1970. L-R: Roy Cobb (who about this time punched out, without the aid of an angle grinder, the bowl of the Simon Verity font in Clifton Cathedral), David Sole, the Author, Clarence Riman, Robert Smith, Ilay Cooper.

CLIFF STONE / 155

and carvers have chosen Pond Freestone for its fine working qualities. The quarry also supplied lettered panels for the Royal Festival Hall and the British Museum, and a retrospective memorial commemorating 17th century Digger, Gerrard Winstanley. At the other end of the social and political scale is the Duke of Windsor's ledger slab at Frogmore. Carvings include the Tregonwell stone outside the Bournemouth International Centre, and stones for a Common Ground arts project. Perhaps the most far-flung was Lord Craigmile's headstone, delivered to Knoydart by helicopter.

SHEEPSLEIGHTS

By the late 19th century a small quarry had been developed here worked by the Browns. They also operated variously East Winspit, Halsewell, an inland quarry (employing, by Purbeck standards a lot of men) in Captain's Field and a Marble quarry down Crack Lane. They worked Sheepsleights intermittently but never failed to do some work there each year in order to retain possession. The owner was Squire Calcraft of Rempstone. The quarry was pushed in from the side of the combe, producing an underground, since obliterated. The stone tends to be small. Billy Brown was known for making 'dots', which are like pitchers but of regular squares rather than oblongs. When he had a biggish order Buff Bower and others would sometimes give him a hand. Billy's 'dots' were something of a joke amongst that generation. Areas of such Cliff stone 'dots' remain, probably of Sheepsleights origin. Sites include Corfe Rectory courtyard, an alleyway by the Poole Arms off Poole Quay, the hard standing

Quay Hill, Lymington, Hants. Cliff stone; possibly Billy Brown's 'dots'.

machines at the quarry. He thought it suitable to call the place St. Aldhelm's rather than Alban's. Masonry work done by him using stone from this quarry includes Blue Bit for the Winfrith Atomic Energy Security block and the altar in the Mary Magdalene chapel in Chichester Cathedral. Other work in Pond Freestone includes the almond-shaped east window in All Saints Church, Swanage, and paving in the Temple Church, London. Lettered memorials by him include the Dru Drury tablet in Corfe Church and Keeper Murray's headstone in Langton's Old Cemetery. His son Chris continued to resist the prosaic, by this time machine-cut, tide. Subsequent lettercutters

Sheepsleights quarry, plant about 1925. Photo taken by British Geological Survey group.

Sheepsleights, Worth Quarry Co., 1926

for the hackney carriages that awaited passengers arriving at Swanage pier. The small sized block which this quarry tends to produce lent itself to such work in a way that the more massive block of Seacombe and Winspit did not. However, these other quarries were producing such small stuff to an extent. In the railway era and subsequently, Sheepsleights was better placed geographically for access, an advantage that became even greater as lorries took over completely.

In 1923 a group of businessmen including A. H. Scammel, brother of the lorry manufacturer, bought the quarry, forming Worth Quarries Ltd, with Thomas Webber as manager. At that time Poole Harbour Commissioners were considering the construction of the Training Bank and Scammel had an eye for the contract. As it turned out he did not get it; the Dorset Quay Co., formed about the same time, supplied the stone, mostly by sea from Seacombe. A considerable fanfare surrounded the launch of the new Worth business.[68] A lime kiln and crushing plant were installed, photographs of which were taken by the geological survey with which this expansion coincided. The idea was to crush the Spangle and dig the Freestone for masonry or lime burning. Some of the old hands warned that it wasn't good enough and so it turned out.[69] The blocks were generally small and flawed and the lime, when used as plaster, tended to blow after application. However, for a while quite a lot of men were employed, including some who left Seacombe *en bloc* following a pay dispute. Happily a photograph of a group working at Sheepsleights was taken in 1926. In the course of developing the business they built a ramp at the Swanage Gas works off Victoria Avenue. It allowed for lorries to tip directly into railway trucks. In 1933 the company went into liquidation. William David of the Dorset Quarry Co had talks with Scammel but nothing came of it. A scrap dealer bought the plant and then sold it back to some of the old directors plus a new man from Wales, Thomas Lant. He started a new company, calling it Swanworth Quarries.[70]

War work included the supply of hard core to, amongst other places, Thruxton Airfield.[71] Lant's nephew, Ronald Waters, took over in 1946, expanding the quarry enormously as a source of aggregates and sea defence armour stone. Machine mounted drill rigs allowed for wholesale blasting of all the beds, including the cherty series, right down to the Portland sand. Edward Pushman spent most of his working life in the office or on the road as a salesman for the company. The business also sold walling, rockery, crazy paving, fireplaces etc., the stone for which mainly came from their quarry at Fratton Ground, where the Middle Purbeck beds were dug, mostly by Harold Bonfield.

Large orders requiring more help were also subcontracted to Harden's quarry and Edward's brother John's quarry in Eastington Cowlease, where Alf Meader did the banker work. Tom Samways was foreman in the post-war days, which saw a massive expansion in aggregate production. Several of his sons followed him, including Michael, who worked nowhere else after leaving St. George's School, Langton Matravers, until retirement. I guess he got more stone out of the ground than anyone else in Purbeck ever (with a bit of help from Alfred Nobel's invention, gelignite). When busy they were pushing out about 3,000 tons per day.[72]

A consortium which included the landowner, the Encombe Estate, seeing the quarry prosper, attempted in 1968 to open a rival quarry across the combe to the northwest. However, it was turned down following a planning inquiry. In anticipation of the Inquiry Inspector's site visit, the crushing plant was run night and day to produce a massive stock. This decision in effect gave a Purbeck crushed stone monopoly to Swanworth, which was soon acquired by a big national firm, Tarmac; Tarmac in turn by a multi-national. The land with potential across the combe to the northwest from the Encombe Estate was bought by Macalpine. The rock in that direction is shallow, without the problem of overburden, whilst to the east it becomes progressively deeper and therefore more costly to quarry. Preliminary planning soundings met with a vociferous and successful 'Stop' campaign by local residents. Envisaging the cessation of quarrying, a restoration scheme which includes some waste disposal has been put in operation. When completed this quarry's most interesting feature, a vertical cliff, will be reduced to a slope, perhaps a suitable monument to our homogenized risk-adverse culture. But what if that had been in place when Winspit, Seacombe, Tilly Whim *et al*. ceased work? The site has in recent years been acquired by local operators, Suttles, who are also exploring the idea of developing the northwest area for further production. Edward Pushman's son, David, has produced several titles, including *Swanworth, a History of the Quarry*.

LONDON DOORS

There are two quarry-cut rock faces at the head of the Encombe valley, the western of which was called London Doors. Harris mentions it in 1893: 'There is a quarry called 'London Doors' a little way inland, but used only for estate purposes – private property'. Several lengthy masonry-lined tunnels supply water to the lakes on the Encombe Estate. This quarry could well have been a source for this sort of work. My father said of the men who built the church that they were disparaging of the stone from this quarry. Cut into the Portland beds, it is not productive of big blocks, but was used for work such as Kingston churchyard wall, where some has frost-shattered badly.

KIMMERIDGE

Now a car park above the village, the cliffstone beds there were dug for a considerable height including the Cherty series. It was of no use for masonry other than low grade rubble. Some was dug by Italian prisoners during the 1939-45 war.[73]

GAD CLIFF

The useful Freestones are thin or even absent, but incredibly, there are three stones bearing pit marks and a scappled-out D trow in the undercliff close by Smugglers' Cove. The tumble of great boulders is both geologically and in configuration similar to the St. Aldhelm's Head undercliff, and similarly there is no question of a pier. They surely had a way of getting heavy stones into a boat across this most difficult terrain. One left, bearing pit marks, is about six feet long and could have been intended for a field roller or post. The cove has changed significantly in my life time. Its small beach of pebbles, formerly big enough for a stone boat to land, is now covered by big boulders, and the secret walled up cave, mentioned in Lilian Bond's *Tyneham: A Lost Heritage*, has collapsed.[74]

WORBARROW

Here the beds of stone run into the sea and could easily have been loaded into boats. In contrast with Durlston Bay, they lie at a steep angle and most are reduced in thickness. For example, the Feather, two feet thick in Durlston, has gone entirely. The New Vein, nearly 5 feet in Durlston, is reduced to a mere three inches.[75] The beds in the Rag/Freestone part of the sequence are difficult to identify, but also much reduced. However, the Downs Vein bucks this thinning trend, remaining at about three feet, much the same as it is further east, whilst the Burr runs to 4 ft 6 inches. Is this the source of the mysterious Harp Stone near Bradle, which, standing 7 feet out of the ground, with no doubt quite a lot more hidden, is a fine block? The top of the best Burr bed is exposed for 50 feet or so near water level along the Worbarrow Bay side of the Tout. The Burr also outcrops quite near where the Harp Stone stands, but to have quarried it there would have almost certainly meant digging a lot of stone before such a big one was found.

Where the Burr rises out of the shore the edge of the layer tends to lie back at a less steep angle than most of the other beds. This suggests that some has been quarried. It would be easy to prize a block free, letting it slide down to the shore. Several large ones lie there, one with a row of four pits cut in it. Thomas Webster (1815) mentions the new quarry at Worbarrow, so something was happening then. But work was stopped, as reported in the newspaper, *The Advertiser and Visitors List*, Sept. 9th 1881:

> 'The curious Tout was once quarried but this was very easy work for the strata came right down to the shore, and as the end was cut off more slipped down by its own weight, and all the men had to do was to cut it off and ship it to Weymouth. Luckily the owners saw how the Tout would ultimately be damaged, and put an end to it before the work of destruction had gone too far'.

In the southeast corner of the bay several layers of Marble form reefs, visible at low tide. Obviously they once extended up out of the shore and have been taken. But the blocks do not compare in size or quality with what we see at Peveril. The steep dip produces a narrow exposure and precludes any significant quarry development. A specific reference to its use comes in the accounts for building the new Catholic church at Lulworth in 1786-7. These include quarrying stone at Bindon Warren, which lies between Mupe and the cove: 'taking down stone at Bindon Abbey' and 'Warbarrow stone for the plinth'. The church plinth and elements of the gate piers to the park are of Marble. Worbarrow, the corner of Mupe Bay or Lulworth Cove are all possible sources. The main part of the church fabric is Portland.

On the western side of Worbarrow Tout gypsum (alabaster) is exposed and falling down to the shore. It occurs in discontinuous masses that are associated with faults, rather than even layers, so as the cliff retreats the same horizon can be productive of a lot, or perhaps none at all. In the 19th century in Durlston it was being burnt for plaster. No significant amount is now revealed there. Perhaps Worbarrow gypsum was similarly burnt, but that it was also considered for dimension work is recorded in an astonishing letter:

'MR. ARTHUR ROODS TO SIR JOHN THYNNE. ABOUT PURBECK STONE

1549 6 June

Thys shal be to advertyse yr. Mastershyppe after whatt sort the stone lyeth att Purbecke, and whatt order I have taken there. Fyrste in the south partt of the Iland, at a poyntt calyd Sayntt Aldomis from the wyche pointt ij myles towards the west end of the Ile lyeth the towyche [touch] stone yn ij shelffs endlonge towards the see very neer levell by estymacyon iij or iiij foote in length devyded with dyvers joyntts, some one stone iiij loods and many of them ij and iij loods apece and but one cowrse of stones yn every shelffe: the bredth vii or viii fote, the thyknes betweene xij ynches and xv ynches, the nerest end off the shelff towards the land ys at the lo-water mark att refe tyed, so hytt cannot be broken butt att sprynge tyed.

The alabaster ys a myle and a halfe from the towyche, att th'est end of the Ile att a place calyd Worbarrowe, falen owtt of the wydest clyffe wyche ys 30 fadom hye, and lyeth att full see marke in rownde pecys of viii or ix to wne a pece: the utter partts of them being of whyte alabaster and full of craks; wyche woll not ryse in breadth passing xij ynches square wyth a small thyknes; and inwards towards the myds of the pece ys ij other cowlors of stone, one somewhatt blaker then the other, much lyke unto a grey Marbull of the wyche I wyll brynge a sample unto my Lord's grace withyn thys vij dayes; wyche stone wyll ryse to iij fote in length and xviij ynchys in breydth and vi or viij ynches thyke, so thet I have sett 2 workmen upon brekyng of the same att soche tyme as they canott worke for the water upon the towyche that I heve also appointed them to breke. – From Wolfhalle vi June,

Your humble sarvytour, ARTHUR ROODS.
To the right worshipful Syr John Thynne Knyght
Att Brainford. [Brentford.][76.]

Sir John Thynne was Edward Seymour (the Lord Protector Somerset)'s steward during the reign of Seymour's nephew, Edward VI. Wolf Hall, the family seat near Burbage in Wiltshire, was in the process of being rebuilt at the time, and is now destroyed. Sir John Thynne went on to build Longleat, and his descendants live there still.

What did they use the 'towyche', surely the oil-rich black

Sample of alabaster/gypsum.

band, for? The Romans used it extensively for amulets, tesserae and even elegant furniture. Beyond simply burning it I have not seen it put to any post-Roman use, but one of the limestone beds that occurs within the Kimmeridge shales appears as steps in the medieval part of Tyneham House. This particular bed occurs in the shore at two locations: northern Brandy Bay and near Rope Lake.

MUPE

The steeply sloping shelf at Bacon Hole has been cut away at the level of the Upper Portland beds. Its walls bear both drill and pit marks. On the landward side, where the cave has been walled up by the quarrymen, stones are arranged to form a dock, which has holes to hold a gibbet. The exploited Portland beds differ from their Portland and Purbeck equivalents. Some of the stones that form the dock are of a Cap-like bed that lies beneath the New Vein. This bed, in the Cherty freshwater series, is thicker here and of better quality than in eastern Purbeck, where it was called the Flint and of no use.

In 1826 James Marsh of Swanage and Thomas Lander of West Lulworth, Stone Merchants, took out a 25 year lease on 'All that stone quarry, Vein or Stratum of Stone situate at certain rocks, these called Mupe Rocks'. It is perhaps safe to associate most, even all of this working with these men. They must have made the first breach just above water level, which would have been difficult in a layer almost seven feet thick. But from then on, the advance up the 40 degree slope would have allowed each loosened piece to slide down into the dock area relatively easily. This first bed, lying above a layer of flints, may well correspond to the Pond Freestone plus other overlying beds of eastern Purbeck. However, it is markedly different. One important characteristic is its relatively greater abundance of blacks (stylolites), some running vertically, which I have not seen in quarries to the east at all. In one place punch marks follow either side of one of these stylolites. The quarryman was trying to determine how weak it was. The next layer, about

Worbarrow Bay with Mupe rocks in the foreground. Portland Beds form the isolated rocks at right, Purbeck beds striated at left with Arish Mell a gap in the chalk behind. The steeply tilted Portland and Purbeck beds form Worbarrow Tout and Gad Cliff in the distance. In the centre, with chalk cliffs to the left, is the low tapering cliff of the Wealden beds, with the Marble outcropping where they meet the sea at right. The walls of Bacon Hole, behind the photographer, show drill marks. Close by, stones were arranged to form a dock and holes cut to form a gibbet, now all in disarray.

three feet six inches thick, has also been taken. Below that only a sump has been broken out, which suggests their intention was to go lower, but they gave up. Small stones flooring Bacon Hole are mostly, if not entirely, their waste from dressing. They include bits of D trows, sinks and staddle stones broken in manufacture, i.e. the normal early 19th century Cliff stone fare; what a place for a banker! An area of Lulworth Castle paving re-done in the 19th century includes two small heavily-stained stones exhibiting stylolites. If they were sourced from this quarry, which is likely, the suspicion is prompted that they are offcuts and that therefore this sort of stone should occur in more demanding elements of that building or others.

There is a nice row of pits not set off, plus others that have burst out ineffectually. Radiating shattering shows that they were using gunpowder in the drill holes. The loading wharf at about a 100 foot seems unnecessarily long, but that was dictated by the distance between the cliff proper and a solid reef of Cypris beds between which it was built. The stones are jammed in, each on end to the sea, three courses or more wide and two high, with much of the top course now demolished. The larger range, weighing about three tons, give testament to the mens' skill in handling the stone with only a crowbar, for I guess it was all done in that way and not with the benefit of cranage. Dislocated and broken stones contain a square sinking about 18 inches square by 10 deep, surely cut to hold a gibbet king post. In storms there would not have been a safe place for it to be removed to other than possibly the back of the cave, and I guess the building of the internal wall with its now missing door would have been to do with that.

SIX
Uses

PAVING AND STREETWORK

Apart from expensive mosaic or other patterned forms, there are two straightforward ways of paving, either with random rectangles or gauged squares. Random rectangles are the cheapest to make, as they involve less waste and require less care. Each raw slab is dressed to make the biggest oblong it can contain. A disadvantage is that such random shapes do not fit together easily. One solution is either to cut them to a gauged width whilst leaving the length random, and lay the result in courses, or to select courses from a random load on site. Squares are more costly in that a stone can be well over size but still make only one. This can be mitigated by having more than one module. Leaving aside aesthetic considerations, the dilemma is perennial: lower cost of shaping but more trouble required to fix random, against greater production cost but ease of fixing of squares. Hawksmoor's St. George's, Bloomsbury, has a lot of Purbeck paving in the undercroft, long hidden under stacks of coffins. In my opinion, it is an example of the fixer sorting out the random paving into courses as best he could. St George's is probably a typical example of cheap floors of the time, that is, entirely random sized stones being shipped from Purbeck, leaving the courses to be organised on site.

The basic medieval square is 12 inches by 12 inches. Perhaps it is not a coincidence that such a size one inch thick weighs 14 pounds, that is, one stone in weight. One inch is thinner than a typical paving, but some stone measures were, depending on the commodity, greater, even up to 24 pounds. It prompts the suspicion that the unit of measurement by weight is linked to the standard 12 inch square paving. The next size larger is approximately 17 inches by 17 inches (the diagonal of a 12 inch square, which is not a round figure), whilst the largest is 24 inches by 24. These three sizes produce a face size sequence of 1, 2, 4. Later, it seems, there was a departure from this convention and squares of other sizes were made.[1]

Survivals of medieval 12 inch squares are the most common, perhaps because with concurrent demand for large brass indents, they were a way of utilizing small pieces that would otherwise go to waste. Winchester Cathedral nave and Lady Chapel have both 12 inch and 17 inch squares of Purbeck and Sussex Marbles. Salisbury has 12 and 24 inch squares that would seem to be medieval, but also similar areas of both 19th and 20th century work.

Chichester has one area of 12 inch squares at the west

Chichester Cathedral. Medieval flooring, between nave and south aisle, showing relationship between twelve and seventeen inch squares. Mostly Marble, the lesser size laid arrace-wise.

cloister door, more in the south aisle, including a block south of the Arundel Screen. Some of these are of the local Sussex Marble, but Purbeck dominates. Norwich Cathedral gained a new Purbeck stone floor in the 18th century. Nave monuments placed within the width of the arcades have, in some cases, Marble squares of the two usual, lesser sizes filling the spaces around them. They are surely medieval survivals. Westminster has twelve inch squares in the North Ambulatory, opposite the tomb of Edward I. St. George's Chapel, Windsor, has twelve inch squares in both Lincoln and Beaufort Chapels. The latter is 1506, and it would seem the paving is of that date. How early are the first? Perhaps they begin as early as Marble quarrying, that is, around 1160. What is certain is that in 1312 Adam Le Marbrer was paving St. Paul's with squares of Marble, whilst in 1355 John Canoun and John Mayow were supplying 1,200 pieces of Marble, which suggests squares, for paving Westminster. Southwark Cathedral has approximately 12 inch Marble squares that are probably medieval, but also others of Downs Vein, plus others that are modern. Several East Anglian churches, notably Covehithe, Aldeburgh and Southwold, Suffolk, have surviving areas, but I believe it accurate that not a single medieval square is to be found anywhere in the Isle of Purbeck!

Many church floors have been rearranged and old stones destroyed, moved or recut to allow for the introduction of

USES / 161

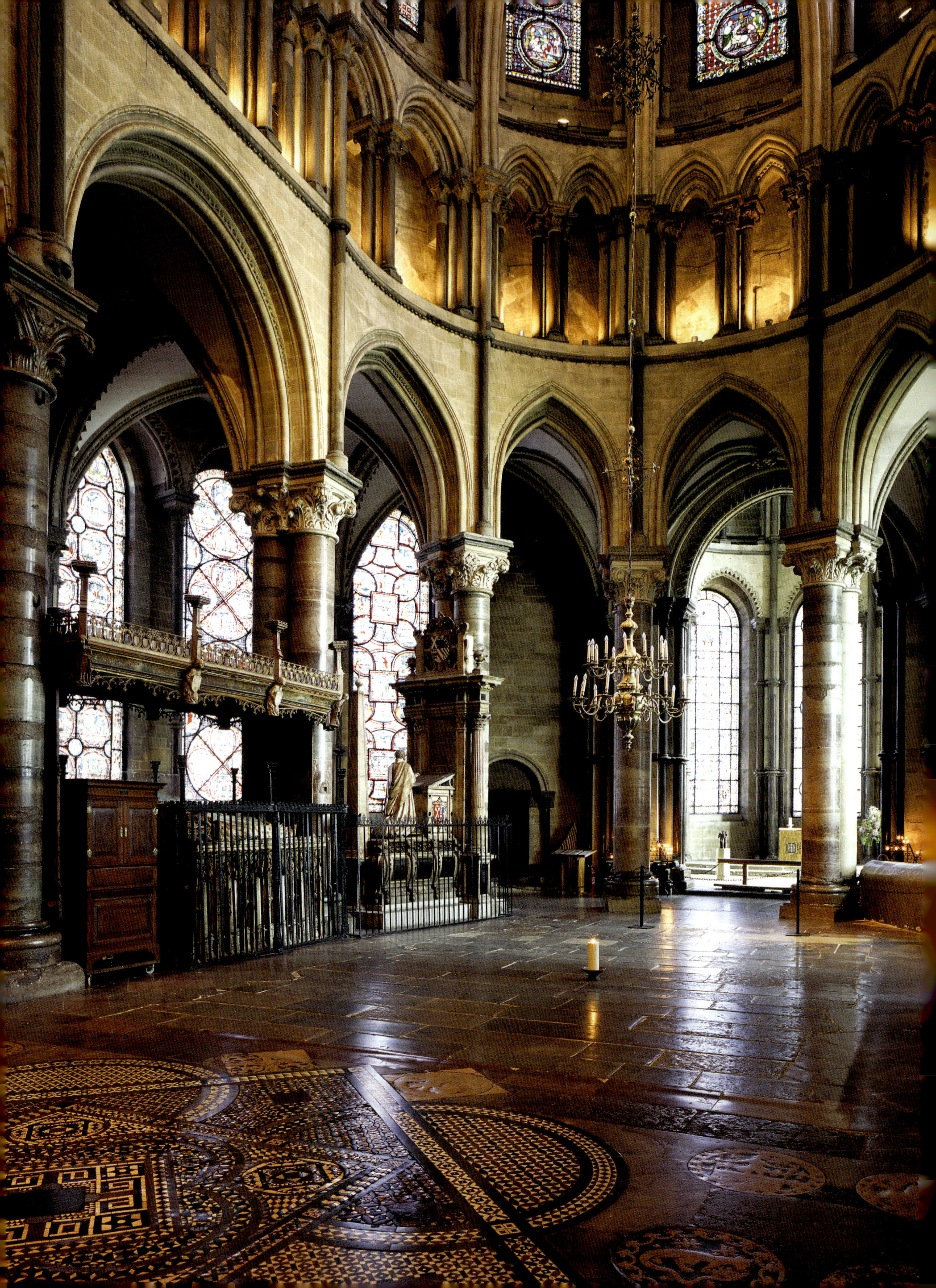

ABOVE Canterbury Cathedral. Floor at site of Thomas Becket's shrine, showing relaid steps amongst wider courses.

OPPOSITE PAGE Canterbury Cathedral, Trinity Chapel, including Purbeck Marble elements; late 12th century. St Thomas Becket's shrine was placed there in 1220, and destroyed in 1538.

post-medieval ledgers, heating ducts, etc. Plain odd-sized Marble slabs are common. However, the distribution is such as to prompt the suspicion that they are not just ordinary paving, but relatively cheap tomb slabs. Were they once painted? I have never knowingly seen an unaltered medieval Purbeck floor of a random arrangement. Did such a thing ever exist?

Such an altered floor, occupying the site of Becket's shrine at Canterbury Cathedral, consists of the shrine's original steps relaid sometime after its destruction in 1538.[2] The several course widths range from about 15 to 20 inches and their arrangement contrasts with the highly decorated areas which include a Purbeck element, all around where the shrine once stood. Canterbury's north quire aisle, and the quire itself have large areas of Purbeck Marble squares of the standard two sizes, surely the largest medieval area of such remaining in the country.

Medieval floors of Purbeck stone rather than Marble seem almost non-existent. However, the fact that stone was being quarried for roof tile from as early as the 13th century would imply their existence, for the digging of one is likely to produce the other. A floor retaining what would seem to be original Purbeck Marble and Purbeck stone but now much altered by insertions of ledgers, heating systems, etc. lies in the north eastern nave aisle of Westminster Abbey. Perhaps it dates from soon after the re-building in the 15th century. There is a practical logic in leaving the paving until last. A Langton Wallis court record of 1423 tells of almost certain quarrying of paving stone going on at the same time as the certain production of roof tile.[3] The record is not entirely clear, but there can be little doubt that a small amount of stone paving was being made. However the court records of tile production continue over decades without further mention of paving. It would seem output from that estate, and therefore probably others, was then small.

Some of the Westminster north eastern aisle slabs are of Downs Vein, such as occurs close to the surface on Langton Wallis. From this floor westwards both aisles, plus the nave, are one concept, completed between 1507 and 1517. The nave, but not yet the western towers, were almost finished by 1496. These floors, consisting of twelve inch squares, contain repairs, but the mass would appear to be original. Downs Vein of a Langton Wallis / Gallows Gore type dominates, but there are also other beds, including Vie bed and Laining Vein, the latter of a distinctive sort such as outcrops near Spyway Farm, Langton.

If the Windsor Chapel marble floor is of 1506, which seems likely, we can perhaps see a seamless shift from marble to stone production in these first years of the 16th century, though some marble went on being dug for a while yet. Stone floors, of almost certainly late 15th century date, survive at Athelhampton, Dorset. The Porch, Great Hall and Oriel have squares of approximately one foot five and a half inches set diagonally, producing triangles against margins formed by stones of random length in straight courses. Each floor is discrete to its room, medieval fashion. They are of Downs Vein, exactly such as is produced around Gallows Gore. Another early non-ecclesiastical floor existed on the Real Tennis court at Canford. A document of 1542, in the public Record Office, describes it as being in disrepair and made of 'hard stone that came out of Purbecke'.

Downs Vein ledgers crop up in the 16th century. Those selected stones imply the production of paving as well. City of London Ordinances of 1509 laid down minimum thickness and breadth of 'Frestone Bourdou' and minimum thickness of 'Frestone paving rough as it commethe out of the quarry'.

St George's Chapel, Windsor. Beaufort Chapel, 1506. Purbeck Marble floor in twelve inch squares.

USES / 163

King's Bench Walk, London. Purbeck pitchers at left forming pavement, pavers at right, 1677-8.

Though not stated, it seems likely that some, perhaps all, was Purbeck. Early Tudor London was perhaps for the first time acquiring external pavements, though the requirement to improve standards suggests use had been going on long enough for problems to have emerged. One wonders whether even a scrap from this date remains in place. A reasonably secure date for surviving London Purbeck street work seems not to come before the 1677/78 part of Kings Bench Walk. Other areas of obviously-early Purbeck paving survive, tucked away in the Inns of Court, whilst all across London, York stone now dominates. It is tempting to conclude that the York is post-railway. In 1574 large quantities of Purbeck stone were being used at Windsor, and in 1580 the London masons were making 'special provisions for a new stone becoming popular in the city called Purbeck'. The queen's surveyor was Humphrey Michell, which has prompted, wrongly in my opinion, the idea that he gave his name to Mitchel paving.

The Oxford dictionary definition of 'Mitchel' quotes Neve from 1703: 'Purbeck-stones for Paving pick'd all of a Size, from 15 inches square to 2 foot.' What is meant is squares of a set size, from as small as 15 inches to as large as 24 inches square, not rectangles. Happily we have evidence of the use of the term in Purbeck. The Melmoth inventories of the 1680s include '50 foot of muchells' (John's) and Phineas's mentions £3s worth of 'muchells and step'.[4.] The compiler of the Bankes Estate quarry returns for 1726 included on an odd scrap of paper: 'Muchels pay 1s. per hundred (foot) as other stone.' From the landlord's point of view, the royalty rate was the same whatever the shape.

I suspect this clue tells us not of Elizabeth I's surveyor but of a much older origin. The Oxford Dictionary gives 'Michel' as 'Great, with reference to size, bulk or stature', and a quotations from Chaucer: 'A wonder wel farynge knyght of good Mochel and right young thereto'

Medieval Purbeck Marble paving survives in the regular square forms of 12 and 17 inches. The latter would seem to be the original muchel. Was there a name for the smaller other than perhaps a stone? Less commonly, 24 inch squares also occur in early paving.

Another floor of regular 17 inch Downs Vein squares, probably of about 1576, can be found at Buckland Abbey near Plymouth.[5.] In 1603 Thomas Sackville paved his Great Hall at Knole in Kent with 12 inch square chequers, the dark of Marble, the light of Downs Vein, making it one of the last, if not the last, 'grand floor of Purbeck.' The accounts record the use of more Purbeck: '1609 to Thomas Wilson, mason, paving the great beer cellar with Purbeck', and 1612 'Mason has paved cross walks with Purbeck'. 'A. Kerwin for 500 ft of Michell stone for finishing the walk in the garden at 4d per foot, for 70 ft of Purbeck stone at 4d per foot and for water carriage'.[6.]

Kerwin was also supplying Oxfordshire stone, but by the ton, not foot. His Purbeck supplier could have been Robert Codd, Mayor of Corfe, and a Freemason rather than a marbler, as his Will and Inventory record in 1617. He left quarry tools, rough paving and healing (roofing) stones. He must surely have been digging Downs Vein. His will was witnessed by Anthony Vye and Susan Cole, both signing with marks, both from families which figure prominently in the stone trade that was to follow.[7.]

Subsequent alterations make dating of many floors difficult, but another, also of Downs Vein, would seem to be all of a piece with the installation of pews and a gallery in Puddletown church, Dorset, in 1635. Inigo Jones' new Banqueting Hall was finished in 1622 with Nicholas Stone carrying out the masonry. An illustration of an ambassadorial reception there in 1660 (called 'The Embassy') shows it to have had a floor of large dark and light squares laid in staggered courses producing chevrons rather than the usual straightforward chequers. That floor has gone, but that Purbeck was used by Jones in the Palace is known and has resulted in a new Purbeck floor in the restored undercroft.

Ham House, Surrey, has a hall floor of foreign black and white marbles that is generally thought to be of 1610 when the house was built. However part of an area of mostly Purbeck paving outside the north front consists of sixteen and a quarter inch squares, laid in courses rather than diagonally. It makes little sense to lay expensive squares in such a way and the external occurrence is rare. This prompts the suspicion that these squares are from the original hall floor and that the present black and white chequers result from the later reordering of 1637, or even 1672. Nicholas Stone and his contemporary Master Mason of the King's Works, William Cure, were Renaissance men versed in continental marble. Cure, a member of the recently defunct London Company of Marblers, was of foreign extraction. James I commissioned him to make his mother's monument. Every bit of it is from abroad. In 1620 there was a new survey of work at Windsor to the value of an estimated cost of £1,547. 3s. 10d, the largest single item of which was 'paving the terrace with Purbeck stone'.[8.] In 1625 the platform for the ordnance of the Weymouth blockhouse was made of Purbeck stone. A 17th century fort, complete with the Purbeck paving forming the gun platform, survives in Jamaica.[9.]

By the time of the formation of the Joint Stock Company in 1698 it is clear that paving production was the bread and butter trade for Purbeck. Some idea of its scale is provided by records published by the Wren Society. Wren was using Portland ashlar for his cathedral and city churches: various 'marbles', including a hard, dark, polishable limestone from the Isle of Man, and Oland stone (from Sweden) for his 'showy' paving elements, but also Purbeck stone in the more work-a-day areas. The 18th century pattern was set. Southern houses of pretention frequently have Carrara marble or, at second best, Portland, for the hall and main staircase, Purbeck in the servants' quarters.

The Wren Society Publications give an indication of its frequent use in and around London:[10.]

'St. Bennet Finck, Threadneedle St.
1675-76. Cartwright for Paving the Churchyard with Purbeck Stone. £2-6-0. (Churchwarden's Accounts.)

St. Dionis Backchurch, Fenchurch St.
1672 Pave the Alley with Purbeck stone.
1673 Bill of John Thompson, Mason, and for Purbeck stone, 9d the foot. (Vestry Minutes)

Royal Hospital, Chelsea.
1686. To Thomas Hill, Mason. For Work done in the South front over ye Porticoe, […]

Ham House, Surrey. Area of outside paving under portico, including Purbeck squares, probably from a previous arrangement.

Dunshay Manor. Approach path, probably 1642, consisting of seventeen inch Downs Vein squares, set diagonally.

For 5:4 of Purback Step, there rubd at 2s 6d p foote   13s 4d
For 5:4 of rough Purback Step there at 2s p foote   10s 6d
1687 Thomas Hill, Mason: in the Hall and Chappell,

Neve, talking of marble other than Purbeck, says: 'Some Pavements, (as in Foot-paces before Chimneys) are laid all of one sort, or colour, and in one entire Stone; others of two Colours laid square, or Chequer-ways, the side of one by the side of the other; others are laid Arrace-wise, of two Colours, laid Angle to Angle, and this last is the neatest way; but there may be divers Forms contriv'd to lay them in.'[11.]]

Royal Hospital, Greenwich.
1706. … that the Cellars under the West building next Fryer's Rd be paved with rough Purbeck Stone.
1716. Cellar floor paved rough purbeck and passages ground floor with rubbed Purbeck, Mitchells.

Whitehall Palace. In Her Majesty's Chappell Closett.

USES / 165

Langton Matravers High Street. Well curb outside Street Well Cottage.

Swanage, near the pier head. Streetwork, 19th century. From top: kerb (broached), gutter sole, pitcher.

Langton Matravers Museum, Trapstone to cover drain hole.

survives in Langton High Street outside Street Well Cottage. The central hole is sufficient to allow for a bucket, and the top surface is weathered (sloped) away from the hole to prevent dirty water entering.

In the course of 19th century reorderings paving, much of it Downs Vein, found its way into many churches. Another common product was steps, cut to a standard size, about twelve inches by six inches by a minimum length. Some can be found at least as far west as Ottery St. Mary, Devon, where shop doorways still have them.

This streetwork continued. By the late 19th century kerb had replaced paving as the main product. Indeed it was the trade's mainstay, particularly through the recessionary 1920s, but concrete was soon to largely replace it. As late as the 1950s my father was supplying kerb, of various widths but standard at about twelve inches deep, quadrants, pitchers and gutter soles all still wrought out of the rough without the aid of a saw. In his 80s he recalled the weights of various categories, important to know when loading railway trucks at Swanage depot:

Pitchers, 1 ton 6' width @ 6' deep equalled 55ft run
Gutter soles, 60ft run
[This difference is accounted for by the fact that pitchers were left off the punch whilst gutter soles were chiselled flat. The sole formed the base of the gutter, between kerb and pitcher, its smooth finish allowing for easy flow of water and cleaning.]
Kerb, 1 ton 5' wide x 12' deep equalled 35ft run
Kerb, 1 ton 6' wide x 12' deep equalled 30ft
Kerb, 1 ton 8' wide x 12' deep equalled 25ft
Kerb, 1 ton 9' wide x 12' deep equalled 20ft

For speed, this sort of work was measured with a line of known length (c.20ft). The kerbs of variable lengths were generally stood on end and one end of the line was held up against the bottom of the first piece, marking the length at the top with the fingers of the other hand. Then the 'upper' holding finger position on the line was offered up to the next piece at the bottom, and so on along the length of the line. In wet weather the line was checked for length before and after loading, by measuring it in a similar way against a two-foot gauge. No bits of paper, no arithmetic. Many yards, even miles of this streetwork, even though in good condition, has been replaced by concrete. I was astonished to see the entire length of Greasehead, virtually all in good condition and dressed by Thomas Bonfield, scrapped. Hounslow Council was doing the same thing as recently as 1996, even in a conservation area.

In the partially-mechanised depot of the 1930s, when they had a floor to do, my grandfather would more often than not get Albert (Fiddler) Bower and Albert Phippard to go through the common paving, of which they carried a stock brought from the quarries, and organise it in courses. This involved minimal re-dressing of the joints and the need to avoid waste in general. They would also refine by tooling the top face. If a random arrangement was required the stones would be laid out as they progressed. On completion a drawing was made and

168 / PURBECK STONE

North Street, Langton Matravers. Underside of Downs Vein paving. Mark at centre is measurement indicating six superficial square feet. Mark at top right represents course No 3. Lighter 'W' mark is the personal mason's mark.

Kimmeridge churchyard. Downs Vein headstone, 1779 with measurement mark on the back representing nine and a half square feet.

numbers painted on the undersides so the fixer could follow without confusion.

The men at the quarries generally produced common paving marked on the underside with the superficial measurement to the nearest half a square foot in a Purbeck version of the Roman system. The measurement was all important, for it was the basis on which payment was made. Working to the nearest half foot could cause contention. Men rounded up more often than down, according to the merchants. My father said that Harry Burt, who did the measuring in the depot, had to contend with Josiah Harris, who would trudge to Swanage to argue the toss over a half foot or so quite regularly. It seems that the usual system was to mark a stone in each load with one's personal mark. I guess it was sufficient to mark just one stone in each load for the merchant to know whose was whose! Virtually all of these marks are straight for speed of cutting, quickly chopped in so they reveal the width of the chisel used. Brian Bugler has spotted a rare exception to this: a Downs Vein paving bearing a mark consisting of both full and half-length strokes, the latter achieved not by the use of a narrow chisel but by holding the same chisel so that only one corner bit in. The course marks also follow the same Roman type system as the measurement mark, as do some personal marks, which can cause confusion. Rarely, a slab can exhibit all three. Two strokes in a stone of two square feet may tell of its size, but alternatively it may indicate that it belongs to Number Two course. Yet more confusion is caused by the addition of the horizontal mark representing a half being added left or right of the units. Course marks tell of preparation at the merchant's or quarry rather than the arrangement being left to be done on site. Gauged work like big ledgers or standard squares did not receive measurement marks, there was no need. A Kimmeridge headstone of 1779 exhibits 'VIIII' on its rough back, which tells us of adaptation from the original intention for use, which perhaps explains the plain square top. This sort of thing is possibly not unusual. West Alvington, Devon, has two unmarked Purbeck stone slabs on very modest external chest tombs. Both stones possess roughly dressed edges, as was the normal treatment of paving.

USES / 169

The rediscovered Marble supports show it was about nineteen feet long! This is surely the slab for which Adam De Corfe, Marbler, was paid 50s. in 1311, 'to place at the high table of the King', in Westminster Palace. Edward II had been on the throne four years.[19] However archaeologist Philip Emery concludes that the evidence suggests that the great stone was nearer thirteen feet long but with extensions. The re-discovered supports that pre-date Adam's top have been re-assembled in their original positions. As so often with things medieval, it is not easy to be certain.

However, what must be certain is that size availability influenced design. Whoever carved the Wadham tomb of a soft Freestone in Ilminster church in 1452 could hardly have done so before being sure he could get its 11 feet long top slab. I guess it was worked first. Imagine doing all the soft stone work; having a go at the Purbeck top and then knocking a corner off, leaving it too small. The freestone carver ordered the biggest Purbeck that quarries could get, his client being wealthy, before designing the chest to suit it. The medieval tombmakers were responsive to the materials as available.

With the exception of a few hand-sawn 18th and 19th century Cliff stone examples, all pre-1900 Purbeck slabs were smoothed off by hand. So the face is invariably of the colour and fossil content possessed of that particular layer near the bedding plane. They did not hew off more than they had to! In the case of one of the green Marble beds lots of distinctive fossil unios cluster near the upper bed surface, hardly any at the other. Should the marbler have selected the first, the resulting slab would present a unio rich face, if the other, a unio poor one. What may appear to be two different beds on the evidence of only one visible face are in fact one and the same.

Christchurch Priory stands almost alone in possessing several medieval slabs of Purbeck beds other than Marble. One is puzzling, but just could be New Vein from Durlston Bay. The shape of the missing brass suggests a date around 1400, John Savage (1773) having been added later. The others are a group of probably eight which are definitely Cliff Blue Bit. The precise number is difficult to tell, for they have been recut and moved to fit re-arrangements. In my opinion they are almost certainly from the St. Aldhelm's Head undercliff. The least mutilated bear peripheral Lombardic inscriptions to Prior Borard (1397) and John Wodenham (1377). It would seem they are all of this late 14th century period. Why did not others find their way elsewhere around that time?

The next Blue Bit example seems to be Bishop Goodrich (1554) in Ely. His brass survives, and so do most of those in what is probably the next, Sherman (1583?), in Ottery St. Mary. Perhaps the same merchant supplied the next that also occurs in Devon, the Cary/Helier ledger (1607) in Exeter. It has a medieval style peripheral inscription, plus more text cut bookwise later. In the 18th century a branch of the Carys became owners of Renscombe, by coincidence the manor on which lies the headland productive of these slabs. Their ledger bears on its escutcheon three roses. One wonders whether there was a connection with the Rose family who were in possession of Rempstone and a Swanage manor with active quarries. Their seal, similarly consisting of three roses 'slipped proper',

appears on the Joint Stock Agreement of 1698. Near this Cary/Helier slab in Exeter is another of Marble commemorating, in a peripheral black letter inscription, Sir Richard Helier (1446). Both now bear lead filled letters which cannot be original, but surely are examples of a 19th century re-cutting. This sort of thing may not have been uncommon. Certainly some Salisbury slabs have had their inscriptions deepened relatively recently. Perhaps this is a solution to the problem of loss by wear – keep the letters going down with the surface. It may not be ideal, an awkward task for the letter cutter, but better than a total loss.

After the restoration of Charles II other beds of Purbeck stone became commonly used as ledgers. Exeter, Salisbury and Winchester Cathedrals, plus Romsey Abbey and Christchurch Priory have the largest assemblies. Outside England there was a traffic to the American colonies. The precise identification of many is difficult, but not all. Comparisons between these major groupings are interesting, and no doubt tell us of particular Swanage merchants supplying particular monumental masons who were also dealing with, or competing with other monumental masons using stone from other sources. Those main competitors in the south of England are Portland, and what continue to be called until recently, in a rather loose way, Belgium Black, plus others more locally restricted, such as Lias and a type or types of Wiltshire Glauconitic sandy limestones, often called Chilmark. As well as the sandy limestones, the Purbeck beds also occur in the Chilmark region. This Wiltshire 'Purbeck' has obvious similarity with Purbeck from Purbeck, but yet is distinctive.

There is a similar difficulty with the Purbeck that outcrops in the Dorset Ridgeway. Settlements such as Dorchester and Puddletown have lots of it in the form of rubble, but it was also used for more demanding elements in 16th century Wolfeton House, somewhat earlier Athelhampton and Old Kingston Maurward House. Most of this stone is easy to distinguish from Purbeck Purbeck. The one bed that can be identified in both regions is the Cinder. It is of little use but does turn up in rubble. In my opinion an area of floor in the pub only a short walk from the quarries in Upwey is Purbeck Downs Vein – not from the adjacent quarries. This is reinforced by an advertisement for Upwey stone from 1889, which does not mention paving.[20] Similarly, Athelhampton contains paving that is surely from Purbeck, and some of the stone in the house itself is very much like Purbeck Burr, but may not be.

It is probably safe to say that most post-medieval ledgers were dispatched from Purbeck in a plain condition, and that the inscriptions were cut locally. This is certainly true of some Channel Island 17th century Grub examples, for they bear a local granite style of crude raised block lettering, quite unlike anything found in southern England. However, where skills were lacking there were exceptions. In a description of the dire straits that affected recessionary Poole in 1843, there appears:

> 'The Newfoundland fisheries have been of great importance to Poole. I saw a curious specimen of free-trade while in that town. A trader had received from Newfoundland a consignment of salted cod. The payment was to be a shipment of goods, partly made of clothes and partly of grave-stones. The grave-stones were in process of manufacture, the letter of advice specified the length

ABOVE St Lawrence, Jersey. Ledger slab, Swanage Grub.

BELOW Trinity, Newfoundland. A mixture of Purbeck and Portland tombstones.

and breadth and thickness of the stones, and gave the names, ages, dates, and so on, of the parties to be commemorated; with the addition, that all of them must have four or more lines of religious verse at the bottom, the verses to be made in Poole. 'You see,' said the trader, 'what we can give in exchange for human food, when we are allowed to bring it in. The Newfoundlanders would go without tomb-stones were we not to take their cod, for they have nothing else to give us; but as we are allowed to import their cod-fish, we can give our stone-cutters a job; perhaps if we were allowed to take corn in exchange, we would supply some other part of the world with grave-stones; at all events, we would supply some other portions of our workpeople with work.'[21]

These slabs may or may not have been of Purbeck, but it seems highly likely.

The fact of inscriptions being arranged to be cut across the Atlantic when the only connection was by sail is surprising. When I visited Newfoundland I found about thirty Purbeck headstones, all of the 18th century. The biggest assembly is at Trinity, the harbour used by one of the biggest cod fishery merchants, Lester of Poole. Rather more common, and more widely distributed, are Portland headstones. One of these, at Brigus, is signed by George Bonfield, surely the Swanage merchant. A grave at Trinity is marked at head and foot by two almost identical Portland stones. I was told that the dead

USES / 173

St Brelade, Jersey, three identical headstones. One, Maugen, (1780), is Purbeck, the other two Portland. Surely the local men cut all three?

man's widow ordered a stone from England which failed to arrive; she sent a repeat order, and ended up with two. So, not to be wasteful, she had both set up!

What distinguishes the Newfoundland Purbeck group, and indeed 18th century Purbeck headstones in England in general is that, though there is an obvious genre, few of the top shapes are exactly the same. Obviously the cutters did not have face moulds that they used time and again. This variation was probably partly driven by the fact that the stones differed in size. One of the Trinity Downs Vein stones, James Pottle (1781), 'Native of Christchurch Hants' has what is almost certainly a measurement mark on its back. Gauged work was not normally marked, for it was sold by the piece, so it seems these stones left the quarry as paving but were adapted. However from a practical point of view there was not much sense in this. Why dress a stone into a neat rectangle only to knock the corners off one end later as required by a typical headstone shape? If this is what was done there would have been a natural reluctance to cut away, and thereby waste, too much. This could be why some 18th century Purbeck stones exhibit relatively square tops. Will Jones (1778) of Trinity, Newfoundland, is an example. His stone is doubly interesting for it is Downs Vein, whilst his wife's, dying only two years before, is Portland, but the lettering is similar. This is surely the work of the same man.

In 1708 Freemason Thomas Sweet of Chilmark, Wiltshire, requested a 'Purbeck paving tombstone very good and large and to have letters cut in it for me.' He left 12 pounds to cover its costs and those of his burial.[22] Some inscriptions possess a charming naivety, others lack much interest. The best are wonderful, both in terms of design and execution; a few echo the medieval masterpieces when the best artists were working in a Purbeck medium. Dating pitfalls remain, with some commemorating several people all recorded at the same time, whilst others had inscriptions added over time. Almost all ledgers, particularly the biggest ledger assemblies in the cathedrals, are under threat from trampling feet.

It is a boyhood memory of mine, helping my father measure ledgers in Salisbury that had decayed to the point of being dangerously uneven. Introducing underfloor heating forced the lifting of much of the Salisbury pavements and provided an opportunity to get rid of the worst stuff. Most of these dangerous rotten slabs were either medieval Grey Marble indents or Laining Vein Rag, or New Vein ledgers of much later date; it is never easy to be sure in that the inscriptions had gone, but circumstantially of late 18th and early 19th century. A point to be made with all the beds is that some just do not crop up at all as ledgers because they do not occur in big enough blocks, others only occasionally. These tell of other work absorbing the small stuff. It makes sense to, say, dig Downs Vein for paving, setting aside the occasional big stone for something special like a ledger.

Problems of identification remain with all. Even the Blue bit, with its big distinctive Trigonia bivalves, can be confused with stuff from the Chilmark district, which has the same fossils in spite of being somewhat older. The polishable stones from the Weald present another challenge of identification. The best known are from Petworth, Sussex and Bethersden, Kent, less so Laughton and Charlwood, sometimes called Winkle stone; the beds occur higher up the succession than Purbeck, at the top of the Weald clay. They must be later by a few million years. Though not relevant to ledgers, there is a somewhat similar problem in the separation of Isle of Wight stone from Burr. It is later in date, with all the Wealden plus Chalk separating the two. Most of the Isle of Wight beds are easy to tell at a glance, but some, particularly that which gets called Quarr stone, is similar. Another problematic stone crops up around Aylesbury. It is Marble-like, but not from the Purbeck beds of that region, rather from lower in the Jurassic, below the Kimmeridgean.

Downs Vein is about three feet thick and subdivided into several different beds. The mangy bed part, common and distinctive in paving, was not much used for memorials because of the soft trace fossil pockets that despoil the face, but other more problematic bits of the Downs Vein were. The Clear All bed is so bland, fine grained and free of obvious shell that it could be mistaken for Portland, and was favoured for monuments. It has the occasional black shell, of a species that cannot occur in Portland, but it really can be difficult to tell. Another helpful clue is that some tight vents (they must be tight to withstand the dressing process) can have a rusty stain associated. No Portland has anything like it. Other parts can be of an open pinholey texture, easily confused with inland Freestone, which does not occur as ledgers, being too small on plan and generally too thick in bed height. The top part of the Downs Vein is quite different, dark enough to be confused with Thornback or even Grub. Thornback, which generally has a scatter of small black shells, is fairly easy to identify, but some stones of the Oxford area are superficially similar and can deceive. What can put them beyond doubt is the presence of a scallop, which no Thornback can possess. It has been suggested that the small black oyster, characteristic of Thornback, is in fact from the Cinder bed, which was being eroded in one area as more beds, including Thornback, were accumulating elsewhere. It would explain how a marine species got into a lagoonal environment, but more than that, it brings home how complicated Purbeck geology can be!

Downs Vein was being dug as early as the 13th century, as

evidenced by its use then as roof tile, to the modern era. In general it does not occur in big pieces and quite extensive recent quarrying has yielded hardly a stone over four feet long, though bigger slabs were found in the past. The most common usage was as paving, but large selected stones were made into ledgers from as early as the 16th century. Two similar crudely cut, pre-Reformation altar tops of Downs Vein at Church Knowle (*see page 76*) and Arne probably belong to this period. All the other 25 or so Purbeck medieval altars are of Marble (with the possible exception of Boxgrove). There are few brasses set in Downs Vein, perhaps its light colour was a deterrent to use, but a slab now only possessed of rivets in Norwich Cathedral's South Transept is an example. Winchester has two early Downs Vein ledgers, whilst hidden under the nave chairs is the charming William Lambe, 'Singinge Man' (1631). Foolishly I almost missed this as being Portland, but of course it is too early to be Portland main stream. Another quite exceptional slab is in St. Andrew's, Norwich. It once bore a brass and has an inscription added in 165? It looks like Downs Vein, but at over eight feet it is almost unbelievably big for that layer and, as a non-Marble medieval indent, rare in the extreme.

Lying immediately above the Downs Vein is a bed called the Leper. West of Acton it is about seven inches thick, at Belle Vue only about four. It is extremely hard and dense, lacking obvious shells, and blue hearted, though this blueness does not extend to the actual bed surface. Hence it could be tooled over to produce a face without the blue being exposed. Recently quarried Leper has all proved to be quite small, but some modest 17th century ledgers are made of it. Surface working of Downs Vein would force its removal; underground they sometimes took it, if only to build the legs and provide more headroom, (or should it better be called shoulder room?); sometimes it was left up as the ceiling. Richard Claville's brass plate (1637) at Kimmeridge is set in a piece five feet three by two feet four inches. But soon after this date they began finding better stuff.

A whole series of second half of the 17th century ledgers are of a good lasting, dark, shelly Purbeck that in my opinion is Grub from the Swanage district. They include the best post-medieval slabs. We can be sure they are from there in that elsewhere the bed is very different. For example, close by the Worth road north of Eastington, the top half is small, thin broken stuff, the bottom ceiling bed part more shale than stone, with only the dense, hard, middle two inch bed good; certainly not a source of big slabs. In the Acton area around the Priest's Way it is almost non existent as a solid stone, but northwards towards the hamlet it develops as thin, flakey beds of stone with lots of partings. By the Kingston road it has thickened. The bottom is of poor quality, termed the Ceiling bed, as that is what it was in most underground quarrs of that area. Above that there is a separate, dense, hard bed, about two or three inches thick, and very good. Above a gingery brown parting there are several beds of good quality but marred by lots of discontinuous clay patches. Northwards from the Kingston road these clay patches fade out, leaving a good, clean stone, of which virtually none has been dug in that this bed was left up as the ceiling. Westwards it changes again. At Gallows Gore the ceiling bed improves whilst the top part becomes more mealy and the blocks are generally small, so there are no good ledgers from this district either.

In the California and Mutton Hole district, south of Swanage, the gingery brown parting is also prominent, a good example of a distinctive bedding plane extending over miles. Above it the stone is rather poor, unevenly bedded and of little value. But below it the good, hard, dense bed is grown on to the ceiling bed which, unlike at Langton, is good. It is this lower half of the Swanage Grub that produced excellent slabs. The under side is of a general grey/brown colour dominated by lots of black shells, the upper part a dense blue black with a pure white shell concentrated in one very thin layer, a distinctive death assembly that extends over miles. So within a few inches of thickness this rock changes considerably, and different ledgers of the same bed can present quite different faces, depending on whether the slabs were inverted or not, or how much was hewn off to achieve a good face. As with green Marble, what may appear, on the evidence of only one visible face, to be two or even three different beds, is in fact one and the same layer.

Recent quarrying has revealed some Swanage sections of the Grub. At Mutton Hole the good bottom part is about four inches thick, the blocks generally too small to make ledgers. To the south it thickens to about seven inches and the blocks are bigger. Westwards in California it thickens more and beautiful blocks are produced, but continuing westwards across Belle Vue it thins again and is not much use. Eastwards across Southard it reduces to six inches or so and the blocks are generally small with many lists, whilst in Durlston Bay it is down to about four inches or so and very broken. What few pieces there are to be found in the waste piles west of Round Down reveal it to be even thinner there. However, somewhere in the wider Swanage district, sometime around 1650, they began to dig considerable quantities of Grub, using the biggest stones for ledgers, a number of which survive. Salisbury Cathedral has 14, including the most splendid, which bears a brass commemorating Alexander Hyde (1667), and flawlessly measures nine feet five inches by four feet three, a serious rival to the great medieval brass indents. Most bear inscriptions rather than brasses, many as good as when cut. Winchester has 21, with dates between 1655 and 1713, interestingly Chichester and Westminster, none. But others got as far afield as rural Norfolk (ledger to Will Bullock of 1693, Lessingham, complete with nice fossil bone) and in Suffolk, at Barsham, a headstone to Thomas Edward (1695), plus a remarkable assembly of three (all late 17th century) at Raveningham, Norfolk. At least one has made it to the continent. Curiously lacking an inscription, it lies outside the Gruuthuse, Bruges, amongst slabs of the local blue stone. Another, at Portsmouth bears: 'Here lieth y body of Sam. Ive who departed this life the 8 of Aug 1667 Being the Master Carver belonging to the dockyard'. Locally, Steeple church has Sarah Collens (1675), Eliz Bond (1674), Nath Bond (1728). Lady St Mary's, Wareham, has William Bond (1669), and another commemorating Robert Coombes (1714), plus others including Richard Haines (1754). It is perhaps relevant that last amongst the 142 artisans who signed the Joint Stock Company agreement of 1698 was Thomas Coombes, before five gentry who included 'Richard Hains'; perhaps this same Richard. What involvement those men had with the company and quarrying is not clear, but the association must have been close.

In Swanage the slab to Brune Cockrum (1710) is another probable piece of Grub, as is at Kimmeridge the loose headstone to a member of the Foote family (1693); but as with all heavily patinated external stones, it is difficult to be certain. A clear pattern thus emerges of the exploitation of Swanage Grub between 1650 and about 1720. Many of these ledger slabs are around six feet long, which is bigger than any blocks I have had the luck to dig at Southard. However Grub tends to run bigger where shallow, and saucer-like dips tend to be productive of big slabs rather than the obverse dome-like forms that I have encountered. In the second half of the 17th century somewhere south of Swanage, possibly around where Bon Accord Road has been developed, plus virtually certainly California, men were finding fine, big slabs from shallow ridden holes rather than underground. But, no matter how good, any quarry would surely have been also producing stones too small, or of the wrong shape, for ledgers or even headstones. They would perhaps have been too thick for the main item of trade at that time, paving, but a convenient thickness for articles like steps and gutters.

A quite exceptional and probably unique monument made of Grub is the plain tomb chest to the Rev. W. Watkinson (1702) in Sturminster Marshall. Another is the splendid slab outside Langton church. It must surely have been one of the monuments recorded in Hutchins, but chucked out, with others, punched all over, before being put in the path by the Victorians. They have a lot to answer for! I guess the most likely is that it was Rector George King's 'flat blue stone' (1709).[23] That others in the curved path rearrangement were originally larger is revealed by pit marks on their edges.

Above the Laining Vein there are several hard bluish beds, separated by clays, which were also used for ledgers from the 17th century onwards, and for a few brass indents before that. Excavations to allow a barn to be built at Greyseed Farm revealed an old ridden hole largely comprised of small and odd-shaped bits of one of these excellent beds. The old hands had clearly taken it where it was shoaling, and I suspect they did along much of Greasehead and eastwards as far as Durlston Bay, where big slabs of it are falling on to the shore. It is much less common than Grub, but examples of its use include the splendid slab in Salisbury Cathedral's north transept commemorating Ann Dear (1720). Medieval usage would seem to be rare, but a floor slab in Cawston, Norfolk, bearing rivets indicating a missing brass, must be one example. Laining Vein proper occurs as post-medieval paving and tomb stones, but I have poor knowledge of these, mostly blueish, beds. Rarely, they crop up as a wall tablet; in Kentisbeare, Devon, Edmund Crosse's record of bequests with its Beer stone surround, is almost certainly an example.

Another dark possibility is the Feather. What we currently quarry at Belle Vue would have been of little use in pre-easy-saw days in that neither surface is good, clean stone, suitable to bearing an inscription. One is flaky, the other hard but marred by soft spots; to cut down to a good face would have been a lot of work. However, some blocks at Belle Vue tend to split. Where they do, a good face could be more readily achieved. Such monuments are rare, but Ambrose Carter (1753) in Romsey is surely one, if not from Belle Vue then from somewhere where the bed is similar.

Several beds below the Cap have flint nodules. They are most striking in the Cap and Brassy bed, but also present much less noticeably in the Feather. Such a slab, dark, dense, plain, but with small raised flint clusters, lies in Swanage church north aisle west of the slab to Joan, wife of stone merchant Thomas Chapman, not a ledger but a pointer to the possibility of others. A bed about five inches thick at Belle Vue, splits off the bottom of the cap. It is fine grained, has small flints and a polygonal shrinkage pattern not only in relief but within the sediment, so a worked slab continues to show this highly distinctive patterning. I have only seen one such ledger, in Rye church, before the altar rail in the southeast chapel, commemorating Edward Wilmshurst (1718). Cap itself is generally thick, so is hardly to be expected to serve as a ledger, but Alice Scott (1708), in Christchurch, is a piece. Another rarity is the Brassy bed, whose coarse composition suggestive of concrete would tend to make it unsuitable for lettering; however, some cutters managed to overcome this difficulty. There is a large slab of it adjacent to a monument to Max Warren in Westminster Abbey cloister walk. Such a size would suggest a monument rather than mere paving. Perhaps the inscription has been entirely worn away? Another is John Welshman (1698), in Christchurch Priory. This stone is good, but other New Vein beds have failed badly. They are mostly White Bit, which at best is about borderline, at worst poor, and Tomson bed, which serves only to give Purbeck a bad name. Presumably the name corrupts from Tombstone, but it is not suitable. Another failure is the Laining Vein Rag such as occurs at Southard. A slab of this has been recently removed from Steeple church. It commemorated Roger Clavell (1687). It was already undecipherable by 1850 and worn to the point of being dangerous by the 1990s. This bed is bluish and has plenty of shells, but it seems the matrix has a clay component that inexorably breaks up.

Though these beds have failed, there are more that are good. Perhaps best of all is Langton Thornback. Around Acton it tends to be hard and rough on the upper surface (hence its name) where a rotten scurf bed either can be 'grown on' or, if lucky, slips off freely. It generally tends to become somewhat softer towards the underside, where a thin 'sad' bit adheres. This 'sad', 'sat', 'zad' or 'zat' bit can be a mere crust, or it can thicken to at least two inches thick as in Alf Benfield's Kingston road quarry. Immediately to the south of Acton the Thornback is thin, about five inches, but very hard right to the underside, which has a generous scatter of black shells; smoothing off this surface produces an excellent face. Towards Burngate the underside is much softer. This underside is invariably used as the face, in that the other side, even if the scurf does slip off freely, is marred by soft clay-like patches.

Ernest Norman would tease my Uncle Frank by calling Thornback 'the Pride of Purbeck', knowing as he did that Frank did not think much of it. 'Never seen one without a clay patch' was Frank's retort. Some ledgers have worn and the inscriptions have been lost because they are of the soft sort. The rate of wear will slow up, for they get progressively harder away from the bed surface. If such a stone was to be cut now with the benefit of modern machinery it would be easy to saw it in the optimum place. However, the best, such as those quarried in east Eastington Cowlease, Highlands and Long Close, are really good, deserving, in my opinion, Ernest's label. One of the last from this especially good area we cut in 1996 for John Ralph Bankes' headstone. Inscribed by John Andrew, it stands outside the southeast corner of Studland church. Westwards of a line running north from Eastington they are thicker, much softer and generally small, so not ledger material.

There are some 18th century Thornback headstones which show the natural underside of the block as the back. These, I suspect, were ridden from quarries so shallow that this generally homogenous bed split on bedding planes, which happens where it lies close to the surface. Roy Cobb told me that he ridded shallow Thornbacks not far northwest of Eastington that went over in beds in this way. Winchester has five Thornback ledgers cut between 1671 and 1709 (against 21 Grub), Salisbury has two plus two Wetsun beds, (against 14 Grub). These crude samples would suggest that in the late 17th and early 18th century Swanage men were digging more Grub than Langton men Thornback. Local Thornback examples include Christopher Goss (1698) in Worth Matravers church, Francis Swaine, daughter of Roger Clavel (1701) in Kimmeridge church, and James Gould, Rector of West Stafford (1708). One of the furthest afield commemorates Ralf Greedier (1696) in St Nicholas at Wade, Kent. It has a somewhat unusual white list which is surely a clue to its source.

Current quarrying south of Priest's Way to the south of Acton produces blocks with such lists, and suggests a source in that direction. Swanage church has a large paving in the central nave aisle close to the chancel steps which has a blurred blue heart. This is exactly like the Thornbacks in the Belle Vue region of Herston where this bed tends to include small clay clasts, which diminishes its quality from a letter-cutter's point of view. Wetsun beds, particularly the upper part, can be very like Thornback, and a problem to differentiate, but they do tend to be more fractured, so big stones are less likely. Unlike Grub, Thornback and Wetsun are quarryable underground, so they continued to be available after the shallow stuff got worked out and underground working increased. Unlike Grub, they continue to crop up on through the 18th and 19th centuries.

West of Acton and in Eastington Cowlease, the underpart of the Wetsun bed which is of a quite contrasting sediment can adhere to the top without any cleavage plane at all. In some areas it slips off freely, where it can be about five inches thick. It tends to be a light buff, with odd black shells and often blue hearted, and it may account for some of the problematic stones difficult to identify. Kevin Keates coined the name 'grandma bed' for his. We cut the back of the memorial seat at St. Aldhelm's Head from it (quarried at Turnpike). Benjamin Jesty's headstone in Worth churchyard may also be of this lower part of the Wetsun bed. My father remarked that the Wetsun or 'Sugar' bed, as the Swanage men called it, was about the most

Studland churchyard. Thornback headstone to J. R. Bankes, 1996.

Langton Matravers. St George's. Wetsun bed. Lord Tovey's memorial tablet.

variable bed. Be that as it may, two plaques serve to show how different it can be within a short distance: the 1960s wall-mounted war memorial in Langton's Village Hall's Memorial room, dug 200 yards or so southwest of Acton compared with Lord Tovey's tablet in Langton church, dug due south of Acton, just north of Priest's Way.

Amongst these difficult slabs are some which are rare because

ABOVE Freshwater, Isle of Wight. Purbeck headstone, to Robert Shutler, 1715. Note treatment of 'J' in 'joyful'.

LEFT Worth Matravers churchyard. 'Turner style' headstone, 1850.

the general run of block was too small. However when the quarrymen found a fair sized stone they took advantage of it. One such rare bed is the Vye Bit. Westminster Abbey's cloister south walk has Mary Medley (1783 + later inscriptions). It is over six feet long, has a list and a vent, is asymmetrically blue-hearted and has the distinctive small, tough, silicified white shell which resists wear and therefore sticks up. Weathered stones in the field walls of Belle Vue, Verney and westwards show the same shell etched in relief. This Medley slab is surely a Vye Bit, almost certainly from the Swanage rather than the Langton district. I have quarried tons without ever finding one as big.

Amongst the Cliff stone beds only the Blue Bit splits thin enough and big enough to provide natural slabs suitable for ledgers. Where used inside the result is good, but where outside in a saturated situation recumbent slabs can be frost-shattered. The Spangle below it tends to be much more broken and venty, and I have never encountered it as a ledger. The Cliff Freestone beds are thick and quite the wrong shape. But they can be sawn to produce fair-sized slabs, and there are post-medieval examples, which are difficult to separate from Portland. Medieval use of Cliff stone in general is rare and the Christchurch Priory Blue Bit assembly stands out as being exceptional. A few Cliff Blue Bits continue after 1700 but are also relatively rare. Ann Brown (1713) in Studland, remains protected from wear in a sanctuary position and in good condition.

Other later 18th century Blue Bit examples include a series of three to the Bennell family (1755) at Coombe Keynes. Tilly Whim is definitely not a possible source, nor East Winspit. Other cliff quarries remain just possible, but in my opinion St. Aldhelm's Head is the almost certain source, the undercliff for the early ones, the quarr for those after about 1700. At Chichester the Bishop's kitchen has steps of Blue Bit which are just like what we currently quarry at St. Aldhelm's Head. I suspect that these, which are probably 18th century, are also of St. Aldhelm's Head provenance. At Chichester there are ledgers of Cliff Freestone that could only have been produced by sawing. One, in the west cloister, is laid adjacent to three Portland examples. It is worn, the date is gone, but William W??LL is still evident. The north chapel, east of the door, contains two Portland type ledgers. Of these Bridget Shore is Cliff and again sadly the date is worn away, but the lettering style, similar to neighbouring Barbara Briggs, would suggest c. 1735.

For what it is worth, the 18th century Punch House in East Street, Chichester, has a splendid Blue Bit threshold, sculptured, with wear. It seems someone in or near Chichester was dealing with a Purbeck merchant who dealt in Cliff stone. Winchester has a Cliff headstone; Margaret wife of John Jolliffe (177?), now sadly languishing as a paving stone. Hand sawing of this sort of stone for headstones continued from the mid until the late 19th century in Worth Matravers, where several such were worked by the Turners of Port Arthur, Winspit. A number of their stones are of the same pointed top style.

Lichens make the identification of headstones more difficult than internal ledgers. Perhaps the best clue to look for first is whether the back is rough or not. Virtually all old inland Purbeck headstones are, for they were made from split slabs, whilst most Portland are not, as they are a product of sawing. As far off as Woolverstone, Suffolk, where Purbeck is getting thin on the ground, James Sewell (1713), stands out for this reason. Examination reveals a good fine grained face suggestive of Portland, but it is Downs Vein, probably from around Gallows Gore. Purbeck stone examples seem to begin with the Restoration. Many south coast churchyards have assemblies consisting of a few 17th century stones plus many more of the 18th century. Langton, the source of so many, does not have a single pre-18th century example! The 18th century was the most productive time, with odd stones getting as far afield as Tenby (Robert Salter (1761), master of a sloop, of Emsworth). There are also Portland examples from this pre-machine period, and during the course of the 19th century, perhaps to do with the introduction of mechanisation, they seem to win out in the competition, such that they dominate numerically, even in Purbeck at, for example, Langton's old cemetery.

178 / PURBECK STONE

Another complication in terms of making identification is the mixing by monumental masons of stones from different sources. Alverstoke, Gosport, has a box tomb, Henry Abraham (1709), with a Portland top on Purbeck sides, but there are greater oddities. A *c.*1800 brick box tomb at Happisburgh, Norfolk, has a Marble top with rivet holes which once secured a brass. Canford Magna has a similar survival, which in my opinion was an altar top. Both are surely medieval, as are virtually all such usages of Marble of apparently 18th and 19th century date.

TILE

In the recent past roofing stone seems simply to have been called 'tile' or 'stone tile'. Earlier references also called it 'Healing Stone', but that term has gone out of use; the occupation of hellier (slater, tiler) derives from the word. The word 'slat' crops up in some old Purbeck references, but it too has gone out of use. However the term is used in Portland for some of the overlying Purbeck beds because of their fissile qualities. It can be seen on a few Portland houses.

'Slat', used to mean splitting, may have only recently died out. Arthur Hancock related that old Thomas Haysom would emerge from the Black Swan the worse for drink, swing around a lamp post and say 'Ah, me zun, thes cusunt slat a Cap!' Cap tends to consist of big homogeneous blocks which can only be split (or slatted) with considerable skill.

Corfe Castle village, the Bankes Arms. Mid-20th century example of expertly-laid graduated Purbeck stone roof, with largest courses at the bottom and smallest at the ridge.

My father was of the opinion that stone tile roofs, largely confined to the local district, were in the main a spin off from the paving trade. Quarrying for paving, particularly Downs Vein, also produced layers which were too thin and flimsy, and could be made use of for roofs. Certainly a lot of Downs Vein was quarried from about 1500 until about 1900, and it seems likely that most of the roofs we see were dug during that period. He was probably right to a degree, but it is not the whole story. What has recently emerged is that quarrying of tile (and virtually nothing else except Marble) was being pursued on a considerable scale on at least one manor, Langton Wallis, during the 15th century.[24]

There is evidence of yet earlier use. Archaeologists have recorded tiles from a number of Roman sites. Perhaps of particular interest are the finds made by Titus Lander at his Gallows Gore quarry between 1931 and 1949. J. Bernard Calkin records: 'short lengths of wall foundations still remained in place. Nearby, we sometimes found roofing stones. Some were rectangular, others had pointed ends, while not a few retained their nails, which had rusted up in the holes.'[25] This shows evidence of Romano-British use of stone tile right on the possible source, for the Downs Vein runs out of the ground here.

The Building Accounts for Corfe Castle record: 1282, 9-15 August, 'For the service of Henry of Wool the roofer who roofed the chamber above the gate by task 14s. For 2000 of pegs to fix stones onto the roof of the chamber made by task by Geoffrey le Byke 4 ½ d.'[26] In 1285 Edward Brandon was paid for 500 stones for the roof.[27] Repairs or additions were ongoing more than 300 years later. In 1616 'To the hellier for worke by him done about the Castell this yere and for Laughts and Nayles, 18s.' In 1618, 'To the hellier for worke by him don about the Castle 11s. 7d.'[28] However it is to be remembered that most of the castle's roofs were of lead. A survey of 1635 refers to 'all the leads aloft'. In describing the manor of Lutton, in West Purbeck, Ida Woodward says 'The chief interest of the place is the barn, the roof of which was taken from the banqueting hall at Corfe just before the castle was slighted.'[29] By a circuitous route some of these Lutton tiles have ended up on Eastington Farm. The post war dispersal of masonry items from the army ranges is a deplorable story.

In 1358-61 Edward III built four lodges in the New Forest 'of timber roofed with Purbeck and Cornish slates'.[30] The accounts for the palace at Bishop's Waltham record the use of slate and clay tiles produced in local kilns. However in 1401 a part was rebuilt 'with a roof of Purbeck slates'. In 1415, at Durrington, slates were brought from Chilmark (surely from the Purbeck type beds), although tiles and 'Purbeck stone' (or slates from Purbeck) were also used.[31] Lady Down, near Tisbury, was a source of roofing stone until as late as 1900, and medieval exploitation of thin Wiltshire Purbeck beds from there must be certain.[32] The separation of Purbeck from Purbeck Wiltshire stone, particularly in old roofs including Roman villas, is difficult, but possible under close inspection.

As with the fissile Wiltshire Purbeck beds, some Cornbrash and Forest Marble splits to convenient thicknesses when also quarried close to the surface. These stones were available from a wide area and used on a considerable scale. In my opinion both Purbeck and Cornbrash from an unknown source occur in old roofs at Wolfeton House (near Dorchester), the latter characterised by beautifully clear ripple marks which are rare, but not entirely absent in Purbeck.

At Winchester College there is a bill from 1399 for Purbeck slates for £9 3s 4d. Later, in 1417, Thomas Ywayn of Wareham supplied 100 Purbeck 'Sklat' delivered at Hamble for 13s 4d.[33] The Southampton Port book for 1435-36 records a 'boat of Poole' bringing 10,000 slates into Southampton. It is by no means certain that this cargo was from Purbeck, but it seems likely.[34] The account for Holt amongst the Bankes Estate papers is illuminating:

> 'Kyngeston Lacy 1428
> And on 6,000 stone tiles purchased at Poole for the aforesaid roofs, 1,000 at 10s. 63s
> And on carriage for the said stones from Poole as far as the aforesaid manor that is with 24 carts at 12d per cart, 24s.
> And on the expenses of Simon Helyer and an overseer riding as far as Poole and Purbeck on 3 occasions to inspect and purchase the said stones, 2s.
> And on 26 stone tiles called Crestyles purchased to roof both the chamber of the lord King and other houses within the said manor, 1d a piece. 2s.2d.'

Cutting ridge tiles ('Crestyles') is highly labour-intensive and calls for a quite different sort of stone; probably Burr.

Presentments to the court at Langton Wallis show that manor to have been a source of tile at about the same time. In 1419, 5,000 were sold from Robert Wylton's holding, another 4,000 from John Tresshere's, each man paying one shilling per 1,000 as royalty. The retail value would have been several times this. In 1423 the records show: '3s of land to Henry Vyport [this name later becomes Phippard, prominent in the trade until the recent past] and John Gylet on La Yulde for 4,000 stone tiles at the end there'. Two years later: 'William Dennyng pays 12d to extract 2000 stone tile and Thomas Rede 8d for stone taken out at the end of the said quarrying operation'.[35] Eleven years later Henry was still acting for the Lord (i.e. the Court), paying in to the court 4s. for the sale of another 4,000 tiles. The next year he paid in for 4,850 tiles in small lots, ranging from 350 to 1,500. He was Haywarden and collecting these monies from the various tenants: John Harding Junior, John Wastell Junior, John Smyth, Joanna Smyth and Edward Warmewell, as well as paying for himself. Of these holdings, Edward's included a meadow in Taketon (Acton), as did John Wastell's father's holding.

During 1437-38, 14,000 tiles were dug. In 1441-42, 3,000 were dug from the lord's land for payment of 1s. per 1,000, whilst another 2,500 came from the tenants' land at half that rate, 6d per 1,000. During 1448-49 output from the tenants was down to only 500 but still 7,000 were quarried from the lord's. Forty years later tenant/quarrier Henry Smyth took 1,500 stone tiles and paid the court 9d. Two years later he dug another 1,000, as did a fellow tenant, John Spycer, who also took the same amount the next year. You could dig tile on your own tenancy for so much (6d per 1,000) but you paid twice as much to do so on the lord's land. I guess the logic was that a tenant was already paying rent and also that he was causing damage to the agricultural value of his own holding and not someone else's. Treswell's survey of 1585 spells out the convention on Langton Wallis; 'That every tenant may make a quarry of tile stone in his ground, paying to the lord for every load thereof one penny.'[36] The use of the term 'load' rather than a numerical quantity of tile noted in the medieval accounts may suggest a shift from a fixed tile size to varying sizes, as in all extant rooves.

Unlike adjacent Eastington, where Downs Vein and other beds productive of tile run shallow across parts of Broadmead, Nunbarrow and Cowlease, it is difficult to identify obvious shallow tile deposits in Langton Wallis, and therefore where La Yulde and the other various quarries lay. Quarry may hardly be the right word, for much of their digging was probably shallow, exploiting fissile beds already split by subaerial weathering just beneath the 'clot'. There is an added difficulty in knowing just what land area came within the Court's jurisdiction at the time. Possible sites include where the Laining Vein outcrops south of Priest's Way where undulations mark quarry activity in this layer just west of Spyway Barn. Perhaps a more likely site lies further south, where the Roach shoals more or less in an east-west line south of Sea Spray cottage; or perhaps the most likely is where the Grub shoals where the hamlet of Acton now is. Just possibly, the New Vein right at the top of the ware, was a source, but for most of this manor, short of going underground, the Cinder would have made this vein difficult to get. Downs Vein would seem not to be the stone in question if the workings were surface only.

Where it actually outcrops on this estate, at least as revealed by Bob Harris above Hedbury in the 1950s, it has thinned out almost to nothing. However if underground working had developed by this date other areas become possibilities. In particular a recent sudden collapse revealed old Downs Vein underground workings in Acton Field, now a camp site. The whole field is characterised by quarry humps and hollows, some certainly, all possibly, to do with shallow underground rather than surface working. It lies exactly in line with the pre-1700 holloway that runs northwards from Castle View, which was possibly the way that the tiles went. What is certain is that digging was going on on several tenancies plus the Lord's land, on an estate probably subdivided then much as when surveyed later by Treswell in 1586.[37.]

This hard documentary evidence of tile being dug on Langton Wallis in the 15th century prompts the suspicion that the same thing was happening on other manors where the geological prospects were as good or better. It probably tells of concurrent and earlier working on Eastington, Worth, the spread of Swanage manors from Sentry to Herston, in particular the area around Round Down, the westerly series from Dunshay to Bradle, and even the few this list leaves out.

The Victoria History of the County of Dorset includes Poole Port records: 'Early in the reign of Edward IV [crowned 1442], a foreign ship with a Dutch or Flemish master took out 30,000 stones called 'sclatte stones' valued at £4.[…] Another foreign ship about twenty years later took on board 30,000 'helyng stones' worth 45s.'[38.]

The evidence of sending roof tiles to the continent is surprising, but there were also other English sources. Clifton Taylor writes of Devon: 'The largest quarry (of slate) was at Charleton, close to the Salcombe estuary, whence […] a great deal was exported, especially in the 15th century, to Holland.'[39.] I suspect medieval Purbeck roof tile is to be found in Holland, or Flanders, if not on a roof, at least in a museum.

Mottistone Manor, Isle of Wight, built in 1567, has what from the ground looks like a roof consisting of an upper half of clay tile, a lower of Purbeck stone tile. There must be a degree of uncertainty as to whether it is original or not, but it seems likely that it is. Another, as Pevsner puts it, 'once-important' Elizabethan house with a stone roof which probably dates from the original building, is Uvedales in Corfe. However this house has a complicated history. Recent tree ring dating shows the timber work of its exceptionally steep roof to be post Civil War which leaves us guessing as to just when the tiles were made. One important consideration is that for thatch to be effective a steeper angle (about 60 degrees) is required than that for stone (about 45 degrees). The steeply-pitched barn roof at Renscombe (Worth) possessed a stone tile roof until the 1950s when the stones were taken to Winchester College. Was the barn previously thatched, and were the timbers re-used for the tile roof? It does seem to be clear that as the years went by stone found its way on to more humble dwellings,

Privy roof at Gallows Gore, built by a quarryman Corben (mid-1800s) on top of existing field wall. Note nearest long roofing slab, heavily distorted by dinosaur trampling.

replacing thatch, though probably with or without alteration of roof pitch.

Archaeological investigations at Corfe Castle have revealed clearly unbroken tiles of, by modern Purbeck standards, remarkably small size. One five by fifteen inches, several three and a half by nine inches. The position of the fixing hole and the dubbed edges indicate that these small stones were made as we find them rather than subsequently broken. Were they part of a graduated roof?

Another eight inch square is corner hung. What is its date? The Romans used corner hung gauged tile with pointed bottom edges which produce a fish scale-like effect. The several medieval references to numbers of tiles prompts the thought that their roofs may have similarly consisted of standard sizes. But all extant roofs, without exception, are of graduated sizes, with the biggest stones at the bottom. Such a system is the cheapest, in that the quarrier simply squared each stone more or less as big as he could make it, leaving the hellier to sort them out and put in the fixing hole. In some instances these holes were cut, with either a sharp pointed hammer or hammer and punch, at the quarry, but this called for the quarrier to provide each course in proportion. This random method can result in stones as big as five feet by three! (on the 19th century Kingston lodge). These large stones are incorporated in running courses. Some flat dormers were resolved with as large or larger special stones. They are heavy to the point that sufficient muscle power on the scaffold may have been the limiting factor. In considering the practicalities of producing a fixed size type roof in Roman style as against a modern graduated roof, to produce a small standard size would have meant breaking the big stuff – not easy to do without waste.

A conventionally graduated roof of such large pieces produces more lap than strictly necessary to exclude the wet. The quarr houses in general and some outbuildings of local cottages, often the privies, are covered with undressed slabs, without so much wasteful lap. The result is much more free handed. Such roofs are typically of big stones, of thicker than average tiles and of a much flatter pitch than 45 degrees, making pegging unnecessary.

The quarryman dressed or 'dubbed round' the raw stone with a hammer, whilst holding it on edge. Such a dressed edge takes on a characteristic section and becomes easy to tell apart from undressed. It results in a central ridge. Some Romano-British tile edges are not like this. They exhibit a splayed edge, such as results from the application of a narrow chisel/pitching tool to the side; a risky business. These differences may be helpful in differentiating between Roman and later tiles. The risk of breakage by striking the stone square with a pitching tool can be reduced by applying something solid like a hammer head to the opposite side of the slab. This reduces the stress carried through the slab. The recent quarryman made the biggest rectangle he could, though missing corners at the top of the finished tile to be did not matter, indeed is sometimes an advantage when the stones are being laid. They were dressed by eye. Harry Tatchell told me that, being a novice, Bob Harris put him alongside Flinger Bower dubbing tile for a water pumping station on the Stour. Cautiously he was applying the square. 'The virst thing thee can do is chuck thick thing away,' said Flinger.

The finished tiles were sold by the load, a load being measured with the stones stood on edge in a mass eight feet long, two feet wide and on average two feet high. This height was important. If some courses measured less than two feet, others had to be higher to compensate. With good thin tile a load may have held perhaps 16 to 18 courses. Half an inch thick is about the minimum, one and a half inches about the maximum. Thicker stones would have meant a smaller area covered per weight, a recipe for dispute. A quarryman's load roughly corresponded to a builder's square, that is ten feet by ten feet laid on the roof, and was about the capacity of the average 18th century farm cart. There was therefore no need to mark them in the normal way of things. Marks are therefore extremely rare. 'H 1806' found on the underside of a stone tile at Knitson Farm is therefore probably a roofer's rather than a quarryman's mark.

A Worth Church Book from the 18th century records the purchase of tile from Stephen Purbeck who held several fields in Worth, as well as a tenancy in Langton, which included the field called Judas.[40] This is a possible source. In Judas at its shallowest, the Downs Vein only gets to within about ten feet from the surface in the southeastern corner. If that was Stephen's quarry, he was underground. On the other hand, a shallow Laining Vein source cannot be entirely ruled out.

1739	1 ton healing stones	6/s
	1 load healing stones	7/s
1740	1 load healing stones	7/6d

In 1725, the agent for the Bankes Estate, itemises 'Healing stones after being battered are worth upon the place 7s 6d per load, that is a tun and half.' Bankes' agent was specific about the weight of a load, but Stephen Purbeck's comparative values of loads as against tons would suggest a load was rather less than one and a half tons. Whatever, the 'builder's square' of tile laid on a roof weighs at least a ton, and usually more. Neve says: 'For this sort of coursing [he is discussing Horsham stone, similar to Purbeck] the timber ought to be considerably stouter and stronger because a square of this sort of stone is almost as heavy again as a square of Tyling.'[41] The Bankes estate quarries were producing large quantities of paving. Tile must have been coming out in quantity as well. Perhaps the Estate which claimed one load in four, as revealed in Mr. John Bankes' own hand, was buying the rest as well. They were certainly using a lot at that time on, for example, West Mill, Corfe and at 'Farmer Brown's house in Corfe Castle': '6 load or more of stone tyle for y stables', etc. It is an especial pity that West Mill has been demolished, for detailed accounts of its building in 1730 survive. Edmunds delivered a load of healing stone in May; during July, Matthew Gover, Thomas Smith and Edward Dampier four more. Amongst a lengthy list of workmen employed at the Mill appears John Stockley, Hellier paid 18/9d. to July 18th. Of these hauliers, Dampier was farming Eastington.

The interesting admixture we see to this day in Corfe, of stone and thatched rooves, perhaps relates to differing estate ownership, thatch being replaced by those who had the resources to do so. But the local vernacular is not the whole story, for some tile, particularly in the form of eaves courses, was travelling beyond the bounds of Purbeck around this time. Christchurch Priory has an extensive stone roof of unknown date but which could be medieval. A lot of the courses are not particularly big, only showing about seven or eight inches high. Bere Regis church is partly covered in stone, almost certainly Purbeck, but of unknown date.

Wareham and Christchurch have good examples of vernacular buildings with stone eaves courses. They are usually combined with clay tiles or, less commonly, Welsh slate. Some consist of just one course (actually two, because of the need of a lap), others two or three courses, whilst some are of stone for half the height. One wonders why? It would seem to me that it must be easier to resolve the problem of forming generously overhanging eaves with big slabs rather than little clay tiles. However, Richard Spillar points out that whilst clay tiles require modification to a timber roof built to carry thatch, stone tile, used at the lower part only if in short supply, does not. Contradicting Richard some other builders claim that the consideration is that stone is heavier than the alternatives, but this does not much matter at the eaves where the weight rests directly on the wall. Whatever the reasons, they were surely functional rather than aesthetic. Iron fixing nails rust, oak pegs become 'cold', battens rot. Few roofs stay on for much over a hundred years, so all these roofs which, on the face of it, are 18th century, have virtually certainly been relaid, bringing the likelihood of modifications. It must therefore be certain that is there is no undisturbed medieval or Tudor roof left.

Some builders claim that when a thatch roof is replaced by stone tile there is a need to raise the masonry of the gables. Several tiled houses in Swanage and Corfe show such a break in the stone work, which is possibly evidence of this adaptation. However this may be deceptive. Often in building a gable it was brought up to almost roof line before being then left to be completed <u>after</u> the roof was on. This produces an often obvious break line in the rubble walling but is not necessarily evidence of a change in roofing material. One of the cottages close to Worth church retained a thatch roof until at least 1919.

Corfe Castle village, East Street. Mix of thatch and stone tile rooves.

Now no examples remain in Worth, Langton or Swanage other than at Ulwell. Conversely no Kimmeridge cottage has gained a stone roof, only the 'up market' Parsonage and farm, together with its barns.

Even the most solid beds will tend to split where they occur near the surface, within the effects of subaerial weathering, particularly the penetration depth of the Ice Age permafrost, about ten feet below present contours. Opportunism results in any suitably thin stuff being used, so we can perhaps expect Romano-British and medieval tiles to have been gathered from shallow outcrops of almost any bed other than Cliffstone, Marble, or Burr. However, by far the most fissile in most areas are the Downs Vein, Laining Vein and Roach, hence these are the most important tile sources. Of these three, the Downs Vein is arguably the best and most used. 'In most areas' can hardly be over-emphasised, for there are exceptions: from Acton to Swanage the Roach readily splits into several beds, but at Gallows Gore, none at all. Other beds that can also split thin at some locations include New Vein and Button. Thomas Webster specifically mentions the latter as a source of tile.[42] It consists of a few thin layers mixed with shales lying directly beneath the Cinder. His comment tells they were taking it underground, but in some later Cap quarries they left it up as the ceiling. Thomas Collins told me his father didn't like whistling whilst they worked. 'You'll 'ave them Buttons down' he said. My father thought the aversion to whistling lay in the fact that sometimes as a ceiling bed separates there can be a sucking sound. It was something best to be on the alert for. Even Thornback, which is generally homogenous, can split where really shallow. Bobby Cobb found a shallow patch in Eastington Cowlease, where it went over in paving thicknesses, whilst at Belle Vue it has yielded some beautiful thin roof tile.

The Roach is generally harder and more brittle than Downs Vein, but more frost vulnerable, at least the lower Pink Bit part. Downs Vein from the Acton-Gallows Gore-Worth road region makes durable tile. Of the Swanage district, W. M. Hardy says: 'Around these hills (Round Down) the Purbeck beds come close to the surface, so that the quarrymen could get their stone without going underground. An immense quantity was obtained, especially walling and tiling stone. The quarries in the upper part of Newton Manor were supposed to be the best for tile.'[43] He is almost certainly referring to Roach rather than Downs Vein, for in the Belle Vue, Swanage region, of which I have experience, the Downs Vein is hardly productive of any tile whereas the Roach is. New Vein White Bit from some areas tends to split thin enough for tile, but does not endure half as well. By contrast the roof of 10 North Street, Langton Matravers, has been recently relaid without any loss at all, its Downs Vein being as good as when first laid. Across most of Purbeck the Roach and the Downs Vein split freely, even when quarried at depth. However, mostly the partings are a few inches apart, so any one block produces several pavings and perhaps only a couple of tiles. But in parts of Worth's Quarry Close (formerly Nunbarrow, west of Broad Mead, north of the Worth road) the Downs Vein at about two feet thick 'went over' in 22 beds (R. Bower) or 19 beds (A. Lander), all beautiful tile. These men had quarries about one hundred yards apart.

Perhaps the medieval hellier suppliers, and indeed the Romans, found such shallow, highly tile-productive outcrops. That they did so is made more likely by the fact that had they been digging beds that produced both paving and tile thicknesses, then surely they would have utilised the paving and we would find it. The earliest floors of Downs Vein seem to begin in the late 15th century. I suspect that the Downs, the fields above Scoles, Afflington and Dunshay, could have been sources of tile such as that used as early as the 13th century on Corfe Castle. Exploitation of Round Down, and other shallow eastern outcrops, could have been equally early but have since

USES / 183

been confused by subsequent activity. I suggested to Steve Paine when he was quarrying at California that most tile is a spin off from the paving trade. He proved me wrong in that context; he told me of finding a shallow patch where only the Roach, all thin stuff, had been taken, nothing below. What was the date of that digging? Knowledge gained recently from Langton Wallis court records suggests medieval.

Compared with Roach, Downs Vein is tough without being too brittle. This makes it easier to dress and knock the peg holes through without so much risk of breakage. Whether this difference influenced the choice of bed much is doubtful, but there were 19th century times when thin Roach was not particularly sought after, as evidenced by Townsend underground quarries dug at that time, where it has been left up as the ceiling. As some ceilings now tend to collapse, beautiful potential tile is falling to the floor. Perhaps it was the arrival of ubiquitous Welsh slate that killed off demand. Kingston Old Church (rebuilt 1833), and St. Aldhelm's Head coastguard houses (1834), are examples of it in Purbeck. However there are later stone roofs and they include Kingston Church (1873-1880), much of the Downs Vein being dug by Albert (Fiddler) Bower somewhere near Gallows Gore. My father said of him that he had such a good tile hole that he could work Mondays and Tuesdays and drink the rest of the week. It is therefore puzzling to read the contemporary newspaper account of the opening of the church reporting that the oak and stone slates were sourced from the Eldon estates in Gloucester.[44]

A recent secular roof is Maen House (1903), Dorchester, stonework supplied by Stevens. Other examples include the Voysey house at Woodhouse Hill, Studland, built by Parsons and Hayter in 1896, and a house in Scotland at Curradale from about 1930, built for one of the McAlpine family of contractors. Thomas Bonfield was one of those who helped rid the Down Vein in Eastington Cowlease for my grandfather for the McAlpine work. The lead hand was Teddy Corben, who would not let anyone touch the stuff with a punch. Instead they cleft it using a hammer-headed chisel. George Hancock went to Scotland to work on this roof. Grub also produced tile from this field. After visiting St. David's Cathedral, Pembrokeshire, I reported that if I had been nearer home I would have said the tower louvre slabs looked like Purbeck, and was astounded to hear my father say that Ambrose Bower had dubbed them around for him in Eastington Cowlease.

My father would cite the rebuilt Bankes Arms (Corfe Castle) roof as a good example of how stone tile should be laid (c.1950). William Weekes, on fixing the eaves course, remarked that they had laid the 'heel of the roof'. What would he have thought of the modern fashion of slubbing up all the joints with hard Portland cement? Not much, I suspect. Traditionally a little soft lime mortar was used so that the tiles did not rock, to eliminate pressure points and to prevent draught and snow blowing in. It should not show. Torching, the Cotswold practice of plastering over the undersides after fixing, seems not to have been done, at least in the recent past.

I am indebted to Mr. Nelson Bower for tile terminology, but dismayed at finding inconsistencies in my notes made at the

Langton Matravers Museum. Oak pegs from which stone tiles are suspended on battens. These are c. 4 inches long. They were fixed in from the outside of the tile with a light hammer.

time of more than one conversation. He said a typical cottage roof was graduated in one and a half inch increments. This contrasts with Cotswold Forest Marble roofs, which can have as little as one eighth of an inch decrease per course.[45] Such roofs often contain by current Purbeck standards very small stones, some as little as five inches long. Usually the average cottage eaves course measured two feet six inches from the bottom edge to the peg hole, and was called a 'Twelve'. The next course up, two feet four and a half inches to the hole, was an 'Eleven', and so on, with a 13½ inch therefore being called a 'One'. Curiously, the 12 inch high stone was therefore a 'Short Five' making the 'Long Five' a 19½ inch tile. Lesser courses were simply called 'toppers'. The normal under-eaves course was about 21 inches to the hole, with the eaves course normally showing about 14 inches. This is less than is strictly required for weather proof lap but is a benefit for subsequent even gradation.[46] In these graduated roofs do we see a post-medieval development from the Roman model? Tilers made use of a rod which had a peg at one end and a series of marks at one and a half inch intervals at the other, starting at 12 inches from the peg – the Short Five, marked with a Roman 'V'. One of these surviving rods has no marks at less than a Short Five, whilst another in Langton Matravers Museum is marked for a further six inches, also at inch and a half intervals. The plain marks vary in length. Exceptionally larger roofs may require greater sizes to start with and, Cotswold-like, a slower rate of gradation.

My father was amused by roofers such as Jim Ball being jocular about Short Fives, and was mystified about what was meant and how the system had arisen. It is interesting to learn that stone roofers in other parts of England also had courses called 'short', but no Short Five.[47] Presumably relatively isolated helliers of each stone tile producing area developed their own nomenclature, but use of the term 'Short' suggests a common origin. The varying nature of the rock would have affected this, Purbeck being distinctive in that the stones are on average large, which gives its roofscapes a particular character.

Kevin Keates informs me that the eaves course on Swanage Church is three feet to the peg hole. Neil Harding found Millpond cottage roof tiles 42 inches to the peg hole. This size variation was of course driven by what was coming out of the ground. It was no use specifying a high course if the quarry could not produce it, but conversely it made sense to keep the stones big when possible. The Churchwarden's book for 1793-1828 includes purchases of tile stone over the entire period from several quarriers, including some in Langton. It seems incredible that work on the roof, with what that entailed in terms of scaffolding, etc., was going on for so long. The explanation could be that piecemeal replacement of lead by stone was going on as money allowed, for whereas Hutchins describes the nave as being lead covered, the Rev. J. Colson's drawing of 1837 shows the whole covered in stone tile.

'Dec. 1793, paid for Tiling stone, 7s [the value of 1 load]
April 1808, paid J. Harden for tiling stone for the church, 7s
March 1808, paid James Galley for [?] tiling stones, £2. 16s.
June 1809 ' ' ' for turnpike for tiling stone
Dec 1816, to Thom. Stickland Heling stone, 10/s carrige 1/s
March 1818, to Turnpike for Helingstone for the church, 3/s
Oct 1822, Carrige for a load of healing stone from T. Brown at Langton to S. Church, 8/s
Oct 1822, Carriage from Swanage Field half load Healing Stone from William Phippard, 4/s
Oct 1822, Paid William Coastfield for Thomas Brown Corbin Tilling stone, £1.4s
Oct 1823, paid Moses Farwell [the builder] for William Phippard Tyling stone bill
Aug 1825, William Corben load tile stone, £1.4s'

Claridge, in 1793, splits the costs down: 'The tilling stone is worth at the quarry 5s 4d per ton, and delivered at Sandwich at 8 shillings'.[48.]

Keeping roof valleys watertight presents a difficulty now

ABOVE RIGHT Stone tile hung to exhibit lapping: around are various tools, including hammers and tiler's rod.

RIGHT Langton Matravers Museum. Tiler's rod leant against crab stones.

BELOW Swanage, Church Hill: swept valley showing coffin-shaped stones.

USES / 185

Swanage, the Mill Pond. Early 20th century, showing stone tile roof with 'swept' valley, shedding rain straight onto the porch over the door; also cheek stones on side of dormer.

resolved by the judicious use of lead. However this can be achieved by using narrow, long tapered 'coffin stones' that jam in the intersections to form a swept valley. Purbeck examples are rare, but the dormers on the Purbeck Hotel at Swanage (known as the White Harte when Francis Haysom built it) exhibit them. The method is to close-butt the under-eaves course at the intersection then lay a tapered 'coffin'-like stone at the eaves course level about seven inches long at its narrow bottom edge, and so on. It sounds easy enough, but I got into a mess attempting it.

186 / PURBECK STONE

WALLS

The stone-bearing part of Purbeck is defined by a network of walls. In contrast to the seemingly almost haphazard mosaic of the adjacent Wealden Vale hedgerows, they are in the main, particularly in Rowbarrow Hundred, in a regular grid of rectangles. In this eastern half of Purbeck in particular their long axes run north to south, as do the long, narrow manors they define. Though there have been later additions many are of pre-Enclosure Acts date. Elsewhere in England similar semi-regular field configurations have been shown to be pre-medieval, even Bronze Age.[49]

Dating is difficult. Early evidence for Purbeck walls is recorded in the Manorial Presentments for Langton Wallis in the medieval period: one example from April 23rd 1484 says 'William Latyn is presented to the Court for allowing the hedges and walls of his property at Aketon to become a public danger'.[50] Evidence from the Tudor period may be provided by Treswell's maps of 1585, which show boundaries that are almost certainly walls dividing up Sir Christopher Hatton's manors of Verney, Langton Wallis and Eastington; most of these boundaries remain to this day. Some have gone, whilst new walls have been built since, particularly in the western half of Langton Wallis, south of the Priest's Way, which Treswell shows as just one big field. Comparison with another survey of the same period show additional walls 'appearing'.

Some surmount, so post-date, old quarry undulations. One wall running east to west along the Cinder outcrop at Benlidge (Benlease) is particularly striking in this way. It is just possible that the alignment predates quarrying, that it was rebuilt as the quarry tide passed, but that seems unlikely. A farming acquaintance suggests the alignment was chosen so that stock could enjoy a measure of protection afforded by the undulations on both sides. It presents another puzzle where it impacts Verney to the west, for there the otherwise reasonably straight north-south boundary kinks. It would appear men digging from the Benlidge side pushed through. This sort of thing was going on elsewhere during the Bankes' Estate sequestration; 1645 to about 1660. If this kink in the wall does reflect that event, it puts those quarries back to a rather earlier date. The fact that waste piles are spread across another boundary, that between Tom's Field and Cole's Ground in Langton Matravers, between Hart's and Bankes' land, is similarly curious. Is this for the same reason?

Under many miles of walls the immediate substrate is clay rather than hard rock so they tend to fall. No doubt just how long each lasts depends on various factors, including the skill of the builder and the quality of the stone. What is difficult to tell is just how old are the oldest 'goads' currently standing. This unit of measure, about 14 feet, was that of a spiked pole long enough for a ploughman to prod his oxen with. Its linkage to wall construction may tell of them being built at a time when oxen rather than horses drew the plough and, of course, the simple fact that each farm would have possessed one.

The 'life' of a wall varies enormously. Some only recently rebuilt are already falling. Conversely I suspect that those that are well bonded, wide, battered, of good stone in terms of both good shape and durability and on a good footing, may last centuries. In its early years ivy may serve to stitch the stones together, but if allowed to get high beyond the reach of sheep so that the wind gets hold of it, it can act as a sail and cause a disaster. In rebuilding a fallen shart (which corrupts from shard – as fallen gaps are called), stones that were at the bottom can be re-used at the top, and vice versa. Freshly added ones can be put at the bottom rather than on top, and so on. The result can be an enigmatic mix of stone types and style of build that is a puzzle to date and a beauty to behold. From a quarry history point of view they are informative on two counts. Firstly, they can contain quarry by-product. Secondly, before the on-going restoration campaign that began about 1982, stone to build them was usually only taken short distances so the walls are, or rather were, reliable indicators of what outcrops fairly close by. This has since changed, with two or three quarries southwest from Acton providing material for repairs as far off as Belle Vue and Durlston, so lessening their distinctive character. Some contain large stones set in the ground on edge, showing on one face of the wall only. These may be pre-wall manorial boundary marker stones. Such markers occur between Langton Wallis and Langton Matravers, and between Langton Wallis and Eastington. There are also occasional exotics such as an Iron

Ralph Treswell's 1585 map of the Isle of Purbeck. Many of the boundaries shown between manors probably consisted of walls (Dorset History Centre D/BKL/E/A/3/1/0).

Age sandstone quern built into a wall near Spyway, Langton. Worn kerb stone incorporated into walls about Verney tell of the tenant farmer's engagement with Council work in the 1960s, when perfectly serviceable stones were replaced with concrete.

Material to build, repair or extend walls has been sourced in three ways: by being ploughed up, by being quarried deliberately, or as a by-product of quarrying for stone of greater value. The beauty of stone turned up by the plough is that only the good durable stuff is so produced, it having stood the test of time lying close to or at the surface. This contrasts with quarry by-product, which can often contain low quality stone that will not weather well. This is particularly applicable to the white rock sometimes called 'shards' which overlies the Downs Vein. Ridding Downs Vein from shallow surface workings would have produced lots of it in good shapes for walling, which would have been tempting to use. Some walls being currently built or repaired just will not last.

A bed of stone that can, in my opinion, be reliably identified as being produced by the plough only is the Flint, from the Cherty freshwater beds. This fine grained mudstone, full of flint nodules, lies beneath the lowest most useful beds of New Vein, so there is never a reason to dig it off to get at something better underneath. This is at least true of eastern Purbeck; to the west it thickens and improves in quality, and there is evidence of it being deliberately dug for something other than walling above Devil's Staircase, Blackmanston and at Bacon Hole. It can be confused with Cap or even flinty Cliff stone, but it tends to become more distinctive as weathering destroys the matrix, leaving projecting flint nodules in characteristic rotund, pudding-like shapes. Where it shoals to the surface, particularly west of Gallows Gore onwards to Bradle, the walls are full of it. It also shoals out on the top of the ridge that forms West Man, but is less given to forming the pudding shapes there.

Another silicified and hence durable rock, but of no use for masonry, is the Earth Rock. This layer caps the Cliff stone, hence its name, and is productive of fossil wood, particularly in the west at the celebrated fossil forest at Lulworth, but also in eastern Purbeck. A bed that also produces petrified wood, but of smaller girth, occurs further up the sequence just above the Downs Vein. Other horizons yielding vanishingly rare amounts include the Dun Cow and Cap. Of the latter we have turned over many tons, so far finding one piece! Along much of the cliff the advance of the sea into the Portland scarp has yet to reach the Earth Rock outcrop, but where the quarries have been pushed further into the hill it has been exposed. These include Dancing Ledge, Hedbury, Seacombe, Winspit and St. Aldhelm's Head, so all are possible sources of Earth Rock, but in the main I suspect that what we see in the walls has been ploughed up. This applies to where it surfaces only a few yards from the coast path between Hedbury and Seacombe, Seacombe to Winspit, Winspit to Buttery Corner and on a wider outcrop line from St. Aldhelm's Head quarry inland to Sheepsleights and thence westwards. These siliceous beds are usually of a poor shape from a walling point of view, but are so resistant to weathering that no matter how many times a wall may fall, the stones remain to be built up again. One wonders how many generations of wallers some have been handled by.

In contrast the Cinder is a bed of generally rotten quality. But within its mass of ten feet or so a few inches are of relatively resistant well-cemented mussel shells. This part also crops up in field walls. Quarries going for the Cap and New Vein underneath sometimes dug well into it, such as we see in a lengthy heading still extant at the top of the ware east of Hedbury. But what Cinder occurs in field walls is, in my opinion, more probably from the plough. Bits occur in what is almost certainly immediately-post-Conquest rubble in Corfe Castle, together with bits of Flint Bed and Vie bed. All three crop up in walls around Kingston and their presence in the fortress suggest ploughing of that area at that time.

Without being entirely certain as to what is original and what is not, Norman rubble in Worth church seems to be mostly Downs Vein with some New Vein, particularly Vye Bit. Both could have been ploughed out within a quarter of a mile of the church. The original rubble of St. Aldhelm's Chapel, whatever its date – probably 12th century – is almost entirely Shrimp. This poor quality stone occurs in the cliff top only yards away. Other beds now visible in the Chapel walling are mostly, if not entirely, the result of later patching.

Evidence for deliberate quarrying to provide for field walls can be seen where the Cliff stone outcrops south of Kingston. This rock does not make ideal wall stone shapes, but where the Spangle, and to a degree other beds, shoal just beneath the clot, the effect of Quaternary freezing (which penetrated to a depth of two or three metres or so below current contours) was to shatter the stone into flattish cornflake-shaped fragments. Two fields south of Kingston Barn there was a shallow Spangle quarry of this, now filled in. The adjacent walls are of this distinctive stone and differ thereby from those that extend southwards towards Chapman's Pool. These more southerly are of the underlying Cherty series, plus Portland sand beds, which typically are of a more rotund shape and thereby surely more challenging to the builder. They are also distinctive for supporting a bearded lichen that only grows on flint nodules, or a silica rich matrix, and is therefore absent from most Purbeck walls. There is no question of these walls being a by-product of quarrying for something better. They were either a product of ploughing, or dug especially from a number of holes that can be seen around the top of the hill slopes above Hill, Coombe and Pier Bottoms and Encombe.

The filled-in Spangle quarry was strategic in that it provided for an area some way away from any of these hill edge sources. On the one hand they lay some way off to the south; on the other the nearest Purbeck bed quarries were too far away to the north. It is perhaps instructive in pre-tractor farm logistics! The bed immediately beneath the Earth Rock, Shrimp, tends to come out in good shapes for walling, but is highly frost vulnerable and if saturated will break up when frozen. But where perched up in a well-drained dry wall it may serve reasonably well. There is such a wall immediately above White Ware quarry, surely of stone from there, now interestingly pockmarked by lengthy exposure. However, if it should fall to the soggy ground, winter frosts will break it up. A head of Shrimp is exposed near the badger sett in Abbascombe Bottom. It tells of deliberate quarrying for it alone, for they went no deeper. Opposite lies a ruined wall, much of it Shrimp, and frost-shattered.

The cliff quarries proper did not provide much walling material, for what came out of most of them went away entirely by sea. White Ware is reachable by horse and cart, which explains the small amount in the nearby wall. There was a capstan at West Hedbury which perhaps explains the presence of Cliff stone in the seaward end of both Cliff Fields walls, but in the main those walls that descend the Wares are dominated by beds of stone dug at the top rather than the bottom. It is, of course, easiest to take stone downhill! Across the plateau sometimes thin flat bedded walling dominates, telling of Laining Vein, Downs Vein, Vie bed, Roach and, around Round Down, Rag. But Round Down Rag, with its tendency to split thin, is atypical. More often it is thick and open textured, giving rise elsewhere to rotund shapes which can be difficult to tell from Burr. Both are durable and take on, over time, 'water-worn' shapes when close to the surface. Such weathering of these and other relatively resistant beds can suggest the action of the sea, but is not. In my opinion Burr of this sort that can be seen in post Conquest Corfe Castle rubble has not been sourced from the sea shore but simply from shallow quarries. Rounded Rag tells the same story of lying just under the grass.

Some Langton walls now lie ruined to the point of disappearance, some have recently been deliberately removed. One still remaining that appears on Treswell's survey separates the manors of Matravers from Wallis. In and near the village all sorts of things have happened to it, including changes in alignment, but both north and south of Priest's Way what seems to be old work survives. On plan it rather weaves about, suggesting antiquity. In elevation a lot is built at a deliberate slope between horizontal ground courses and a horizontal coping. Some parts appear to lack the horizontal foundation work but this is probably present but hidden below grass level. On parts of another manorial boundary between Eastington and Worth, this horizontal work extends to a height of a foot or more before the sloped courses begin. This mode of construction cannot have been merely whimsical, nor aesthetic. That it makes it more difficult for sheep to get over has been suggested. Another consideration is that such a method may be stronger because the weight is transferred differently. A horizontal stone only presses downwards. If tilted it not only bears down against what is below but also its neighbour. In turn it is under pressure from its other, higher, neighbour. Perhaps it was just plain easier to do it that way, rather like in dressing a stone it is easier to broach diagonally than it is to work parallel. However, wallers who have recently attempted this sloped method tell me that it is more difficult.[51.]

Around the course of this wall separating the Langton manors, part of the Laining Vein is distinctive in that it contains in abundance the pond snail typical of Marble. There is paving made from it from as early as 1510, and, lo and behold, not only is there a lot of this bed used in the wall, but also bits of paving broken in manufacture. So it is with other walls, stretching from Swanage to Worth. They contain a scatter of broken bits of paving, channel and roof tile, even bits of troughs, each one an annoyance to the quarrier who had put fruitless work into it, but who then made the best of a bad job by chucking the reject into rubble destined for walls, whether cottage or field. Some such evidence is obvious, some much less so. The more cryptic includes stones exhibiting mere bulbs of percussion, but this clue is confined to 'quick' natured beds such as Cap, Marble and Cliff Freestone. These distinctive fracture surfaces tell of the rough dressing of blocks with a heavy biddle. The wall running inland from just east of St. Aldhelm's quarry has lots of such spalls exhibiting characteristic conchoidal fracture surfaces.

For the most part the typical wall stone gives no such clues as to how it came by its shape, but what is certain is that, in digging for paving, lots of low-value bits suitable only for walling would have been produced. None of this gives actual dates of building, only the knowledge that quarry by-product was finding its way into the walls either being new built or repaired. It is not unreasonable to link the construction of some

Belle Vue, Herston. Dry stone wall, showing a mix of horizontally and diagonally-laid stones.

with the development of the paving stone trade, as opposed to Marble production, getting going in the 16th century. Possibly medieval are those in the north part of Langton Wallis and at Dunshay, which are of waste Marble and Burr but perhaps built later than the time of digging. This could apply to the few pieces of Marble rubble, some certainly quarry waste, which have found their way into the wall by the car park for Spyway. This is ¾ of a mile away and uphill from the nearest possible source, Wilkswood, but formerly part of that same manor. The apparently rather pointless wall that weaves westwards through the wood west of Wilkswood Farm is also of Marble and Burr quarry waste. Such Burr tends not to exhibit tool marks to the degree that the harder Marble does, but bits of Burr within this wall have definitely been struck off by the use of heavy hammers.

An account recording work done on the Hatton (latterly Bankes) Estate in 1616 includes:

'For making part of the wall about Langton Wood item, est £12
For 300 foot of stone sent into London for her Ladyshippe's use £7'[52.]

What is interesting is that though the stone immediately to hand is Laining Vein and Burr, the mass of these walls around the southern part of the wood is Downs Vein, including Leper and including again bits of paving broken whilst being dressed. The account nicely links 'Her Ladyshippe' getting paving for her London property, Ely Place at Holborn, latterly Hatton Garden, with the building of a rough wall on her Purbeck estate. In 2006 the very dilapidated southern wall was restored which has considerably lessened its archaeological value. In underground Downs Vein working, the Leper was either left up as the ceiling or, if taken, used mostly for the legs. Either way not much was brought to the surface. Some of the Leper in these walls is permafrost affected, which tells of shallow surface working. The nearest such outcrop is roughly half a mile away in the northwest corner of Broad Mead, which is on the Hatton Estate. In spite of alternatives occurring near to hand, it was carried what I suspect was exceptionally far. Surely the compelling reason was that quarries going for the value added stuff, paving, were at the same time producing lots of excellent wall stones, so they made use of them; it was also

Knitson. Gate posts with holes at top for a bar and slots below for timbers, to control the movement of stock.

downhill.

Whether this was new build or not is uncertain. The wood is certainly older, for in 1491 ten tenants were paying 4d per annum for the freedom to take underwood for fuel. One wonders just how old the most venerable ash mocks are. Evidence that some walls were old enough to be in decay by the time of the Hatton family's ownership of the estate is provided by the only sheet of the Langton Court book that has survived from the 17th century:

> '1612 We do present that the pound walls is in decaye and is to be repaired by the tenants, the walles by the coppeholders and the dore by the farmer to be amended'

In the margin is added, 'by midsummer 6ft high'. Quite a wall.

Proof of rebuilds, additions and possibly new building of walls appears in the Bankes Estate disbursements during the 18th century:

> 'Farmer John Brown has made 110 Goad of walling in Verney at 15 ft per goad. Bilt 4 foot high under 'ye coping' [...] All made to be viewed'.
> 'To view ye fences [walls] at Eastington and inquire at how much per goad a man will repair those that are [...] in decay, And how many goad of such fences John Brown charges [...] 242 goad of walling at Eastington at 1/8d per goad.'

From about 1710 until 1725 John Brown held Bankes' southern farms and collected the dues from the quarries there:

> '1771 Paid Mr. Lander for a load of Coapers used at north part of Broad Mead.'
> 'Paid Gabriel Bower for 2 load of ditto used against Nichols Down'

These are larger than the normal walling stone, big enough to span the wall in one. 'Nichols', 'Nicholas', 'Necklas' variously, is the coastal field west of Seacombe which marches with Worth. Stone such as we see in this wall is much easier to access on the Worth side, which suggests Gabriel's quarry was on East Man, where many holes have been filled in in my life time. Neither he nor Mr. Lander appear amongst the names of Bankes Estate quarrymen around that time. However Samuel and Thomas Lander were working on the Worth Estate about then. They were probably just over the Broad Mead wall in French Grass, where that family certainly were working more than one quarry one hundred years later. It is interesting that Bankes was prepared to buy from adjacent quarries rather than depend on his own when circumstances called for it.

Gaps in walls quite frequently had pairs of stone posts on either side. Some footpath examples supported iron bars to make stiles, while some wider gaps had slots to accommodate wooden bars. Alternatively plain posts held swinging gates. Gate posts seem not to crop up in royalty returns nor have I seen them beyond the bounds of Purbeck, but they appear in Rev Austin's Economic Geology list for 1852, when they cost 4s. each. I would expect a degree of range in price in that some needed no more than a drill hole to take a leaded-in hinge whilst other have beautifully cut and more costly slots to take individual timbers, the usual arrangement being three or four, which allows for some stock control: removal of the lowermost lets sheep through but bars cattle, etc. Some examples have a round hole to take a pole at the top rather than a slot. Billy Winspit said the old hands often made them out of Blue Bit. Certainly that bed at St. Aldhelm's Head tends to run long and narrow, almost readymade for posts. Several examples remain of these and of the same bed from East Winspit, which is distinctive. However there are others of several inland beds, including Thornback and White Bit, both of which can also run to the necessary length, around about seven feet. Uncommonly, they were utilised in hedgerows rather than walls, examples remain near Church Knowle and Slepe.

LIME AND PLASTER

Limestone and alabaster (gypsum) were both dug to produce lime on the one hand and Plaster of Paris on the other. They were burnt in kilns. Lime was used either for mortar for building construction or for agricultural use. Lime fresh from the kiln was called quicklime; it is volatile and reacts strongly with water. It was used for whitewashing and for sanitary burial. When water is added, slaked lime is formed; this was used for mortar. Recent research now suggests that owing to the slow-setting nature of slaked lime mortar, some medieval projects were built while the lime was in the hot reactive state, during slaking rather than after the reaction was complete: this is known as a 'hot mix'.[53.]

Corfe Castle building accounts from the 1280s record

several purchases of lime from Poole and Bindon:

June 1282 6 quarters of lime bought at Bindon along with carriage of the same.
June 1282 3 quarters of lime bought at Bindon 2s
May 1282 6 quarters of lime bought at Poole
Aug 1282 'For canvas and sacks bought and hired for carrying lime for all the same works both on sea and by land 2s. ½d'
Sept 1282 '6½ quarters of lime bought at Poole'
Aug 1285 'For 7 bands to hoop a cask for lime'[54.]

It is likely to have been quicklime that was being transported. In such condition the rock is about third or half of the weight of the unburnt rock. Slaked lime putty is even heavier than the original material, therefore the risk of carrying such a volatile material in a boat must have been outweighed by the relatively light weight of the cargo.

In June 1285 there is a reference: 'Hauling lime from the old kiln to the castle with 2 horses for 2 days' before a lengthy entry from July 1285 itemising the building of a new kiln at Ower by Adam de Crawford, which includes:

'2 boats hired to bring stones from Fawley to the kiln, 12d.
For the service of men hauling stones from the water and the boats to the kiln, 3d.
or the service of 2 stone layers making a wall around the inside of the pit, 6d.
For a hundredweight of firewood to ignite the fire under the charcoal, 5d
For the carriage of that charcoal from Branksea to Ower, 8d'.[55.]

They possibly burnt coal as well or instead of charcoal, for in 1291 the accounts record: '80 quarters of coal of Newcastle on Tyne were bought at Ore for £4-0-0.' On the face of it Fawley, if it is the Southampton Water Fawley, seems an unlikely source of stone of any sort, but it had, and still has, a Stoney Point. It may be that this rock has heat resistant properties and was used in the construction of the kiln rather than for burning. The greater puzzle is the geology of the source rock for the lime they had been bringing from Poole and Bindon, and what were they burning at Ower? Why not have the kiln at Corfe and burn the chalk the castle stands on? The simple answer is that chalk does not produce good quality lime mortar for masonry purposes. Whatever their materials and methods were, they were successful in producing a strong mortar, as evidenced by the lumps of masonry that lie in the stream still intact after bouncing down the castle mound from high above. However Pam White points out that Corfe Castle mortars vary. That in the Norman keep is strong, whilst the Gloriette (*c.*1200) is poor, at least in the core of its walls. Perhaps they were using chalk where they thought it mattered less. But another possibility is that in the core location, the full hardening is prevented by deep burial.[56.]

'Bindon' surely refers to a source within the lands held by that Abbey, which then included Mupe and Lulworth Cove. Lulworth is celebrated for its wide range of rocks exposed in a small area. Mupe has the same. They include Chalk and both Purbeck and Portland Limestone beds. All, at least theoretically, are possible source rocks for lime. Perhaps most likely are some of the Purbeck beds which, by trial and error, had been found to be best. Strength of a mortar is affected not only by the type of limestone burnt, duration, and temperature achieved but also by the lapse of time between slaking and use, even indeed the amount of water used in the slaking process. Medieval, as opposed to modern factory-made lime, is complicated stuff. Neve, in the early 18th century, says: ''Tis a great Error in Masons and bricklayers to let the lime slacken and cool before they make up their mortar and also to let their mortar cool and die before they use it'.[57.] Perhaps the medieval builders used it whilst still hot! One way to achieve this is to mix the ground up quicklime with sand then water and use it immediately. In 1291, 20s. was paid to bring oyster shells from Poole to 'Ore' (a large sum, so surely a large quantity). These can be burnt to make lime, but are a less than ideal size.[58.]

In the Swanage depot they had two kilns, but scrapped them when Worth Quarry Co. built theirs at Sheepsleights in the 1920s. They burnt stone of different beds from various quarries and were in a position to learn what was best. My father only had a hazy memory of this sadly lost knowledge. He did say that each bed of stone made a lime of a different quality. Neither Cliff stone nor Burr were particularly good, but soft (soapy) Inland Freestone was. Best of all was Downs Vein. He was thus interested to read, late in life, Claridge (1793), which confirms the same finding: 'this (tiling) stone is sometimes burnt as lime, which is preferred by plasterers to any other in the kingdom and is sold at 7d per bushel or 14d per cwt.'[59.] Praise indeed!

However, what a plasterer looks for in terms of quality may not be the same as that of a castle builder looking only for strength, durability, and possibly setting speed. There were more than these two sorts of application for lime; in 1243 the whole keep at Corfe was whitewashed. How eye-catching that must have been! With that sort of usage in mind, my father remarked that one problem with the Worth Quarry Co. lime was that it tended to go on blowing after application. The Grosvenor Hotel did not appreciate pieces popping out of the plasterwork months after the work had been completed.

With regard to what was mixed with the lime to make mortar, he also recalled talk of a Swanage builder, Smedmore, who would gather the ground-up road surface from the High Street as the iron-tyred carts reduced it to dust. Smedmore had to sieve it of course, but as the ruts were forever being filled with fresh scars he was getting limestone dust with, I guess, some clay and organic material. *A propos* Corfe Castle, the mortar colour may be explained by the use of sand from the nearby Wealden beds. This could also be why odd bits of Wealden stone occur in the rubble cores; they are a by-product of digging the sand.

More evidence of the good quality of Downs Vein for lime is provided by the late 18th century Ramsgate Harbour building accounts. Sam Warren, who had a quarry in Durlston Bay where the Downs Vein runs to the shore, was supplying 'Lyme stone'. This is surely Downs Vein rather than Lias from Lyme Regis, which was, confusingly, much used for cement.[60.]

There was a kiln at St. Aldhelm's Quarry, which was destroyed in about 1932 when William David reopened the quarry. Beyond a patch of Shrimp and Blue bits being taken before that time, the quarry was not developed much, so presumably it was the Shrimp that was being burnt. It does not make a good lime for masonry, which suggests it may have been used on fields nearby which, surprisingly are acid because of leaching and the high percentage of silica in the cherty series.

Another lost kiln is indicated in John Lampard's late 18th century royalty return for Eastington and Langton Wallis farms: 'Received of Mr. George Baker for ½ an hundred of lime, 7½d'.[61.] Downs Vein was the most exploited layer there then, so it is probable that this best stone was being used. Evidence of the relative cost of lime mortar in the 18th century is provided by cottages at Ulwell which are of rubble stone set in clay, with only the exposed faces exhibiting a shallow mortar pointing. A curious and apparently mysterious feature of old lime mortar such as is used in local rubble walls is swirled shapes that develop on the weathered surface.

Trink Bower's quarry kiln at South Barn has been restored. Another, complete with a building, remains amongst old quarries west of Kingston. North of Church Knowle, also with an adjacent building, are the remains of a kiln that obviously burnt chalk; there is a similar one at the foot of Corfe Castle. In the late 18th century the population of Corfe included just one lime burner at the same time as 10 quarriers, 16 masons (builders) and 64 labourers.[62.]

In a wood east of Blackmanston a kiln has been built against a head of Burr. This may show an opportunistic use of an older quarry, using other beds outcropping above the kiln, rather than the Burr itself being burnt. Construction against a bank in this way is typical of these more recent kilns. It allows for the heavy stone and fuel being loaded easily in at the top, the burnt lime drawn from the bottom. However kilns of the earlier pit type may have continued in later use as the archaeologists investigating the Wytch Farm oilfield concluded with regard to the kiln discovered on Wytch Heath.[63.]

Parts of a kiln remain at the foot of the chalk in Lulworth Cove. Thomas Webster's view of Durlston Bay (*see page 99*) shows a smoking kiln close to the shore. This could be burning gypsum for plaster rather than stone for lime.[64.] Gypsum is listed in later royalties paid by quarriers in that bay. There is no income to be made from gypsum there now, as there is only one piece to be seen east of the rocks which form the massive sea defence scheme. Gypsum, also known as alabaster, occurs in discontinuous masses associated with faults. It seems that at present in Durlston Bay the advance of the sea has hit a relatively sterile patch. The same geological horizon, exposed on the east side of Worbarrow Tout, is similarly devoid, but in sharp contrast, on the western side, large masses are exposed and falling to the shore. This productive horizon lies about midway between the Portland beds and the New Vein, so the exposure extends over miles.

Medieval references to plaster would seem to mean burnt gypsum rather than burnt stone. Plaster of Paris was carried from Purbeck to Clarendon in 1288. 'Plaster of Corfe' occurs at Windsor in 1362, and 'burnt plaster of Purbyk' at Porchester in 1397.[65.]

The fuel used in the depot kiln was called 'culm' (anthracite), brought in by rail, but the last Purbeck kiln at Sheepsleights continued with coal. Geoff Hooper, who worked on it, told me there was an optimum size of stone, no more than about nine inches diameter. The men breaking up the rock with spall hammers were supplied with a metal plate with the right sized hole in it that the stones had to pass through. Conversely, small stones were no good, as they tended to block up and stifle the draught. The kiln had a cone, point up, in the centre, with four draw holes at the base. It was lit with faggots, but then burnt coal for months at a time. They generally used Freestone, the harder Spangle being kept for other uses such as tarmac. They usually had two draws a day of about one ton each. The well-burnt lime was light and had a feel and 'ring' to it, whilst the partly burnt stuff was heavy. This was discarded, but 'blew' on the tip. At night the draught was sealed up with dust. Chert turned to glass. Shillingstone chalk pit beat them on price and quality, and as the demand for crushed stone grew in the late 1950s, lime production was given up.

There is current revival in the use of lime mortars following years of Portland cement domination. When cement arrived first is uncertain, but by the late 19th century houses in Langton were built with the intention to render with hard, waterproof cement rather than it being used in a remedial way to cure damp walls. Cement-lined underground cisterns were also built in the late 19th century. Perhaps cement became commercially available with the arrival of the railway.

SEVEN
Technology

TOOLS

What distinguishes Purbeck from some other stone producing places is that there was no real distinction between quarrymen and stonecutters or banker masons. The average Purbeck quarryman was both. He would dig his own stone and then dress it into finished items. Of course where several men worked together there was often a division of labour, but typically men would acquire both skills. It was quite usual for young men, having started in the quarries and 'got to know the tools', to go off to London or anywhere masons were wanted. John Mowlem was therefore quite typical and it is a myth that the quarry community were enclosed and inbred – though many had a powerful sense of place. Some more able Purbeck men achieved responsible positions. Charles Edmunds, for example, starting as a boy at Hedbury, became foreman of masons on Manchester Town Hall, Victorian Gothic at its height. My father would say, with a twinkle in his eye, 'They all went away, and if they were any good they stayed away, if not, they came back,' which may explain a few things about Purbeck.

SAWING

Despite evidence of the sawing of Purbeck Marble during the Roman period and the delicate form of some components of medieval masterpieces such as the shrine at St. Albans which suggest the use of saws, there was not much sawing of Purbeck stone before the modern era.[1.] Purbeck, both 'Marble' and stone, being generally hard, made it just too laborious, so men exploited nature as best they could. Slabs were obtained from beds that split, cuboid forms from those that did not. However, in the post–medieval period there was some sawing of the Cliff stone beds, particularly for the production of headstones, before the first powered machines arrived in about 1900.

Fred Audley, who lived at Acton Field but laboured in the Swanage depot for years, remarked to my father that he 'sawed down big [staircase] landings for Grocer Burt [Henry Weeks Burt] from Ambrose Bower's Freestone at Seacombe.' I suspect that the block was sawn in such a way as to produce two or more useful stones without offcuts such as we moderns, with the aid of diamonds and cheap power, produce so profligately. Fred's landings could very well be part of the staircase of Seacombe stone that includes landings in the Sedgewick

Drawings of saws from W.H. Pyne's *Microcosm*, 1806.

Museum, Cambridge, built by Sir T. G. Jackson between 1904-1911. Burt had a powerful reason to cut the block in this laborious way. It could not be severed into slabs with wedges. To saw such Seacombe Under Freestone would be only marginally more difficult than the average Portland, and large quantities of that were sawn by hand during the 18th and early 19th centuries. Some monumental masons went on cutting Portland block in this way well into the 20th century.

A telling account was given me by Mr. Weeble who began work under his grandfather Beck in Winchester in the 1930s. They were still employing hand sawyers, mostly army pensioners. Their saw took the form of an H with a plain blade of steel at the bottom about one tenth of an inch thick. This was tensioned at the top by either a Spanish windlass or, in the case of the Beck tool, a bottle screw pulling in the top, which put tension on the blade. The H frame came apart so that cross bars and blades of differing lengths could be used and the cross bar could be inserted at differing heights. Thus different depths of cut could be achieved. When in action it was partly supported by means of a counterweight hung over a pulley supported by shear legs. The sawyers sat in a little weatherproof sentry-box-like shelter, pushing and pulling the saw to and fro all day, cutting blocks up to six or seven feet long. Water was fed into the cut from a barrel over corrugated roof sheets laid horizontally, which served to spread the trickle which flushed sharp sand down onto the blade. Their yard had a pub close by. It was said that on one hot day a sawyer managed twenty pints of bitter!

In the 1930s Winchester still had roads pitched with flint. The iron tyres of wagons ground this and rain washed these sharp fragments into the drains. Mr. Beck used to buy this sand from the men who dug out the gullies. He sieved it to achieve an even particle size. This sand was the all-important cutting agent. The fine waste produced from sawing was also kept and used later in the rubbing smooth of the slabs, the saw tending to leave coarse striations. I describe this at some length, as no doubt Grocer Burt's saw was similar and because Mr. Weeble's account so well illustrates the lot of the artisan, his perspicacity and toil. Latterly my father used Bridport beach sand for his engine-driven machine. Purchase gives a description and drawings of such a handtool, mentioning that a good man could cut fifteen or even twenty square feet of Portland in a day. What I find puzzling is how the sand particles got under the blade.[2.] Perhaps the motion of the saw was slightly rocking. Later power saws had vertically corrugated blades to provide for this (and they had a lifting action) but the hand-operated blades were straight.

The 18th century Portland nave floor tiles in Canterbury Cathedral are in fact offcuts (what a thought!), for on the underside some reveal a scappled surface and even the odd 'dog hole', which only makes sense when we realize that the slab now bearing it formed part of a much larger block. They provide nice evidence of how the result of hard labour was not wasted. In fact they prompt the thought that where it was possible so called 'offcuts' were cut off of sufficient thickness to be useful. 18th century Cliff stone octagons combined with smaller dark blue squares in the sanctuary at Horton, Dorset, could also perhaps be seen in the same light.

In Freshwater churchyard, Isle of Wight, there is a headstone that exhibits on its back striated surfaces about one third of the way in from each side, with a rough centre. It is clear that the sawyer cut in part way, turned the block over before cutting in part way again. Then, rather than grind on to the bitter end, he took a chance and broke the block. Mostly such evidence of method is destroyed by the face being worked over smooth, as of course the front has to be. Luckily this 18th century sawyer, by skimping the work, has left this telling evidence. Also at Freshwater churchyard the Crestwell slab is of Cliff stone, whilst Chichester Cathedral has two 18th century ledgers of Pond Freestone such as is quarried at St. Aldhelm's Head. It is possible that these slabs were worked from thin single blocks such as rarely occur naturally, but I suspect sawing to be a virtual certainty. Similarly, the series of Cliff stone headstones made by John Turner of Worth must have been sawn. So too were rare Cliff stone pavings in some cottages at Kingston (c.1830), which are surprisingly of Seacombe stone, not stone from quarries on the Encombe Estate.

In 1831, in the course of the work on Clavell Tower, Kimmeridge, Jeremiah Bower specifically charged the Rev. J. Clavell for the use of his saw. Late 18th century Worth Estate records reveal William Browne to be working a cliff quarry, surely part of Winspit.[3.] His usual output was harbour wall work, rollers, sinks, etc., but in 1792 his list includes the

Worth Matravers churchyard. William Bowers' sawn Cliff stone headstone, 1794. He 'drowned by being upset in an open boat' in Swanage Bay, aged 33.

unusual item of 202 square feet of headstones. With a typical headstone of the period measuring about ten or square feet, he was making quite a few. Perhaps he was newly equipped with a saw and was working it hard to get the money back. Patination makes the identification of external headstones difficult, particularly the relatively fine distinction between Portland and Cliff stone. William Bower's late 18th century headstone on the west side of Worth churchyard is virtually certainly of Cliff. He was drowned in Swanage Bay and is perhaps one of the William Bowers working another part of Winspit at the same time as William Browne.

For sharp sand to cut effectively it must get under the blade, so the blade has to lift off the workpiece at the same time as the sand particles find their way down corrugations in the blade walls. Some time in the 19th century powered saws based on this principle were developed. A blade was tensioned within a horizontal frame, suspended at each corner by pendulums. This was rocked or swung to and fro by a connecting rod attached to a crank and flywheel. Worm screws driven by belts from the same power source slowly drove the pendulum supports down the corner support columns to provide a controlled cutting speed.

When Charles Burt took over the depot in about 1910 he brought with him from his yard in Liverpool a primitive version of such a swing saw, together with its operator, Mr Brown. My father tried to explain the ingenious mechanism that converted the to-and-fro motion into the downward movement, which could be varied according to hardness of the

194 / PURBECK STONE

stone, but I failed to understand it. I suspect that headstones such as Maria Hussey's (1915) in the Nonconformist section of Langton Matravers cemetery were cut by it. Her stone is Thornback, relatively thin and smooth both sides, difficult to achieve other than by sawing.

Charles Burt's ex-Liverpool machine is therefore almost certainly the beginning of mechanised stone sawing in Purbeck. Burt also brought to Swanage the first planer, a Coulter. This could produce both flat surfaces and straight moulding. The workpiece was clamped to a steel table, which was driven to and fro on a bed of rollers. An adjustable arm was mounted over the table in which a chisel was held at an inclined angle to the work surface. The arm carrying the tool canted over so that the chisel cut on both back and forth strokes of the table. Burt's two machines, plus a chaff cutter for preparing the feed for the wagon horses, were all powered by a single gas engine that produced about 50 horsepower. It was started on Town Gas, but switched over to gas produced by burning anthracite once it was running. Later Burts developed a tarmac plant, the crushed chippings being brought from Mutton Hole.

Their Coulter planer had tempered steel chisels, but some time in the 1930s tungsten carbide tipped chisels became available. My uncle Frank remarked that they were providing stone for the house on Furzey Island, which included a long moulded mantlepiece. He was machining a piece of Bill Tomes' Belle Vue Thornback, which was hard. The new tungsten carbide cut it in a way that would have been much more difficult with mere tempered steel. Presumably tungsten was also being used for banker tools by this time. Its introduction was a blow to the blacksmiths, as tungsten does not need forging.

These late 19th century machines remained the only stone-processing machines in the depot and the whole Purbeck area up until the 1920s, as Burt and Burt became the Purbeck Stone and Trading Company. However, when Haysoms took over the depot they quickly installed a bigger, more efficient saw, built by Smiths of Keighley. It was capable of cutting blocks up to about ten feet long, powered by a 25 horsepower Tangye engine, supplemented by an oil engine of the hot bulb type. The cutting agent was sometimes steel shot but more often sand from the beach at Bridport. There were scores of these swing saws in the Portland yards, presumable all using Bridport sand. The cut surfaces produced were characteristically striated. Coarse particles of above average size would produce a deeper scratch and thereby a nuisance in a surface that needed to be rubbed smooth.

A yard at Chesil was equipped with steam saws by 1877, some thirty years or more before Purbeck's first powered saw.[4] Haysom's saw was newly installed and working when Anthony Haysom visited the yard and stood watching it. It was said of him that 'he could not read or write but my god he could reckon'. 'Wa's' think of that, Hantney?' someone inquired. 'Thick thing is comfort to no man' he said. Haysom's also installed a circular saw, operated by Bert Tomes, which had a 30 inch carborundum blade. About this time, the 1930s, they were supplying stone for St. Francis' Church, Charminster Road, Bournemouth. True to the Arts and Crafts ideal, evidence of how the stones were cut was left, so the masonry exhibits not only hand tooling but surfaces produced by both sorts of saw.

St. Aldhelm's Quarry (Haysom's). General view of workshop, 2020. The yellow machine is a saw doing a similar job to those featured in Pyne's *Microcosm*.

The sharp sand readily wore away the steel blades. As the wear developed, so the blade was turned over, so that both edges wore down to such a point that, finally, the blade broke. A broken end of one of the blades remains in the Langton Matravers Museum. The blade would have been, when operational, about fourteen feet long. A major disadvantage with these saws was that they required an operator to feed the sand all day.

In the 1920s the Dorset Quarry Co. equipped their yard by Wareham station with both frame and circular saws and planers. In their Seacombe quarry they also set up a nail saw for rough trimming of the blocks. Its concrete foundations remain close to the cliff edge, towards the western end of the quarry. The circular blade was armed with replaceable hardened steel pins. It was operated by Mr. S. Causon and could be heard, according to my father, 'up Tilly Whim'. A broken blade of this type can be seen in the Portland Museum. It is likely that this was the first circular saw in Purbeck. It was an innovation that, with the introduction of diamond-tipped blades after the Second World War, would revolutionise stone working.

DRILLS

The tools a cliff quarryman needed to get the stone out would have included drills. These were usually held and turned in one hand and struck by a four to seven pound hand hammer in the other. Modern air driven drills are either chisel ended or star bit faced; that is, the cutting edges form a cross shape. Such drills produce a flat bottomed hole, but old remaining drill holes still to be seen in the cliff quarries are slightly pointed at the end, showing the drill had a single cutting edge that was brought to a blunt point. Knocking a drill hole in by hand is difficult in that the waste dust produced tends to jam the rotation. This is less of a problem when drilling horizontally than vertically, but

Plug and feathers.

it puts a limit on easily accessible depth. At both Seacombe and Sheepsleights during the 1920s, longer drills were employed to 'bump down' deeper holes, one man holding and rotating the shank while a second struck it with a biddle. The advent of pneumatic drilling with flushing air being introduced down a hollow shanked drill ended the clogging difficulties, but such drills did not arrive in Purbeck, at Seacombe, until about 1924.

The last hand drills were used by a few men as late as the 1960s when electric drills became the norm. One trick with the manual system which helped to keep the hole clear was to add water: each blow of the hammer threw up a spurt of water together with the waste. But this could splash in the face. To get over this some men fitted a circular disc of rubber on the drill to suppress the squirt. The power of compressed air allowed for more speed and larger diameters. Such holes can be seen at Seacombe and West Winspit. Another result of easy, rapid drilling was the general application of 'plugs and feathers'. They were to replace the old skill of cutting pits for wedges by hand and were probably invented in Vermont USA marble and granite quarries in the early 19th century. They had been in use in British granite quarries for some time.[5] A pair of sleeves, or feathers, serves to convert a round section hole into a rectangular section, into which a tapered wedge, or plug, is driven. A series of such wedges acting in a line of holes can be used for lifting a block off its bed or for secondary splitting. They were possibly introduced into Purbeck at Seacombe with the first pneumatic drill in the 1920s,

KIBBLE

There is some evidence of the possible cutting of wedge pits with a kibble, and the tool is mentioned in 17th century inventories. It is synonymous with Portland, and John Smeaton the civil engineer gives a graphic description of the prowess of the men handling it there. It is not known to have been used in Purbeck in the recent past, but appears in 18th century inventories. Grimm (*c.* 1789), illustrates one in use in a cliff quarry, and it is probably the tool mentioned by Hutchins in his description of work at Seacombe.

The Portland men used the pointed end to pick out the long slots they cut to take wedges to split the blocks free. These cuts would run continuously the length of a block, unlike cliff quarry pits that were almost invariably cut separately for each individual wedge. An exception are those in underground on the east heading at Dancing Ledge, where long almost continuous pits have been cut by hammer and punch. St. Aldhelm's Head undercliff has just one block exhibiting a long, continuous Portland style cut, which suggests the use of the kibble. My father obtained a kibble, but Thomas Bonfield and Jack (Rippy) Norman, highly proficient men, could not get on with it, preferring a hammer and punch and biddle.

Marks left by hammer and punch on the one hand, a kibble on the other can be confusingly similar. Some 18th century Portland headstones exhibiting what looks like a punched back are in fact the product of the kibble. The norm in Portland was for the raw blocks to be squared up by the kibble to avoid hauling unnecessary waste. Such a block sawn into headstones, produces an outer slab bearing a kibbled surface. However similarly squared up blocks left at Dancing Ledge and Seacombe bear what are certainly punch marks. One minor snag of the kibble is that had to be removed from its handle when taken to the blacksmith to be sharpened.

In some early references the word seems to mean a nail; Corfe Castle Accounts (1282): 'For 2000 kevels' bought for stones 3d. [Fixing roof tiles][6] Exeter Accounts, also in a roofing context (1316): '1000 *kevillis* 1d.' Scholars have translated *kevillis* as 'wedges' but surely these are nails.[7] However, not much later, 'kevyll' appears in a 1404 list of tools at Durham. Can a certain wry humour be detected in this later change of meaning from a little nail to a heavy tool, the use of which raised a lot of sweat?

PUNCHES AND PIT CUTTING

Unlike on Portland, Purbeck wedge pits have overwhelmingly been cut using a hammer and punch. Punches were simple points of varying lengths, generally about nine inches, They are much used for preliminary dressing, but sometimes for finishing. When driven across a stone at an angle in parallel lines or drokes they produce a surface called 'broached', characteristic of much 18th and 19th century Purbeck work. Broaching can typically be seen on bridge or harbour wall work, where a straight face was required, but not so refined, and therefore not as expensive as tooled or chiselled ashlar. The sequence for producing a fine rubbed face is to go from punched, to clawed, to chiseled, to abrasive rubber. In working

Fort Cumberland, Portsmouth. Example of late 18th century broaching work.

Walter Harden using hammer and punch, c.1950.

hard material like Marble a short punch is best in that it has less tendency to 'dance'. If too short, the scars coming off the work piece can strike the side of the little finger, producing a painful chap. Ralph Bower used to wear a little finger leather to protect his. More commonly men would wear a thumb leather around the base of the thumb, which is in constant contact with the punch or chisel and where chaps also tend to develop. For cutting pits or hollow work like sinks longer punches were needed. As tools became dull they were 'whet out' on a piece of grit stone called a rubber. These days a piece of the ubiquitous York stone is used, but such abrasive stones were formerly obtained locally.

Bobby Norman, who as a young man worked in the Durlston Bay quarries, was in charge of the stonework on Herston church, (1869-70), and latterly foreman to Thomas Stevens in his Tilly Mead yard. He would take a dinghy and row across Swanage Bay to the sandstone ledges that appear at low water towards the northern side, and there split off bits for use as rubbers and whetstones. No doubt he would have known the properties of the various ledges: New House, Tanull, and Phippards. Repeated whetting out resulted in the tapered punch becoming more and more 'stiff' until it was returned to the blacksmith for sharpening. It also resulted in wear and tear to the whetstone

Hammer and punches.

unless care was taken. The groove created was called a 'droke'. In the Co-op's workshop by Acton road Reggie Pickles (Bower) put a notice above the whetstone: 'DON'T DROKE THE RUBBER'.

The blacksmith would heat the blunt punch until cherry red and 'draw it down' by hammering. Such a newly drawn out punch was then tempered and became 'fire sharp'. The art of tempering was to harden the point so that it cut, but not so that it broke off, a considerable skill. The blacksmith played a vital role. The 1687/8 will of Swanage blacksmith Thomas Collins of Swanage informs us about his material goods, including tools and stock in his shop. They include Welsh, Spanish and 'Sweeds' (Swedish) iron and steel, 'a kiwell, 2 peckaxes, 4 twie bills'.[8.]

Newly fire-sharpened punches cut the best, but being finely drawn out were most likely to break. In cutting a deep pit a more averagely worn punch was used to do most of it, the final 'topping out' being achieved using one that was fire sharp and keen. The cutting of these pits demanded skill, and care had to be taken in doing the final topping out, for it was vital that the wedge, when driven, 'bit' close to, but not on, the bottom. If it 'pinched' too close to the top then the sides just flushed off uselessly; if it touched the bottom, when struck, it would tend to fly out of the pit ineffectually. Most men of the last generation of pit cutters seem to have sunk them to a fine point, but numerous medieval examples revealed in old Marble workings at Quarr are relatively flat bottomed, almost 'U' rather than 'V' shaped, which suggests the use of thin steel plates or 'scales' lining the pit. The cliff quarries exhibit many

TECHNOLOGY / 197

Splitting Stone by Gads, Gordon Bower, 1987 (Langton Matravers Museum). Seacombe, 1920s. Using wedges to sever a large block of Under Freestone. Once achieved, the split surface exhibits the characteristic pit marks as seen on the front edge of the stone below the man on the right. The marks are large for wedges, smaller for gads, and smaller still for punches. These are clearly wedges.

examples of beautifully cut pits, particularly where the block was big or tight. The spacing and depth was dependent on the resistance of the block to be split. The recent exposure of an almost certainly circa 13th century Marble quarry face has revealed many more cut in that harder stone, clear evidence of medieval blacksmiths forging excellent tools. The walls of these pits exhibit striated diagonal punch marks which were made by the quarryman commencing at the far end of the proposed pit and working back towards himself, leaving the characteristic marks within a typical asymmetric 'U' shape.

Exceptionally, much longer punches were needed, for example for cutting the socket holes to mount jibbets. These holes, such as can be seen on various loading rocks, demanded skill in that it is vital to keep the punch attacking around the outside of the hole. If, as it deepens, the verticality of the walls is lost, it cannot be regained. This was brought home to me in the working of the two stone flower vases in Langton church. Cyril Haysom worked one, Thomas Collins the other. Lacking a core drill they cut these relatively deep container holes by hammer and punch alone; a difficult task.

PITCHERS

Another tool for rough dressing was the pitcher, or pitching tool, somewhat like a heavy, blunt faced chisel, it was used for bursting off waste. Early rubble walling usually had any face bulges roughly chiseled or 'jagged' off. It became a fashion in the late 19th century to leave the face of dubbers 'off the pitching tool'. Especially if the courses are high this can be productive of a lot of protruding 'rock', such as is exhibited by the railway bridges and Corfe viaduct. Any tool marks left on a rock face were frowned on by this Victorian school of thought. Innumerable wedge pit marks were dressed off, which from a modern perspective would add to the interest of a wall. Langton Church (1876) is an example of this later fashion. The Village Hall opposite (1845) is a good late example of what went before. An example of difficulties with quality control from the middle of the 20th century concerns Jobey Cobb, whose dressed walling was not of the neatest. Merchant Jacky Harden delicately inquired as to which was the face on one particularly poorly-shaped piece. 'Ruggle 'im round on banker til the back's lookin' at yer, then tother side's the face,' said Jobey.

GADS

In addition to the big wedges for lifting and splitting large blocks, the quarrier would also have had small wedges, known as gads, for splitting smaller stuff, and short, worn out punches for yet smaller. The meaning of the word 'gad' seems to have changed over time. From Knoop and Jones comes: 'At Beaumaris Castle, winter 1316-17, one smith and assistant employed making big gads and little gads. Working at task he was paid 2d to sharpen each iron and ½ d for shaping each gad.'[9.] These payments are for tools for the hewers, layers and quarries. The cost of sharpening suggests a cutting tool rather than a wedge. ½ d against 2d suggests a punch, as compared to a wide chisel. It has been suggested that Gad Cliff looks wedge-shaped viewed from the east.

BIDDLE AND OTHER HAMMERS

Large wedges were driven with a heavy two-handed long-handled hammer called a biddle. It was two faced. One rounded face was hardened to strike steel, the other, of a different temper, with a square or slightly concave cutting face, was used for striking stone. Later biddles were made of steel, but earlier ones were of iron, with a hard steel face bonded on. Such an old tool was found underground at Winspit by Bob Harris when he cleared away a founder.[10.] Similar hammers, but with both faces designed for striking stone rather than steel were known as spall hammers, and the large waste pieces produced by such hammers, spalls. Heavy, two handed hammers of this type were in use in the Middle Ages, for many spalls, exhibiting a typical bulb of percussion, can be seen amongst the Marble waste debris in Talbots Wood. Reopening old workings at Quarr in the summer of 2004 revealed a lot of medieval waste together with large blocks bearing a variety of tool marks. These include lumps obviously struck off by the use of a narrow-headed heavy tool rather than the biddle as we know it, as well as 'normal' biddle blows. They suggest a tool more akin to the modern Portland kibble. Smaller waste fragments, produced by the punch and pitching tool, are called

Seacombe Quarry, 1920s. L-R, Victor Short Bower, Bob Turner (behind), Buff Bower, Billy Winspit Bower, Jack Corben. The men are employing wedges to sever a large block of Under Freestone. Once achieved, the split surface exhibits characteristic pit marks, as can be seen on the front edge of the stone below the man on the right. The marks are large for wedges, smaller for gads, and smaller still for punches, the choice being dependent on the resistance of the rock. These are clearly wedges.

scars, formerly sometimes gallets. My father remembered older men saying 'chuck a gallet under him' when milling (rotating) a stone about on the banker, but scar was the usual term.

BARS

For loosening and moving stones, bars were all important. The mechanical advantage gained by a long bar acting on a fulcrum positioned close to the load makes it possible to move stones weighing tons. Our heaviest bar took two men to pick it up. Jammed under the end of a tight block with two of us jumping on it exerted a lot of leverage. Of course much smaller more manageable bars were used for most work. A front-edge to heel length of two inches on a five feet long bar gives a mechanical advantage of 30-1. A reasonably strong man exerting a hundredweight effort can therefore move one and a half tons. The biggest bars are difficult to move. To alleviate this problem the Dorset Quarry Co had one at Seacombe equipped with a roller fixed under the heel.[11]

Whatever the size, they had to be straight; 'as useless as a bent bar' was an expression. The importance of the simple straight bar can hardly be emphasised enough. It is singled out in early inventories such as Robert Codd's, (1616), freemason of Corfe: 'one quarre barre other quarr and mason tools', and Hugh Hort's (1693), 'marbler of Sanwich': '2 quarr barres and a kevill 15s. 0d.'[12] The use of bars was central to workings like Hedbury and East Winspit. The only cranage employed was for dropping the finished work into the boat. In inland underpicking, sharp chisel ended bar-like tools called 'paddles' were driven by a hammer whilst 'gussers' were specific to the similar task in Downs Vein quarries.

MEASUREMENT

In addition to quarry face tools, men would have had a two foot gauge for measuring and marking out, which was a wooden rod with the inches marked on with scratch lines and/or nails such as those used in hobnailed boots. This was sufficiently accurate for most work. When I started work in 1959 my father was making use of a factory-made folding boxwood rule, but Jack Norman still had a handmade 'Two voot', as it was called. I guess he was the last to do so.

A good description is given by Thos. B. Groves, F.C.S.:-

'The rule used for this testing, as well as for measuring all kinds of stone as to breadth and depth at or from the quarries, is a piece of wood 24ins. long, 1¾ins. wide, and ¾in. thick. It is marked at every inch with a cut or notch, and at every 3ins. with holes burnt in – in much the same way in fact as the iron rule in use at Portland. This rule is made by the mason or quarrier and is called the 'stick of inches".[13]

There is a good example in the Langton Matravers Museum collection. David Lovell, in his capacity as stone dues collector for the Bankes Estate in the recent past, had an example with brass terminals. Mr. W. M. Hardy informed Mr Groves that

Langton Matravers Museum. L- R: Two foot measuring stick, tiler's pick (note removable head). gusser lacking its wooden handle. Both the cutting tools are now blunt; when in use they were kept sharp.

TECHNOLOGY / 199

Langton Matravers Museum. Metal 90 degree square and 135 degree mitre square.

it is also called a 'tuvvot'. This is surely the same tool which puzzles Salzmann and other medieval scholars, a 'twyvete'. i.e., two foot. Hardy also noted that it has an evil reputation owing to its being used across the backs of loitering boys 'gone too long after father's dinner, or stopping about when sent after the donkey'[14.]

This may be the appropriate place to include a playground chant my cousin, John Haysom, recalls from his days at Mount Scar School, Swanage in the 1940s:

'Wher'art gwain?
Up quarr
What for?
Veather's dinner
Wha's got?
Teaties an' beans
Gi'e I a bite?
No! veather'd miss en.'

Other essential tools included a square and a pair of compasses, sufficient to mark out a staddle leg or design an entire cathedral. Most important of all is the 90 degree square of a variety of sizes. Several medieval illustrations show the master holding such a square that is out of parallel. That is, though both inner and outside edges form 90 degrees, the width changes. Matthew Paris' *Life of Saints Alban and Amphibalus* illustrates a good example.[15.] Brian Bugler has suggested that it is not poor draughtsmanship on the part of the artists concerned but shows the instrument as it really was; that the angle of displacement was 3 degrees, and therefore that it could function as a protractor. The medieval variety is illustrated in *Batisseurs au Moyen Age*.[16.] The illustration shows that external edges are at 90 degrees, but not the internal, which I find astonishing. When working on the banker it is far better to make use if the internal rather than the external edge of a square. For it not be 90 degrees seems totally mysterious.

A variant on the modern square is the adjustable sinking square. The length of the arm can be altered, essential in working sinkings of restricted depth. A variant on this is the double sinking square, which has an additional arm, also adjustable. It can reach around corners, so to speak, but is seldom needed.

Less vital were trammels. There are two sorts: one for scribing parallel lines, the other for describing circles of a larger radius than compasses expand to. The latter consists of two pins that can be variously adjusted along a batten. Curves of a radius greater than this call for a cord. The other trammel is of an L shape with a short pointed foot and an extended vertical that is broadened to a hollow that fits around the shank of an average chisel. With the two gripped together the chisel head can be drawn along the edge of a curved piece of work so that the trammel point describes a parallel line at the required interval. The basic marking tool is a scriber, simply a sharp point for scratching in lines.

Straight edges were used, of various lengths, both wooden and steel. As well as being necessary for marking, they were constantly in use for testing the workpiece in the course of its preparation, particularly with tooled surfaces. Titus Lander had an unusual wooden one with a gap. This was useful in the working of rustic Latin (straight-armed) crosses in particular. They present a problem in that to achieve a straight arris across the arms requires a gap to accommodate the raised rock face in the centre of the cross.

Moulds were seldom required in the quarries, but they would have been needed for working sections of moulding, such as we see on the various manor houses. Recently these have been made from zinc sheet. Presumably before its introduction similar thin sheet of other metals was used, even perhaps thin wood board. My father was, I suspect, typical of men not given to waste, in that he would cut zinc moulds again and again until only scraps were left. Hence few of that sort survive, alas and none of the earlier type. Plastic sheet that can easily be cut with scissors has largely replaced these hard materials, but it brings a disadvantage. It cannot be scribed around. The benefit of a good hard scratch line is that it becomes the actual arris of the finished piece. Moulds were only ever marked on one side. Imperfections in making apparently-symmetrical moulds mean that in practice they never are. This is not a problem so long as the mould is applied one way round on one end of the work piece and the other way round on the other. Hence the expression in masonry, 'lines up, lines down'.

Another necessary mason's tool was the mitre square. Carpenters usually resolve moulded mitres by cutting a joint at the intersection. This is bad practice in masonry as the feather edges so produced are liable to break. Return mouldings are therefore worked in the solid on the same piece. Having worked the long side first, the difficulty of drawing a guide line across the moulding is resolved by a combination of mitre square with mitre board, and/or 90 degree square with mitre board. The mitre square is of plate metal with an angle of 135 degrees, which is needed for a 90 degree return. The board is simply a piece of straight wood typically about two feet six inches by half an inch.

To execute designs such as tracery windows requires that they be set out full size, the jointing arrangement decided on and full size face moulds cut for each stone, other than those that repeat. There must have been Purbeck provision to do this on a flat surface somewhere. The 14th century stone cutter who fashioned the Burr canopy and curvilinear window in the Turberville Chapel, Bere Regis, surely had access to such a tracing floor. Worth Matravers church east window has identical geometry, but is bigger. Each would have needed a separate set of face moulds. One of only two such medieval floors that survive in England is hidden away in York Minster. When Burts provided the east window for Langton church, James Haysom set it out on the floor of the room of the Swanage Congregational church, of which he was a member. Setting out work of this size would have called for a string line. Similarly, my father made use of abandoned huts at RAF Worth Matravers, plucking a taut string charged with chalk powder.

If the Turberville Chapel work required setting out full size, what of somewhat simpler earlier forms such as the 13th century tracery windows at Church Knowle? I imagine they did too. Going back further what of the dogtooth arches at Worth and Creech Grange, formerly Holme Priory? Each arch probably required striking out full size on the ground using no more than a length of cord and a pair of pins such that a voussoir face mould could be cut. But what distinguishes these 12th century arches is that the voussoirs vary. They do not all conform to an exact size, as Victorian copies usually do. However, it is possible to use a face mould to give the basic shape, particularly the rake of the radiating joints, but not to be inflexibly controlled by it. The masons could have adjusted the position of the mould, both resulting in some variation in the widths of the individual voussoirs and the angle of each zigzag.

This artisanal approach distinguishes early masonry from what comes after the evolution of the modern architect; 'hands on' men often produced apparently quirky but practical solutions. What of Worth's chancel arch? Why the single, large voussoir low on the north side? Did the builder get started, only to find the general run of stones coming out of the quarry to be rather smaller than anticipated? Alternatively, it is possible that, without using moulds at all, they offered each stone up in turn on the centering, and 'fudged' their way around. Arguably the most difficult is 'circle on circle'. The arches in the round part of the Temple Church in London demonstrate a beautiful 12th century solution.

MASONRY WORK

For banker work, the masons would have had more punches of various lengths and shank size, and claw tools, which are serrated chisels. Much medieval Marble work in general, and the 13th century Marble drums of the piers in Salisbury in particular, exhibit marks from such fine, keen claws. There were chisels of different widths from an eighth of an inch up to four inches, including round or bull nosed chisels of various radii for working hollow mouldings. Wide chisels, called 'boasters', or 'bolsters' were used for the final finishing of flat surfaces and marks left by them are therefore common. Such tooling can be done very neatly (the number per inch can be specified) or the work can be bashed over roughly. With all these cutting tools

ABOVE Bere Regis, St John the Baptist. Window canopy in Turberville Chapel.

BELOW Worth Matravers, St Nicholas. Chancel arch with irregular dog-toothed Burr voussoirs.

Langton Matravers Museum. Stone-working tools.

Langton Matravers, St George, showing measured batting on column: the capital is left 'off the chisel', ready to be carved later.

the blacksmiths, who were rarely the quarrymen themselves, played a crucial role. For as wear caused the tools to become 'stiff' they had to dress them time and time again. To get an even temper along the wide edge of a boaster is difficult. All these tools gradually reduced until too short for use. In the case of punches, when worn out they were sometimes converted into little gads, but with a point retained.

DRESSING

Identifying the difference between surfaces wrought by chisel on the one hand, axe on the other, is difficult. Marks left on medieval Burr ashlar in Corfe Castle (13th century) and Langton's 15th century church tower are almost certainly left by the axe. It is safe to say that all somewhat-similar marks on post medieval paving have been left by the chisel. There are problematic surfaces, such as Corfe's (1285) Outer Bailey (eastern turret). The tool marks run obliquely in a puzzling way. What characterises such a typical paving surface is that following an initial draft along a long edge, secondary drafts were worked along each end before the whole surface was worked across in the same direction as the first draft. Each draft was systematically tested and corrected by straight edge before the next was driven. The result is that tool marks all go in one direction except at the ends. Though there is some variation, the chisel can be applied off square etc.; most post-medieval paving conforms. However, the soffits of long vaulting slabs in work of 1285 in Corfe's Outer Bailey are not like this. The tool marks run obliquely. However it was done, the mason was not testing each draft end to end. In tooling with a chisel, the chisel is held at an angle so there is a slight difference between the entry and escape side of each mark. Heavy, measured corduroy-type tooling can call for two or even more blows per 'scoop'. In contrast some of the Corfe medieval surfaces show that the tool was applied dead-on rather than at an angle. I guess those are from the axe. Some are fine and similar in appearance to surfaces certainly left by the chisel and so can be easily confused. But other medieval Corfe marks are different: great bold swipes sometimes producing chevrons obviously made from an axe held at an angle. Of course, striking a hard stone will give a different result from striking a soft. The bold marks tend to be on reasonably soft Burr.

There is a difference between chiselling a surface to achieve a shape, and a deliberately finished 'batted' face. Langton church nave pillars provide good comparisons. The intention was to carve the caps, but this was never done, so they remain left off the chisel or 'boasted for carving', whilst the pillar below exhibits neat measured batting as intended. Other elements such as the base mouldings are rubbed.

Kingston church (1875) exhibits consistently fine perfect tooling. No doubt the architect, G. E. Street, specified so many strokes per inch. Not only does the width between the strokes vary but it is possible to see where some men dipped the chisel a bit deeper in places in an attempt to take out a too deep punch mark, therefore skimping, taking the whole surface down a bit more. Street would not have let them get away with it. At risk of reinforcing a calumny, the term 'a Swanage dip' was in parlance in the Portland stoneyards. It was applied in jest to such imperfections as if Purbeck men made more of them than the Portlanders did. There is a paradox in that, with today's mechanised way of doing things, what was once the more expensive type work is the easiest and therefore cheapest to replicate. Langton's imperfections can only be reproduced in a more contrived way.

Another less refined finish was termed 'broaching'. When in

Kingston, St James. Perfect tooling, 1875.

Langton Matravers Museum. Beech wood mallets; note heartwood 'beat' at left.

Langton Matravers churchyard. Decorative broaching on back of headstone.

the form of ashlar this was usually about 40 degrees off the vertical. It was cheaper than tooled (that is chiselled). Each stone was taken out of twist by being given a tooled margin, but the panel punched only, rather than refined further. Many old Purbeck headstones were left rough backed, but some were broached. Some, to achieve symmetry, were broached to the centre line. Row paving, neat enough for external work, was also left broached only. However some seemingly original broached paving is the result of the deliberate roughing of old slabs worn smooth. In the 1950s, Walter Norman sat on a sack bag and worked his way up a section of Swanage High Street roughing up the stones with a punch.

Pitching tools and punches were struck by a longheaded hammer, which gives a better blow than a lump hammer of the same weight. A softer 'more of a push' blow is better when chiselling, so these were more often used in conjunction with a wooden mallet. Such mallets were generally of apple, but though round in shape, they were not made the way of the tree. Instead the grain crosses the round shape, which gives a hard heart wood 'beat' on two opposite sides. It is important to strike on the beat as the other parts of the mallet are softer and liable to damage. Many men cut a small notch in the handle to accommodate the little finger so that as they grasped it they could feel, without looking, when it was in the right position.

Banker masons and carvers also occasionally used drills, even in hard Purbeck Marble. Some were small, such as those used by the Stanton Harcourt shrine carver in 1300 in his representation of hair (see page 49). Many capitals, notably those in the Salisbury Cathedral triforium, have holes cut above the bead to introduce lead into the joint between shaft and cap.[17] This contrasts with the 19th century dowel solution at Kingston, which has left shafts that waggle.

The masons did not use gouges, Purbeck stone being too hard. Quirks, that is, fish-tail ended chisels used for cutting narrow grooves such as water bars, were part of a mason's kit, but not most quarrymen's.

RUBBING AND POLISHING

To produce a smooth or rubbed face abrasive sandstones were rubbed over the chiselled face until the tool marks were obliterated. The first rough rubbing was done by coarse stones or loose sand, finishing with finer. Though not much rubbed face work was produced at the quarries, the faces of headstones were brought to a fine rubbed finish before lettering. John and James Haysom, Swanage letter cutters, used pole rubbers. One sort consisted of a hinged clamp on a long handle that held an abrasive stone, the other, a similar long handle attached by a hinge to a heavy perforated iron tray that held water and sharp sand. The slab to be rubbed was laid flat and the rubber pushed to and fro by means of a long handle.

Neve gives a description of this sort of polishing: 'An old experienced Mason tells me, that he has observ'd Stone-cutters polish Marbles for Hearths in this manner, viz: By laying three or four of 'em in a row as even as they could, and then with another of these Stones fix'd to a broad Beetle, with a Handle put in at Oblique Angles, (and with Sand and Water) by moving this upper Stone too and fro on the lower ones, they wrought off the Strokes of the Ax, and afterwards with Emmery and Putty they polish them.'[18]

Polishing Purbeck requires three grits: coarse, medium, fine followed by another stone: 'snake', before final polish. How long has that natural stone been used? The first three have now been largely superseded by carborundum or other synthetics. The Victorians finished off with various potions, including shellac and sperm whale oil; Scott used both in his work on the medieval Purbeck Marble in Westminster Abbey.[19] Another treatment was linseed oil, which my father continued to use in his work on the Temple Church. Experience must tell us that, excepting in ideal, perfectly dry environments, Purbeck Marble should be treated like iron, that is, it requires protection of some sort. The current best solution is applications of microcrystalline wax. The effect of acid was known long ago. In the *Metrical Life of St Hugh of Lincoln*, written about 1200: 'This stone [Purbeck Marble] disdains to be tamed with steel until it has first been subdued by art for its surface must first be softened by long grinding with sand and its hardness relaxed with strong vinegar.'[20] This sequence is rather puzzling but it is clear that acid was utilised.

CRANAGE

For lifting or moving heavy stones, gibbets and capstans, essentially medieval machines, remained in use; the former until about 1880, the latter until the 1950s. The 'Hykerell' location at Wilkswood in late medieval Court Presentments suggests possible evidence for cranes in medieval Purbeck quarries.[21] In around 1910 Burts had a requirement for Cliff stone. They obtained a hand-operated Scotch derrick for Webber's Dancing Ledge quarry. It was the first of this new generation of cranes

TECHNOLOGY / 203

in Purbeck. It was soon removed to Swanage and set up in the depot, where it was positioned to offload wagons and place blocks on the machine tables. This type of derrick was a considerable advance. The jib, greatly increased in length compared to the old gibbets, could be raised and lowered, allowing for a much greater working area. No doubt such machines were in use elsewhere well before Purbeck. A view of J. Mowlem's Guernsey granite quarry shows one in use in 1883. In Portland such cranes began to be used about 1825.[22] Before that all lifting, other than on the piers, was done solely by bars and jacks.

A lot of these modern derricks were utilised during the first half of the 20th century, the average Purbeck one having smaller capacity than those on Portland. The king post, with the jib attached by a pivot at its base, was free to rotate but supported by bracing timbers set at 90 degrees to each other, so the jib actually reached over an arc of 270 degrees. The braces were triangulated to the king post by horizontal ground timbers. So long as these were firmly fixed to the ground the crane remained secure. The easiest way to do this was to pile heavy weights on them, so photographs of such cranes in operation invariably show a stack of stone trapping the end of each brace. Within the stack the bolts linking brace to ground timber rusted and became difficult to take apart. When they took their cranes away George Hancock and George Lander, at Greyrock and Wilkswood respectively, left these parts – where they remain to this day. Most such cranes used in Purbeck had the king post split, with the winding gear mounted across the gap.

Cliff quarry type gibbets were probably once in widespread use. These early cranes consisted of a fixed king post with a movable braced arm mounted beside it on a pivot held up by a hinge at the top. This arm, the gibbet, could be rotated through 90 degrees or more. About ten feet back from the king post a pair of timbers, also mounted in holes, supported a windlass mounted in a horizontal plane; this drum could be rotated by means of a large spoked wheel. A rope wound on the drum passed via fair leads on the top of the king post to the end of the gibbet, from which the load was suspended. The holes cut in the rock to hold these timbers therefore take the form of an isosceles triangle with the apex close to the water's edge.

The biggest is on the loading rock at Seacombe, 21 inches by 21 by 24 deep! Some still retain the iron bearing, offset about seven inches, which supported and at the same time allowed the gibbet to rotate. The pair of holes, cut to support the winding gear or jenny, are set back from the king post, usually away from the water's edge. Sadly, the Dorset Quarry Co. appear to have destroyed the jenny holes that served this massive Seacombe gibbet when they levelled the ledge to take their more advanced crane.

It is worth bearing in mind that these machines were not required to lift a load to any great height. It was simply just lifted off the quarry floor or cart, swung out over the cliff and lowered. Nor, I believe, was the windlass laboriously rotated by the operator whilst lowering. But I suspect he could have jammed the wheel and let the rope slip around the drum. In this way quick lowering would have been possible, a necessity with a boat rising and falling in any swell. A photograph of Michael Bower's gibbet, taken after its wheel had gone but with the drum still remaining, shows it scored as if by rope burns. Though primitive these cranes, only employed for controlled lowering, would have remained relatively efficient. Their capacity would have been dependent on the strength of the timbers and the rope or chain. The load would tend to pull them over, and to resist this they were braced, as indicated by sloped holes cut in the rock close to the windlass mounts to accommodate timbers, or they were tensioned by block and tackle, anchored to arches cut in the rock (often wrongly identified as holes for mooring the boats).

We know of the form of these medieval cranes from the Pouncy photograph of Michael Bower's gibbet at West Hedbury, complete with winding gear (*see page 125*), and the splendid painting of Lander's at East Hedbury, by Henry T. Wells (*see page 126*). Both William Masters Hardy, in his book, *Old Swanage*, and Harry Pouncy, giving a lecture to the Society of Dorset Men in London in 1913, used the terms 'Jenny Jibber' rather than 'Whim', which it has been suggested is the name of this primitive type of crane. Such simple machines, with the winding gear fixed either horizontally or vertically, were common in medieval England on construction sites and docks. Harwich retains one, built in 1667, complete with a winding gear under a tiled roof. Brian Bugler has made a scaled down working model. However, some surviving socket holes are not simply a plain isosceles triangle. The arrangement east of the Cheese Rock, Winspit, tells of a combination of gibbet with capstan. Thomas Webster's 1812 engraving of Tilly Whim (*see page 140*) shows a capstan being worked, without the use of a gibbet, drawing up timbers from the loading rock. A gibbet appears in a view of St. Paul's in the course of construction. It is recorded that Wren also used 'sheers', or 'sheer legs', that is, three stout trees triangulated like a wigwam. Sheers can be immensely strong and, unlike the gibbet, free of the tendency to topple over, but of course, lacking in freedom of movement. It is doubtful that they were ever used for quarrying.

The Portlanders made use of a simple screw jack from as early as 1790, for one appears in a view by Grimm. My father got one and Thomas Bonfield made some use of it underground. It is now in the Langton Museum. Some measure of what can be achieved with such simple gear is illustrated by Ken Lynham's account of his father's involvement in moving a 70 ton block to form the seaward side of Durdle Pier, Portland. They managed to push it sideways and into position on railway rails. Seven jacks are visible in the photograph showing this being done. Once on steel a stone would slide relatively easily, but wow![23]

However that was Portland. In Purbeck they formerly relied entirely on bars. As derrick cranes came into general use in the inter-war years and after, Ambrose Bower made up one out of telegraph poles more or less on the lines of the old gibbets, the winding gear being a factory made crab. Such crabs were equipped with two gear speeds and were of various sizes. Some were used underground to draw loaded carts up inclines, but they failed to replace the capstan 'up top'. One remains in Sheffy Harris's Burngate underground. When such machines first appeared in Purbeck is obscure, but a bill from R. Vining, charged in the course of building the Clavell Tower at Kimmeridge in 1831, reads 'use of iron crab, blocks and chaines and ropes, 1 rope destroyed'.

An oddity was the crane brought from Portsmouth dockyard in about 1860 and set up on Randell's banker. It had a jib fixed to a king post that was free to rotate through 360 degrees. Being unbraced this type is inherently weak and the jib has a limited reach. It appears in both Craft's painting of stone loading in Swanage Bay (*see page 223*) and various photographs. The Swanage pier of 1859 had two somewhat similar fixed jib cranes one 'inshore' by the side of the pier, and another at the end. They had a maximum capacity of five tons; this was still insufficient, as one toppled over into the water, drowning the operator, Frank Coleman.[24.]

The blocks were gripped by what were called 'nips' or 'lifting dogs'. These required a pair of holes to be punched in opposite ends of each block, which the nips, held on a triangulated chain, got a bite on. Blocks left at Seacombe, and others tipped over St. Aldhelm's Head, exhibit these characteristic nip holes. Some medieval illustrations of building work show big stones being craned into position, gripped by a big pair of scissor-like pinchers. They would surely also call for the cutting of opposing nip or dog holes. Their disadvantage, compared with the use of chain nips, would be that they allow for little size variation. The beauty of both, for a fixer, is that they would allow a stone to be lowered on its mortar bed without hindrance.

Another way of hoisting stones are lewises. Though not much used in Purbeck, several examples indicating their application remain in cut slots at Seacombe and Winspit. Lewis tools, stout quirk-like chisels, were used for cutting slots for the lewis pins. A three-legged lewis consists of two tapered outer legs that are spread apart, after insertion in a dovetail-like hole, by means of a central parallel pin. The three are linked by means of a through bolt, which also carries a shackle for attachment to a crane. Once joined, if properly fitted, the lewis cannot be withdrawn. The beauty of them is that a stone so suspended can be lowered on to its mortar bed without the hindrance of a supporting rope or strop. They were therefore most commonly used in the fixing of large stones, where they are invariably cut at the centre of gravity. However, they were also commonly used in the Bath underground quarries for they allowed purchase on a block with only the top exposed. Unlike Purbeck, the cutting

Three-legged and two-legged lewis.

Seacombe Quarry, April 1930. Bottom Freestone block suspended by lifting 'nips'. Samuel 'Short' Bower, centre, William Jeremiah Bower, ('Billy Winspit') right.

of lewis slots in Bath stone would have been relatively easy and quick. The slots that remain at Seacombe and Winspit were anchor points for pulley blocks to change the direction of pull of a crane, or temporary fixing points used to pull a heavy underground crane into position.

They do not appear in any pre-Dorset Quarry Co. (1924) work in the cliff quarries. However, knowledge of them existed before. On sections of Portsmouth front (circa 1800) heavy Purbeck coping stones have lewis holes. Each one is plugged with a neatly fitted little 'mason'. Heavy 13th century Purbeck marble capitals in what was the monks' lavatorium at Beaulieu also have them, as does the wonderful marble screen (c. 1200) at Southwick, Portsmouth. They are evident only thanks to the demolition of the stonework they formerly supported, and I dare say that most heavy medieval capitals have them. It would have been difficult to cut such holes in hard Marble, but well worth it where the use of pinch bars in final fixing would have risked damage to the face edges, precisely the case where a cap rests on a free-standing column. These Portsmouth and Beaulieu lewises were probably of an earlier two-legged

Beaulieu Abbey. Purbeck Marble capital in the monks' lavatorium. The lewis hole in central position (pen for scale).

TECHNOLOGY / 205

Seacombe quarry. Dorset Quarry Co Cranes, 1920s. Billy Winspit talking to the lorry driver. The waste pile, hidden by the lorry, produced by swinging skips around by using the crane, became much higher before the quarry was abandoned.

rather than a three-legged type. These needed a similar dovetail hole but the jambing effect was achieved by triangulation. A clever 20th century invention is the split pin lewis, which jambs tight in a cylindrical drill hole. Its invention made lewis chisels obsolete at a stroke. Many got adapted into punches. Another way to suspend a load that requires the use of a drill rather than a lewis tool is by drilling a pair of holes rather than a single. They need to be as far apart as possible. A pair of pins inserted in the stone are linked by a triangulated chain which thereby provides grip.

The Dorset Quarry Co. installed both hand and, an innovation, steam driven Scotch derrick type cranes at Seacombe. Not only could these pick up greater weights than the old-fashioned jibbets, but they spanned a wider area, as the jib could be raised or lowered, increasing or decreasing the radius of the 270 degree arc. Their capacity varied according to jib angle. The maximum, with the jib right up, was about ten tons. Underground they put in cranes of a Bath quarry type that were fixed between floor and ceiling and could rotate through 360 degrees. Round holes mark where the king post pin entered the ceiling, each with an adjacent lewis slot that provided a fix for a temporary block and tackle or endless chain that was used to haul the crane into an upright position. These cranes were hand-operated, but were strong and could pull a heavy block free of the active face.

In the 1930s, '40s and '50s a number of quarries acquired cranes of the more modern type, as men tended to give up underground and began ridding from the surface; Burts was the first. This would fit with the family's go-ahead character. Ernie Burt's crusher at Mutton Hole was also probably the first, though Worth Quarry Co at Sheepsleights developed this sort of business more fully at about the same time. Burt and Burt also installed the first telephone. The number was Swanage 1.

Discounting the railway trains, the Purbeck steam age was short-lived, covering just the interwar period. There were steam cranes at Seacombe and steam lorries taking the block away, particularly to the Wareham yard and Swanage station, where the Dorset Quarry Co. had installed a crane for handling rough blocks only. There was also Ernie Burt's single steam crane at Mutton Hole.

MECHANISATION

There was no lathe on the Swanage bankers or at the depot; my grandfather used to make cylindrical columns entirely by hand. However, concentric tool marks on some of the circular Kingston church capitals tell of the use of one in the 1870s. Setting aside known Roman use, perhaps it was the first in Purbeck. The question is frequently asked as to how all the medieval shafts were made. It is possible by multiple chamfering, and nook shafts in Westminster Abbey that retain a ridge on the hidden corner were certainly so made. Evidence of lathe use by William of Sens appears in the Gervase account of the rebuilding campaign beginning in 1175 in Canterbury: 'made stones into shapes by a lathe with his inborn talent.'[25.] With the need to turn a number of columns for the post-war restoration of the Temple church, my father installed a lathe in the St. Aldhelm's Quarry. Sometime in the 1950s he converted the frame saw, circular saws, planer and lathe to electrical power, all formerly powered by a diesel Tangye engine, and bought the first diamond tipped saw blades.

The rubbing of flat surfaces was semi-mechanised by the introduction of a handheld flexible drive polishing machine. About 1958 my father added a 'Jenny Lind'. This machine, consisting of a polishing head that can be steered about on an articulated arm, presumably dates from when the 'Swedish Nightingale' was at her most celebrated, almost one hundred years earlier! Incidentally, the name was also applied to a type of steam engine built between 1847-1860.

The banker mason's kit has retained several old tools, in particular chisels. One significant innovation was to drive them pneumatically. Such a tool has the advantage of delivering lots of rapid light blows per minute rather than relatively few, heavy blows. My father used such chisels on the Temple church work, particularly the capitals, but his masons, excepting his brother Frank, displayed the typical conservatism of the craftsman and would not use them. About 1985 a Dutch stone carver appeared, intent on working a piece of Purbeck. He produced various grinders and disappeared in a cloud of dust. Within a few hours he emerged, having produced an 'abstract' form complete with through hole, in a style then popular. Grudgingly, the advantage of the angle grinder has to be recognised. It is versatile and as highly effective in cutting checks as in simply getting rid of waste. In that regard, to a degree, it replaces the punch, at the same time being capable of precise cuts. It instigated a new genre of decorative plates, bowls etc. In this new angle-grinder age it is easy to lose sight of the skill of previous generations who lacked them. The 19th century piecing of Salisbury's shafts leaves one gasping with admiration.

About 1965 William Lander installed the first hydraulic guillotine in Purbeck. Other quarries quickly followed. The production of split faced walling was greatly speeded up as the relatively slow and skilled task of cutting wedge pits was eliminated. A few years later, tractor mounted breakers were first used for reducing blocks. They have largely done away with plugs and feathers. Perhaps the most significant change has been the introduction of hydraulic excavators capable of digging not only overburden but block stone as well. The ratio of 'efficiency' (as compared with the earlier bar and wedges technology) can be measured in several tens to one if not hundreds, with all the social consequences that result. In the 1970s William Lander also introduced the first lettercutting machine. This allowed for relatively easy cutting of 'v' section letters, guided by stencils. Subsequent developments include sandblasting lettering machines which produce a 'u' section cut, and finally computer – controlled saws and routers that can produce complex three-dimensional shapes, to the elimination of the craftsman.

Some quarries mechanised little, if at all. The Hancock brothers continued in the Swanage Railway yard until they ceased trading without installing saws. Most of their work consisted of garden ornaments and boulder-like memorials worked from small blocks of Inland Freestone rather than slab, which made this possible. The Wessex Division War Memorial at Wynyards Gap was worked out of the rough (other than its Portland Paving) by Jimmy Chinchen whilst in Thomas Hancock's employ. It must be one of the last projects on that scale, medieval technology prevailing until the 1950s.

QUARRYING METHODS

Most tools in a stone cutter's kit have remained much the same for centuries. Mallets, formerly of wood, are now nylon, tempered steel chisels are tipped with tungsten carbide, but Henry Yevele would still recognise them. However, masonry methods of working and extractive quarrying itself have been transformed. Significant change began with the mechanisation of some processes in the late 19th century, followed by the application of diesel engines, diamond saws, etc. Quarrying for centuries was opencast and consisted of the use of picks, shovels, wedges, levers and windlasses. At some time, certainly by the mid 17th century if not before, Purbeck quarriers adapted to underground working. At the cliff quarries this was assisted by the introduction of gunpowder. Both of these important dates are difficult to establish but in the case of the latter surely after first use by the military.

Really big changes for inland quarries came in the late 1940s, when bulldozers and draglines were first used to clear off a patch of overburden before the stone was dug conventionally. Of course the logic was for machines both to strip off the top and to take out the stone itself, and this soon followed. The traditional art of quarrying was superseded.

MARBLE QUARRYING

Although complicated by folding and faulting, the basic structure of the Marble outcrop is that of a dip to the north. The Marble shoals at the surface, becoming deeper northwards. The overburden consists of a clayey shale. It would seem that, at least initially, any quarrier would first find the outcrop at the surface and then begin following the bed northwards. As he did so he would have had to remove an ever increasing amount of shale. But how did they get waste and large blocks up out of an ever deepening hole? The idea of the wheelbarrow is known in Western Europe from the 12th century.[26.] Panniers, baskets carried on heads, or rope systems are possible methods, as are carts or boxes drawn out by means of capstans or windlasses of various sorts. The configuration of remaining holes and waste piles give us clues. It is easier, when possible, to follow stone up rather than down a dip slope. It is therefore very likely that, after the initial difficult breach down the slope, the quarryman would continue either left or right along the outcrop at the bottom first, though this would entail risk.

Large blocks were reduced by being cut by wedges. In my opinion claims that the rock was deliberately split by using freezing water or by plimming up wood are entirely fanciful. The size of some Roman Marble components suggest that they were sourced from quarries of some depth. There is archaeological evidence of workings of Romano-British date at Wilkswood. Presumably these holes remained until the big 12th century development.

Running from Crack Lane to Dunshay Lane, close to the stream, is one continuous medieval quarry defining the outcrop. The humps and hollows we now see, masked by woodland, suggest a scatter of separate quarries. However, it is possible that they represent the more or less wholesale removal of Marble down to a depth of twenty feet or so along the entire distance. In an ideal situation, once an initial area has been dug out, a surface quarry can begin to roll over; that is the overburden can be returned to the exhausted hole left behind as the face is pushed forward. But in practice the medieval quarries did not enjoy an ideal situation. They were hemmed in by a stream and a hill of overburden. Heavy demand required the opening of several diggings at once, almost certainly resulting in overburden being dumped where it could later prove to be an obstacle to further digging. West of Wilkswood, the stream widens into ponds formed by flooded diggings. Lanchard Hill rises quickly to the north, so they did not have much option to dispose of waste in that direction. The stream, which seldom completely dries, must have bedevilled progress. How did they cope with extracting Marble from well below its bed level?

About 300 yards east of the boundary with Quarr, a deep cutting, now choked with hollies, ascends the Lanchard scarp. It is surely the track out of the series of diggings that lie to the east and may well have extended much further, even connecting with the Court Pound sunken track. Immediately beneath this cutting there is a waste pile about 100 feet across by about ten feet high. One wonders whether this pile, and others like it, conceal Marble *in situ*, reachable before its construction but effectively sterilised since. It would have been daunting to manually shift the whole lot twice.

To the east, close by the stream, there is a particularly splendid bifurcated oak. However old it and others equally venerable are, the workings they grow on are obviously older.

Further east lies a waste pile that could be the key to how other less clearly defined heaps were made. It is in the form of an almost symmetrical dome, about 50 feet across, steep on all sides. There can be no question of wheelbarrows being used to make this. It suggests the use of a rope system, with suspended panniers, discharging more or less at one point. If this point was moved in the course of constructing the heap then the shape resulting would become more complicated. This is surely what we see in other waste heaps, such as the long examples flanking the Dunshay Manor drive. Superficially similar cones of waste rock at Seacombe were made possible by the use of cranes possessed of lengthy jibs: they had a long reach. The medieval piles were certainly not made in such a way, but are similarly the product of tipping at one spot.

At the eastern extremity of Talbots Wood the footpath leading to the bottom of Crack Lane runs through a pair of similar mounds. Each has an adjacent hole lying to the southwest. The way out for the blocks would have lain in that direction, away from the obstructing waste piles. Sadly this side of the wood has been much altered by material being dumped there over the past 80 years and more.

Further evidence of final dressing at source is provided at Dunshay, where discoveries of column fragments were made. Recent falls on the Durlston Bay side of Peveril Point reveal that the Marble bed has been dug out, the void filled mostly with shale overburden, which contains pieces of waste Marble, some bearing telltale tool marks, much as at Quarr. The Peveril material, which is probably 12th century, includes off-cut bits of paving thickness which exhibit shallow continuous chases rather than pits of sufficient depth to take wedges. They suggest a different method, since lost from oral tradition, that of weakening the slab sufficiently to snap it where desired by delivering a series of sharp blows along the base of the groove, the groove serving to get rid of the soft sediment adjacent to the bedding plane.

Once the blocks are loosened they can be forced further apart by means of bars, in the case of Marble extraction the wedges and bars being applied between the blocks rather than below them in that they readily slip on the smooth bedding planes. To get the blocks out of the hole called for some sort of windlass. It is curious that the steeply inclined surfaces of quarry shafts were called 'slides', in spite of the fact that the stones were rested on a wheeled cart before being drawn up by means of a capstan. They did not actually slide, but is the name indicative that they once did? Does it hark back to the medieval Marble quarries where the blocks were slid up the dip slope on the slipping shale or a timber arrangement of which we found evidence at Quarr? W. M. Hardy is trenchant: '1700 they began to mine and make shafts about 120 ft deep. At first they were at a very flat angle and they called them slides, because the first carts had no wheels, but merely a flat piece of board with a stout rope fastened on and around a capstan, which was pulled around on top, sometimes by a horse, or an ass or a person, using a little water to make it slip. The next thing was a wooden bed with four wheels'.[27] Some of this sounds hardly plausible; how was such a loaded board drawn along underground to get it to the mouth? However, his 'wooden bed with four wheels' is identifiable as a cart. A typical survivor of the last carts used has a flatbed bounded by iron with four wheels. Harold Bonfield said that about 1929 Charley Oates, who lived at Herston, built one for about £5.

Israel Bower used a cart in his Marble quarry at Oatridge (variously Oak Ridge) which had rollers rather than wheels, as did the Squibbs' at Woodyhyde. This was because there was no hard floor to run on. Presumably those specialist carts were built without the central thar pole. There would have been an imperative to keep the cart strong but also as low as possible. Typically a six inch thick frame mounted on twelve inch diameter wheels under a two inch bed gave an overall height of about one foot two inches. If Marble quarr cart rollers were less than 12 inches in diameter the bed could have been proportionately lower – a great benefit in restricted head room.

UNDERGROUNDS

Presumably the first undergrounds were somewhat like the Freestone quarry still worked by Frenchy Bower in the 1930s, about 200 yards southsouthwest of Worth gate. The stone had been shallow enough to rid from the surface, but as the dip made it run in deeper, he gave up the muck shifting and drove in underground. The result was so flat and shallow that he could almost back the donkey in underground! The quarry was wet, and just inside the mouth on the side of the lane he dug a sump that filled with water. He lived not far away on the southwest corner of the hamlet of Acton, and drew his water from the sump. Jack Norman said that sometimes the water was coming in so fast that, whilst underpicking, Frenchy would jam up a galvanised roof sheet to keep the worst of it off. 'If you saw a ball of clay walking up the road, it was him', said Jack.

The use of wet quarries as water supplies may have been more general where they were close to home. Sybil Sheppard, née Lander, remembered visiting her grandmother of the Brownsea Bower family at Castle View. To make a cup of tea the old

Swanage district. Quarry shaft, October 1911, looking straight down the chain. The pipe is indicative of a problem with stale air. The walls flanking the shaft tended to move, hence the wooden struts.

lady first took a jug underground to get the water. This quarry remains open west of the cottages.[28.] In the other direction Sunshine Norman's wife visited him underground in the quarry he had newly opened. He had a job to push her, heavily pregnant with twins as it turned out, back up the shaft.[29.]

When shafts proper first developed, the quarrymen must have quickly found that there was an advantage in them being at a steep angle. It is more difficult to cut a shallow angle and keep it supported. This is particularly true of getting down to the Freestone, because much of the overburden is unstable clay. They resorted to building up the sides with stone and putting in arches, but the inherent instability remains, only reduced by the angle being as steep as possible. But this brings the disadvantage of making the hauling harder and the access more hazardous, though I guess that did not influence things much. Father mentioned that one of the Normans was nicknamed the Iron Man because, missing his footing one dark morning, he fell the entire way down a deep shaft, only to pick himself up and go on in underground to work. Where the ground slopes down to the north, most shafts were dug southwards. This meant the shortest distance to reach the desired stone. Curiously, Lewis Tomes' shaft at Belle Vue quarry is an exception to this, and one wonders why.

A depth of 120 feet deep, as given by W. M. Hardy, was exceptional. Most shafts, especially those around Langton, were nearer half that. Jimmy Chinchen's in Greasehead, recently filled in, was about 80 feet deep to the Freestone, and he, or Isaac Stickland, or Henry Haysom before him, had pushed on down to the Downs Vein, but not deeper.

All underground quarries had a capstan. Old surface workings which dip downhill also probably required one. The direction of pull was always only one way and so long as the crab and bearing stones were well held, and the rest of the gear commensurately strong, high levels of strain were possible. A shaft was sunk at an inclined angle down to the usable vein, and the stone was drawn up it by means of the capstan. This was set back at a sufficient distance from the shaft edge for a donkey, horse, man or, sometimes woman, to walk around in a circle at the end of a long pole or spack. Dr. Bell was grieved to see two young women pushing round their father's spack, 'up to their ankles in mud and clay'.[30.] The length of this pole, together with the girth of the drum, would have dictated the mechanical advantage of the machine. Benfield makes the point that a steep slide called for a smaller, therefore lower-geared capstan drum.[31.] When his eldest brother was born, his father Charles planted an ash that would grow with the boy and serve as his spack. He was killed on the Western Front. I guess spack has the same root as spoke. In William Barnes's 'Father Come Hwome' he has the child say:

'O, Mother, mother! Be the teaties done?
Here's father now a-comen down the track.
He's got his nitch o'wood upon his back,
An' such a speaker [spack] in en! I'll be bound,
He's long 'ough to reach vrom ground
Up to the top ov ouer tun; [chimney]
'Tis jist the very thing vor Jack an I
To goo a-colepecksen [apple picking] wi', by an' by.'[32.]

Herston Field quarry. Almost certainly George Hancock, ducking under the spack as the horse goes round.

Langton Matravers Museum. Capstan, showing drum, chain, spack, collar board and crab stones braced with stone slabs.

The capstan consisted of a windlass with the drum mounted almost vertically, held in position by being rested against a hollow in a horizontal wooden collar board. This in turn was set in slots cut through a pair of crab stones buried in the ground and braced with stone slabs. The crab stones were set square to the direction of strain, which would have pulled the neck of the drum hard back into the hollow in the collar board. The bottom of the capstan drum simply rotated on a gudgeon pin resting in a hollow bearing, leaded in a stone buried in the ground. Elm was a good wood for the drum; ash for the spack and oak for the collar board. In the 1930s Horace Norman, retiring after many years on the banker at Portland, whimsically made a drum of stone. It never worked properly, one difficulty being that only a relatively small hole could be cut to take the spack, which was therefore not strong enough. It remains at his Herston Field quarry.

A long spack was needed for heavy loads, but too great a strain risked breakage or pulling the capstan over. This risk was at its greatest when the chain was at the top of its movement up the drum.

Another danger was posed by the risk of breakage of the chain attaching the animal to the spack. If this should happen with the loaded cart part way up the slide, the spack whirls round with terrible force. To eliminate this risk most, but not all, capstans had a ratchet and pawl fitted, which allowed for rotation in one direction only. When the empty cart needed to be lowered back down, the pawl was flipped over, which allowed the drum to spin the other way. Hauling would have been accompanied by the 'click click' sound of the pawl as it fell from each tooth of the ratchet in turn. Breaking of the main chain was less dangerous in that it did not affect anyone up top. Thomas Bonfield escaped relatively unscathed one day as he came up from underground with a loaded cart, taking advantage of half a ride. He had one foot on the cart whilst hopping up the steps on the other. In the moment the chain broke the cart and block together plummeted away, throwing him off balance, so he followed them on down, arriving in a heap at the bottom. The cart was undamaged, some measure of how robustly they were.

The tending of the donkey, mule or horse was often the boy's job. Some were worked too hard, others looked after well. When Thomas Bonfield worked for 'Hantney' Haysom, about 1930, the number of men in the quarry and the rate of production were too much for just one horse to cope with. They used one in the morning, another during the afternoon. After turning it loose one evening it described a circle, as though still restrained by the capstan, before sinking to the ground. Hantney remarked: 'We'll know where to find 'ee in the morn'. On one market day, knowing the Farmer Horlock to be away, they attached one of his big carthorses to the capstan, dragging up two carts at a time. Warren, pronounced 'Warny', Bonfield must have had a kinder attitude to his mule, for he took the trouble to set up a headstone over its grave and those of other pets. A slab of self-faced Roach bears 'Beneath this stone lies our mule. She was a faithful creature drawing up the stone from this quarry for 32 years. Died aged 34 years.' They must have known one another pretty well. Glen Bower, maker of the capstan set up on Lighthouse Road, had the job when a boy before the war, of looking after his father's donkeys. They sometimes used two side by side on the spack in their quarry close to Worth Gate. Glen had to catch them before going to school, sometimes having to go 'ver' near up 'Edbury'. I guess two donkeys were cheaper to keep than one horse.

There is no evidence of medieval underground Marble working other than a single record that might imply it. In 1268 a coroner's court recorded the death of Walter de Vel and Hugh le Mochele in Peter de Clavile's quarr.[33.] At this time Peter de Clavile held Woolgarston, and almost certainly the manor of Quarr, for his son and heirs were in possession for generations. It is most likely that this was the location of the quarry (probably Marble) where they were digging, according to the record, with a certain tool called a *besca*, valued at 6d. The verdict was misadventure. The Latin term used in the Court Record is *oppressi*, which translates as crushed. Its suggestion that this was underground working is, in my opinion, misleading. Where a big block disappears under a depth of twenty feet or so of overburden there is a great temptation to undercut in order to free it, rather than laboriously but safely shift tons. Marble overburden consists of a shale that can stand virtually vertical, but then suddenly fail. I have seen it happen. Those

Haysom's quarry, Gallows Gore. Quarr cart carrying Cliff stone sink.

men were probably buried by just such a sudden collapse of the overburden mass confronting them, rather than a roof fall.

Downs Vein underground quarries are usually about three to four foot high. Freestone quarries are usually, but not always, much higher. If all the beds from and including the Freestone and Roach are taken, the resulting space is generally about seven foot high. Around Gallows Gore the Roach is poor and they left it up, so a six foot man bangs his head. South of Acton Joby Ball Bower and 'Phea Brownsea Bower both left up the Roach and the Thornback as well. They were only taking the Wetsun bed and the top part of the Freestone, thereby creating a space only about three foot high in which to work. In 1929 'Phea was supplying pitched faced dubbers to the depot for St. Francis Church, Charminster Road, Bournemouth. His Wetsun bed was very good quality, hard and crisp but small, as such stone usually is. The Thornbacks in that area are hard and thin with the scurf 'growed on'; to make use of them would have been difficult for him. Subsequent opencast work by Les Lock and Roger Bonfield in turn has obliterated his underground. Harold Bonfield saw it when opened out and remarked: 'I ain't seen a Freestone quarr like that: sitting on the floor my head was touching the ceiling!'

The waste could be got rid of by the use of wheelbarrows, especially easy where it could be tipped away down a bank. A lot of old quarries along the wares in general, and Round Down in particular, show a cut dug into the slope with an adjacent tip spilling down the hill below. They were probably all made by the use of wheelbarrows, even the most massive such as that lying on the northern flank of the top of Hawcombe more or less north of Round Down. These tell of the loaded barrows being pushed on the level or, at the most, only a bit uphill. But the suspicion that some waste heaps accumulated uphill by the use of barrows cannot be entirely discounted. Sometimes to get a heavy headstone up a sloping churchyard we would attach a rope to the front of the barrow, so that the man in front could provide propulsion whilst the man behind kept the load up. I doubt whether this was a day to day way of doing things in the quarries but there were no hard and fast rules. Wheelbarrows may well have been used a lot, but it is worth bearing in mind that a quarr cart can be converted to carry muck by jamming a post in its 'eyes and ears' to support boards, forming a box.

In underground work, the first task was underpicking. The whole block had to be freed of the underpicking dirt before it could be 'drawn' (extracted). A clue as to the size of the stone being uncovered was, in some quarries, provided by changes in the colour of the dirt, it being blue in the middle of a stone, lighter where oxidization has occurred around the joints, where it also tended to be softer, another clue. Some men claimed to be able to tell the size of the stone confronting them to the nearest few inches by sounding it with a hammer. But I doubt it. In a Downs Vein underground the penetration was achieved by digging away the underpicking dirt (hence its name), with a gusser. This was a light chisel-ended bar of iron with a wooden handle that according to Jack Norman was thrust with the hip, rather than struck, the underpicking dirt being a soft clay, at least in the Gallows Gore area. Sam Short Bower had one with a cutting edge about one and a half inches wide. Where the Leper is left up in the Gallows Gore undergrounds, marks left by this tool can still be seen.

Downs Vein quarries are only about three to four foot high, so in a crouching attitude the hip was at about the right height to drive the tool. But there was more than one way of doing things: Thomas Bonfield, when underpicking Downs Vein, actually used a mattock-like pick axe. Towards Swanage the underpicking dirt tends to get thinner and harder and I guess the gusser may not have been suitable. In a Downs vein quarry the underpicking dirt lay under the ceiling. With it out of the way the topmost bed was lifted, drawed, and slid down onto the cart before going on down to the next layer. Only beds below cart bed level had to be heaved up.

In the Freestone vein the underpicking dirt was harder and cut away with a paddle. The chosen layer of clay for the initial penetration varied from quarry to quarry, depending on ease of removal. At Gallows Gore it lies between the Freestone and Wetsun beds. Eric Benfield describes underpicking between the Grey Bed and Roach. In some other Swanage quarries, perhaps where that layer of clay gets too thin, they went under the Freestone. In most quarries it was easiest to attack under the Grub. A typical Freestone quarry paddle was a plain straight bar about half an inch across, struck with a hand hammer. The chisel cutting edge of about three quarters of an inch was kept sharp. Thomas Bonfield would whet his out on a sharpening stone. The various paddles which have ended up in museum collections are no longer sharp, as when in use. The greater width of a Downs Vein gusser is indicative of how different the underpicking dirts are, the Downs Vein layer being a soft, almost, slimy clay. A shorter tool is easier to use than a longer, so clearing a patch would begin with a short paddle, but as the cut deepened so a longer one was brought into play. Eighteen inches was about the right length for the first paddle, for it had to be held up. As the cut deepened a longer one could be rested, so its greater weight did not matter. In order that the cut should not taper, the paddle had to be driven in, alternating between high and low angles. This meant that in underpicking the Grub, seeking to achieve the bottom cut, the head of the tool was tight to the ceiling, which made it difficult to hit with a hammer without the risk of touching the ceiling, resulting in a deflection and a skinning of the fingers.

'Bower's quarry' at Acton. Quarr cart with posts jammed in the 'eyes'. This may suggest that there was a downward slope in the lane below ground, with the attendant risk of the load toppling forward.

Acton quarry about 1910, with good view of a wooden wheelbarrow (rather than a truck barrow). It would have been used for running the scars (waste from dressing the stone) out to the scar bank. Also of note is the pair of rafters which are railway line.

In Verney, a thin Sly Bed split off the bottom of the ceiling, which gave a few more inches to swing the hammer. When father and son, Thomas and Harold Bonfield, worked there in the early 1950s, they reckoned on digging a patch of about six feet by eight feet each week, six feet being the penetration depth of their longest paddle. This rate of progress, about 25 ton, included splitting up the Roach into crazy paving, working the Thornback and the top lift of the Freestone into kerb, cutting out the rest of the Freestone to sell on to a monumental mason or to make bird baths, and building up the supporting legs and all other necessary work. It is a faster than average speed of advance, for the Bonfields were particularly strong and proficient. Dependent on the amount of time required to make the end product, others would usually have progressed more slowly. One of the Tomes, for example, made trap stones. They were small and fiddly, cut through to take a grating set in a rebate or an arrangement of small holes made with a punch. Langton Museum has an example which is twelve inches square by about two inches thick *(see page 168)*. A man

TECHNOLOGY / 211

would not have made many of those in a day. Perhaps it is not wildly wrong to suggest that the average man in the average underground was going forward at the average rate of about ten ton per week. It would have been much faster in quarries like Boss Burt's Freestone quarry at Cowleaze, Swanage, where men were kept digging full time.

Jack Norman told me that when he worked in Alf Benfield's quarry close by the Kingston Road with, variously, his grandfather Alfred or his father Jack or brother Fred, they reckoned to be doing well to dig and pull out four carts in a morning, roughly three tons. The horse could then be let out to rest. Then Alf or Jack Senior would 'cut up' during the afternoons whilst Jack Junior would 'go in on banker'. They would sometimes continue cutting and dressing next day rather than dig more. Kerb was the staple, and they were sometimes selling the Thornback as scappled block to the depot. I never saw any man work faster with hammer and punch than Jack Norman.

When a head of stone is left over time the underpicking dirt squeezes out. This can make it difficult to resume work later, so where this was anticipated, men jammed in lumps of stone to prevent it from happening. Where such stones are found now they indicate that the plan was for that particular face to be left for a while, but that the intention was to come back to it in the future. The loading on a leg is very concentrated. Lacking mortar, the individual stones bear on pressure points. They can fracture with a load bang, such as is produced by splitting stones with modern hydraulic guillotines. Roger Bonfield mentioned the alarm of hearing this for the first time whilst working underground. His father just carried on as if nothing had happened. The strange underground world which resulted from the work of generations of men is now utterly dark, silent but for the sound of occasional drips, the dropping of a crumb of underpicking dirt, but then without warning, a sudden bang. Unlike Portland, where natural underground fissures have opened up as a result of blocks of land slipping apart, Purbeck seems not to have caves. However, at least one fair sized chamber is indicated by warm air coming out of a natural fissure at St. Aldhelm's Head.

It was easier to work up a dipslope rather than down, for then gravity aids dragging the loaded cart to the mouth. At first the advance away from the mouth was relatively slow, for everything had to come out, but as working room developed waste such as the underpicking dirt, clay from between the joints, scurf, etc., was left where it did not impede. The essential thing was to keep a lane open wide enough to get the loaded cart out to the mouth. More often than not, as patch by patch was taken, the route of the open lane followed, the rest of the void becoming choked to the ceiling with waste.

Working down the dipslope forced another method, for when the floor slopes downwards away from the mouth it becomes impossible for a man to pull a laden cart uphill towards it. This had to be done by employing the capstan up top, leading to the development of a permanent lane called a runner. Typically the chain was made to pass through a block fixed at the bottom of the slide, which provided for the necessary direction change. Some men had blocks that came apart. As the cart reached the block, Tommy Bonfield could strike out the pin, freeing the chain so that the cart swung round and on up the slide in the new direction, without the horse even stopping. Such a runner could be kept in use for years as the stone to left and right was brought in to it across the dipslope by manpower alone. Runners requiring the capstan were invariably straight but others where the loaded cart can be pulled along manually can twist and turn. Both sorts were usually walled up on each side to ensure long term stability of the ceiling, and they frequently developed well worn ruts from years of use. To a degree these assisted in steering the cart, but became a problem if too deep. One remedy was to lay a length of old chain along the groove. Such grooves were sometimes welcome when they held water, for it served to keep the wooden wheels plimmed up and the iron tyres tight. In Harris's Verney quarry, recently reopened, the grooves are quite deep, for there they had left much of the Freestone layer down, leaving the soft section to serve as a floor. More often, at least in the Acton area, men took more of the Freestone layer, leaving only the hard bottom part, called the 'White Horse', as the floor. This would not so easily develop ruts. Benfield makes the point that it was necessary to leave the White Horse to provide the good solid floor needed to support the legs, as well as to run the cart on.[34] Jack Norman encountered a difficulty in trying to do this at Alf Benfield's quarry. He found the Freestone developed false beds that ran out of level within the overall block height. It became difficult to take the best upper part of the Freestone only and leave a good level floor. This is classic current bedding, proving to be a quarryman's headache. Beneath the White Horse lies the 'Dun Cow' which is unfit to sell. Fortuitously, the bottom part of the Downs Vein is similarly not as good as the upper parts of the layer. For that reason, and to retain a hard floor, it was left down.

All quarries have a limit to their lives, in that the ever-increasing distance from the mouth gets to a point when it is better to sink a new shaft rather than drag each stone a long way out to the entrance. Nevertheless some achieved a considerable size. Boss Burt's Cowleaze quarry, surveyed by Brian Bugler, is more or less the size of a football pitch and all running downhill from the mouth. An undulation in the north-sloping strata meant that the runner chain, when under strain, bit hard on the ceiling, so they fixed up a roller overhead. Such a long chain was more than a capstan could take. They must have separated it, used the entire chain for the first haul, unhitched the runner end half, brought back the other half by unwinding the capstan before attaching that to the cart for the last haul out to the top. Some old crab stones bear striations, telling of carrying an excess of chain. Of course a big drum, combined with widely spaced crab stones, would hold relatively more chain than a lesser machine. But it would have called for a longer spack, heavier section collar board, the need for a horse rather than donkey, etc. Harold Bonfield remarked that one glance by the old hands at the capstan and its chain capacity would tell them how deep the quarry was.

Each quarry was different and presented individual problems. Harold remembered seeing a big section of tree jammed horizontally under the ceiling at a change in slope-

Herston Field and Cowlease quarries. Photographs by E.W. Ralph, August 1914.

A. Herston Field. George Hancock's quarry. George at left, Jack Corben centre, and George Edmunds right, posed by loaded cart. Note position of candle to right.

B. George Edmunds pushing on the main chain with his foot as the horse draws the cart out of the mouth of the quarry. There is obviously some problem with the alignment.

C. Herston Field: Mr Turner 'in on banker', dressing kerb with a mallet and boaster.

D. George Hancock using a biddle and wedges to split a layered block, probably Roach. Notice hand hammer resting on it.

E. Herston Field: George Hancock with his horse Topsy. Note cows in the distance escaping the flies on a hot August day on the top of Harris's scar bank.

F. Swanage Cowlease quarry: loading the wagon. The finished stone is stacked behind the stooping man (left), the wagon is mostly hidden behind the raised loading banker which he stands on.

TECHNOLOGY / 213

angle position in Jimmy Chinchen's Greasehead runner. Its function was to act as a brake when the runner sloped steeply downhill towards the mouth. To prevent the loaded cart taking charge they passed one turn of chain, which was twice the length of the steep section and equipped with a hook at each end, around the tree. The chain bit hard, so with time and wear the timber was turned into an hourglass shape. On each trip the empty cart was pushed back uphill towards the head but on its return one end or other of the chain was always lying ready at the critical place. When the empty cart was inched over the roll stone its steep descent down the mouth was controlled by the lowering chain (brake) which pulled against the drum. When working alone the trick was to manoeuvre the cart onto the roll stone and leave it teetering, then walk to the capstan, standing on the chain all the way, so as to restrain it and the cart. The quarrier then grasped hold of the lowering chain, stepped off the main chain and gave it a flick, so as to topple the cart and start its descent down the shaft in a controlled way. Repeated use of the lowering chain resulted in a deep groove being worn in the capstan drum. However, getting the empty cart on along a much less steep runner was a different matter. To do so meant pulling out an ever increasing amount of clay-caked chain through one or more blocks and over the roll stone as well as rotating the capstan drum back up top. It was probably best to get up a good speed to start with – literally to run! One or two men tried crabs underground, including Sheffy Harris at Burngate and Jesse Lander east of Gallows Gore.[35.]

Two accounts of this underground way of life have been given by men who experienced it. They are Eric Benfield in his book *Purbeck Shop*, (1940), and James Corben, who, in his autobiography written in 1880, described his youth underground between 1826 and 1837. The manuscript was in the possession of Australian descendants who brought it

Worth Matravers. Walter 'Joby' Ball Bower holding onto a slack main chain. The quarry is possibly at the site which became the Observer Corps on the Worth road. Note roll stone with roller in foreground. The roll stone is placed at the pressure point where the loaded chain changes direction from the vertical to the horizontal. The capstan was behind the photographer.

Belle Vue underground. Unknown quarrymen dragging loaded cart along runner. Note worn grooves in floor and boy assisting by pushing.

Cover for Eric Benfield's *Purbeck Shop* (1948). The men are L-R, Jesse Lander, Michael Bower, William Bower (Billy Winspit).

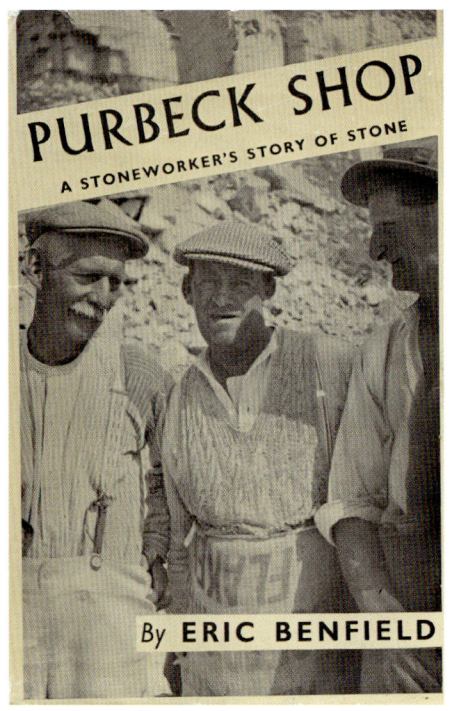

back to Dorset.[36.] His descriptions graphically illuminate the harshness of the life. Young James was first set to work with his uncle, George Harden, in Swanage, but after a short time he was with another uncle, John Corben, in Langton Matravers. His description of the quarry identifies it as almost certainly being in the Freestone, the underpicking 'clay nearly as hard as stone' and 'four courses of stone, ten inches to one foot three inches' in thickness.

John does not appear on a comprehensive list of quarries active on the Bankes Estate in 1825. However, the list reveals that Thomas Corben, possibly John's brother, was working a quarry in Long Meadow: perhaps that is where James worked. Young James' relationship with his uncle was more than strained. He gives an account of pushing the loaded cart from behind with murder in his heart while his uncle dragged it from in front. This was how thousands of tons were got out to the mouth of the quarry: the man in front going backwards with a rope around his waist, and controlling the speed of the cart by holding back when on steeper sections of the lane, the boy helping by heaving from behind with a bar on level or uphill sections.

Harold Bonfield described it thus: 'You pulled the cart by going backwards with the bridle chain around your back, each hand holding the chain so as to slew the cart to left or right', the only light being a single candle on top of the load (a candle at waist height gives the best light for working in). Illustrations showing the quarryman pulling facing forwards are misleading.[37.] Roger Bonfield added that they loaded the cart so that it was back end heavy which made it easier to steer. His father would wrap a sack bag around the bridle chain to give it some padding. One of its hooks was small enough to pass through the eye and back on the chain, so that the length could be adjusted when long slabs overhung. Sometimes they were forced to switch the bridle chain to one side in order to drag the cart back on course. How they managed in low Downs Vein holes, where it is impossible to stand, I do not know.

Eric Benfield wrote several books, ranging in subject matter from the semi-autobiographical to a description of Dorset. He devotes *Purbeck Shop* to the stone trade and the culture surrounding it, and it remains a unique account of working methods and traditions. Recently re-issued and added to by his grandson, Brian Bugler, it provides an insight into the mind of a craftsman/quarryman of the generation that experienced the shift from a horse to an engine-powered technology. Though not specifically focussed in the same way, some of his other titles, including *Saul's Sons* and *Southern English*, are almost equally informative of that culture, as a quote from the latter may serve to show: 'One thing is certain: school [up to 14 years old] did not encourage us to think that there was any chance in the world without hard grinding work, and in that it was right'. The two accounts both describe working underground and convey what hard and potentially dangerous work it was. But at least men in the Freestone layer enjoyed the 'luxury' of being able to stand upright. This was denied those toiling in the Downs Vein. In the light of his own experience in a Freestone quarry, Harold Bonfield remarked on how important the height issue is. It is much easier to place a heavy stone high up whilst building a leg if you can stand upright. G. F. Harris, visiting Swanage in 1893, talked to George 'Boss' Burt, who said: 'My health has been ruined by underground work in the quarries and made an old man of me before my time'. Harris adds: 'In working, the men underground have frequently to lie down, and as the ground is always wet they easily contract rheumatism'[38.] Boss's quarry is still open. Parts of it flood to the ceiling for much of the winter.

In 1813 Sam Phippard and James Summers were killed in a roof fall described in detail by Hutchins. In the early 19th century when Swanage parish had over 90 quarries, every year, on average, one man was killed. In 1823 the rector of Swanage, the Rev. Thomas Oldfeld Bartlett, alluded in his sermon to the 'awful death of Matthew Benfield, killed instantly by the falling in of the roof of his quarry last Tuesday'. The Rector continued to record more fatalities. George Haysom, 1830, aged 57, Sam Norman in 1831 and John Harden 1832, aged 54, Robert Keats, aged 27, all killed by 'founders' (a collapse of the ceiling).

Another near fatality was reported in the *Salisbury and Winchester Journal*, 24/8/1829:

'A serious accident occurred Saturday last to a poor man, name of Cross [in 1820 the rates record a Thomas Cross in partnership with Joseph Bower], who, when at work alone in a quarry, a stone, supposed to be ½ ton weight, fell upon him and crushed his left arm in a shocking manner, in consequence of which amputation was declared indisputable; the operation was performed by H. D. C. Delamotte, Esq. and his assistant Mr. Wilson, through whose skill and attention we are happy to say that the poor man is likely to do well, notwithstanding his advanced period of life, being upwards of 60 years of age, and his great loss of blood, occasioned from him remaining more than 4 hours before he could extricate his shattered arm from under the stone.'[39.]

Thomas Collins told me of the death of his grandfather,

Langton Matravers, closed cemetery. Memorial to 11-year-old Frederick John Harris, who 'was accidentally killed at the quarry' in 1888.

Old quarrymen. Walter Haysom thought they might be J. Brown or Michael Cooper, with Walter Tomes. Thomas Bonfield thought them to be Reuben Bower and Frank Seymour. Frank Seymour's quarry was at Greasehead, where it was later operated by Alfred Norman.

Walter, in the early years of the 20th century at his quarry in Lanchard, Herston. It was caused by the sudden failure of an unnoticed weak vent in a block of Cap they were moving. He was 69. Other fatalities incide a Phippard killed by the fall of a Thornback block in Eastington Cowlease; a Norman in 'Shilling' Norman's quarry in Belle Vue; 'Sunshine' Norman's eldest son in Nelson Burt's father's (formerly Squibb's) quarry north of old Eastington Road gate about 1910; a second tragedy struck that family with the death of the second son on the Western Front. Another boy killed in France was Dick Gad's son, Ernest. When call-up started Dick Gad resisted, for Ernie had been maimed by the spack as a boy, but it made no difference. Perhaps the last was 'Swelly' Burt, killed in a quarry near Worth gate. His body was brought up on a sheep's hurdle.

Thomas Bonfield had a close scrape in the New Vein at Verney, whilst working with Bill Haysom, nicknamed 'Bubbles'. Crusty Norman came in underground where they were and remarked; 'a lot of room in yer', which was to say there was a lack of supports. Tom remembered: 'Soon after it came in, the vlint making a tearing noise'. As it happened they were close to the face and unhurt, the roof falling behind them. They began to dig their way out. The men up top sent for help. Amongst those who responded was a Webber, who, though still strong, was not good on his feet and couldn't cope with the steps so they lowered him down the slide on the cart. When Bill gained the light, he retched. He was one of several Purbeck men past call-up age with experience of underground working, who went to Corsham during the Second World War. They were employed on conversion of the spacious underground quarries for workshops, stores, etc. He was killed there by a roof fall.

Lesser accidents were more common. Billy Winspit lost some toes, as had his father and grandfather, Jeremiah, before him. One of the cliff quarry Corbens suffered an injury for which Jeremiah had little sympathy. Broadly his attitude, and that of generations, was that if you got hurt it was your own fault. When he in his turn was injured, he too received little sympathy. 'It's your own words, Jeremiah,' became a catchphrase.

Though it is important not to belittle the risks of quarrying in general, and underground working in particular, in the event many men spent their lives at it and lived to tell the tale. Billy Winspit said that when his father was off work because of injury they abandoned working at Seacombe for a while. Billy went to work for his elder brother, Ambrose, in one of his Acton quarries. He was given the task of underpicking a patch and warned that as the cut increased he must keep a 'spall' in the gap. This was a nuisance as the action of raking out the underpicking dirt tended to dislodge it. He let it fall. He was warned again but let it happen again. Suddenly he was struck hard from behind by one of the older men who had come up behind him in the dark. 'Now you'll remember,' he said.

By the late 19th century, possibly earlier, men digging the New Vein in the Swanage district took things a stage further. They would take out an area of New Vein first before coming back and taking the next beds immediately above, that is the Cap and Feather. First they would underpick above the Vie Bed using a heavy paddle, called ironically a feather paddle, one man holding it while another struck with a biddle. Clearing a patch allowed them to draw the Vie Bed, which is generally fairly small, enabling them to get on top of and cut the White Bits and Brassy Bed, which run big. Having dug a patch in this way, built the legs and filled in between the legs with the waste, they would bar out the top of one or two legs, which would let the Cap above drop. They would run the cart in on top of the waste, which of course did not provide a firm floor. But, Thomas Bonfield explained, they got over that by making use of a pair of railway lines laid sideways, the cart wheels running in the hollow. Knowingly or otherwise, they were reverting to the earliest railway track use, such as at Middlebere Clay tramline of 1806, which used a non-flanged wheel. One of the Edmonds' shafts in Burngate, recently renovated by the National Trust, has the upper section of the slide formed by such a pair of rails.

In the latter days of underground working one or two men installed rails to take a flanged wheel cart, but it did not work particularly well. Such rails can be seen above ground at Sunshine Norman's Castle View quarry and at Burngate, formerly worked by Ambrose Bower. Returning to the working of some Swanage New Vein quarries, next the Feather was dropped, then the legs taken on up to catch under the Button bed, before advancing again. This method was made possible by the fact that above the Button bed lies the Cinder, which is massive and which holds up well. The reason was that to take the New Vein and Cap and Feather all in one go would have required impossibly high legs. Impossible is perhaps not the right word. They could, at least in theory, have placed something to stand on in order to reach up, but obviously it was not practical. It was a method fraught with risk but brought financial reward for those with the nerve to do it.

Jack Norman told me one of his earliest memories was of being carried down underground by his grandfather in his New Vein quarry in Greasehead: 'He sat I on the cart out by the mouth and lit several candles in through'. This was unusual, it being normal to work by the light of just one. Then he barred out the furthest leg before coming back and barring out the next one and so on'. I am not sure how many Jack said, but more than one. 'Then he came back, sat wi' I on the cart and waited for them Caps forming the ceiling to begin to drop.' The trick, of course, was to get them cut up and out of the way and the legs extended on up to the Button before that too started to come on down.

Some men used temporary legs of timber, which advanced with the quarry face, being replaced by permanent legs of stone when there was enough space. One such timber leg, with a small stone jammed on top, appears in the photograph of Scurry Bonfield and his boys underground.[40] Thomas Bonfield was heading up cliff early one morning for a prowl around with his gun when these three came up from underground and set off home, having worked all night. Men, absorbed by their work, sometimes lost track of time underground and especially, I imagine, when tackling some of the challenges they did. The regime of working to fixed hours that became the norm after the establishment of the railway with its timetables, was alien to these men's working lifestyle.

Odd timber struts have been left in some old undergrounds. Bob Harris made the probably exaggerated remark that the quarrymen once enjoyed the freedom to cut what wood they wanted 'north of the turnpike', that is, in Langton West Wood. Perhaps this was as much to do with the possible tenants' right to take wood for fuel as for use in the quarries. Seacombe has many wood chocks strutted under the ceiling. Most are probably from the Dorset Quarry Co. episode rather than earlier.

Strong legs call for fair sized pieces. Some such stones exhibit horizontal pits that on the face of it seem nonsensical. However, this tells of those stones being split in half so they could be lifted into position in two manageable pieces rather than one excessively heavy one, before being put back together. John Ivamy Bowers' quarry in Burngate has several. In effect, all this underground work was achieved by the use of bars, sometimes combined in the cliff quarries with a stout timber. There is a photograph in *Discover Old Swanage* of a block and tackle fixed up in an underground, but its use was exceptional, and it is not clear from the photograph how it is being used.[41] Limited headroom, the need to shift position frequently and confined space, all precluded it. What astounds me is the realisation of just how big some of the blocks were. A five ton Cap is not unusual, but as Jack Norman remarked of Alfred: 'Grandfather was as cunning as a rat underground'. By the way, there were no rats underground in Purbeck – there was nothing for them to eat. Men complained that the 'fluttermice' ate their candles, but they were wrong; these were probably mice, venturing in to where the candles were kept, just inside the mouth.

Swanage New Vein quarries were the deepest sunk in Purbeck. Bad air was a problem in some, particularly in summer. They called it 'the damps'. Candles would go out. Anthony Haysom would resort to lighting a fire at the bottom of the shaft to get a circulation of air going. Alfred Norman fixed up pipes from the surface for the wind to blow down. Where possible, they broke through into earlier workings to get a draught, which in this situation was a benefit, in others not, for it makes a candle burn too quickly and give a poor light. Thomas Bonfield told me that after working in such an atmosphere it felt as though you were being stifled; symptoms for which the Swanage doctor, Dr. Rees, would prescribe quinine! The problem was caused by an accumulation of carbon dioxide rather than methane, as in coal mines. Stagnation was seasonal, not occurring in the winter when cold surface temperatures cause an exchange of air. During calm frosty mornings remaining shafts can betray their presence by gently steaming as the warm air escapes upwards.

Open-sided sheds were built to work in during wet weather; when facing away from the wind they can provide reasonable comfort. William Melmoth, of Sandwich, left one in 1689, for his inventory includes: 'and timber of the Quarr House'.[42] There must have been sheds of some sort in the medieval period: illustrations in Nicola Coldstream's *Masons and Sculptors* suggest open-sided thatched structures.[43] The majority of later sheds have been pillaged for the sake of a few wallstones or their roofing slabs. But there are lucky survivals such as Trink Bower's at Gulley and Frank Tomes' at Belle Vue. Neither now retain a stone roof which they possibly once had. The walls were of rubble, with fine scars or dust in the core to lessen draughts. The arrival of corrugated iron in Purbeck is probably post railway: a substantial early example is the Swanage Drill Hall (1886). Quarry photographs of c.1890 show virtually none with corrugated iron roofs; by the 1920s, most have them. Subsequently, corrugated iron has made a clean sweep, walls included. However, Bob Harris went against this fashion with his post-war machine sheds at West Winspit, which were of dressed stone and brick. An example of a possible earlier type of quarry shed is provided by a photograph of Port Arthur, Winspit, from c.1900, which shows a stone shelter covered in what appear to be hurdles, carrying a thin layer of thatch. As with all Cliff quarries, that quarry would not have been readily productive of thin slabs for its shed roof.

As the stone was dressed, waste scars were tipped close by and accumulated to form banks. In some instances, when the wheelbarrow distance got too long, they gave up pushing too far and let scars build up close by. This forced the raising of the capstan, roll stone and even sheds. Lewis Tomes' quarry is a good example, with its crabstones now well above the surrounding fields. On the face of it is daft to add to the depth of the shaft, but of course it made sense in practice. The accumulating scars were sometimes integrated with a vertical wall of large stones (often of poor quality that would not be sold) to form the loading banker. These may now be the only evidence of a former quarry.

CLIFF QUARRIES

Some late medieval and 16th century monuments provide evidence of the taking of stone from St. Aldhelm's Head. This was probably from the undercliff, where good material lay loose for the taking. But perhaps from quite early on it was also dug from the cliff top as well, for here the usable beds are easily accessible. Stone right on the cliff is relatively loose and easier to dig, hence Jack Edmunds of Hedbury's maxim, related to my father: 'keep between the deep [the hill being the deep] and the shoal [the cliff edge]'.

The way of working that had developed at most cliff stone quarries at least by the 18th century, but not St. Aldhelm's Head, was to penetrate by attacking the bed immediately above the Lower, or Bottom Freestone. Hence its name, the 'Underpicking Cap'. It is not always clear in the third edition of Hutchins (1874) what period is being described, but in 1796 digging the Underpicking Cap at Seacombe was described as 'always blown up with gunpowder. Formerly, and but a few years since, it was picked out by a kind of pickaxe – a tedious process.'[44] This suggests the introduction of gunpowder to Purbeck in the late 18th century. However, the first edition of Hutchins (1774), describing the Cinder, says: 'no tools can work, gunpowder alone can affect it, very ponderous but of no use', suggesting at least some use of gunpowder in Purbeck by this date.

Neve describes the use of gunpowder in quarries in 1726. Methods seem much as employed here later, and perhaps at the time: 'Some in drawing stone make use of gunpowder [...] By making with a fit instrument a small perforation into the rock, which may reach a pretty way into the body of it [...] at the further end of this perforation there is placed a convenient quantity of gunpowder and then all the rest of the cavity is filled with stones and rubbish strongly rammed in (except a little place left for the train) the powder being fired, the impetuous flame being hindered [...] cracks the rock into several pieces, most not too unwieldy to be managed by the workman'.[45]

Most of the Cliff quarries present evidence of how explosives were used, usually in the form of radiating shattering. Typically

Chilmark quarry, a typical drill hole used for gunpowder.

a hole, approximately one inch in diameter, was drilled into the Underpicking Cap, dipping slightly below the horizontal, to a depth of two feet or so. This angle was a good one at which to swing the hammer. A charge of gunpowder (about an egg-cup full) was inserted, fused, and in the recent past stemmed with clay before it was fired. Clay rather than small stones was used perhaps after the introduction of damp-proof fuse wire. Care had to be taken not to use too much powder, and shake either the Freestone below or the ceiling bed above. The broken rock was prised away with bars and the operation repeated until a patch of Bottom Freestone was uncovered. West Winspit was the last quarry to be worked in this way, but by using gelignite, before Bob Harris packed up there about 1956.

The next step in a cliff quarry was to loosen the Freestone by inserting wedges in pits cut horizontally at its base as well as in the natural joints. Big blocks were subdivided by the same method. Cutting deep horizontal pits at floor level is difficult, especially if the block bulges out in 'a bunch', making it hard to get close. Once loosened, bars were used to lever the block onto a cart before it was dragged into the light for working. *In situ* standing stones were left to support the ceiling, hence its name, the House Cap, or sometimes 'legs' were built up. In most quarries, when a fair area had been undermined in this way, the supporting legs were blasted away with gunpowder. This controlled collapse was termed 'having a founder'. The mass of stone above would fall, loosened, to the quarry floor. The men would sort through it. The good was 'worked up', the waste tipped into the sea until the quarry shelf got wide enough to accommodate it. East Winspit shows such an accumulation of waste. This Purbeck method, therefore, differs entirely from that used at Portland, where no undermining was ever done until recently. It is important to bear in mind, when looking at the wide quarry platforms of Dancing Ledge (not the lower ledge, which is natural), Hedbury and Winspit, that this was how they were created, not by digging down from the top, layer by layer.

This underpicking method was slow, but a founder produced a bounty of loose stone. However, there are snags in all things. Overlying the topmost usable beds is about ten feet of useless Shrimp. This would have come down in a founder, and been a thorough nuisance. Quarries which were pushed further into the cliff encountered ever increasing amounts of additional useless beds. This is the reason for the cessation of work at about the line we see at East Winspit. The puzzling configuration of the loosened heaps there, some of which are foundered masses that have not been gone through, can probably be explained by this Shrimp nuisance. In a well-controlled founder the upper part of the mass tends to fall the furthest out. Where this was Shrimp there was no point in shifting it all unless it was burying something worth having. The temptation would be to leave it and go around to get at the Pond Freestone behind. Worthless Shrimp was not an issue where most of these quarries were started out on the cliff edge, for in only a few places does it extend that far. The bowl shape of West Hedbury shows this graphically: no Shrimp at the seaward start, but the full height plus earth rock at the back of the quarry. Only at the eastern ends of Hedbury and Dancing Ledge did they push in further.

Another factor acting against deeper penetration into the hillside is that the joints tend to get tighter, and the bedding planes more firmly attached. An idea of the problem may be gained by examining old quarry floors. Where they are uneven or exhibit many wedge marks the quarrymen were struggling. The worst-case scenario in attempting to lift a block with wedges is for the split to run up rather than level. Not only does it spoil the shape of the block but on its removal the quarryman is faced with a worthless sloped lump still attached to the floor, that has to be got rid of before the next block can be attempted. We sometimes found this a problem at the Head, though with the advantage of pneumatic drills we could break out the residual 'root' reasonably easily. Unlike most of the cliff quarries we were lifting the Pond rather than Under Freestone, but the problem is much the same. Some blocks could be fairly free, though uneven flints lying at the bedding plane level always added to the difficulty as they act like dowels, whilst other blocks were so tight that we had to force them off with a lot of plugs and feathers. This variation in adhesion could be patchy, tight blocks lying adjacent to freer ones.

Long cuts were made or heavy blocks lifted by a row of wedges acting in concert. Latterly plugs and feathers were used to do the same thing. Rows of drill holes at Seacombe and Winspit tell of their use there in the 1920s and 40s respectively. In my opinion all earlier cliff quarry single drill holes indicate the use of gunpowder.

Brannon (1858), in his account of quarrying methods, uses the term 'ridding', especially with reference to Dancing Ledge. This is misleading, as the account may well be in other ways too. For example, his view of a shaft shows steps flanking the slide on both sides. Not a single quarry was like that. One flight was sufficient. To 'rid' simply means surface as against underground working. Hence such shallow surface quarries are 'ridden holes' worked by 'ridding'. Harry (nicknamed 'Ton') Chinchen, an underground man, disparagingly remarked to me: 'There ain't no quarries left today, only a few ridden holes up Langton'. Once in wider use, the term crops up in the Rev. Kilvert's diary in his remarks about a Shropshire quarry. In 1435, as quoted in Salzman: 'Thomas Goldesburgh and four others employed ridding, clearing and stripping fifteen rods of quarr at Huddlestone'.[46.] An early Purbeck reference comes in a Hatton estate account of 1618: 'to one workman for cutting of nettles, ridding of stones [...] in the castle [...] 5s.' This term hardly fits the cliff quarries. To have worked a face such as we see at Dancing Ledge by any opencast method would result in 'benching', which none of the old cliff quarries exhibit. The opposite is true, in that they are almost all undercut. Even on some of the smallest excavations like Platter, where hardly any digging was done, they had already begun to undercut.

Following loosening of the block, it was moved by means of bars. These levers were the only means they had of moving stones free of the face and on to the cart. There was no cranage other than the gibbets mounted on the cliff edge, which were solely employed for lowering the finished stones away to the boats. This did not change until the 20th century. The gauge of worn trackways still visible at Blackers Hole, Dancing Ledge and Winspit show that a different, wider cart than normal was

Seacombe Quarry, April 1930.

Seacombe Quarry, directly below previous image. Probably the first pneumatic drill in Purbeck. Samuel Short Bower and Billy Winspit at Bottom Freestone level.

used in these quarries: approximately two feet six inches as against one foot six. A photo of Seacombe (c.1910) shows one of these wider carts in use. From the chance remark of one man, Jack Edmunds, who as a youth worked at Hedbury, we know of the use of yet another sort: the horn cart. One is illustrated in Thomas Webster's drawing of East Winspit (1814). However, the usual inland quarr carts were also used at times 'up cliff', particularly by men who switched from quarry to quarry. One appears in the painting of Hedbury by H. T. Wells (*see page 126*). A. Close examination of the Winspit trackway that leads out to the central dock, and the eastern fork of the Dancing Ledge track, shows the presence of a third rut consistent with an inland cart gauge.

Evidence of how the boats were loaded from the cliff remains in holes cut in the rock to accommodate crane timbers. They reveal the type of primitive crane employed until the end of the 19th century. They were not superseded until the introduction of the Scotch derrick around that time. The gibbet was necessary to reach the load out over the cliff. Their reach was fixed and limited, unlike the cranes that replaced them. The horizontally mounted jenny was surely more practical than a vertical capstan for this task. These gibbets would have easily been dismantled and moved. More often than not the configuration of the cliff meant that the stone had to be lowered to a shelf at the cliff foot before being picked up again and swung into the boats. Dancing Ledge has by far the widest of these shelves, such that a cart was used to carry the stones between the two gibbet positions. The crane could not have been left on the water's edge or heavy weather would sweep it away. On the day of loading, the quarry edge gibbet would have dropped the king post, gibbet arm and jenny on to the cart below. This would have been run out to the water's edge, the king post reared up into its socket, the arm attached by its single hinge fixed at the top of the king post and rested on its bearing that remained permanently leaded into the rock. The windlass or jenny was set up in its pair of holes and the rope reeved; all ready for action, in minutes. Just two of the fixed iron bearings yet remain in place.

The natural configuration of the cliff differs from quarry to quarry. In some they had no choice but to lower the stone from quarry floor straight into the boat, even when this was fifty foot or so below. In others, there was no choice but to drop it to a low, even sea-washed ledge, before then picking it up again and swinging it aboard. That there was a net benefit in this alternative, even though on the face of it this meant more work, not to mention the need for a second crane, is revealed in places like West Dancing Ledge. There they used the low ledge option even though the other also existed side by side. Winspit was notoriously difficult for loading, mid-Hedbury good, and Seacombe almost as good as a man-designed wharf, whilst White Ware and Reform look horrendous! All, however, would only have been possible in relatively fair weather.

TRANSPORT

BY SEA

It is frequently claimed that one of the factors affecting Purbeck Marble and stone's pre-railway usage was the advantage provided by its coastal location. The major medieval projects where it was used in quantity such as Canterbury, London, Exeter, Ely, Lincoln *et al.*, are on rivers and reasonably close to the sea. The route by which Salisbury was supplied remains uncertain. The oft repeated claim that it was by the Avon remains in doubt, as it had numerous barriers to navigation.[47] The route to other destinations also remains guesswork. Presumably Marble for Worcester went via Land's End and the Bristol Channel, but what of the effigy in Carlisle? Perhaps the North Sea followed by a short cross-country haul is most likely. Two more or less random samples relating to location are revealing. Of twenty odd coastal churches in north Norfolk almost all contain medieval Purbeck of some sort, mostly brass indents, whilst in a sample of similar size in Bucks only about fifty percent possess any Purbeck. However though sea transport is definite in the cases of a font in the Scilly Isles, effigies in Dublin, columns and tombs in Normandy, some Purbeck was also reaching the more inaccessible interior of England, such as Ashbourne, Derbyshire.

A tantalizing glimpse of overseas trade is offered in the Patent Rolls.[48] In 1205 King John granted a license to the Abbot and canons of Sori, (Italy) to carry away English Marble to build their church and 'not to take away from our kingdom any more than victuals for the sailors.' Another Purbeck-related order from the King hints at disputes. 'To all the Bailiffs of the seaports of Dorset: Know ye we give license to the Venerable Father Simon, Bishop of Chichester, to carry his marble from Purbeck to Chichester to permit them to pass through your bailiwicks.'[49]

Setting aside trade to the Americas, post-medieval distribution was more restricted; quantities of paving and tomb stones were shipped east and west, and south to the Channel Islands. Harbour wall 'front' went east in quantities; westwards in a very small amount. Many south coast churches and churchyards have big collections of late 17th, 18th and early 19th century Purbeck headstones and ledgers, but beyond London they become scarcer. By north Norfolk they are rare. To the West paving reached St Mawgan, near Falmouth, but not much rounded Land's End. The wider distribution of Marble centuries earlier is a measure of former prestige – never regained.

OWER QUAY (POOLE HARBOUR)
The ongoing payment of a pound of pepper by the marblers for right of way at Ower suggests that it was the most important shipping place in earlier times. Its antiquity as a port is illustrated by the payment of 'one pound of pepper as an acknowledgement in order to preserve the company's right to the way or passage to Oure Key according to ancient and usual custom.'

This custom of paying in pepper was already established in Purbeck, when in the 12th century the chaplain at Wilkswood Priory was paying a pound in weight of pepper as part of an agreement to do with land adjacent to the Marble quarry. If pepper was a valuable commodity in 17th century England, it is likely that it was at least as valuable, relatively, in the 12th.[50.] By the late 17th century most of the traffic was going through Swanage.[51.] Within a few years the use of Ower ceased entirely. Swanage's dominance at the time is revealed in the document of 1687: all the signatories are men of Langton and Swanage.

Ower is the nearest point to Corfe on Poole Harbour, where a channel capable of taking a sea going boat of reasonable size comes close to the shore. It was thus medieval Corfe's port. Materials for the castle were landed there, including heavy items such as a 32ft long log for the bridge in 1285.[52.] Whatever provision was made at Ower for handling such weights (it could hardly have been less than three tons), no evidence has been left.

The causeway that extends to Green Island, interrupted by the South Deep channel, has been shown to be Iron Age.[53.] I suggest that there never was a medieval pier at all; either here or what is now called Ower Quay; that wagons were driven out into the water, as was the practice until late 19th century in Swanage, thanks to the ancient hard causeway surface. The top of the causeway consists of irregular but fitted small slabs of Purbeck stone.[54.] Presumably they date from about 250 B.C. as the timber support piles certainly do. The sea level has risen by one, possibly two, metres since construction, so when first built the causeway was dry around mid-tide but flooded regularly.

By the time of the medieval marble traffic the all-important 100 metre long hard surface was hidden by mud and water. Provided the edges were marked by posts to prevent going off, the Swanage method of horse and cart entering the water would have worked, even to the point of loading fair-sized seagoing vessels directly from the causeway.

The Ower agreement of 1695 does not relate to the whole route from Corfe, only to the land of John Collins's of Ower:

> For and in consideration of A Pound of Pepper and a Foot Ball to be paid by the said company of free marblers on the next day following shrove Tuesday or in four or five Days after except sabbath day then to be paid the next day following to be paid to the said John Collins his Executors Administrators or Assign's at or in the New Dwelling house of the said John Collins being at Ower abovesaid all which being perform'd and paid by the free marblers abovesaid, they shall have, use, occupy and possess the way which was formerly allowed to the said company, without any hindrance, trouble or molestation of the said John Collins His Heirs or Assign's: The bound of the way being as followeth:
>
> Beginning at the said house of John Collins at the East side Down along the lane to the strand and so to the Quay

The three witnesses, Joseph Hort, Thomas Chapman and William Cull, were all prominent in the 1698 Joint Stock Company. 'New dwelling house' is probably the east end of Ower Farm house, which is late 17th or early 18th century. The strand is probably the southern shore of Cleavel Point. At this point small stones strewn across the open mud contain a high percentage that are Marble, whilst current erosion at the extremity of this Point is exposing not only oyster shells in quantity but bits of Marble buried at some depth. This location is some way from the few remaining wooden posts said to be the quay that extend into the mud close by the cottage called 'The Quay', but near where South Deep comes closest to the hard shore. The bay east of Ower is called Newton, from the failed, and probably Marble-traffic-related, 14th century settlement. Treswell's map of 1585 shows it as The Hope, which means an inlet, as Church Hope Cove, Portland.

Whatever was done at Ower, stones must have been stocked somewhere before shipment, unless the loaded wagons were timed to coincide with the vessels' arrival, meaning that unloading could be done direct into the boats from the causeway. Is it possible that the natural banks rising above high tide mark near Cleavel Point were used as 'bankers'? Were there once masonry walls providing a hard edge to these banks that have been taken away since abandonment?

There is plenty of evidence that stone was taken from Peveril for building Poole. Abandoned stones at a place like Ower, easier of access than Peveril much of the time, would have been tempting to take. Alternatively did they manage without bankers and simply let the heavy loads down to the ground? It seems unlikely. Archaeologically Cleavel is dominated by Iron Age features but there are a few that are medieval, notably a 'ditch' more or less in line with the causeway, about four metres wide. Is this evidence of a cart track across the end of the peninsular to the causeway?[55.] A significant change affecting the Ower shoreline and adding to the causeway's concealment was the arrival of the hybrid cord grass, spartina, in the 1930s. Its subsequent massive spread reached a maximum in the 1980s since when it has retreated by about 50%. It has a big effect in trapping sediment.

REDHORN QUAY (POOLE HARBOUR)

Evidence for an old stone quay, now almost entirely gone, is provided by C. E. Robinson in a description of Poole Harbour sailing in 1882. 'Anchoring off the mouth [of a channel] which leads with a twisting course of nearly a mile to a rude 'banker' of Purbeck stone called Redhorn Quay, one of the places whence that material seems to have been formerly shipped before the vessels employed in the trade were stout enough to bear the brunt of bad weather in Swanage Bay'. I suspect that this speculation is wrong, for there seems no logistical sense. Rather, in my opinion, it was built for use by the market boat, which was the means by which Swanage was provisioned before the railway arrived in 1885.

The Redhorn quay's almost complete disappearance is instructive. Just one course remains, extending for about 50 feet in length, plus a few loose blocks. Curiously, those that remain are all Cliff stone, sticking out of the mud below high tide mark. In good weather the market boat brought commodities such as flour, sugar and tea directly from Poole to Swanage. In bad, it was forced to stay within Poole Harbour, leaving its cargo at the nearest point to Swanage, Redhorn, on the eastern shore of Brand's Bay. Marky Tomes, variously quarryman and

Leland's 'Peere', Swanage, showing steps and parapet of Cliff stone from Tilly Whim or Hawcombe added by Morton Pitt in the 1820s.

coxswain of the Swanage Lifeboat, inherited his nickname from his father who had served for years as Master of the market boat. My Aunt Dorothy told a story about Redhorn Quay. She was descended from James Summers, killed in a quarry roof fall in 1813, neither of whose two sons went into the quarries. One, Charles, became a tranter. Once, crossing the heath in the fog near the Agglestone on his way to collect from the market boat, he blundered into a bog, only saving himself by using the buoyancy of the air trapped in his bowler hat!

WAREHAM

Gervase, the Canterbury monk, describing William of Sens' rebuilding campaign, mentions Wareham as being a noted port. Perhaps it was the home of some of the vessels employed in that campaign. It certainly was later. The great master Henry Yevele became embroiled with one in January, 1374. He stood surety for the *Margarete* of Wareham after it was arrested at Poole. Of 48 tons burthen and 'laden with 2 high tombs of marble for the Earl of Arundel, and his deceased wife Eleanor, a great stone for the Bishop of Winchester and other things of theirs', she was released and taken to London.[56.] Could a vessel of that size negotiate the River Frome as it is now? Formerly, in order to maintain a channel of sufficient depth for the ball clay vessels using Ridge wharf, a chain was sometimes dragged astern during low water ebb; this stirred up mud, which was carried away in the concentrated flow.

Langton Wallis Court Accounts for 1448/49 show 3000 stone tiles at 5s per 1000 and 10/s for carriage to Wareham, probably when it was still a port of embarkation for the stone trade. Around this time large quantities were being shipped abroad out of Poole. Further evidence of the use of Wareham as a port exists in the form of exotic rubble in several of its walls. It is surely discharged ballast and includes Devonian Limestone.

SWANAGE

Around 1540, John Leland makes no mention of the stone trade when describing Swanage. This is perhaps not surprising for about that time Marble usage was fading out, and the exploitation of other beds was at a low level of output. He says 'a fisher town called SANDWICHE has a PEERE and a little fresh water'. Leland's 'fresh water' is Boil Well that continues to break out close to the shore east of the quay. It was significant for mariners as a source of safe drinking water. It has been suggested that Monkey Beach got its name from the powder monkeys whose job it was to fill the water casks of Royal Naval ships.[57.]

Leland's pier is surely the quay. Though repaired and added to, notably by Morton Pitt, the core structure may be medieval and therefore Marble trade related. It literally occupies a key position at the end of the High Street. Is it possible that the depth of water was sufficient for small medieval craft to get alongside at least on high water springs? Be that as it may, this was not how things worked after then, when a tidal range of about six foot maximum would have precluded stranding the vessel upright at high water alongside the quay wall before loading her directly from carts when the tide was out.

The post-medieval handling solution at Swanage involved horse-drawn carts being driven into the sea so that their loads could be transferred to small boats, and the construction of cart-high bankers above the shore for the stocking of stone awaiting shipment. They allowed for it to be manhandled off the carts arriving from the quarries and then back on to the carts that went out into the sea without letting it down to the ground, from where it is difficult to get it up again. The trick with manhandling is to keep the stone up or at least on edge. The old hands used to say: 'keep it lively,' 'never let a stwune down dead,' 'keep 'im on edge,' etc. Surprisingly large stones, particularly shapes like paving, can be walked or 'trotted' about by adept men.

These seagoing carts had bigger wheels than the normal farm cart. The discrepancy must have been a problem for in building the banker to an ideal height it could not be exactly level with both types of cart! They are referred to in two wills of Swanage merchants. Thomas Pushman in 1738 left his three horses, 'cart boater' and all his bankers to his son John, whilst in the same year James Keats' inventory includes 'The banker going to Brooke, boat cart, ankers etc.'[58.] A relic of the Swanage seagoing carts remains in the form of a summer-room table adapted from one of the big wheels by another big wheel, George Burt.

The first pier, built in 1859, was for the shipment of stone. Horse-drawn trams running on rails (a lengthy section of which remains), linked the pier to the various merchants' bankers. It had a crane at the end. It seems cranes on Swanage pier were ill-fated, as not only was this crane overloaded and pulled into the water, but a later steam crane, placing large blocks of Portland Roach at the end of the masonry, was similarly pulled over, drowning its operator, Harry Hixon. The pier must have been advantageous, but it did not put an end to the old ways

ABOVE Painting of loading stone at Swanage Bay by William Craft, early 1860s. Note the old method, employing horses and cart going on at the same time that the recently-built tramway is in use. Note measurement marks on paving in the boat in the foreground. Note also tram on rails on tramway.

BELOW Harbour Grace, Newfoundland, built 1831. The windows are of Rag and Swanage Freestone.

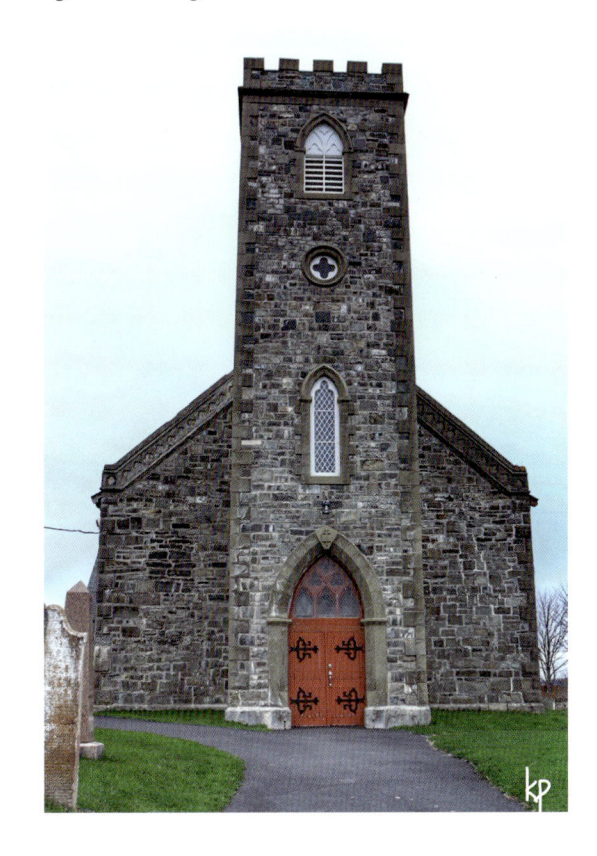

of doing things, partly because some merchants would not pay the tolls. So it was that Thomas Hardy was able to sketch 'Loading stone – Swanage' in 1875, which shows a horse and cart in the sea with a stone boat alongside. Just ten years later the railway arrived and the trade moved away from the shore to the railway yard and what became known as 'the depot' near Court Hill, which had its own siding.

TRANSATLANTIC DESTINATIONS

Purbeck paving used in the Governor's house in colonial Williamsburg, Virginia, was shipped from Bristol. Presumably a coasting vessel took it there before transfer to another of ocean-going capacity. It seems another James Keats was involved with similar transfers, some of which did not go smoothly, for in 1752 a complaint is made about him in Poole: 'a large flat stone has remained on the quay for near 3 years, it belonging to James Keats of Corfe castle'.[59] The inventory of the earlier James includes stone left at Poole and Wareham. From Corfe to Wareham is not much further than Corfe to Ower, which had ceased to be used by this date. Perhaps there were circumstances, loading big vessels in Poole in winter maybe, when it made more sense to haul to Wareham for transit to Poole by river, rather than risking the open sea route via Swanage.

The 17th and 18th century transatlantic traffic was considerable. Headstones, ledgers and paving remain from as far south as Jamaica and Barbados to Newfoundland in the north. One particular transaction is nicely described by Revd. Harston, visiting Swanage in about 1830. He noticed a little church, built on the bankers, to be exported to Newfoundland on a Poole Trader: 'Our cutter took it to Poole'. This could be the church at Harbour Grace, Newfoundland, which has Purbeck stone window dressings combined with the local hard stone in the plain walling.

A glimpse of the riskiness of the passage is provided by a letter to do with the supply of paving to Mr. Carter in 1730s Virginia. Some of his cargo had to be dumped at sea. How extreme was it for the ship's master to have to dump cargo? Paving was packed in tight on edge, to take one out would loosen the rest. Imagine what was going on to get sizeable stones out of the hold and over the side in a heavy sea.[60] Some

TECHNOLOGY / 223

stone even found its way to St. Helena in the South Atlantic, for East India Company records include 'the landing place steps being very dangerous with many accidents happening to boats and people, gave orders to lay a flight of Purbeck stone into the rock 1772'.[61]

Stone may have served as ballast in the form of paving or steps. In addition, examples of inscribed headstones have been found in Newfoundland, apparently finished in England, and presumably carefully packed for transit. The fact that soft plants were used as dunnage may explain the presence of species of English heather now growing over there.

SHIPPING

Most of Purbeck's output over centuries could be handled without the need for cranes, but exceptions included big slabs used as brass indents. The largest examples include Salisbury's Bishop Wyville slab at more than 13 feet long. These big indents are probably about nine inches thick, which makes them about four tons weight, perhaps more. These, and many more almost as heavy, were loaded into boats either in Swanage or Ower. This would have been done with timbers and bars. A few other large slabs, including several from the 14th century in Christchurch Priory and notably Ely's Bishop Goodrich (1554) indent, were almost certainly loaded off the highly exposed St. Aldhelm's Head undercliff. The 'Blue Bit' Cliff stone bed from which they come is about 12 inches thick, so these slabs, though not as big on plan as some of the Marble examples, could be almost as heavy. Seaworn Marble rubble in the 12th century Constable's Lodge at Christchurch could only have come from Peveril Point or close by in Swanage Bay. It must surely have been put in the boats there. The Marble we see in one of the first big projects, William of Sens's work at Canterbury, also 12th century, has an abundance of thick calcite veins, just as we see at Peveril Point, but not to the same degree in Marble quarried further west. It must be a safe conjecture that it too was loaded in Swanage.

Some idea of the size of 17th century vessels can be gained from London Masons' Company records. Particularly informative is 'An Accompt of the search of Purbecke stone June 4 1671'. It lists the masters of the 'Barkes' arriving, with the measurement in 'Ffootes', together with the London 'Debitours'. The stone is paving, of which 50 square feet weighs about a ton. Assuming that no other items of significant weight were being carried, we find Mr. Wise, with his 'Smale Barke', brought about 50 tons, whilst Edward Phippard carried about three times that amount, the rest ranging in between. From June 1671 to February 1672, 47 vessels made the trip, carrying an average of about 80 tons each.[62]

Some of these masters sound like Purbeck men: Mr. Cull, Robert Butler, John and Richard Masters, Thomas, William and Edward Phippard; but others not. If this is so, it is like the pattern that continued in the late 19th century before the railways killed off that way of life; that is, locally based boats employed almost entirely in the stone trade, but others joining in as well. That it was a free-for-all for the right sized vessels is shown by an advertisement placed by merchant Timothy Chinchen in 1775: 'Notice is hereby given to all masters of vessels from 20 to 200 tons that they may meet with constant employ in carrying stones to the new works at Portsmouth at 2/1d per ton exclusive of customs house charges. N.B. They may depend on quick dispatch in the delivery as there is considerable more depth of water made and 3 cranes erected'.[63]

PETWORTH CONSIGNMENT

Presumably the 17th and 18th century London masons had wharves on the river where stocks were kept, as was certainly the case later in the 19th century before the development of the railways. As that happened riverside locations generally were given up and premises taken in or near the railway yards, mirroring similar changes in Swanage. A glimpse of how things were sometimes arranged appears in a letter given by the Duke of Northumberland to his mason concerning the supply of stone to his house at Petworth:

> 'These are to certifye that the Bearer hereof William Sares is a Stone Cutter and has been many Years, & is at this Time employed in my Buildings and Works at Petworth in Sussex, [...] And is an Inhabitant and House Keeper in the Town of Petworth and is now Sent by my order to the Island of Purbeck to Buy Stones for my said Buildings and Works. You are therefore desired to Suffer him to Proceed thither and to Returne back to my House at Petworth without Interuption or Molestation. Given under my Hand And Seale this Twenty fifth Day of March 1727'.[64]

LONDON CONSIGNMENT

A record of prime costs of an unknown project in or near London reveals that getting the Purbeck paving to the site cost rather more than half the value of the dressed stone itself:

> 'At the quarry per hundred [this is 100 square foot of paving probably averaging about three inches thick and therefore round about a two tons; 'quarry' probably means the Swanage bankers] £1-0-0d.
> Freight from Purbeck to London   8s.0d
> Lightridge from below the bridge to Scotland Yard   1s.0d
> Warfage and carting from Scotland Yard to the work 3s.0d.
> Total   £1.12.0 per hundred foot'

Scotland Yard, close to Whitehall palace on the river, from the time of Inigo Jones housed the official residence of the Surveyor of Works to the Crown.

RAMSGATE HARBOUR

The 18th century saw the biggest job supplied from Purbeck; Ramsgate Harbour wall. It was to forge several Purbeck connections such as the following:

> 'Some time before, Charles Vye came to Ramsgate in charge of a consignment of stone for the harbour. His wife Sarah came too. They liked Ramsgate and settled. First child Mary was born 1790. A frequent visitor was Capt. James Bartlet Kelsey part owner of vessills *The Resolution* and *Swift*. Kelsey married Mary Vye and established a chain of shops later absorbed by Liptons.'[65]

THE RESIDENCE OF THE REVD JAMES HAMMOND, UPPER BELGRAVE PLACE.

H.E.KENDALL JUNR ARCHT. MESSRS J & F.HAYSOM, BUILDERS.

LOADING

Great grandfather John Haysom worked for a while in the 1840s in London on the rebuilding of the Palace of Westminster. Such was the traffic between Purbeck and the capital, that he could walk on Sunday to the wharves near London Bridge and usually find someone on a vessel from Swanage to have a yarn with. This latter generation of stone vessels were mostly gaff rigged ketches sailed by two men and a boy. William Masters Hardy refers to rigging 'Swanage gear', preparatory to loading. The Wells painting (*see page 126*) appears to show the men using a block attached to the mainmast. It would have been essential for lifting stones of more than a hundredweight or so up out of the stone boat lying alongside. Small stuff was not laboriously craned in this way, but passed from man to man. Even in the 1950s and '60s, when we were still often loading lorries by hand with stone from off the ground, Bert Norman would say 'belly and breast 'im', that is, lift the piece up on to the chest before giving it a final push up on to a high load.

When a boy I was taken to have a formal tea with my great uncle, Captain Albert Masters. He was a retired mariner, who had begun his sea-going life on his father Joseph's vessel the *Ginevra*, in those last years before the railway branch line

A composite advertisement for H.E Kendall, 'Junr. Archt.' and 'Messrs J&F Haysom, Builders', c.1845. The new 'residence', which was evidently a joint project, was in what is now Buckingham Palace Road, while the builder's yard was actually located elsewhere, in more industrial surroundings by the river. The detailed drawing shows block being craned out of a vessel with the use of a gibbet-type crane and nips. The masons are sawing the block and dressing the stone in the yard with mallets or hammers.

arrived. He said when the heavily laden stone boat drew alongside their vessel, the shout to him (the boy) was 'Jump aboard and chuck your own weight out quick'. Once those first few hundredweights were safely in the vessel they could have a breather.

The all-important link in this method of loading that prevailed in Swanage for at least 250 years was the humble stone boat, pronounced 'Stwun Bwut'. Good detailed illustrations do not exist, only rather distant views including Craft's painting on the previous page and William Daniell's 'Swanage' (*see page 253*). W. M. Hardy gives an account of them: 'the strongly-built but inelegant stone boats, which were pointed at the stem and the stern, and capable of carrying from six to nine tons'; this seems too much for the boats illustrated.[66] However, they were still light enough that they could be pulled up by a capstan in bad

TECHNOLOGY / 225

Etching by Alfred Dawson: 'View of Swanage from corner of the Grove', in C.E. Robinson (1882), *A Royal Warren or Picturesque Rambles in the Isle of Purbeck*. The almond-shaped boats drawn up on the shore at centre are surely stone boats. The several thwarts would have been necessary to stack stone such as paving against. Note that they are impeding the use of the tramway: is there a turf war going on?

The *Ripple* of Swanage. Her Master was William Smith, nicknamed 'Billy Ripple'. This is typical of this last generation of late 19th century sailing vessels.

weather, at least in Swanage where most, but not all, were kept.

The remains of the 23 feet long boathouse at Hedbury, built close by the jibbet, show that a fair-sized boat could have been kept there. Photographs taken around 1910 show it to have been a good quality building complete with date stone and stone tile roof. The beauty of the Hedbury situation is that except during storms a boat could have been kept on the lower level loading rock. It must surely have been easier to launch, indeed load, boats in general from a relatively low position like central Hedbury, where the men on the jenny could better see, or at least hear, what was going on at water level. Where the cranes were mounted high up the men turning the wheel would have been completely blind to what was going on down at the boat. It must have been a bit dodgy to occupy a small boat as a heavy weight was swung out fifty feet or so overhead. Presumably they did most of the lowering with the boat pulled clear, for the restricted arc covered by the jib gave little scope to keep the load at a safe distance and yet remain within the swing. The vital moment must have come when the stone was still suspended but making intermittent contact with the boat as it rose and fell. Though 'strongly-built', the boats may not have been particularly heavy-duty, any more than the carts provided by the farmers were. No doubt the gunwales were protected by iron where it mattered like modern pot hauling boats, but beyond that, and some good stout bottom boards and good fendering provision, they may hardly have differed from the average fishing boat in terms of their strength of build.

BOAT MONEY

There must have been a considerable benefit in keeping a boat available at one of the western cliff quarries like Hedbury, for the alternative was arranging for one to be brought from Swanage. But to have had one where needed must have been a great advantage, and it must be this arrangement that John Bankes was alluding to in 1724 when he wrote: 'the tenant has liberty to open quarries of stone allowing me [...]1 tun out of 20 of freestone [this is cliff stone] [...] with necessary boats by assignment'. Evidence that one was kept for a while at Winspit is contained in that estate's papers. For the early years of the 19th century the various Worth quarrymen simply paid royalties to the estate. Then, in 1825, some also began to pay 'boat money' for the hire of the squire's boat at Winspit. At the same time the estate was in receipt of rent for the government boathouse there.[67] The western half of the existing cottage had been built as a coastguard house not long before. Clearly the coastguards kept a boat. However there is no evidence of any 'boathouse' which is large enough for a boat, but perhaps the necessary gear was stowed in a small stone shed just above the cove. This shed has since been vandalised, but the flight of steep steps to it still remain. To improve the dock would have required work, probably done by the Government. It is likely that the estate then cashed in on this asset by keeping their own boat there, for which they charged. There are two categories of payment for boat money, either 5d per ton or 3s. per trip to Swanage. The rate per ton was when a vessel was anchored close by, that is, as close as the master could get. In 1827-8 William and Edward Brown paid for 216 ton plus four boats to Swanage.[68] They were the main players, and were definitely working the cliff quarry; William was also being paid to keep the stone account and another of the family lived in the cottage semi-detached from the coastguard.

The location of the other quarriers is uncertain but it seems that James Lander, for one, was inland. The strong indication is that he was working on East Man and shipping his stone from Winspit, whilst the group of other Worth estate quarries around Gallows Gore were surely sending their stone to Swanage via the turnpike road. It is unfortunate that in most years the accountant only lists the bare income from each man, without indicating where the quarries were. But in 1800 he went into more detail, which reveals that William Brown, Joseph Chinchen and Thomas Bower were working Winspit, all the other men worked paving quarries. There could be a clue as to their whereabouts in their order in the accounts. Henry Bower and Richard Keates, both making paving, come first, probably with quarries in the Gallows Gore area. Then come the Cliff trio, followed by Sam Lander, Ed Barnes and Will Corben, all again making 'paving' only. The notable absentees from paying boat money are the Chinchens, who were certainly working the cliff, but not it seems using the same boat the others. They had their own (as included in Nathan's will of 1836) kept, probably sometimes at the boathouse at Hedbury, sometimes at Swanage. Hedbury is perhaps the front runner in that the Swanage Rate Assessment of 1820 shows the Chinchens paying on quarries and bankers there, plus two sloops, the *Swanage* and the *Portsmouth*, but with no mention of a boat.

Chapman's Pool too had a boat house. Robinson writes: 'A little stream trickles [...] a few fishing boats drawn up on the beach around the roofless lifeboat house, lately dismantled.'[69.] A photograph, presumably from the same period, shows this lost building in the same condition. Between 1866 and 1880 a lifeboat was kept here. The station was closed due to threatening landslips and the difficulty of launching in a southwesterly gale. However this would not have been a determining factor in the case of a stone boat, which would only have been used in clement conditions. This prompts the suspicion that the 'lifeboat house' was originally built for a stone boat to serve the quarries at Pier Bottom and St. Aldhelm's Head Undercliff.

SHIPPING FROM WINSPIT

The dock at Winspit is now choked with boulders, to the extent that the high tide crane position is rendered useless. Eighty years or so ago Billy Winspit kept it clear of big rocks arriving in the winter storms by blowing them up with gunpowder. Since then more and more have arrived from the southwest. Somewhere below what we see now is, I suspect, a shelving surface of relatively small stones up onto which the Preventive men and the estate hauled their boats. That the boat definitely belonged to the estate rather than the quarrymen is indicated by a lament of a member of the Brown family when the boat came to a sudden disastrous end. 'Oh my legs and caps!' was his bewail. This became a catch phrase and referred to the loss of his cargo, sunk somewhere between Dancing Ledge and Blacker's Hole: it was not the boat, surely of greater value, which was on his mind, but the staddles. According to Billy Winspit he did not get much sympathy. Divers have found an assembly of such staddles in about the right place.

That Winspit quarrymen kept a boat there before the squire supplied one is suggested by the death by drowning in Swanage Bay of William Bower. His Worth headstone records: 'Upset in an open boat   Aged 33 in 1794'. Two Williams, father and son, were paying Winspit royalties in 1790. Smaller fishing dinghies carried on at Winspit until the 1950s when the last, George Waller's, finally ended as fuel for a barbecue.

The shipping of stone at Winspit from inland quarries may well explain the construction of the flat platform produced by walling up the east side of the stream right at the seaward end. It was let as an extra piece of garden to Ambrose Bower in 1882, but such a use could hardly have justified all the work involved in its construction in the first place. The platform lies at the end of a track that goes up on the east side of the stream (formerly called 'the lake'), close by and on a level with the cottage. A dotted line on the tithe map of 1840 shows the track passing the cottage and terminating at the cliff edge shed, relics of which remain. Now lost in bushes, the track squeezes by the eastern side of the garden. About half way up to Worth a break in the series of horizontal lynchets allowed a way down from the Long Ledge and East Man paving quarries.

The carts only conveyed a ton or so at a time, but the vessels needed perhaps 70 or more for a load. So there was an imperative to have stacking room close to the crane position, for when the vessel arrived speed was of the essence. The platform does not end in a vertical drop to the water but tails off in a slope of about the same angle as the natural cliff below. Below this a uneven natural ledge, devoid of cart tracks, extends out into the water. At its southernmost extremity, washed by the sea, lie a configuration of at least six post holes plus two mooring holes cut about 15 feet apart from one another. They reveal the position of a gibbet, with its jenny set further back than most because of a big fissure, square to the dock, which would have allowed clear space for stone arriving from the north. A jib reach of seven feet or so would put the load right in the middle of the boat position as indicated by the bow and stern mooring holes.

The problem with this loading position is that there is no way a cart could have been brought to it. To have resorted to some timber arrangement would surely have left evidence in the form of fixing holes which are entirely lacking. Seatings for short planks spanning joints at Winspit and Dancing Ledge show that timber was used to a degree to overcome obstacles. More substantially at Seacombe, seatings for sleepers tell of a railed track between the quarry and loading rock crane position, but it was only a few feet long. There is no evidence of this sort of thing on this eastern side of Winspit dock. The solution is revealed in another stout post hole lying further out than the crane position. What is remarkable about the Winspit hole is how low it is to sea level. It scarcely dries from one spring tide to another. Someone worked hard and fast to cut it, a task made more difficult by all the lumps of flint he had to get through.

Its alignment would allow for a strong rope (possibly steel by this date), attached at the other quarry end up on the platform area, that spanned to and across the jibbet position. The suspended paving could have been zip-wired down and across the sloping cliff plus uneven ledge obstacle in one go. Arriving at water level, its sling chain could have been detached and put on the gibbet. A few turns of the jenny and it was again airborne and swinging into the boat, whilst the men up top were pulling the empty block back up. A couple of sling chains would have kept things going quickly. It seems that the system was similar at Dancing Ledge, where the anchor post for another rope system lies in a similar relationship to a jenny gibbet. The span at Dancing Ledge is much longer and post holes reveal an intermediate pylon. Possibly the load was suspended in such a way that it could pass over such a pylon.

SAILORS AND LOADERS

The boats were propelled by one or two men standing, plying long sweeps. Some had a sail stepped forward, leaving clear cargo space. When that was paving, as it often was, it was leant against the thwart. A clue as to where some were probably built is provided in an agreement of 1855 between the Trustees of Ilminster Free School and 'Robert Barnes boat builder, a parcel of land with boat house, workshops and saw pit on the north side of Swanage bridge between the Turnpike road and the sea'. According to W. M. Hardy (1908), the last remaining boat, at Chapmans Pool was in a rotten state.[70] He gives a graphic account of life endured by the sailors and loaders. John Mowlem endorses the hardship of it: '19 Dec 1845. Wind W, strong. [...] Heavy showers. Several vessels in the bay, all loading stone, the men wet through, nothing on to keep them dry except duck which is wet through in a few minutes; no improvements, the men have no idea of comfort.'[71]. Hardy, a Nonconformist teetotaller, also criticised the custom of paying these men, at least in part, with beer:

> 'In addition to paying the loaders' wages he (the ship's master) was compelled to pay the objectionable beer bill. Just think of it, that for loading a vessel of 110 tons he had to pay for 75 to 80 pints of beer, not for his own benefit in the least, unless he belonged to the feathered tribe; and what good it did the loaders to pour this river of brewer's concoction down their throats I fail to see, as it was neither food nor physic; but in many cases it was stated that it was for no one's good, bur for the good of the house, and so the riddle is solved.'[72].

Payments of beer ceased in Swanage with the end of sea transport except for the requirement of apprentice boys to provide a quart on Shrove Tuesday, which continues. But the custom was an old one. Knoop and Jones refer to payments of beer for work done as early as 1311 at Leicester, whilst the London Bridge accounts record the payment of beer, value 3s. 4d., to the bridge workers or masons and carpenters on Ash Wednesdays from 1404 – 1418. Samuel Keats was receiving beer for compiling the Corfe Parish stone accounts in the late 1700s, whilst Jeremiah Bower charged the Revd. Clavell for the beer he gave the boatmen who handled the Clavell Tower stones at Kimmeridge in 1831.

In 1805 a Swanage Poor Rate record lists the merchants, including their boats. Although ten men paid for a banker, and can therefore be identified as being merchants, only two of them, Thomas Randell and John Pushman, had boats, which is puzzling; Thomas had two boats, John five! Presumably they hired them out to other merchants, except perhaps the Chinchens. The Chinchens are known to have had a boat at Hedbury which would not have been rateable for Swanage Poor Rates. On November 22 1824, the Rector recorded the loss of two boats. 'Last night and the whole of the day it blew at tremendous gale from the S.W. The sea in the bay ran higher than ever was before remembered, doing much damage. Two vessels' stone boats were driven out of the bay and lost, all the people perished'.[73]

It is astonishing they were putting to sea in such conditions. Later, in 1846, Robert Burt had at least one stone boat, which John Mowlem recorded as being lost, laden with paving. Two years on, describing the regatta for which he brought fireworks from London, John Mowlem wrote: 'All this (the greasy bowsprit, duck hunt, etc.) finished with four stone lighters being rowed by two men each. William Butler, who is 70 years old, was the first boat, his brother George the next'. These men were marblers and had quarries in Durlston Bay; one was nicknamed 'Admiral'. Such freemen handled the stone right until it got to the vessels. Evidence of the bygone loaders and mariners remains in the form of broken clay pipes which continue to wash up on Swanage beach. They range in date, but some are certainly pre-1700.[74]

Stone boats also had to be used in Durlston Bay, Pier Bottom and the cliff quarries, where the vessels could not safely get alongside. The normal practice was for the master to manoeuvre as close to the cliff as he dared get before anchoring. Claims that the boats were stranded at low water and then loaded before being lifted off by the next tide are doubtful in the extreme, at least as far as the cliff quarries are concerned, though not impossible at Durlston Bay. Great uncle Albert Masters said that on one occasion at Hedbury, the conditions being favourable with a light northerly breeze, his father took the risk and put his vessel, the *Ginevra*, capable of carrying about 70 tons, right on the cliff. After first anchoring he took a warp to the cliff, by the dinghy, with which he pulled her in, paying out on the kedge anchor warp as he did so. At Hedbury the loading rock spans a cave, so the quarrymen would have been able to drop the stones straight into the hold; quite a saving in time and effort. Boy Albert was amused by the bewhiskered faces that peered down on them from around the piles of stone awaiting shipment to 'the Uplyme job', as he called it, the mansion at Rousden, being built by Sir Henry Peek. On completion they drew the vessel seaward by using the kedge anchor warp, getting her clear before safely setting sail. The exposed position of the cliff quarries meant that loading could only be done in relatively good weather, usually the summer. However, John Mowlem noted on 24 November 1845: 'one vessel was laden for Durlston Bay, one ditto at cliff, this is very remarkable at this season of the year, and shows what a demand there is for stone'.[75]

The cliff quarries had defined loading places equipped with a gibbet. Durlston Bay was different, with a shelving shore of small rocks and ledges. They managed by getting the stone boat in close before leaning a timber 'ladder' from shore to gunwale. The loaders, standing in the water beside it, manhandled the stones along. Presumably the boat was tied on, and there would have been some places more advantageous than others, but it seems the method was workable virtually anywhere along the bay, though it must have been difficult in any sort of swell. W. M. Hardy gives a description:

> 'The methods of loading in Durlston Bay were somewhat different from those adopted at the cliff. Here the stone boats were hauled close in to the shore, and an inclined portable stage placed near it, on which the stones were slid or rolled and lowered

into the boats, and trotted to their proper resting-places by the loaders. These loading operations had sometimes to be conducted breast high in the water all day long, and in the cold weather it can be guessed with what pleasure the men would knock off and indulge in a crust of bread and cheese and a pint to keep them going till the end of the day's work.'[76].

Risks attended them afloat. The Rector, Rev. T. O. Bartlett, included in his diary: '21 Aug. 1836, stone boat sunk in Durlston Bay with crew of 3. Norman, his son and Harden. Norman and Harden rescued by the coastguard boat, but young Norman, who was to be married tomorrow, sank and rose no more.'

STONE ANCHORS

Divers have also found several stone and marble anchors that may have been lost by stone trade boats or vessels. They have holes that accommodated a pair of wood tines in addition to a third hole to take the chain or rope. One made of marble, found not far from the position of the former pier at Pier Bottom and bearing a mark, is displayed at the Dorset County Museum. Perhaps it is from the wreck of a stone boat there; fisherman and quarryman Sid Lander knew its position. He would remark on shooting a pot: 'Let's see if there's a lobster in the bwoat.'

VESSELS

Llewellyn Hardy had an account book of Thomas Masters which gives details of earnings of the *Purveyor*. She was built 1812 and part-owned by Thomas between 1838 and 1868, before being lost in 1912. The other owner was William Tomes, described as 'quarryman' in his will of 1843, who left his half to his wife while she lived and after her to his son, another William. William (Senior) also left a half share in another vessel, the *Sygnet*, to another son, George, who was already her 'commander'. In the days before insurance vessels must have been a high-risk investment for relatively small men like William Tomes. Llewellyn's book also includes earnings of the *Brisk*, between 1851 and 1852, and the *Rising Sun*, before 1859, when she was also lost. She was bought in 1836 for '£78 - 4 + repairing £73'

9 April 1831 has: 'Southampton, Mr Garrett. Due to Thomas Masters, Left Due £7 - 1.' [The Southampton masonry firm of Garrett and Haysom, who fitted out the marble bathrooms on the liner *Queen Mary*, was wound up in the 1960s.]

19th May has: '1000 ft of paving at 7s 0d per hundred [foot] £3 - 10 - 0. 5 tons of pitchers at 3/6d per ton 17/s. 1 sink of 11½ peck 1s'; also mysteriously 'man for putten stone back 1/s.' As a rough estimate she was carrying about 25 tons. Some vessels were considerably bigger. John Mowlem had a schooner built for his Channel Island granite trade capable of '245 tons with a good bold side.'

Joseph Masters was perhaps a typical mariner in that he had his 'beat': Falmouth in the west, Channel Islands to the south and London in the east, and he did not go much beyond. His mate for years was a Brownsea. Brownsea was

John Mowlem (1788-1868). Mowlem was born in Swanage and went to London as a young man, beginning the construction company that until recently bore his name by paving streets with Purbeck stone and granite from his Channel Island quarries.

illiterate, but had an intimate knowledge of the coast; he knew every sea mark, clump of trees, church tower, etc. between Swanage and London Bridge, and could even tell where they were when below. Joseph's son Walter passed on one anecdote illustrative of the hazards. When he was yet a boy they ran into heavy weather off the Downs, just managing to get into Ramsgate without the harbour master even seeing them! Everything was carried away, so Joseph had to send home for money to buy fresh sails so they could carry on to London.[77] But sometimes the best knowledge wasn't enough. Joseph's relative, master of the *Champion*, was drowned after striking the shingle bank off Hurst Castle in a fog. There was a heavy ground swell, which often accompanies fog. It seems they tried to get the anchor away from her in the hope of pulling her clear, but were thrown out of the dinghy. The Swanage Rector organised a collection to benefit the widow, left with young children. Enough money was raised to buy her a mangle so she could take in washing and support herself.[78] Some men went further afield. Thomas Hardy, brother of W. M., had a part share with Mrs. Thomas Randell in the fast, high rigged *Excell* that was finally lost in 1927, off Anglesey. He would take a load of stone to London before continuing on up the east coast to Newcastle for coal. Purbeck vessels were doing this from the 18th century, if not earlier. On one such return passage, heavily laden, beating westwards from the Needles, he fell in with a race of gentlemen's yachts out of Cowes, and gave them a good run for their money. So impressed was Lord Linlithgo that he put in to Swanage to make enquiries about the vessel with a view to purchase.

TECHNOLOGY / 229

An engraving of a sailing vessel in one of the cliff quarries. Note the similarity to the painting of the revenue cutter below. The artist is unknown, and the painting, which is on linoleum and fragile, formerly hung in the White Hart Inn at Swanage.

ENGRAVINGS

A number of sailing vessels are engraved at several cliff quarries, along with initials, tally marks, portraits, dates (1736 at St. Aldhelm's Head and 1829 at East Winspit amongst the most striking) and mysterious symbols. Most are cut on vertical surfaces, though curiously the only one at Dancing Ledge is on the flat, and most are concentrated where the dressing was done. They are of a variety of rigs, but gaff cutters, some towing dinghies or stone boats, predominate. Others include a Bermuda rig cutter, fore and aft gaff ketches and schooners, plus others with square topsails, a 3-masted barque flying union flags and, most bizarrely, a Viking ship. This oddity was probably inspired by a replica that was sailed along this coast in 1893. In the main the rest are probably contemporary with the working of the quarries and cut by the men working there. With the probable exception of the barque they could be showing vessels employed in the trade; but the high proportion of high rigged cutters with long bowsprits, including a group of 12 at Winspit, prompts the suspicion that some of these are Revenue cutters. The distinction between a sloop and a cutter is fine, with a sloop being more of a work horse. James Chinchen's two vessels were listed as sloops. Winspit has the most engravings; curiously Seacombe none, perhaps because the 20th century expansion cut away faces that bore them. Sadly modern graffiti has been imposed on some of the best at Halsewell. Hedbury has a lot. Reforn, White Ware and Scratch Ass a few. Curiously Tilly Whim, with its plethora of other graffiti, has only a gaff-rigged ketch.

FINDING A HAVEN

A problem with Swanage is that it provides no haven in an easterly gale. My uncle used to say: 'the wind that bloweth from the east is neither good for man nor beast', which I bet would have struck a chord with generations of men and horses. Shelter was sought in South Deep, Poole Harbour, or according to Robinson, sometimes Studland:

> 'Rounding the point [Handfast] into Studland Bay and steering at first for the wooded village at its head, we pass the quiet anchorage, where a pilot cutter or two, and on Sundays a small fleet of craft engaged in the stone trade are usually to be found, for the shelter here is more complete than in Swanage Bay. The 'stone-hackers' [elsewhere Robinson also calls them 'hookers'] are left quite alone by their crews, who tramp over the hills to their homes in Swanage on Saturday nights. Even if a gale arises fierce enough to drive them ashore, little harm is usually done, as the spot where they touch the ground is a bank of soft sand.'[79.]

A greeting we were discouraged from using as children, but still in parlance, was 'Wucher me old acker' (What cheer, my old hacker?). It must have come across the waters of Swanage Bay so many times as the 'Stwun Bwuts' neared the newly-returned and waiting vessel. These men had to be looking at the sky and taking decisions all the time. In uncertain weather conditions, was it to be the greater safety of South Deep but a longer walk home, or the lesser walk from Studland but more risk? Sometime in the 1780s a vessel running for shelter, laden with 300 tons of stone, struck on a shoal off the entrance of Poole Harbour and foundered; the crew were saved, but the vessel and cargo remain to this day at the bottom.[80.]

Exploring this wreck and retrieving some stones, plus a quantity of deer antlers, we found its load of pavings, which included Roach of the sort dug south of Acton, neatly stacked on edge on top of solid Cliff Stone steps lying in the bilge - clear evidence of a merchant putting together a load from more than one quarry. A 13th century marble cross dredged up in Brownsea roads which is now in Poole Museum may tell of a much earlier wreck. An assembly of scappled blocks also of marble, lying off Lepe Beach in the Solent, must surely also be a medieval wreck. They lie east of a spit, suggesting she drove ashore in an easterly.

There was tension between the Purbeck mariners, who had sought the safety of the South Deep channel within Poole harbour without payment for centuries, and Poole which, over time, had grown to dominate the harbour. The tipping point was the Poole Quay Act of 1756 which, in spite of resistance from Wareham, gave Poole the right of dues on goods shipped through the harbour. Purbeck mariners were left grumbling. Brownsea and the other islands remain part of Purbeck.

RAILS

The arrival of the railway branch line in to Swanage 1885 effectively put an end to the sea traffic. One of rail's promoters, George Burt, advised his relative, Joseph Masters: 'sell the vessel and put the money in the railway company'. However, stone was taken by sea for Luton Hoo (1910) and the Training Bank (1920), both conveyed from the cliff quarries by steam-tug-towed lighters. Also about that time, or later, my grandfather William supplied stone for Lord Iliffe's house on Furzey Island and for a substantial house on Brecqhou in the Channel Islands, subsequently demolished and replaced by a castle built of Spanish stone. My father was not sure, but thought that some had gone by Poole Quay, rather than Swanage Pier. It seems an era ended unnoticed.

Neither plans to link the railway to the bankers and pier in Swanage nor the idea of a tramway running as far west as Langton along the route of the Priest's Way came to anything. The tramway which was constructed for the pier in 1859 connected the bankers from the parish slipway to the pier. Man-propelled skips running on rails were in operation at Mutton Hole, Seacombe and Sheepsleights (1920s), St. Aldhelm's Quarry (1930s), West Winspit (1940s), inland quarries at Castle View and Burngate in the 1950s, all with flanged wheels. Rails used with flat-wheeled carts remain in Edmunds' underground at Burngate.

The arrival of the railway also promoted the development of two quarries to provide hardcore. In the First World War one was opened to the south of Gordon road, where German prisoners were employed digging broken stone for the Holton Heath Munitions Factory. A second quarry for the same need was at modern Day's Road, a short horse-and cart haul down Washpond Lane to the railway line: presumably the stone was thrown over the bridge in to the waiting trucks below.

OVERLAND

HUMAN TRANSPORT.

In a rather confusing appendix Hutchins includes an account given by a James and Robert Scates, quarriers, of a time when the stone was conveyed from the quarries to the bankers on men's backs, especially perhaps at the end of the day, if the bankers lay in the same direction as home.[81.]

Thomas Collins was apprenticed at the Quarry Co-op at Acton in the 1920s. Walking there to work from Swanage, he would often fall in with Bill Galley, who had a quarry close by. He told me Bill paved out a yard near the Black Swan, at Swanage, carrying a single stone two miles home each evening rather than pay the transport! In the 1950s, Douglas Bower, named the 'Purbeck Sledgehammer' as he took on all comers at fairground boxing booths, did something similar. Whilst working in his quarry at Queen's ground, Langton, he carried home each evening a coping stone for a garden wall. Carrying such a weight was, for him, part of his training regime.

Swanage sea front, looking East towards the stone quay. Tramway rails, built in 1859 relaid in modern paving, between the parish slipway and the pier.

CARTING

The 'standard' 18th century farm cart generally carried rather more than a ton. Roof tile was sold by the load, a measurement deriving from such a cart. The carts introduced in the later 19th century by the merchants carried rather more, up to three tons, requiring more horses. In 1847 John Mowlem wrote in the course of his improvement to Swanage High Street: 'I am busy carting stone for the street here, the road is soon cut up. I find there are 1,500 tons of stone taken through this narrow street with waggons with 3 and 3½ tons in each, with 3' [width] wheels.'[82.]

W. M. Hardy suggests traffic to the bankers was about 60 loads a day of about three tons each. The carts had a 'back stick' or heavy timber which material such as kerb was leant against, the stones being loaded in and out over the sides of the cart. On steep descents like Court Hill some carts had a 'drug' to slow them down. This was an iron shoe suspended in front of a wheel, which when required was lowered so the wheel rode onto it and jammed. Another braking device was a 'bat'. This was a flat shoe, forming part of the iron tyre. As the wheel rotated it banged on the ground, making a distinctive sound. At a steep descent the wheel was held by a chain at the critical point on the rotation so that the bat was in contact with the ground and took the wear. Either way the wheel dragged rather than rolled freely. For most if the Swanage quarries it was more or less downhill all the way, both to the shore or, later, the railway depot. In 1881, about the time the switch from shore to depot was occurring, Mr Grant's carter, Pitcher, was fatally injured by his wagon carrying four tons of stone, drawn by three horses, going over his legs. 'The tackle for tying up the hind wheel broke'.[83.]

TECHNOLOGY / 231

The wear and tear of the tracks on steep descents would have been considerable. The problem was more acute on Portland, where blocks had to be got down to the pier. A solution illustrated by Grimm, about 1790, was to have a team of horses pulling a big block, carried on a wheeled wagon with a smaller block resting on a sledge attached behind to act as a brake. The weight of the greater helped to pull the lesser at the same time as the lesser helped to control the greater. One shudders to think of the fate of the horses in front if the link between cart and sledge gave way. Grimm's view shows additional horses attached behind the sledge resisting the forward momentum. It must have been difficult for the carters to get the balance of effort right over a distance where the angle of slope changed.

It seems improbable to me that sledges were used on long level hauls like Corfe to Ower. However, there is one piece of good evidence for the use of medieval sledges. In 1859 O.W. Farrer contributed a paper to the newly-formed Purbeck Society entitled 'The Marblers of Purbeck'. In mentioning the Shrove Tuesday pepper payment he includes 'Marble used to be drawn on sledges from Wilkswood to Ower'. On more certain ground, the tracks worn into solid rock at the cliff quarries (Dancing Ledge, Winspit, *et al.*) are certainly **not** the product of sledges, but of iron-tyred carts.

TO AND FROM CORFE

Trackways crossing Corfe Common indicate a considerable traffic converging on Corfe. There must have been a point where it made overwhelming sense for stone or Marble in the west to go to Ower via Corfe, that in the east to Swanage. By the late 18th century, when Ower was no longer in use, this watershed was as far west as Gallows Gore, for we know that Downs Vein quarries were active there then, and their stone was going to Swanage. This dominance is made clear in an advertisement for Downshay Farm in 1793: 'replete with stone quarries and at a distance of about four miles from Swannage from whence all the Purbeck stone is shipped, to which there is a good turnpike road, and where there is a most excellent shore, much resorted to for bathing'.[84] The construction of the turnpike in 1766 would certainly have affected choices of route.

It seems that in the 13th century the watershed was further east, even as far as Crack Lane. The equation is not straightforward: Ower is safe in any weather, but further from the quarries than Swanage; Swanage is unusable when the east wind blows. Lady Elizabeth Hatton's 1618 Purbeck accounts for stone for her London house show that she was using both ports: 'For cariage of stuffe from London to Poole and from Poole to Ower - £1 9s. 4d. For ditto by carte from Corffe to Sandwich to be sent to London 4s. 4d.'[85]

If the Corfe Common trackways are related to the medieval marble trade, they are astonishing in scale. Their relative absence eastwards (between the Common and the quarries) is in marked contrast, but this could be the result of agricultural improvements. Terry Lucas remarked that his grandfather had him stone picking a line that crossed their Quarr manor land: this could have been one of the old trackways. Improvements of this kind happened over time on cultivable land, whilst on the Common the tracks have been fossilised.

A Langton Wallis court presentment of 1423 refers to the poor condition of the 'king's road south and west of the garden of Wylcheswode'.[86] It was surely the way out of the quarries for Marble destined for the royal works at Westminster, a project that began in the 13th and continued into the 15th century. Remnants can still be traced. Just a short section remains in current use, about 200 yards of the track that leads westwards out of the farm yard. At that point the active track swings south into the open field; the lost road follows a decayed wall westwards into the wood, where it follows old coppiced maples now being killed by overtopping ash trees. It then bears northwest, crosses the stream, passes on the east side of a splendid bifurcated oak as it ascends Lanchard Hill through a 15 foot deep cutting, choked with holly trees. From its crest the going westwards to Quarr, Haycrafts and Corfe is relatively easy. Another such track similarly ascends Lanchard further west, close to the boundary with Quarr, where it joins the same route to Corfe. It was surely the way out for the most westerly West Wood quarries.

In the other direction what is conceivably also the route of the lost road extends eastwards of the farm buildings, close by and south of the course of the stream. In this western part of Talbots wood, between what is probably the route of the road and the stream, sections of decayed wall remain. In this part of the wood east of the farm, the space between stream and quarry undulations is wide and undisturbed, allowing plenty of room for a level road, but eastwards stream and quarry evidence converge. A massive waste pile now virtually blocks the continuation of the possible road eastwards. At that point, and only that point, the stream bank has been walled up. At the risk of being too fanciful I suggest that it all spelt trouble. I suspect the scenario may be recognisable in the presentments of 1482, when John Jerard, Thomas Trearther and John Talbot were given notice to repair their walls and hedges and the 'raised road' abutting them.[87] The Marble lay close to the road and the sloping site made it much easier to tip the waste downhill towards the road rather than the more difficult uphill way. They pushed their luck too far and part of the tip subsided, as evidenced by a step, which brought tons and tons of waste shale and worthless bits of Marble almost right across the track. Men reliant on getting their Marble out from further along were not happy and complained to the court.

The men named were not certainly known to have been Marblers, though Talbots certainly were, 200 years later, and the name remains attached to that wood. The presentment that mentions the road 'south and west of the garden' in 1423 reveals that John Lychett, Edward Kene and John and Thomas ByBy (Rigby?) were each fined 2d because it was 'in a dangerous state of repair adjacent to their lands'. These men quarrying Marble were, it seems, endangering the road which they were required to maintain. This remaining section of the road veers away from the stream, avoiding big quarry holes. The geological imperative was to pursue the Marble vein right to the stream and even under its bed, an activity that threatened the road and forced a diversion. It was not particularly in the interests of Edward Kene *et al* to do work on the road adjacent to their own quarry, so long as they could get their own marble out. They neglected the task and got fined for it. The record is reminiscent of recent disputes that arose on the National Trust estate at Acton where separately operated quarries abut. One man could be back filling an area which his neighbour, and rival, needed to keep open as an access road; a Gothic scenario if ever there was one, but now a thing of the past.

Another long abandoned holloway links to this 'king's road'. It runs from Court Pound northwards through Langton West Wood, where it follows the eastern boundary before joining up near the stream. Half way down its descent through the wood another track converges on it from the southwest, and it reaches a depth of five feet or more. If evidence of quarrying, it is of stone, not Marble, which was being taken from the Acton area to Ower rather than Swanage, so it must be pre-1700. What is somewhat odd about it is that on the face of it they could have used a more direct route to Corfe, which prompts the suspicion that on reaching the crest of Lanchard rather than turning west to Corfe the route was to Knitson and then Ower, but this is highly unlikely. It has been suggested that the deeply worn trackway ascending the down above Knitson, which lies due south of Ower, could relate to it, but there seems not to be evidence of a linkage to the Marble quarries.

As for other sunken tracks at Blashenwell and Woodyhyde, which it has been claimed are 'Marble routes', it is likely that these are ancient trackways which pre-date the medieval quarries: in neither case do they commence where the marble was quarried. However, near Windmill Hill a crudely shaped (unfinished?) Marble cross of unknown date has been found, also broken mortars, which may tell of this being a route rather than, as has been suggested, a workshop site.

HAULAGE

Medieval transport records are few, but the accounts of Andrew de Kilkenny's executors, completed 1316, reveal that whilst the plain slab of Marble cost 13s. 4d., the cost of a cart to fetch it to Exeter was 10s. The extant slab, still bearing a damaged cross brass, probably weighs about two tons. It seems that in this case it was carried all the way by road in the same cart. Why did it not go by sea, as other Marble destined for the cathedral fabric at that time certainly did?[88.]

In the 18th century farmers did the haulage from quarry to shore or quarry to inland destination which gave them a stake in the trade. An advertisement of the lease of Worth Farm 1813 makes reference to this custom:

> 'And also find and provide sufficient carriages with horses to carry stone from the several quarries on the said premises for the use of the quarriers working the same at the usual price or prices or permit them to employ other persons and carriages for that purpose.'

But as with the truck system, Brannon was a critic:

> 'Not less mischievous is the system by which the quarrier is compelled to employ the wagon and team of the farmer on whose land his quarry is. For the former suffers in such a compulsory system, and the latter too often neglects agriculture in attending to this advantageous source of income.'

Like so many reformers, Brannon is jumping in with both feet without realising the wider consequences. But he wasn't the first. Hutchins (1774) includes: 'Inattention to agriculture too much prevails in the neighbourhood of Swanage, as the farmers are principally employed in the carriage of stone'. He adds: 'Custom House Records for Poole Jan 1764 to Jan 1771 amount to 94,000 tons' and more was shipped than recorded.

Agriculture may have suffered but the custom was beneficial in terms of a good relationship with the quarrymen. However, about the time of Brannon's criticisms, the 1860s, things changed, for some of the Swanage merchants acquired teams of horses and wagons with which they collected stone from the quarries. My father related that his grandfather had been critical of this development because it cut out the farmers. They no longer got anything out of the stone trade, only spoliation of the ground, a recipe for disputes. Another effect was that the farmers who had kept their tracks in repair, by using by-product scars, gave up bothering. Therefore the ruts got worse and relations between quarrier and farmer deteriorated. One farmer let a sudden flood of water into a quarr, threatening those underground with drowning. The friction culminated in the trial of George Lander in 1904, with its financial ruination of the Company of Marblers (*see pages 265-269*).

Not all stone went by sea. In 1797 a receipt given by Thomas Kent shows that £452 was paid by Thomas Corme for paving stone for the County Hall in Dorchester, the stone to be delivered at Wool Bridge. This is the Shire Hall in High West Street by Thomas Hardwick. It has a façade of austere Portland ashlar but internal Purbeck paving. There is a telling letter related to this transaction, from Joseph Willis at Encombe, addressed to the Rector of Corfe, the Revd Thomas Bankes l'Anson:

> Sir, Am sorry to say its not in my power to attend the Vestry as I intended – hope the Farmers in the North division will have no objections to carry stones enough to fullfill Mr. Cormes order – I think it's a duty incumbent on them. I believe there is or will be delivered by tomorrow morn 2100 [feet]
> Viz
>
> | | |
> |---|---|
> | Mr Pitts Team | 450 |
> | Mr. Sansoms | 300 |
> | Mr. Hopkins | 300 |
> | Mr. Kents | 300 |
> | Mr. Culls | 300 |
> | Mr. James | 450 |
> | | 2100 |
>
> If the undermentioned will undertake to carry one load each I think will complete the order:
>
> | | |
> |---|---|
> | Mr Garland | 150 |
> | Mr Davis | 150 |
> | Mr Furmage | 150 |
> | Mr Rose Smith | 150 |
> | Mr Gover | 150 |
> | Mr Burden | 150 |
> | Mr Polden | 150 |
> | Gould | 150 |
> | Roe | 150 |
>
> Any time that's most convenient for them within a fortnight will fullfill my agreement [89.]

ABOVE Langton-Kingston (turnpike) road. Probably Alfred Benfield's quarry, the loading banker of which remains. Merchant's wagon being loaded with kerb.

BELOW Steppes Hill, Langton Matravers. Carter William Masters with Burt's stone waggon *en route* to Swanage with a load of approximately three tons of kerb stones; c. 1900.

Mr Rose Smith was the farmer at Woolgarston, Davis at Challow, Gover at West Wood, Gould at Ower and Cull at Blashenwell, while the carter Burden was at Scotland Farm. Wool Bridge is about half way between Corfe and Dorchester. It seems that the Purbeck farmers took their consignments one day's travel (there and back), leaving other carriers from elsewhere to complete the distance. This stone is almost certainly from quarries around Gallows Gore, where Samuel Keats was working, as well as compiling the parish stone account for that same year of 1797. Kent's receipt and Willis's letter, afford a tantalising glimpse of a pre-railway arrangement. Though it brought with it the obvious disadvantage of extra handling, with the attendant added risk of damage, perhaps such staged journeys were normal. One wonders what happened at Wool Bridge. Was the stone dumped and left, or transferred cart to cart?

In 1758 James Warne built Turner's Puddle Farm, purchasing his paving stone from James Keat. Warne's diary tells of his team of six horses collecting both paving and tile from Wareham rather than the Purbeck quarries. Presumably this was the usual way of doing things with stone going inland.[90.] Where was the Wareham depot and did it possess anything equivalent to the Swanage bankers? It seems likely that it was the open working area at Wareham Quay, now the car park, and Purbeck farmers probably dropped off their loads to the ground. We are left puzzling with how they coped with heavy stones such as the Charlton Marshall monoliths (See Cliff Stone), for which Wareham also served as a stage.

Fewer horses were needed to manage journeys within Purbeck, such as that from the Langton quarries to Swanage, almost all downhill except the short ascent of Steppes Hill out of Putlake and the modest rise at Newton Knap. That obstacle could not have been too much of a problem or they would surely have used the Priest's Way more. Evidence from pictures and records suggests that the early (medieval and post medieval) carts and wagons were smaller than the standard farm wagon of the late 18th century and that the wagons the 19th century merchants employed were somewhat bigger again. Of the last generation the most photographed was Ambrose Bower's, used in the course of the George Lander row (*see page 265*).

Steam lorries out of Seacombe hauled stone to Wareham and Swanage stations during the 1920s. By the 1930s Mutton Hole, Haysom's and Harden's had petrol lorries, whilst some stone continued to be taken away by rail. By the end of the Second World War the shift to road transport for all stone was almost complete. Possibly the last railway truckload was a consignment of bird baths, despatched by Thomas Hancock in the 1950s.

EIGHT
Trade Organisations

ALTHOUGH A NUMBER OF individual medieval marblers are known from wills, building accounts and contracts, there is a lack of documentary evidence of a guild or company existing in Purbeck before 1651. That year, in the aftermath of the Civil War, the 'Company of Marblers inhabiting within the town of Corf Castell' [...] 'renewed and confirmed' [...] 'as they are drawn out of their ancient records', ten 'articles' or rules. The ancient records referred to are sadly lost, Hutchins says in a fire in Corfe in about 1680.[1.]

Knoop and Jones point out that 'Medieval stone building operations were essentially large undertakings which in nearly all cases were carried out by what we should now call 'direct labour', by the Crown or the Church, the two chief building employers in the Middle Ages'.[2.] The Westminster Abbey building records are illuminating: John Mahu, 'Marborer of Corfe' and John Russe were appointed by Richard II in 1393:

'The King's workers of marble columns in the church of St. Peter to take personally and by deputies in Dorset, at reasonable wages, the necessary masons, workmen and servants of that art, and ships, wains and carts for carriage of the said work.'

Mahu supplied ten of the main nave columns for £40 each.[3.]

Works in Purbeck did not only consist of big projects like the Abbey. Right from its mid-12th century beginning, individual fonts, tombs etc., were also its stock in trade. Small quarry workshops would have been capable of those. John Harvey says: 'As a general rule, mediaeval craftsmen with their own businesses were small capitalists in trade [...] They both made the objects within the competence of their craft skill and also sold them'.

We know that there was movement across the skill levels and that the quarries were a natural nursery for masons, the relatively rough nature of most quarry work providing a grounding for men who went on to develop more delicate skills. This was very much the state of Purbeck affairs into the 20th century, with quarry boys, having picked up the basic skill of 'how to use the tools', commonly going off to Portland or London where finer work was being done. The medieval Marble trade required a considerable skills range and there is archaeological evidence that unskilled stripping off of overburden on the one hand and finely moulded work on the other was going on in close proximity.

At the top of the skills ladder were men like Marbler Thomas Canon of Corfe. Whilst working in London, he was paid £30 6s 8d for making thirteen stone images of kings for Westminster Hall; these can still be seen. At that time a labourer was getting 3d per day. In a perhaps unusual case he bought an apprentice in 1382: 'John Shepeye, barber, has taken Thomas, son of Hugh Le Peyntour of Durham, as his apprentice for seven years by indenture dated 1 April and now sold to Thomas Canoun, Marblerer, all his rights to his apprentice.' The son of an artist with experience of anatomy became a stone carver![4.]

The Guild of Marblers was enfranchised in London in 1485. From at least this date, a guild of marblers who mainly worked in Purbeck Marble existed there. They were accorded the right to elect two wardens who had powers of inspection and of the seizure of work 'not sufficiently wrought'. Their authority extended to 'every person occupying the said craft within the Franchise of the said city that maketh any stonework of marbyll, laton or copper werke belonging or perteynyng to the same crafts'. More evidence that these men calling themselves marblers were also working in other materials, particularly brass, is provided in wills such as John Lorymer's made in 1499:

'That Henry Lorymer should complete and sell such marble stones and latin werke thereto belonging which I have with in the precinct of the black Fryers.'[5.] This appears to be John Lorymer instructing his son to complete his contracts.

Just a hundred years later these London Marblers lost their identity when they were absorbed into the Masons' Company. Cornelius Cure and twelve others 'had beene humble suitors of the Court [of Freemasons] that as wel in respect of the greate decaye and dysabyltye of their said Company'.[6.] Jon Bayliss, in describing the Renaissance period which effectively saw the virtual extinction of Purbeck Marble in London, comments: 'The London Marblers were faced by two major problems during the latter part of their company's existence. First, they had to decide how to deal with the presence of immigrant craftsmen [such as the Cures; Cornelius' father had arrived from the Low Countries as early as 1540; Cornelius went on to become the Queen's Master Mason]; secondly, the larger Free Mason Company wished to see the marblers become part of their company because they shared some of the same skills'[7.]

These London marblers had had close connections with Purbeck. At Westminster Abbey in 1292 no fewer than four are called de Corfes (Edmund, John, Hugo and Peter). Another, Adam, who died in 1331, left a city workshop, plus two tenements in Corfe. He is known from several paving contracts and the supply of a great Marble table for the king. Pieces of this remain in Westminster Hall.[8]

Although records are lacking, it must be reasonable to assume that a guild of some sort also existed in Purbeck from at least as early as in London, and that it was similarly organised.[9] But by 1560 things were at a low ebb, as revealed by a Patent Roll:

'March 14, 1560

Grant to the mayor, burgesses and commonalty of the borough of Corff in the isle of Purbeck, co. Dorset, of the right to hold a market every Thursday and two yearly fairs, on the feast of St. Philip and St. James and the feast of St. Luke; rendering yearly 13s. 4d. At their suit: they hold the said town by service of castle-guard, whereby they are to defend the castle adjoining the town for 40 days in time of war at their own costs; but they are impoverished because they live by the working of marble, which art is in decay because it consists in the manufacture of sepulchral monuments and other monuments now not in use.'[10]

Purbeck Marble had lost its prestigious position. Grand monuments, formerly almost the preserve of Purbeck, were being made out of foreign marble by foreign craftsmen such as Cure. The long line of sepulchral monuments, beginning with 12th century effigies, was coming to an end in the late 1500s with a series of modest wall plaques bearing brasses.

THE 1651 ARTICLES

The common practice of re-using earlier slabs, which often meant reworking the face, makes the tracing of the later Marble trade by examining the monuments difficult, but it is clear that by 1651 most of the 86 signatories to the Articles were quarrying stones other than Marble. Quarr Farm's fireplace, displaying the very date, 1651, is made of Cliff stone, surely cut by one of these men.[11] Though this shift was occurring, the label 'Marbler' went on being applied, even in the 18th century, by which time almost all were stonecutters and the Marble trade was effectively dead.[12]

After beautifully writing out the ten articles and assertion, the 1651 scribe adds the names of the wardens. They would surely have been first in the list of signatories, but are no longer at the top. It seems other names have been added over successive years. Amongst these later additions are the Corfe mayors, Anthony Ffursmann signing in 1655, and Will Okeden, who served from 1657 to 1659. The 85 or so names therefore include those agreeing in 1651, plus more enrolling over an unknown period of successive years. Of the wardens one was entitled Town, meaning Corfe, the other Country, meaning the rest of Purbeck. Respectively they were Edward Vye and Will Cull.

Some of the signatories crop up in other almost contemporary documents, such as the Protestation Returns of 1641, Hearth tax levies of 1664 and Parish registers. From them it is possible to assign some men to their parishes, and gain some idea of how the trade was spread at that time. The following imperfect table is an attempt, based on information in the above returns and other documents. The 'X' marks between some of the names indicate that the name was written by a scribe, with the Marbler making his mark. Authorial notes in square brackets provide further corroborating information; this ranges in date from 1615 to 1682.

SWANAGE

William Cull (Warding)
Thomas X de Virge
Edward X Cole
Thomas Chapman
Tho.Verge Jun. [born 1623]
Robert X Colman
Thomas X Beale
Henrey X Tarey
Bartholomew Pike [born Swanage 1615-1677]
George x Pushman [born 1624]
William Melmoth
John X Cottrell

CORFE

Edward Vye (Warding)
Thomas X Rose
John Horsy
John X Harden
William X Bower

LANGTON

Samuel X Tarey
Thomas Hall
John Chenchen
John Howard
John Corberett

WORTH PARISH

John X Bower

UNATTRIBUTED

William X Bower
Elihu Benfelld
Richard Benfeilld
John X Melrose
John x Chinchin the elder
Thomas X Ash
Richard X Melmer
Robert Elery
Gorg Cobb [the suspicion must be that the three Coobs/Coob variously are the same family as Robert Codd, described as 'Freemason' in his inventory of 1616]
Will X Bonfild
John X Vey
Will Gibbs
Henry X Gibbs
Phinnes Mellmer
William X Hedgcok [Highcock? buried Swanage 1679]
Edward Cole
Thomas X Gover

Robert Bondfild
John X Combes
George Weekes
Robert X Banfeld
Thomas Hort
Thomas X Ellery
John X Hort
John X Cull
Anthony Serrell
T Thomas Pushman [church warden]
Henry Serrell [buried 1682]
John Tarry [buried 1680]
Peter Melmoth [buried 1680]

Thomas Horsey
John X Bush
John X Gover
Lewis Gover [church warden]
Antho ffursman Maior Anns 1655 [Mayor in 1655]

William Bondfield eldr.
John Bower
Wm Cobb
John Coob
William Chinchin

William Chinchin

George X Gardner
Edward X Cull
John Horsey
Hugh Hort
Henry X Meeller
Jered X Colman
Robert Roper
Josiah Hort
Thomas Tollen
Samuel Tarry
Will X Banfeld
John X Bouer
Robert X Bonfell
James X Chinchin
Thomas Brodwai
Henry X Hort
John Hancoke
John ....
John Bond
John Melmoth
Philipp Ninam
Joseph Hort
Moses X Pushman
William Dollinge

236 / PURBECK STONE

The marks are usually based on the first letter of a Christian name, placing it in the gap between first and surname, e.g. John I Combes, Edward E Vye. Those signing for themselves, without a mark, appear to be literate, though caution must be applied in interpreting this evidence. Both Thomas Chapman and Henry Serell do this. Setting aside the 'unattributed' signatures, the numerical evidence suggest the domination of Swanage in the stone trade.

One man, Thomas Horsey, can be identified with a specific job, for in 1688 he was paid 2/6d for 'writing on Mr. Abbots tombe'. A small piece of the inscription, in Marble, survives as a shelf in a blocked up doorway in Corfe church.[13]

To what extent the Company had a total grip on the trade is obscure. For what it is worth the Swanage Registers record the burial of some 'Marbellers and Quarriers' between 1679 and 1682 whose names seem not to appear in the articles, but had they been members we may possibly expect them to have done so. They include 'Quarriers' Thomas Dolling, Luke King, Henry Hayward, Sam Melmouth and Thomas Alford. A Herston cottage contains, over the fireplace, Thomas' name and mason's mark and the date Jan 21 1674. 'Marbellers' include Peter Melmouth and John Abbot. One wonders what distinction the Rector was making between 'Marbeller' and 'Quarrier', or whether the titles were interchangeable. Little if any Marble was being worked.

From at least as early as the 15th century the London Masons' Company had been exercising the right of search; that is, inspecting stone arriving within their jurisdiction. By the 17th century this quality control measure meant the systematic inspecting of shipments of paving arriving from Purbeck. They tried to get the Purbeck men to pay for the inspections, to which they objected. In 1687 certain Marblers and Stone Merchants of the 'parishes of Sandwich and Lanckton' (though not Corfe) made a declaration refusing to pay:

'Whereas wee whose hands and seales are hereunder-written and fixed being inhabitants of the severrall parishes of Sandwich and Lanckton within the Isle of Purbeck and County of Dorset Marblers and Merchants in the seid Trade, haveing received information and intelligence from the Citie of London that the Masons and Cittizens thereof does pretend and intend to put us to unreasonable and unusuall Trouble and Charge in and about our Stone Trade in Purbeck, To wit to procure a searcher to search every hundred of Stone by us sent to London and make us pay the charge fourpence per hundred for the searching our owne goods whiche was before never done agitated or heard of Wee therefore Taking this unusuall matter and also unreasonable Case into consideration and consultation have thus agreed upon That is utterly to deney and refuse the payment thereof as being very prejeditiall to our dealing and Trade here in Purbeck to subject ourselves to such new impositions and exactions and extortions which in ffuture Times may usher in greater Toles and Tributes And it is further agreed upon by and betweene us and every of us to and by these presents in manner ffollowing That is to say that if any or either of us shall bee sued at the Law arested vexed or attacked either in Body or goods to his or their losse dammage or detriment whether it come to a suite and Tryall in Law or not to a suite or Tryall in Lawe That the rest of us shall assist beare and contribute our or their proportionable parte That is according our Abillitie and Tradeing for and towards his or their loss detriment or dammage if any be for and by reason of any such

Herston, Swanage. Thomas Alford's tablet. Was 21st January 1674 the day he moved into his house there?

Trouble vexation mollestation or suite of Law And we doe further binde ourselves and every of us each to other And especially to the warden of the Company ffor the time being in the poenaltie and forfeiture of ffortie pound Lawfull money of England to be paid unto the warden of our said Company for the time being as aforesaid for non performance the above agrements, the same to be imployed and bestowed to the use and uses above mentioned And this is and shall bee our Act and deede irrevoakeably Witness our hands and seales this   of Aprill in the Third year of the reigne of our Sovereigne Lord James the Second.

It was signed by the following: George Weeks, Thomas Verge jun., William Camell, Charles Weeks, Tho. Chapman jun., John Bower sen., Edward Cole, Thomas Bower, James Hall, George Dolling, Ederd   EB barnes, George Bondfeild, Joseph Hort, William Dolling, John Bower jun., with the mark of John X Bishop'[14]

It is not known whether the Purbeck men's solidarity paid off. Perhaps this experience inspired the formation of a Joint Stock company a few years later, in 1698. Some of the same signatories are there, with the exception of John Bishop.

Records of the London Masons' Company are informative, for they tell us of the buyers in London, of the problem of quality control and even the dates and loads of individual shipments, from which it is possible to make approximate estimates of the carrying capacity of the vessels of that time.

A document of July 1691 suggests that the London Masons' Company accepted the disputed cost of the search of shipments which the Purbeck Marblers had rejected in 1687, agreeing 'to go on board of said vessells to search y said stone whether it be merchantable stone or not to pay for y search of y said paving four pence for every hundred foot . . .'

The same document includes an extract relating to individual shipments, the London buyers and the cost of searches.
'The amount of quantity of stone searched for y company of masons London July 1691 Edm. Strong on vessel of Purbeck stone
5200 foot of P. paving at 4d per ft 17/4d
400 foot P. step of 8d. per ft 2/8d.
400 foot P chanell of 4d per ft 1/4d
(approximately 126 ton total)
July 1691

TRADE ORGANISATIONS / 237

Mr. Warden Stanbrow's vessell of P. stone
2400 ft pavings at 4d per   8-0d
100 ft step at 8d per   8-8d.
(approximate total weight 50 ton)
Mr. Charles Martins vessell ditto
4400 ft paving ditto
Mr. Tho. Staynors vessell
4000 ft paving
150 ft step
July 1691
Mr. Charles Martins vessel
4400 paving
300 step
Warden Stanbrow
2400 p
100 step
+one more similar vessell.
October 1691
One vessell '[15.]

Probably most of this traffic was carried on through Swanage rather than Ower and within a few years all of it certainly was, but in 1695 John Collins of Ower drew up an agreement with 'the quarriers or men called marblers… concerning their privileges at Ower Quay'.[16.] The three marblers who signed were Joseph Hort, Thomas Chapman Jun., and William Cull. It seems Ower was already practically obsolete, but these men wanted to retain their traditional rights.

THE JOINT STOCK COMPANY, 1697/8

By the end of the 17th century trade was bad. In an attempt to control matters the Marblers reiterated their Articles and went on to form a Joint Stock Company. It tried to reduce their number by regulating further the taking of apprentices and controlling the price.

In compiling the Joint Stock agreement they set out some new terms. The three points made in the first article are, with some small change in wording, the same in both 1651 and 1697/8 versions. Both versions are set out below for comparison.

'1651 First That no man of the Company shall set into his fellow tradesmans Quarr to worke there without his consent within twelve monethes and a day, nor to come into any part of that Ground within a hundred foote of his fellow tradesmans Quarr upon the forfeiture of ffive poundes to be paid unto the Owner of the Quarr unto whome the offence shall be doun Neither shall no man of this Company worke Partners with any man except it be a free man of the same Company upon the forfeiture of ffive poundes.

1698 Imprimis It is agreed that noe person being a member of the said Company shall sett into his fellow Tradesmans Quarr to worke there without his consent within twelve months and a day nor to come into any part of that ground to worke or digg or draw any stone within one hundred foote of his fellow Tradesmans Quarr upon the forfeiture of ffive pounds to bee paid to the owners of the said Quarr to whome the offence shall at any time bee soe given nor shall any member of this Company worke in partnershipp with any orther person (except such person be free of the said Company) upon the forfeiture of ffive pounds to bee paid to the wardens of the said Company for the use and benefitt of the said Company.'

But in No. 2 there is a change. The taking of apprentices is further restricted.

'1651 Seconly That no man in the Company shall take any Apprentice but that he shall keep him in his owne howse uprising and downe lying for the Terme of Seaven years upon the forfeiture of ffive poundes To be paid unto the Wardings of the Company for the use and benefitt of the whole Company

1698 2ly That noe person of the said Company shall take any apprentice for less time then the terme of seaven yeares and such apprentice shall live in his Masters howse uprising and downe lying for the said terme upon forfeiture of ffive pounds to bee paid to the wardens for the use and benefitt of the said Company. And because the Dealers in the Stone Trade are exceedingly multiplied of late by the takeing of fforraigne apprentices to the greate impoverishing of the said Company It is now by an unanimouse consent agreed that for ffourteene yeares yet to come noe person shall bee at liberty to take an apprentice un-lesse such apprentice bee the sonn of a member of this Company under the forfeiture of paying the summe of Tenn pounds to the Wardens of the said Company for the use and benefitt of the said Company.'

There was obviously a benefit to the master in having an apprentice but not to the trade in general to have too many men in their industry. The Londoners imposed a limit of one apprentice at a time in 1521. They similarly attempted to control the arrival of 'Forrens' to whom an Act of Parliament had granted freedom. This Act was intended to keep wages down but, in response to pressure, was repealed after one year. 'Forrens' to the Londoners meant people beyond the jurisdiction of the City, to the Purbeckians surely anyone from outside the island.

Articles 3, 4, 5, and 6 remain essentially the same in both versions.

'1651 Thirdly That no man after his apprentis shall take any other Apprentice in the whole terme of Seaven years upon the forfeiture of ffive poundes for every moneth ffor as many monethes as he shall keepe him And to be paid unto the Wardings for the use of the Company.

1698 3ly That noe person haveing served his time out as an apprentice shall bee capable of taking an apprentice for and untill hee hath worked for himselfe seaven years from the expiration of his apprenticeshipp upon the forfeiture of ffive pounds for every month hee shall keepe such apprentice to be paid to the wardens of the said Company for the use and benefitt of the said Company.

1651 Fowerthly That no man in this Company shall sell or make sale of any stone within this Island unto any man but by its owne proper name Upon the forfeiture of ffive pounds To be paid unto the wardings for the use of the Company [Some transcribers have read 'its' as 'his', but that that is wrong is made clear in the 1698 version] That no man of our Company shall undercreep his fellow tradsman to take from him any bargaine of worke of his trade upon the forfeiture of ffive poundes To be paid to the Wardings of the Company for the use and benefit of the whole Company

1698 4ly That noe person of this Company shall by himselfe or by any other for him sell any stone within this Island but by the known name of such perticular sort of stone upon the forfeiture off ffive pounds to bee paid to the wardens of the said Company for the use and benefitt of the said Company And that noe person

238 / PURBECK STONE

of the said Company shall undercreepe his fellow Tradesman in order to take from him any bargain of worke on any pretence whatsoever upon the forfeiture of ffive pounds to bee paid to the Wardens for the use and benefitt of the said Company.

1651 Fivethly That every man in our Company upon notice from the wardings of the Company by the Stewards to appeare at any place appoynted, and do not there appeare according to order shall paie for his neglect Three shillings ffower pence To be paid unto the wardings for the use and benefit of the Company, without a very lawfull excuse, And that noe man of our Companie shall take any apprentice that is base borne or of parents that are of loose lyfe or that the said servant or apprentice is or hath been a loose Liver upon the forfeiture of ffive pounds To be paid to the wardings of the Company for the use and benefit of the whole Company

1698 5ly That every person being a member of the said Company that shall at any time be summoned by the Steward to the said Company by order or warrant from the Wardens of the Company and shall refuse or neglect to appeare att the place appointed such person shall for such refusall or neglect forfeite the summe of three shillings and fower pence to bee paid to the said wardens for the use and benefitt of the said Company (always provided that such person have noe lawfull excuse such as shall bee approved by the said wardens and Company) and that noe person being a member of the said Company shall take an apprentice being a base borne child or of parents that are of a loose life and conversation or the apprentice himselfe being a loose and wicked liver upon the forfeiture of ffive pounds to bee paid to the Wardens of the same Company for the use and benefit of the said Company.

1651 Sixthly That upon any acceptance of any apprentice into the Company He shall paie unto the wardings for the use of the Company sixe shillings eight pence (this equals 1/3 of £1, or ½ a mark or 1 noble) a penny loafe and twoe potts of beere That no man of the said Company shall set a laborer aworke upon the forfeiture of ffive poundes.

1698 6ly That every person that have served out his time as an apprentice shall pay unto the wardens at the time of his being made free six shillings and eightpence to the use and benefitt of the Company. And moreover shall pay for one penny loafe of bread and one flagon of drinke to be given to the wardens and Company then present and that noe person being a member of the Company shall emply a labourer to worke in his Quarr upon the forfeiture of ffive pounds to bee paid to the wardens for the use and benefit of the Company'

In the 1698 vesrion of 7 they bring in the Ower Agreement.

'1651 Seaventhly That any man in our Company the Shrovetewsdaie after his marriage shall paie unto the wardings for the use andd benefit of the Company twelve pence and the last married man to bring a footbale according to the custome of our Company.

1698 7ly That every person being a member of the said Company shall upon the Shrove-Tuesday after his or their marriage pay to the wardens of the said Company Twelve pence for the use and benefitt of the said Company and such person as was last married over and besides his Twelve pence shall bring with him a ffooteball for the diversion of the said Company which said ffooteball shall within six dayes after bee carryed to Oure as allsoe a present to bee then and there made of one pound of pepper as an acknowledgment in order to preserve the companyes right to the way or passage to Oure Key according to antient and usuall custome.'

Articles 8, 9 and 10 remain essentially the same.

'1651 Eightly That upon any appointed meeting at any time or at any place together ther shalbe any noyse hindrance or disturbance to the company upon the command silence from the wardings and not observed, the man in default shall paie twelve pence to the Wardings for the use and benefit of the Company.

Ninthly That the warding of the Country shall have the Companyes stocke, alwaies provided that the warding of the Towne shall have securytie for the use and benefit of the Company.

Tenthly That if any of our Company shall at any time reveale or make knowne the secrettes of his company or any part thereof upon notice given, and just proofe be made, he shall pay for his default to the wardings for the use and benefit of the Companie ffive poundes.

1698 8ly That if any person or persons att any publick or appointed meeting of the Company shall make any noyse whereby to hinder or disturbe the buisness of the said Company and the warden or wardens shall command sylence and such person shall refuse to bee sylent accordingly that is default thereof every such person shall pay downe one shilling for the use and benefitt of the said Company.

9ly That the wardens which are to bee chosen yearely according to usuall and antient pracitce shall have power by and with the consent of the said Company to putt out any part of the Companyes stock remaining in their hands from time to time at Interest uppon good and sufficient security for the advantage and benefit of the said Company.

10ly That noe person being a member of the said Company shall at any time reveale and make known the secretts of the said Company or any thing relating thereunto and in case any person shall offend herein such person shall upon due proofe made thereof before the wardens and Company forfeite the summe of ffive pounds to bee paid to the said wardens to the use and benefitt of the said company.'

Here the general similarity ends. The 1698 Joint Stock Company document sets out the reasons for the company's creation and appointment of seven managers. It sets prices and agrees to pressurise company members to join.

'And for the future improvement and better management of the decaying Trade of the said Company and to prevent the many greate and growing evills that have and doe dayly attend the severall dealers in the Stone trade who by reason of the deadnesse of the said Trade have of late yeares made it their practice to carry their said Stone to London in small quantities haveing but little stocks And in order to dispose thereof have and still doe endeavour to undersell one another to the infinite prejudice of the Stone Trade by meanes whereof the price and value of the said Stone is soe lessened and beate downe that scarce anything can now bee gotten by it and consequently the wages for labour in drawing and working the said Stone is reduced soe very lowe that many of the members of the said Company are thereby rendered uncapable to support their ffamilys by their said Trade which mischeifes and inconveniencyes if not timely prevented will send to the greate impoverishment if not the utter Ruine of the said Company wherefore it is hereby further agreed and consented unto as followeth (vizt.)

Imprimis That from henceforth all and every the members of the said Company which now are or hereafter shall beemade appeare to bee worth in substance ffifty pounds and their Debts paid, shall from time to time bee obliged that what quantity of Stone shall bee by them provided or made in order to send to

London shall bee brought into a Joynt Stock to bee agreed and settled at Sandwich in the Isle of Purbeck and that no paveing or other Stone shall bee by any of the members of the said Company sent to London but what is sent in the said Joynt Stock which is hereby intended to bee erected and sett upp, upon the forfeiture of Twenty pounds to be paid by every such member as shall offend herein (whither such member be qualified to come into the said Joynt Stock or not) unto the wardens of the said Company for the use and benefitt of the Company.

2ly That the said Joynt Stock soe erected shall be mannaged by seaven persons that shall bee chosen at the Generall meeting of the Company upon Shrove Tuesday next By the name of the Managers of the Joynt Stock for the more effectuall carrying on of the Stone Trade in the Isle of Purbeck, which persons shall bee men of knowne integrity and honesty and being soe chosen shall continue to bee managers of the said Joynt Stock Trade for ffive yeares to come before any others shall bee chosen in their roomes unlesse in case of the death of any of them when a new person shall bee chosen to supply his place on the Shrove Tuesday that shall then next happen. And the wardens and Company haveing mett this present Shrove Tuesday in pursuance thereof have unanimousely chosen Thomas Chapman James Hall Charles Weeks Joseph Hort the elder Samuel Prestly Alexander Petten and Henry Serrell to bee the managers of the said Joynt Stock Trade accordingly who shall bee and are hereby declared to bee the persons wholy impowered to mannage and governe the said Joynt Stock Trade for the benefitt and advantage of the Company and every member concerned therein and the said Managers shall have power to receive any quantity of Stone that shall bee made good and merchantable (and if found otherwise to cause the same to bee broke) into the said Joynt Stock from any member of the Company quallified as aforesaid delivering and tendering the same att the waterside where the price of the said Stone shall bee allwayes taken and accounted to bee of the value of Sixteene shillings for every hundred foote of paving Stone soe delivered which price is hereby declared to bee established and meant to bee the selling price of the said paving Stone and of all other Sorts of Stone after the same rate at the waterside for the better support and maintenance of the poore labourers employed in the drawing and workeing the said Stone, [side bracket at left: 'Price agreed att the waterside to bee sixteene shillings for every hundred ffoote for the incouragement of the poore'] and the said Managers shall cause the same imediately to bee charged in the Companyes Joynt Stock books to bee kept for that purpose and may and shall order the shipping of the said Stone for London att what tymes and seasons they shall thinke fitt and there sell and dispose of the same or any part thereof att such prices and rates only as shall bee agreed and settled by the said Company to bee the selling price of the said Stone [side bracket at left: 'Price agreedd to bee ffouer and Thirty shillings for every hundred ffoote and not to bee sold for lesse nor without ready money at London'] and shall allsoe receive the monyes ariseing and growing due for the same which monyes and every part thereof shall as soone as received bee applyed to every particular members account in equall proportion to the quantity of Stone such member had and then stood charged on his account in the Joynt Stock bookes of the said Company at the time of the Sale of such Stone in London.

And for the better carrying on of the Joynt Stock Trade and the making it more effectuall for the good and benefitt of the Company the Managers shall have full power and authority to order and direct the contracting and paying for all fraights wharfeage and other reasonable and necessary expenses as well as the settling of the Clerkes and servants and paying them their wages   All which charges (except ffraight and the charge of shipping) shall not exceed in the whole upon every hundred foote of Stone above Two shillings which the Managers shall deduct from each members account out of every hundred ffoote of Stone in proportion to the quantity sold and disposed of in the Joynt Stock for his use so allso the ffraight and charge of shipping according to the Contract made and paid for the same.

(The ffraight is calculated not to exceed Tenn shillings for every hundred ffoote of Stone to bee sent to London winter or summer which if it should happen to exceed, the managers may in such case raise the price of the Stone in proportion to what it shall pay more)

And uppon the paying and cleering of every members account which shall bee done twice in every yeare at least the Clarkes shall make out and deliver to each member a duplicate of his particular account as it shall then stand in the books of the Joynt Stock Trade that such member may bee apprized of all the deductions out of his account and what the balance that remaines does amount unto and all the contracts for ffraight and agreements for wharfeage with the other expence and charge shall bee daily entered into a booke to be kept separate and apart from the other books and accounts of the said Joynt Stock Trade all which books and accounts shall and may bee viewed and examined by every member concerned therein att all seasonable times for the Information and Satisfaction of all and every the members of the said Company.

That if any member of the said Company shall att any time or times refuse to come into the said Joynt Stock Trade and such member bee proved to bee worth in substance fifty pounds (when his debts are paid) that then and in every such case none of the members of the said Company shall worke for him or sell him any Stone under The forfeiture of paying for the same the summe of Ten pounds for every such offence to bee paid to the Managers of the Joynt Stock Trade for the use and benefitt of all the persons concerned in the said Joynt Stock and that noe person shall be admitted to take his freedome in the said Company untill such person shall give his consent to this agreement by first signeing the same.

5ly That every one of the Managers chosen to manage the said Joynt Stock Trade shall before his being admitted to act give security in the penalty of one Thousand pounds to the wardens of the said Company (for the time being) by his owne Bond faithfully to performe and discharge the trust reposed in him without favour or affection and make due and true.

Accounts of all his proceedings in the management of the said Joynt Stock Trade to bee rendered to the wardens for the time being and their successors and the said Company att the generall meeting every Shrove Tuesday if thereunto required. (The Bonds to bee entered into to the wardens of the Company for the security of the Joynt Stock)

6ly and lastly because it is intended that neither the members of the said Company nor any other persons whatsoever shall have it in their power to send any paveing or other Stone to London but what shall bee sent in the Joynt Stock Trade It is further agreed noe member shall sell any paveing or other Stone to any master of a shipp or vessell or any other person which shall pretend to shipp the same but every such member of whome such Stone shall bee soe bought shall bee obleiged that the party agreeing for the same shall enter into sufficient security to the Managers of the Joynt Stock Trade that such Stone soe to bee shipt nor any part thereof shall bee carryed within Thirty Miles of London upon the penalty that every Member of the said Company offending herein shall for such his offence pay to the managers of the said Joynt

Stock the summe of Ten pounds for the use and benefitt of the said Joynt Stock Trade.

WEE whose names are hereunder written being members of the said Company of Marblers Doe by these presents bynd ourselves and all and every of us Respectively Joyntly and severally in the Summe of Twenty pounds of lawfull money of England that wee and every and either of us will observe performe maintaine support and abide by the above mentioned Articles and oppen the breach of them or any of them wee doe hereby agree consent uphold and maintaine that the offender or offenders shall bee punished according to the severall ffynes in the severall Articles mentioned and expressed for such his or their offence and offences and further such person shall bee put by his Trade and noe member of the Company shall deale with him untill hee shall submitt himselfe to the said Wardens and Company and give sattisfaction for such his offence as afoesaid. For the performance of all which Clauses Articles and Agreements as before mentioned and expressed wee doe by vertue of these presents bynd ourselves our heires Executors Administrators and Assignes and all and every of us prespectively to the wardens of the said Company for the time being and their successors to performe fullfill and keepe the same according to the true intent and meaneing hereof in the penall summe of fifity pounds to bee leavyed uppon our goods and chattles IN TESTIMONY whereof see have hereunto putt our hands the day and years abovesaid the seale of the said Company of Marblers being hereunto first affixed

[The list of signatories follows. Some names are illegible, others very difficult to read; a few more have been recently revealed by using ultra violet light. Probable misreadings include, for example John 'Keann', who is quite likely Keates. Wardens George Dolling and Richard Keate sign first, followed by the managers: Thomas Chapman, James Hall, Joseph Hort senior, Charles Weeks, Alexander Petten, Sam Prestly and Henry Serrell.]

The rank and file were:

George Franklin
Anthony Serrell
James Brown
John Corben
Benjamin ffoott
John Cook
John Vye
William X Cull Sr.
Giles Grove
William Tubb
John X Warren
John X Dowland
John X Pushman
Charles X Vye
John Gill
James X Chinchen
Stephen Dowland
Thomas X Gover
John Phillips
Caleb Weeks
William Sabboth (?)
William X Seward
Roger X Savage (?)
Peter X Hancock
Anthony ?
John Haysome

William ?
Thomas Bland
Joseph X?
Henery Master
Josiah X Hort
John X?
Edward X Barnes
John X Cobb
Thomas Collier
Thomas X Browne
Steven Shepard
John Weekes
William Cole
John Cook
George X Cobb
(column 2)
John Talbot
Walter X Wakely
John X Meader
Robert X Bonfeild
James X Best
Lewis Gover
Peter X Gover
John Sumers
Alex Melmoth
John X Barter

John X Bower sinior
John Harris
William Bower
Josiah X Nineham
Joseph Hort Juner
John Bower Juner
Anthony Serrell Jr.
James Chinchen
John Dolling
Jerrard X Steevens
Thomas Bower
James X Thickes
John Bonfield
Robert Bonfield
Robert Bonfield Jr
George X Harding
John X Thoms
William X Balham
Thomas Bonfild
Georg Weeks
Thomas Wellman
Alexander Bonfield
mas X Eidbury
William Canmell
Robert Burt
Thomas X Cobb
Alexander Steell
Thomas X Hort
Thomothe Hosee
Joseph X Speer
Emanuell X Gover
Robert X Seymour
Edward Benfeld
Elias Benfilld
Thomas Coomes
(column 4)
John X Chinchen
Will Bower
John Devenish
Robert X Benfeild
William X Corben
John X Corben
Edward X Hancocke
John Clark
Thomas Cull
Robert X Bush

Samuell X Tarrey
Peter Melmoth
John Edmonds
Edward Cole
Edward X Bush
[At this point William Culliford (?) writes:] 'The before mentioned persons being in number according to the severall Collumes before amounts unto 142 persons signed the same in the presentes of us
Will. Culliford
Richard Kaines
Henry Saunders Mayor
John Culliford
Nath Smith'
(column 5) There then follow a further 22 who apparently didn't attend that day, and signed later.
James Turner
The mark of Edward Webber Junr
John Bower sen
Lewis Tubb
The mark of Edward Webber sen
Thomas Pushman
John Dolling
The mark of Robert Bower
Thomas Dowland
Robert Turner
Henry Vye
The mark of Abell Bonfield
Francis Steele
John Keann
William X Carter's mark
George Bondfeild
William Melmoth
George Banester
William X Gray
William Cook
The mark of Thomas Webber
The mark of Josiah Hort Jun

The wardens and managers who signed first are surely the men who drove the company. 133 more sign up to the end of the fourth column: these are the '142' mentioned at the end of the fourth column by the 'witnesses' drawn from the ranks of the local gentry. These were: Will Culliford of Encombe, M.P. for Corfe, with his son John, Richard Kaines (St. Mary's, Wareham, has several ledgers of this family, including one commemorating Jane, widow of Richard, Gent., who died in 1754, aged 80), Nath Smith, who appears in the Swanage Register for 1680 as Justice and Henry Saunders, Mayor, not it seems of Corfe, but probably Wareham.

The document is stamped with a seal of the Rose family of Rempstone. William was Rector of Swanage between 1667 and 1690, where he held land that including quarries. His ledger slab, close to the font at Swanage and getting badly worn, bears the same escutcheon 'on a pale three roses slipped proper'. Hutchins III comments: 'to one of them (the 1698 document) is attached a seal purporting to be the seal of the Company'. I guess it was simply the Rector's, used to give the document *gravitas*.[17] As with the 1651 Articles, the document belongs to the Company of Marblers, who deposited it for safe keeping in the Dorset History Centre. Before the Second World War the documents were held by one of the wardens, but in the postwar years they were kept at Lloyd's Bank, Swanage. Archivist Margaret Holmes' advice was that conditions were less than ideal, hence the remove.

Numerical comparison of the number of men in the industry as stated in 1651 and 1697/8 documents are difficult, but it is clear that numbers working in the quarries had increased a lot over 47 years and that this was a problem. However it perhaps comes as a surprise to learn of the 'deadnesse of the trade' from the Joint Stock Agreement only 30 years or so after London's devastating fire. However well the agreement may or may not have operated, the Londoners were not satisfied, for in 1702 they ordered the clerk to write to various persons, including 'the marblers of Swanage' and to two men at Portland with regard to the badness and undersize of the stone sent to them. One wonders what was meant by 'badness'. It was probably to do with both quality of the stone itself and the way it was worked. On examination, virtually all old handmade paving has the bottom of the joint roughly pitched off, which leaves a reduced width needing to be worked properly. It means a saving in time but is arguably skimping the job. Certainly with small pavings it would mean they tended to rock. It is the sort of thing that would have caused contention.

None of the Joint Stock books survive, nor hardly any other marblers' records from the 18th century. Judging from the monuments, the trade then was generally buoyant, but the cooperative effort did not last. We are left guessing just how long the Joint Stock Company persisted. Perhaps it is safe to say that for a few years at least at the turn of the 18th century virtually all Purbeck stone dug and supplied to London went through the company. However, its members were still free to trade outside London. The building accounts for Antony, a substantial house near Plymouth built between 1710-21, provide an interesting example of a known Purbeck supplier working independently of the agreement. In September 1713 Richard Harden supplied 700 feet of Purbeck Stone (surely paving, with a weight of about fourteen tons). Two months later John Harden was paid for another two cargoes. This could be the same John as the one who joined the Joint Stock Company in 1697 and was in trouble with the court on the Manor of Worth for digging in 'Calles Common' (Gallows Gore).[18] By 1726 the pattern of trade was still that of small individual quarries, but they were supplying competing merchants, not a single organisation. There is no further evidence of a cooperative effort again until the 1920s.

RIGHTS AND 'ROYALTIES'

Both sets of articles shed little light on what relationship the marblers had with the various estates they worked on. In 1725 John Bankes wrote that his tenants had the right to dig stone, paying him a percentage.[19] Perhaps this was the custom right across Purbeck, as it seems it was for the tenants in Portland. But what if someone who gained a tenancy on good quarry land was not a freeman of the Company? Did the benefits of membership invariably mean that such a man, wanting to quarry, invariably joined? Some light on how things were structured a bit later is provided by details of the sale of Worth in 1771. Following a list of tenants a footnote reads: 'There is on this manor divers quarries now working of different sorts of stone which the lords of the manor are entitled to and are excepted out of the tenants leases. The present annual value of the quarries is uncertain but they are capable of great improvement. There is payable out of this Manor a Cheff Rent of £4-2-0 per annum to John Banks Esquire as Lord of the Manor of Corfe Castle on the said Isle of Purbeck.'[20]

So far as his own freehold was concerned, John Bankes also in his 1725 document claimed ownership of one load in every four of roof tile, which was surely a heavy burden on the quarry men. But it got worse. Under the terms of licences imposed in the early 19th century the estate got half! This prompts the suspicion that the estate was not insisting on royalties for every category of stone. This suspicion is reinforced by many 18th century royalty returns that mention nothing but paving. However, that interpretation may be wrong by 1809, when Henry Bankes' seven year agreement for West Hedbury with Joseph Chinchen included every category of output:

Front and scapled backing, 6d per ton
Rough backing or block stone, 4d per ton
Ashlar and step stone, worked to my particular order, 2s per 100 ft
Paving and Channel, 1s per 100 foot
Tomb stones or grave stones, 1s each [what is the difference? Is he making a distinction here between upright stones and ledgers?]
For every 30 peck of troughs and sinks, 1s
Rollers, 1s per ton
Legs and cap, 1s per set of 9

Detailed accounts of vessels, wagons, purchasers, etc. had to be kept and the quarry worked by a 'sufficient number of competent workmen and labourers'.

Poor old Joe. The squire had him on the rack.

An insight into royalty implementation from the owner's point of view appears as comments in a comprehensive list of Bankes Estate quarries of 1825:

'Some of the Proprietors of the Inland Stone Quarries have increased their Ground Rents and both Taylor and Cull are of opinion that the quarriers cannot afford to pay more for the quarries than the old reserved Rent for altho' the Price of Stone is higher than it was 2 or 3 years ago yet it is not so high as it was when the Rents were fixed. Mr. Cull's statement that the Rents might be increased 1/4th was made on the principle that Stone is now selling at 34/s per Hundred and two years since for only 18/s but it appears that at that time the ground Rent was paid by the Parish and that many of the quarriers received parochial relief. Two Quarrymen belonging to the Calcraft quarries, the one an Inland and the other a Cliff quarrier confirmed the above statement. The selling prices to the merchants for the Stone taken out of the Cliff quarries are the same now as they have been for the last 30 years with the exception of 2 or 3 years when the prices were lower.'

One of the first references to the payment of royalties, as described by Bankes, and which is the system that has continued to operate, appears in the will of Edward Cole of Langton, Marbler, made in 1714. He was old enough to have grandchildren, and was about to marry. He makes his son, also William, executor and continues: 'also the quarr after which he hath now broke up paying nothing for the ground of it to her [his wife to be], except the Lord.' 'Ground of stone' becomes the standard term in later estate records. It was a percentage of the finished value and not always the same.

In 19th century documents that relate to the row over the Swanage manor of Eightholds it is stated to be 1/30th of the value of the stone 'when wrought'. But it was not firmly fixed as such. For example, in the competitive struggle for the Ramsgate work, rivals would reduce the price of the finished stone whilst retaining the same level of payment to the landowners.[21] Presumably this royalty system was how things operated many years before. Leland recorded that Alice de Brewer, who held Worth, including Downshay, gave 'all the marble to the church (Salisbury) for ten years.' She surely had the freedom to sell it on some royalty or rental basis if she had chosen to do so rather than make it a gift.

Recent transcriptions of Langton Wallis Court presentments provide clues as to how things were organised in the late medieval period.[22] In the case of Marble, they were paying the Lord of the Manor (the absent Wallises) rent per year, but in the case of roof tile, so much per tile. In October, 1479 'John Russe and Stephen Atkyn were granted rights to quarry marble in the north part of the Prior of Wilkeswood's lands for a year from Christmas for themselves and six other men for a rent of 40s.' 40s. was a large sum, the cost of a complete Westminster Abbey pillar, which an earlier John Russe, previously mentioned, was helping to supply in 1393. The dates would fit with Russe junior and Atykyn completing the last westernmost pillars of the nave.

About the same time men were paying the court for the freedom to dig roof tile. In 1491 Henry Smyth and John Spycer both dug 1000 tiles on each of their tenancies, paying 6d, whilst others, digging on the lord's land, paid double that rate. The Haywarden, Henry Vypart, was collecting the money for the court (much as woodman Robert Thorn continued to do on the same estate 400 years later!).

In 1481 Atkyn is presented again, this time to 'pay for an acre of land next to the road which he had taken'. He failed to pay and was fined 6s. 8d. About sixty years before 'John Lychett has sold one hykerell on the south side of Wylcheswode to Edward Kene, Thomas Edmunds and John Rigby for 13s. 6d. Also 3s. 4d. of land at the end of the stone pavement (a working area?) with two men for one month to Thomas Edmunds and 20d of land at the same place to John Canon with one man for one month'. Entries such as this are puzzling and suggest sub-letting. If fully understood, these Court Presentment records could offer great insight into the workings of medieval quarries.

Of these surnames, two or more generations of William Canons were supplying Exeter Cathedral with finished marble columns.[23] In 1385 Thomas carved the figures of kings still to be seen in Westminster Hall.[24] In 1424 a John Canon was appointed master carpenter to Queen Katherine for all her Essex manors. Is this the same John, switching to another craft? The Edmunds family continued to figure in the trade until recently.

In the 18th century, on both the Calcraft and Bankes estates, the relationship between landlord and quarries was straightforward, that is, landlord was in receipt of royalties (sometimes confusingly called rents), paid by the quarryman according to the stone taken out. This was surely typical of Purbeck in general, but there were a few exceptions. One example from a little earlier, is Onesiphorus Bond who in 1664 sold 19 acres of his Carrants Court Farm to Thomas Chapman of Swanwich, marbler, who later acquired the remaining portion. This manor included Court Cowlease, which lies southwest of the Priests' Road – High Street junction, and which has been much quarried. Thomas therefore became the freeholder of stone-bearing land and it must be a safe assumption that he operated quarries there on his own freehold. He was of considerable substance, leaving legacies to several relatives, including his son, also Thomas. One of the beneficiaries built the Manor House, latterly the Victoria Hotel. Thomas Chapman Senior signed the 1651 articles, Thomas Junior both the objection to the Londoners' stone search (1687) and the Joint Stock Agreement of 1697/8. Both Chapmans have ledger slabs in Swanage church. Joan, wife of Thomas, who died in 1727, has a ledger slab of Grub, probably from their own quarries.

Returning to the more recent past, Claridge, in 1793, gives an account of the 'rents': There is a ground rent, paid to the owners of the land, in nearly the following proportions:

6d per ton for front walling
3d for scalp back
2d for scalp rough
2s per 100 feet of ashlar
2s per 100 feet of steps
1s per 100 feet of pavements
1s for a set of rick staddles.

It is interesting to compare the number of men employed [400 dig and work, 50,000 tons shipped annually] with the Norden pipe clay industry, where about 100 men dig 11,000 tons annually, and on Portland, in the King's quarries, 30-40,000 tons.'[25]

What complicates matters in 18th and 19th centuries is that is that whilst the quarrymen paid royalties on the stone dug, hence recognising the landlord's ownership, they willed and sometimes sold the actual quarries. Useful evidence for this is the 1814 will of Henry Bower which well as his quarrying tackle, tools and implements includes a gift to his son Isaac of 'all my right title estate and interest of in and to All those my two stone quarries now or late in my occupation respectively called or known by the names of Seacombe and Idbury situate at Cliff within the parish of Langton Matravers'[26].

What the quarrymen were buying and selling was termed 'labour'. If, for example, a man invested a lot of non-productive work into sinking a shaft (on average about six weeks of unpaid work), building a loading banker and sheds, setting up crab stones etc., then for some reason wanted to leave, he

TRADE ORGANISATIONS / 243

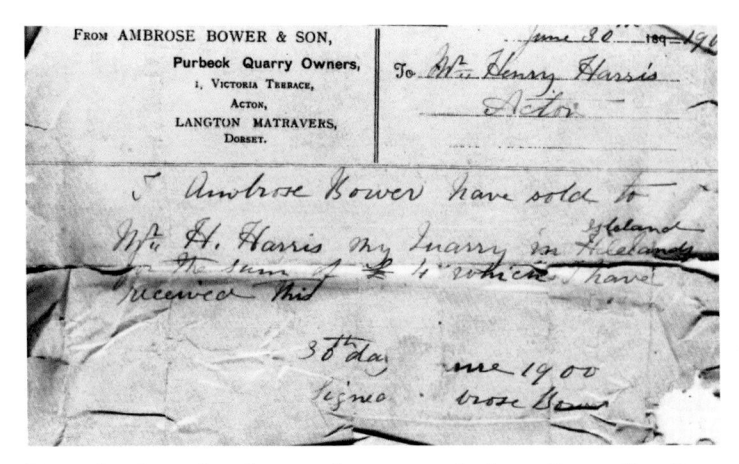

Example of transfer of quarry from 1900: Ambrose Bower (Junr)'s quarry in the field which lies south of the hamlet of Acton. Ambrose was obviously uncertain as to whether the 'H' applied or not.

would agree a value for this 'labour' with any other freeman wishing to take over. Of course the labour value would vary, and paradoxically in a typical inland underground quarr, the value would drop the more work was done. For as the head (the working face) of stone underground retreated away from the shaft, so the hauling distance increased until finally it became so great that the quarr would be uneconomic. Such an exhausted quarr had no value; no man would want it. In such circumstances, of course, it made sense to sink again, but this brought with it the difficult question of what constituted a quarry. Where did it end? Even recently, many Purbeck quarrymen would claim that they, as freemen of the Company of Marblers, had the right, granted by Royal Charter, to dig where they wanted. Evidence of men seeking permission to open new quarries exists, for example in an extract from a letter to Squire Calcraft from Thomas Bartlet, Wareham 5 July, 1786:

> 'Dear Sir, Titus Chinchen has applied for leave to open a quarry in the clift on the east part of Winsprit quarry where he thinks and hopes he shall be able to make and vend a large quantity of stone, Pray may he have liberty or not? I am, Dear Sir, Your most obedient servant, Thomas Bartlet.'[27]

It seems that over time a general custom of the island emerged that men sought permission to sink quarries, and having gained it, went on enjoying possession without time limit, which accords with Article 1, the 'year and a day rule'. What this first article does not inform us of is how quarries were sunk in the first place. The fact is relevant that the Articles were drawn up during the Commonwealth, when certainly the Bankes Estate and possibly others were subject to sequestration. Were royalties or rents paid in this period, and if so, to whom? I heard a quarryman tell his son that he should join the Company of Marblers because then he would be able to dig anywhere on the Bankes Estate! Vic Bower made a remark typical of the quarrymen: 'there aint a field up southward the old hands 'aint been in', implying the right to dig anywhere that was once enjoyed. The idea of possessing quarry 'rights' became very strong. It is telling to see in the Dorset Quarry Co. papers that, in their attempt to gain control over the cliff quarries in the 1920s, they agreed rents with several men –

notably Reg Bower, Jack Edmunds and the Lander brothers, all at Hedbury – 'sitting' on their dormant quarries, rather than, or as well as, with the landlords.[28] However, to add to the confusion, some landowners were imposing time limited licences from as early as 1719.

An extract from the diary of the Reverend Oldfeld Bartlett, Rector of Swanage, in 1824 illustrates one aspect of the relationship between landlords and quarries. The men referred to were working in the Glebe, and the Rector was in the habit of giving them a Christmas treat: 'January 2, in the evening, entertaining quarriers who pay me stone dues, with beef and mutton pies and strong beer. Number of quarriers 13, of singers 25.' The following year: '14 Feb. in the evening, entertaining the singers and quarriers 32 in number with beef and plum pudding.'[29] Those were the days!

The Bankes Estate papers reveal in 1726 that some men held quarries on the estate as well as premises on the shore in Swanage, where they stocked other men's stone as well as their own. The distinction between merchants on the one hand and quarrymen on the other was blurred. Men doing both, occupying quarrs in Eastington and Langton Wallis as well as a Swanage banker were: Alex Corbin, Giles Speare and William Chinchen. Other merchants buying from other quarrs on those manors and possibly occupying quarrs on other manors as well were: Thomas Pushman, James Keate, William Melmouth, Sam Serrel, Henry Vye, John Marsh, Peter Corben, James Benfield and Mr. Chapman. But there may have been other merchants who do not appear in the Bankes Estate papers because they were not involved with it. Some, perhaps all of these competing merchants, if old enough, had been parties to the Joint Stock Agreement of 1698; the certain ones being Alex Corben, Will Melmouth, Sam Serrel, Henry Vye and Mr Chapman, who was one of the managers. Another almost certainly is Thomas Pushman. 'Mr.' denotes Thomas Chapman's superior status.

Until recently I would have assumed that all those men were involved only in production, not fixing, but in James Keat's case at least this is wrong. In 1758 he supplied paving for the kitchen floor at Turner's Puddle farm, and lodged there with his son, also James, for three weeks or so. [30, 31] The Warne diaries also tell us of James and his son James ' ...at Bindon cutting out post stones for cow pens.' This suggests that they had supplied the posts 'blank' and was cutting out the rail holes to the farmer's specification on site.[32]

MERCHANTS AND TRUCK

In 1749 what is almost certainly a comprehensive list of merchants appears in Mr. Preston's report on the set up in Purbeck *apropos* the building of Ramsgate Harbour. 'All the men who have served their time in the island become free, and have the right to work the quarries. These workmen are dependant from time to time for supplies on others, which are called Merchants, and must also be Freemen. The names of the Merchants are Tim Chinchin, Howard Serrel, William Chinchin, Henry Vye, John Pushman, Francis Warren, John Melmer, William Melmer, John Cole, John Collins, John

Harding, John Marsh, Math. Benvil, and these are the persons most proper to treat or make contract with.'

Minutes of meetings of the Ramsgate Harbour Trustees reveal how competitive these merchants were between themselves, not forgetting that they were also up against would-be suppliers of other sorts of stone from the Isle of Wight, Portland, Folkestone and Maidstone.[33] Merchants continually undercut one another's prices. Two offers of ashlar at 9 shillings per ton could not compete with John Chinchen's 6 shillings 'provided the gauge of the ashlar should be from 11 inches to 2 ft and their contract should only oblige them to deliver stone sufficient for 100 running feet of peer'.

Chinchen's point about the gauge is important. The more relaxed the specification so the cheaper the price. One wonders if the trustees were always comparing like with like. Unless there was hidden collusion these men were in sharp competition – their fathers' Joint Stock Company co-operation a thing of the past.

Mr. Calcraft's agent, in a 1770 rent book's marginal note, tells of a measure of affluence enjoyed by the quarriers, but predicts a coming downturn. 'The right of this heath (Newton, near Ower) for cutting turves for firing has been formerly worth 4d per year to supply the people of Lankton and Swanage but for about 15 years past they have a good trade in the stone business and the vessels in return bring a plenty of coals from Newcastle, whom the merchants have obliged them to take in exchange for their stone. Though it is now lighkly that the stone trade will fail, which if so the heath will again be worth its rent.'[34]

Hutchins also describes these improved conditions in Swanage in 1794:

'There is an appearance of affluence, especially on Sundays, in the inhabitants of this town. They earn great wages, and lay out a greater proportion of their pay in the articles of food and clothing than is practised in the neighbouring places; yet the people are improvident, and spend all they get, and when any accident happens in the quarries to the father of a family, or he falls ill, causing only a short suspension of work, they instantly apply to the parish for relief. The rates have increased surprisingly of late years. The only disadvantages at Swanwich to counterbalance very material advantages are, scarcity of fuel for the poor, and the practice, already mentioned in the description of Langton, of masters not paying their workmen in ready money, but compelling them to take goods from their shops. Most of the poor women and children are employed in spinning flax for the Kingston manufactory, and are assiduous and industrious.'[35]

Hutchins' 1796, describing Langton, says:

'The inhabitants are mostly quarriers, the women and children knit stockings or spin. Fuel for the poor is scarce in this parish and a practice almost universally prevails here of keeping a running account with the work-people instead of paying them wages in money. Most of the masters have shops on purpose and compel the people to buy every article of them; in fact it is paying them in truck though they find means to evade the law. Cottages for the poor are very much wanted, many quarriers and labourers cannot obtain habitation […] and are compelled to take refuge in the parish poor houses, where it often happens that several families are crowded together; the industrious and decent forced to associate with the idle and dissolute…'.

One of my grandfather's earliest memories was of being carried on his father's shoulders down to Randell's store and being sat up on the counter whilst Sally Bradford dealt out flour for the quarrymen from a tub. In those pre-railway days that and other commodities, were brought in to Swanage from Poole on the market boat. Brannon was a critic of this system:[36]

'The merchants take the stone of the quarriers but they must receive the return in goods of the quality and price the merchant choses, and such may not be always what could be described whilst the apparent kindness of credit in winter and in dull times reduced the former to a condition of absolute bondage.'

Pub landlords were often also quarrymen. Such was the steady demand for common paving, a quarryman might well carry a piece to a pub where the landlord added it to his stock in exchange for beer or 'baccy'. W. M. Hardy's 'ponderous pence' account of this sort of exchange is somewhat overdrawn.[37] Little girls lugging heavy stones to exchange for a stamp was hardly the norm, but strong men carrying stones on their backs to exchange for beer, bread etc. were to be seen.

Exceptionally, the culture of barter went on into the age of lorries. When the weather allowed, Billy Winspit and Buff would break off quarry work and put out a few lobster pots from Winspit. Sometimes they sold their catch to 'Hantney' Haysom, who would walk along the cliff to collect them to take to his shop at Herston Cross. Sometimes he paid in goods, particularly stuff not selling well, rather than cash. From off Seacombe, Buff saw the familiar figure approaching along the cliff top. He stood at the oars and yelled 'No socks tonight'. It became a catchphrase.[38]

BANKERS

Most stone from the inland quarries was conveyed by wagons to dumps on the shore prior to shipping. To aid handling, without the benefit of cranage, these dumps consisted of platforms raised to cart bed height, called 'bankers'. Underground quarry sites usually had a similar loading banker, where the finished stone was stacked ready for transfer to the wagon. Even heavy stones could be walked or 'trotted' from banker to wagon, wagon to banker, thereby avoiding the difficulty of getting them up off the ground. As described in Hutchins III:

'Swanwich was originally a landwash, where all the stone made from the quarries in the Isle of Purbeck is now landed; the landing-places are called bankers, being banks built by a dead stone wall about three feet high, or thereabouts, in order to receive stone from carts and convey it more conveniently into boats, in order to be carried to stone vessels; banks were raised round the bay. About sixty years before the time of the account being given by two persons, of the names of James and Robert Scates, quarriers, the stone was conveyed from the quarries to the bankers on men's backs. No acknowledgements were paid before these banks were raised, from which time acknowledgements of 2d. a hundred were received by the different builders or proprietors of them; and if the stones were carried immediately to the boats, the proprietors claimed the privilege of conveying them in carts kept for that purpose, and their accustomed demand was 1s. a hundred, and then no acknowledgement was paid for lodging the stone on the banker.'[39]

TRADE ORGANISATIONS / 245

The continuator of Hutchins has added:

'The land lying on the bay (at least on the south and south-west) is supposed originally to have belonged to Sir William Phippard as waste ground of his manor of Swanwich; shortly after Mr. Chapman's purchase in 1721 he instituted a suit for the recovery of the several bankers erected on the shore or wastes of this manor, but, in consequence of the length of adverse possession in the then proprietors, the suit was discontinued.'

This account reveals the bankers to have been well-established by 1721. The earliest specific reference to the stocking of stone on the shore comes in the inventories of William Melmoth of Sandwich, who died in 1689 and John Melmoth of Herston, who died in 1685.[40.] Both men agreed the Articles of 1651 and would appear to have enjoyed considerable material status. Both, together with other Melmoth inventories from the same period are very informative. John's includes 'stone on the North Banker' and on the 'South Banker', as well as a stock of stone at his quarry. This would appear to be the earliest known reference to the bankers. William's includes stone 'at the strand', while Phineas Melmoth's (1686) stock is 'by the waters side'.[41.] These inventories show that some bankers were clearly in existence by this time, but that it is possible that men like William were managing without them. I would read stone 'by the waters side' to also mean Swanage bay, but in the case of Alexander Melmouth's inventory it could mean Hawcombe.[42.]

These inventories are of such importance, that William's is quoted in full below:

'Inventory of the goods and chattells of William Melmoth late of Samwich in the Isle of Purbeck and County of Dorset, Marbler, who departed this life 1689.

In the hall
2 table boards and a form
6 chairs and other lumber   2 – 0 – 0
the rack and meat upon it   1 – 0 – 0
9 powder dishes   1 – 0 – 0
4 brass pots, a warming pan, 3 skittolls, a small flagon, 3 small
tinnon candlesticks and a chamber pot   2 –10 –0

In the Buttery
4 Barrels 2 bottells and salt
A powdering tub and other trifles   1 – 0 – 0

In the other room.
A small furnice and coal   1 – 0 – 0

In the hall chamber.
A feather bed and beds
And all furnishings belonging to it   5 – 0 – 0
2 Chests 2 boxes a trunk and a ..   1 – 0 – 0

In the Buttery chamber
2 feather beds and all the furnishings belonging to them 8 – 0 – 0
A chest a dresser and a chair   10 – 0

At the quarr
Plain paving   12 – 0 – 0
For rough paving   1 – 5 – 0
For ashlar at quarr   6 – 0 – 0
For 10 reasonable tomb stones   5 – 0 – 0
For round gutter and stepp   2 – 0 – 0
For quarr tooles   2 – 0 – 0
For 4 planks and 3 wheelbarrows and
Timber of the quarr house   1 – 0 – 0
For the quarr and labour   5 – 0 – 0

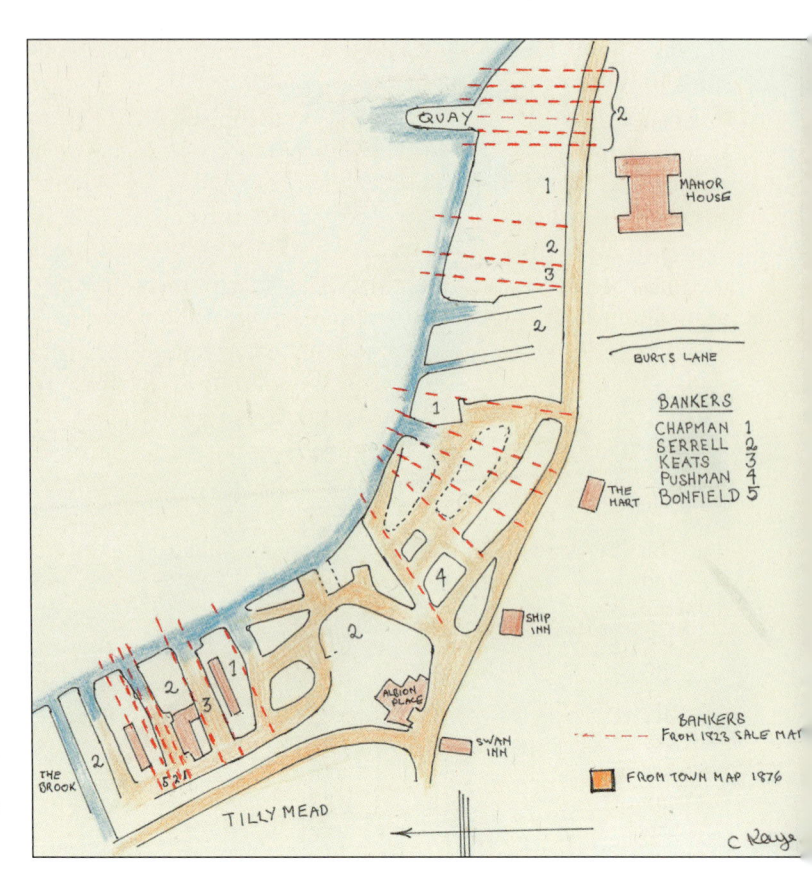

Plan of Swanage bankers in 1763, drawn by Chris Kaye.

At the strand
4000 ft plain paving   24 – 0 – 0
100 ft of stepp   2 – 0 – 0
50 ft of gutter   1 – 0 – 0
tomb stones and other small stones   15 – 0 – 0
100 grinding stones   6 – 0

for the house by the millpond   2 – 0 – 0
for the house called the George   15 – 0 – 0
for the house he lived and died in   6 – 0 – 0
in moneys debts and disperate debts   80 – 0 – 0
his wearing apparell   5 – 0 – 0
                                                           208 – 1 – 0

Witnessed: Nicholas Coffin (3), Joseph Hort, Anthony Serrell'[43.]

In 1763 controversy over the ownership of land and houses adjoining the foreshore in Swanage resulted in a memorandum recorded by Howard Serrell. What emerges is a complicated pattern of ownership, surely indicative of antiquity:

'Following is a Memorandum of what ground Bankers or Boat Hall is my property and right on the shore at Swanage. This 13 day of dec 1763 Howard Serrell.

First one boat hall bounded by Mr. Chapmans Boat hall or banker on the east and Mr Keats boathall on the west.

2 One Banker opposite the apothecary's shop and lane from Mr Hardens and Hurlorks houses by various house bounded on the east by Mr Keats Banker and on the west side by Mr Chapmans formerly Verges both the above were the property of my late Grandfather John Howard.

3 One triangle piece of ground where I use to keep hauling* stones laying between the two roads opposite Mr Chapmans Great house on the south and Mr Vyes or Pushmans Boat hall or

246 / PURBECK STONE

banker was the property of my father Samuel Serrell. [*This could be healing stones (tile)]

4 One banker on the north side of the Swan now Bests' formerly Brines and bounded on the north by the banker belonging to Mr Chapman and on the south by a banker belonging to Mr Pushman, I bought of John Weeks grandson of Charles Weeks.

5 One large banker farther north and was given to my father Samuel Serrell by his relation Mrs Verge about the year 17--on the north by half banker the property of Mr Chapman and on the south by y banker belonging to Mr Keats y ground on west side against y meadow

6 Half banker whole about 22 foot from the north side bounding William Benfields Banker formerly Clerk Dollings, south side or half Mr Chapmans as mentioned above the half my father purchased of William Cull of Langton.

7 One banker I bought of George Pushman and his mother Elizabeth Pushman the ground on the west side to the meadow bounded on the north by the banker belonging to Mr Pushman formerly Vyes and on the south by the banker now Benfields formerly Clerk John Dollings.

Further particulars might be found in some papers and church books delivered to the late William Templeman attorney at law on account of an action at law by Chapman against Pushman and others and against Mr Cochrane as Church warden to recover the houses of Brine and Smedmore held under the church of Swanage

Which books and papers are now in the Hands of his son Mr William Templeman attorney at Dorchester.

Whence there about 6 weeks past witness

Howard Serrell'[44.]

Samuel Serrell, 'Gent' of Coombe Keynes (born 1666), bought lands in Langton, Worth and Beulige (Benlease) in 1721. Acton Thornback ledgers, recently moved, mark his and his wife's graves in Coombe Keynes church. His son was also Samuel, and his grandson became the Rev. Samuel Serrell and married Lord Digby's sister Harriet. However, whether either Samuels I or II were the Samuel of this memorandum and/or of the Joint Stock Company, is open to doubt; what is clear is that earlier Serrells, Henry and Anthony, appear as Purbeck Marblers in the articles of 1651.

Men with boat hauls (slipways) and bankers stockpiled and arranged the loading of stones produced by others. Vagaries of weather, if nothing else, would have dictated timing of shipments in the uncertain security of Swanage Bay. Those men with premises on the shore were best placed to become merchants. In the recent past some quarrymen, particularly with reference to the truck system, would talk critically of the old merchants, as if poor, hardworking quarrymen were being exploited by these dealers. Perhaps there was a measure of truth in this, but the distinction between the two was always blurred, and it seems to me that, with one or two exceptions, few of the merchants made much money. Allowing for the considerable scale of the trade for a lengthy period, Swanage, at least in terms of well-to-do houses, has little to show for it. The exceptions include John Chapman's house, later the Royal Victoria Hotel and Anthony Serrell's 'New House' (latterly 'Magnolia'). There were times of severe hardship, others of modest affluence, at least in terms of quarriers' income compared with other artisans. Good evidence is provided by the splendid census of Corfe commissioned by philanthropic Mr. William Morton Pitt, MP, in 1796. It is a record, not only of all the inhabitants, but also their weekly incomes, excepting those with independent means. The following list includes all the 'quarriers', as the compiler calls them plus some ancillary occupations:-

'James Keats Quarrier Sons John and Joseph (aged 18 and 11, both quarriers)
Weekly pay   15/s, 10/s, 6/s.
John Howard, Lime burner   7/s
Charles Keats, Quarrier   15/s
William Gould, Mason   9/s
David Hibbs, Mason   7/s
James Gould, Mason   9/s. Lodger Joshua Benfield, Mason
Richard Keats, Quarrier   15/s Son Thomas aged 10, 4s.
James Keats (lodging with W Davey) quarrier 15/s [45.]
William Corben, Quarrier   15/s
Samuel Keats, Quarrier   15/s
James Edmunds, Mason   7/s
James Edmunds, Mason   9/s
Oliver Vye [46.]. Quarrier,   13/s [Joseph aged 13 gets 4/s]
John Hibbs, Mason   9/s
John Roe (shoe maker) Lodger George Roe, Mason   9/s
William Kitcat, Mason   9/s
Samuel Welsh, Thomas Roe both lodgers and masons labourer 3/s and 2/6.
Edward Webber, Quarrier   4/s
James Smith, Stonecutter   15/s
James Beere, Mason   9/s
Thomas Bushrod, Mason
William Cutler, Mason
John Edmunds, Quarrier   15/s
Total
Quarriers Masons Stonecutter Limeburner   Labourers
9+ boys   10   1   1   64 (including agricultural)

Builder as an occupation does not appear. 'Mason' must be the equivalent, but possibly also included men shaping stone for the quarriers. All are less well paid than most quarriers, with the exception of James Smith, the one and only stonecutter. Was he doing fine work such as window mouldings, etc. and perhaps letter cutting, giving him a similar status to the quarriers? The category of 'Mason' may also have included men working for the better paid quarriers. It is significant to note young Thomas Keates at a mere 10 years old earning more than mason's labourers.[47.] The least well-off quarrier, Edward Webber, was probably old or infirm.

The 1851 Census for Langton gives interesting parallel information. There were no less than 103 quarriers with 28 stone masons, plus 8 away. This time the category of builder does appear, but there is only one. As with Corfe, 50 years or so earlier, there was just one lime burner, but another new occupation is given, 3 bricklayers. The writing was on the wall! Of the all-important blacksmiths, there were 6.

APPRENTICES

During more affluent times the Marblers relaxed the restrictions on the taking of apprentices. However, later in the 19th century, presumably during recessionary conditions, the restriction of apprenticeships to the sons of freemen was again rigorously applied.

The arrival in Purbeck of the Manwells and their entry into the stone trade, was recorded by George, brother of the better known 'Swanage Philosopher' Thomas. Their carpenter father had come from Winterborne Stickland but died in 1723, leaving them as infants. Within a few years both were apprenticed to quarrymen, one aged 8, the other 11.[48] Writing to his son in 1814, Joseph's grandson, described what he knew of their family and included, 'After London was burnt some years and the city began to be rebuilt and flourishing, there was an uncommon call for Purbeck stone, and paving was sold at so high a price as 30 s per hundred. This, of course, attracted the notice of the neighbourhood round, and numbers of boys from different parishes at the distance of twenty miles, were apprenticed here to the stone trade and premiums given. This increased the inhabitants greatly.' Premiums were an added incentive to take on an apprentice boy. Thomas's exceptional gifts were recognised by the Revd. Bell.[49]

For most stone workers, perhaps all, an apprenticeship was the only way into the trade. For some it was not a matter of choice. Poor boys were put off the Poor Rate by the overseers by placing them in apprenticeships as soon as they could. Records survive for Corfe.[50] Perhaps Cornelius and George Webber were brothers. Fate separated them in 1783 when George, only eleven years old, was placed with marbler Joseph Collins of Swanage, whilst the other was destined for the fogs and icebergs of the Newfoundland trade, in the employ of Mr Tory. Perhaps Joseph Vye knew his fate better, for his master bore the same name:

> 'This indenture made the TWENTY FORTH day of JUNE in the TWENTY SIXTH year of the reign of our Sovereign Lord GEORGE THE SECOND by the Grace of God, of Great Britain, France and Ireland, King, Defender of the Faith and soforth; and in the year of our Lord One thousand seven hundered and FIFTY TWO Witnesseth that ROBERT ROE and Thomas FISH Church-Wardens of the Parish of CORFE CASTLE in the COUNTY OF DORSET and JOHN KENT and RICHARD PHIPPARD overseers of the poor of the said Parish by and with the consent of his majestys justices of the peace of the said COUNTY whose names are hereto subscribed, were put and placed, and by these presents do put and place JOSEPH VYE a poor child of the said Parish, Apprentice to JOHN VYE OF THE PARISH OF CORFE C. AFORESAID with him to dwell and serve from the day of the date of these presents, until the said apprentice shall accomplish HIS full age of TWENTY ONE YEARS During all which Term the said Apprentice HIS said MASTER faithfully shall serve in all lawful benefits, according to HIS power, wit and ability; and honestly, orderly and obediently in all things demean and behave HIM self towards HIS said MASTER and all HIS during the said term And the said JOHN VYE for HIM self HIS executors and administrators doth covenant and grant to deal with the said Church-Wardens and Overseers, and every of them, their and every of the executors and administrators and their and every of their successors, for the Time being by these Presents That the said JOSEPH VYE the said apprentice in THE ART OF A MARBLER WHICH HE NOW [?] SHALL TEACH AND INSTRUCT and shall and will during all the Term aforesaid, first provide and allow, unto the said Apprentice, meet, competent and sufficient Meat, Drink and Apparel, Lodging, Washing and all other things necessary and fit for an apprentice. And also shall and will so provide for the said apprentice, that he be not any way a charge to the said Parish, or Parishoners of the same, but of and free of charge shall as well have the said Parish and Parishoners harmless and indemnified during the said Term. And at the end of the said Term shall and will make, provide, allow and deliver unto the said apprentice double Apparel of all sorts, good and new (that is to say) a good new suit for the Holy-days and another for the working days. In witness whereof, the Parties aforesaid to these present Indentures interchangeably have put their hands and seals the day and year above written.
>
> Sealed and delivered in the Presence of
> THOMAS HOUNSELL
> THOMAS FISH
> THE MARK OF JOHN + VYE
> We whose names are subscribed, Justices of the peace
> COUNTY aforesaid
> Do consent to the putting forth of the aforesaid JOSEPH VYE apprentice according to the intent
> And meaning of the above Indenture.
> W THORNHILL
> SYDn WILLIAMS'

Despite the evidence of the Corfe census, which shows that at least some quarry boys were being paid, the indenture makes no mention of wages. It seems young John and his fellows went out into the world with nothing but the skills they had learned and two fresh suits of clothes. James Corben describes an almost unbelievably harsh experience which may not have been unusual.[51] I can attest that working for one's father can be difficult, and Harry 'Ton' Chinchen remarked to me: 'My father was a crabby man', with all that that implied. Thomas Bonfield mentioned how, as a youth working alone, he had got a loaded cart jammed in an awkward, tight place, and asked his father for a hand. The response was: 'You got it in there, you get it out'. Behind this culture of treating the young hard lay the stark reality that life was harsh, and one had better learn that lesson early on.

Thomas Collins told how 'Shilling' Norman got his nickname. His family worked the quarr south of and close to Belle Vue farm house, and the relationship between them, possibly father and son or, at any rate, Senior and Junior, was bad. In anger Senior hit the boy. He lay still and quiet in the dark. Alarmed Senior said 'Speak boy'. Silence. 'Speak boy!' Silence. 'Speak boy, I'll gi' thee a shilling.'

Coming of age with its freedom from an often tyrannical master must have meant a lot. Farrer describes free boys being allowed to kiss any women of their fancy as they gained their freedom, many of them parading with a band through the streets of Swanage and Corfe. It is said the overly-rough ringing by the boys of Langton church bells cracked two of them.[52]

In the recent past some men, during or after their apprenticeship, fashioned what were often elaborate pieces for their own amusement. Most popularly these took the form of a clock case; some designed to take a fob watch, so

'Apprentice piece' made by Albert or Arthur Harding, early 20th century. A clock case made of 'soapy' inland Freestone, probably from the Castle View region. It was designed to take a fob watch.

providing a safe visible place when it wasn't being worn. Perhaps there may once have been a formal requirement for some sort of apprentice piece. Articles such as the clock cases were made to show evidence of newly acquired skills, a usefulness combined with ornament, a reminder on the mantelpiece that though the day to day reality may be the hard graft of churning out relatively plain work, one could also manage the fiddly stuff. Another demanding variant was to work a length of chain with the links free from one another, the stone ending up longer than when started! The Portland Museum has such a piece made by a John Bower.

Whatever the rights and wrongs of the apprenticeship system, it had the benefit of being simple and of no cost to the tax or rate payer. Judging by the example of Kingston church, who is to say that the achievements of current college trained craftsmen are superior to those of their predecessors who learned on the job? My apprenticeship experience was one day per week at college, the rest at work. I cannot claim to be more proficient than my father, who had no college experience at all, or indeed grandfather, who left school at twelve or so. Nor indeed great-grandfather John who, if Swanage church is anything to go by, knew what was what. His resolution of the internal arch moulding, as they take two or three courses to emerge, is elegant. Having said all that, there may be some benefit in a 'taught' environment. I do not know when the Purbeck men first experienced it, but Hubert Harding may have been one of the earliest. He won successive prizes in 1920-22 at Weymouth Engineering and Technical School in the evening class. He had to work as well! In each case the award was a copy of G. R. Barham's *Masonry*. He gave one to his brother.

POOR RATES

Old age was often harsh. People did not support the poor from outside their own parish. Those likely to become a burden had to prove they 'belonged', which could be difficult without the right papers. They were 'examined' by magistrates. Presumably John Corbin had worked away for such a long time that no-one knew him when in 1772 he faced examination in Corfe. He said he had heard his father Thomas Corbin say that 'he was settled in Langton […] that he lived with his parents as an apprentice according to the custom of the Company of Marblers, but he was never bound by any commit, indenture or agreement.'[53.]

In attempts to relieve hardship, money collected locally from rates was redistributed by the overseers acting for the Vestry, the precursor of local councils. The overseers also provided help by other means, such as paying for sharpening of tools, enabling the recipient, if fit enough, to work. The aim, it seems, was to help men to continue in work if possible when they could not pay their bills. Though the system was considerably older it seems it was not until the late 18th century that documents revealing its working *apropos* the stone trade appear.

In November, 1795, the Swanage Poor Book recorded that increasing numbers of quarrymen were applying for relief: 'by reason of having no vent for their stones'.[54.] The Vestry agreed they should allow '4s. per week for each man, 2s. for his wife, and 1s. for each child.' The parish would take the stone he produced, to be sold when the opportunity arose, at which times any surplus owing to the amount paid in relief be returned to the quarrier. In some instances the overseers paid the hard-up quarryman's rent for him. It must have all been very fraught, with the merchants who were in the category of those paying significant rates competing with one another in dealings which included the sale of stone produced by men paid by the overseers who were in receipt of the rates! Perhaps Aaron Bower (died 1853), who was both a merchant and a Swanage overseer, did not burn the Swanage Poor Books entirely by accident! It seems that, following the defeat of Napoleon and the removal of the threat of invasion, the Government cut back on military spending, including fortifications around Portsmouth. This affected the Pureck stone industry.

In April 1815 Mount Tambora in Indonesia erupted, causing famine, disease and unrest around the world. Henry Bankes MP, unaware of the eruption and its effects, wrote in his diaries:

'September 1816. A general calamity, extending over the whole continent of Europe as well as of America – most unseasonable weather and a deficient harvest. The grievous effects were felt throughout the kingdom. Never remember so long a continuance of wet weather during the whole summer and Autumn, which delayed everywhere the carrying in of crops, prevented the corn coming to maturity and in many counties rendered it unfit for the food of man. Farms were relinquished and abandoned even without any notice. In the Isle of Purbeck, upon my own property the stone trade threw a very large proportion of the labouring class wholly out of employment.'[55.]

The Swanage Poor Book of 1822-8 has numerous entries that reveal how the system worked. During the first years,

TRADE ORGANISATIONS / 249

parapet wall pieced with quatrefoils) at 11s per foot: almost as much as 100 foot of rough paving! He added: 'for the use of my trucks, cro bar, saw and wedges for 21 weeks'; also he includes '4 boatmen 1 pot of beer each, 6 boatmen 1 pint of beer each'. All those costs were at the quarry end of the operation, though perhaps not his tool hire. The builders were charging the freight, cranage at the Kimmeridge site etc. plus the rubble and, the only Portland element in the building, the 'geometrical stone steps'. The tower has recently been rebuilt by the Landmark Trust, with missing components of Portland rather than Purbeck Portland.[61]

THE VICTORIAN PERIOD

An advertisement in the *Salisbury and Winchester Journal*, November 11 1843, announced that:

> 'Mr Bonfield has received instructions from the Proprietor to sell by PUBLIC AUCTION all that very important BUSINESS PROPERTY' know as BANKER LAND or Deposit for stone, with the Cottage and Sheds thereon and the privilege of shipping stone and entitling the owner to all charges for all business done thereon.
>
> The whole property was let many years ago to Messrs. Marsh and Burt at the low yearly rent of 27*l* and is now considered to be worth considerably more than that sum. To be viewed on application to Mr. Francis Haysom of Swanage.'

Francis Haysom was an old man living nearby.

By 1880 the number of merchants had shrunk to Thomas Stevens, W. G. White, H.W. Burt, Emily Randell and George Burt Esq. Nathaniel Chinchen's business had devolved firstly to Nathaniel Chinchen White then latterly to William Grove White. It was on a considerable scale, for John Mowlem recorded in Nov. 1848: 'Mr. White has discharged 40 or 50 men, not one I should say has been provident to provide for a day ahead. This will be a hard winter for them.'[62] Thomas Randell junior had become an attorney but continued the business with John Haysom managing it. Luckily a photograph showing the men employed there survives. A crane John brought back from Portsmouth dockyard identifies Randell's banker in other photographs, as it does in Craft's painting.

Around that time the bankers extended not only from the quay to the stream, but also north of it, for in 1855 the landowner, the trustees of Ilminster Free School granted a lease to: 'Thomas Randell, stone merchant to demise and let that land called stone bankers lying on the north side of Swanage bridge [...] Yearly rent of 4 [...] land bounded by a garden of Mrs. Bower and another banker of William Grove White.'[63] The school also granted another agreement for a banker with George Stickland, again on the north side of the bridge. This was just before the building, for the stone trade, of the first pier in 1859. A more ambitious scheme proposed a tramway linking the quarries from as far west as St. Aldhelm's Head to the pier, but only the pier part was realised. John Haysom was in charge of the pier's stone work, then of the masonry of the church rebuilding, before working for Randell. Both church wardens at the time of the church rebuilding were leading stone merchants, Thomas Randell and William Grove White.

The first pier was linked to the bankers by a railed tramway which was carried on bridges from banker to banker in order to leave 'boat haul' gaps for each merchant to retain his access to the shore. These gaps have been walled up but are indicated by straight joints in the masonry. Just one of the old boat hauls is left in this part of the bay, Parish slip. Though they began using the pier, loading by the old method, employing high wheeled wagons driven into the sea, continued. There was a reluctance to use the newfangled pier and to pay the tolls! The innovation of the pier brought the first significant change in 200 years or more, but a much more radical one was soon to follow, with the opening of the railway branch line in 1885. Just before that happened a colourful description of Purbeck was given in a local area publication:

> 'Everything is very still just now among the quarries, and we can examine the curious places from which most of the stone that once paved London is taken, and where the work is very slack at present, and we can almost see, too, the immense masses of stone called 'bankers' that line Swanage shore, spoiling that otherwise lovely little watering-place, and giving it the appearance of an overcrowded churchyard. The bankers extend one side of the bay, and thence the stone is shipped into carts with enormous wheels, that go far out into the sea to the barges, whence the stone is again shipped into vessels – a costly process, that it is believed the coming railway will do away with.'[64]

The advent of government inspectors and the railways brought an increasing number of 'foreigners' with an outsider's perspective on the Purbeck stone trade; another report, in a newspaper from 1880, also includes the inhabitants of Portland in its comments:

> 'The 'islanders' of Purbeck and Portland as remarkable in their habits and having a settled idea that the workings of the quarries in those localities is a privilege of their own, and they not only resent the intrusion of other workmen but go so far as to qualify the latter and, indeed, the whole world outside Purbeck and Portland, by the approbrious title of 'foreigners'. The Purbeckians of Swanage maintain that this privilege is secured to them by an ancient charter providing that no person may establish himself in their trade who is not a direct descendant of some local quarryman.

Boat haul at Swanage showing tramline spanning gap between bankers, after the time of the construction of the first pier. Note sinks in foreground. The bridge was high enough for a horse and stone cart to pass underneath.

252 / PURBECK STONE

View of Swanage Bay with Victoria Hotel at right, quay at centre. Stone being transferred from cart into boat: Marine Villas behind.

The principal merchant at the turn of the 20th century was Burt and Burt. In the previous generation, Robert Burt's business had had its origins on the shore, but after arrival of the railway, transferred to land owned by Mrs. Serrell of Langton Matravers, establishing what became known as the 'depot'. By that time it was being run by Henry Weeks Burt, known as 'Grocer', who was joined by a relative, Frank Burt, brother of George. George had played a principal part in the expansion of his uncle John Mowlem's business in the capital, becoming Sheriff of London. Frank, returning to Swanage, took a share in the business for his son Fred, thereby forming Burt and Burt by 1889. They acquired quarries in Durlston Bay and a 'lighter' to carry stone away from them. Frank built Gordon Villas in the London style he was used to, and maintained a voluminous diary, which can be found at Swanage Museum and Heritage Centre.[65.] Descendants developed the Poole based building firm Burt and Vick, recently wound up. Henry had three brothers: Billy, who had a Cap quarry in Herston Field; George, with a quarry in Court Cowlease, known as 'Boss' but not to be confused with George in London; and Charles, who had a stone yard in Liverpool. Best known of these men is 'Sheriff' George Burt (1816-1894), who, having made a fortune in what continues as Mowlem's, retired to his native town. He acquired the Sentry Estate, built Durlston Castle, Great Globe, etc., and a new Purbeck House, now the Purbeck House Hotel. Thomas Hardy called George the 'King of Swanage'.

Fred died and Henry retired in about 1908, Charles, with his son Ernest, sold up in Liverpool and took over in the Swanage depot. They brought two machines back with them: a primitive sand-fed frame saw and a Coulter planer, both driven by a Town Gas engine. These were the first stone processing machines in Swanage. The industrial revolution had arrived! Though a small quantity of stone continued to be shipped, particularly for work in the Channel Islands, the arrival of the trains spelled the end of the old order.

The shift from shore to railway left a vacuum. 'Sheriff' George Burt set out to acquire the land lying south of the stream, but was frustrated by one merchant, probably Nathaniel White, who would not sell at any price. Burt duly succeeded by buying through a third party. His redevelopment plans included enclosing some sea between the quay and Boil Well (a spring). The fishermen complained that this would affect their seine netting, and appealed to the fishernmen's board, who upheld the objection. Reading between the lines I suspect it is indicative of the considerable antipathy he aroused. Remarks, such as that he 'hoped the sound of tools would be silenced in Swanage', may have struck a chord with others who shared his vision of a genteel future, but not all. Frustrated, Burt built the coal stores on the site of the old bankers. Here coal, brought in by rail and then transferred by horse and cart, was dumped to fuel the steamers, the old tramway being used to get it out to where they lay alongside the pier. This coaling operation was generally done at night in order not to interrupt the programme of daily sailings.

Two ledger books covering the years 1878-1888 and 1890-1895, now in the possession of Dorset County Council, belonged to a railway era merchant. Unfortunately the owner is not readily identifiable, but was probably Henry Weeks Burt. The later one has missing pages before records of customers' names, of which this is a sample:

'1891 May Item 1 Messrs William Poate and Son builders, Westbourne, Emsworth, Hants. 20 steps 66 ft run delivered in truck at Havant station at 1/2d per ft run £3-17-0
Right angle quoins, Jambs, Window sills, ashlars to make out sills, angle stone to make out sills for bay, 8 angles, double jambs, sills, mullions, etc.'

Streetwork accounted for a big slice of the business, but not

TRADE ORGANISATIONS / 253

all. In about 1930 the depot would send out on average two or three eight-ton trucks each day. Some of this was walling, rockery, etc., but dressed kerb dominated.

The other ledger book bears the stamp of George Hardy, builder, but otherwise seems to have no connection with that firm. It records payments to several men for various sorts of worked stone and the hire of capstans and/or chains. One could perhaps expect that every quarryman would possess this essential equipment, but some obviously did not. The rental was 3d per week for a chain, 6d for a capstan and chain at a time when James Phippard earned 12/s in a week, Joseph Weeks 10/s. Burt's had wheelwright's and blacksmith's shops in the depot, where these capstans were probably made. At £3-10-0 (roughly six weeks wages) they were a considerable expense, but Thomas Phippard bought his outright in 1894.

Men renting capstans in 1878 included James Norman, Philip Edmunds, William Collins, John Tomes, Charles Phippard, Robert Norman, Sam and George Squibb. The following year Joseph Brown and James Norman Sen. join the list, and so on. Some rented for a short while only, perhaps while their own capstan was being repaired.

There is an index of quarries, each with a page number, where entries are made, recording payments. They give some indication of the vein being dug. James Phippard was making half squared flatners at 5/s per ton, squared flatners at 6/6d per ton, plus horse pitchers; nothing thick, which suggests a Downs Vein hole. Albert Norman, however, was supplying coping, one foot eleven inches by one foot six inches in section! This just could be Freestone, but Cap is much more likely. Richard Stickland was probably in the Cap as well, for he was paid 6/s, half a week's wages, for 'one large stone' three feet by three feet by one foot six. He was also making coping of the same dimension as Albert, plus jambs, cills and grating stones. The index includes individual quarry operators, Joseph Brown, James Haysom, Charles and Albert Norman, James, Peter, Joseph, Henry and John Phippard, Richard Stickland, Richard and John Card Tomes, Joseph and Arthur Weeks, plus two quarries called by other names, which would seem to be in the possession of the ledger's owner, Henry Burt, and which he was letting out to others. These are 'Hardens' in Swanage Field, occupied by Sam and George Squibb, and 'Blowhole' in Chesters, occupied by George Norman. George produced kerb and block only over a fifteen year period.[66.] My father talked of this quarry. It was in what he called the Rotary camp at Townsend. It was deep, and bad air was a problem. It is probably the quarry with the chicken shown in the photograph used by Brian Bugler for the cover of the re-issuing of his grandfather's book, *Purbeck Shop*.[67.]

By 1903 Kelly's *Directory* listed the stone merchants in Swanage as John Warren Bonfield, Burt and Burt, 'Chinchen, White and William Collins', Albert Harris and Stevens (Thomas and Son). James and John Haysom appear as 'Monumental masons' and Henry John Rose, also as a monumental mason. William Haysom (my grandfather) appears as a stonemason at the railway yard. John and James Haysom had worked as managers for the bigger merchants, but by this time were doing memorials on their own account. They had been allowed to build a small workshop in the railway yard northeast of the church, on what is now the site of the Fire Station. They did local memorials in a thick and thin style of lettering, the business being continued by James's son Louis. When he in due course retired, Hancocks continued on the same premises. In their time James and John did most of the lettering in Swanage, and sometimes further afield.

In the 1850/1860s John Haysom was manager of Randell's banker. He employed non-members loading stones on the pier. This prompted a delegation which included Reuben Short Bower, Langton Warden, who told him that unless he stopped those men he would 'warn the trade' and stop everyone from supplying Randell's. I suspect the new-fangled pier had created a 'grey area' that had not formerly existed. On land the stone had only been handled by freemen of the company, whose domain ended at the shore. Was the pier land or water? Several boys, not sons of members, were apprenticed on the

Swanage, probably Grandfather's Knap quarry. c.1900.

building of Kingston church, but on its completion could not find employment in the local stone trade. One, a Kingston boy called Damer, went to London and in due course developed his own business in a yard close to the railway line between Clapham and Waterloo. The advertising sign has in my lifetime changed from 'Damer' to 'Harvey' to 'Stone West Cox'. Fred Smith, of the fishing family, and Frank Hardy both wanted apprenticeships, but were prevented. Young Smith went away to Southampton in order to start as a mason, so inflexible were the quarrymen.

The quarriers were equally rigorous in the application of the 'base born' rule. Alfred Norman, Warden between 1924-32, had an elder brother who was born before his parents wed, and was therefore debarred. He went to sea instead. This inequality of opportunity naturally caused resentment. In particular, the growth of Swanage in the late 1800s created jobs 'on the building'. Sometimes these were filled by quarrymen, but their builder fellows could not conversely get employment in the stone trade. The quarrymen could switch jobs if they liked, but it did not work both ways. The somewhat derisive 'Queen Anne' label was applied to the quarrymen at this time by the builders, particularly 'Patch' Hardy. An earlier name applied to men in the stone trade was 'Turk', perhaps because of their outlandishness. Ida Woodward, in her book *In and Around The Isle of Purbeck* (1908), refers to Swanage men being call Turks perhaps 'on account of that ignorance of things in general and commerce in particular'. Does Turks Lane, Lilliput, have a stone trade connection?

Examining the stone work of Richmond Bridge I noticed a sign advertising 'TURKS LANDING'. Enquiries revealed that a waterman family of that name had worked on that part of the river for generations. Perhaps the first arrived with a consignment of stone. One of the Swanage Butlers was known particularly as 'The Turk'. His father had a quarry at the eastern end of Durlston Bay. His mate was Frank Tomes of Swanage, whose descendant Frank Venables told me that the two young men ran off to London 'to avoid the music' after the young Turk pushed, or allowed to fall, his father's quarry donkey over the cliff. Care of the donkey or horse was generally part of the boy's work. This Frank Tomes went on to become manager of Trollope and Colls stoneyard in Vauxhall in the 1880s.

THE PURBECK MARBLERS

In 1859 O. W. Farrer, Chairman at Wareham County Petty Sessions, published his account of the Purbeck Stone industry. He wrote that about thirty years previously the box belonging to the Purbeck Marblers had been removed to Swanage. A general meeting had been opened at Corfe and adjourned to Swanage. An altercation had taken place and since that time the town and country meetings had always been regularly held at Corfe and Langton respectively. He added that the Mayor of Corfe had formerly attended, but his presence had of late been discontinued, though the bailiff of Corfe still continued to attend.[68.] This is surely the same row that W. M. Hardy graphically described in *Old Swanage and Purbeck*:

'At the time they were building the hotel [this was the conversion of the old manor house into the Victoria Hotel, commenced soon after Mr. Morton Pitt bought that Swanage estate in 1825] Mr. Corben, foreman of the stonemasons, and a member of the Ancient Order of Marblers, was chosen as warden, and in that capacity had the custody of the old oak chest, the oracles and charter. At their meeting on Shrove Tuesday the marblers elected another warden and Mr. Corben was requested to hand over the oak chest to the new warden. This he refused to do, being evidently piqued at being deprived of office. Now this chest was looked upon by some of the quarrymen as little less sacrosanct than the Ark of the Covenant was to the Children of Israel [...]So one morning, about nine o'clock, they all came down from Worth, Langton and Herston and joined the Swanage men, forming an army of about 400 men.'[69.]

They broke in by the bedroom window, found the chest and carried it off in the direction of Langton. This old oak chest is sadly lost and, it seems, its successor, for in 1845 the minutes record: 'carried to bank £4-0-0 remaining 12s.10d kept in part payment of a box ordered to be made'.

When my father 'paid his money' and expressed an interest in the papers in 1925 the two wardens were Alfred Norman, Swanage, and Alfred Benfield, Langton. At that time Alf Norman was working in what had been his co-warden's quarr, right on the Langton and Worth parish boundary, close by the Kingston road. He was walking there from Swanage each day. Alfred Benfield lived close by and by arrangement they all met at his home for, in order to open the box, which had two locks, both wardens, holding a key each, had to be present. Amid claims and counter claims, I have not been able to discover who had the box last or what happened to it.

What appears to be the one and only 18th century document belonging to the Marblers has recently come to light. A single sheet of watermarked paper has the 1651 articles copied verbatim in an elegant copperplate hand. What follows tells of Shrove Tuesday meetings held at Corfe that had probably gone on since the 17th century, but without a record being kept. In a very different hand appears 'Article 11, Town Hall Feb 23 1830.' The Company are unanimously agreed that 'no man shall work in the Western District unless he has paid his freedom at Corfe Castle.' Following this, in a different hand again: 'Article 12. It is also agreed by the consent of the Company that from after this present Shrove Tuesday (Feb. 16) that every Member of the Company who shall omit or neglect to pay his accustomed fee of six shillings and eight pence, and shall not during life pay the same, his children shall not be considered as entitled to be admitted Members of the said company – 1836. such Members to have notice from this date and this article to be in force. 1837'

It can be no coincidence that the earliest Minute Book in the possession of the Company of Marblers commences that same year. But it is not concerned with 'the Western District at all', just Swanage alone. It opens with the 1651 articles, followed by the Ower Agreement of 1695, copied out in the same hand. The first minute is headed Swanage, Shrove Tuesday, and what follows is a record of annual meetings that, for about the next thirty years, take place in various Swanage pubs (usually the Black Swan, occasionally the New Inn, less often the Mason's

Arms and Royal Oak). There is a formulaic preamble: 'At a meeting of the Company of Marblers this day held at the [name of pub] being the anniversary of the said company it is agreed to admit the following persons who have served their lawful apprenticeship as freemen of the said Company of Marblers by paying the sum of six shillings and eight pence together with one pot of beer and one penny loaf according to ancient custom', followed by a record of the names of newly admitted freemen, their marriages, the appointment of two wardens and a steward, sometimes disbursements and fines and occasionally other matters.[70] In the first year the costs were 'Room 2/6d, Pepper 2/6d, Steward 2/6d, Ball 1/s, Book 7/0, Paid for writing 2/6d. Expenses to Wareham 3/8d.' Wareham had the nearest bank, later the company banked their money with Mrs. Serrell at Durnford Manor, Langton. Both wardens were from Swanage. They were George Bower and Robert Burt, who probably wrote the minutes, and the steward was Charles Mowlem, nephew of John who made a fortune in London. The stewards were invariably newly admitted young men, for their job, usually lasting only a year or two, was to do the leg work, taking 'warnings' of meetings to each quarry.

The 1837 book is at first a record of Swanage meetings only, and makes no mention of Langton before 1864 when, at a meeting at the Royal Oak, Herston, further west than the usual venues, they admitted men from Langton for the first time. Presumably Langton, Worth and possibly Corfe men were also meeting on Shrove Tuesday, but at Corfe, as had been done for centuries but without a record being made. The Swanage men paying for 'journey with pepper' must surely tell of them going to Ower in that first year, but there is no such cost for the ensuing years.

The second Minute Book began as a record of disbursements, for it begins 'Henry Burt, James Lander and John Haysom in account with the Wardens and Committee of the Company of Marblers Isle of Purbeck 1866'. Which is odd, for the Swanage warden at that time was Henry Seymour and, as such, his name could be expected to appear. It began to be used for minutes in 1876, recording both Swanage and Langton affairs. At this time the record of pepper payments becomes annual. The Royal Oak meeting was an important one. The Company reduced to one warden, admitted 31 new members. Some paid the cash, 3s 4d, others the same value in stone taken. Joseph Haysom was fined £1 'for Breach of one of the articles'. This would seem to be the episode referred to by Sir Stephen Collins in his reminiscences written in 1915: 'On one occasion my father, who was a quarry owner, differed from the committee on some small matter and was threatened by a fine [...] hundreds of men, led amongst others by a brother of my father, who was a leading member of the Guild, came to the quarry to enforce the fine in kind. I can see now my father as he sat upon the stone to be taken.'[71]

The annual recording of meetings at Corfe, does not commence until some years later, from when the two books run in tandem, a physical manifestation of a continuing schism. So the two books continue, the earlier only recording Swanage admissions, appointments and fines, the later, both Swanage and Langton with Worth admissions, appointments and fines plus names of the two separate committees, plus expenses. Each warden was keeping his own book, but whilst John Warren Bonfield, known as 'Warny' restricted himself to Swanage matters, William Saunders of Langton included both committees in his recording. As wardens came and went the handwriting changed, but it is false to assume that the writing was always the warden's own. My father remarked that his grandfather John, who never served as warden, sometimes wrote on the warden's behalf.

Similarly it is misleading to assume that all the newly admitted were young men just out of their apprenticeship, though the overwhelming majority were. In 1895 John Ernest Mowlem paid for himself and his dead father Thomas Joseph at the same time. Thomas, a nephew of John, founder of Mowlems, London, had painted a fine view of Swanage Bay in 1869. Here was a new category of membership, that of men with freeman ancestors, but not active in the trade themselves. A few years later, sons of Richard Webber and Henry Corben of the firm of that name with a yard in Clapham, London, were all admitted together. The father to son tradition of membership gave them an automatic right, but as the numbers of that sort of entrant tended to grow proportionally over time, the identity of the order also tended to change. Perhaps there is a parallel with what happened to the London Livery Companies; these evolved from being trade or craft based to their present state.

My father remarked that all through the First World War a few men continued to attend at Corfe and maintain the customs. In the immediate aftermath of the war a committee meeting of considerable consequence was held:

> 'having recommended that the Quarrymen join up with the operative Stone Masons Society with a view of improving the prices and conditions. This action was endorsed, a committee instructed to carry out the necessary arrangements'.

The following year, for the first time, the Langton book recorded in detail events that occurred over the course of that year. The Marblers committee applied to the Society of Old Stone Masons for their help and co-operation. At a Swanage Labour Hall meeting 13 quarrymen joined the Masons Society, followed by 12 more in Langton, and five more at another Swanage meeting. A resolution was passed that Brother J. Murrey of the Masons Society 'enter into negociations on their behalf with the Stone Merchants to ensure the schedule of prices as sent in'.

It was the beginning of what emerged as the Co-operative, or 'Purbeck Co-operative Stone Industries Ltd'. After this inaugural year the Minute Books give no more specific information about what became a business organisation that for a while included a majority of Purbeck quarrymen as direct employees, or as independent quarrymen but supplying it, or as investors; notably the local Purbeck men working in the Portland stoneyards. It was the first attempt at a form of collectivism since the Joint Stock Company of 1697/8. With nearly all stone being despatched by rail in the early 1900s, the Purbeck Stone & General Trading Co., with its railway depot, created a virtual monopoly. The quarrymen almost generally resented it. This, perhaps together with a sense of solidarity, the experiences of war and a general collectivist *zeitgeist*, were reasons which led to the formation of the Co-operative.

The Co-op built a corrugated iron workshop on the Bankes Estate just off the Acton approach road, where masonry work was done without the benefit of machinery, with Reg 'Pickles' Bower as foreman. They took space in the Swanage Railway yard for loading trucks, street kerbing being the staple product. The Co-op failed tragically, the secretary taking his own life as the finances became more desperate. Beyond attending the inaugural Labour Hall meeting, newly demobbed, my father had no involvement with it, and other than gossip, heard little of what went on. Members, or the sons of those involved, told me various versions, all spun to a greater or lesser degree! One problem was that of divided loyalties, with some men part in the Co-op, part competing for the same customers in their own right. Another was the committee management style, and another lack of investment. But the times were extremely difficult; not only did the Co-op go down around 1930, but also Worth Quarry Co. operating Sheepsleights, and the Dorset Quarry Co. operating Seacombe, both big employers. Job prospects must have been bleak indeed! After closure the Co-op's matchboard office was used as a shop, whilst Bob Harris and finally Landers Quarries, occupied the main shed.

The old Swanage Minute Book continued until 1936, when it was decided to appoint one joint committee rather than two. It had become pointless therefore to continue with two books, so the Swanage one ended the following year. This left blank pages, some of which were used to record later committee and some Shrove Tuesday meetings. Admissions, appointments and some matters of import continued to be recorded in the Langton book.

An issue arose with Mr. Bankes' agent, Mr. Lodder. In 1921 'he was determined to have dues on all stone quarried'. This was to do with the sale of scars for which, with projects such as the construction of the Valley and ferry roads, there was a growing demand. In the past, beyond the farmers patching up their tracks, there had not been much call for this by-product. Over time banks of it had accumulated. The Estate, waking up to this potential income, which was quite considerable for a while, demanded a royalty. Some quarrymen thought this unjust. Scars were, after all, the laboriously made waste from stones on which they had already paid royalties.

The Estate saw it differently; royalties had indeed been paid on the finished stone, but not on this waste; it was theirs, and they saw money in it. Another 1921 minute tells of how things become obfuscated. The quarrymen persuaded Mr. Lodder to reduce the rent on empty quarries. This would suggest that it had been traditional to charge rent on quarries, which was hardly the case. Though the term 'rent' had been often applied it was based on output and not a fixed sum. For many years throughout Purbeck virtually all quarries had been worked on such a royalty basis. The year and a day rule, dating from at least 1651, had meant that a quarrier, wanting to keep his claim on a quarry but not needing to work it all the time, would make a point of doing a few days work there. He would produce a few stones and pay the appropriate royalty. My father talked of quite a few men doing this from time to time. Examples were: James Brown, who worked several quarries, among them

Corfe Castle, Town Hall. Shrove Tuesday meeting, 1923. Jimmy Ivamy Bower holding the football at centre. The four men holding quart jugs of beer are probably the four apprentices admitted that year; they were William and Hedley Lander, Fred and Harold Norman.

Sheepsleights; months could go by without a need for what that quarry could produce, but he never let a whole year pass; another was Joby Webber who, late on in life, would borrow Josiah Harris's cart and do a bit in his quarry up at Blackers Hole ware. This is the quarry where the slide stones remain out on the open knap. Chatting about this with Harold Bonfield, he told me that according to his father they dragged the cart towards the quarry upside down, so making it obvious to the farmer that they had been up there! Indicative, I suspect, of a certain tension.

The next step in this evolution from royalties to rent was that some men, particularly those holding undergrounds which no longer had a working capstan, would offer a nominal royalty but not bother to take any stone at all. By 1921 the Bankes Estate possessed more quarries where this was going on than any other. Its agents accepted it and had begun to call the payment 'rent'. As the years went by they added it to the list of items on their standard royalties return tickets issued to and made out by each quarryman.

Years elapsed without most of the landlords ever visiting their quarries, but about this time Ralph Bankes, on coming of age, showed an interest. The charabanc from Kingston Lacy Hall duly arrived at Alfred Norman's quarry near Worth gate. This was perhaps chosen because Alfred was one of the current wardens and his quarry was convenient to get to. His grandson Jack said that Alfred spent days tidying up in advance of the visit.[72.] The young squire was shown around underground, then, according to Jack, his grandfather missed a trick, for Mr. Bankes asked: 'Where do you keep the horse?' Alfred said: 'On the common' (as the field south of Acton was called then) 'it can take an hour catching him some mornings'. 'Why not keep it in this field?' "Tis alright,' said Alfred lamely, to his lasting regret. Included in the celebrations of young Ralph's majority, the quarrymen were invited over to the Hall, where food was provided in a marquee. Confronted with a range of delicacies, which included jelly, one said 'I'll 'ave zome of thic shaken pudden please'.[73.]

By 1925 trading conditions were bad and the Marblers, as

The Company of Purbeck Marblers.
Swanage and Langton Matravers.

PRICE LIST
from 1st January, 1948.

WHITE C...	34/- per ton.
CRAZY PAVING, other than white	28/- „
WALLING STONE (reasonably graded)	13/- „
ROCKERY	18/- „
HARD CORE	4/6 „
SCARS, in Bank	2/3 „
KERB, 9in.	3/1 per ft. run
„ 8in.	2/10 „
„ 6in.	2/3 „
„ 5in.	2/0½ „
„ 4in.	1/8 „
SQUARED FLATENERS	2/3 per ft. sup.
SQUARED PAVING	2/6 „
6in. PITCHERS	40/6 per ton.
GUTTERSOLES	1/3 per ft. run.
TILE	£6 15s. per load.
BLOCK FREESTONE	4/- per ft. cube.
BLOCK THORNBACK	4/- „ „
JOINTED DUBBERS	15/9 per yard super.
COMMON DUBBERS	13/6 „

Wages as Building Trade:
Quarrymen - 2/7½ per hour.
Labourers - 2/4¼ per hour.

All previous lists cancelled.

Purbeck Marblers' 1948 Price List, showing pencil emendations; from the archive of Arthur Hancock.

an institution, under stress. On the one hand they agreed 'that a letter be sent to Depot and Co-op (the two main merchants) requesting them not to buy any more stone from Joseph Harris and Harry Bridle [both obviously the sons of freemen], until they have paid their usual fee'. On the other hand they voted 'that no one shall be admitted in the Company for a period of 5 years'. They would not, perhaps could not, stick to it, for two years later they admitted three new members, the next year four more!

The wider Purbeck reality was even more bizarre. Besides the depot and Co-op, the biggest operators by this time were the Dorset Quarry Co. at Seacombe and Worth Quarry Co. at Sheepsleights. Both were owned, managed and staffed to a degree by people from outside Purbeck. The Marblers had no power and little influence over these companies. Perhaps because of these realities there was apathy and a low attendance at Corfe on Shrove Tuesdays. But some men did continue to attend the annual meeting. The wardens retrenched to a position in which they concerned themselves with the inland rather than cliff quarries, where they continued to adjudicate in disputes. In one such, newly admitted freeman Robert Harris, quarrelling with Sam Bower, appealed directly to the Bankes Estate, who responded by reinforcing the authority of the wardens: 'Major Lodder desires both parties to abide by the decision of the Wardens re sinking, measurements to be taken by the Wardens in the presence of Thomas Lovell, Steward. Findings; R. Harris not to sink' The 100 foot rule was still alive, the Bankes Estate giving the Marblers oxygen. Perhaps it was causing side effects, for in 1937 they began to call their Company the 'Ancient Order', a label that appears first in W. M. Hardy's *Old Swanage and Purbeck*, 1908! A possible influence in this change was that many men, particularly those at Seacombe in the 1920s, joined societies such as the Order of the Moose. Billy Winspit had his certificate of membership framed on the wall.

The church bell summoning the Shrove Tuesday meeting was still being rung in 1940, but not for the ensuing war years, as its ringing was reserved for a signal of invasion. The pepper continued to be provided throughout the war, but who got it when Ower Farm had been evacuated for military purposes is unclear.

In the post-war recovery new members were again admitted, and the big issues, prices and wages, tackled at Shrove Tuesday and general meetings. Nationalisation was in prospect. Some likened the Order to a Trade Union. On the wages front an attempt was made at definitions. In 1946 the minutes record: 'It was unanimously agreed that for the purposes of defining a quarryman as distinct from a labourer, the former shall be able to lift and cut a block in a cliff quarr, or underpick and cut the same in an inland quarr, in both instances working in safety to himself and his fellow workmen'. This was pursuing a will of the wisp. How relevant was it to talk of underground skills when by this time almost all were working up top? Technological change would in twenty years or so entirely replace the old time-honoured quarry skills.

The thrashing out of a revised price list went on each year. This included provisions to maintain the merchant system. It allowed 'that a margin should be fixed between the prices wholesale to local merchants and retail to the casual purchaser who may come into any quarry to obtain stone and carry it away on own vehicle.' A battered example survives from 1948, with amendments in pencil which may be evidence of proposals for prices in 1949. Rail transport of stone petered out during the 1930s. More efficient lorries, coupled with the fact that most of the active quarries were in the Worth and Langton area, imposed a new geography, with a new generation of merchants emerging.

Landers, Hardens and Hancocks, quarrymen who had bought small freehold lots when the Worth Estate was sold off in 1919, were the main players, but they were, as the merchants of old, also members of the Order with which they sometimes found themselves in negotiation. So it was that a number of small quarries could continue to exist by supplying a merchant who could, if need be, add their stone to that supplied by others, and thereby undertake large jobs beyond the capacity of any one quarry. That was the main benefit of the merchant system, as it always had been. But the maintenance of a fixed price list was often under strain. The first general meeting I attended centred on this. It became clear that, only days after agreeing to abide by an approved price, some men, for reasons of Byzantine complexity, sold below it. It marked the end of the price list. Lorry flexibility was driving change. More and more individual builders or garden centres *et al* would find an individual quarry giving a better price and go to it rather than to a merchant.

Another factor propelling this change was increased output driven by mechanisation. In particular, the introduction of the hydraulic guillotine in the 1960s meant that production of split faced walling, the staple output, could be speeded up. So equipped, one small quarry could produce sufficient for an average house in a reasonable amount of time. The merchant system that had survived the shift from sea to rail, and for a while from rail to lorry, finally petered out.

1946 saw the introduction of honorary memberships, for lifetime only. I suspect it was part of Robert Harris's vision of a revived Order. Elected as Langton Warden in 1945, together with John Pushman (of Worth but retaining the title of Swanage Warden), he steered the Order for over ten years. The Rector of Corfe, the Rev. Yorke Batley, was appointed chaplain. One of the first 'Honourable' members was Rural District Councillor Geoffrey Warner, who pressed for stone to be used for the Capstan Field council houses. Another was artist Elizabeth Muntz, who designed the 'guild emblem' which became available as proof of membership.

The Order entered into negotiations with the Bankes Estate in an attempt to get more land released for quarrying. This in due course led to quarrying of a hitherto almost untouched field known variously as Kings or Queens ground. Other fields were also considered, but Queens Ground was selected, not for good geological reasons but simply because, being on a relatively distant part of Eastington Farm, the tenant objected less than he did to nearer alternatives. It was a sign of things to come. The current so-called 'preferred areas' (for quarrying) have been identified for reasons of landscape location, not the nature of the rock. The 1947 Town and Country Planning Act, plus other new provisions, brought in planning and government officials, working at both local and national level. Preliminary test holes in the new Queens Ground revealed shallow stone at its southern extemity, but this was within the newly identified half-mile-wide coastal belt, where future quarrying was to be banned. A worrying new culture of external control was emerging.

In 1949 Fred Bower asked at the Shrove Tuesday meeting about the proposed visit by the Stone Controller. He was told: 'we should welcome such a visit as, in these days of restrictions and controls generally, the Stone Controller could undoubtedly become our greatest friend and ally.' Warden Bob Harris, a strong Labour Party supporter, may have thought he saw a light at the end of the tunnel, when in fact it was more like an approaching train. As a precursor to full nationalisation, the Controller required each quarry to obtain a government licence.

The modern era of planning law began with the post-war Labour government. Consultant John Lawrence reported to the relevant authority (in those days what has become Purbeck District Council, rather than the County):

'PURBECK MARBLERS. 6 MAY 1948.

Today the demand for stone from this area is mainly for ornamental purposes such as rockery and crazy paving which is most easily obtained by open cast working rather than the old shaft mining used for the production of monumental stone.

Thus the old shaft workings have more or less disappeared as working concerns and sporadic open cast workings have taken their place. The geological formation makes these two distinct types of working require different areas of operation. Therefore the area of land to operate has changed and at the moment the Marblers are attempting to work the ground in the areas of the shaft mines as there is considerable opposition to their taking new land to meet the new circumstances.

Within the last month or so the local Council have undertaken the building of Council houses in stone and have so put a new demand on the Marblers. As the Marblers are working inefficient open cast workings they are afraid that the cost of production of stone will cause them to lose their newly found demand.

To meet this change in circumstances and demands, the Marblers wish to open up new fields which are more suitable for meeting the new situation, but appear to face considerable opposition from landlords and tenants.

Thus the request for them to produce their five year plan has caused considerable consternation as their methods of operation are in a period of change.'[74.]

Lawrence's first paragraph fails to paint the full picture. His report marks the inauguration of what has become a self-serving bureaucracy. Sadly vision seems inexorably to give way to such.

The continuing emasculation of the Marblers as an organisation since the 1947 Act was brought home to me at a meeting with mineral planning officers held in the course of a further tightening of planning law in about 1990. It included a 'presentation' with 'art work' showing an old photograph of Harry, nicknamed 'Ton', Chinchen, standing by his capstan, and went on to show us how to operate our quarries, Thornback in one neat stack, Freestone in another, etc. 'Are we being perceived as being complete twerps?' I thought. The days when the government had no involvement, the wardens sorted out rows, etc., seemed far off indeed, and yet there were men present who could remember them well. There we sat – by any standard our jobs being pretty arduous, each facing the daily challenge of competitive hard work, being pushed around by government functionaries knowing only the comfort of a warm office and steady salary! A culture once so vibrant and colourful, was being extinguished. Change was of course much wider, including the acquisition of the old quarrymen's cottages as holiday houses. Fisherman-quarryman Alan Lander observed: 'Once Purbeck was for the workers, now 'tis for the shirkers'.

During the first part of the 20th century most of the trade had continued through Swanage. The biggest merchant, Burt and Burt, was based in the Court Hill depot, which had its own railway siding. Others were William Collins, in Kings Road West and Thomas Stevens' yard in Tilly Mead. Thomas had been a paragon of the work ethic, each day riding between his three farm tenancies before arriving at this stone yard and going through the post with his manager, Robert Norman. In his latter years Robert suffered from phlebitis, or some such condition, brought on, it was said, by hours of semi-immersion

Haysom and Sons depot between the wars, Back Row, L-R, Sam Florence, Fred (Sheppy) Lock, Fred Haysom, Phil Brown. Middle Row, L-R, Walter Haysom, Bert Tomes, Albert Phippard, Arthur Bonfield, John Haysom, Jimmy Chinchen, Harry Phippard, Bert Norman, Front row: Frank Haysom, holding chain nips, Harry Gillingham, Harold Haysom, Charlie Coleman, Harry Tomes, Teddy Corben, Arthur Corben, Sid Cooper. Some men are missing, as they would go to the Black Swan at lunch times. The nips dangle in front of the bed of the Coulter planer and the frame saw can be seen behind the main group.

loading stone in Durlston Bay when he was a young man. He packed up full time work about the time Thomas died. Thomas left the business to his hard drinking brother, Jack, who lived at one of the tenancies, Eastington Farm. Jack promptly sold the stoneyard to builders Parsons and Hayter, who employed masons preparing stone for their own projects as well as continuing in business as general stone merchants. My father Walter began work there in 1914, aged fifteen, as an informal apprentice. The stone side of the workforce at that time consisted of about a dozen men, with his father William as manager. Of his older brothers one was working away in London, others volunteered for the army. Less closely related and working in the same stoneyard were other Haysoms. Another Walter, whose father was landlord of the New Inn, had been crippled as a result of his ankle being crushed in an underground accident. Alfred Haysom was soon to be killed in the trenches. Others masons included Billy Harding, nicknamed 'The Gent', who had spent most of his working life in London, and his nephew Albert, of Langton. Another was Thomas Phippard, also from Langton, who rode to work each day in a donkey cart, for he had been born 'hurdle-footed' and was crippled. He had been apprenticed on Kingston church, where the rigorous exactitude of that training left him unable ever to work in a quicker, rougher way. He is not to be confused with Thomas Phippard of Swanage, known as 'Tommy Tilly', who had a quarry in Herston field. Others were Frank Turner, Thomas Turner and Joby Webber, deaf George Brown, Albert Brownsea Bower, George Dowland, George Norman, and the other apprentice boy, Jimmy Ivamy Bower, whose father worked in partnership with Charles Harris in their quarry in Burngate, near Acton. Bobby Norman continued to come in a few days a week. Most had worked for Thomas Stevens. The one job my father mentioned they had done was Maen House, Dorchester, but when he started they were busy with work for Bournemouth Corporation, Herston school (his older brother cut the name stone), the Royal Yacht Squadron at Cowes, and a floor of diamond-shaped paving, cut entirely by hand from bottom caps dug by Peter Manwell from his quarry close to present day Southard House.

In 1914 the slogan was 'business as usual'. Young men volunteering left grandfather short-handed. Two old men came out of retirement to help out: Charlie Coleman, father of 'Cack-handed Charlie' who was paid extra for his left handed proclivity, and, yet older, Samuel Collins. Both Coleman senior and Collins had worked on the rebuilding of Chichester Cathedral spire by Sir George Gilbert Scott and his son, George, after its collapse in 1861; and so my father worked alongside men who had worked under Scott! As the war went on, all masonry stopped. My grandfather was put in charge of German prisoners of war who were marched each day from 'the Cage' at Godlingston to Washing Ground to dig hardcore for Holton Heath munitions works. Washing Ground lay just south of Priests Road, opposite Gordon Road. Women living nearby had been in the habit of spreading their washing out to dry on the bushes there. It would have been the nearest source of this sort of of material to the depot with its railway siding. When this hole was exhausted the prisoners, paid volunteers, continued to work at Greasehead, about where modern Days Road has been constructed. Did any of these ever know where the stone was going?[75.]

Another early 20th century merchant was Billy Collins, who employed about six men, including Billy and Sam Tomes, in his yard on the site that became the laundry in Kings Road. He made the Palgrave Cross on Church Hill out of block from Turner's quarr, Port Arthur, Winspit. Billy Collins had started in the quarries but 'had his head screwed on'. He acquired Chinchin and White's merchants' business from old Nat White and also Randell's on the retirement of John Haysom.

After the war, and by 1920, Collins had amalgamated with Burt and Burt, Ponds, who had two brickyards, Parsons and Hayter, builders, and Walter Masters, who dealt in coal, to form the Purbeck Stone and General Trading Company.[76.] Ernie Burt was appointed managing director, but was sacked. He moved out to Mutton Hole by 1923, forming the 'Newton Stone Quarries', on the site of what is now the Swanage Holiday Park. He took one of the Town Gas engines to power a stone crusher or 'cracker'. There he made a cutting through several of the veins of stone, and set up a steam crane. The days of the horse drawn capstan were numbered! He installed a weighbridge, which remains, and proposed a ropeway supported on several pylons to convey stone from the quarry to the railway line, crossing over the High Street at Newton Knap; that particular idea never got off the drawing board. By 1935 the name was changed to 'Swanage Quarries Ltd.', probably at the time when it was acquired by Mr Crew. They crushed the Rag, worked the Grub into kerb and Roach into crazy paving etc. They made tarmacadam and road kerbing. Fred Lovell was the foreman. The business continued until the 1950s. A few years later J. Suttle revived quarrying there again.

Billy Collins' son Arthur was appointed manager of the Purbeck Stone and General Trading Co. in Ernie's place, but was also sacked. He claimed possession of the Fernery quarr down at Winspit, but actually continued with a New Vein quarry close to Compact Farm, subsequently worked by the Cobb family before being filled in. This move was probably the result of coming to an accommodation with the new owners of Worth and Compact farms, who did not want further quarrying at Winspit. Meanwhile, back in the Swanage depot, Harry Burt, foreman of the masons, semi-retired. William Haysom was appointed in his place.

About 1927, with the lease about to expire, the principal P.S.G.&T.C. shareholders, with a view to building houses on the site, as they had done at Steven's yard, decided to wind the company up. The liquidator burnt piles and piles of papers that had accumulated in a loft over the office. One weeps to think of what may have gone up in smoke that day. Templemans, one of the leading Bournemouth masonry firms, stepped in by buying a controlling interest. They decided to keep the stone yard going, retaining William as manager, and changed the name to Haysom and Sons. This continued until the next war, when the yard was sold to Swanage Town Council. Not long before this, Sam Florence was taken on as an apprentice. His father had a small stone business in Bournemouth, and advised him: 'Purbeck

G & T Lander's Gallows Gore quarry 1931.
Top L-R: Frederick ('Darky') Bonfield, George Lander (Snr), Titus Lander, Edward Stockley. Lower, L-R, George Lander (Jnr), William Webber, William Lander, Richard Stockley, K. William (Karl Bill) Lander.

TRADE ORGANISATIONS / 261

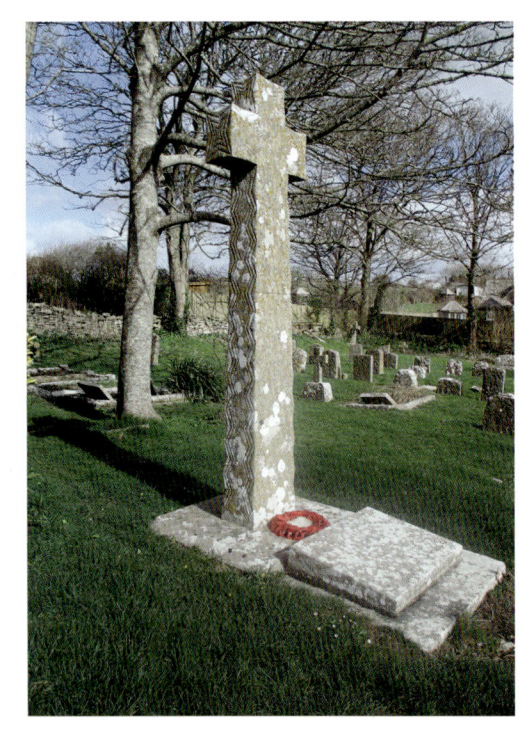

Worth Matravers Churchyard. Memorial cross, pre-1914.

Highlands, Acton. Fred Wellman, 1970s (photograph by Jed Corbett).

Thornback, is soft as Bath stone one side, hard as granite the other. If you learn to work it you can cope with anything. Get on over to Swanage.' The train fare absorbed most of his pay! [77.]

It should not be assumed that fine work was confined to these 'main players' in Swanage. Though the run of work at the quarries was generally quite rough, like street kerb and row ('rough') paving, some men employed highly skilled masons, notably Ambrose Bower, who had William Bower and Ike Vye working for him, both after long experience in London Yards. One of the jobs they did was the cross in Worth churchyard. It serves as the war memorial but pre-dates the First World War. They also prepared the masonry for the new north-east wing of Dunshay Manor, commissioned by Captain Marston and designed by Philip Sturdy. Ambrose, half brother to Billy Winspit, was also Mr. Sturdy's mason for the building of Trigon House (c.1927), using both new stone and that salvaged from the medieval and Georgian Wareham bridge over the Frome, newly demolished. My father said that Ambrose also sold out to the P. S. & G.T. Co., but I am not quite clear what he sold, in that his principle interests were quarries operated under custom on the Bankes Estate. Phillip Bower (grandson of Martin) said of him that in his lifetime Ambrose had worked twelve different quarries! This is likely to be an exaggeration. Another independent was Anthony Haysom who, in the interwar years sometimes had as many as sixteen men working in Lane, the quarry close by the Priest's Way at Verney.[78.] They supplied the stonework for the Swanage Bandstand. Another was Albert 'Trink' Bower, who had the lime kiln quarry by South Barn, the quarry close by the main road at Gully, plus a third in Burngate. His skilled masons included Frank Ivamy Bower and Tommy Harding.

The immediate post war period saw other rapid changes. Outside interests with capital acquired both Seacombe and Sheepsleights. But perhaps the most significant event was the dismemberment and sell off of the southern half of the Rempstone Estate, including the whole of Worth in 1919. Small freehold parcels of stone-bearing land came, perhaps almost for the first time, within reach of quarrymen. Titus and George Lander, Bert and George Harden, George Hancock and his sons, all Co-op. men at the time of its formation, acquired small lots adjacent to the Kingston road near Gallows Gore. Lorries were beginning to prove more effective than rail. With the main concentration of active quarries and stone reserves on the neighbouring Bankes Estate, these men were best placed to be the new generation of merchants.

DISPUTES

Though the stone trade may have been of mutual benefit to quarriers, landowners and farmers alike, as well as ancilliary trades such as blacksmiths, seamen, etc., disputes arose. These often involved lawyers, which led to the production of documents. The resulting records therefore tell of a disproportionate level of conflict; eras of peace go relatively unrecorded.

In 1725 farmer Edward Dampier 'ordered to fill up Math

Benfield and John Dowden's (surely Dowland) quarr in the meadow'. This is almost certainly Broad Mead.[79]

Ten years later, in 1770 John Bankes wrote to Mr. Filliter, lawyer and mayor of Wareham, complaining about the activities of another Benfield, Robert, who had illegally been opening up and selling off quarries. Bankes was surprisingly lenient: 'But as he is represented to me as a poor idle fellow with a wife & Family, I shall out of compassion to them, & the Parish of Corfe, only require him to satisfy me for the Injury done; to level the Ground; and to dig no more upon any part of my Estate in Purbeck.'

In 1778 Mr. K.B. Dampier, the new owner of the Swanage manor of Carrants Court, took a quarrier, Cooke, to court on a charge of trespass. A newspaper reported a 'case between a person who rents a quarry in the Isle of Purbeck and Mr. Dampier. On the part of the renter of the quarry it was maintained that the custom was that any person who was licensed by a proprietor to open a quarry there held that right as long as stones could be produced. On the other side it was admitted that a custom did exist, but it was proved that the custom insisted on by the renter of the quarry was not that custom and a verdict was accordingly given to Mr. Dampier.'[80] Dampier was awarded £1 damages, plus £40 costs. With wages at about 10s to 15s a week, this must have been a blow to Cooke. It seems he was insisting on an interpretation of the year and a day rule (Article 1) that the owner and court did not agree with.

In the early 19th century things were complicated on the Swanage Manor of Eightholds. The Dean and Chapter of Exeter Cathedral had demised the manor for 21 year periods. About 1753 William Morton Pitt Esq. sold his interest to Mr. William Taunton, whose heirs continued to receive the profits. In 1803 the Dean and Chapter woke up to the fact that they should have been getting the royalty income. It was complicated. Eightholds is a small, narrow manor extending from the Swanage stream to the cliffs. It was divided into eight tenements (hence 'eight holdings' corrupting to 'Eightholds'), where about 14 quarries were being worked. The lawyer noted that most of them had been open longer than anyone living could remember'[81] For about fifty years the Tauntons had been mainly absentee landlords, leaving affairs to a steward. In an attempt to sort things, in 1805 L. Taunton served 'several notices to quit on such of the Quarrymen as the attorney could catch outside of their holes' What a scene! The quarriers claiming the right to remain in occupation under the year and a day rule, disappearing underground when they saw the lawyer approaching! Setting out the case for Counsel's consideration, the situation is described:

'This manor of Swanage consists, besides some minute portions of waste, of 8 ancient Customary Tenements demised and demisable immemorially by Copy of Court Roll for 3 lives, the life of the longest liver, not at the will of the Lord, as appears by the Older Court Rolls, therefore probably of the Tenure of ancient demesne great quantities of stone are dug in numerous quarries in Swanage Parish by Persons pretending to hold their quarries by a Peculiar Tenure viz by a Parol Grant or Licence to dig paying certain ancient prices or sums for the stone they raise according to the quality viz:

For paving stone per 100 Ft super	1/s
Gutter Do	2/s
Step Do	2/s
Block per ton	3d
Edging stone per load	6d
Every grave stone	1/s
Columns Rollers per ton	1/s
Rick Haddles per load	4/s
Hollow work Troughs per 60 pecks	1/s

being about one thirtieth part of the value of the stone when wrought, they say that their interest is not determinable by notice, is descendable to the next of kin, attainable and only determined by entirely omitting to work for a year and a day'

Taunton 'commenced an ejectment and obtained a conditional judgment against about 8 of them since which he has done no act to recognise the tenancy of any of the persons served with notices' A survey of 1805 showed eight inland quarries, all more or less north of Bon Accord Road. Did one or more of these men go to court, for in the following year Taunton imposed a licence for his quarry at Tilly Whim? t was probably this dispute, continuing into 1806, which occasioned the newspaper report:

'At the above assizes (Dorchester) a case of considerable importance came to be tried, respecting certain ancient rights of the Company of Free Marblers of the Island of Purbeck, which we understand is to undergo a discussion next Michaelmas Term in the Court of King's Bench.' One wonders what happened; I have not been able to find out.

In 1853 Thomas Stevens, George Stickland, Henry Haysom and William Tomes were tried at Wareham for trespass and carting away stones. The dispute centred on Mr. Bridle's Field. Ann Bridle of Worth had inherited the Newton Estate, Swanage, and was presumably trying to get these quarrymen out. The magistrates dismissed the case 'for want of jurisdiction'. Henry Haysom may have left then, for later he had a quarry in western Greasehead, subsequently worked by J. Chinchen. But others continued and in due course clashed with the next owner, Sir Charles Robinson, who was surveyor of the Queen's pictures from 1882-1901, and art advisor to the South Kensington Museum, later to become the V&A.

In 1875/6 Mr. Robson reported on the condition of the Bankes Estate. He included:

'The benefits derived from the Stone Quarries are totally inadequate to the losses sustained by damage to the surface of the land, and trespass by the Quarrymen, as well as through the augmentation of the parochial Rates [...] The Tenants to Eastington and Wilkswood Farms complain bitterly of the lawlessness of the Quarrymen, and their difficulties in depasturing their stock, and the Trespass and annoyances are deteriorating the letting value of the Farms, and it really seems necessary that the rights of the Quarrymen should be lawfully defined, and though great difficulties would arise in closing the Quarries (as important interests in the neighbourhood would be seriously affected in so doing) it may nevertheless be advisable to reconsider and increase the Royalties, as an endeavour to lessen the losses to which the Estate is subject, and allow the Market value of the Stone to be realised, but the change could not be effected without litigation and tumult.'[82]

The storm clouds were gathering.

Soon after, Mr. Bankes, with the other major landowners, John Hales Calcraft, the Earl of Eldon, Mrs Serrell and Charles Robinson, sought Counsel's opinion. In a document headed 'Mr. Ralph Bankes Esq. and the Stone Quarries', it was stated that the quarrymen claimed to have a charter allowing them to open the Land for getting at the Stone and when they are once in possession and have worked at the quarry they cannot be dispossessed if they pay the accustomed royalty.'

The document went on to list various leases from the 1820s, pointing out that the quarrymen had long done much as they liked, even selling quarries despite their being covenenants against their doing so:

'An instance has just occurred in which one Richard Benfield had sold a quarry which had not been worked for years to George Lander for £5 who now works it. He had Notice that he was trespassing but treats that with contempt and the Agent of Mr. Bankes who gave the Notice has received no Ground Rent or Royalty as although offered by Lander he declined to receive it (no specific amount was tendered) treating him as a trespasser.'

In response Bankes' agent, T. T. Kent, ordered Lander to keep off the Bankes Estate or risk being taken to court. But he was not the only one guilty of withholding royalty payments:

Another Case has just occurred in which a Michael Bower sold his quarry to a man who works it but no royalty is received.

Thomas Phippard who holds no Lease has also leased his quarry for 2 years without consulting Mr. Bankes.

There is also the case of Martin Bower an old man who has taken possession of an old quarry which had been worked by his Ancestors but had been closed for 30 years and filled in by Mr. Salway, Mr. Banke's Tenant of Eastington Farm, and in his occupation Martin Bower was served with a Notice similar to that before set out.

Another Case of a man of the name of Barnes who took possession of an old hole which had been filled in by the same Tenant (Salway) many years ago (it is said at least 30 years) but claimed to be worked by Barnes on the ground of the quarry having been once worked by his forefathers.

It was decided to bring actions for trespass and ejectment on the grounds that they would be the best method of legally defining the relative rights of both the owners and the quarrymen.

On the Bankes Estate things festered. The Earl of Eldon clashed with the last quarry operators, Burt and Burt, on his Peveril Estate. After a wrangle which must have had a certain piquancy with their cousin Sir George owning the neighbouring estate, the Burts gave up in 1889. Sir Charles Robinson, seeking to develop his Newton and Eightholds estates, was frustrated by the presence of a number of quarrymen who would not leave. He resorted to direct action, employing outsiders who had come as labourers on the railway construction to go at night and fill in the shafts. It was not unusual to keep a few chickens or grow some vegetables at the quarries. Chemister Norman, one of the quarriers and a Company of Marblers committee member, had such a patch of spuds which Robinson's shaft blockers grabbed, together with anything else ready to hand, and threw it down the shaft. It earned Robinson the nickname of 'Tatey Greens'. Feelings ran high. Fights ensued between the 'foreign' labourers and the quarrymen. The row was going on when Thomas Hardy visited with his new wife in 1875. She wrote: 'the men are talking in groups, the quarries all neglected. Mr. R. has bought the land and raised the rent of the quarries. Five women went to meet the steamer, but he came by land to Wareham and got safely home'.[83.]

Robinson's new nickname provoked yet further trouble. In August 1876 his eldest son responded to being called 'Tatey Greens' in a Swanage street by striking a quarrier called William Saunders with a stick. The outcome was an appearance in court and a charge of assault, for which he was fined £1.[84.]

Sir Charles was unwilling to let the matter rest, writing letters to the press complaining about the lack of police in Swanage, calling the quarrymen 'lawless', and claiming that 'My own life has been threatened, and the peace and comfort of my family seriously disturbed.'[85.]

Sir Charles won, of course. The quarriers were evicted and where they had toiled he laid out his new roads, coining names from the manor's past: Cluny, St.Vast, Taunton, Exeter, etc. This choice of names is indicative of Sir Charles's scholarship. No hint of this row is suggested in his son's *Picturesque Rambles in the Isle of Purbeck* (1882), which gives a sympathetic account of the stone industry.

Mrs. Serrell seems not to have clashed with the quarrymen in the same way. Perhaps she was more aware of how difficult life was for the less well off. There are two small Laining Vein quarrs in Langton in Cole's ground and Dry Meadow in which, according to Ambrose Bower, Ma Serrell employed out of work quarrymen.[86.] Perhaps too, she had no development aims that conflicted, in the way Sir Charles had.

The apparent quietude on the Bankes Estate was broken by George Lander junior breaking open a quarry on land farmed by John Stevens, brother of Thomas, who was both a farmer and stone merchant. On 4 November, 1882, Thomas Stevens wrote to Bankes' agent H. O. Chisslett:

'We write to inform you there is 2 new quarrys opening on Eastington Farm which we cannot alow as all the best part of the farm. If men are let alone to do as they like will be all quarry holes and scar banks. If this still continues to grow which way can we pay you our rent. The men opening a quarry is Richard Bower and George Lander junior. The other is Thomas Brown Bower and Joseph Brown Bower please see this is put a stop to and the present fresh holes filled up and oblige us'.[87.]

The pressure to get out must have already been applied to the Brown Bowers, and they conceded, for almost in the same post Thomas wrote:

'Just a word to say I have not been to work in the hole; against Job Bowers quarry since the day Mr. Penney was here and likewise filled it up. I must here state that I was not the first to open it.

p.s. I should not have had anything to have done with it only my quarry is wet not fit to work in nor yet this month past'.

It seems the Brown Bowers went on struggling with their difficult quarry for another five years before seeking permission to reopen another old quarry in Highlands in 1887: 'it is in an old hole near the road but amongst the furze . . .'

The Brown Bowers touched the forelock, but whether Richard

Bower and George Lander prevailed is not clear. However, 21 years later George prompted another letter of complaint from Stevens. In what seems to have been an increasingly febrile atmosphere the Marblers minute book of 1889 recorded: 'Mr. Calcraft Esq. has made it known to the Company that all quarries on his estate is worked to General Custom according to Royalty Raised'. In 1904 Bankes instructed his steward, Robert Thorn, who was the woodman at Wilkswood and dealt with the quarries on a day to day basis, collecting the dues, etc., to tell Lander to stop. So the matter had finally come to a head.

Warden Saul Bower kept a record of the meetings which the ensuing row provoked. Most were held at Greasehead, the best midway point for men walking from Swanage on the one hand, Langton on the other.[88.]

> 'February 13 1904 A general meeting of Members was held at Henry Seymour's Quarry Greasehead when over 200 were present to hear the affidafits Sworn to by John Stevens (Tenant) of Eastington Farm and W Ralph Banks owner of Same regarding a Quarry that has been reopened in a Meadow Called Broad Mead after being Closed for over 40 years by George Henry Lander this Quarry was reopened without the Company being Consulted. After a Lengthy discussion it was Unanimously agreed to Support George H Lander in the action taken by the Plaintiffs
> A Resolution was passed authorizing the Warden to Engage a solicitor to write the Plaintiff's Solicitors stating that the Case would be met before the Threatened Injunction was Issued'

Solicitors were appointed, but it soon became apparent that nothing could be done to stop the proceedings against Lander and that Ralph Bankes was determined to test the Marblers rights as a Company. In due course a group of the oldest members gave sworn affadafits:

> 'March 29 1904 The warden went to Poole with G.H.Lander Isaac Bower aged 83 James Bridle 75 George Lander Father of the Defendant affidafits were sworn and information given to the Solicitors as to Ancient Customs & usages with regard to the reopening of old Quarries.'

> 'March 29 1904 Called at Swanage for Mr. Powell to take 6 Photographs of the Quarry reopened by G H Lander and the Surrounding Holes & Banks as the Plaintifs State in their Afidafts Broad Meadow was a Plain Pasture Field '

ABOVE The first of three of William Powell's photographs taken in the course of the George Lander row. Ambrose Bower's cart being loaded in Broad Mead. Note the presence of women and girls, and a large group of fellow quarrymen.

BELOW The cart on its way to Swanage, on the turnpike road, with Gallows Gore cottages visible at left. It is being drawn by the men and boys, using a quarry main chain. The figure riding on the stone is either George Lander or one of the Brownsea Bowers, who decked himself out as if for a Whitsun procession. Sitting in front of him is Thomas Tilly Phippard, who was born lame.

Photographs which survive show various stages of the conveyance of a load of stone to Swanage, possibly in early summer, rather than all being devoted to views of the field.

None of the Swanage merchants would send their wagons to collect the stone George Lander prepared, because to do so meant driving into the field and thereby getting involved. Lander had made a new gap in the wall for access, which Stevens blocked up again. What stone was dispatched was taken away by Ambrose Bower's horse and cart. For some reason for one load they dispensed with the horse but instead attached a main chain to the wagon, which was dragged by a number of men and boys down to the Swanage depot. Photographs were taken at various points on the journey. They show one of the senior Brownsea Bowers, perhaps too old to walk, decked

The group on arrival at the Court Hill depot; stone merchant Henry Weeks Burt in top hat, facing, at centre. He was reluctant to provide a wagon to carry away Lander's stone from Broad Mead, and thus become embroiled in the row.

out as was done for Whitsun outings, and Thomas Phippard, crippled from birth, as well as George Lander, riding on the cart. The final scene at the depot includes the group being met by Henry Weeks Burt, with deaf Teddy Corben looking at left. They constitute a unique record of a gathering of quarry men before the disaster of 1914-18.

Events ground on. The Company's solicitors made it clear that George Lander was in danger of imprisonment if he did not stop working the quarry, after it was agreed that all the members would save a shilling a week to help meet the costs of his defence.

In the course of trying to construct a defence the quarrymen's lawyers had learned from the Bankes lawyers that the Bankes Estate had granted ten or more time-limited licences 100 years before. The Estate named some of the recipients: Barnes, Bower, Squibb, Bridle, Chinchen, Corben, and most tellingly, Thomas and Edward Lander. Ten quarries may not have been the full number working on the Estate at that time, but was a very significant fraction. The agreement was for a term of 14 years, paying a shilling for every 100 square feet of paving and channel, 2s. per 100 foot run of step, 1s. per load (8 feet by 2 feet) of healing or tiling stone etc. The defence was seriously weakened.

George Lander insisted that members of the Company of Marblers and Stonecutters had the right to re-open old quarries, evoking Article I, but Isaac Bower went further, claiming:[89.]

> 'According to ancient and immemorial custom the said Company of Marblers have the exclusive right to dig and quarry all stone in the Isle of Purbeck in lands not being gardens orchards or woodlands such right having according to tradition been granted to them their heirs and successors for ever for services performed by them in defending the Isle of Purbeck and the Coast from invasions.'

In his affadavit George Lander stated that both he and John Stevens were members of the Company of Marblers and Stone Cutters and:

> 'The quarry which has been recently opened up by me in the field known as Broad Meadow in Eastington Farm in the Isle of Purbeck is an old quarry which was formerly worked as I am informed and verily believe by my grandfather and also by my great grandfather [...]
>
> I had previously to opening the said Quarry on the 16 March 1903 informed the plaintiff John Stevens of my intention to do so and he then said he did not mind how many old quarries were reopened as he should have £2 a year taken off his rent for each quarry so opened.'

Lander described the underground workings and how he found the old quarry working still in existence. He also found the remains of old quarry tools. He had clearly re-opened an underground. He went on:

> 'The Members of the said Company have always so far as my recollection goes claimed the right to re-enter upon any disused quarry and work the same. I remember my father in the year 1872 opening up and working an old quarry upon the Estate of the present plaintiff Walter Ralph Bankes. His right to do so was then disputed and the steward of the Estate refused for some years to take dues from my father but ultimately my father's right was conceded and the dues were accepted and the quarry was afterwards worked (without any interference) by my father and my brother.
>
> About 18 years ago I reopened an old quarry at Wilkswood Farm on the Estate of the plaintiff Walter Ralph Bankes and I worked

266 / PURBECK STONE

the same for several months and then sold the rights to my fellow tradesmen James Benfield who afterwards sold to Messrs Burt and Burt who worked the quarry for many years.

I deny that I have caused the plaintiffs damage by my works I have simply used the Old path for the Conveyance of the stone and the old scar bank round the quarry has been made higher by the deposit of the waste from the quarry'.[90.]

Another senior quarryman, Richard Bower, confirmed Isaac's statement and added a list of men re-opening old quarries without hindrance from the landlord. However, he did not cite any cases of men breaking open new quarries without permission. Two different things were being claimed: the freedom to re-open old quarries; the freedom to quarry *per se*.

The Bankes' side were in communication with other landlords. Their agent, Mr. Lodder, was informed of disputes on other estates. He wrote: 'Have seen Captain Rogers (the owner of Durnford, Langton) respecting the quarry on his estate that was stopped. He said it was John Stevens who claimed the right to work it, having bought it off another party'. John, it seems, was running with the hare and hunting with the hounds. Another case mentioned was the Earl of Eldon and William Edmunds (farmer) v. Henry and Anthony Haysom (father and son):

'Haysoms had entered upon a field belonging to Lord Eldon in the occupation of Mr Edmunds and began to open out a quarry. The action was brought in the Chancery Division of the High Court and asked, first, for an injunction to restrain the defendants from continuing to work the quarry or from entering on the land, Secondly, damages for trespass, and thirdly, for costs.' One defendant appeared but offered no defence, the other did not appear 'and accordingly judgement was entered in terms of the claim'.

The Minute account continued:
'May 24 Went to Poole & had an interview with the Solicitor, Edwin Bower of Worth going with me, we Stated that the Leases refered to above must have been granted to the various members named. Unbeknown to the General members of our Company, it being against all rules and Usages for a Quarry to be Worked on those conditions Several Quarrymen having to our knowledge to Forego working when the Company found that a lease was to be taken.
The Solicitor stated their agents had done their utmost to find a Copy of the said Charter but nothing relating to such a document could be found, and requests us to forward to them More Ancient records and Customs also Cash.'

Edwin Bower's assertion seems astonishing in the light of records held by the Bankes Estate. Indeed it seems there was a collective amnesia. A systematic list of all the estate quarries made in 1825 shows that with the exception of three, expired, all 23 of them held 14 or 21 year long licences, some from as early as 1809.[91.]

It would seem men agreed such time-limited licences, but somehow conflated it in their minds with the year and a day rule. Joseph Chinchen's 1809 agreement for Mr. Bankes' part of West Hedbury is a good example of such a time-limited licence, going into considerable detail, given its early date:

'18 August 1809 Henry Bankes to Joseph Chinchen, Bankes' part of West Idbury, already occupied by Chinchen.

Term of seven years, Rents
Front stone and scapled backing, 6d per ton
Rough backing or block stone, 4d per ton
Ashlar and step stone or stone worked to any particular order, 2s. per 100 feet
Paving and channel, 1s per 100 feet
Tomb stones or grave stones, 1s each
For every 30 peck of troughs and sinks, 1s
Rollers, 1s per ton
Legs and cap,s 1s per set [9 legs and 9 caps]'

The lease required detailed accounts of the stone quarried, the vessels or wagons by which it was taken away and details of the purchaser. The quarry had to be active, and be worked by a 'sufficient number of competent workmen and labourers'.

The Lander row rumbled on: 'June 7. Called Committee meeting to hear report from our Collector, Thos Saunders and found that t was not every satisfactory.'

Amongst Lander case-related papers is an undated list of people: it must surely be Thomas Saunders' record of contributers. Quarrymen overwhelmingly dominate, but there are a few other signatories, notably Mrs. Serrell, Mrs. Randell, a Mr. Whit (White is surely intended?), their social status indicated by the title not given to other contributors. They may well have donated more than the shilling asked of the quarriers. Another oddity is Nath. Haysom. I am not aware of a quarryman of that name, but there was a clergyman named Nathaniel Haysom who often visited Swanage at the time. The sentiment of those supporters is perhaps caught in an anonymous letter sent to Mr. Bankes:

'Sir, I feel it my duty to drop you a line concerning Lander I don't think the man is fairly dealt with as there are others opening quarries at the present time and nothing said about them because the man is open and above boarde he is dispised but Sir please remember the little ones For inasmuch as ye have given a morsel to the least of these ye have given it to Me

From one of The Company.'

The contributors were: (asterisks indicate those whose surname was in fact Bower. 'Joseph Baker' is actually Joseph Baker Corben)

William Saunders
William Phippard
Alexander Corben
Isaac Bower
James Ball*
Charles Saunders
Reuben S Bower
Henrey Whit
Thomas Bower
Isaac Bower Combe
Aaron Bower
John Bridle
Rich Benfield
Titus Bower
Charles Bridle
Isaac Bower Acton
H. Stickland
Mrs. Serrell
Titus Phippard
James Bridle
John Ball*
Michael Corben
Thos. Phippard
John Curtis
Jacob Bower
John Saunders
James Webber
John Prestone*
John Turner
Ambr Bower
Timothy Brown
Job Corben
Jos Geo Harris
Joseph Baker
William Squibb
Joseph Seymore
Hireham Bower
John Squibb
Frank Seymore
Reub Bower

TRADE ORGANISATIONS / 267

Thomas Bower Jr
Mrs. Randell
Joseph Benfield
Seth Brownsea*
John Haysom
J. Whit Bower
John Phippard
Mr. Whit
Charles Bower
James Corben
George Keates
Albert Brown
Nat. Haysom
Thomas Stevens
J. Cake Bower
Agustes Bower
Henrey Burt
Thomas Brown
John Harding
John W. Bonfield
Seth Benfield
Jeremiah Bower
James Galley
James Haysom
Robert Squibb
George Mussellwhit
James Saunders
Joseph Lander
Job Edmunds
William Turner
William Brown
William Tomes
Henrey Bridle
Samuel Lander
Henrey Tomes
John S Bower
Henrey Lander
Walter Tomes
Thos. Phippard Jun
Thomas Lander
Richard Tomes
Richard Bower
Samuel Harding
Frank Toms
Nat Tomes
John Harries
Thomas Phippard
? G. Bower
Alfred Harries
Joseph Phippard
William Vinsent
John Chinchen
Petter Phippard
Henrey Ball*
Jesse Bower
William Weeks
James Cake*
Amos Bower
Samuel Cross
Edward S. Bower
Job Bower
Frank Stickland
William Bower Comb
Michael Bower

Charles Colman
George R Weeks
George Bower
James Colman
Frank Bower
George Corben
Joseph Phippard
Albert Saunders
Thomas Webber
John Phippard
George Long
William Nye
John Weeks
Edward Bower
Charles Corben
Isaac Collins
Thomas Corben
Samuel Corben
Henrey Cooper
Jesse Bower
Isaac Brownsea*
Henrey Manwell
George Bess
James Meader
Bengman Bower
William Stevens
John Tomes
Thomas Stevens
Charles Edmonds
Charles Bonfield
John Corben
Emmanuel Turner
Joseph Manwell
Lot Corben
William Cooper
Henrey Bower
George Corben
William Chinchen
William Cooper
James Dowland
John Meader
George Cooper
George Turner
James Haysom
Joseph King
George Norman
Robert Stickland
John King
William Burt
Thomas Haysom
George Bonfield
Howard Collins
Thomas Bower
George Harris
Joseph Galley
Charles Phippard
George Corben
Henrey Haysom
James Norman
Isaac Stickland
Henrey Haysom
Henrey Gover
George Collins
Thomas Harris

Charles Edmunds
James Butler
Isaac Bower
James Corben
James Norman
James Brown
Walter Bonfield
John Dowland
William Short*
John Haysom
Henrey Cross
Charles Allen*
Stephen Haysom
John Norman
Ed. Phippard
Frederick Haysom
Robert Norman
James Bower
Walter Benfield
George Kets
Marting Bower (infirm)
George Harding
Alfred Toms
George Burt
Frederick Edmunds
George Chinchen
Frank Haysom
Isaac Toms
Isaac Haysom
Robert Chinchen
Henrey Seymore
Henrey Haysom
Chas. Stickland
John Norman
Thos Squibb
George Squibb
Charles Harris

Thomas Squibb
Philip Edmunds
Isaac Collins
Frederick Bower
William Collins
George Bower
Henrey Edmunds
Frank Turner
Mark Hibbs
James Brown
Christopher Haysom
(infirm)
James Collins
Walter Brown
Charles Harding
Joseph Bonfield
James Collins
John Stickland
Thomas Norman
Joseph Brown
Henrey Hancock
Frank Norman
George Short*
Walter Collins
John Cooper
George Brown
Samuel Brown
Robert Norman
George Collings
Charles Harding
Peter Manwell
Robert Collins
John Stevens
William Collins
George Norman
William Burt

92.

The list includes virtually all the independent quarriers plus most of the men working for them and the merchants, even those who had reservations about the wisdom of the action. It would have been difficult to stand out and not produce a shilling. John and Thomas Stevens' names are puzzling: could these be the men central to the row?

'June 21 Received notice that G H Lander was being taken from the Quarry by the Policeman and an officer sent by the Court, to London. This was done as he declined to obey the order made by the Judge to Stop Working till after the trial.

June 25 A General Meeting held at Henry Seymour's Quarry Greasehead when it was Unanimously agreed that the Warden Draw the Cash from the Bank and proceed at once with the Solicitors to do all they can to get Lander's discharge from Brixton Prison as soon as possible and that the Subscription be handed over to the Collectors

It was also agreed that the Documents & papers held by the Warden be handed over to the Solicitors they having made application for them

The Langton Warden called the names over with the exception of 2 they were answered.

A Resolution was passed and agreed to that fines should be taken from those who refused to pay the Collector'

It obviously difficult to collect more money and the solicitors were threatening not to act further unless paid. The subscription collector resigned. It was resolved that each quarry owner or employer should collect from the men employed by him. The solicitors agreed to reduce their outstanding bill to £12. On March 7 1905 they were sent a postal order for £1. The Company of Marblers had spent all its banked savings plus what they had collected specifically for the defence. Not until 1914 did they get enough together to pay off the remaining debt and recover their papers from the lawyers. The Minute Books entries cease. George's offence was Contempt of Court. To defy the judge as he and the Committee chose to do was folly. In terms of the rights and wrongs of the case, nothing was proved either way. One wonders how Mr. Bankes viewed this outcome. Bob Harris said to me that on George's release Bankes ordered 'That man is not to be seen on my estate off a footpath.' In due course of time his four sons continued quarrying on the neighbouring Worth Estate, acquiring freehold plots of land following its sale.

George attracted sympathy as being a 'hard working' man suffering for his convictions. Perhaps the Estate's attitude softened, for the half century that followed saw the concentration of quarrying there and an acceptance of custom, particularly the year and a day rule, well after all the other estates had ceased to recognise it.

Other disputes arose which were dealt with by the wardens. The 100 foot rule meant that you could not start a quarry within that distance from one already established, but, of course, once begun, both could head towards one another and sometimes even meet. Apart from the major point about who got what stone, this could cause a draught that made the candles burn quickly. Quarrels often erupted:

'April, 1904. The Warden received notice from Richard Bower [known as Dick Gad] to call the Committee together to decide how far Reuben Short Bower had encroached on his Head of Stone the Committee found that he was three feet to far with one range as determined by the Swanage & Langton Committee some time Previous. A Mark was affixed as to R S Bowers limit by the Committee those Present being S Bower (Warden) Ambrose Bower, Edwin Bower, Charles A Bower Henry B Bower with a Number of the Swanage Committee who were the Previous Committee'.

Just to put this in context, Reuben Short Bower's banker remains by the main road just to the west of 'Weathertop' near Acton.

But their quarrel continued:

'June A General Meeting called By Reuben Short Bower Complaining that Richard Bower had Broken through on his Head of Stone [this is underground] it was Unanimously decided by those present that Reuben S Bower was in the wrong has he had exceeded his bounds by Several feet on Richard Bowers Stone, as determined by the Committee on April 27th A mark was again put as to how far he was to go, and a Resolution declaring that the the one that worked against the Company decision should be fined the Full Penalty on the next occasion'

Whatever the complications of this upset were, at least those concerned were working on the same level. Harold Bonfield told me of a dispute between Shilling Norman and Frank Tomes that arose when Shilling drove in the Downs Vein under Frank's Freestone workings at Belle Vue. Frank's concern was that if Shilling caused a founder it would bring down his quarry. I wonder how the wardens sorted that one out. My father said that his father, who not having a quarry was seen as non-partisan, would sometimes be asked to make measurements, by the aid of tape and compass, when such issues arose between neighbours.

Farm tenants were sometimes aggrieved by the action of quarrymen, sometimes it was the other way around. County Petty Sessions, 1865 included Henry Spicer of Coombe Farm, Langton Matravers, being summoned by George Bonfield 'for unlawfully and maliciously throwing down a certain wall fence to his quarry, called 'Chop Hayes,' and injuring the said quarry, to the value of £4' – for which he was fined £2. 2s., including the damage to the wall and costs.'

One wonders whether, magistrate J. Mowlem, Esq., with his quarryman antecedents could have been entirely even-handed in a case like this.

Keith Bower, latterly farming the same Chop Hayes in Verney, told of a perhaps similar circumstance. They had cut the thistles in summer and left them lying. Heavy autumn rains floated them down the sloping field until they began to pile up against a wall. This served to block the crannies that normally let the water through. The water began to bay up to such an extent that the wall was threatened. Keith barred a break in the wall allowing the water to escape in a sudden torrent.

ADMISSIONS LIST – COMPANY OF MARBLERS

(numbers relate to the number of times the name appears

1837-1936   BOOK 1   SWANAGE

Alford, 3	Hancock, 10
Benfield, 13	Harden, 10
Best, 1	Harding, 4
Bonfield, 29	Harris, 12
Bower, 15	Haysom, 38
Bridle, 2	Hibbs, 2
Brown, 8	Horlock, 1
Burt, 31	Keats, 9
Butler, 4	King, 6
Chinchin, 19	Lander, 4
Cole, 1	Manwell, 5
Coleman, 8	Meader, 9
Collins, 38	Melmouth, 3
Cooper, 10	Mowlem, 8
Corben, 21	Musselwhite, 2
Cross, 8	Norman, 41
Curtis, 2 1896	Parsons, 1
Dowland, 14	Phippard, 21
Edmunds, 12	Pushman, 6
Galley, 5	Randell, 2
Gover, 3	Seymour, 10

1876–1925 BOOK 2 LANGTON AND WORTH

Benfield, 4
Bower, 79
Bridle, 6
Brown, 13
Burt, 4
Chinchin, 2
Corben, 6
Coleman, 1
Curtis, 4
Dowland, 1
Edmunds, 3
Galley, 2
Harden, 6
Harding, 3
Harris, 11
Hobbs, 1
Keats, 2
Lander, 24
Lewis, 1
Norman, 3
Saunders, 3
Squibb, 2
Stevens, 2
Thorn, 1
Vye, 1
Webber, 7

WARDENS

commencing 1837, as recorded in the Minute Books.

SWANAGE

1837	Robert Burt	George Bower
1838	Robert Burt	George Bower
1839	Robert Burt	Thomas Keats
1840	Robert Burt	Thomas Keats
1841	Robert Burt	Thomas Keats
1842	Robert Burt	Thomas Keats
1843	Robert Burt	Will Butler
1844	Charles Chinchen	Thomas Randell Jn.
1845	Charles Chinchen	Rob. Burt Sen.
1846	Rob. Mowlem	George Stickland
1847	Rob. Mowlem	George Stickland
1848	Rob. Mowlem	George Stickland
1849	Rob. Mowlem	George Stickland
1850	Rob. Mowlem	George Stickland
1851	Thomas Stevens	W. C. Burt
1852	Sam Bonfield	Moses Webber
1853	Sam Bonfield	Moses Webber
1854	Moses Haysom	Moses Webber
1855	not recorded	
1856	not recorded	
1857	not recorded	
1858	Isaac Collins	Will Cooper
1859	Isaac Collins	Will Cooper
1860	not recorded	
1861	not recorded	(Hutchins III of 1861 refers to the Joint Stock Co. document as being in the possession of 'the only member of the Company now resident in Corfe and one of the wardens'. This must be John Webber, whose name seems not to appear in the books)
1862	not recorded	
1863	Isaac Collins	Will Cooper
1864	Henry Burt	Sam Collins
1865	Henry Seymour	
1866	Henry Seymour	
1867	George Collins	
1868	George Collins	
1869	Will Bower	
1870	Fred Harding	
1871-1875	John Warren Bonfield	

(The record of Swanage wardens continues: the record of Langton wardens begins in 1876)

SWANAGE		LANGTON
1876	John Warren Bonfield	William Saunders
1877	Isaac Stickland	William Saunders
1878	Henry Cooper	George Lander
1879	Henry Cooper	George Lander
1880	Henry Tomes	Joseph King, George Lander
1881	Walter Tomes	Joseph Baker Corben, George Lander
1882	Walter Tomes	Frank Bower
1883	Thomas Stickland	Frank Bower
1884	Thomas Stickland S	eth Benfield
1885	Thomas Stickland S	eth Benfield
1886	James Brown	George Lander
1887	Michael Cooper	George Lander
1888	Michael Cooper	Ambrose Bower
1889	Michael Cooper	Ambrose Bower
1890	Michael Cooper	Ambrose Bower
1891	Sam Squibb	William Turner
1892	Sam Squibb	Reuben S Bower
1893	Thomas S. H. Phippard	Reuben S Bower
1894	Thomas S. H. Phippard	Reuben S Bower
1895	Thomas S. H. Phippard	Reuben S Bower
1896	Thomas S. H. Phippard	Reuben S Bower
1897	Richard Tomes	Reuben S Bower
1898	Richard Tomes	James Albert Brown
1899	John Haysom	n/r
1900	James Chinchen	
1901	James Chinchen	James A. Brown
1902	James Chinchen	James A. Brown
1903	James Chinchen	James A. Brown
1904	James Chinchen	W. W. S. Bower [Saul]
1905	Albert Tomes	Saul Bower
1906	Albert Tomes	Saul Bower
1907	Walter Norman	Saul Bower
1908	Walter Norman	n/r
1909	George Burt	n/r
1910	George Burt	n/r
1911	George Burt	n/r
1912	James Chinchen	
1913	James Chinchen	C. Bridle
1914	Fred Meader	T. Webber
1915	Fred Meader	T. Webber
1916	Fred Meader	T. Webber
1917	Fred Meader	T. Webber
1918	Fred Meader	acting wardens J. Chinchen and F. Seymour
1919	Charles Benfield	n/r
1920	Charles Benfield	John Ivamy Bower
1921	Charles Benfield	John Ivamy Bower
1922	Charles Benfield	John Ivamy Bower
1923	Charles Benfield	John Ivamy Bower
1924	Alf Norman	Alf Benfield
1925	Alf Norman	Alf Benfield
1926	Alf Norman	Alf Benfield
1927	Alf Norman	Alf Benfield
1928	Alf Norman	Alf Benfield
1929	Alf Norman	Alf Benfield
1930	Alf Norman	Alf Benfield
1931	Alf Norman	Alf Benfield
1932	Alf Norman	Alf Benfield
1933	Albert Chinchen	Hedley Lander
1934	Albert Chinchen	Hedley Lander
1935	Albert Chinchen	Hedley Lander
1936	Albert Chinchen	Hedley Lander

1937	Albert Chinchen	Hedley Lander
1939	End of Swanage book	John Pushman
1940		John Pushman
1941		John Pushman
1942	Away on war service	John Pushman
1943	Away on war service	John Pushman
1944	Away on war service	John Pushman
1945	Away on war service	John Pushman
1946	John Pushman	Robert Harris
1947	John Pushman	Robert Harris
1948	John Pushman	Robert Harris
1949	John Pushman	Robert Harris
1950	John Pushman	Robert Harris
1951	John Pushman	Robert Harris
1955	John Pushman	Robert Harris
1956	John Pushman	Robert Harris

FIRMS AND MEN OF PURBECK ORIGIN WORKING ELSEWHERE

Some of these are listed solely on the evidence of Purbeck names, others on more certain ground.

ALBION STONE YARD in Merton, London, started in 1920s by Alfred BOWER and Thomas THORNE + a third Langton man. (Thomas was son of Robert Thorne Bower, woodman at Wilkswood.)

BARNES Stone yard in Portland employing about 70 masons in the 1920s. The foreman was 'Catchem' Corbin of Langton. Tom Corben and ? Phippard did the block selecting and cutting out; that is, still cutting with wedges. Walter Haysom had a summer there. Every Friday Catchem tapped someone on the shoulder; 'out'. There were always others waiting for work.

BENFIELD & LOXLEY. Masons and contractors, formerly in Bullingdon Road, Oxford, latterly trading as Joslins, Long Hanborough, Oxford

BENFIELD AND SON. 106 Scrubs Lane, Willesden, London

BOWER, Albert. Had stone yard in Finchley.

BOWER, Albert. In charge of Portland night shift for years after the First World War, returned to Langton on retirement.

BOWER, Albert. In charge of night shift in Bath and Portland's yard in the 1960s. (He was Dick Gad Bower's nephew). Nicknamed 'Nutty'.

BOWER, Jack Gad. Brother of Dick, Hiram and Levi, was working in Barnes Yard, Portland, in 1920.

BOWER & FLORENCE. Granite firm, Aberdeen.

BOWER, Thomas Rabbit. Brother of Sammy Coffin Bower (usually known as Sammy Rabbit). Went to Portland to work as a young man, then Brighton, then London, where he worked on St. Paul's for twenty years or so, the Clerk of Works at that time being Mr. Lynge, a relation of Joby Ball Bower. Was presented to George V and Queen Mary in recognition of his long service there.

BOWER, William. Worked mostly in London. Latterly for Ambrose Bower on such jobs as Dunshay Manor in about 1906. Built 'Maycroft' in Malthouse Lane.

BROWN, Abe. Worked on water reservoir construction on top of Table Mountain, South Africa.(Father of Pat, Gunner and O.C. O.C.'s speech affected by a bayonet thrust through his jaw).

BROWN, Walter. Worked as a mason in London.

BURSLEMS, Tunbridge Wells. Harold Haysom did War Grave work there. They called the local sandstone 'Kettle and brick' (because those were the 2 tools you needed to work it)!

BURT, Albert. Worked with Mat. Rose in Eardley Road, Streatham, 1922-1956, making garden ornaments, memorials etc. Son of William (1844-1903), a brother of Henry Weeks and George (Boss) and Charles (see below). About 1903 Albert worked in Liverpool for a while with his cousin Ernest. Before leaving Swanage he helped his father with supplying Swanage sea wall, including the date stone. (Information from John Burt, his son). His father, William, had a Cap quarry in Herston Field, where Albert started work before going to London.

BURT, Charles, brother of Henry. Had stone business in Liverpool. One of the Cake Bowers worked for him there.

BURT, Charles. Son of 'Swelly', who was killed underground. Apprenticed in the depot, worked with Harold Haysom in Holloway's yard, London where they worked on the Cenotaph.

BURT, Frank. Began work as a young man with his brother George in their uncle John Mowlem's yard in London. Later in life moved to Swanage, becoming a partner with Henry Weeks Burt, so forming Burt and Burt. Kept a daily diary from 1852 to 1898, part of which covers his Swanage days. Owned a vessel called the 'Susie', named after his daughter, which was occasionally used for pleasure trips. The Durlston Globe was brought down from their Greenwich yard in her. He owned a share in the 'Brisk' in 1887. Served on the pier committee when they decided to remove the old crane. Attended the opening of the Tilly Whim tunnel in 1888.

BURT, Harry. Worked in Winchester for Blackwell & Moody before the 1939-45 war, then Vokes & Beck afterwards. He lettered the war memorial in Langton church.

BURT, George. 1816 – 1894. Nephew of John Mowlem. Having started life in the Swanage quarries, went to London 1835. He expanded his uncle's business in London. In partnership with Mowlem & Freeman (Mowlem, Freeman and Burt) 1844. Became Sheriff of London. Operated stoneyards in Greenwich and White Square, London. Acquired Sentry estate and planned large scale development, only part if which was built. Built Durlston Castle, the Great Globe and a new Purbeck House, currently the Purbeck House Hotel, where he lived in retirement.

BURT, Robert. Foreman of Parish of Lambeth. Dismissal 1848. (John Mowlem's diary). David Lewer suggests he was Sheriff George's younger brother.

BURT & VICK. Builders of Poole, founded by Charles, born 1865, son of Frank

COLLINS, Sir Stephen. Son of Swanage quarryman, born about 1844, started work in a Swanage quarry, before going to London. Developed business in yard under railway arches at Vauxhall, mostly working Portland. William Haysom worked for him there. Involved with property developers called the 'Liberators', supplied stone work for the Savoy Hotel. Became Liberal MP for Kennington. Also a Congregational preacher.

Was made a Knight. Gave Portland window for Swanage Congregational church (United Reformed), worked in his yard in London.

Active in the Society of Dorset Men in London, arranging an excursion to Swanage by special train in 1908. Made speech at Grand Hotel where he regretted to see so much brick in new Swanage buildings. Edward Barnes, Dept. Lieutenant of City of London, proposed toast, mentioning various jobs Collins had done: Hotel Cecil, Hyde Park Corner, Charlton Hotel, etc. This is surely a Dorset Barnes, possibly of the Purbeck quarry family or of the masonry yard on Portland. It is curious his list of work done does not include the one job my grandfather mentioned, the Savoy. Sir Stephen recited a poem: 'The home of his birth which he left when a boy'.

In 1916 and in 1919 he contributed 'The Swanage of My Boyhood' to the Society's year book. He mentions attending a dame school at top of Church Hill, that school was a luxury given to few, that many contemporary lads worked in the quarrs from aged 7, that the stone trade was at its zenith before the construction of the pier, that the 'Quarryman's Guild' rigorously enforced its rules.

CORBIN, 'Catchem'. Was foreman under a manager called Hawkins in Barnes yard, Portland, after 1918. They had about eight frame saws and about 70 men altogether.

CORFE. Knoop and Jones mention several Corfes working at Westminster in 1292, including Edmunde, John de, Hugo de and Peter.

CURTIS 'Buster'. Working in Webber and Corben's White Square stoneyard at Clapham about 1920.

DAMER. Kingston boy, apprenticed on the church. He could not get a job in the quarries, and went to London, developing a business in Clapham, which became HARVEY DAMER, and later successors.

DOGET, John. Marbler, (fl.1287-1294). One of the Masters of the work at Vale Royal Abbey, Cheshire. Held Whiteway in Purbeck.

EDMUNDS, Charles. Foreman of masons on Manchester Town Hall. He built Cluny Crescent, Swanage. He worked at 'Uplyme', the mansion at Rouseden, Devon, built 1874-1878 for Sir Henry Peek. Later in life worked for Frank Tomes, in Trollope & Colls', Vauxhall yard. London.

EDMUNDS, Isaac. Apprenticed on the 'Uplyme' job; he was later in charge of what is now Lloyds Bank, Swanage; also Swanage War Memorial using Rag dug at California, and a section of Swanage sea front. He became foreman mason for H. & J. Hardy when they extended Swanage church about 1910. Hardy's 'subbed out' the rose window to Henry Rose, who had a workshop up at Townsend, above the Black Swan.

GARRET & HAYSOM. Southampton masonry business founded by a Swanage Haysom about 1860. Continued for two or three generations until wound up about 1964. They fitted the marble bathrooms in the Queen Mary. The Pilgrim Fathers memorial, 1913, signed by them.

GILLINGHAM, Nathan. Chinchen Italian marble monument in Swanage church, (1840), is signed 'Gillingham, Winton'. Is there a possible connection with Henry Gillingham Senior, stone merchant of Swanage, around 1800?

HARDING. Paviour of Westminster.[93]

HARRIS, Fred. Worked mostly in London. After I had been working for some weeks in Benfield & Loxley's yard, Bullingdon Road, Oxford, in 1962, an old Scots mason, who kept himself to himself, came up to me and said: 'You are one of those quarry slaves from Purbeck, aren't you?' He went on to say that the finest mason he ever worked with was Fred Harris. He said that as he got older Fred could not stoop, so the boss made sure an apprentice worked near him to retrieve from the floor any tools he might drop. Fred was in Foster & Dixie's Yard, London, before 1914 and later foreman on the House of Commons refurbishment. Albert Haysom and Douglas Norman worked under his supervision there.

HARRIS, William George. Working in London in 1893. Father of Herbert John Harris of Langton.

HAYSOM?. Had a stone yard in Greenwich, about 1900.

HAYSOM, Albert. Son of William. Apprenticed under him in Parsons & Hayter's yard, Swanage. After the First World War worked all over the place, including New Zealand and Sydney harbour bridge. Work shop foreman on Southampton Town Hall, with a lot of other Purbeck men working there. Also worked at Haysom and Sons, Swanage and for their competitors, the Dorset Quarry Co., Wareham. He was supervisor during conversions of the Bath stone underground quarrs during the 1939-45 war. After the last war worked on bomb damage at Canterbury and for Bert Adams at Portland and also supervisor on U.S.A.F. war memorial, Runnymead.

HAYSOM, Arthur. Son of James. James was manager of Burt's in Swanage, around 1876, when they made Langton Church's East Window. Arthur was sent as a boy to work for relative Frank Tomes at Belle Vue quarry, rather than being apprenticed on the bankers. He left for London and seldom came back; he worked as manager for Higgs at Loughborough junction, then for Higgs and Hill, where another Swanage man,? Meader, was foreman.

HAYSOM, Frank. Son of James. Went to London, worked as mason, only returned on holidays.

HAYSOM, Fred. Had monumental masonry business in Finchley around 1900. Son of William, who was son of Christopher, killed by fall in Durlston Bay. Fred's brothers, Steve and Joe, continued in a quarry close to Swanage Hospital. Joe was blinded by accident there, struck by flying punch. They supplied stone from that quarry for the house at the top of Hopabout Lane, now called Queen's Road.

HAYSOM, Frederick. A Commercial Directory of 1841 lists Joseph and Frederick Haysom, Builders, Statuaries and Masons, Upper Belgrave Place, Pimlico. Fred is probably the Fred born in 1811 who, fled Swanage to avoid arrest for smuggling. They had contraband hidden in a hollow stack of stone on the bankers. In attempting to bribe the Preventive Officer Fred revealed his identity. He returned many years later incognito, but made himself known to author W. M. Hardy. Hardy used his reminiscences for the core of his book: *Smuggling Days in Purbeck,* referring to him as Mr. F. H.

HAYSOM, Harold. Son of William, apprenticed under him in Parsons and Hayters yard, Swanage. Left Swanage at 17 to work for Tomes and Wimpey, London. After 1918 worked for Burslems doing war grave work and for Holloways, about the time they did the Cenotaph. He also worked for a while in Haysom and Sons, Swanage. Went to Sydney to work for Lang's, building the harbour bridge. Lived at 'Granite town' in Sydney. Supervisor of (mostly Scots) granite masons. Went on to Auckland University, New Zealand. Later taught at Kidbrooke (technical school). After 1945 assisted Walter Haysom (brother) with Temple Church restoration, in particular the quatrefoil Marble collars, the interlaced arcading and the piecing together of the shattered medieval effigies.

HAYSOM, James. Son of Moses. Worked on Kingston church, went to Liverpool. His son Peter spent almost his entire working life on that cathedral. Known as 'the naughty man'.

HAYSOM, Joseph Henry. See Haysom, Frederick. Died of pneumonia working on Buckingham Palace.

HAYSOM, Nat. Mason on Buckingham Palace. Would sometimes bring home leftover puddings, etc. from the palace kitchens!

HAYSOM, William A. Son of Moses, who was brother of Frederick, who fled Swanage to avoid arrest for smuggling. William spent most of his working life in Sheffield and London.

HIBBS & BOWER. Masonry firm on Portland, joined Bath & Portland group but continued to trade independently after 1918. Walter Haysom worked for them for a short while in 1922 when they were making the Bournemouth War Memorial.

HYLLARY, John, Marbler of Langton, Witness in a trial (1580) (Pope's Dorset Suits, Vol. 6). Surely this is same family as Ellary, John, marbler, in 1698 and ELERY, Robert, Marbler 1651, and Ellary Monumental masons, established in Ryde, Isle of Wight, 1847, taken over by Banks, in turn by Hoares of Bournemouth.

KING. Thomas Bonfield spoke of three brothers who had a Cap quarry near South Barn. They barred the arch out and went to Australia. The result of their action was that the sides of the shaft would soon to begin to fall in, rendering the quarry inoperable.

MAHU, John (13th century) Supplying Purbeck Marble columns at £40-0 each for Westminster Abbey.

LANDER, Ben. Foreman in Bath & Portland's Easton yard, Portland, in the post war years.

LANDER, (brothers) Edward and George (1797-1861). Became established as monumental masons at Kensal Green Cemetery soon after its opening in 1833. Their father was Thomas (1754-1804) who had married Mary Chinchen and had eleven children. They lived in Langton High Street just west of the Scout Hut. Another brother, John (1795-1877), moved to Salford, where he worked as a mason. By 1851 George was employing sixteen men. He died in 1861, leaving an estate variously valued at between £1.8 and £5.2 million in today's money. Successive generations continued at Kensal Green but Philip Henry moved to Hove and established another monumental masons firm there. John's son, Titus, is remembered on a plaque in Harrow School chapel for his work at the school. His son, James Brook Lander, (1838-1912) became mason to the Palace of Westminster. By 1878 London-born Joseph Pushman, of Purbeck extraction, was manager of what had become 'Lander and Co., Monumental Sculptors'.

The showroom, bearing the title 'E.M.Lander Ltd.' has been threatened with demolition, which the Friends of Kensal Green and other groups are resisting, it being the sole survivor of several showrooms which once clustered around the gates of the cemetery.[94]

LANDER, Fred. Brother of Ben. Formed Smith & Lander Portland that became Easton Masonry Co.

LANDER, HENRY. Had quarry near Preston, Weymouth. One of the Bowers who worked for him there was known as Billy Preston. Also had other quarries of stone, in particular marble, at Orchard in Purbeck.

LANDER, Jimmy. Foreman for Foster & Dixie's, London, before 1914. They worked on County Hall, London. Later he was foreman on the restoration of House of Commons. Albert Haysom and Doug Norman worked under his supervision.

LANDER, Joby. Brother of fisherman Frank of Worth, working in Webber & Corben's stoneyard, White Square, Clapham, in about 1920.

LANDER? (Possibly Ned). Worked on supply of Farmington (stone) for Temple Church, London after the war. Account by Freda Derrick, in her book, *A Trinity of Craftsmen*, describes the Farmington quarry in 1948, with quotes from 'Mr. Lander of Purbeck'.

MANWELL, Henry. Son George, b.1787. Went to Portsmouth as a stonecutter, aged 17, and to later to Calshot Castle. He worked at Greenwich and Woolwich Arsenal. Became schoolmaster under mentor Dr Andrew Bell, before being elected rate collector for Marylebone.[95]

MANWELL, George. Brother of Henry, born 1791, married Sarah Mowlem. Became 'Government Mason' (1830-40). Office of Works Contracting Mason for London District. Succeeded in this position by John Mowlem.[96]

MEADER?. Worked as foremen for masonry contractors Higgs & Hill, Loughborough Junction, London. Foreman about 1920 at Swanage.

MOWLEM, John (1788-1868). Swanage Quarry boy left aged about 17, worked on Norris Castle, Isle of Wight, then for Henry Westmacott in London, becoming his foreman, aged 28. Established in 1823 paving roads for the Vestry of St. George's, Hanover Square. He had a yard and offices at Paddington. He went on to develop granite quarries in Guernsey, and a considerable business in London. In due course he returned to his native Swanage, where he kept a diary. In the main he was using granite, but one diary entry tells of Purbeck. 1849 'Schooner, the *Gulf of Parma*. Weeks, master, with a cargo of kerb for us from Mr. Burt got on shore between Christchurch and Hurst and is totally lost. A loss of £40. Thank God the crew is safe.' His nephew, George Burt, continued the business. The Mowlem firm was still extant in 2003, and made profits of approximately £45,000,000. (*The Independent*, March 2004). They produced a house journal called 'London John'.[97]

MOWLEM, Joseph. Brother of John. Went to Mexico, hence nickname 'Mexican Joe'. Painted views of Swanage Bay.

NORMAN and BURT. Masonry contractors, London and Burgess Hill, Sussex. Did work on one of Chichester cathedral's western towers.

PUSHMAN, Walter and family. Left Swanage to work at

Webber & Corben's Kensal Green Cemetery masonry works. His son Ralph was apprenticed there (five years followed by three years as an improver for 7s 6d per week, most of which he gave to his mother.) He envied the bosses' sons' pennyfarthing bicycles. He left to work on the Law Courts. The union struck for an increase of 6d; the bosses offered 3d. The offer was refused, so the men were locked out. German masons were brought in to complete the work. Ralph sailed to Australia, joined by his wife. The climate did not agree with her and she returned to Enfield. He continued in Australia, but the economy collapsed due to the failing of the Knickerbocker Trust. Ralph took ship to Cape Town, got a job with Ab. Brown working on the Table Mountain Water Reservoir. He returned to England and took over the shop in Worth with his wife. He had two sons: Edward, who worked for most of his life for Worth Quarry Co., latterly Swanworth, and John, who ran the shop and what had been Fred Burt's quarry on Eastington Cowlease and served as warden for lengthy post war period. (Information provided by both).

SEYMOUR. One had a stone yard in Chichester.

SEYMOUR, Lydia, made a declaration in 1878, 'wife of William Seymour of DRUITTS stone works, Mile End, Middlesex., stone mason'. She was 63 years old, born in Swanage, daughter of Thomas MARSH, who was brother of Jane BUTLER of Swanage.

SEYMOUR & SONS. Monumental masons, Wimbledon (closed about 1963).

SEYMOUR. William Bankes' mason at Kingston Lacy Hall about 1850.

SMITH & LANDER, Portland. Started after the First World War by Fred Lander, brother of Ben (who was manager of Bath & Portland's yard in Portland), descended from Sam, brother of George, son of Henry (see above). Firm became Easton Masonry Co.

TILLY. A firm of monument and general masons in Brighton, removed from London three generations ago. Possibly of Purbeck origin?

TOMES, Albert. Brother of Frank, who had a quarry in Belle Vue. Worked on Randell's banker where he appears in a photograph. Learnt letter cutting there from his father-in-law, John Haysom, and went on to cut many of the inscriptions at Durlston for George Burt; in particulatr the extract from 'The Tempest', cut in the cliff. During the 1880s had a stone yard in Bromley.

TOMES, Alfred. Monumental masons, founded 1896. Park Royal Road, North Acton, London. Alfred went to Belgium to select slab for grave of the Unknown Soldier in Westminster Abbey.

TOMES, Eugene, brother of Thomas. Stone mason. Laid out streets of Accra, Ghana 1910.

TOMES, Ernest. Foreman of masons on Waterloo Station. Son of Frank (see below).

TOMES, Frank. Manager of Trollope & Colls' yard in Vauxhall (about 1880). Frank went off to London when a young man with his mate, one of the Butlers, who was running away rather than face the music after letting the donkey fall over the cliff in Durlston Bay.

This Frank Tomes is not to be confused with another Frank of roughly the same generation who had a quarry in Belle Vue.

TOMES, Samuel. Son of William, who was the master of the market boat. Samuel had worked at Aberystwyth before returning and becoming Billy Collins' foreman (Billy, had taken over Randell's and Nat White's business). They did the Palgrave Cross on Church Hill, Swanage.

His brother was Thomas (known as 'Marky', from the market boat). Marky had a limp from breaking his leg underground. He took over as cox of the lifeboat after the hiatus that followed Frank Smith putting the boat on Peveril Ledge and Jack Giant (Smith) similarly bumping the Berry, a patch of rock hidden at high tide. These humiliations left no one prepared to be coxswain.

TOMES?. Mason in charge of Corfe Church during 19th century restoration.

TOMES & WIMPEY. They began as street work masons in London, before splitting up. Tomes continued with masonry, Wimpey with general contracting (this grew enormously).

TOOPE. Pevsner includes in his description of Swanage church: 'Plate, a fine set of 1692, given by Mrs. Abraham Story, the wife of the distinguished London mason.' A particularly splendid example of his work is the Croft memorial, Little Saxham, Suffolk. He had married Eliz. Toope in Saint Olave's, Southwark in 1656. She was surely a Swanage girl, perhaps the daughter of John, born there in 1622, or of Henry, who also had an Elizabeth, born 1619. Perhaps it tells of John or Henry being business associates of Abraham, who lived in Pall Mall. Lady Ranelagh was a neighbour and Robert Boyle, the physicist of Boyle's Law fame, a sometime lodger. Evidence of Toope's quarrying in Swanage later is provided by an 1806 map of Eightholds that shows Edward's quarr about where Queens Road has been constructed.

VYE, Ike. Worked most of his time in London, came back and worked for Ambrose Bower. Worked new windows for rebuilding of Dunshay Manor north east wing (1906), with another mason of long London experience, William Bower (not to be confused with all the other William Bowers). Also before the First World War worked on the cross in Worth Churchyard.

WARREN, of Wareham. Signed marble tablet East Stoke church. Kath Warren married Christopher Haysom at East Stoke, 1750.

WEBBER, John (1806-1893). Worked on restoration of Corfe church, poet, said to be last marbler of Corfe. Exhibited at the Great Exhibition. Son of Cornelius, a poor boy of Corfe, apprenticed to the Newfoundland trade in 1783 but who must have come back. Chief Clerk of Clay Merchants Messrs Pike, part time letter cutter. According to a *Morning Chronicle* report, a man of considerable standing; 'Mr Webber is an understanding man. He knows more about us than we do ourselves. He keeps us right. Whenever we get into difficulties we always go to him'. When men said of him that he was the last Corfe marbler, what was meant was that his ceasing work saw the final depletion of what had once been a large Corfe contingent. It left no-one living in Corfe yet still working in the trade. Since then other Corfe men have found jobs in the quarries but the continuity has been broken.

Webber communicated with Turbulant Squibb and someone with the pseudonym 'Steinschmatzer' by means of poetry. John Mowlem's new Institute prompted the following in 1862:

'To Steinschmatzer at Peverel Ledge.
A child's amang you taking notes
        And faith, he'll prent it.
 Dear Sir, in 'taking notes' of late
Of things deserving mention,
A building of the present date
Attracted my attention.
But being situated near
Your old established dwelling,
It will be nothing new I fear
The story I am telling.
It is erected near the strand
That bounds your lovely bay
(Not with foundation laid on sand
That can be washed away).
If winds arise and waves rave
The ocean it will mock,
Firm as 'Old Harry' rock.
Its plan of elegant design
Well lit, capacious too-
Pray who hath raised this structure fine
I asked of those who hew.*
'Why brother you have heard no doubt
'That wonders never cease,
'The Town of Swanage has turned out
'A justice of the peace.
And as his worship had no place,
'Except a room quite small,
'Wherein to sit and try a case
'He built himself this Hall.'
Thus answered one-another then
Joined in the conversation,
Saying 'He thought with many men
T'was for a railway station.
But having both a gallery,
A lobby and a porch
Seemed more appropriate to be
For chapel or church'
'You both are wrong,' a third replied,
It is a kind of college
Where all may freely be supplied
With good and useful knowledge.
 Where folks may study, and read the news,
And hear sometimes a lecture,
And quarrymen with hob-nailed shoes
Be welcome as the rector.
It is a free unfettered gift
Intended by the donor,
To benefit the poor and lift
His fellow men to honor.'
He needs not to record his worth
A marble pillar high
This will perpetuate henceforth
His memory said I.
And I feel proud to let you know
That from my natal place
Nine centuries at least ago
His pedigree we trace.
 'De Moulem' royal architect
Appointed was of old,
Our ancient Castle to inspect
In history we're told.
Thus while these buildings represent
The present founder's name,
Corfe Castle stands a monument
To those from whom he came.
Corfe Castle, October 3, 1862.
*Quarrymen, hewers of stone.

(The last verses refer to the claim that the Mowlems descend from Durandus, the Conqueror's carpenter). The original building was rebuilt in the progressive 1960s, but continues to bear the name.

WEBBER and CORBEN. Masonry contractors with a yard in White Square, Clapham, (earlier pre-railway yards were on the river, like Trollope & Colls at Vauxhall and Mowlem at Greenwich.) Taken over about 1914 by Mowlems but continued to trade as Webber & Corben for some more years. In 1920 several Langton and Worth men were working there, including Ike Vye, Amos Vye, 'Buster' Curtis (of Gallery quarry family), Joby Lander (brother of Frank, Jesse, Hubert and Miller) when my father had a few months there. The Langton/Swanage schism was even reflected in the London yards, with Langton men tending to look for a job with Webber & Corben, Swanage men with Frank Tomes at Trollope & Colls. 'Blind' George Webber, returning from London, built Virginia House, High St., Langton, in London style.

In 1903 the Langton Wardens' book recorded the admission, into the marblers, of three sons of Mr. Henry Corben of London, Fred, William and Frank. At the same time Walter Webber, son of Richard of London, also joined, all for the sum of 8s 3d rather than the usual 6s 8d. Presumably the extra was to cover the cost of a quart of beer and, perhaps, their marriage shilling, which suggests they were not present. These children of the diaspora were maintaining their Purbeck connections!

DOCK & HARBOUR BUILDERS

A lot of Purbeck names crop up in the church registers of Ramsgate, Portsea, Gosport, Devenport and Dove between 1728-1823. [98.]

Appendices

PERSONAL MARKS CUT ON THE UNDERSIDE OF PAVING, SEA WALLS AND OTHER WORK.

1. Woolland Manor, Dorset

2. Mount Scar House, Swanage
   Whiteways Manor House

3. West Creech Farm (several)

4. Eastington Farm, several on various layers, including Freestone and Wetsun Bed

5. Eastington Farm

6. Eastington Farm

7. Eastington Farm, also on a piece of channel: Antler wreck, Hook Sands, Poole Harbour entrance: Encombe House, internal paving, Downs Vein

8. Eastington Farm, several, all on Downs Vein: Orchard Hill Farm, also Downs Vein

9. Eastington Farm, several

10. Eastington Farm

11. Talbot Cottage, Langton

12. South Egliston, Kimmeridge

13. Ditto

14. Kimmeridge Home Farm

15. Ditto

16. Church Knole Farm

17. Ditto

18. Victoria Hotel, Swanage

19. Ditto (two on Downs Vein)

20. Victoria Hotel, Swanage

21. Orchard Hill Farm

22. Orchard Hill Farm, Downs Vein (could this be the same person as 21?)

23. Orchard Hill Farm

24. Arundel Terrace, Langton

25. Arundel Terrace, Langton; is this Titus Chinchen's, who built it?

26. Manor Farm, Steppes, Langton.

27. Ditto.

28. Chapel Cottage, Langton.

29. Antler Wreck, Hook Sands, Poole Harbour entrance.

30. Number 2, North St, Langton.

31. New Buildings, Langton, several.

32. Ditto.

33. Langton Rectory Coach House.

34. Ditto: Flagstones, Durnford, Langton.

35. Hatfield House, Hertfordshire, Downs Vein.

36. Ditto.

37. Wilkswood Farm.

38. Ditto, several, Downs Vein.

39. Flagstones, Durnford, Langton.

40. Afflington Manor House, Corfe, most, if not all, Downs Vein.

41. Ditto.

42. Stratton Mill.

43. Woodsford Castle, Dorset, Downs Vein.

44. Powder House, Chapman's Pool, Downs Vein.

45. Unknown

46. Afflington Manor, most unusual, with the letter strokes foreshortened by holding the chisel at an angle.

47. St. Aldhelm's Chapel, Worth Matravers, Downs Vein.

48. Ditto: Barn, West Orchard, Corfe Castle.

49. No 6 North St, Langton.

50. Ditto.

51. No 6 North Street, Langton, Downs Vein.

52. Woodsford Castle, Downs Vein: Dorset Reclamation, soft Thornback.

53. Rollington Farm, Downs Vein.

54. Unknown

55. No 6 North Street, Langton, Downs Vein.

56. Ditto.

57. Portsmouth Cathedral.

58. Ditto.

59. Stratton Mill.

60. Box cottage, Langton, several, Downs Vein.

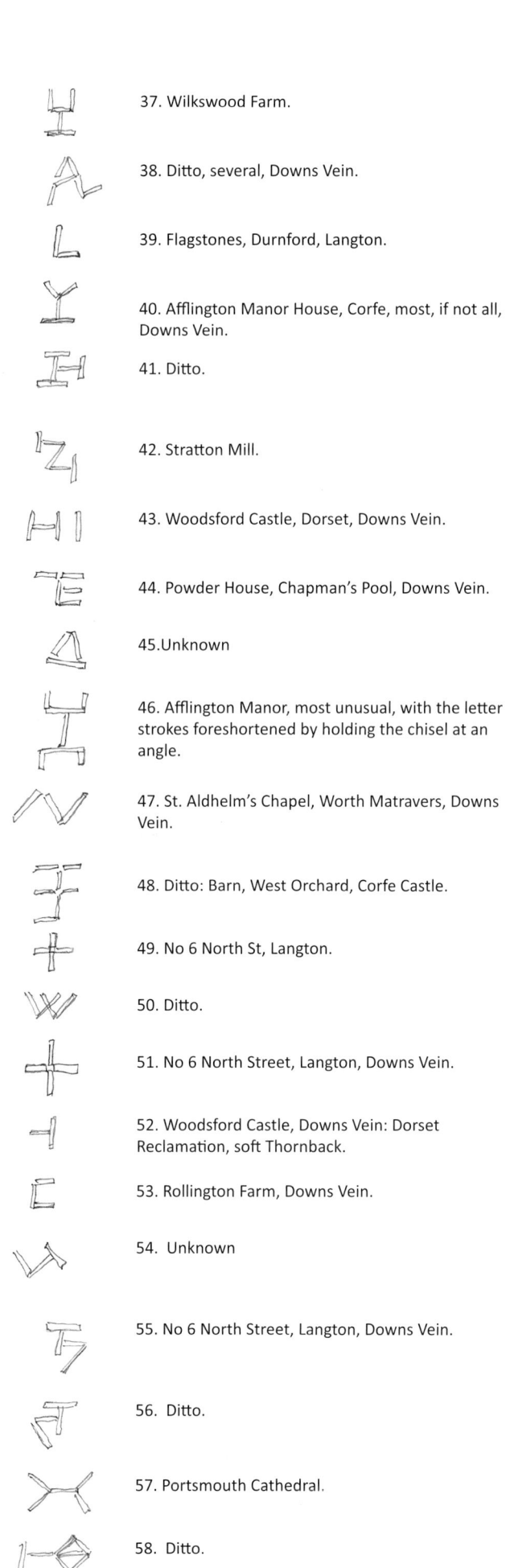

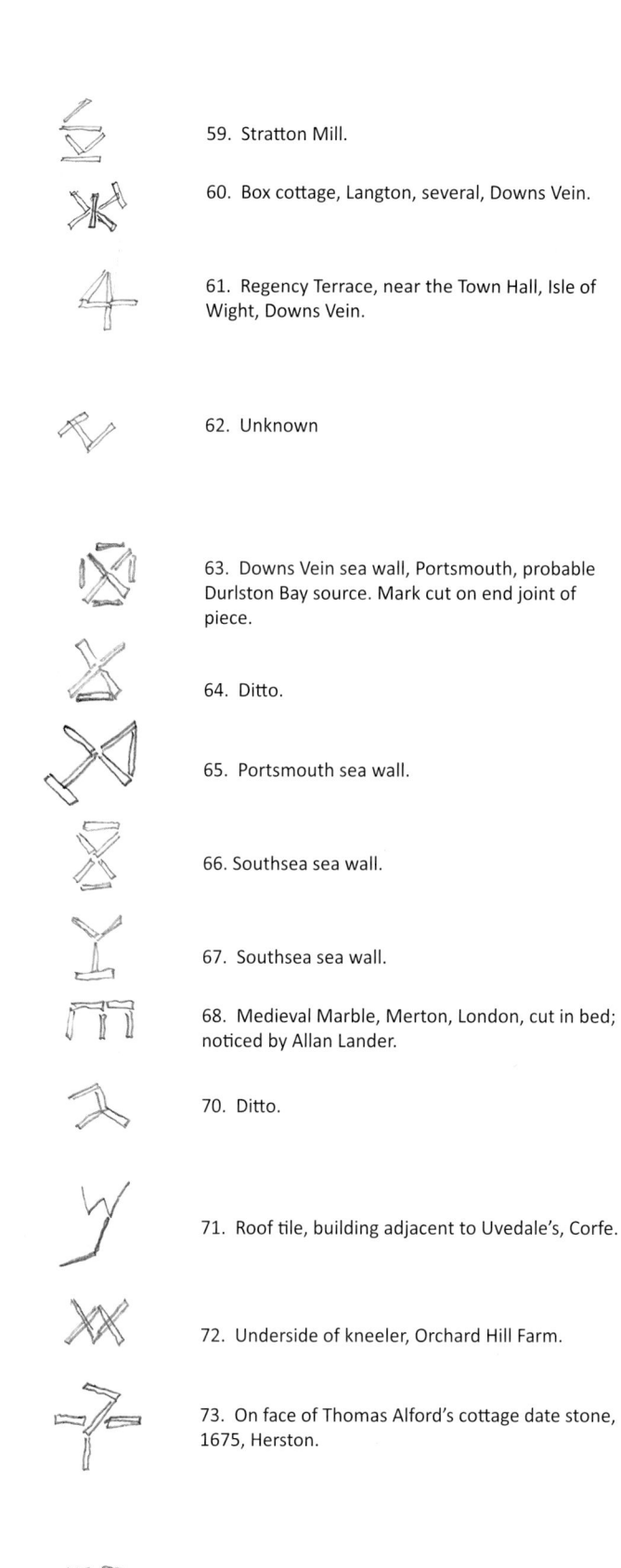

61. Regency Terrace, near the Town Hall, Isle of Wight, Downs Vein.

62. Unknown

63. Downs Vein sea wall, Portsmouth, probable Durlston Bay source. Mark cut on end joint of piece.

64. Ditto.

65. Portsmouth sea wall.

66. Southsea sea wall.

67. Southsea sea wall.

68. Medieval Marble, Merton, London, cut in bed; noticed by Allan Lander.

70. Ditto.

71. Roof tile, building adjacent to Uvedale's, Corfe.

72. Underside of kneeler, Orchard Hill Farm.

73. On face of Thomas Alford's cottage date stone, 1675, Herston.

74. Roof tile, Knitson.

75. Morton's House, Corfe, external on porch.

APPENDICES / 277

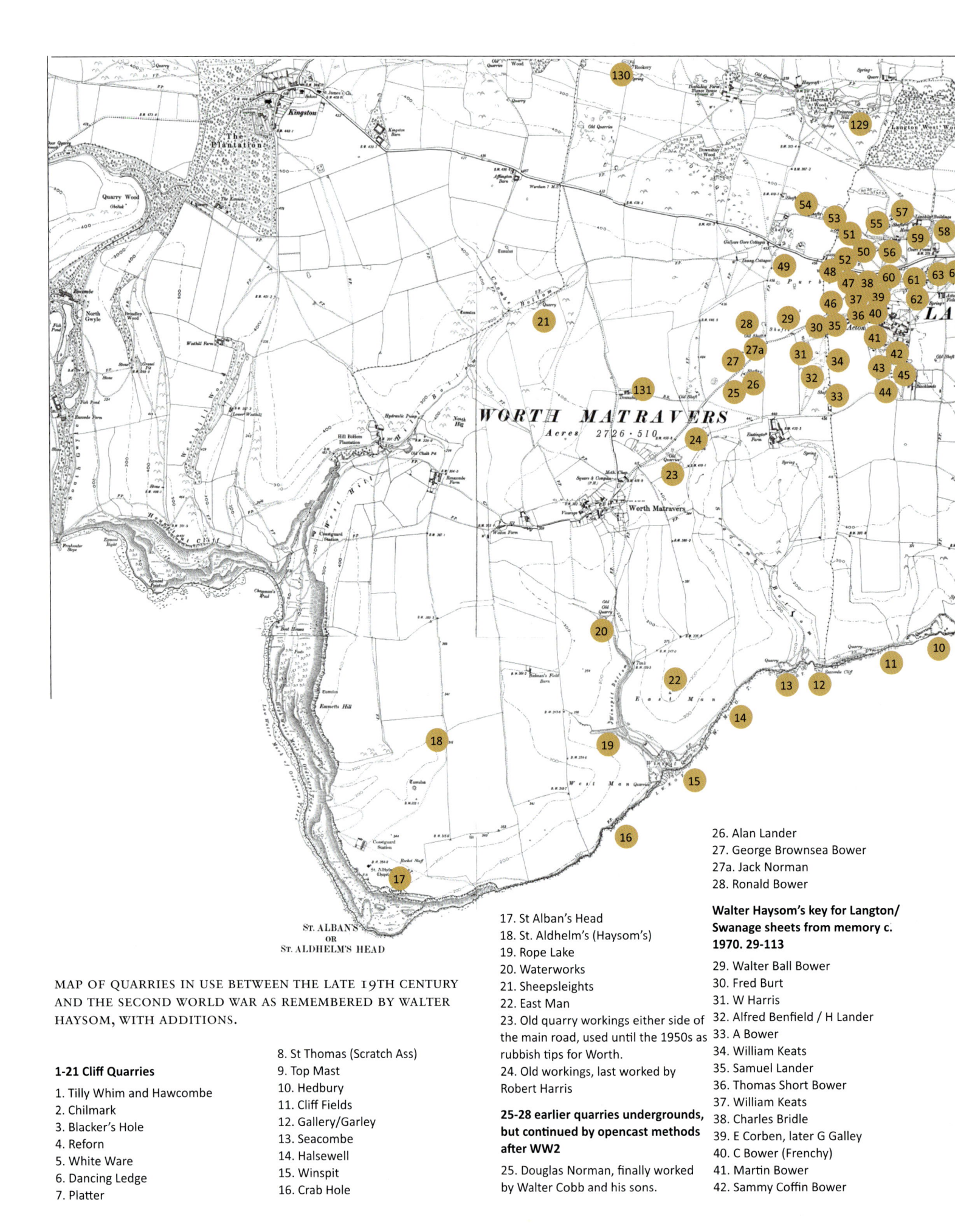

MAP OF QUARRIES IN USE BETWEEN THE LATE 19TH CENTURY AND THE SECOND WORLD WAR AS REMEMBERED BY WALTER HAYSOM, WITH ADDITIONS.

1-21 Cliff Quarries

1. Tilly Whim and Hawcombe
2. Chilmark
3. Blacker's Hole
4. Reform
5. White Ware
6. Dancing Ledge
7. Platter
8. St Thomas (Scratch Ass)
9. Top Mast
10. Hedbury
11. Cliff Fields
12. Gallery/Garley
13. Seacombe
14. Halsewell
15. Winspit
16. Crab Hole
17. St Alban's Head
18. St Aldhelm's (Haysom's)
19. Rope Lake
20. Waterworks
21. Sheepsleights
22. East Man
23. Old quarry workings either side of the main road, used until the 1950s as rubbish tips for Worth.
24. Old workings, last worked by Robert Harris

25-28 earlier quarries undergrounds, but continued by opencast methods after WW2

25. Douglas Norman, finally worked by Walter Cobb and his sons.
26. Alan Lander
27. George Brownsea Bower
27a. Jack Norman
28. Ronald Bower

Walter Haysom's key for Langton/Swanage sheets from memory c. 1970. 29-113

29. Walter Ball Bower
30. Fred Burt
31. W Harris
32. Alfred Benfield / H Lander
33. A Bower
34. William Keats
35. Samuel Lander
36. Thomas Short Bower
37. William Keats
38. Charles Bridle
39. E Corben, later G Galley
40. C Bower (Frenchy)
41. Martin Bower
42. Sammy Coffin Bower

278 / PURBECK STONE

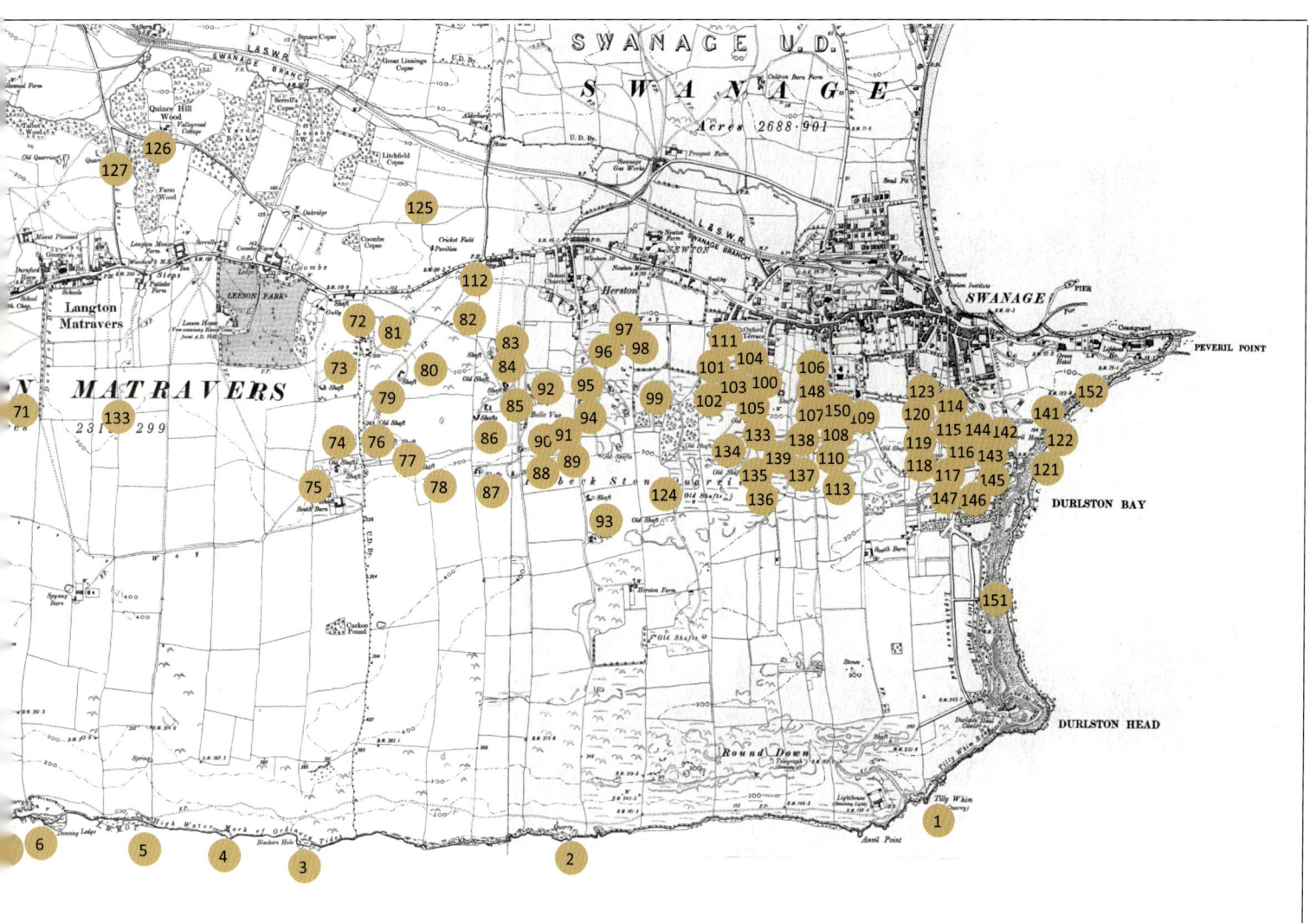

43. Sammy Coffin Bower
44. Alphaeus Brownsea Bower (Phae)
45. Walter Ball Bower
46. H Burt (formally Squibb)
47. Saul Bower
48. Alfred Benfield
49. George Lander (in dispute)
50. Albert Bower (Trink)
51. John Ivamy Bower and Charles Harris
52. George Vye
53. F Burt
54. F Norman
55. Seth Brownsea Bower
56. Ambrose Bower
57. Seth Brownsea Bower
58. Fred Norman (sunshine)
59. Stephen Bower
60. Reuben Short Bower
61. Richard Gad Bower
62. Hiram Gad Bower
63. Richard Gad Bower
64. W Brown
65. Thomas Webber
70. Titus Bower
71. Saul Bower
72. Albert Bower (Trink)
73. Teddy Corben
74. Josiah Harris
75. Albert Bower (Trink)
76. W. Bonfield (Scurry)
77. Webber and Stevens
78. Anthony Haysom
79. Alfred Norman
80. W Bonfield (Scurry)
81. Albert and Jimmy Chinchen (2 shafts)
82. Frank Seymour
83. Anthony Haysom
84. Richard Tomes
85. Alfred Norman
86. William Collins
87. W and Lewis Tomes
88. George Harris (Whistle)
89. Walter Tomes
90. Frank Tomes
91. 'Shilling' Norman
92. Warren Bonfield (Warny)
93. William Collins
94. George Hancock
95. W Harris
96. A? Harris
97. Horace Norman
98. Thomas Phippard (Tilly), late (previously) W Burt
99. Samuel Phippard
100. George Burt (Boss)
101. Charles Benfield
102. Fred Bower
103. Walter Brown
104. George Burt (Young George)
105. Fred Meader
106. W Norman
107. Alfred Norman
108. Fred Haysom
109. F Haysom, late W Haysom family quarry
110. John Haysom, formally Isaac Haysom
111. Rag dug during WW1
112. Rag dug during WW1
113. Peter Manwell

114 – 120. From Eight Holds Manorial survey 1806: probably not worked after this.

114. Joseph Foot
115. Thomas Randal
116. Timothy Warren
117. Geog. Bonfield
118. Moses Chinchen (Nath and James?)
119. Will Cole
120. Edward Toop
121. George/James Butler, latterly, before closure, Burt and Burt
122. Thomas Benfield, latterly, before closure, Burt and Burt
123. Samuel Squibb
124. Newton quarries (Mutton Hole)
125. Isaac Bower
126. Walter or William Brown
127. Dorset Quarry Co.
128. George Lander – Burr
129. Hedley Lander
130. Squibb - Marble
131. Arthur Collins, latterly Walter Cobb and Sons

133 – 150. Quarries marked on Dampier Estate sale map in 1823

151. Quarry in sale details (1823) occupied by Thomas Randal

152. Quarry in sale details (1823) occupied by John Pushman

APPENDICES / 279

Glossary

Terms included are Purbeck specific

ARCH Some quarry entrance shafts were reinforced by the construction of an arch built from side to side. This was necessary where thick layers of unstable clay occur between the various Rag Beds. One, less often two, are common in Freestone quarries.

ARRACE 17th and 18th century references to paving 'laid arrace – wise' means an area of squares turned to produce triangles at the margins. Such triangles with acute corners would have been almost impossible to make without resorting to sawing of a diagonal cut. Word linked to *Arris* (below).

ARRIS Edge at intersection of two planes. If the junction is less than 90 degrees it becomes a 'feather' edge. To damage an arris is to *flush* it.

ASHLAR Fine-jointed, closely-fitted facing stone of various finishes.

AXE or ADZE I have no practical experience of tools of this sort and their usage seems to have faded out in Purbeck at least 150 years ago.

BACKING Not usually a bed as such but undressed, or very roughly dressed, stone fit for filling in behind dressed harbour wall work; more commonly known today as 'hard core'. Also applied by Bonfield in Hutchins (3rd Ed.) to a particular poor quality bed, lying between the Laining Vein and Ryal.

BACKSTICK In the 1830s a boy was punished for stealing the bolts and washers for a backstick on Wilkswood Farm. My father said that kerb and paving stones were leant on edge in the cart or wagon against the backstick.

BANKER Stone bench on which stone is dressed. In addition to this ubiquitous type used by masons generally, many Purbeck quarries had a loading banker. This consisted of a level raised area made up with waste produced from sinking the shaft, extending from the mouth of the quarry to a vertical edge alongside the access track. The finished stone was stacked on the loading banker, which was roughly level with the side of a wagon. In the absence of any cranage, this facilitated loading.

A number of former underground quarries are now only recognisable by the survival of their loading bankers, as is the Co-op banker alongside the Acton approach road. However many old workings, particularly on and around Round Down, lack them. They may have been subsequently pillaged, but it is possible that they were operated without a banker. As late as the 1960s stones were still being manhandled into lorries using a stout plank, a hard working solution that has been around for a long time.

On the shore each Swanage merchant had such a raised platform for stocking stone on arrival from the quarry. This general area, extending from the quay to north of the stream, was known as 'The Bankers' as a result. The term has caused confusion: a 19th century critic of the truck system as operated by some of the banker- owning merchants mixed up stone 'bankers' with financial bankers.

BAR i) Steel or iron lever of varying lengths, c.2ft-8ft long, for most work round about 3ft. The lower end is brought to a blunt chisel end with a curving 'heel' below.
ii) Hard, dense, discontinuous layers within open-textured Burr. No similarly-textured Freestone contains them, so their presence can be diagnostic in old masonry.
iii) Billy Winspit referred to 'the bar' at Seacombe quarry which prevented progress in that direction. The rock in question is faulted, tight and bonded with calcium carbonate.

BARGE (As in Thames barge) This term is now frequently erroneously used to describe sailing vessels. Most vessels taking stone out of Purbeck in the latter days of sail were gaff-rigged ketches. The only barges/lighters in the history of Purbeck stone were steel-built, towed by steam tug, taking stone away from the cliff for the Luton Hoo job and Training Bank (see Dancing Ledge and Seacombe), relatively brief and insignificant events.

BAT i) To tool a surface with a wide bolster/boaster.
ii) Reinforced section of iron tyre on a stone wagon. When braking, the wheel was fixed with the bat in contact with the ground. Such wagons made a distinctive sound as they went along unbraked. Was this like the sound made by the mason with his mallet and chisel whilst 'batting'?

BD This abbreviation in 18th century references to paving surely means 'best dressed'.

BEAT The hard heartwood part of a mallet. Though round, masons mallets do not conform to the round shape of a tree, for the handle is inserted square to the grain. This produces two beats. The tool should be gripped so that only the hard part strikes the chisel.

BED A distinct and separate layer sometimes dividing into Bits. Hence a bed, called Titonites by geologists, at St. Aldhelm's Head becomes four Blue Bits rather than Blue Beds. Some beds are only referred to by the single name, e.g. Thornback, is never Thornback Bed or Bit for example, but conversely Wetsun Bed always has the label 'bed' attached.

In sedimentary limestones the shells almost invariably lie flat, indicating the bedding direction. Some, such as many of the Marble snails, can be only partially filled with sediment, so they indicate which way up the rock lay when deposited. However, a few fossils can be preserved in life positions rather than fallen. A very limited area of Thornback from southwest of Acton contained a single layer of hazelnut-like neomiodons held in this way. A modern altar top at Shaftesbury Abbey exhibit them well. The Red Rag in Durlston Bay contains similar assemblies, superb in their preservation.

The term 'False beds' refers to discontinuous weak layers, some mere clay patches a few inches across, others involving larger areas, sometimes connected with current bedding. Within a given layer these can run out of level: a quarryman's nightmare.

BENCH Step in quarry face produced by open cast quarry methods that developed during 20th century.

BESCA Tool, generally translated as spade used in digging Marble. One is specifically mentioned in a Coroner's Court record of 1258. Medieval shovels and spades usually had wooden blades tipped with iron.

BEVEL See Shift Stock.

BIDDLE Two-handed heavy hammer of about 14lbs, one face square for striking the stone directly, the other round for driving wedges, paddles, etc., the handle usually cut somewhat shorter for working in confined spaces underground. Those of recent manufacture are made of steel but earlier ones were of iron with 'steeled' faces. One of these was found when underground workings were opened during the War at Winspit.

BIT Subdivision of Bed.

BLACKS Thin, dark, often faint layers in Cliff Stone. Some run flat so as to suggest bedding planes but they are in fact stylolitic in origin. They become more obviously stylolites where they are crinkly, as in the Titanites beds. Some in the Freestone can run out of level, and can become weaknesses. These are called slivers. Blacks are fairly common in the Cliff stone beds of Purbeck, even more abundant in the same beds quarried at Mupe, but entirely absent in Portland. They are therefore diagnostic.

BLOCK 1. Stone in raw state intended for further working.
2. (as 'block and tackle') Conventional block and tackle were used to tension king posts. A specialised sort which came apart was employed as a direction-changer in underground quarries.

BLUE-HEARTED Some light coloured beds have darker centres, caused by oxidisation from the joints. This feature is valuable in the study of ledgers in particular in that the extent of colour change indicates the original shape of the raw block, the lighter oxidised area roughly following parallel to the natural joints. Lighter areas extending into the heart of a slab can indicate water/oxygen penetration along flaws. Shallow stone is more penetrated by this process than that lying deep or in tight-jointed situations. The same layer can be a whitish colour when quarried from a shallow source, but blueish from a deeper one. Dense beds are more resistant, so Marble, for example, remains dominantly dark with typically only the outer one or two inches or so changed to a lighter brown, whilst at the other end of the porosity scale the Cliff Freestones are white.

However where extracted from the deepest part at Seacombe the largest blocks proved to have blue hearts. It suggests that at depth all the Cliff stone mass becomes blue. It seems that Portland pre-oxidisation was also once blue, as was the chalk. King John's marble effigy in Worcester has brown extremities at both ends, telling us the block was only just long enough. The extent of the brown is an indicator of the depth at which the block lay, round about ten feet, I would hazard, for the king. A different phenomenon, lacking a name, is some sort of staining, possibly caused by hydrocarbon residues. Some Wetsun Bed from Queen's ground exhibits it, and Freestone from the Acton Preferred Area, now dormant.

BOASTER/BOLSTER Wide chisel.

BOAT Pronounced 'bwoat' or more fully 'Stwun bwoat' used to convey stone between the shore and the larger vessels in Swanage, or between the cliff quarries and vessels anchored nearby. According to W. M. Hardy, they were capable of carrying six to nine tons. They were propelled by 'a bit of sail' or by standing men pulling big 'sweeps', taking a step back and forward with each stroke. Some of the boats were almond-shaped. John Mowlem called them stone-lighters.

BOILS Generally rotund bulges measuring from a few inches to a couple of feet across, protruding from the underside of several different layers. Now generally recognized as reptilian footprints.

BONING IN See WINDING

BROACHED A finished surface produced by driving the punch in parallel lines about one inch apart, roughly diagonally.

BRIDLE Chain for pulling quarr cart. Approx. 8ft long with hook at each end for quick attachment to two 'eyes' at the front of the cart.

BUMP (verb) Applied to heavy shaping work such as 'bumping kerb'.

BUNCH Protruding mass; lump on side of otherwise straight block.

CALLUS Hard brown outer surface of blocks; not an accretion but a change of the actual stone.

CAP The name for a particular inland bed, characterised by being very fine grained with chert nodules. In addition, some Cliff beds are known as Caps, i.e. Underpicking Cap, House Cap and Brown Cap. Surely derived from the fact that they come above the Under Freestone. Similarly inland Cap rests on top of the New Vein. (See Legs and Caps below)

CAPSTAN Windlass with the drum mounted almost vertically.

CART Typical quarr carts were of wood bounded by iron, forming a flat bed usually about 4' x 2ft 6ins x 1ft 2ins high, mounted on four wheels of about 12 ins diameter. The wheels were set in underneath on a rectangle of about 1ft. 9ins. by 1ft. 4ins., a gauge therefore of about 1ft. 3ins. A low centre of gravity gave stability. The flat top allowed for stone of any size. The small distance between the wheels meant that the cart could be pulled around corners without any movable axle. It could be tipped up on its side in order to load stone on to it. It had wooden iron-tyred wheels, or sometimes one pair of such wheels and a second pair of wholly iron wheels. A pair of lugs (sometimes referred to as staples) on the sides of the frame for attaching chains were called 'ears', a pair at each end called 'eyes'. The central wooden timber in the frame was called the Thar Pole. This was removed and the wheels replaced with rollers in Marble quarries.

CATCH UP To catch up the ceiling with a 'leg' was to support it. Having decided where the critical point for support of the ceiling needed to be, often where two stones meet thereby supporting both, the trick was to hold a small stone at that point before dropping it; where it landed was the place to start building your leg. In the course of underpicking, a small stone called a 'catch stone' was sometimes inserted into cut as a precaution against sudden collapse. They were a hindering nuisance and therefore often dispensed with, though this could be risky.

CHAMFER Bevel or decorated edge made by taking off the edge of a right-angled surface.

CHANNEL Paving cut to a shallow hollow to form a gutter- shape. Used in stable and farmyards.

CHECK Notch or rebate.

CHERT Geological term for silica nodules which the quarrymen call Flint.

CHIPS or CHIPPINGS Not used other than to describe small broken marble or glass chippings spread on graves.

CHISEL Tempered steel banker tool of various widths used in the later stages of working a stone, latterly sometimes tipped with tungsten carbide. The widest is termed a 'boaster' or 'bolster': these can be two to three inches wide, exceptionally more. The narrowest chisels go down to a quarter of an inch for fine work such as letter cutting. The metal head was usually shaped to be struck with a mallet (mallet-headed), less often, for some usages, chisels were hammer-headed. An even rarer variant was cup-headed which some carvers claim brings advantages when used with an iron dummy. Hollow mouldings required round-nosed (often called bull-nosed) chisels of different radii, but seldom gouges. In some awkward situations 'bent' chisels were used.
Although hardly applicable to mainstream Purbeck, masons cutting soft stone such as Bath used wooden-handled chisels. They also used narrow chisels for getting rid of surplus stone, hence they call them 'wasters.'

CLADDING Thin crazy paving applied as a veneer to wall surfaces. In vogue in 1960s.

CLEFT/CLIFT Weak bed where a split can be made; particularly applicable to land Freestone.

CLIFT Cliff. Note its use at Ramsgate.

CLOSURE Last stone (cut to a dimension) in a running length. End stone in course of paving or top of a column. What we see in such arrangements is every stone cut to its maximum length except possibly the last, the closure.

CLOT Surface earth; topsoil

CLUNCH Basal chalk, suitable for masonry. No known medieval exploitation in Purbeck. However, the Neville screen masterpiece in Durham cathedral is of Dorset Clunch. Its designer in about 1374 was almost certainly Henry Yevele, who held the wardship of Langton Wallis, and gave security for the sailing ship, the 'Margaret' of Wareham around that time. Could Pondfield (Ponfill) Cove under Ballard be the source?

CLUTCH This term was used by Billy Winspit to describe how his gads and pitching tools all tended to acquire an out-of-square head which then made them 'clutch'. He must have always struck them off-centre.

COCKS AND HENS Rough walling stones usually placed on edge serving to cap off a wall. A good way of utilizing awkward shapes difficult to incorporate in the wall proper. Some, neatly dressed, have triangular profiles, alternating 'cocks' (higher) with 'hens' (lower).

COMPASSES Tool used to describe circles and transfer measurements between drawings and stone.

COPERS Term used in 18th century Bankes Estate field walling accounts. Refers to above average size pieces laid flat, used to cap off the top of the wall.

COPE To 'cope around' was to bring a slab to a particular shape. This could involve cutting off large amounts of surplus with gads or punches, or more often, lesser amounts with a pitching tool.

COMMON Waste material thrown back as the quarry advanced. In underground working, once the shaft was sunk, useless material was thrown behind 'in common'. This waste was built up vertically to ceiling height, with open lanes left for the carts to run to the mouth. Similarly, in surface working, the men threw any unsaleable material back behind them. Sometimes rough walls were built to prevent this rubbish from falling back into the working space. As the face advanced, these walls became lost in the common mass; some old commons recently revealed still contain good walling stone. When Jack Norman took over Alfred Benfield's underground quarry he decided to go in a direction the Benfields had blocked off with waste. 'We had to cut their common' he said.
In the recent past the much-quarried land south and west of Acton was referred to as The Common.

CORDON Projecting bull nose course about twelve inches high. Incorporated in Napoleonic forts around Portsmouth.

CRAB 19th century factory-made geared winch unit wound by hand. Also used on the shore for pulling up boats.

CRANE About 1900 the first of a new generation of cranes was introduced into Purbeck. Often called derricks, these cranes differed from the earlier gibbets in that the winding gear was fixed on a vertical king post (often split) that held up a jib that could be raised or lowered. The king post in its turn was held up by two inclined braces that allowed it to rotate within three quarters of the full arc. The one exception was an ex-dockyard crane that was free to rotate 360 degrees, and thereby inherently unstable. It was brought to Swanage in 1850s and set up on Randell's banker. Almost all of the later cranes were the braced, three-quarter arc type, only varying in lifting capacity and whether man-operated or engine driven.

CRAZY PAVING Natural paving as dug, without any shaping beyond punching off the worst bumps. Two categories emerged, brown and white, with white commanding a higher price. I am not aware of any pre-20th century usage but it can perhaps be anticipated in the use of irregular polygonal walling in the late 19th century.

CRISP Descriptive term referring to the working characteristic of a stone.

CROP Brimless cap worn underground. Benfield says it was sometimes adapted from a woman's hat.

CRUSHERS Small pieces of stone. Blocks can be damaged by heavy impact when being turned over on a hard floor. A good precaution is to place small stone crushers in little piles that absorb the blow at the critical spot.

CUT OUT A term used to describe cutting the raw block into the approximate shape of the finished article with wedges. The next step was to take the stone to the banker for final dressing. In the production of items such as street kerb the cost more or less broke down into equal thirds: digging, cutting out and working.

DAMPS 'The Damps'. Stale air present in some deep Swanage underground quarries in Summer.

DEPOT Stoneyard on Serrells Court estate, Swanage. Established with its own siding by Burts (not Sir George) following the arrival of the railway. It served as Swanage Town Council yard in the post-war years.

DEW POND Rustic stone container similar to a bird bath, but without stand.

DIPSLOPE Slope in strata of stone.

DOG'S NEST Soft patch in otherwise solid stone, often just a honeycomb, but sometimes an open hole which may be filled with clay from the adjacent joint, varying in size from a few inches to a couple of feet wide. Common in Thornback and Freestone from Acton Highlands and Eastington Cowlease and in Gallows Gore Grub.

DOGS Alternatively called nips. A pair of right-angled hooks held on a triangulated chain, used to pick up blocks with a crane. To secure a firm grip, a pair of opposing small holes (hence 'dog' or 'nip' holes), were punched into the block to be lifted.

DOT Approximately four inch square cubes; similar to 'pitchers' in that both were intended to cope with wheeled as opposed to foot traffic. Particularly made at Sheepsleights by Billy Brown around 1900. In the 1890s the London and South Western Railway Co. purchased a quantity of them, together with channel stones.

DRAUGHT In dressing a flat surface, the chisel is driven in a series of straight draughts, each tested with a straight edge before progressing to the next. Many 19th century dressings were left natural or 'rock-faced' but with a 'draughted' margin. Arthur Hancock recalled that when he started work in 1930 the corner of pitched faced quoins had to be 'draughted' and how easy 'we moderns' have it now, since that requirement has gone.

DRAW Verb meaning 'to dig.' This old term was specific to underground work: 'Then we drawed the Thornback'. The act of freeing each block involved drawing it sideways. However, it was also applied to the act of quarrying in general.

DRESSED WALLING A rougher and therefore cheaper form of walling than dubbers, at the same time being suitable for cavity construction. As with dubbers the face was left rough i.e. ' off the pitching tool' but, unlike dubbers, the beds could be out of parallel and the joints out of upright so long as still reasonably square. However, the distinction between dressed walling and common dubbers is quite a fine one. Some men's dressed walling was just as neat as the rough dubbers of 'yore'. The term was 'born' during negotiations between Council officers and the Marblers re: the building of local council houses the late 1940s. It became the main product for most quarries for nearly fifty years.

DRILL The most common sort in use, before the advent of pneumatic straight chisel and star bit types, had a chisel end brought to an obtuse point. It was struck by a hand hammer. The resultant holes which are common in the cliff quarries, rather than being flat-bottomed, characteristically end in a blunt point.

DROKE Grooved line as produced by a punch when driven across a surface. Similarly a groove worn in a whet stone or rubber. Possibly derives from stroke or 'drolk'- colloquial word for a ditch.

DRUM Component of cluster column, usually circular, laid in bed, hence load-bearing.

DUBBER, to DUB To dress roof tile, some hammers so used were called Dubbing hammers. Tiles are dubbed square by being held on edge and hammered vertically, a treatment that produces a characteristic ridged edge and minimises the risk of breakage. From this it is possible to distinguish dressed from natural edges. Presumably dubbers, a form of rubble walling, were produced similarly by being knocked into shape by a hammer only, but in the recent past have been mostly shaped by using a hammer and pitcher, or hammer and punch, or even the most neatly worked, which were called jointed as against common, with mallet and chisel. Presumably the word has the same root as the action of conferring a knighthood. Post-War variants include sea wall dubbers (basically big) and fireplace dubbers (basically more neatly dressed than average).

EDGE STONE 18th century term for street kerb. By the 20th century it had come to mean thin stuff, one inch to two inches thick, with one straight edge, used for flower borders and paths in gardens when set on edge.

EASTER SEPULCHRE A canopied space over a tomb chest, in the chancel of a church.

ENGINE John Melmoth of Herston's inventory of 1685 includes the quarry tools and also 'an Engine to pull out the stone' which is worth £1 10s. This is almost certainly a capstan and a rare use of the word before fuel-powered machines.

ENTASIS A slight convex curve in the shaft of a column, introduced to correct the visual illusion of concavity produced by a straight shaft.

'EYES' and 'EARS' See CART.

FERN PATTERN Common on inland Freestone vent surfaces. Rare or non-existent in other beds. Not fossiliferous, but dendrite.

FIXER Mason who sets stone in place.

FLAGSTONE A term not traditionally used in Purbeck.

FLATNER In the 18th century street work specification it seems to be an alternative term for pitcher or small rectangular paving. Horse flatners were similar, but deeper (about six inches) and restricted in width to maximum of five inches to provide plenty of joints and therefore grip for horse traffic. However in the recent past it was applied to paving of larger size, left self-faced or punched.

FLUSH To flush means to damage an arris.

FOUNDER Fall of overlying material in underground working; sometimes by accident, sometimes by design. Deliberate founders were caused in New Vein holes and in the cliff.

GAD Small wedge used for cutting; usually several employed in a row, driven into slots called pits cut out with a punch. However, medieval accounts suggest a cutting tool rather than a wedge, or even nails.

GALLET Not a term much used in Purbeck, but characteristic of a style of building in Sussex and Kent, where small flakes or gallets are set in the joints of larger flints. My father heard men say 'Chuck a gallet under 'im', probably indicative of them having worked with flint-knappers.

GATE POSTS They seem not to crop up in royalty returns nor have I seen them beyond the bounds of Purbeck, but they appear in Rev Austin's Economic Geology list for 1852, when they cost 4s each.

GAUGE A two foot long measuring stick. (see 'TWO FOOT')

GAUGED WORK Stones cut to a particular size, as opposed to *range* work.

GIBBET Type of crane consisting of a braced arm mounted to rotate about a fixed king post, used in combination with a jenny.

GIRT (adj) Great or big.

GLARE Same as 'list', of the white sort.

GLASSY Descriptive of nature of stone. Same as 'quick'. Cap is glassy, Burr the opposite.

GOAD Unit of length of wall, about 14ft., named from the pole that was long enough for the ploughman to prod his lead oxen.

GOUGE A hollow curved metal tool suitable for working soft stone, seldom employed in Purbeck.

GOUSER/GUSSER A paddle-like tool with wooden handle. (see Underpicking). No example complete with handle has survived. Even the steel part is very rare. They were specific to Downs Vein quarries where the underpicking clay is soft, so that it could be dug away using a tool not needing to be driven with a hammer. Presumably, as with paddles, they would have been of more than one length. Langton Museum's example has a dull cutting edge but when in use it would have been sharp. Some underground ceilings exhibit marks left by such a really sharp tool, fresh as if cut only yesterday.

GRIPE To undercut, cut down at a slant, undermine.

'GROWED ON' When beds are bonded together, rather than free-splitting.

GUDGEON Steel pin fixed in the underside of the capstan drum. It was free to rotate in a metal bearing leaded in a stone set flush with the ground slightly forward of the crab stones. Also used similarly to give free rotation of the arm on a gibbet. Some were wrought with fishtail-like extensions to provide good attachment to the timber.

GUTTER As CHANNEL.

GUTTER SOLE Flat stone forming base of gutter set between pavement kerb and a course of pitchers. Chiselled rather than left 'off the punch' for ease of cleaning and water flow.

HAMMER Most hammers used were long-headed with two faces, rather than lump hammers. The weight ranged from 3lbs upwards. Made of steel with a wooden handle.

HAMMER HEADED A flat end on a metal tool suitable for hitting with a hammer. All pitching tools and virtually all punches were hammer-headed, but few chisels.

HAULING Applied to using some type of windlass. The Corfe accounts of 1282 make a clear distinction between 'hauling' and 'carting': 'For the reward of one man hauling 500 stones to roof the building, 8 pence. For the service of one man carting the said stones to the castle for 2 days, 12 pence.'

HEAD or HEADING 1. The quarry face that confronts the quarrier. Pits cut into the head are head pits and, in this same sense, a pit cut into the edge of a stone as opposed to its horizontal bed is a head pit, even when the block is out and no longer part of the head. Greasehead, now more often called Days Road, perhaps corrupts from 'Greys Head' from Badgers digging their setts under an old quarry face.

2. Alternative name for lintel. Jack Norman said the 'old hands' reckoned that the thickness should be increased by one inch for every one foot increase in span, starting at about six inches for a stone four feet long. However there is big variation in the local vernacular. The average cottage door or window opening requires a stone about four feet long. They can be as flimsy as four inches or as thick as twelve. Supply was dealt a blow by the introduction of steel lintels in about 1970, which result in rubble without visible means of support.

HOLLOW WORK Sinks, troughs ('trows'), dewponds and bird baths: anything hollow.

HONE Obsolete. Applied to what is now called white rock.

HORN CART Used in the cliff quarries. None survive but there is an illustration of one at East Winspit by Thomas Webster (1814). It was equipped with a T handlebar, hence perhaps its name.

HORSE'S HEAD Derogatory term for ill-shaped lump of stone. Also applied by some to irregular, edge-bedded stone incorporated in standard walling. There was a fashion for this method in the 1960s.

HUNDRED FOOT RULE The first Article of Agreement for 1651 includes '…nor to come into any part of that ground within one hundred foote of his fellow tradesman's quarr.'

HYKERELL A location at Wilkswood mentioned in medieval Court presentments. Almost certainly a crane.

JACK Quarry tool little used in Purbeck. My father got hold of an old Portland one, now in the Langton Museum, for Tom Bonfield to use underground, but he found it of no particular advantage.

JENNY Horizontally mounted windlass rotated by means of one or sometimes two large wheels used in conjunction with a gibbet for lowering stones down the cliff.

JENNY LIND Articulated machine used for polishing large surfaces. Not introduced into Purbeck until about 1957. Perhaps some wag thought it made a noise like the celebrated Swedish singer who, incidentally, John Mowlem heard perform.

JIM CROW A vice-like tool used at Sheepsleights to straighten or bend rails or bars when cold.

JIBBER, JIBBET see GIBBET

JIT (verb) To move a large stone by using a bar, in small incremental movements. Noun means a small movement of a large stone.

JOINT The cracks between blocks are joints, but in addition a fault, where the strata jumps or folds, is a joint. A quarryman saying 'I have hit a joint' is talking about one of the latter.

JUMP Break in level. Same as fault or joint.

JUMPER 1. Within a wall, a high stone combining two or more thinner courses of rubble. The convention, since strayed away from, was that a jumper should never be shorter in length than its 'heighth', in other words never less than square.
2. A drill struck by a hammer, not to be confused with a weighted drill which was bounced rather than struck - unknown in Purbeck to my knowledge. Surviving jumper drills are rare because, as pneumatic drills replaced them, they were made into punches.

KEEL In the Purbeck context, usually a vertical ridge on an otherwise-rounded pillar. Some of the 12th century Purbeck pillars at Lincoln have keels whilst others lack them. They prompt the question whether they exist for practical or aesthetic reasons. It is easier to apply a plumb-bob to a flat keel rather than a rounded surface.

KIBBLE / KIVEL Two handed tool for rough trimming blocks. It is perhaps best described as a cross between a biddle and a pick axe, with one hammer face and one point face.

KING POST Part of gibbet (crane). Timber post secured in a deep vertical socket, 6ft-10ft high, to which swinging gibbet arm was attached. Used extensively in cliff quarries for loading boats until late 19th century. Also vertical part of a 20th century derrick crane.

LABOUR Value of work invested in a quarry that was bought or sold when a quarry changed hands. (See : Trade Organisation)

LADDER 1. As recalled by my father some of the ' old hands' referred to the timbers laid across the floor of an upper level quarry to cover over the shaft going on down to a lower vein as the ladder.
2. W. M. Hardy's use of this word is also surprising, to describe the strong timber employed to load boats in Durlston Bay. It spanned from shore to boat, which required the loaders to stand in the water in order to manhandle the stones along.

LAKE/LEÄK One of several terms for a calcite vein. The more common term for such a vein is list. A stream of water is a 'lake' in southeast Dorset.

LANE Underground route kept open for the cart to travel from face to shaft, All around was usually back-filled by waste, but lanes, being semi-permanent were strongly walled up. Also used in Purbeck ball clay mines for initial tunnel which left clay *in situ* to left and right for subsequent digging.

LAINING Name of vein of stone lying below the Toads Eye above the Rag. Perhaps from the family of that name living in Purbeck in the 17th century and possibly earlier (John Lanning of East Lynch, yeoman (1685) for example). But more likely from its layered characteristics (see Beds). Lane and End, Leaning and Lanning etc. are all attempts by observers such as Thomas Webster to make sense of what they heard.

LEG Usually a built support in undergrounds, but in some Cliff quarries they are rock left in situ. James Corben uses the term Pillar, which is odd. (See also Legs and Caps).

LEGS and CAPS often known as STADDLE STONES or RICK STONES A mushroom-like structure consisting of two parts, a round champfered 'cap' resting on either a truncated cone 'leg' with a smooth tooled finish , or a punch-finish tapered square leg, the former being more expensive. The original meaning of 'staddle' is a tree of a certain size. These staddle stones, generally called 'legs and caps' by the quarrymen, were used to keep granaries or ricks free from rodents or damp. They were usually sold in a set of nine, sufficient for the average rick or granary.
  LEWIS Three types of implement for fitting into top surface of wrought stones in order to lift them by crane without damage.

LEWIS TOOL The cutting of lewis slots called for a particular sort of chisel, similar to a *quirk* or bricklayer's plugging iron, but wider. Following the split pin lewis invention, most were turned into punches.

LIGHTER Name applied by Thomas Hardy to the stone boats. Also by Burt and Burt to the vessel they used in their Durlston Bay quarry. This is surely metropolitan influence.

LINE String. Apart from use in construction and setting out curves beyond the limit of a trammel, but also used for measurement. Random length items such as kerbing were not individually measured and tallied up, but a line of known length, usually about 20ft was applied to the stones by moving the fingers progressively down its length.

'LINES UP, LINES DOWN' Expression used in applying moulds to a stone.

LIST Vein caused by calcite infilling crack.

LOAD Roof tile was sold by the load. At the quarry the stones were measured by being set up in rows, bottom edge down, to form a mass eight feet by two feet by an average two feet high to the peg hole. Stones below two feet in height had to be compensated for by stones above two feet. The weight of this mass was rather more than an old ton and was the capacity of the average farm wagon. Laid on the roof, such a quarryman's load usually more or less corresponded to a builder's square (ten feet by ten feet lapped) but of course thicker stones produced less cover per weight, a source of contention.

LOWERING CHAIN Short length of chain which served as a brake on a capstan. It was attached to the collar board at one end, held at the other by hand. A single turn around the drum provided sufficient friction, at least when dry.

LUTCH Inlet of the sea. Particularly applied to those of the Kimmeridge ledges which develop at low tide.

MAGGOTY Term used to describe Thornback with distinctive holes unique to the area around Quarry Close, Eastington farm.

MALLET. Wooden Tool used for striking chisels. Often of apple wood.

MARK There are three main types, personal, fixing and measurement. Personal marks are almost all cut with single strokes of the chisel, thereby displaying its width. Fixing marks are similarly cut either to indicate location in an arrangement, particularly in a course of paving, or to show which way up the stone should go in the case of pillars. With measurement marks, the Roman numeral system can mean different things. The same mark on a paviour indicates superficial feet, on harbour Front cubic feet; on hollow work such as sinks it represents pecks. There are also what must be tally marks in the cliff quarries.

MASON In the late 18th century the content of the Morton Pitt census at Corfe suggests that 'mason' meant a builder in stone: paid less than a 'quarrier'. However, by the early 20th century the term 'mason' applied to men shaping stone on the banker. Also applied to a neatly fitted piece of stone forming a repair.

MILLER Any scrap stone on which a piece being worked could be rotated.

MITCHEL A square paving stone of contested proportions. The word has fallen out of use in the 20th century.

MITRE SQUARE A metal plate with one angle at 135 degrees used in conjunction with a mitre board and/or a 90 degree square to draw the intersection line across a moulding. Therein lies the difference between masonry and carpentry methods. Carpenters can put their joints in the mitre, hence have no need for a mason's sort of mitre square.

MORE THAN ALL An expression quoted by Benfield to describe getting the best from any stone by 'letting go' requirements that are not strictly necessary e.g. the bottom back edge of a solid step can be missing without any detriment. Some of the apparent quirkiness of medieval masonry can be explained by men driven by this expediency which may be seen in features such as irregular door and window jambs. In brief it was best value for money, with common sense being applied. This is a concept very difficult to get across to those used to modern materials, readily available in big standard sizes. I was required to supply a carver with an exact, sawn six-sided piece, complete with corners, only for him to reduce it to a rotund shape. I could hear the ghosts of generations of practical men groaning.

MOUTH Entrance to underground quarry. This term was used more than the word 'shaft'. Memory suggests that the last generation of real underground quarrymen did not use the word 'shaft' at all.

MUCHEL See MITCHEL

NIPS See DOGS

NISH Soft

NITCH A collection; applied to punches when taken to the blacksmith, or withies for lobster pots.

PACE Obsolete. It appears in the Richard Beauchamp tomb contract of 1453, meaning the raised step surrounding the chest (eighteen inches wide by six high), if not the whole platform. John Cook, Marbeller of Sandwich (1699), includes 'channel and half paces'. Neve says of 'footpace', 'Or as some call it *Half pace* [...] after 4 or 6 steps, you arrive to a broad place, where you may take two or three paces before you ascend another step, thereby to ease the Legs.' More recently, such steps were called 'landings'. They are big, at least four feet square and usually more, and therefore expensive. However, Neve also mentions 'chimney foot paces, 2s per foot', which suggest hearths. The term was still current in the 19th century, for Jeremiah Bower lists two hearth paces in his Clavell Tower bill of 1831.

PADDLE Chisel ended bar of varying length (from about eighteen inches to six feet long) used to cut away underpicking dirt. Usually struck with a hand hammer. A heavier sort called a 'feather paddle', was sometimes used, particularly in New Vein undergrounds. This was struck with biddle, with two men working together, one holding the paddle, the other wielding the biddle. In 1908 Burt and Burt, who employed blacksmiths, sold one of 4lb weight to Edwin Bower of Worth. This was probably for use in his Freestone rather than his Downs Vein quarry.

PAPERY Descriptive of some sorts of stone, in particular the lower part of the Roach, Pink Bit, which decays. Derogatory.

PAWL A form of brake attached to most capstans. When engaged with the toothed ratchet it allows for rotation in one direction only.

PAVING (not called Flags)

PEABODY Billy Winspit's term for a poor, unsafe ceiling. particularly referring to part of his family's quarry at Seacombe.

PEAK ENDED Term for acutely shaped end joint on walling or ashlar with excessive amount of its back corners missing. Where such a stone butts with a good square stone it can be acceptable, but two peak ended stones together are a weakness. Where such walling is sold by the face area there is a temptation to let such stones go. To dress the peak off means more work and at the same time less face and less money. Such things caused contention between quarryman and merchant.

PECK Unit of measurement by volume for hollow work. Equivalent to two gallons or a quarter of a bushel.

PERCH This unit of measurement is rarely used in a Purbeck context, but appears in a bill for walling stone used in the Clavell Tower of 1831. Whether this is a linear, square or cubic measurement in this context is open to question, but the stone referred to is the Yellow Bed (sourced from the shore close by), which is of a relatively consistent thickness.

PICK 1. Pickaxe. Large two-handed tool with wooden shaft usually used in conjunction with a shovel for loosening clay and smaller stones. Also used uncommonly for underpicking.
2. Tiler's pick. A small version, wielded with one hand, used in creating fixing holes in roof tile. It needed to be regularly sharpened by the blacksmith, hence it was designed so that the wooden handle could be easily detached from the head. There is a good example in Langton Matravers Museum.

PINCH BAR Short metal bar used for moving small stones.

PIT Slot to take wedge. More often than not several were cut in a row, superseded by 'plugs and feathers' in the 20th century, the number and depth dependent on the resistance. Cliff quarry examples cut as deep as a hand tell of big wedges being driven in hard. Most expert quarrymen cutting them in the recent past made a neat fit for the wedge or gad but medieval examples suggest the use of thin 'steels' or 'scales'. These lined the pit with the wedge driven between them.

PITCHER/PITCHING TOOL Chisel-type tool, usually about two inches wide, with a thick (quarter of an inch) c.90 degree cutting edge. Struck with a hammer and used for bursting off waste. A category of walling stone dressed in this way was termed 'pitched face'. 'Pitchers' are also a Purbeck term for cobbles, small roughly squared blocks four inches to six inches deep for laying in stables and courtyards, to accommodate heavy wheeled traffic. Rev Austin (*A Guide to the Geology of Purbeck* 1852) lists 'Pitchers, unworked' and 'pitchers worked'. The more neatly dressed pitchers were sometimes called 'gauged' and the rougher sort 'common'.

To 'pitch in' stone is to fit roughly or lay an area of rough or semi-dressed material such as hard core for a road base or exposed work such as boat slipways.

PLACE Flaw. Same as *vent* or *shake*.

PLATNA A category of hard, flat Purbeck stone used in the 18th century for public building projects such as the prison at Clerkenwell, Middlesex in 1787, and Chertsey bridge. In the 18th century context it seems to mean large flat blocks such as were used for wharves and bridges, but by the 20th century men working at Mutton Hole were applying the term to paving stones.

PLIM UP (verb) Expand (usually used of wood, by water).

PLUG AND FEATHERS The plug is a long thin wedge used in conjunction with a pair of sleeves (i.e. feathers) that serve to convert a round drill hole into a rectangular shape. Typically employed in a row of holes to achieve a split. Not used in Purbeck before the advent of pneumatic drilling about 1920. All earlier quarry drill holes tell of the use of gunpowder.

POINT Alternative name for *punch* not much used in quarry parlance. However, Nathaniel Chinchen used the term 'pointed' to describe a rougher alternative finish to tooled. He almost certainly meant 'broached'.

POUND An expression meaning 'help with a task'.

PRICKLE Protrusions on the underside of some Cliff stone beds. The underside of the overlying layer was eroded, rather than the top of the bed below; this is explained by phreatic conditions prevailing long before present land forms.

PRICKLE BED Usually called the Puffin bed. Also called 'Prickle Bed' because of its rough surface. Best seen in the form of the wide expanse of Dancing Ledge.

PRINT Expression used by Thomas Bonfield describing the neat exactitude of much old work. 'They, the old hands, used to print their work'.

PROMISCUOUS PAVING Former term for random rectangular paving, therefore the cheapest. Neve's 'The City and Country Purchaser' from 1726, cites promiscuous paving, costing 6d., 7d. or 8d. per square foot, whilst mitchels (squares) cost 1s. 10d. per square foot: more than twice the price of the 'promiscuous' paving.

PRONG A garden fork - like tool, but with the tines wider, and bent such as to allow a load to be held. When used for cleaning up scars it leaves the smaller to be shovelled up separately.

PUNCH Tool with cutting edge forming a simple point, struck with a hammer. Used for hewing off waste to near finished surface, to be followed by claw and then chisel. If driven in straight lines to produce a finish it is termed *broaching*. Also used to cut pits and rough out hollow work. The range of surface finishes left by a punch can vary a lot from very fine 'sparrow-pecked' to coarse.

PURL To turn over. 'Gi'us a purl over' was to ask for help in turning a heavy stone.

QUADRANT Quarter circle stone incorporated into kerb at street corners.

QUARR 'Quarr' is interchangeable with quarry.

QUARR HOUSE Usually open-fronted shed at quarry, used as shelter for dressing stone.

QUARTER Obsolete. Unit of measurement of sand or lime that appears in the Corfe castle 13th century building accounts. Also applied to Freestone, which probably informs us that the stones were only roughly dressed. 8 bushels or c. quarter of a ton.

QUEEN ANNE Term for a Purbeck quarryman (see Turk).

QUIRK Fishtail - like chisel for cutting grooves. Its flared out corners allow for free cutting where a standard chisel tends to bind. Similar to a Lewis tool.

QUICK Descriptive of working properties: similar to glassy. Burr is at the opposite end of the scale, being woolly.

RAILS Probably first used in the Purbeck stone trade in the tram line that connected the bankers with the pier of 1859. The first use in quarries would appear to have been the sleeper-less pairs. Later, at both Seacombe (1920s) and Winspit (1940s) fixed rails carried flanged wheeled carts out from underground. Railed skip lines were also used at St. Aldhelm's and at Sheepsleights. Some men installed rails in their underground quarries, notably 'Sunshine' Norman and his sons at Castle View where they remain to be seen.

RELICT Relating to much-diminished presence of a particular bed of stone, usually near the edge of the outcrop; a surviving trace.

RICK STONES see LEGS and CAPS

RID To extract stone from the surface as distinct from underground, hence 'ridden holes'.

ROCK Protrusion on pitched-face work, characteristic of late 19th century walling and later. Two inches is a generous amount; Northbrook railway bridge (1880s) has a quoin which is the record-breaker at five inches!

ROLL or ROLLER Hollow wheel set at the top of the slide to provide direction change for the main chain feeding horizontally from the capstan before going down the steep shaft angle. It was critical to get the arrangement right so that the loaded cart moved freely up and over the roll.

ROW PAVING (pronounced to rhyme with cow) Purbeck term for paving slab.

The roughest paving is crazy paving, which was virtually undressed; not much sold before the 1920s. Before that the cheapest paving was 'Row' or rough paving, made up of stones, each jointed into the biggest rectangle that the raw slab would contain, the top face either left self-faced (natural) or if necessary just ' taken out of winding' with the worst bumps punched off. The root is the same as for rough. In 1494 building accounts for Woodstock distinguished between 'Fre' and 'Row Masyns'. The eastern of the two Purbeck hundreds is Row Barrow. In early 17th century Corfe Castle Accounts it appears as Roughborough.

RUGGLE Term used by Eric Benfield to describe moving a stone around on the banker or getting it onto the cart with the aid of a bar.

RUBBER Term for abrasive stone used in the polishing process, formerly of natural sandstone, latterly (since 1930s) of carborundum and/or other synthetic materials including compounds containing acids. To wear away chisel marks quickly calls for a relatively coarse abrasive. To get rid of coarse scratches left by such a No 1 rubber calls for a finer grade and so on, No 3 producing a fine finish ready for a natural stone called 'snake' which leaves a virtually polished finish ready for, in the 19th century tradition, a coating of linseed oil. This tradition does not include the use of acidic materials, but the practice is an old one.

RUBBLE Walling stone of various degrees of refinement. When entirely undressed, as in field walling, sold by the ton, but when dressed, sold by the superficial square yard. In a dressed state, the Purbeck term for this walling stone is 'dubber', latterly 'dressed walling'.

ROTTED Term used to describe poor quality stone, particularly applied to such lying close to the surface.

RUNNER A lane running down or across the dipslope. If down, the capstan was required to pull a loaded cart out. All such runners therefore ran in a straight line from the mouth towards the active face. (In the Purbeck ball clay mines a runner was the miner who pushed the cart from face to shaft so that meaning is different.)

RUST SPOTS Not an old term, but applicable to iron pyrite nodules common in some Rag, particularly Devil's Bed. Very rare in Leper.

SAMSON POST Alternative name for KING POST.

SAND BOX Shallow wooden box filled with sand, sometimes used when working small or delicate pieces. It stops them 'dancing' around and avoids breakage.

SCANTLING Sometimes shortened to 'scant'. Blocks only roughly squared up. Latterly applied to sawn slab before squaring.

SCAR A relatively small chip or waste piece produced by dressing stone with hand tools.

SCRIBER Sharp point for scratching lines around moulds.

SCURF Loose, most specifically applied to the layer on top of the Thornback. Neither clay nor stone, so worthless.

SEARCH Term used for inspection of stone entering London. Ordinances of 1481 gave powers of 'Search'. In the 17th century a row developed when the Londoners tried to impose the cost of it on their Purbeck suppliers.

SELF-FACED Type of surface left natural, usually of paving, without tool
marks (sometimes now called 'Riven').

SET OFF To force open a row of pits with wedges.

SHAFT 1. Access to underground quarries usually cut to 45 degree angle.
2. Long, slender column.

SHAKE A weak crack or flaw, same as VENT.

SHART /SHARD 1. Gap produced by a section of field wall falling over.

2. 'Shards': useless layers between Freestone and Downs Vein, more often called 'White Rock.'

SHELLAC Used in repairing imperfections in 19th century marble work. Examples can be seen in Kingston Church. Sometimes the Victorians used it more lavishly as a surface coating rather than a mere filler. Scott applied it to Purbeck and Reigate stone in Westminster Abbey, all since cleaned off. Generally superseded as a glue by synthetic resins in the 1950s. Portland masons called this new generation of glues 'German' from its source.

SHIFT STOCK Like a sinking square but with adjustable angle.

SHOAL (verb) To outcrop, to come to the surface.

SHOPHAYES/CHOPHAYES This field name occurs on the manors of Verney and Afflington. The unlikely suggestion has been made that it is to do with quarry workshops.

SINKINGS Hand-made depression in a stone surface: for example, the top 'bath' of a bird bath.

SINKING SQUARE Square adjustable for depth, fixed at 90 degrees, useful for cutting out sinkings.

SLAT Applied as a verb 'to split' or, on Portland, to overlying Purbeck beds sometimes productive of thin roofing stone. It also appears in old Purbeck roofing tile references.

SLIVER (to rhyme with driver) Weak flaw, sometimes open, running at approximately 45 degrees, common in most cliff quarries. Some, perhaps most, are stylolites. They are a major disadvantage in that they make the block more difficult to dig, and the resultant three-cornered shaped stones less valuable than rectangular. Also present in some inland beds such as the Downs Vein and Grub from near Gallows Gore where they appear to be typical slickenslides.

SLY Unreliable, hence potentially dangerous joint or Bed. Bristow (1884) called the underpicking dirt above the New Vein 'sly bed'. Benfield (1940) described his ceiling bed 'grubs' as being 'sly-jointed' i.e. not easy to see. Roger Bonfield, describing the Grub ceiling in Verney, said it had a 'sly bottom part that sometimes held on and sometimes let go unexpectedly.'

SNAIL CREEP A Portland rather than Purbeck term, but in parlance in the 1960's to describe polygonal (usually face bedded) walling in vogue for a while. The Portlanders use the term for veins akin

288 / PURBECK STONE

to Purbeck lists. Portland snail creeps tend to wander more than typical Cliff stone lists and are usually more blurred.

SNAKE Naturally occurring abrasive stone of mottled appearance suggesting snakeskin.

SNAP New term following the introduction of the guillotine, describing saleable offcuts made by it.

SOAPY Descriptive of fine grained soft sort of Langton Freestone.

SODER Applied to calcium carbonate deposits filling the joints and thereby bonding the rock.

SPACK Pole for capstan (*see illustration opposite*).
SPALL (noun) Piece produced by spalling waste off a block with a biddle or spall hammer; larger than scars. Can exhibit a bulb of percussion. (verb) To break stone off a block as above.

SPUR i) Post-like stone set at the corner of buildings to protect them from wagon wheels, sloped and of a height that the wheel rim rather than hub impacts.
 ii) Term used for bad result when, in attempting to split a block straight, the break actually shears to one side. It is said to 'spur out.'

SQUARE i) The all-important 90 degree tool with arms of differing lengths used for setting out and/or the working of all close-fitting masonry.
 ii) Builders' superficial measurement unit of roof tile or paving equalling ten feet by ten feet. In the case of the former, it is of the stone as laid, therefore including the lap.

SQUINT Splayed quoin other than 90 degrees.

STADDLE STONES see LEGS and CAPS

ABOVE Unknown Purbeck quarry. Donkey attached to the pole, or spack, for the capstan. The spack could be easily slipped out of the drum (right). The stone braces and drum resting against the collar board show that the quarry shaft is out of view to the right. The short length of chain on the drum indicates that the cart is underground.

STANDING Stone in situ.

STAPLES U-shaped lugs fixed to quarr carts, more often called 'eyes and ears'.

STEEL SHOT Sometimes used as an alternative to sharp sand as cutting agent on (now obsolete) frame saws. One snag was that unless care was taken to wash away every piece of shot, unsightly rust stains could develop on the stone.

STIFF 'Blunt', applied to any cutting tool in need of sharpening.

STREETWORK Kerbs, gutter soles, pitchers, channel, paving; i.e. All things pertaining to pavements and streets.

STUN A pale bruise mark left by percussion of chisel or punch, most noticeable in dark beds, particularly marble: a polisher's bane.

SUET Discontinuous fine-grain blob-like forms characteristic of Burr.

SUPER Abbreviation of superficial - a surface measurement rather than cubic, an important distinction when reading old documents. All measurements of Purbeck paving were by the 'foot super' whereas Portland measurements were by 'foot cube'. More confusion lies in the fact that some measurements were linear. Considering the Rev Austin's *Economic Geology* (1852) whilst his pavings are 'foot super' his kerb and steps surely 'foot linear' similarly his landings

GLOSSARY / 289

and tombstones are 'super' whilst his gauge stones are 'cubic'.

SURLY Descriptive of a stone's working property: bad natured.

SWANAGE STONE General term for Purbeck stone in the Channel Islands.

TILER'S PICK See PICK

THAR POLE Centre member of quarr cart.

THE DAMPS See DAMPS. Stale air present in some deep Swanage quarries in Summer.

TOOLED Name given to surface left off the chisel which can vary considerably from very fine to wide strokes. Such wide measured tooling is sometimes called corduroy work.

TOP OUT The action of finishing the bottom of a wedge pit to achieve an acute point.

Training Bank Rocks placed outside the entrance to Poole harbour in 1920s to promote scouring of the navigable channel.

TRAMMEL i) Two sorts, one used for scribing parallel lines, the other for describing circles of a larger radius than compasses expand to. It consists of two adjustable pins on a length of batten.
ii) Used with chisel. L shape with a short pointed foot and an extended vertical broadened to a hollow that fits around the average chisel.

TRAP STONE Drain cover.

TRIG / TRIG UP To prevent a cart moving by jamming stones at its wheels. Also to support a stone in a desired position in a temporary way. When driving off waste with a punch it becomes somewhat easier if the surface being worked on is inclined away. This can be achieved with a small 'trig' under the workpiece.

TROW Term for trough. A common sort took the shape of the letter D hence 'D trows'.

TRUCK BARROW Wheelbarrow with flat bed and head board, lacking sides. Used for jobs such as running finished work from 'in on banker' to 'out on loading banker'.

TRUCK SYSTEM Payment in kind rather than cash by merchants for stone or labour.

TURK Term for Purbeck quarrymen.

TWIE BILL Hammer-like pick held in both hands with both cutting ends pointed, similar to kibble. Not in use in Purbeck in recent years but both kibble and twie bill are included in a late 17th century Swanage blacksmith's inventory.

TWO FOOT Term for two foot long gauge (still used by Jack Norman in the 1960s) for measuring and marking out stone, sufficiently accurate for most work.

UNDERPICKING The initial penetration in underground working. In the cliff quarries this was done by cutting away the bed lying above the Under Freestone, in the inland quarries by taking out a layer of 'underpicking dirt'.

UNIO White fossil shell about the size of a limpet. Abundant in green Marble, particularly towards the top of the layer, less common in the blue and absent from the grey. Also common on the top of the Burr.

VENT Weak crack in a stone. Common, particularly in the thicker beds like the Inland Freestone. Few large stones can be got from those blocks, even when they appear large at first sight.

VERGE Medieval term for rod, stick or shaft. (a verger carries a long staff to drive dogs out of church, same root). 'Virga' appears in payments for Queen Eleanor's Crosses 1291-1294 (P.R.O.) Is the family name Verge (John and Robert, both buried in Worth in the 1590s, and Thomas senior and Thomas junior, Marblers, in 1651,) derived from ancestors who made verges?

VERNE In 1292 a log of alder was provided 'for the machine which is called Verne' at Corfe and Hugh the Smith paid 9d. for making straps for it. This must surely be the drum of a capstan, or the equivalent part of a jenny. In the recent past elm, which is difficult to split, was more often used. Verney in Purbeck and Verne, Portland, are both high ground. Is there a possible connection?

VIEWER Obsolete. One was regularly paid 12d in the Corfe Castle accounts for his services during the 13th century works at Corfe Castle when the labourer was getting one or two pence per day. This term for an inspector continued until the 18th century, for the Bankes Estate papers include walls when finished 'to be viewed'.

VILL Obsolete term: appears in Corfe Castle 13th century building accounts. Refers not just to the built town or village, but to the surrounding area of the parish as a whole.

WARE Sloping coastal field.

WET OUT (verb) Sharpen cutting tools by rubbing on a gritstone.

WHIM-WHAM Chamfer of varying width enriching soffit of 19th century door and window heads.

WINDING A twisted or uneven surface is 'winding'. To take a stone 'out of winding' as on the top surface of a paving, is to work it into a flat plane.

WINKLE STONE Term for Petworth and Bethersden Marbles.

YERK W. J. Bower's term for the major joints or faults along the cliff; Green Point 'Yally Hole' east of Dancing Ledge, being one of the largest. He said: 'There are twelve girt yerks along clift' between Durlston and St. Aldhelm's Heads. This is a simplification. There are many more if those of a throw of only a foot or two are counted.

YARD Dubbers and dressed walling were sold by the superficial or square yard. As the stones were dressed they were set up or 'yarded up' in rows nine feet long by two feet high, each row therefore two square yards.

ZUENT Straight, plain, sweet, smooth

Notes

ONE: THE STONE

1. J. Hutchins, (1st edition, 1774), *The History and Antiquities of the County of Dorset*. London. The third edition has more detail on the Purbeck Stone industry. p.606.
2. John Aubrey, (1656-91), *The Natural History of Wiltshire*, Various Reprints.
3. Thomas Webster, *Transactions of the Geological Society*, London, 1824.
4. Revd, J.H. Austen (1852), *Guide to the Geology of the Isle of Purbeck*: Damon, R. (1884), *Geology of Weymouth, Portland and Coast of Dorsetshire from Swanage to Bridport-on-Sea with Natural History and Archaeological Notes*. Weymouth. New and Enlarged Edition (2nd Ed.), Weymouth, R.F. Damon, London, Edward Stanford. 250p. With a colour geological map of part of the Dorset coast, and including a log of the Purbeck strata of Durlston Bay, Swanage, by H. W. Bristow and Prof. E. Forbes.
5. R.G. Clements, (1969) 'Annotated cumulative section of the Purbeck Beds between Peveril Point and the zig-zag path.' Published in Torrens, H.S., (Ed), *International Field Symposium on the British Jurassic Excursion No. 1 Guide for Dorset and South Somerset*, University of Keele, pp.A1-A71.
6. P.C.Ensom, (1985) 'Annotated section of the Purbeck Limestone Formation at Worbarrow Tout.' *Proceedings of the Dorset Natural History and Archaeological Society*, 1985.
7. W.J.Arkell, Names of the strata in the Purbeck and Portland Stone Quarries, *Proceedings of the Dorset Natural History and Archaeological Society*, 1945.
8. Dr G. Dru Drury, 'Use of Purbeck Marble in medieval times.' *Proceedings of the Dorset Natural History and Archaeological Society*, 1948.
9. Ed.D. Lewer, (1990), *John Mowlem's Swanage*, Wincanton Press, Dorset Publishing Company.
10. J. Aubrey, (1656-91), *The Natural History of Wiltshire*, Various Reprints.
11. E. Benfield, (Revised 1990), *Purbeck Shop*, Southampton, Ensign Publications.
12. Thomas Webster, (1816), 'A description of the principal picturesque beauties, antiquities and geological phenomena of the Isle of Wight' in Englefield, H.C. (1816) *The Isle of Wight*, Payne and Foss, London.
13. Ed. Lewer, *John Mowlem's Swanage*.
14. Dr Buttin, Pers comm.
15. Fred Wellman, Pers. comm.
16. Ruth Farnon, Pers. comm.
17. Vince Giavarini, (2007), Report for the National Trust. In his opinion there are yet more to be identified.

TWO: MARBLE

1. Prof. M. Biddle, *The Antiquaries Journal* 45 (1965), p.260.
2. Dr. Geof. Blacker, Pers. comm.
3. J. Hutchins, (3rd Edition, 1861), *The History and Antiquities of the County of Dorset*, Vol. 1, p.466, ftnt.b.
4. Jeremy Powne, Pers. comm.
5. Ed. R. Gem (1997), *St Augustine's Abbey, Canterbury*, T.Tatton-Brown, Chapter 6, 'The Abbey precinct, liberty and estate', London, English Heritage, p.121.
6. Eds. J. Blair and N. Ramsay, (1991) *English Medieval Industries*, London, Hambledon Press p.47.
7. M. Thurlby, (2013), *The Herefordshire School of Romanesque Sculpture*, Logaston Press, p.132.
8. N. Pevsner, D. Lloyd, (1967) *Hampshire and the Isle of Wight. The Buildings of England*. Penguin Books, p.710.
9. Mr. R. V. Davis, Pers. comm.
10. N. Pevsner, (1952), *South Devon, The Buildings of England*, Penguin Books, p.42
11. Rochester contains approx 1,000 tons of Purbeck Marble. Brian Bugler, Pers.comm.
12. Roy Spring, Pers. comm. (ex. Clerk of Works, Salisbury Cathedral).
13. H. Colvin. (1971) Building *Accounts of King Henry III*, Oxford, Clarendon Press.
14. Roy Spring, Pers. comm.
15. Laurence Stone suggests that this date is incorrect; it should read '25 Hen VI', which would be 1447, when the accounts show Bourde at work in the chapel. L. Stone, (1955), *Sculpture in Britain. The Middle Ages*, Penguin Books, p.266, Note 47.
16. The tomb is discussed in Eds. R. G. Marks and P. Williamson (2003), *Gothic Art for England 1400-1547*, London, V&A Publications.
17. Ed. H.M. Colvin, (1963), *The History of the King's Works*, London, HMSO, Vol. I, p.250.
18. Westminster Abbey Official Guide, p13.
19. N. Pevsner, rev. B.Cherry, (1981), *Wiltshire, The Buildings of England*, Penguin Books.
20. I am indebted to Dr Tim Palmer for spotting this.
21. Philip Lankester, unpublished lecture on Purbeck Marble Effigies given in 1996 to the Church Monuments Society.
22. W. R. Lethaby, (1906), *Westminster Abbey and the King's Craftsmen: a Study of Mediaeval Building*. London: Duckworth & Co..; W. R. Lethaby, (1925), *Westminster Abbey Re-examined*. London: Duckworth.
23. a2252 Nottingham, Nottingham University Library, Middleton MSS, Mi 6/174/58.
24. Blair and Ramsay, *English Medieval Industries*, p.51.
25. M. Norris, (1965) *Brass Rubbing*, London, Studio Vista. Sally Badham. Pers. comm.
26. Church Monuments Society lecture London c.2004. Dr Geoffrey Blacker. (Nidderdale)
27. Ed. J. Alexander, P. Binski, (1987) *Age of Chivalry. Art in Plantagenet England 1200-1400*. Royal Academy of Arts, London, Weidenfeld and Nicholson, p.289, Fig 225.
28. Tim Tatton-Brown, Pers. comm.
29. Yevele was Master mason to the King and Black Prince, Warden of London Bridge 1368 to 1369. He was granted Wardship of Langton Wallis 1375. See J.H. Harvey, (1946), *Henry Yevele, 1320-1400: The Life of an English Architect*, London, Batsford.

30. L.F. Salzman, (1968) *Building in England down to 1540. A Documentary History,* Oxford Reprints, p.134.

31. David Hinton, Pers. Comm. See also Ed. D. A. Hinton, *Purbeck Papers,* (University of Southampton Department of Archaeology Monograph) (2002).

32. Ed. A. D. Mills. (1971) *The Dorset Lay Subsidy Roll of 1332.*

33. Devon and Cornwall Record Society accounts of the fabric of Exeter Cathedral, 1279-1353. A. Erskine 1981.

34. Transcription of Corfe Castle Building Accounts 1280-1285 commissioned by the National Trust from Public Record Office document E101/460/27.

35. BBC TV 'Time Team', October 2008, broadcast February 2009.

36. These names have been picked out from John Harvey's *English Medieval Architects* and *The Dorset Lay Subsidy Roll,* A. D. Mills, Dorset Record Soc. (1971).

37. See Drury, Leach, Blair etc.

38. R. Morris, in Ed. F. Kelly, (1991), *Medieval Art and Architecture at Exeter Cathedral,* British Archaeological Association Transactions, Volume 11. Maney Publishing.

39. My thanks to Mrs. M. Godfrey (widow of Walter Godfrey) for access to her husband's papers.

40. Adam White, Pers. comm. drawn from City of London Record Office, Guildhall Repository.

41. J. Baylis, Pers.comm. and 'Decline of the Marblers' article – Church Monuments Society Journal.

42. Jerome Bertram, Journal of Church Monuments Society.

43. D. Sibun, (1974), *Dorset Brasses,* The Abbey Press, Sherborne, p.42.

44. M. Pitt-Rivers, (1966), *Dorset. A Shell Guide.*

45. A Strahan, (1898), *The Geology of the Isle of Purbeck and Weymouth,* HMSO.

46. Revd. J.H. Austen, (1852) *Guide to the Geology of the Isle of Purbeck and the South Coast of Hampshire,* Blandford, London.

47. W. J. Haysom, Pers. comm.

48. Uncle Albert Haysom, Pers. comm.

49. Strahan, *The Geology of the Isle of Purbeck.*

50. Bankes Estate Papers, Dorset History Centre.

51. Dr. Mark Forrest, one time Archivist at the Dorset History Centre, and R. J. Saville, a local historian, have done extensive work in transcribing and translating these medieval Court Rolls, which are held among the Bankes Estate papers at the Dorset History Centre. Extracts, some relating to stone extraction, were published in Journals of the Langton Matravers Local History and Preservation Society between 2004 and 2010.

52. O. Rackham, (2006), *Woodlands,* Collins, London.

53. Wilkswood Priory Records, Nottingham University.

54. Roy Spring, Pers. comm.

55. Ed. W. Page, (1908), *Industries – Quarrying, The Victoria History of the County of Dorset, Volume Two,* London, Archibald Constable and Co Ltd., p.332, ftnt 10.

56. J. Aubrey, (2007 reprint), *The Natural History of Wiltshire.* Bibliobazaar.

THREE: INLAND QUARRYING

1. Ed. A.M.Erskine, (1983) *The Accounts of the Fabric of Exeter Cathedral,* 1279-1353. Part 2: 1328-1353, Devon and Cornwall Record Society.

2. F. P. Pitfield, (1985), *Purbeck Parish Churches,* Sherborne, Dorset Publishing Company, p.24.

3. Pevsner N., Newman, J. (1972) *Dorset, The Buildings of England,* Penguin Books.

4. RCHM, *Dorset, Vol II, South East, Part 2,* p.321.

5. I am indebted to Michael Lebas for showing me these pieces.

6. RHCM, Ibid. p.269. (Steeple), p.279 (Studland).

7. Dorset Natural History and Archaeological Society Proceedings, *A Study on the Work of Preservation of the Church of St Nicholas, Studland, Dorset,* William Masters Hardy, Vol.12., (1891), pp. 164-179.

8. I am indebted to Debbie Handy for pointing out the discovery of the masonry in the wall.

9. In R. Damon, (1884), *Geology of Weymouth, Portland and Coast of Dorsetshire from Swanage to Bridport-on-Sea with Natural History and Archaeological Notes.* Weymouth. New and Enlarged Edition (2nd Ed.), Weymouth, R.F. Damon, London, Edward Stanford. 250p. With a colour geological map of part of the Dorset coast, and including a log of the Purbeck strata of Durlston Bay, Swanage, by H. W. Bristow and Prof. E. Forbes.

10. J. Hutchins, (3rd Edition, 1861), *The History and Antiquities of the County of Dorset.* London, Vol. 1, p.495.

11. Public Record Office, *Corfe Castle Building Accounts,* 1280-1285, (E101/460/27) Recently translated and supplied by the National Trust.

12. In consideration of names and spellings, Bonfield adapts from Bonvil (or variants), a change more or less effected by the end of the 17th century: also Benvyle/Benfield.

13. Erskine, (1983) *The Accounts of the Fabric of Exeter Cathedral.*

14. Erskine, Ibid.

15. J. Harvey, (1954), *English Medieval Architects,* London, Batsford, p.239.

16. Dorset Record Soc. Vol. 4 Lay Subsidy Roll. A. D. Mills.

17. Salzman, L.F., (1968) *Building in England down to 1540. A Documentary History,* Oxford Reprints, p.132.

18. Salzman (Ibid.), p.133.

19. Langton Court Presentments, 20th October 1425, in Journal 8 (2004), Langton Matravers Local History and Preservation Society.

20. Tim Tatton-Brown, Pers. comm. based on abbey accounts.

21. RCHM (MCMLXX), *An Inventory of Historical Monuments in the County of Dorset,* Vol II (South East), No. 22 is numbered 112, p.92.

22. RCHM (Ibid.), No. 23 is numbered 89, p.91.

23. *Dorset Wills and Administrations,* 1568-1799, (1900) published by British Record Society.

24. Hutchins, (3rd Ed.), p.686.

25. W. J. Arkell, (1945). 'The names of the strata in the Purbeck and Portland stone quarries.' *Proceedings of the Dorset Natural History and Archaeological Society,* 66.

26. W.M.Hardy, (1908) *Old Swanage, or Purbeck Past and Present,* Dorchester, Dorset County Chronicle Publishing.

27. This deposition is in the collection of papers made by Mr Bankes' lawyers in anticipation of George Lander's trial in the early 1900s. Bankes Papers, Dorset History Centre.

28. D. Lewer, D. Smale, (1994), *Swanage Past,* Chichester, Phillimore and Co., pp.42-3.

29. Rempstone Estate papers (D/RWR), Dorset History Centre.

30. There are numerous quarrying references in the Bankes Papers (D/BKL). This particular quotation is included in the National Trust archaeological survey, Martin Papworth (1994). Bankes Papers, Dorset History Centre.

31. Information taken from map of Bankes estates at Langton Wallis and Easington; (c.1725) a revision of the Treswell map of Bankes tenancies in the area from 1585.

32. I am indebted to Mr James Lindsay and Judy Longman for permission to view it.

33. Purbeck Marblers' Papers. Published in Hutchins, (3rd Edition, 1861). This edition includes "The present price of 100 foot of paving stone which weighs about 1¾ ton when put on board is

1*l*. 13s; ...freight to London per ton 7s." It would seem the cost was inflating. p.688.

34. Ed. J. F. James, J. H. Bettey, (2014), *Farming in Dorset. Diary of James Warne (1758)*. Facsimile Reprint, Dorset Record Society, Hobnob Press.

35. Ed. I. Atherton, *et al*, (1996) *Norwich Cathedral. Church, City and Diocese. 1096-1996*. London, Hambledon Press.

36. Reg Saville, Pers. comm.

37. W .J. Haysom, Pers. comm.

38. C. Beddington (2006) *Canaletto in England*, Newhaven and London, Yale University Press, p.101-2, 108.

39. Dorset History Centre, DA/I/1689/76.

40. Dorset History Centre, DA/I/1703/48.

41. Mr Willis Hart, 'Gentleman of Wimborne' married Betsy Franklin at Langton Matravers in 1759; the land would have probably come into his possession through that marriage. Her grandfather (?), George Franklin signed the Joint Stock Company agreement in 1698. Mr Hart's freehold included several scattered stone-bearing fields. Those quarried include what are now Tom's Field and Acton Field campsites and another surrounded by Burngate; each an island in a Bankes sea! John was working a quarry on Hart's land but driving underground beneath Bankes'; both landlords knew of and accepted the situation.

42. Dorset History Centre, D/RWR E16 14/15.

43. Dorset History Centre. Encombe Estate Papers.

44. W. J. Haysom, Pers. comm.

45. Dorset History Centre.

46. Dorset History Centre, PE-SW/CW/1/2a (Churchwardens' Accounts).

47. From a letter forming a part of collection relating to stone supplies for the forts, compiled by Bruce Chandler and Judith Roebuck of English Heritage (unpublished).

48. 'List of Purbeck Stone Mines worked under the Metalliferus Mines Regulation Act, in Dorset, during the year 1896' from the Tables compiled by Jospeh S. Martin, H.M. Inspector for the South Western District in his report for 1896. (Peak District Mines Historical Society Ltd).

49. From the report for 1877 of Dr. C. le Neve Foster, Her Majesty's Inspector of Mines, p.446.

50. E. Benfield, (Revised 1990) *Purbeck Shop*, Southampton, Ensign Publications, p.59.

51. Jim Norman, Pers. comm.

52. Jack Norman, Pers. comm.

53. Ed. Paul Hyland, (2009) *Written in Stone: New Writing from the Isle of Purbeck*, Artsreach.

54. D. Gardiner, (2nd Ed. 1943) *Companion into Dorset*, London, Methuen.

FOUR: PEVERIL AND DURLSTON BAY

1. John Blair produced this after I rashly claimed that there was virtually no post-medieval marble quarrying before the 19th century revival!

2. C.E. Robinson, (1882), *The Royal Warren or Picturesque Rambles in the Isle of Purbeck*, London, The Typographic Etching Company.

3. Clements (1969) 'Annotated cumulative section of the Purbeck Beds between Peveril Point and the zig-zag path.' Published in Torrens, H.S., (Ed), *International Field Symposium on the British Jurassic Excursion No. 1 Guide for Dorset and South Somerset*, University of Keele pp.A1-A71.

4. The Hatcher Review, Vol.V, No 45, (1998) T. Haysom, *Extracting Purbeck Marble*, p. 53.

5. Quoted in D. Lewer, D, Smale (1994) *Swanage Past*, Chichester, Phillimore, p.64.

6. D/SEN/28/1/1/14 Dorset History Centre.

7. A. Strahan (1906) *A Guide to the Geological Model of the Isle of Purbeck*, Memoirs of the Geological Society, Great Britain.

8. Lewer and Smale, *Swanage Past*, pp.3, 4.

9. For expenses, see Lewer and Smale (Ibid), p.8, ftnt 10.

10. Brannon, P. (2nd Ed,1860), *The illustrated historical and picturesque guide to Swanage and the Isle of Purbeck with a clear digest of the geology and a minute description of the coast from Bournemouth Bay to White Nore*. Poole and London, p.54, footnote quoting Charles Kingsley.

11. Llewellyn Hardy, Pers. comm.

12. Lewer and Smale, *Swanage Past*, p.3.

13. C.E. Robinson, *The Royal Warren or Picturesque Rambles in the Isle of Purbeck*, p.98.

14. Dorset History Centre, Eldon papers.

15. John Mowlem's diary. Ed. D. Lewer, (1990) *John Mowlem's Swanage*, Wincanton Press, Dorset Publishing Company.

FIVE: CLIFF QUARRIES

1. Dr. W. Townson, 'Lithostratigraphy and Deposition of the Type Portlandian.' Quarterly Journal of the Geological Society. Vol. 131.

2. Jo Thomas, Pers. comm.

3. J. Hutchins, (3rd Edition, 1861), *The History and Antiquities of the County of Dorset*. London, Vol.1. p.687 ftnt. b.

4. RCHM (MCMLXX), *An Inventory of Historical Monuments in the County of Dorset,* Vol II (South East), Part 2, p.410.

5. Archaeological work by Dorset Institute of Higher Education, 1980/81.

6. RCHM, as above.

7. *Celia Fiennes, (1702), Through England on a Side Saddle in the Time of William and Mary*. (Reprinted London, Penguin Books, 2009)

8. D. Defoe, (Penguin Classics, 1971), *Tour Through The Whole Island Of Great Britain*, London.

9. Accounts in C. Busson, (1985), *The Book of Ramsgate*, Ramsgate, Barracuda, and letters and meetings of Trustees in records at National Archives, Kew.

10. Hutchins, (3rd Ed), Vol.1., p.537.

11. J. Claridge, (1793), *A General View of the Agriculture in the County of Dorset, with Observations on the Means of its Improvement*, London.

12. C. Beddington, (2006) *Canaletto in England*. Yale Centre for British Art, New Haven and London.

13. P. Brannon, (1858), *The illustrated historical and picturesque guide to Swanage and the Isle of Purbeck with a clear digest of the geology and a minute description of the coast from Bournemouth Bay to White Nore*. Poole and London.

14. J. Harvey, (1954), *English Medieval Architects*, London, Batsford.

15. W.M. Hardy, (1908) *Old Swanage, or Purbeck Past and Present*, Dorchester, Dorset County Chronicle Publishing, p.9.

16. Alexander Melmouth, (1703), Dorset History Centre, DA/I/1703/48.

17. Dorset History Centre.

18. Bankes Papers, D/BKL, Dorset History Centre.

19. C. E. Robinson, (1882), *The Royal Warren or Picturesque Rambles in the Isle of Purbeck*, London, The Typographic Etching Company.

20. Evidence for this comes from a map in the Dorset History Centre which is a survey done in 1806 on behalf of W.P.Taunton, who leased the manor of Eight Holes at that period. Dampier is

recorded as holding the land on the West side.

21. H.C. Englefield, (1816) *The Isle of Wight*, Payne and Foss, London. Plate 33.
22. From a special version of Hutchins, 2nd Edition, Vol. III, 'Extra Illustrated', Dorset History Centre.
23. Bankes Papers, Dorset History Centre.
24. M. McGarvie, *Somerset and Dorset Notes and Queries*. G.F.Harris, (1893) *Stone Quarry Notebook* 3, I/969, Dorset History Centre.
25. Treswell surveyed Sir Christopher Hatton's newly-acquired Purbeck estates and his map of 1586 provides much detail. Dorset History Centre, Bankes Archive. Ed. Forrest M. et al, (2017) *Treswell's Survey of Purbeck 1585-6*, Dorset Record Society, Volume 19.
26. Bankes Papers, Dorset History Centre.
27. Brian Bugler, Pers. comm.
28. Contemporary account recorded in Hutchins, J. (3rd Edition, Vol. II, 1863), *The History and Antiquities of the County of Dorset*. London, p.67.
29. *Dorset County Chronicle* 28 May 1840.
30. Identification by descendant, Mr David White.
31. Dr Martin Ayres, notes on D/BKL: 8B/88 relating to Dorset Quarry Co.
32. Woodward's survey of the Bankes Estate is in D/BKL at the Dorset History Centre.
33. *Somerset and Dorset Notes and Queries*.
34. Bankes Papers, Dorset History Centre.
35. A Swiss National, Grimm was commissioned by Sir Richard Kaye in the last decades of the 18th century to make a topographical record of Great Britain. His view of Seacombe is called 'Quarry at Peveril Point, Swanage'!
36. Hardy, *Old Swanage*, p.21.
37. Laurence Keen, (2012), 'Chantmarle, Cattistock: Sir John Strode's account of his building, 1612 to 1623, and the consecration of his oratory or chapel', *Proceedings of the Dorset Natural History and Archaeological Society*, Vol.133, 37-41.
38. Bankes Papers, Dorset History Centre.
39. M. McGarvie, *Somerset and Dorset Notes and Queries*.
40. Nelson Burt, Pers. comm.; also *The Times and Directory*, April 9 1927.
41. Bill Hancock, Pers. comm.
42. 'The Purbeck Co.operative Stone Industries Ltd' as listed in *Kelly's Directory* 1923.
43. Nelson Burt, Pers. comm.
44. Roy Cobb, Pers. Comm.
45. Bankes Papers, D/BKL: 8B/88, Dorset History Centre.
46. Calcraft Papers, D86/M9, Dorset History Centre.
47. Filliter Papers, Dorset History Centre.
48. Calcraft papers, as are all quarry returns for Winspit.
49. *Somerset and Dorset Notes and Queries*, 2004, 'Portland Stone Trade' by J Davies.
50. Letters (Ref. MA/G/CBF/245-257 and MA/G/CBF/312) held in the London Metropolitan Archive (spotted by John Haysom).
51. 'Worth Matravers, Dorset'. Auctioneers' brochure for a sale on September 30th 1919. Copy in Dorset History Centre.
52. I am indebted to Penny Huntley for spotting and photographing this for me.
53. Taylor, Sue *A Short History of Affpuddle*.
54. E.Benfield, (1940) *Purbeck Shop*, Cambridge University Press.
55. Alan Lander, Pers. comm.
56. Fred Wellman, Pers. comm.
57. For four of these maps see Barker and Le Pard, (2004), *Proceedings of the Dorset Natural History and Archaeological Society*; for the letter; see section on Worbarrow below.
58. John Harris, Pers. comm.

59. Hutchins, (3rd Ed), Vol I, p. 699.
60. Dorset History Centre, D-FRY/11/12, Map of the Manor of Renscombe, 1737.
61. I am indebted to Mr Charles Mc.Veigh for the opportunity to view the interior of Encombe house.
62. F.P. Pitfield, (1985), *Purbeck Parish Churches*, Sherborne, Dorset Publishing Company, p.112.
63. H.C. Englefield, (1816) *The Isle of Wight*, Payne and Foss, London, Plate 41.
64. (Bob) R.W.Wollage, (1976), *Slatts and Slubb. Portland People Customs Sayings*, p.56.
65. Photocopy of photograph of cottage in *Langton Matravers in Photographs*, 1850-1900. LMLHPS Booklet 26, p.35.
66. Dorset History Centre.Ref: D FRY/11/12.
67. *Taunton Courier*, March 1810.
68. W. J. Haysom, Pers. comm. His father attended.
69. Ted Pushman, Pers. comm.
70. Ibid.
71. Hubert Beavis, Pers. comm. His father was for many years this quarry's blacksmith.
72. Mick Samways, Pers. comm.
73. Major Mansell, Pers. comm.
74. L .Bond, (reprint 1984), *Tyneham. A Lost Heritage*, Wimborne, Dovecote Press, pp. 71-2.
75. See P.C. Ensom, (1985), 'Annotated section of the Purbeck Limestone Formation at Worbarrow Tout.' *Proceedings of the Dorset Natural History and Archaeological Society*.
76. *Wiltshire Archaeological Magazine*, XV (1876), pp. 182-3.

SIX: USES

1. R. Neve, (1726), *The City and Country Purchaser and Builder's Dictionary*, David and Charles reprints, Newton Abbot, 1969, p.217.
2. M. Sparks, (2014), *Handbook for Cathedral Guides*.p.47. T.Tatton-Brown, (1981), *The Trinity Chapel and Corona Floors*, Canterbury Cathedral Chronicle, 75. pp.51-56.
3. Dorset History Centre, D/BKL.CC1 and 2: Bankes Manorial and Hundredal, transcribed and translated by Dr Mark Forrest. Extracts were published by R.J.Saville in Langton Matravers Local History and Preservation Society's Journals 2004-9.
4. John Melmoth, (1685), Dorset History Centre, BC/I/M52 [BC = Bristol Consistory Court]: Phineas Melmoth. (1686), DHC, BC/I/53.
5. Brian Bugler, Pers. comm.
6. Knole Archive.
7. Dorset History Centre.
8. Ed. H. M. Colvin, (1963), *The History of the King's Works*. London, HMSO.
9. Eric Robinson, Pers. comm.
10. I am indebted to Lady G. Wilson for those extracts from the Wren Society Publications, Vols. XlX, XX, Vll, X.
11. Neve, *The City and Country Purchaser*, pp.217-8.
12. Ibid, p.228.
13. Daniel Defoe, (1724 -1726), *A Tour thro' the Whole Island of Great Britain*, Penguin.
14. The Salmon reference is contained in an authoritative description of 18th century London's paving by Sally Jeffery, *Association for Studies in the Conservation of Historic Buildings; Transactions*, Vol. 13, 1988.
15. Southampton Record Series Vol. XXXI.
16. Notes on Paving: Portsmouth Record Office PU51/1.
17. J. Claridge, (1793), *A General View of the Agriculture in the County of Dorset, with Observations on the Means of its Improvement*.
18. Corfe Castle Papers, Dorset History Centre.

19. *Times* report June, 2006.
20. Jo Thomas, (1998), *Stone Quarrying*. Wimborne, Dovecote Press.
21. From Alexander Somerville, (1852, Ed. K.D.M.Snell, 1989) *The Whistler at the Plough*,
22. T.P.Connor, (2014) 'A Standing Tombe of Stone', *Church Monuments*,Vol XXIX, p.79.
23. J. Hutchins, (3rd Edition, Vol. 1, 1861), *The History and Antiquities of the County of Dorset*. London, p.642.
24. Dorset History Centre, Bankes Papers, Langton Wallis Accounts D/BKL CC 3/1.
25. J.B.Calkin, (1968), *Ancient Purbeck*. Dorchester, The Friary Press, p.46.
26. All medieval Corfe Castle quotations from: Public Record Office, *Corfe Castle Building Accounts, 1280-1285*, (E101/460/27) Recently translated and supplied by the National Trust. This extract, p.36.
27. Ibid. p.59.
28. Bankes Papers – Hatton period, Dorset History Centre.
29. I. Woodward, (1908), *In and around the Isle of Purbeck*, London, John Lane, The Bodley Head, p.112.
30. Ed H.M.Colvin (1963), *History of the King's Works*, Vol III, Part i.
31. J.N. Hare. (1991), *Medieval Archaeology* 31.
32. J. Palmer. *Dorset Natural History and Archaeology Society Proceedings*, (2009).
33. I am indebted to the late James Sabben-Clare for these references which he found among the work of John Harvey, and the *Annals of Winchester College* (1892), by the Bursar of that time, T. F. Kirby.
34. David Hinton, Pers. comm.
35. D/BKL.CC1 and 2: Bankes Manorial and Hundredal, as above.
36. Ed. M Forrest et al, (2017) *Treswell's Survey of Purbeck 1585-6,* Dorset Record Society, Volume 19.
37. D. Lewer, D. Smale, (1994), *Swanage Past*, Chichester, Phillimore and Co. p.53.
38. Ed. William Page, (1908) *The Victoria History of the County of Dorset, Volume Two*, London, Archibald Constable and Co Ltd., p.336.
39. B. Cherry and N.Pevsner, (1989), *Devon, The Buildings of England*, Penguin Books, section 'Building Stones' by Alec Clifton-Taylor p.14.
40. Worth Church Book – Churchwarden's accounts from 1721 [?], Dorset History Centre.
41. Neve, *The City and Country Purchaser* p.164.
42. T. Webster. (1826) 'IV.—Observations on the Purbeck and Portland Beds'. Transactions of the Geological Society of London, S2, 2, 37-44.
43. W. M. Hardy, (1908) *Old Swanage, or Purbeck Past and Present*, Dorchester, Dorset County Chronicle Publishing.
44. Quoted in F. P. Pitfield, (1985), *Purbeck Parish Churches*, Sherborne, Dorset Publishing Co., p.40.
45. Arthur Price, Pers. comm.
46. Neil Harding, Pers. comm.
47. I am indebted to R. Mason (RIBA) for drawing my attention to M. Aston, (1974) *Stonesfield Slate*, Oxford County Council.
48. Claridge, J. (1793), *A General View of the Agriculture in the County of Dorset, with Observations on the Means of its Improvement*.
49. O. Rackham, (1986), *The History of the Countryside*, J.M.Dent. Plate XIII shows Iron Age and Roman field systems at the Dengie peninsula, Essex.
50. Journal of Langton Matravers Local History and Preservation Society, (2005), p.11, clause 21.
51. Graham Marsh, Pers. comm.
52. Bankes Papers, Dorset History Centre.
53. *SPAB Briefing* (2015) *Lime* SPAB Magazine supplement, p.17.
54. Corfe Castle Accounts, 1280-1285.
55. Ibid, p.51.
56. *How hydraulic lime binders work* and *Charlestown Limeworks Research and consultation*. Scottish Lime Centre Publications.
57. Neve, *The City and Country Purchaser,* p. 200.
58. Abe Shaffer, Pers. comm.
59. Claridge, *A General View of the Agriculture in the County of Dorset*.
60. Public Record Office; Ramsgate Harbour Building accounts.
61. Bankes Papers, Dorset History Centre.
62. J. Hutchins, (2nd Edition,2 Vols, 1796/1803) *The History and Antiquities of the County of Dorset*. London.
63. P.W.Cox, C.M.Hearne (1991), *Redeemed from the Heath: The Archeology of the Wytch Farm Oilfield (1987-90)*, Dorset Natural History and Archaeological Society, Monograph Series No 9, pp.104-7.
64. H.C. Englefield, (1816) *The Isle of Wight,* Payne and Foss, London. Plate 30. (Drawings by T. Webster).
65. L.F. Salzmann, (1968) *Building in England down to 1540. A Documentary History,* Oxford Reprints. p.156.

SEVEN: TECHNOLOGY

1. J B. Calkin, Pers. comm. and publications.
2. Wm R. Purchase, (1917), *Practical Masonry,* London, Crosby, Lockwood and Son, pp.4-6.
3. Dorset History Centre, Rempstone Estate papers.
4. S. Morris, (1985) *Portland. An Illustrated History*, Wimborne, Dovecote Press, p.102.
5. Dr P. Stanier, Pers. comm.
6. Public Record Office, *Corfe Castle Building Accounts*, 1280-1285, (E101/460/27) Recently translated and supplied by the National Trust.
7. Ed. A.M. Erskine, (1983) *The Accounts of the Fabric of Exeter Cathedral, 1279-1353. Part2: 1328-1353*, Devon and Cornwall Record Society. New Series, Vol 26.
8. Dorset Wills, Dorset History Centre.
9. Knoop and Jones (1967) *The Medieval Mason*, Manchester University Press.
10. Fred Wellman, Pers. comm.
11. Jack Corben, Pers. comm.
12. Dorset Wills, Dorset History Centre.
13. T. B. Groves, (1894), 'Some Local Stone Marks'. *Proceedings of the Dorset Natural History and Archaeological Society*.
14. Ibid.
15. N. Coldstream, (1991) *Masons and Sculptors,* London, British Museum Press.p.11, Fig 9.
16. T. Hatot, (2001), *Batisseurs au Moyen Age*, Editions L'Instant Durable, Clermont-Ferrand, p.75.
17. Gordon Tucker, Pers. comm.
18. R. Neve (1726), *The City and Country Purchaser and Builder's Dictionary*, David and Charles reprints, Newton Abbot, 1969, p.195.
19. Mike Burley, Pers. comm.
20. Quoted in S. Murray, (2014), *Plotting the Gothic*, Chicago and London, University of Chicago Press, p.147.
21. Dorset History Centre, D/BKL.CC1 and 2: Bankes Manorial and Hundredal, transcribed and translated by Dr Mark Forrest. Extracts were published by R. J. Saville in Langton Matravers Local History and Preservation Society's *Journals* 2004-9.

22. Michael Marshall, Portlander, Pers. comm.
23. Ken Lynham, Pers. comm.
24. Commander J. W. King, R.N. (1874) *The Pilot's Handbook*, Potter.
25. Rev R. Willis (1845), *The Architectural History of Canterbury Cathedral*, London, Longman.
26. Coldstream's *Masons and Sculptors* contains pictures of medieval barrows.
27. W.M Hardy, (1908) *Old Swanage, or Purbeck Past and Present*, Dorchester, Dorset County Chronicle Publishing.
28. Sybil Sheppard, Pers. comm.
29. Susie Norman, Pers. comm.
30. Dr Bell, Rector of Swanage from 1801 to 1809.
31. E. Benfield, (Revised 1990) *Purbeck Shop*, Southampton, Ensign Publications, p.86.
32. Ed C. Wrigley, (1988) *William Barnes. The Dorset Poet*, Wimborne, The Dovecote Press, p.123.
33. Ed. W. Page, (1908), *The Victoria History of the County of Dorset*, Volume Two, London, Archibald Constable and Co Ltd., p.332.
34. *Purbeck Shop*, p.66.
35. Alan Lander, Pers. comm.
36. Ed. R. J. Saville, *A Langton Quarryman's Apprentice, 1826-1837*, Langton Matravers Local History and Preservation Society Publication.
37. See D Haysom (2010), *Discover Old Swanage*, Frampton, Roving Press, p.85, Fig 3.8 shows a photograph of the dragging process.
38. M. Mc Garvie (G.F. Harris,) (1893), 'Purbeck Quarries in 1893', *Somerset and Dorset Notes and Queries*.
39. Dr Delamotte is commemorated by a tablet in Swanage Church.
40. *Purbeck Shop*, p.51.
41. *Discover Old Swanage*, p.85, Fig 3.7.
42. William Melmoth, (1689), Dorset History Centre,DA/I/1689/76.
43. *Masons and Sculptors*, pp.10, 54.
44. Continuators were the people who added to Hutchin's Editions II and III.
45. *The City and Country Purchaser*, p.252.
46. L. F. Salzman, (1968) *Building in England down to 1540. A Documentary History*, Oxford Reprints.
47. T. Tatton Brown, Pers. comm.
48. T. D. Hardy, (1835), *A description of the Patent rolls in the Tower of London; to which is added An itinerary of King John, with prefatory observations*, London, Eyre and Spottiswoode.
49. Ibid.
50. Undated, circa 1200, Wilkswood Priory records, Nottingham University, Reg Saville, Pers. comm.
51. Records of the Purbeck Marblers and Stone Cutters, Dorset History Centre.
52. Corfe Castle Building accounts.
53. E. Wilkes, 'Green Island and Ower' in B. Dyer and T. Darvill, (2010), *The Book of Poole Harbour*, Wimborne, Dovecote Press, p.66-8.
54. Mike Markey, Marine Archaeologist and diver, Pers. comm.
55. P. Woodward (1987), 'Excavation at Ower', *Romano-British Industries in Purbeck*; Dorset Natural History and Archaeological. Society Monograph.
56. G.Dru Drury,(1948) 'The Use of Purbeck Marble in Mediaeval Times', *Proceedings of the Dorset Natural History and Archaeological Society*, Vol 70, pp.77-98, p.76, quoting J.H.Harvey (1944), p.32.
57. Harold Haysom, Pers. comm.
58. Dorset Wills, Dorset Records Society.

59. C.N. Cullingford, (2003), *A History of Poole*, Chichester, Phillimore.
60. Marcus M. Key Jr., Robert J. Teagle, and Treleven Haysom. (2010) 'Provenance of the Stone Pavers in Christ Church, Lancaster Co., Virginia.', Quarterly Bulletin of the Archeological Society of Virginia 65, no. 1: 1-15, p.7.
61. I am indebted to John Haysom for unearthing the St Helena records.
62. London Mason's Company Records, Guildhall Library, MS 5329y, London.
63. *Sherborne and Yeovil Mercury*, 10th April 1775.
64. Reference courtesy of John Haysom, not now found.
65. C.Busson, (1985), *Book of Ramsgate*, Town Books, Quotes Ltd.
66. Hardy, *Old Swanage*, p.20.
67. Rempstone Estate papers, Dorset History Centre.
68. Rempstone Estate papers, DHC, D-RWR-E-12-1-4509.
69. C. E. Robinson, (1882), *The Royal Warren or Picturesque Rambles in the Isle of Purbeck*, London, The Typographic Etching Company.
70. Hardy, *Old Swanage*, p.25.
71. Ed D.Lewer, (1990) *John Mowlem's Swanage*, Wincanton Press, Dorset Publishing Company, p.39.
72. Hardy, *Old Swanage*, p.25.
73. Diary of Revd. Thomas Oldfeld Bartlett. (unpublished).
74. Perry Barnes, Pers.comm.
75. Ed D. Lewer, (1990) *John Mowlem's Swanage*, Wincanton Press, Dorset Publishing Company, p.34.
76. Hardy, *Old Swanage*, p.21.
77. Walter Haysom, Pers. comm.
78. Mrs Bert Norman (descendent of drowned seaman), Pers. comm.
79. Robinson, *The Royal Warren*, p.155.
80. Ibid, p.180.
81. J. Hutchins, J. (3rd Edition, 1861), *The History and Antiquities of the County of Dorset*, Swanwich, Appendix 1 p.682.
82. Lewer, *John Mowlem's Swanage*, p.87.
83. *Dorset County Chronicle*, October 1881.
84. *Sherborne Journal*, 1793.
85. Bankes Papers, Dorset History Centre.
86. From R.J.Saville, Journal of Langton Matravers History and Preservation Society, (2004), p.10.
87. Ibid, (2005),p.11.
88. John Blair, Pers.comm.
89. Encombe Estate Papers, Dorset History Centre.
90. Ed. J. F. James, J. H. Bettey (2014), *Farming in Dorset. Diary of James Warne* (1758). Facsimile Reprint, Dorset Record Society, Hobnob Press, p.66.

EIGHT: TRADE ORGANISATIONS

1. The originals remain in the ownership of the Purbeck Marblers but in the care of the Dorset History Centre.
2. D. Knoop, and G.P. Jones, (3rd ed. 1967) *The Medieval Mason*, Manchester University Press.
3. W.R. Lethaby, (1906) *Westminster Abbey and the King's Craftsmen: a Study of Mediaeval Building*. London: Duckworth & Co.; J. Harvey, (1954), English Medieval Architects, London, Batsford.
4. Harvey, *English Medieval Architects*.
5. M. Norris, (1978), *Monumental Brasses, the Craft*, Faber & Faber.
6. Adam White, Pers. comm.
7. Jon Bayliss, *Decline of the Marblers' Company*, Monumental

Brass Society Bulletin 1983.

8. For information about the London Marblers (Adam et al) see G. Dru Drury, (1948) 'The Use of Purbeck Marble in Mediaeval Times', *Proceedings of the Dorset Natural History and Archaeological Society*, Vol 70, pp.77-98; R.Emmerson, (1978), 'Monumental Brasses, London Design, c.1420-1485', *Journal of the British Archeological Association*, 131, pp.50-78; J. Blair, Chapter 3, 'Purbeck Marble' in: Eds. J. Blair, N. Ramsay, (1991) *English Medieval Industries*, London, Hambledon Press; Harvey, *English Medieval Architects*, L.F. Salzman, (1968) *Building in England down to 1540. A Documentary History*, Oxford Reprints.

9. Dru Drury, 'Use of Purbeck Marble in Medieval Times'. Also Ed. H.M. Colvin, (1963), *The History of the King's Works*, London, HMSO.

10. I am indebted to Jon Bayliss for findng this.

11. My thanks to Mr T. Lucas for allowing me to view the fireplace.

12. Swanage Parish Registers are particularly informative in relation to this.

13. RCHM (MCMLXX), *An Inventory of Historical Monuments in the County of Dorset*, Vol II (South East). Also Corfe papers, PE/COC Dorset History Centre.

14. The Purbeck Marblers have copies, but not an original of this document, which is at the Dorset History Centre.

15. Guildhall Library, London. Masons' Company Stone Search record 1669-1691, 5329.

16. Purbeck Marblers Papers, Dorset History Centre.

17. One wonders how Hutchins got sight of it. J. Hutchins (3rd Edition, (1861-70)), Vol I, *The History and Antiquities of the County of Dorset*. London. Appendix 1.p.682.

18. Rempstone papers, Dorset History Centre.

19. Bankes Papers, Dorset History Centre.

20. Calcraft papers, Dorset History Centre. Cheff rent (also 'chevage') = Poll tax which was payable in the medieval period on villeins in neighbouring manors. This seems to have lingered on, certainly in this manor, and possibly others too.

21. Ramsgate Harbour Accounts, PRO.

22. Several issues of the Langton Matravers Local History Preservation Society Journal include extracts, particularly numbers 6, 8 and 9.

23. Ed. Audrey M. Erskine, (1983), *The Accounts of the Fabric of Exeter Cathdral, 1279-1353. Part 2: 1328-1353*, Devon and Cornwall Record Society.

24. Harvey, *English Medieval Architects*, p.51.

25. J. Claridge, (1793), *A General View of the Agriculture in the County of Dorset, with Observations on the Means of its Improvement*, London.

26. Henry Bower, DA/W/1818/26, DHC.

27. Calcraft papers, Dorset History Centre.

28. Bankes Papers, Dorset History Centre.

29. Diary of Revd. Thomas Oldfeld Bartlett, (unpublished), Swanage Heritage Centre.

30. Ed. J. F. James, J. H. Bettey (2014), *Farming in Dorset. Diary of James Warne (1758)*. Facsimile Reprint, Dorset Record Society, Hobnob Press.

31. Ibid. p.71.

32. Ibid. p.55.

33. Ramsgate Harbour Minutes, PRO.

34. Calcraft papers, Dorset History Centre.

35. J. Hutchins, (2nd Edition,2 Vols, 1796/1803) *The History and Antiquities of the County of Dorset*. London.

36. P. Brannon, (1858), *The illustrated historical and picturesque guide to Swanage and the Isle of Purbeck with a clear digest of the geology and a minute description of the coast from Bournemouth Bay to White Nore*. Poole and London.

37. W.M Hardy (1908) *Old Swanage, or Purbeck Past and Present*, Dorchester, Dorset County Chronicle Publishing.

38. I am indebted to the late Geoff Hooper who had such an acute memory for all these old yarns. He was educated at St George's Langton during the war, which sometimes meant village children attending during the morning, refugees in the afternoon. Then followed National Service in the Navy, which brought shore runs in post-war Hamburg which awoke an interest in the language of Germany, its literature and the works of the great composers. He read Goethe in the original. Friendship with a visiting student from Strasbourg led on to being more or less self-taught in French and Russian. He composed poetry without writing it down until friends prevailed on him to have it published. He failed to get me to understand the principle of the transistor radio, new at the time. He endured calumnies without too much bitterness; these from a man who was indeed a bounder; a man who, at the height of the wartime emergency, could take a load of hardcore to Blandford Camp, only to exit via a back road without tipping it, in order to book it in a second time.

39. Hutchins (3rd.Ed.), App.1, p.682.

40. William Melmoth, (1689), Dorset History Centre, DA/I/1689/76 [DA= Dorset Archdeaconry Court]; John Melmoth, (1685), DHC, BC/I/M52 [BC = Bristol Consistory Court].

41. Phineas Melmoth. (1686), DHC, BC/I/53.

42. Alexander Melmouth, (1703), DHC, DA/I/1703/48.

43. This inventory was displayed at Dorset Count Museum. Dorset History Centre. D65/T3.

44. Dorset History Centre.

45. One of these James Keats wrote out the Ower agreement and the Articles in his own hand in 1746 at the age of 14. These copies remain in the archives, D65/74 (DHC). They show James to be one of two Window Tax collectors in 1752.

46. A lane in Corfe which goes from the Square down to the Chruch Knowle road bears the same name.

47. Hutchins 2nd Ed. only.

48. D. Lewer, D. Smale, (1994), *Swanage Past*, Chichester, Phillimore and Co.

49. Hardy, *Old Swanage*.

50. CRO Indentures, now at DHC: CRO Indentures, P11/OU/91.

51. Ed. R.J.Saville, *A Langton Quarryman's Apprentice, 1826-1837. James Corben's Autobiography*. Langton Matravers Local History and Preservation Society Publication.

52. O. W. Farrer, *The Marblers of Purbeck*, The Purbeck Papers, 1859.

53. From the Settlement Examinations, Corfe papers, DHC. Apprenticeship papers are also in the same collection - Indentures, now at DHC, P11/OU/91.

54. Swanage Churchwardens' Accounts, (1793-1828) DHC, PE-SW/CW/1/2a.

55. Dorset History Centre, D-BKL/H/H/1/98.

56. Swanage Churchwardens' Accounts, as above.

57. Haysom agreement (1841) – Sentry Estate records, Dorset History Centre.

58. In Ed. D. Lewer, (1990) *John Mowlem's Swanage*, Wincanton Press, Dorset Publishing Company.

59. J. Haysom, '*Wealth of the Chinchen Stone merchants, 1820*' in Somerset and Dorset Notes and Queries, March 2009.

60. I am indebted to David Haysom for drawing my attention to Revd. Harston's 'Sketches for a short autobiography' (1873).

61. I am indebted to Dr Philip Mansel for permission to peruse the Tower accounts.

62. Lewer, *John Mowlem's Swanage*.

63. Leases between Ilminster school and Thomas Randell (1855), Dorset History Centre.

64. *Advertiser and Visitors' List, September 1881*. (Swanage).

65. I am indebted to Mrs C.M. Hercock, née Burt for access to extracts of Frank Burt's diaries.
66. I am indebted to the late Mr Llewellyn Hardy for permission to see these books.
67. E. Benfield, (Revised 1990) *Purbeck Shop*, Southampton, Ensign Publications.
68. Farrer, *'The Marblers of Purbeck'*.
69. Hardy, *Old Swanage*, pp.54-5.
70. This quotation and all others following relating to excerpts from the Minute Books are taken from the original documents in the possession of the Company of Marblers.
71. *Dorset Year Book,* Society of Dorset Men.
72. Jack Norman, Pers. comm.
73. Ronald Bower, Pers. comm.
74. Extract from Planning Consultant John Lawrence's report, Bankes Papers, Dorset History Centre, DBK 8B/209.
75. Walter Haysom, Pers. comm.
76. Kelly's Directory, Swanage, 1920.
77. Sam Florence, Pers. comm.
78. Tom Bonfield, Pers. comm.
79. Bankes Papers, Dorset History Centre.
80. *Western Flying Post* 14th July, 1778.
81. Eight Holds Court Rolls, Dorset History Centre: also following quotations.
82. Bankes Papers, Dorset History Centre.
83. Emma Hardy's notebook, quoted in Lewer and Smale, *Swanage Past,* p.123.
84. *Dorset County Chronicle,* August 1885.
85. *Dorset County Chronicle,* September 1885.
86. Walter Haysom, Pers. comm.
87. Bankes Papers, Dorset History Centre.
88. All following quotations taken from the Marblers' Minute Books held by the Company of Marblers.
89. Extract from affidavit of Isaac Bower, in the High Court of Justice Chancery Division, 1904 (B.No.565).
90. Extract from George Lander's affidavit, Bankes Papers, Dorset History Centre.
91. This can be found among the Bankes Papers in D/BKL/E/C/7/5.
92. I am indebted to the late Mr Norman Priddle for drawing my attention to this document.
93. Ed Lewer, *John Mowlem's Swanage,* (Sat, 22nd November 1845) p32. Harding appears to have been in debt for almost £4,000 at the time.
94. Friends of Kensal Green Cemetery Magazine, Issue 76, January 2015.
95. Ed. Lewer, *John Mowlem's Swanage,* Introduction, pp.15-28.
96. Ibid.
97. Ibid. p 18.
98. Collection researched by Cyril Haysom.

Bibliography

JOURNAL
The Antiquaries Journal, 45 (1965)

BOOKS AND PERIODICALS

Eds. Alexander, J. Binski, P. (1987), *Age of Chivalry. Art in Plantagenet England 1200-1400.* Royal Academy of Arts, London, Weidenfeld and Nicholson.

Arkell, W.J. (1945), 'Names of the strata in the Purbeck and Portland Stone Quarries', *Proceedings of the Dorset Natural History and Archaeological Society.*

Arkell, W.J. (1948), *Oxford Stone,* London, Faber and Faber.

Ed Atherton, I et al, (1996), *Norwich Cathedral. Church, City and Diocese. 1096-1996.* London, Hambledon Press.

Aubrey, J, (1656-91), *The Natural History of Wiltshire,* Various Reprints.

Austen, Revd J. H., (1852), *Guide to the Geology of the Isle of Purbeck and the South Coast of Hampshire,* Blandford, London.

Beddington, C. (2006), *Canaletto in England,* Newhaven and London, Yale University Press

Benfield, E. (Revised 1990), *Purbeck Shop,* Southampton, Ensign Publications.

Eds. Blair, J., Ramsay, N. (1991), *English Medieval Industries,* London, Hambledon Press.

Bond, L., (reprint 1984), *Tyneham. A Lost Heritage,* Wimborne, Dovecote Press

Brannon, P. (1858), *The illustrated historical and picturesque guide to Swanage and the Isle of Purbeck with a clear digest of the geology and a minute description of the coast from Bournemouth Bay to White Nore.* Poole and London.

Calkin, J.B., (1968), *Ancient Purbeck.* Dorchester, The Friary Press.

Cherry, B., Pevsner, N. (1989), *Devon, The Buildings of England,* Penguin Books.

Claridge, J. (1793), *A General View of the Agriculture in the County of Dorset, with Observations on the Means of its Improvement,* London.

Clements, R.G. (1969), 'Annotated cumulative section of the Purbeck Beds between Peveril Point and the zig-zag path.' Published in Torrens, H.S., (Ed), *International Field Symposium on the British Jurassic Excursion No. 1 Guide for Dorset and South Somerset,* University of Keele, pp. A1-A71.

Coldstream, N. (1991), *Masons and Sculptors,* London, British Museum Press.

Ed. Colvin, H.M. (1963), *The History of the King's Works,* London, HMSO.

Colvin, H. (1971), *Building Accounts of King Henry III,* Oxford, Clarendon Press.

Cox, P.W., Hearne C.M. (1991), *Redeemed from the Heath: The Archeology of the Wytch Farm Oilfield (1987-90),* Dorset Natural History and Archeological Society, Monograph Series No 9.

Cullingford, C.N. (2003), *A History of Poole,* Chichester, Phillimore.

Damon, R. (1884), *Geology of Weymouth, Portland and Coast of Dorsetshire from Swanage to Bridport-on-Sea with Natural History and Archaeological Notes.* Weymouth. New and Enlarged Edition (2nd Ed.), Weymouth, R.F. Damon, London, Edward Stanford. 250p. With a colour geological map of part of the Dorset coast, and including a log of the Purbeck strata of Durlston Bay, Swanage, by H. W. Bristow and Prof. E. Forbes.

Defoe, D. (Penguin Classics, 1971), *A Tour Through the Whole Island Of Great Britain,* London.

Dru Drury, G. (1948), 'The Use of Purbeck Marble in Mediaeval Times', *Proceedings of the Dorset Natural History and Archaeological Society,* Vol 70, pp.77-98.

Dyer, B. and Darvill, T. (2010), *The Book of Poole Harbour,* Wimborne, Dovecote Press.

Englefield, H.C. (1816), *The Isle of Wight,* Payne and Foss, London.

Ensom, P.C. (1985), 'Annotated section of the Purbeck Limestone Formation at Worbarrow Tout.' *Proceedings of the Dorset Natural History and Archaeological Society.*

Ed. Erskine, A.M. (1983), *The Accounts of the Fabric of Exeter Cathedral, 1279-1353.* Part 2: 1328-1353, Devon and Cornwall Record Society.

Ed. Forrest M. et al, (2017), *Treswell's Survey of Purbeck 1585-6,* Dorset Record Society, Volume 19.

Fiennes, C. (1702) (Republished 2016), *Through England on a Side Saddle in the Time of William and Mary,* www.folkcustoms.co.uk.

Gardiner, D. (2nd Ed. 1943), *Companion into Dorset,* London, Methuen.

Ed. Gem, R. (1997), *St Augustine's Abbey, Canterbury,* London, English Heritage.

Groves, T.B. (1894), 'Some Local Stone Marks', *Proceedings of the Dorset Natural History and Archaeological Society.*

Hardy, T.D. (1835), *A description of the Patent rolls in the Tower of London; to which is added an itinerary of King John, with prefatory observations,* London, Eyre and Spottiswoode.

Hardy, W. M. (1908), *Old Swanage,* or *Purbeck Past and Present,* Dorchester, Dorset County Chronicle Publishing.

Harvey, J.H., (1946), *Henry Yevele, 1320-1400: the Life of an English Architect,* London, Batsford.

Harvey, J. (1954), *English Medieval Architects,* London, Batsford.

Haysom, D. (2010), *Discover Old Swanage,* Frampton, Roving Press.

Ed. Hinton, D. A. (2002), *Purbeck Papers,* (University of Southampton Department of Archaeology Monograph).

Hutchins, J, (1st Edition, 1774), *The History and Antiquities of the County of Dorset.* London.

Hutchins, J. (2nd Edition, 2 Vols, 1796/1803), *The History and Antiquities of the County of Dorset.* London

Hutchins, J. (3rd Edition, 4 Vols, 1861-70), *The History and*

Antiquities of the County of Dorset. London.

Ed. Hyland, P. (2009), *Written in Stone: New Writing from the Isle of Purbeck,* Artsreach.

Ed. James, J. F., Bettey, J.H. (2014), *Farming in Dorset. Diary of James Warne (1758).* Facsimile Reprint, Dorset Record Society, Hobnob Press.

Keen, L., (2012), 'Chantmarle, Cattistock: Sir John Strode's account of his building, 1612 to 1623, and the consecration of his oratory or chapel', *Proceedings of the Dorset Natural History and Archaeological Society,* Vol.133, 37-41.

Key, M. M., Jr., Teagle, R. J. and Haysom, T. (2010), 'Provenance of the Stone Pavers in Christ Church, Lancaster Co., Virginia.' Quarterly Bulletin of the Archeological Society of Virginia 65, no. 1: 1-15.

Le Pard, G. (2010), *Dorset and the Sea,* Wellington, Dorset Books.

Lethaby, W.R. (1906), *Westminster Abbey and the King's Craftsmen: a Study of Mediaeval Building.* London: Duckworth & Co.

Lethaby, W.R. (1925), *Westminster Abbey Re-examined.* London: Duckworth.

Lethaby, W.R. (Reprinted 1971), *Mediaeval Art, 312-1350,* Freeport, New York, Books for Libraries Press

Ed. Lewer, D. (1990), *John Mowlem's Swanage,* Wincanton Press, Dorset Publishing Company.

Lewer, D., Smale, D. (1994), *Swanage Past,* Chichester, Phillimore and Co.

Eds. Marks R.G., Williamson, P. (2003), *Gothic Art for England 1400-1547,* London, V&A Publications.

Morris, S, (1996), *Portland. An Illustrated History,* Wimborne, The Dovecote Press.

Neve, R. (1726), *The City and Country Purchaser and Builder's Dictionary,* David and Charles reprints, Newton Abbot, 1969.

Norris, M. (1978), *Monumental Brasses, the Craft,* Faber and Faber.

Ed. Page, W. (1908), *The Victoria History of the County of Dorset, Volume Two,* London, Archibald Constable and Co Ltd.

Pevsner N., Newman, J. (1972), *Dorset, The Buildings of England,* Penguin Books.

Pevsner, N., Lloyd, D. (1967), *Hampshire and the Isle of Wight. The Buildings of England,* Penguin Books.

Pevsner, N., (1952), *South Devon, The Buildings of England,* Penguin Books.

Pevsner, N., rev. Cherry, B. (1981), *Wiltshire, The Buildings of England,* Penguin Books.

Pitfield, F.P. (1985), *Purbeck Parish Churches,* Sherborne, Dorset Publishing Company.

Pitt-Rivers, M. (1966), *Dorset.* A Shell Guide.

Public Record Office, *Corfe Castle Building Accounts, 1280-1285,* (E101/460/27) Recently translated and supplied by the National Trust.

Purchase, Wm. R. (1917), *Practical Masonry,* London, Crosby, Lockwood and Son.

Rackham, O. (1986), *The History of the Countryside,* J.M.Dent.

Rackham, O. (2006), *Woodlands,* London, Collins.

RCHM (MCMLXX), *An Inventory of Historical Monuments in the County of Dorset.,* Vol II (South East).

Robinson, C.E. (1882), *The Royal Warren or Picturesque Rambles in the Isle of Purbeck,* London, The Typographic Etching Company.

Salzman, L.F. (1968), *Building in England down to 1540. A Documentary History,* Oxford Reprints.

Ed. Saville, R. J. (1980s?) *A Langton Quarryman's Apprentice, 1826-1837.* James Corben's Autobiography. Langton Matravers Local History and Preservation Society Publication.

Sibun, D. (1974), *Dorset Brasses,* Sherborne, The Abbey Press.

Sparks, M, (2014), *Handbook for Cathedral Guides.* Canterbury.

Strahan, A., (1898), *The Geology of the Isle of Purbeck and Weymouth,* HMSO.

Strahan, A. (1906), *A Guide to the Geological Model of the Isle of Purbeck,* Memoirs of the Geological Society, Great Britain.

Tatton-Brown, T. (1981), 'The Trinity Chapel and Corona Floors', Canterbury Cathedral Chronicle, 75.

Thomas, J. (1998), *Stone Quarrying.* Wimborne, Dovecote Press.

Thurlby, M. (2013), *The Herefordshire School of Romanesque Sculpture,* Logaston Press.

Warren, J.W. (1939), *The Buildings of Old Portland. Part Four: The Isle and Royal Manor Of Portland,* Court Leet and Court of the Manor (of Portland).

Webster, T. (1826) 'IV– Observations on the Purbeck and Portland Beds'. *Transactions of the Geological Society of London,* S2, 2, 37-44.

Willis, R. W. (1845), *The Architectural History of Canterbury Cathedral.* London, Longman.

Wollage, R.W. (1976), *Slatts and Slubb. Portland People Customs Sayings.*

Woodward, I. (1908), *In and around the Isle of Purbeck,* London, John Lane, The Bodley Head.

Woodward, P. (1987), 'Excavation at Ower', *Romano-British Industries in Purbeck*; Dorset Natural History and Archaeological Society Monograph.

GUIDEBOOKS.
Westminster Abbey Official Guide.
Taylor, S., *A Short History of Affpuddle.*

Index

Page numbers in *italic* refer to illustrations

Lists of names of Marblers, Masons, Quarrymen, Wardens *see* 235-6, 241, 247, 267-8, 269-75

Abbascombe, 84, 141, 143, 188
Abbot, John, 237
Acton, 4, 11, 15, 16, 18, 19, 22, 23, 25, 48, 74, 75, 76-7, 79, 80, 81, 82, 83, 84, 90, 91, 92, 116, 128, 137, 175ff, 180, 183, 208, 211, 212, 231, 232, 244, 257, 260, 262, 269
    Bower's quarry *211*
Adisham, Holy Innocents, 46
Afflington, 56, 75, 104
Alben, Bert, 136
Albin, Arthur, 8
Aldeburgh, St. Peter and St. Paul's, 161
Alexander, Daniel, 99, 113, 251
Alexander, Horace, 7
Alford, Thomas, 237, *237*
Alfryngton, *See* Afflington
Alkham, St Anthony, 47
All Hallows by the Tower, 61, *61*
Almer, St. Mary, Dorset, 42
Alverstoke, Gosport, 179
Anderson, Stanley, *170*
Anderson, Tom, *110*, 115
Andrew, John, 177
Antony House, Cornwall, 242
Arkell, William J., 12, 13ff, 16, 17, 19, 78
Arne, St Nicholas, 93, *103*, 103, 175
Arundel Castle, 50, 89
Athelhampton Hall, 68, 75, 163, 172
Atkyn, Stephen, 62, 63, 243
Aubrey, John, 11, 14, 67
Audley, Fred, 60, 193
Aust, Percy, 136-7
Austen, Rev. J., 12, 14, 15-16, 59, 109, 190, 284, 286, 289
Aveton Gifford, Devon, 36
Aylesbury Grammar School, 41, 42
Ayres, Dr. Martin, 8

Baker, John, 63
Ball, Frank, 117
Ball, Jim, 184
Bank of England, 48 56
Bankes Estate, 60, 81, 82, 84, 85, 89, 92, 108, 123, 124, 128, 129, 136ff, 150, 164, 180, 182, 190, 199, 215, 242ff, 257ff, 262ff
Bankes, Henry, 242, 247, 249
Bankes, John, 80, 182, 226, 242, 263
Bankes, John Ralph, 177, *177*
Bankes, Sir Ralph, 79, 117, 128, 257,
Bankes, Walter Ralph, 144, 264, 265, 266
Bankes l'Anson, Revd. Thomas, 233
Barbados, 223
Barham, G. R., 249
Barnes, Ed, 227
Barnes, George, 143
Barnes, Robert, 143, 228
Barnes, William, 209, 251
Barnston Manor, 71
Barsham, Thomas Edward (headstone), 175
Bartlet, Thomas, 244
Bartlett, Edward (Ted), 52, 64
Bartlett, Rev. Thomas O., 99, 150, 215, 229, 244
Barton Stacey, All Saints, 44
Bath, Peter, 9
Batley, Rev. Yorke, 259
Bayliss, Jon, 235
Bayntun, Sir Edward, 56
Beauchamp, Richard, 39
Beaulieu Abbey, 49, 205, *205*
Beaumaris Castle, 198
Beavis, Dr. John, 67
Beccles, Samuel Husbands, 97
Bedingham, Norfolk, 36
    St. Andrew, 36
Belgium, Bruges, 175
    St. John's Hospital, 166
Benfield, Alfred, 26, 91, 176, 212, 234, 255, 270, 282
Benfield, Charles, 90, 209, 270
Benfield, Eric, 15, 89, 144, 211, 214, 215, 282, 286, 287, 288
Benfield, James, 244, 267
Benfield, Matthew, 215
Benfield, Richard, 264
Benfield, Robert, 263
Benfield, Thomas, 86, 99, *134*
Benfield, William, 247
Benvyle, John, 63
Bere Regis
    John Turberville Chapel and slab, 171, 201, *201*
    St. John the Baptist, 49, 56, 57, 70, 182, *201*
    War memorial cross, 144
Bermuda, St. Peter's, 41
Bersone, Benjamin, 139
Bertram, Jerome, 56
Beverly Minster, 37, 51
Bicester Priory, 49
Bincombe, Holy Trinity, 42, 43
Bindon Abbey, 68, 69, 159, 191
Bisham, All Saints, 56
Bishop's Waltham Palace, 180
Blackers Hole quarry, 116-17, 108, 120, 219, 257
Blackmanston, 20, 23, 188, 192
Blair, John, 34
Blandford, 50, 70, 81
Blandford Camp, 145
Blashenwell, 11, 12, 28, 59, 62, 64, 70, 72, 150, 233, 234
Bloomsbury, St George's, 161
Bloxworth, St. Andrew, 71-2, *71*, 171
Blythburgh, Holy Trinity, 56
Boldre, 68
Bond, Lilian, 122, 158
Bond, Onesiphorus, 243
Bonfield, Fred 'Darky', 144, *147*, 261
Bonfield, George, 129, 173, 209, 250-1
Bonfield, 'Mr' (in Hutchins) 12, 13-14, 15, 17
Bonfield, Harold, 8, 24, 91, 92, 125, 136, 158, 208, 210ff, 215, 257, 269
Bonfield, Joe, 24
Bonfield, John Warren 'Warny', 210, 256
Bonfield, Roger, 7, 18, 79, 210, 212, 215, 288
Bonfield, Scurry, 217
Bonfield, Thomas (Tommy), 7, 22, 25, 59, 64, 74, 78, 79, 80, 89, 90, 91, 92, 150, *154*, 168, 184, 196, 204, 210, 211, 212, 216, *216*, 217, 248
Bosham, Holy Trinity, 42
Bourde, John, 39
Bournemouth
    International Centre, 156
    St Francis, 139, 195, 210
Bower, Aaron, 8, 249, 250
Bower, Albert Brownsea, 260
Bower, Albert 'Fiddler', 168, 184
Bower, Albert 'Trink', 8, 22, 192, 217, 262
Bower, Allan ('Uncle Allan'), 125

INDEX / 301

Bower, Alphaeus (Phae) Brownsea, 23, 210
Bower, Ambrose, 107, 118, 121, 131-2, 133, *135*, 138, 143, 184, 193, 204, 216, 227, 234, 262, 264, 265, 269
Bower, Ambrose Jr., 89, 137, 244
Bower, Amos, 146
Bower, Benjamin, 250
Bower, Bill Chaffey, 60, 128
Bower, Bill 'Mart', 7
Bower, Billy Preston, 88, 89
Bower, Charles, A., 269
Bower, Dennis 'Short', *90*
Bower, Douglas, 231
Bower, Edward, 84, 122
Bower, Edwin, 267, 269
Bower, Emmanuel, 251
Bower, Eric, 8
Bower, Flinger, 60, *144*, 182
Bower, Frank Ivamy, 262
Bower, Fred, 13, 29, 89, 259
Bower, Frenchy, 208
Bower, Gabriel, 190
Bower, George, 256
Bower, George Brownsea, 8
Bower, George 'Buff', 134, *135*, 138, *144*, 148, 156, *199*, 245
Bower, Glen, 8, 210
Bower, Gordon, *198*
Bower, Henry, 124, 129, 131, 227, 243, 250
Bower, Henry B., 269
Bower, Isaac, 60, 124, 131, 150, 243, 251, 265, 266
Bower, Israel, 58, 60, 86, 104, 208
Bower, James, 251
Bower, Jeremiah, 131, 194, 216, 228, 251
Bower, Jimmy Ivamy, *257*, 260
Bower, Job, 264
Bower, Joby Ball, 22, 88, 210, *214*
Bower, John, 249, 251
Bower, John Ivamy, 60, 61, 89, 119, 143, *146*, 217
Bower, Joseph, 215
Bower, Keith, 269
Bower, Levi, 143
Bower, Martin, 262, 264
Bower, Michael, 26, 125, 126, 128, *135*, *144*, 144-5, 204, *214*, 264
Bower, Moses, 123
Bower, Nelson, 184
Bower, Phillip, 8, 125, 262
Bower, Ralf, 7, 52, 55
Bower, Ralph, 125, *154*, 197
Bower, Reg ('Pickles'), 127-8, 136, 197, 244, 257
Bower, Reginald Michael, 128
Bower, Reuben Short, 254, 269
Bower, Richard ('Dick Gad'), 216, 265, 267, 269
Bower, Ron, 8
Bower, Sam, 32, 115, 141, 258
Bower, Sam Short, 118, 119, *205*, 211, 219
Bower, Samuel, 251
Bower, Saul, 265
Bower, Thomas, 82, 84, 119, 131, 141, 142, 227, 237, 251
Bower, Vic (Victor) Short, 23, *135*, *135*, *199*, 244
Bower, Captain Whistler, 118, 119, 121
Bower, William, 141, 142, 151, 227, 262
Bower, William Jeremiah, ('Billy Winspit'), 7-8, 19, 80, 83, 88, *110*, 111, 115, 122, 123, 124, 131, 134, 135, *137*, *137*, *138*, 138, 143, 144, *144*, 146, 147, 150, 151, 152, 155, 190, *199*, 205, 206, 214, 216, 219, 227, 245, 258, 262
Boxgrove, St Mary and St Blaise, Sussex, 40, 175
Boys, Thomas, 56
Bradford, Bill, 8, *133*
Bradford, Sally, 245
Bradford, William, 133
Brandon, Edward, 74
Brannon, P., 112, 146, 219, 233, 245
Branscombe, St. Winifred, 48, *48*
Bredon, St. Giles, 56, *57*
Brewer, Sir William, 46, 48
Brewer, Alice de, 46, 63, 243
Briantspuddle, 144
Bridle, Ann, 263
Bridle, Harry, 136, 258
Bridle, James, 265
Bridport, 195, *195*
Brightling, East Sussex, 11
Brine, Henry, 57
Bristow, Henry, 12, 72
British Geological Survey, 21, 134, *156*
British Museum, 50, 156
Brodie, W. R., 97
Bromham, St. Nicholas, 56
Brown, Albert, 144
Brown, Billy, 156, *156*
Brown, Bobby, 99, 130, 136
Brown, Edward, 120, 226
Brown, George, 260
Brown, James, 257
Brown, James A., *139*
Brown, John, 134, *134*, 135, 190, 257
Brown, Joseph, 254
Brown, Martin, *135*, *135*, 136
Brown, Pat, 136
Brown, Walter/William, 60, 91, 142, *142*, 226, 227
Brown Bower, Joseph, 264
Brown Bower, Thomas, 264
Browne, William, 194
Brownsea, George, 8
Bruton, St Mary's, 41
Bryant, Walter, 138
Buckfastleigh, Devon, 34
Buckland Abbey, Plymouth, 164
Bugler, Brian, 8-9, 25, 42, 65, 71, 79, 124, 169, 200, 204, 212, 215, 254

Burgess, William, 149, 152
Burt and Burt, 99, 118, 129, 132, *133*, 133, 143, 195, 201, 203, 206, 253, 254, 259, 261, 264, 267, 271, 285, 286
Burt and Vick, 253
Burt, Billy, 253
Burt, Charles, 138, 194, 195, 253
Burt, David, 8
Burt, Ernest, 128, 133. 143
Burt, Ernie, 90, 91, 206, 261
Burt, Frank, 99, 253
Burt, Fred, 253
Burt, George, 8, 17, 22, 27, 88, 89, 97, 98, 99, 111, 112, 114, 212, 222, 231, 252, 253
Burt, George 'Boss', 212, *212*, 215, 253
Burt, Harry, 169, 261
Burt, Henry, 254, 256
Burt, Henry Weeks ('Grocer'), 60, 118, 119, 193, 194, 253, 266
Burt, Nelson, 86, 92, 115, *146*, 216
Burt, Robert, 87, 228, 250, 251, 253, 256
Burt, Septimus, 9
Burt, 'Swelly', 216
Burtle, Somerset, 33
Buslingthorpe, St. Michael's
    Sir Richard de Buslingthorp slab, 171
Butler, George, 99, 228
Butler, James, 99
Butler, William, 99, 228, 250
Button, Brian, 90-1

Calcraft Estate, 243
Calcraft, John (1729-72), 107, 110, 141, 146
Calcraft, John Hales, 244, 264, 265
Calcraft, William, 156
Calkin, Bernard J., 149, 179
Cambridge, Sedgewick Museum, 193
Canford Magna, 50, 179
    Real Tennis court, 163
Canon, John, 51, 161, 243
Canon, Thomas, 235
Canon, William, 50-1, 65, 74, 243
Canon, William (Senior), 50, 51, 243
Canoun, John, *See* Canon, John
Canterbury, St. Augustine's Abbey, 34
Canterbury Cathedral, 33, 33-4, 35, 43, 47, 49, 63, *63*, 96, 162-3, *163*, 194, 206, 220, 224
    Archbishop Bourchier's tomb, 49
    Archbishop's Great Hall, 48
    St. Augustine's Chair, 49, *49*
    Thomas Becket's shrine, 162, *163*
    Trinity Chapel, *163*
Cardew, Colonel, 86-7
Carter, Ambrose, 176
Carter, Bill, 8
Cary, George, 152
Causon, S., 195
Channel Islands, 172
Chantmarle Manor, 131

Chapman, Joan, 243
Chapman, John, 98, 105, 247
Chapman, Thomas, 176, 221, 237, 238, 241, 243
Chapman, Thomas Jr., 243
Charborough House, 72
Charles I, 79
Charles II, 172
Charlton Marshall, 110, 234
Charterhouse, London, 167
Chaucer, Geoffrey, 13, 164
Chertsey Bridge, *109*, 109-10
Chichester, Punch House, 178
Chichester Cathedral, 34, 41, *41*, 48, 67, 101, *161*, *161*, 175, 178, 194, 260
    Mary Magdalene chapel, 156
Chickerell, St Mary, 171
Chilham, St Mary, 47
Chilmark quarry, 26, 78, 100, 101, 115-16, *116*, 117, 172, 174, 180, *218*
Chilmark, Thomas Sweet (tombstone), 174
Chinchen, Charles, 124, 128, 143, 251
Chinchen, Elizabeth, 143
Chinchen, Harry ('Ton'), 91, 219, 248, 259
Chinchen, James, 117, 142, 143, 166, 229, 250, 251
Chinchen, Jimmy, *134*, 207, 209, 214, 260
Chinchen, John, 82, 83, 129, 245
Chinchen, Joseph, 84, 123, 124, 129, 141, 142, 227, 242, 250, 251, 267
Chinchen, Nathaniel, 142, 166, 252
Chinchen, Timothy, 224, 244, 250
Chinchen, Titus, 123, 124, 129, 139, 141, 142, 244
Chinchen, William, 129, 141, 142, 244, 250
Chinchin, Albert, 89, 92
Chinchin, Jim, 89, 92
Chisslett, H. O., 264
Christchurch Priory, 68, 72, 93, 103, 151, *171*, 171, 172, 176, 178, 182, 224
    Constable's Lodge, 93, 224
Church Knowle, 190, 192
    St. Peter, 27, 56, *56*, 76, *76*, 175, 201
Churchill, Mark, 110
Churchstow, John Maddock Willis inscription, 171
Claridge, John, 167, 185, 191, 243
Clavell, Rev. J., 194, 228
Clavil, John, 56
Clavill, William, 73
Clavyles, John (Herston), 51
Clavyles, John (Worth), 51
Clavyles, John, (at Gloucester Castle), 51
Clements, R. G., 12, 13, 14, 16, 96
Clerkenwell Prison, 166
Cliff Fields quarry, 128-9
Cobb, Bob, 8
Cobb, Jobey, 198
Cobb, Roy, 8, 79-80, *155*, 177

Cocker, John, 57
Codd, Robert, 164, 199
Coffin, Nicholas, 246
Coldstream, Nicola, 217
Cole, Edward, 112-13, 243
Cole, John, 113, 244
Cole, Susan, 164
Cole, William, 112, 141
Coleman, Charles, 129, 260
Coleman, Frank, 205
Coleman, James, 9
Collins, Arthur, 144, 146, 261
Collins, Billy, 144, 146, 261
Collins, Jacky, 91
Collins, John of Ower, 221, 238
Collins, Joseph, 248
Collins, Samuel, 260
Collins, Sir Stephen, 256
Collins, Thomas, 7, 17, 52, 53, 88, 91, 133, 136, 183, 197, 198, 215-16, 231, 248
Collins, Walter, 215-16
Collins, William, 88, 254, 259
Colson, J., 125, 132, *132*
Colson Rev. J., 185
Combes, John, 237
Company of Marblers and Stonecutters, 29, 80, 83, 105, 165, 233, 235, 236-7, 241, 242, 244, 249, 250, 255-6, 257-8, 264, 266-7, 269
    Admissions List 269-70
    1651 Articles signatories list, 236-7, 246
    Purbeck Marblers price list, *258*
Cook, John, 109
Coombe, Langton Matravers, 4, 60, 62, 104, 269
Coombe Keynes, 178, 247
Cooper, Sid, 260
Corben, Andrew, 87
Corben, Arthur, 260
Corben, Henry, 256
Corben, Jack, *135*, *138*, 146, 199, 213
Corben, James, 143, 214-15, 248
Corben, Joe Baker, 88, 267
Corben, John (Gallows Gore), 143, 251
Corben, John Jr., 143
Corben, John (Langton Matravers), 215
Corben, John, (Swanage), 250
Corben, Peter, 244
Corben, Teddy, 103, 184, 260, 266
Corben, Thomas, 86, 215, 251
Corben, Titus, 84
Corben, Will, 227
Corbin, Alexander, 80, *81*, 82, 244
Corbin, Henry, 129
Corbin, John, 249
Corbin, Thomas, 249
Corbin, Walter, 79, 82, *85*
Corbin, William, 142
Corfe Castle, 25, 28, 29, 47, 48, 49, 67, 68, 70, 71, 72-4, 73-4, 75, *93*, 93, 104,
112, 149, 180, 183, 188, 189, 191, 192, 196, 202, 221, 255
    Bankes Arms, *179*, 184
    Dru Drury tablet, 156
    Farmer Brown's House, 182
    Lynch Farm, 107
    Mortons House, 71, 105, 107, 149
    National Trust education centre, 18, *104*, 105
    Rectory, 156
    St. Edward, *104*, 237
    Town Hall, 76, 257
    Town House, 72
    Uvedale's house, *104*, *104*, 181
    village, 4, 21, 28, *28*, 33, 50, 51, 74, 77, *77*, 84, 104, *110*, 110, *179*, 180, 182, 183, 235, 236, 247, 248
Corfe Mullen, 70
Corme, Thomas, 233
Coulson, J., *See* Colson
Court Cowlease, 13, 76, 89, 90, 243, 253
Couse, Kenton, 167
Covehithe, St. Andrews, 161
Cowlease quarries, 15, 82, 84, 86, 88, 89, 92, 129, 158, 177, 180, 183, 184, 213, 243, 253
Clifton-Taylor, Alec, 181
Crab Hole quarry, 19, 149
Crack Lane quarry, 59, 60, 71, *134*, *138*, 156, 207, 208, 232
Craft, William, 205, 223, 252
Cranbourne, 70
Creech Grange, 105, 201
Crickmay, George, 68
Croke, John, 61
Cross, Thomas, 215
Crostwight, All Saint's, 47
Cull, George, 152
Cull, Henry, 107-8
Cull, William, 221, 236, 238, 242, 247 *See also* Cole
Cumnor, St Michael, 56
Cunner Cove, 20
Cure, Cornelius, 235, 236
Cure, William, 165
Curtis, Joseph, 129
Cusyn, Thomas, 74

Dampier, Edward, 82-3, 114, 124, 182, 262-3
Dampier, K.B., 263
Dancing Ledge quarry, 4, 19, 20, 22, 53, 87, 105, 108, 111, 115, 116, 117-22, *118-20*, *121*, 143, 147-8, 188, 196, 203, 218ff, 227-8, 229, 231, 280, 287, 290
Daniell, William, 225
Dartmouth, 48
D'Aubernoun, Sir John, 48
David, William, 128, 134, 137, 138-9, 143, 149, 150, 155, 157, 192
de Bures, Robert, 48
de Clavile, Peter, 210

INDEX / 303

De Corfe, Adam, 172, 235-6
de Crawford, Adam, 191
de Derneford, Nicholas, 51
de Kilkenny, Andrew, 233
de Plukenet, Alan, 49
de Rabayne, Elyas, 73
Defoe, Daniel, 57, 105, 166
Dennet, Anthony, 94
Derneford, William, 51
Dines, Frank, 9
Dinton, St. Mary's, 43
Doget, John, 39
Dolling, Elizabeth, 104
Dolling, George, 241
Dolling, John, 104, 149, 247
Dolling, Thomas, 237
Donne, Samuel, 84, 85, *140*, 141, 146
Dorchester, 172
    Maen House, 184, 260
    Shire/County Hall, 141, 233
Dorchester Abbey, 43
Dormer, Robert, 56
Dorset County Museum, 18, 77, 92, *135*
Dorset History Centre, 8, 85, 141, 142, *143*, 242
Dorset Quarry Co., 119, 128, 130, 134, *134*, 136-9, *136*, 144, 150, 157, 195, 199, 204ff, 206, 217, 244, 257, 258, 272
Dover, 129
Dow, Henry, 57
Dowland, John, 149, 263
Dowland, Sam, 84, 131, 143, *146*
Dowland, Thomas, 139
Dowland, William, 91
Dowell, Freddy, 8
Downshay Farm, 232
Drury, Dr. Dru, 13, 156
Dugdale, William, 39
Dunkeswell Abbey, 46, *46*, 48
Dunshay/Downshay Manor, Harman's Cross, 32, *32*, 62, 76, *76*, 80, 104-5, *107*, 107, 153, 208, 243, 262
Dunwich museum, 50
Durham Cathedral, 51, 196
    Galilee Chapel, 34, *35*, 35
    St Cuthbert's shrine, 49
Durlston, 11, 15, 94, 158, 159
Durlston Bay, 8, 12, 14, 15, 16, 17, 20, 22, 72, 79, 94, *94*, 97, *97*, 98, 99, 115, 129, 130, 151, 158, 172, 176, 191, 192, 197, 228-9, 253, 255, 260
Durlston Castle, 78
Durnford, Ricardo, 51
Durnford Manor, 83, 88, 105, *107*, 107, 111, 117, 128, 141, 256, 267
Durnford School, 111, 126
Durrington, 180
Durweston, 72
Dygenys, Thomas, 47

East Hedbury, 111
East Lulworth, St. Andrew, 43, 93

Eastington Farm, 59, 80-2, *81*, 82, 84, 85, 92, 111, *123*, 123, 142, 180, 192, 259, 260, 264, 266
Eastington, quarries, 15, 82, 84, 86, 88, 89, 92, 129, 158, 177, 180, 183, 184, 244
Ebbesbourne Wake, St John the Baptist, *41*
Edburey. Richard, 117, 122
Edmund of Abingdon, 43
Edmunds, Charles, 125, 126, 143, 193, 272
Edmunds, George, 143, *213*
Edmunds, Gilbert, 107
Edmunds, Isaac, 29, 272
Edmunds, Jack, 60, 123, 128, 130-1, 133, 143, 218, 220, 244
Edmunds, Thomas, 127, 243, 250
Edmunds, Timothy, 128
Edmunds, William, 167, 267
Edmunds quarry, Burngate, 23, 230-1
Edward I, 51
Edward II, 36, 44, 45, *45*, 172
Edward III, 41, 180
Edward IV, 45
Edward VI, 159
Edward the Confessor, 31, 49, *49*
Eleanor Cross, 49
Elmstone Church, Kent, 43
Elsing, St. Mary's, Hastings brasses, 171
Ely Cathedral, 35, 36, 105, 151, 220
    Bishop Goodrich memorial, 101, 172, 224
    Bishop Hotham's tomb, 35, 36
    Chapter House, 35, *35*
Emery, Philip, 172
Encombe House, 27, 57, 101, *106*, 106, 131, 137, 149, *149*, 151, 158
Encombe obelisk, 131, *131*
Englefield, H. C., 94, 114, *152*
Ensom, Paul, 9, 12, 96
Erle, Sir Walter, 72
Essex, John, 39
Eton College, 94, 112, 129
Evelyn, John, 166
Exbury Church, 42
Exeter Cathedral, 29, 36, *36*, 37, 39, 48, 51, 65, 68, 74-5, 105, 151, 196, 220, 233, 243, 263
    Bishop Henry Marshall effigy, 45
    Cary/Helier slab, 172
    Sir Richard Helier slab, 172

Farrer, O. W., 231, 255
Ffursmann, Anthony, 236
Fiennes, Celia, 105
Fifehead Neville, All Saints, 42
Filliter, Mr. (Mayor of Wareham), 263
Filliter, George, 97
Fishbourne Palace, 27
Florence, Sam, 261
Forrest, Mark, 8
Forster, Anthony, 56
Foster, Dr. C. le Neve, 88, 164, 165, 166,

182, 191, 203, 218, 286, 287
Freke, Sir Thomas, 42
Frogmore Estate, 156
Fyfield, St. Nicholas, 43

Gad Cliff quarry, 100, 117, 158, 198
Gad, Dick, *See* Bower, Richard
Gallery/Garley quarry, 129
Galley, Bill, 231
Gallows Gore, Worth, 4, 11, 12, 14ff, 18, 23, 24, 24, 72, 85, 141, 143, 163, 175, 178, *181*, 183, 210, 210, 232, 233, 242, 250, 261
    See also Lander's Quarry
Gardiner, Gerald, *153*
Garrett and Haysom, Southampton, 229
Gerard, Thomas, 57
Gervase of Canterbury, 222
Gibbons, Harold, 139
Gill, Eric, 144
Gillingham, Bill, 170
Gillingham, Harry, 260
Glassock, David, 8
Gloucester Castle, 51
Gloucester Cathedral, 36
    Edward II tomb, 36, 44, 45
Godfrey, Walter, 34, 51, 55
Goodworth Clatford, St. Peter, 43, 44
Greenwich
    Painted Hall, 60, 61, 64
    Royal Hospital, 165
Grimm, Samuel, 79, 129, *130*, 196, 204, 231
Groves, Thos. B., 199
Guernsey, Castle Cornet, 76, 77, 83
Guild of Marblers, 235
Guy, Joe, 147

Hall, James, 74, 241
Halsewell quarry, 60, 139, *139*, 156, 230
Ham House, Surrey, 165, *165*
Hancock, Arthur, 8, 179
Hancock, Edward, 81, 82, 112, 113
Hancock, George, 8, 61, 82, 89, 184, 204, 209, *213*, 262
Hancock, Thomas, 112, 207, 234
Happisburgh, Norfolk, 179
Harden, Bert, 262
Harden, Burt, 60
Harden, George, 60, 215, 262
Harden, Jack, 8
Harden, Jacky, 198
Harden, John, 8, 98, 99, 215, 242, 250
Harden, Richard, 24, 2512
Harden, Walter, 197
Harding, Albert, 249, 260
Harding, Arthur, 54, 249
Harding, Billy, 260
Harding, Hubert, 249
Harding, Neil, 184
Harding, Tommy, 262
Hardwick, Thomas, 233

304 / PURBECK STONE

Hardy, Frank, 255
Hardy, George, 254
Hardy, Llewellyn, 229
Hardy, Thomas, 51, 125, 222-3, 229, 264
Hardy, W. M., 70-1, 79, 112, 114, 115, 130, 183, 199-200, 204, 208, 209, 225, 228-9, 231, 245, 255, 258
Harman's Cross, 4, 21, 105
    Haycrafts Farm, 32
    West Wood Farm, 105
    See also Dunshay Manor; Quarr Farm
Harp Stone, Bradle, 158
Harrietsham, St. John the Baptist, 43
Harris, Bob, 8, 25, 61, 145-6, *146*, 147, 149, 158, 181, 182, 198, 217, 218, 257, 259, 269
Harris, Charles Sheffield (Sheffy), 83, 89, *143*, 204, 214
Harris, Charles, 122, 160
Harris, Fred, 54
Harris, G. F., 120, 125, 129, 132, 215
Harris, Jack, 22
Harris, John, 8
Harris, Joseph, 258
Harris, Josiah, 169, 257
Harris, Robert, See Bob
Harrow School Chapel, 41, 43
Harston, Revd, 223, 251
Hart, Sir John Willis, 117, 128
Harvey, John, 235
Haskell, Richard, 80
Haskell, William, 150
Hatton, Sir Christopher, 186
Hatton, Lady Elizabeth, 232
Hatton Estate, 189-90, 219
    See also Bankes Estate
Hatton Garden, London, 189
Havant, St. Faith's, 44
Hawcombe quarry, 20, 77, 78, 102, 112-15, *113*, 116, 210, 222, 246
Hawley, John, 48
Haycrafts, 62, 64, 232
    Farm, 32, 62,
    Lane, 84, 89
Haysom and Sons, 2-3, 61, 139, 210, 234, 260, 261, 272. 273
    See also St. Aldhelm's Quarry (Haysom's)
Haysom, Albert, 138
Haysom, Alfred, 260
Haysom, Alfred Norman, 26, 60, 68, 79, 89, 98, 125, 138, 144, 168, 184, 206, 269
Haysom, Anthony, 'Hantney', 25, 195, 210, 217, 245, 262, 267, 268
Haysom, Bill 'Bubbles', 216
Haysom, Christopher, 7, 99
Haysom, Cyril, 52, 198
Haysom, David, 8
Haysom, Francis, 8, 12, 99, 186, 251, 252
Haysom, Frank, 8, 54, 176-7, 195, 206, 230 (Uncle), 260
Haysom, Fred, 260

Haysom, George, 215
Haysom, 'Hantney', See Anthony
Haysom, Harold, 52, 146, 260
Haysom, Henry, 209, 263
Haysom, James, 201, 203, 254
Haysom, John, 8, 9, 17, 59, 60, 61, 65, 68, 114, 200, 203, 225, 233, 249, 252, 254, 256, 260, 261
Haysom, Joseph, 256
Haysom, Lewis, 8
Haysom, Dr. Mark, 9
Haysom, Nathaniel, 267
Haysom, Stephen, 9
Haysom, Thomas, 179
Haysom, Walter, 7, 8, 18, 20, 29, 34, 51-2, *53*, 54, 55, 59, 71, 79, 89, 90, 101, 102, 103, 112, 115, 125, 137, 139, 143, 144, 148, 150, 155, 168, 169, 174, 179, 184, 191, 193, 194, *216*, 218, 230, 233, 248, 249, 254, 255, 256, *260*, 260, 269
Haysom, William, 8, 9, 99, 121, 230, 233, 245, 249, 254, 260, 261
Hayward, Henry, 237
Hayward, James, 84
Haywood, Louise, 8
Hedbury quarry, 4, 11, 19, 23, 26, 111, 114, 115, 118, 122-28, 129, 131, 141ff, 147, 181, 188, 193, 199, 204, 218, 220, 226ff, 230, 242, 244, 267
Hennell, Thomas, *170*
Hennock, St. Mary's, 42, 44
Henry III, 31, 36, 41, 45, 48, 56, 59
Henry IV, 45
Henry VII, 45
Henry of Blois, Bishop, 31, 46
Hereford Cathedral, 27
    St. Thomas Cantalupe shrine, 49
Herston, 4, 42, 50, 51, 80, 81, 88, 120, 139, 237, *237*, 246
    Belle Vue, *189*, 214, 248, 269
    St. Marks, 72, 197
Herston Field quarry, 24, 60, 74, 78, 87, 90, 129, *177*, 209, 213, 216, 253, 260, 271
Hill, Thomas (Mason), 165, 166
Hinley, David, 166
Hinton, David, 50
Hinton Martell, St. John the Evangelist, 44
Hixon, Harry, 222
Holmes, Margaret, 8, 242
Holton Heath Munitions Factory, 231, 260
Honing, Saint Peter and Saint Paul, 43
Hooper, Geoff, 7, 154, 192, 297n.38
Hooper, Herbert, 122
Hooper, Mont, 155
Hopton, Sir John, 56
Horsey, Thomas, 237
Hort, Hugh, 83, 199
Hort, Joseph, 83, 221, 246
Hort, Joseph senior, 238, 241
Horton, Dorset, St. Wolfrida, 194

Huntingdon Bridge, 45
Hutchins, John, 11-12, 13, 14, 16, 17, 33, 57, 78, 80, 96, 102, 107, 111, 114, 149, 152, 176, 185, 196, 215, 218, 231, 233, 235, 245-6
Hyde, Alex, 79

Iffley Church, Oxford, 41
Iliffe, Edward Mauger (Lord Iliffe), 231
Ilminster, St. Mary's, Wadham tomb, 172
Ingham, Holy Trinity, 43
Isle of Wight, 16, 42, 43, 68, 70, 86, 95, 131, 174
    Calbourne, All Saint's, 43
    Freshwater, All Saint's, 47, *178*, 194
    Mottistone Manor, 181
    St Catherine's, 131

Jackson, Benjamin, 166
Jackson, Sir T. G., 193
Jamaica, 165, 223
James I, 165
Jerard, John, 232
Jersey
    St. Brelade, *174*
    St. Lawrence, *173*
John, King of England, 44, 220
Joint Stock Company (1698), 80, 81, 112, 122, 149, 152, 165, 172, 175, 221, 237, 238-42, 243, 244, 245, 247, 256
    Agreement signatories, 241, 243, 244
    1651 and 1697/8 Articles, 238-41, 242
    See also Company of Marblers and Stonecutters
Jones, G. P., 197, 228, 235, 272
Jones, Inigo, 165, 224

Kaye, Chris, 8, 96
Keat, James, 233
Keat, Samuel, 84
Keate, James, 244
Keate, Richard, 241
Keates, John, 241
Keates, Phil, 60, 89
Keates, Richard, 227
Keates, Thomas, 247
Keates Quarry, 82
Keats, James, 29, 81, 84, 222, 223
Keats, Kevin, 8, *177*, 184
Keats, Robert, 215
Keats, Sam, 141, 250
Keats, Samuel, 228, 233,
Kene, Edward, 232, 243
Kensington Palace, 166
Kent, T. T., 264
Kent, Thomas, 233
Kentisbeare, Devon, 176
Kerwin, A., 164
Kilpeck, Hereford, 34
Kimmeridge, 20, 23, 27, 71, 103, 158, 176, 183
    Chaffey headstone, 26

INDEX / 305

churchyard, 26, *169*
Clavell Tower, 194, 204-5, *251*, 251-2
  quarry, 158
St. Nicholas, 27, 177
Richard Claville brass plate, 175
King, Luke, 237
King, William, 81
Kingsley, Charles, 97
Kingston, Purbeck, 17, 22, 68, 70, 104, 131, 156, 188, 194
  Lacy Hall, 128, 144, *257*
  Maurward House, *172*
  Old Church, 184
  St. James, 29, *29*, 43, 64, 68, 72, 125, 126, 137, 150, 184, 202, *202*, 203, 206, 249, 255, 260
  See also Encombe House
Knitson, Dorset, 4, *190*, 232, 233
  Farm, Dorset, 99, 182, *190*
Knodishall, St. Lawrence, 44
Knole, 36, 164
  Great Hall, *164*
Knoll House Hotel, 80, 121
Knoop, D., 197, 228, 235, 272

Lampard, John, 84, 123, 129, 192
Lander, Alan, 8, 115, 259
Lander, Allan, 8
Lander, Ambrose, 126, *127*
Lander, Edward, 266
Lander, Frank, 155
Lander, George, 92, 129, 204, 233, 234, 261, 262, 264-5, 266, 269
Lander, George Jr., 264
Lander, George Henry, 265, *265*, 268
Lander, Hedley, 92, 257
Lander, Henry, 65, 115, 116, 251
Lander, Hubert, 144
Lander, James, 226, 256
Lander, Jesse, 112, 144, *144*, 148, 150, 154, 214, *214*, 275
Lander, Jim, 150, 207, 209
Lander, Karl Bill, *261*
Lander, Keziah, 116
Lander, Sam, 227
Lander, Samuel, 190,
Lander, Sid, 229
Lander, Thomas, 65, 82, 86, 125, 126, 159, 190, 250, 266
Lander, Thomas Chinchen, 125
Lander, Titus, 179, 200, 261, 262
Lander, William, 206-7, 257, *261*
Lander's Quarry, 92, 257, *261*
Langton Matravers, 4, 11, 12, 22, 27, 29, 32, 51, 60, 68, 74, 80, 111, 143, 163, 176, 178, 186, 187, 189, 192, 198, 234, 243, 245, 247, 248, 251, 256, 264, 269
  Arundel Terrace, 142
  Box Cottage, Coombe, 104
  High Street, *16*, *168*, 168
  Jasper Cottage, 82
  Museum, 32, 33, 58, 82, *100*, 134, *135*, 136, 142, 168, 184, 185, 195, 198-201, 203, 204, 209, 211
  North Street, 23, *169*, 183
  old cemetery, 27, 29, 116, *155*, 156, 178, 215
  St. George's, 68, *177*, 198, 201, 202, *202*, *203*
  war memorial stone, 146, 177
  See also Durnford Manor
Langton Wallis, *81*, *82*, 84, 111, 113, 117, 122, *123*, 163, 179, 180, 181, 184, 186, 187, 189, 192, 232, 243, 244, 250
Lant, Thomas, 157
Latyn, William, 186
Law Courts, Strand, London, 59
Lawrence, Joe, 170
Lawrence, John, 259
Le Marbrer, Adam, 161
Le Mochele, Hugh, 66, 210
Le Vel, Walter, 66, 210
le Walsh, Joan, 41
Leland, John, 46, 96, 149, 222, 243
Lenard, John, 51
Lessingham, All Saints, 44, *44*
  William Bullock ledger, 175
Letterbox gate, Worth Matravers, 79, 82, 149
Lewer, David, 8
Lincoln Cathedral, 34, 35, 37, 39, 40, 48, 51, 58, 220
Linlithgo, Lord, 229
Litlyngton, Abbot Nicholas, 49, *49*
Llanbadarn Fawr, St. Padarn's, 43
Lock, Les, 91, 210
Lodder, Mr. (Mr. Bankes' agent), 128, 257, 258, 267
London, 163-7, 224, 225, *225*
  Banqueting Hall, Whitehall, 165
  Charterhouse, *167*
  King's Bench Walk, 164
  Scotland Yard, 224
  Whitehall Palace, 165
  See also St. Pauls (Old); Westminster Abbey
London Bridge, 48, 108, 225, 228
London Doors quarry, 158
London Marblers, 235
  See also Company of Marblers and Stonecutters
London Masons' Company, 224, 237-8
Longleat, 159
Looe, St Martin's, 42
Lorymer, John, 235
Lovell, Fred, 261
Lovell, Thomas, 90, 258
Lower Wraxall, St. Mary, 42
Lucas, Terry, 232
Lulworth, 11, 159, 191
  Castle, 160
  Cove, 191, 192
Lustleigh, St. John the Baptist, 43, 170
Luton Hoo House, 118, 119, 121, 230

Lutton, West Purbeck, 180
Lychett, John, 232, 243
Lytchett Matravers, St. Mary, 42, 45
Lyecchet, John, 62
Lyme Regis, 98, 191
Lymington, Quay Hill, 156
Lynch, 13, 19, 20, 28, 51, 59, 61, *61*, 62, 64, 65, 73, 107,
Lynham, Ken, 204

Mahu, John, 235
Maltravers, John, 45
Manchester Town Hall, 193
Manwell, George, 248, 250
Manwell, Peter, 260
Manwell, Thomas, 248
Mappowder, St. Peter and St. Paul, 44
Margate Harbour, 108, *108*, 142
Marsh, James, 65, 96, 159
Marsh, John, 244, 245
Marsh, Samuel, 250, 251
Master Ralph, (London mason), 45
Masters, Captain Albert, 225, 228
Masters, Joseph, 225, 229, 230
Masters, Thomas, 229
Masters, Walter, 119, 136, 229, 261
Masters, William, 234
Mayow, John, 161
Meader, Alf, *158*, 146, 158
Meader, Fred, 91
Meader, James, 139
Melmoth, John, 164, 246
Melmoth, Phineas, 164, 246
Melmoth, William, 83, 86, 217, 246
Melmouth, Alexander, 84, 112, 246
Melmouth, John, 77, 98
Melmouth, Peter, 237
Melmouth, Sam, 237
Melmouth, William, 244
Michell, Humphrey, 164
Milborne Port, St. John the Evangelist, 43
Milford-on-Sea, 50
Milton Abbas, Abbey Church, 55
  Tregonwell tomb, *55*
Minstead, All Saint's, 29, 44
Morden, St. Mary, 102, *102*, 103
Morris, Dr. Richard, 51
Mowlem, Charles, 256
Mowlem, John, 13, 22, 99, 114, 193, 204, 228, 229, *229* 231, 251, 252, 253, 256, 269
Mowlem, John Ernest, 256
Mowlem, Thomas, 256
Much Marcle, St. Bartholomew,
  Blanche Mortimer tomb, 49
Muntz, Elizabeth, 259
Mupe Bay quarry, 11, 21, 65, 159-60, *160*, 191, 281
Murray, Keeper, *155*, 156
Mutton Hole, 22, 88, 90, 91, 149, 175, 195, 206, 230, 234, 261, 287

306 / PURBECK STONE

Newfoundland, Canada, 172-3, 174, 223, 224, 248, 251
    Harbour Grace, 223, 223, 251
    Trinity St. Paul's, 173, 174
Newton Estate, Swanage, 263
Newton Stone Quarries, 261
Norman, Albert, 254
Norman, Alfred, 26, 89, 212, 216, 217, 255, 257
Norman, Bert, 7, 52, 225, 260
Norman, Bill, 7, 53
Norman, Bobby, 8, 197, 260
Norman, Chemister, 264
Norman, 'Crusty', 216
Norman, Doug, 91
Norman, Ernest, 7, 91, 176, 177
Norman, Fred, 91, 212, 257
Norman, George, 9, 88, 254, 260
Norman, Harold, 257
Norman, Horace, 81, 209
Norman, Jack, 8, 26, 91, 110, *110*, 199, 208, 211, 212, 217, 257
Norman, Jack 'Rippy', 80, 150, 196
Norman, Jim, 8, 91
Norman, Michael, 8, 118
Norman, Robert, 254, 259-60
Norman, Sam, 215
Norman, 'Shilling', 248, 269
Norman, 'Sunshine', 133, 209, 216, 287
Norman, Walter, 203
Norris, Geoffrey, 9
Norwich Cathedral, 32, 43, 51, 81, 96, 161, 175
    Windham tomb, 48
Norwich, St. Andrews, Appleyard's slab, 171, 175

Oakford Fitzpaine, 78
Oak Ridge (Oatridge), 19, 58, 59, 60,
Oare, Kent, St. Peter, 43-44
Oates, Charley, 208
Okeden, William (father and son), 107, *107*, 108, 236
Ottery St. Mary, 105, 168
Oxford
    Christ Church Cathedral, 57
    City Museum, 46
    St. Mary's, 56, 57, 171
Ower, 51, 64, 67, 94, 191, 220-1, 223, 231, 232, 238, 256
    Ower Farm, 221, 258
Ower Quay, 220-1, 224, 238

Paine, James, 142
Paine, Steve, 184
Palmer, Alfred, artist, 135, *135*, 312
Palmer, Dr. Tim, 75
Pamphill, Walter Bankes memorial cross, 144
Paris, Matthew, 200
Parsons and Hayter, 8, 260, 261
Payne, James, *109*, 167

Peek, Sir Henry, 126, 228
Peldon, St. Mary's, 42
Pellatt, Thomas, 111, 122
Penshurst, St. John the Baptist, 55
Petten, Alexander, 241
Peveril, William, 46
Peveril Point, 4, 20, 21, 43, 58, 63, 70, 71, 72, 93, *93*, 96, *130*, 208, 224,
Pevsner, N., 42, 43, 181
Phippard, Albert, 168, 260
Phippard, Charles, 254
Phippard, Edward, 224
Phippard, James, 254
Phippard, Joseph, 9, 254
Phippard, Peter, 82, 83, 86, 129, 251, 254
Phippard, Sam, 141, 215
Phippard, Thomas, 87, 112, 224, 254, 260, 264, 266
Phippard, Thomas, 'Tommy Tilly', 260
Phippard, Timothy, 123, 141
Phippard, William, 224, 246
Phipps, J., 98
Piddletrenthide, 68
Pike, John, 79
Pike, Margaret, 79
Pitfield, F. D., 8
Pitt, George, 98
Pitt, William Morton, 94, 96, 98, 99, 113, 152, 222, 247, 251, 255, 263
Platter quarry, 122, 219
Poole, 93, 110-11, 119, 136, 138, 157, 172-3, 221, 222, 223, 230, 233, 245
    Church, 68, 86
    Quay Act (1756), 230
Portland, 102, 231, 242, 243
    Museum, 195, 249
    St. Andrew's, 50, 103
Portsmouth, 86, 98, 99, 141, 175, 224, 249
    Cathedral, *154*
    Fort Cumberland, 86, 87, 196
Potter, Robert, *155*
Pouncy, Harry, 204
Pouncy, John, 125, 204
Powell, William, 115
Prestly, Sam, 241
Preston, Thomas, 107, 108
Priddle, Norman, 8
Puckett, Jim, 104
Puddle Farm, 233
Puddletown, 172
    St. Mary the Virgin, 165
Pulham, St Thomas à Becket, 42
Puncknowle, St. Mary, 56
Purbeck Co-operative Stone Industries Ltd, 256-7, 258
Purbeck, Isle of (maps), 4, *187*
Purbeck Marblers, 258, 259, 263
    See also Company of Marblers and Stonecutters
Purbeck Portland Stone Company Ltd, 144

Purbeck Quarry Co., 146
Purbeck, Stephen, 182
Purbeck Stone and General Trading Co., 133, 143, 195, 256, 261, 262
Purchase, W. R., 194
Pushman, David, 158
Pushman, Edward, 8, 157, 158
Pushman, George, 247
Pushman, Harry, 250
Pushman, John, 8, 158, 222, 228, 251, 259
Pushman, Thomas, 139, 222, 244
Pyne, W. H., 193, *195*

Quarr Farm, 12, 65, 66-7, *66-7*, 105, 236

Rackham, Oliver, 64
Ralf of Chichester, 39
Rampisham, St. Michael and All Saints, 47
Ramsgate Harbour, 107-8, *108*, 119, 141, 142, 152, 191, 224, 243, 244-5
Randell, Ann, 251
Randell, Thomas, 125, 228, 251, 252
Randell, Thomas, Jr., 114, 252
Randell's banker, 8, 9, 58, 59, 125, 205, 252, 254, 261
Raveningham, 175
Red, Nicholas, 62
Redhorn Quay, 221
Redvers, Richard de, 46
Reed, Sir Charles, 56, 57
Reede, Thomas, 62
Reform/Reforn quarry, 20, 117, 220, 230
Rempstone Estate, 109, 134, 139, 156, 172, 241, 262
    Hall, 4, *102*, 102, 141
Rennie, John, 108
Rennie, Sir John, 108
Renscombe, 149, 181
    Manor, 172
Richard II, 235
Richmond Bridge, Surrey, 167, 255
Rigby, John, 232, 243
Ripon Cathedral, 50
Rochester Cathedral, 36
Roberts, Eric, 8
Robinson, C. E., 94, 112, 113, 221, 226, 227, 230
Robinson, Sir Charles, 263, 264
Rogers, Captain Serrell, 111, 267
Rollington, 51
Romsey Abbey, 47, 48, 68, 172, 176
Roods, Arthur, 159
Rose, Henry, 126
Rose, Mack, 107
Rose, William (Rector of Swanage), 77, 78, 241-2
Royal Festival Hall, 156
Rufus, William, 46
Russe, John, 235, 243
Russe, John Jr., 62, 63, 243
Ruzicka, Dr. C., 139

INDEX / 307

Rye, East Sussex, St Mary's, 176

Sackville, Thomas, 36, 164
Salisbury Cathedral, 8, 13, 28, 32, 36, 37-8, 37-9, 40, 44, 46, 48, 51, 63, 63, 64, 65, 67, 79, 128, 161, 172, 174, 176, 177, 201, 203, 206, 220, 243
    Alexander Hyde brass, 175
    Bishop Wyville brass indent (slab), 171, 224
    Tomb of Bishop Roger, 44
    Tomb of Jocelyn de Bohun, 44
Salzman, L. F., 74, 200, 219
Samways, Michael (Mick), 8, 158
Samways, Tom, 158
Sandwich, Kent, St Clement's, 40
Saunders, William, 256, 264
Saville, Reg, 8
Scammel, A. H., 157
Scates, James, 11, 231, 245
Scates, Robert, 11, 231, 245
Schoverwille, William De, 75
Scoles Manor, 50, 62, 75, 76, 183,
Scotland Farm, Corfe River, 107
Scott, Sir Ernest, 137, 150
Scott, George, 260
Scott, Sir George Gilbert, 203, 260
Scott, John, 2nd Earl of Eldon, 106
Scott, John, 3rd Earl of Eldon, 97, 99, 150, 152, 264, 267
Scouyle, William, 50
Scroylle, Phillip, 50, 74, 75
Seacombe quarry, 11, 20, 105, 123, 124, 128, 129-39, 130, 132-3, 135-6, 138, 141ff, 146, 152, 157, 158, 188, 193ff, 199, 205, 205-6, 206, 208, 216ff, 219, 220, 227, 229, 230, 234, 243, 251, 257, 258, 262, 280, 281, 286, 287
Sentry, 22, 97, 99, 181, 251, 253
Serrel, Sam, 244
Serrell, Anthony, 83, 87, 236, 240, 246, 247
Serrell, Frances, 88, 264
Serrell, Henry, 237, 241, 247, 241
Serrell, Howard, 98, 246-7
Serrell Rogers, Captain, see Rogers, Captain Serrell
Serrell, Samuel, 105, 247
Serrell, Rev. Samuel, 247
Serrell, Sheffield, 88
Seymour, Frank, 216
Seymour, Henry, 256, 268
Sheepsleights quarry, 4, 19, 20, 60, 149, 154, 156-8, 156-7, 188, 191, 192, 196, 206, 230, 257, 258, 262, 283, 284, 287
Shepeye, John, 235
Shepherd, Mr., 144
Sheppard, Bertie, 150
Sheppard, Sybil, 208
Sherborne Abbey, 32, 45
    Abbot Clement effigy, 45
Shillingstone, Holy Rood, 47

Short, Thomas (Tom), 118, 135
Short, Sam see Bower, Sam Short
Shoyden, Henry, 50
Shroton, St. Mary's, 42
Sibun, Doris, 56-7
Skerne, John, 56, 57
Smale, Dennis, 8, 80
Smeaton, John, 107, 196
Smedmore, 72, 107,
    builders, 191
Smith, Fred, 255
Smith, James,
Smith, Rose, 233
Smith, William, 226
Smyth, Henry, 243
Society of Old Stone Masons, 256
Sonning, Elizabeth Chute inscription, 171
South Hayling, St. Mary's, 43
Southampton, 87, 180
    St. Michaels, 41-2
Southard quarry, Swanage, 28
Southwark Cathedral, 59, 59, 161
Southwick Priory, 49, 205
Southwold, St Edmunds, 161
Speare, Giles, 244
Spencer Watson, Hilda, 139
Spicer, Henry, 269
Spillar, Richard, 182
Spycer, John, 243
Squibb, James, 86, 150
Squibb, Robert, 58, 59, 84
St. Alban's quarry see St. Aldhelm's Head Quarry
St. Albans Cathedral, 49, 193
St. Aldhelm's Head, 26, 71, 72, 80, 100, 101, 102, 103, 105, 117, 149-52, 177, 184, 190, 196, 224, 227, 229
    St. Aldhelm's Chapel, 104, 119, 152, 152, 188
St. Aldhelm's Head Quarry, 18-19, 24, 25, 52, 53, 101, 105, 106, 119, 137, 144, 144, 145, 149-52, 158, 178, 188, 189, 194, 206, 212, 218, 230, 252
St Aldhelm's Quarry (Haysoms), 150, 151, 152-6, 153-5, 191-2, 195
St. David's Cathedral, Pembroke, 43, 184
St. German's Priory, Cornwall, 42, 43
St. Helena, 224
St. Magnus the Martyr, London, 48
St. Maria dei Frari, Venice, 50
St. Michael Le Belfry, York, 31
St. Paul's (Old), London, 33, 37, 45, 46, 50, 161
St. Paul's (Wren), London, 153, 167, 204
St. Thomas/Scratch Ass quarry, 111, 122, 230
Stanton Harcourt, St. Michael, 49, 203
Steeple, St Michael and All Angels, 42, 70, 70, 70, 71, 77, 77, 175, 176
Stevens, Frank, 9
Stevens, John (Jack), 111, 260, 264, 265, 266-8

Stevens, Thomas, 111, 197, 252, 259, 260, 263, 264, 268
Stevens, William, 129, 250
Stickland, Isaac, 209
Stickland, George, 252, 263
Stickland, Richard, 254
Stockley, Edward, 261
Stockley, John, 182
Stockley, Richard, 261
Stoke d'Abernon, 48
Stone, Nicholas, 165
Stone, St. Mary the Virgin, 37
Strahan, A., 58, 60, 65, 97, 98
Strange, Walter John, 134
Street, George E., 59, 72, 125, 150, 202
Strode, Sir John, 131
Studland, 80, 121, 130, 178, 184, 230
    Bay, 230
    Church Hall, 26, 146
    J. R. Bankes' headstone, 177, 177
    St. Nicholas, 42, 70, 70, 71, 93, 177, 177, 184
    Voysey House, 184
Sturdy, Philip, 262
Sturminster Marshall, 72
    Rev. Watkinson tomb chest, 176
Stuvene, Johan, 51
Summers, Charles, 222
Summers, James, 215, 222
Suttle, John, 91, 261
Swanage, 8, 15, 20, 22, 60, 68, 81, 87, 88, 89, 91, 95-6, 98, 105, 110, 116, 138, 146, 176, 182, 183, 184-5, 185, 191, 197, 221, 222-3, 231, 231ff, 237, 245, 247
    All Saints, 155, 156, 177, 249
    Church Hill cross, 146
    Clifton arcade, 144
    Court Farm House, 104
    Drill Hall, 217
    Eightholds Manor, 243, 263, 264
    Manor House, 105, 113
    Mill Pond, 96, 96, 184, 186
    Mount Scar School, 200
    Museum and Heritage Centre, 253
    Newton Manor House, 87, 87
    Purbeck Hotel (White Harte), 186
    Royal Victoria Hotel, 243, 247, 251, 253, 255
    St. Mary's, 42
    Tithe Barn, 109
    Town Hall, 8, 17
    Virginia Cottage, 105
    War Memorial, 29, 144
Swanage Bay, 21, 70, 71, 91, 95, 95, 116, 119, 146, 154, 194, 194, 197, 205, 221, 223, 224ff, 226, 230, 246, 247, 252, 253
    Pier, 222, 222-3, 252, 252, 254-5
    plan of bankers, 246
Swanage Poor Book, 249-50
Swanage Quarries, 90, 91, 244, 254, 261
Sydney, Sir William, 55

Talbot, John, 232
Talbot's Wood, Langton, 32-3, 232
Tarrant Crawford, 69
Tarrant Monkton, 70, 102
Tatchell, Harry, 8, 182
Taunton, William, 112, 263
Taylor, Isaac, 153
Taylor, Sir Robert, 166
Temple Church, London, 13, 34, 34, 51-2, 53-4, 54-5, 58, 59, 64, 67, 125, 156, 201, 203, 206
Templeman, William, 247
Tenby, 178
Tewkesbury Abbey, 46
Thickes, James, 119, 152
Thickes, John, 152
Thorn, Robert, 243, 265
Thynne, Sir John, 159
Tilly Whim quarry, 4, 112-14, 113, 114, 158, 178, 195, 204, 222, 230, 263
Tolpuddle, St. John's, 45
Tomes, Albert, 9
Tomes, Bert, 195, 260
Tomes, Bill, 195
Tomes, Billy, 261
Tomes, Frank, 8, 11, 217, 255, 269
Tomes, George, 229
Tomes, Harry, 52, 53, 139, 260
Tomes, Lewis, 86, 209, 217
Tomes, Marky, 222
Tomes, Sam, 261
Tomes, Samuel, 144, 146
Tomes, William, 52, 229, 263
Toms, William, 87
Top Mast quarry, 115, 122
Tournai Cathedral, Belgium, 52
Tower of London, 11, 48, 68, 75, 75
    The Cradle Tower, 103
Townson, Geoffrey, 9
Trearther, Thomas, 232
Tregonwell, Sir John, 55, 55
Treswell, Ralph, 81, 84, 94, 117, 122, 149, 180, 181, 186, 187, 189, 221
Trollope and Coll's, Vauxhall, 8, 189, 221, 255
Tully, Gilbert, 112
Turner, Bob, 150, 199
Turner, Frank, 260
Turner, John, 143, 146, 194
Turner, Nathaniel, 59
Turner, Thomas, 260
Turnpike quarry, 28, 177
Tyllie, John, 112
Tyneham, 23, 112, 158
    Tyneham House, 68, 100, 107, 159

Ulwell, 192
Uvedale, John, 104

Vancouver, Charles, 109
Venables, Frank, 255
Victoria and Albert Museum, 48, 263

Vye, Anthony, 164
Vye, Charles, 224
Vye, Edward, 236, 237
Vye, Henry, 244
Vye, Ike, 262
Vye, Joseph, 248
Vye, Sarah, 108
Vypart, Henry, 243
Vyport, Henry, 180

Wade, Kent, St. Nicholas, 177
Wallace, Percy, 150
Waller, George, 227
Walter, Hubert, Archbishop, 46, 48
Walter of Hereford, 39
Waltham Abbey, 43, 50
Warblington, St Thomas à Becket, 40
Ward, Leslie, 135
Wareham, 26, 68, 69, 110, 138, 222, 223, 233-4
    Frome Bridge, 262
    Holy Trinity, 71
    Lady St Mary Church, 26, 46, 46, 69, 71, 93, 175
    Manor House, 26, 26, 72, 72, 105, 107
    St. John's Hill, 69
    St. Martin's, 71
Warmwell, 50
Warne, James, 233
Warner, Geoffrey, 259
Warren, Francis, 108
Warren, Hannah, 98
Warren, Jeremiah, 250, 251
Warren, John, 98
Warren, Kate, 99
Warren, Sam, 191
Warwick, 39
    St Mary, Richard Beauchamp's tomb, 39, 39
Waters, Ronald, 157
Watson, Hilda, See Spencer Watson, Hilda
Webber, Cornelius, 248
Webber, Edward, 247
Webber, George, 248
Webber, Joby, 257, 260
Webber, Richard, 256
Webber, Thomas, 118, 120, 157
Webster, Andrew, 9, 71
Webster, Thomas, 12, 12, 14, 20, 94, 99, 99, 114, 114, 115, 125, 152, 152, 158, 183, 192, 204, 220, 284, 285
Weeble, Mr., 193, 194
Weekes, William, 184
Weeks, Charles, 241, 247
Weeks, John, 247
Welfrich, William, 51
Wellman, Fred, 8, 146, 147, 262
Wellow, St. Margaret's, 43
Wells, Henry Tanworth, 125, 126, 126, 204, 220
West Almer, 70
West Alvington, Devon, 169

Westminster Abbey, 30-1, 31, 32, 35, 36, 37, 39-41, 40, 49, 62, 75-6, 76, 101, 131, 161, 163, 175, 176, 178, 203, 206, 235, 243
    Lady Chapel, 161
Westminster Bridge, 83, 110
Westminster, Palace of, 8, 59, 60, 172, 225
    Westminster Hall, 40, 49, 171-2, 235, 236, 243
Weymouth, 165
    Bridge, 136
White, David, 8
White, Nathaniel, 252, 253, 261
White, Nathaniel Chinchen, 252, 254
White, Pam, 191
White, William Grove, 252
White Ware quarry, 20, 27, 92, 115, 117, 188, 220, 230
Wilkswood Farm, 61, 66, 80, 85, 90, 92, 189, 231, 265, 266
Wilkeswood Priory, 62, 63, 75, 82, 221, 243
Willet, Henry, 97
William the Conqueror, 31
William of Sens, 34, 206, 222, 224
Willis, David, 1
Willis, Joseph, 233
Wilson, Thomas, 164
Wimborne, 25, 103
    St. Julian's Bridge, 25
Wimborne Minster, 34, 39, 68, 69, 69, 72, 131
Winchelsea, St. Thomas the Martyr, 6, 7
Winchester, 178, 194
    Cathedral, 36, 37, 41, 46, 49, 68, 75, 83, 172, 175, 177
    Great Hall, 37, 54, 55
    Lambe, 'Singing Man', 175
    St. Cross, 34, 50
Winchester College, 180, 181
Windsor Castle, 41, 164, 165
    St George's Chapel, 41, 45, 161, 163, 163
Winfrith Atomic Energy Security block, 156
Winfrith, St. Christopher's, 68
Wing, Bucks.
    All Saint's, 56, 171
    Blaknall brass, 171
    'Old Thomas Cotes' brass, 171
    Robert Dormer sarcophagus, 171
Wingate, Bert, 136
Winspit, Billy see Bower, William Jeremiah
Winspit quarries, 4, 20, 26, 61, 84, 101, 102, 105, 111, 120, 121, 129, 131, 139-48, 157, 188, 194, 198, 205, 220, 226, 227, 231, 239, 261
    East Winspit quarry, 11, 26, 60, 75, 100, 100, 101, 103, 108, 133, 139, 141ff, 156, 190, 199, 218, 229, 284
    Port Arthur quarry, 143, 144, 146-7, 147, 178, 217, 261

West Winspit quarry, 20, 25, 101, 126, 128, 129, 133, 141ff, 144-5, 196, 217, 218
Winstanley, Gerrard, 156
Winterborne Stickland, 110, 248
Winterbourne Tomson, 70
Witchampton, St. Mary, 25, 86, *86*
Woodward, Ida, 180, 255
Woodward, P., 60, 122-3, *123*, 128, *130*
Wolf Hall, Burbage, Wilts. 159
Wolfeton House, Charminster, 68, 172, 180
Wolvesey Palace, Winchester, 31
Woodbridge, Suffolk, 109
Woodward, Ida, 180, 255
Woodward, P., 122, 123, *123*, 128, *130*
Woodyhyde, 11, 12, 18, 20, 28, 58, 58-9, 64, 208, 233
Wool, 146

Holy Rood, 50, 68, 71, 72
Woolverstone, Suffolk, 178
Worbarrow quarry, 11, 17, 20, 23, 65, 76, 96, 100, 158-9, *160*
Worbarrow Tout, 17, 21, 100, 159, *160*, 192
Worcester Cathedral, 37, 44, 70
  Tomb of King John, 44, *45*
Worth Farm, 233
Worth Manor and Estate, 141, *142*, 143, *143*, 242
Worth Matravers, 27, 46, 82, 85, 92, 103, 140, 141, 143, *153*, *178*
  Memorial cross, 262, *262*
  St. Aldhelm's Chapel, 27, 70, 71
  St. Nicholas, 71, *71*, 102-3,*103*-4, *103*-4, 177, 188, *194*, 195, 201, *201*
  See also Dunshay Manor; Rempstone Estate

Worth Poor Book, 250
Worth Quarries Ltd, 157
Worth Quarry Co., 191, 206, 257, 258
Wren, Christopher, 50, 105, 165
Wren Society, 165
Wrentham, St. Nicholas, 49
Wymond, John, 51
Wyatt, Benjamin, 131
Wyatt, Samuel, 72, 107, 108
Wynyards Gap, Wessex Division War Memorial, 207
Wytch Farm oilfield, 192

Yevele, Henry, 41, 48, 63, 207, 222
York Minster, 34, 36, 50, 201
  Walter le Grey tomb, 45

The Illustrations

The author is grateful to all those who have helped with providing illustrations. We have done all that is reasonable to trace holders of copyright, but it has not always proved possible. We apologise for any omissions, and will happily make the necessary corrections in all future editions.

It seems invidious to single out any one person, but there are two I must especially thank, Brian Bugler for photographing the stone samples and the use of Purbeck stone in buildings on the Isle of Purbeck, and Dr John Crook for so generously allowing me to take my pick from his remarkable archive of cathedral photographs. More eloquently than anything I can say, these images are the best testament to the skill and craftsmanship of the medieval quarriers and masons, and to the artistic heights of which Purbeck Marble and stone are capable.

My thanks are due to the following:

Dr Martin Ayres: pp. 121 (bottom right), 186.

British Geological Survey: the map on page 21 was created specially for the book by Henry Holbrook and Russell Lawley: Emma Gallagher generously supplied the following photographs from the 1930s, pp. 154 (bottom), 205 (top right) and Cover, 208 (bottom right), 219 (x2), 254.

The British Library (with thanks for their help to Jonathon Vines and Sandra Powlette): Samuel Grimm, Shelfmark Additional Manuscripts, f.64, f.157, f.158), pp. 79, 130 (top left and right).

Brian Bugler: most stone samples on pages 12-19, and pp.26, 29, 46 (middle left), 56 (top right), 57 (middle left), 70 (left), 71 (top and middle right), 72 (top left and right), 76 (bottom left), 77 (middle), 103 (bottom right x2), 104 (top left), 109 (top left), 150, 155 (top right), 169 (right), 183, 185 (bottom left), 190, 196 (bottom right), 201 (top right), 202 (bottom right), 215 (bottom right), 265 (x2) and 266

Ali Burnett, for help with preparing diagrams and maps, and the photograph on p. 96.

Ilay Cooper: p. 107 (top right), courtesy of the Landmark Trust.

Jed Corbett, for help with scanning, images from 'Worth in Pictures' (pp.135(bottom), 144 (top left), 154 (top), 156 (bottom), 157, 199 (top left), and photos: pp. 121(top right), 125 (bottom right), 262(bottom right).

Dr John Crook FSA: pp. 6, 30, 31, 33, 35(top), 36 (top right), 37 (top and bottom right), 38, 39, 40, 41 (top right), 44 (top x 2 and bottom right), 45 (top left and right), 46 (top right), 47, 49 (bottom right), 55 (top left), 59, 63 (left, 76 (top left), 161, 162, 163 (bottom right).

Dorset County Museum (with special thanks to Anna Butler): pp.2-3, 135.

Dorset History Centre; I am particularly grateful to the County Archivist, Sam Johnston, and to Luke Dady for their work on sources and permissions. I would also like to thank Lara Manningham-Buller, Rempstone Estates: pp. 81 (The National Trust), 85 (Rempstone Estate and The National Trust), 114 (top right), 118 (x3), 119, 123 (The National Trust), 127 (bottom left and right), 133 (x4), 140 (Rempstone Estate), 142 (Rempstone Estate), 143 (Rempstone Estate), 187 (The National Trust), 211 (middle right).

Ely Cathedral. The photographs were kindly taken by James Billings, and I am grateful to Lesley Ann Thompson, Director of Communications and Commerce, for allowing access at a particularly difficult time: p. 36 (top left, bottom right).

Bob Gibbons: p. 160.

Guildhall Art Gallery (with thanks to Tanya Dean): p. 126.

Mary Haysom: pp. 100, 185 (bottom right), 199 (bottom right), 209 (middle right).

Sue Haysom: pp. 36 (middle left), 44 (top left), 46 (bottom left), 55 (top right), 56 (top left and centre), 57 (top), 67 (x2), 77 (top left), 92 (top), 102, 125 (middle right), 156 (top left), 167 (top right), 168 (top right), 173 (top left), 174 (top left).

Chris Kaye: map, p.246.

Langton Matravers Museum: pp. 135 (top left), 312.

Cari Laurenson: p. 45 (bottom right)

Peter Lightfoot: p.4 (map), diagrams based on author's drafts, pp. 58, 66, 78, 120 (top right), 127 (top).

London Metropolitan Archive: p.225.

Jan Marsh: Permission to include copy of quarry transfer document, p.244.

Joan Muspratt: p. 197.

Kathi Penney Stacey kindly provided the photographs of Trinity and Harbour Grace churches in Newfoundland: pp. 173 (bottom), 223 (bottom right),

Dr Mary Sparks: Amongst many debts is one for drawing the manors map on page 62.

Westminster Abbey (with special thanks to Christine Reynolds, Assistant Keeper of the Muniments, The Library): p.49 (top right).

123RF: 54 (ID 87195641, Daniel Garcia Villaneuva), 60 (ID 86020742, tupungato) 108 (top and left middle) (ID 19536712, Ian Wool and 439998 Mark Yuill), 109 (bottom) (ID44113833 Matthew Gibson), 164 (ID 31510000, pxl store).

All the remaining illustrations come from the author's own collection, from the Dovecote Press Collection, or were specially taken by Dr Mary Sparks.

'Purbeck Quarrymen' by Alfred Palmer (oil on canvas),
Seacombe, 1920s (Langton Matravers Museum).